ROBERT BERNE
*Graduate School*
*of Public Administration*
*New York University*

RICHARD SCHRAMM
*Department of Urban*
*and Environmental Policy*
*Tufts University*

# THE FINANCIAL

# ANALYSIS

# OF GOVERNMENTS

*Prentice-Hall, Englewood Cliffs, New Jersey 07632*

*Library of Congress Cataloging-in-Publication Data*

Berne, Robert.
  The financial analysis of governments.

  Includes index.
  1. Finance, Public. 2. Finance, Public—
United States. I. Schramm, Richard. II. Title.
HJ141.B44 1986        350.72         85-25787
ISBN  0-13-316233-8

350.72
B52 f

Editorial/production supervision and
  interior design: *Nancy G. Follender*
Cover design: *Edsal Enterprises*
Manufacturing buyer: *Ed O'Dougherty*

Printed in the United States of America

10  9  8  7  6  5  4  3  2  1

ISBN   0-13-316233-8      01

PRENTICE-HALL INTERNATIONAL (UK) LIMITED, *London*
PRENTICE-HALL OF AUSTRALIA PTY. LIMITED, *Sydney*
PRENTICE-HALL CANADA INC., *Toronto*
PRENTICE-HALL HISPANOAMERICANA, S. A., *Mexico*
PRENTICE-HALL OF INDIA PRIVATE LIMITED, *New Delhi*
PRENTICE-HALL OF JAPAN, INC., *Tokyo*
PRENTICE-HALL OF SOUTHEAST ASIA PTE. LTD., *Singapore*
EDITORA PRENTICE-HALL DO BRASIL, LTDA., *Rio de Janeiro*
WHITEHALL BOOKS LIMITED, *Wellington, New Zealand*

*To our families,*

*Shelley, Rebecca,* and *Michael*
*Nancy, Kurt, Katherine, Lisa,* and *Hope*

# Contents

# Preface

This book has grown out of the realization that the methods and information needed to analyze and evaluate government financial well-being are often not available or not especially well-suited to the task, despite the importance of the financial health of state and local governments.

We first discovered this in 1974 as consultants for the Syracuse (New York) Police Benevolent Association and the Syracuse Firefighters Association in a wage arbitration hearing. In assessing the city's financial status and ability to carry higher public employee salaries and benefits, we found that the format and content of government financial statements, the nature and availability of other relevant data, and the existing literature on evaluating government fiscal condition were of very limited help. We were especially surprised at how little guidance the literature provided about what information to look for or what to do with the information once it was found.

Public finance texts of the day, which described and evaluated methods of raising and spending money in government, stressed efficiency and equity but said very little about the resulting impacts on financial condition. Government accounting manuals showed how to develop financial statements but not how to analyze them. Financial management books presented ways to improve financial decision-making but offered little help in determining the government's overall well-being. And credit analysis material addressed the topic of financial condition directly but stressed the investor's point of view and presented ratios and rules-of-thumb without providing an adequate theoretical framework to guide their use and interpretation. What was missing was a book that focused directly on government financial condition, examined existing theory and analytical methodology, and provided guidance for the conduct of financial analysis.

During the 1970s, progress was made in improving the quality and availability of information about government finances, but few advances were made in the framework and methods for analyzing this information. This became most evident when, in 1978, with support from the National Science Foundation and the International City Management Association, we surveyed existing approaches to financial analysis, identified what we felt were their major strengths and weaknesses, and developed an analytical framework for determining a government's financial well-being. These efforts to clarify and extend existing methods and develop an analytical framework, which became the basis for this book, were considerably enriched by our discussion with practitioners during that period.

As the book evolved, we used various chapters in our classes and applied the techniques to a wide variety of governmental organizations. Our students provided helpful suggestions, not only from their classroom study, but also, in many cases, from their experience working in the field of government finance. Work with the American Municipal Bond Assurance Corporation helped test our conceptual framework and methods.

*The Financial Analysis of Governments* is intended for many users: teachers and students of financial analysis; researchers concerned about financial condition analysis from either a methodological or policy perspective; practitioners in state and local government who must understand and monitor the financial health of governments; and employees, taxpayers, private firms, oversight agencies, creditors, and constituency groups with direct interests in assessing the well-being of government.

This book can be used in graduate or advanced undergraduate courses in financial management, policy, and planning, either as a primary text in courses analyzing government finances and financial condition or as a supplementary text in courses that include these concerns as subtopics. While some knowledge of government finance and accounting prior to using this book would be ideal, students without this background will find an early chapter on governmental accounting, financial statements, and budgeting, as well as introductory material and references throughout the book.

This book is also designed for use outside the classroom. Its emphasis on the different stages of analysis, and its inclusion of examples, problems, references, and a continuing case study, are all intended to make it useful and readily accessible to practitioners and researchers concerned with the study of government finances. In this context the book can be used for self-education, as a guide for an actual analysis, or as a comprehensive reference to the methods and issues of financial analysis.

Since this book has been "in the works" for several years, we have benefited from the help of many organizations and individuals. We have already indicated the important role played by the Syracuse Police Benevolent Association and the Syracuse Firefighters Association, NSF, ICMA, and AMBAC. In addition, the Merrill Trust Fund furnished a timely and helpful summer research grant, and the Graduate School of Public Administration at New York University and the Department of Urban and Environmental Policy at Tufts University have provided exceptionally supportive environments for our work.

Numerous individuals have offered substantive criticism and review of our work including Dick Netzer, Leanna Stiefel, Steven Finkler, Helen Ladd, Herman Leonard, and several anonymous referees. Our students at New York University, Cornell, and Tufts have used draft versions of the book over the years and have provided many useful comments and suggestions. It is especially gratifying to get feedback from students who as graduates have applied some of our ideas in their work. Linda Frascino and Nancy Follender at Prentice-Hall helped us with the formidable task of turning our manuscript into a book. Expert typing assistance came from Peggy Andersen, Judy Wade, and Theresa Steinbacher. Finally, throughout the entire process our families and friends have given us the personal support so essential in making this book a reality.

# CHAPTER

# 1 / Introduction

The government sector in the United States is extensive. The combined federal, state, and local government system raised $1,181 billion in revenues in 1982–83, spent $1,351 billion including $314 billion for salaries and wages, and carried $1,836 billion in debt at the end of that fiscal year. Almost half of these revenues and expenditures were generated by state governments and by the over eighty thousand local governments that round out the U.S. federal system of government.[1]

Financial strength of this government sector is essential to ensure the continuing provision of public goods and services. Yet the financial health of governments has been a growing concern over the past fifteen years. Governments in financial trouble have included New York City, Cleveland, Wayne County and the city of Detroit, Erie County (New York), the San Diego School District, several public authorities in New York State, and the recent highly publicized Washington Public Power Supply System. While these examples have received considerable public attention, many other governments are struggling with financial problems with less publicity but similar urgency.

Government financial problems have not reached the levels of the 1930s when thousands of local governments defaulted on their bonds or arranged deferred payments under crisis conditions, but they have become serious enough to be an issue of public concern and debate, spurring legislative hearings, referenda votes, and the institution of restrictions like Proposition 13 in California and Proposition 2½ in Massachusetts.

To assess the financial health or condition of governments, this book analyzes government finances, a task that is far from simple and straightfor-

---

[1] U.S. Department of Commerce, Bureau of the Census, *Governmental Finances in 1982–83* (Washington, D.C., October 1984), Introduction and pp. 5 and 17.

ward. Individual governments differ in many ways: in their purposes, which can vary in scope and type; in the conditions they face in their communities; in the needs for their services; in the legal and political constraints that shape how they meet these needs; in the level and type of expenditures they make to meet their goals; in their sources of revenues and in the resource base that provides these revenues; in their emphasis on borrowing against the future (both debt and pensions); and in the attention they give to their own financial health. All of these differences must be addressed in the analysis of a government's finances and financial condition, and yet the methods of analysis must be general enough to apply to a wide range of governments. The development of methods of analyzing the financial condition of governments with applicability to a wide range of organizations is the task addressed in this book.

In this chapter we begin this task by discussing the types and characteristics of governmental organizations and the type of governments that will be emphasized in this development of financial analysis. We then describe the major goals of governments that play a fundamental role in evaluating government operations and decisions, discuss the importance the goal of financial strength plays in the conduct of financial analysis, and show how concerns about financial health fit in with other concerns of government. Next we present an overview of the analysis of financial condition and discuss the wide range of groups with an interest in the financial health of governments. Finally we present the plan and structure of the rest of the book.

## I. GOVERNMENTAL ORGANIZATIONS

A governmental organization is one that has a public purpose (or several public purposes), is controlled by an elected legislative body representing a particular political (geographic) jurisdiction, and usually has special powers like taxing, tax-exempt borrowing, use of eminent domain, and so forth.

TABLE 1-1   **Government Units, 1962–82**

| Type of Government | 1982 | 1977 | 1972 | 1967 | 1962 |
|---|---|---|---|---|---|
| U.S. Government | 1 | 1 | 1 | 1 | 1 |
| State Governments | 50 | 50 | 50 | 50 | 50 |
| Local Governments | 82,290 | 79,862 | 78,218 | 81,248 | 91,186 |
| County | 3,041 | 3,042 | 3,044 | 3,049 | 3,043 |
| Municipal | 19,076 | 18,862 | 18,517 | 18,048 | 18,000 |
| Township | 16,734 | 16,822 | 16,991 | 17,105 | 17,142 |
| School district | 14,851 | 15,174 | 15,781 | 21,782 | 34,678 |
| Special district | 28,588 | 25,962 | 23,885 | 21,264 | 18,323 |
| Total Governments | 82,341 | 79,913 | 78,269 | 81,299 | 91,237 |

SOURCE:   **U.S. Department of Commerce, Bureau of the Census,** *Volume 1, Government Organizations, 1982 Census of Governments* **(Washington, D.C., August 1983), Table A, p. VI.**

Governments come in many sizes and shapes. Governmental organizations consist of specifically designated governments in political jurisdictions; the federal, state, and local governments with which we are all familiar; plus special, usually single-purpose "governments" created by traditional governments. Table 1–1 presents the number and types of conventional governmental units in the United States for selected years between 1962 and 1982. In 1982 there were 38,902 general-purpose governments (federal, state, county, municipal, and township) and 43,439 limited-purpose local governments (school district and special district governments). While the number of general-purpose governments remained relatively constant over the 1962–82 period, the number of limited-purpose local governments declined by 20 percent. Moreover, the composition of limited-purpose local governments changed dramatically; school districts dropped from 34,678 to 14,851 over this period while special districts grew by 56 percent, from 18,323 to 28,588.

In addition to general-purpose governments and limited-purpose local school and special district governments, there are many public authorities that can be classified as "governments."[2] These are limited-purpose (or single-purpose) public organizations established by one or more general-purpose governments and granted certain public powers, usually borrowing and sometimes taxing powers. These organizations may be interstate (Port Authority of New York and New Jersey), state based (Power Authority of the State of New York), or regional within states (Massachusetts Bay Transit Authority). Such authorities should be included among governmental organizations.

So-called governmental enterprises are included among the governmental organizations described above. Governmental enterprises are usually limited-purpose public organizations or parts of government that produce public goods or services that are sold to the public, with such fees or user charges providing most or all of the revenues to that organization. Although these enterprises sometimes have specific taxing and borrowing rights, they are distinguished by their reliance on fees or user charges to make them "self-sustaining." They are often intended to run without subsidy or even to generate a profit. Government enterprises include, for example, water and sewer systems within local general-purpose governments, public hospitals or utilities run as special district governments, and state or regional transportation authorities.

Many organizations that serve the public, or some part of the public, are not governments. These include a wide range of private nonprofit organizations, such as churches, foundations, colleges, universities, libraries, museums, and hospitals, which have a public or social purpose and are not run primarily to make a profit. While many of such organizations are "tax exempt," they are not governments because they are not controlled by a legislative body or its representatives

---

[2] In fact, only some of these public authorities are included in the census figures listed in Table 1–1. For a discussion of the role of public authorities in the census data, see Annmarie Hauck Walsh, *The Public's Business* (Cambridge, Mass.: MIT Press, 1978), Appendix.

and do not have special taxing and other governmental rights. Although not governments *per se,* many of these organizations are really public entities supplementing governments in the provision of much-needed goods and services.

Many of the methods of financial analysis developed in this book can be applied to these nonprofit organizations. However, since there are some important structural, financial, and accounting differences between governmental and nonprofit organizations, we will focus our analysis and examples on different types of state and local governments and governmental enterprises.

We have decided not to include the federal government in our analysis, since the financial health of the federal government and the entire economy (perhaps even the world economy) are so intertwined, and books on macroeconomics, international economics, public finance, and fiscal and monetary policy providing different elements of this analysis abound. Rather we have chosen to focus on the county, municipal, town, special district, and school district governments and government enterprises and state governments that make up the bulk of the federal government system and have experienced the most financial problems in recent years, and where economics and finance have not been used as extensively to analyze the financial condition of governments.[3]

## II. THE OBJECTIVES OF GOVERNMENTAL ORGANIZATIONS

Governmental organizations provide a wide range of public goods and services—housing, public safety, health services, education, utilities, highways, etc.—and they have several general objectives they hope to satisfy in providing these goods and services. These are normative objectives, what governments *should* strive for, based on various economic and political theories of the role of government. They may not represent what some governments actually set as their goals. But as normative objectives, they can serve as standards to evaluate the actual performance and condition of government—as criteria to judge how well a particular public organization is doing.

First, governments try to raise and spend resources *efficiently*—in the lowest-cost, highest-benefit fashion. This requires that a particular government strive to minimize the levels of resources used, or the costs of these resources, in providing a given set of goods and services. This objective prompts the government to evaluate continually how it is raising its money (taxes, fees, etc.) and how it is spending its money (personnel, materials, equipment, etc.) to keep its use of resources and their costs down. It also requires that the government review the goods and services it provides to be sure it is maximizing the total benefits provided to those it is serving.

---

[3] Throughout this book, *government* refers to all local and state governments unless otherwise indicated.

As an example of the concern for efficiency, consider a government facing choices about how to raise and spend money. Suppose it is choosing between using a property tax and using a sales tax. The more efficient choice would be the one that minimized the costs of raising the same amount of money from either tax, where these costs included administration and collection costs, along with costs to residents in complying with the tax and in the adjustments the tax leads them to make in their overall economic behavior. Next suppose the government is considering spending the money raised on personnel and/or equipment. The efficiency criterion requires that the government seek the combination of these two types of expenditures that minimizes the total costs of wages, interest, maintenance, and so forth, required to provide a given level of public goods or services. And finally, efficiency concerns require that the government use the equipment purchased and the people hired to produce a combination of services, such as public housing and/or fire protection, that maximizes the benefits of those served by the government. The efficiency objective, as we will often see in this book, affects essentially all governmental decisions.

Second, governments try to raise and spend resources *equitably*—distributing the costs and benefits of government activities "fairly" among the individuals and groups they serve. "Fairness" obviously means different things to different people, and governments reflect the sense of fairness of their constituencies. But in the analysis of government actions, "fairness" usually means distributing costs in a manner that recognizes that different individuals and groups have different abilities to pay those costs, and that more of the costs should be paid by those most able to pay them (the "ability-to-pay principle"). Using this same principle, "fairness" implies that the benefits of government accrue to those most in need of them. Other definitions of fairness may also influence government decisions and can be used to evaluate government operations. For example, under the "benefit principle," it is "fair" if those receiving particular public goods or services pay the costs of providing those goods or services, regardless of their income or ability to pay. While other definitions of fairness will be used from time to time, the primary definition used in this book will be the ability-to-pay principle.

The equity criterion does not ask whether costs are minimized or benefits maximized by an organization's actions, but rather whether these costs or benefits are distributed fairly. Thus a government striving for equity would choose either a property tax or a sales tax, or increase either employees or equipment, or provide either more public housing or more fire protection, based on how each of these decisions distributed the costs and benefits among groups where these groups are often categorized by income levels (or other measures of ability to pay). The effects that the combination of all these choices have on individuals with different income levels could be judged in terms of equity.

Third, governments try to maintain a healthy *financial condition*—being able to meet their financial obligations as they come due, in both the short run and the long run, while raising resources and providing public goods and services. Governments are not established to make profits or to amass fortunes, but they are expected to take those steps needed to ensure that they have the financial strength to carry out their public responsibilities.

To illustrate the financial strength criterion, consider a government choosing between financing a program out of current tax revenues or financing it by borrowing the money and repaying the loan from future tax revenues. Each possibility has a different effect on the government's current cash reserves and financial obligations. A choice based on a concern for the government's financial strength would maximize the probability of the government's having cash to meet its current and future needs. Choices between increasing personnel or equipment, or of providing a service where fees can be collected from users or one where they cannot, can be based on financial concerns as well as efficiency and equity, since these choices also affect the government's ability to meet its current and future financial obligations.

Finally, governments have *public accountability* as an objective—responding to the needs of the government's clientele and the requirements of its environment in an open, informative, and involving fashion and being held responsible for its actions. This objective requires that the government develop the information needed to evaluate its operations, put this information into an understandable and accessible form, and provide mechanisms for the appropriate public review of its activities.

These four goals encompass the more specific goals of particular governments. Thus the federal government's concern about national economic growth can be reinterpreted as the goal of using national resources more efficiently, using labor and capital fully and effectively to provide needed goods and services. A state government striving to overcome regional economic problems reflects a concern for equity in the incomes of state residents, the efficient use of its resources, and its financial condition. A local government providing housing for mixed-income groups reflects both efficiency and equity concerns. A school district shutting down school buildings and consolidating its operations is concerned with efficiency, equity (in its choice of what buildings to close), and financial strength. And finally, a local government establishing neighborhood "city halls" may be responding to its need for public accountability.

These broad goals of governments, however, often conflict. Steps taken to increase efficiency may hurt some groups unfairly; the provision of programs for the socially disadvantaged may stretch the government's financial resources; efforts to include community people more fully in government decision making may be costly and time consuming. These conflicts are inherent in government decision making, and financial analysis needs to identify the positive and negative impacts of government operations and decisions on all these goals.

Entire books could be written (and some have) analyzing governments along any one of these dimensions—efficiency, equity, financial condition, and accountability. Because of its importance and the lack of substantial systematic attention in the past, this book focuses on the objective of strong financial condition.

This focus, however, considers the other objectives as well, since the pursuit of financial strength inevitably brings in considerations of efficiency, equity, and accountability.

## III. FINANCIAL ANALYSIS OF GOVERNMENTS

To evaluate the financial health or condition of governments, we need to clarify the goals of the analysis, determine the level at which the analysis will be carried out, construct a framework or "model" to organize the analysis, develop comparative methods that provide benchmarks to judge financial condition and its changes, and identify and secure the information needed to carry out the analysis.

The goal or purpose of the financial analysis of governments is to determine how well the government has met its past financial obligations and how likely it is that it can meet its financial obligations now and in the future. This goal obviously has a time dimension, requiring an assessment of financial condition in the past, present, and future. But what is less obvious is that the goal of meeting financial obligations includes obligations to a wide range of constituencies—taxpayers, employees, suppliers, banks, residents, and local organizations in need of services —not to just a single group such as debtholders. The goal of financial strength is nothing less than having the resources to carry out all the responsibilities of government fully and effectively, and meeting all the financial obligations that this entails.

The level of this analysis is the organization. Many of the data we analyze are aggregate organizational data—total revenues by major sources, total expenditures by major types and functions, total debt by major categories. We ask what is the financial condition of a particular government, not of a particular department or program, although we may in some circumstances examine the condition of major departments or programs in assessing the overall financial condition of the government.

The analysis of a government's finances requires a framework or "model" to organize the questions asked, the data collected, the comparisons made, and the conclusions reached. The approach taken in this book is to assess financial condition by comparing the resources still available to a government with unmet needs for government expenditures ("expenditure pressures"). The greater the difference between the two—the more the available resources exceed the expenditure needs—the stronger the financial condition of the government. This approach requires that the government's revenues and internal resources, and the possibilities of expanding them, be examined to determine the level of available resources, and that the government's operating and capital expenditures (and the factors that determine these expenditures) and the obligations to pay back debt and make pension payments, be examined to determine the pressures to increase expenditures. Only when both available resources and expenditure pressures are known can the government's financial strength be fully assessed. The framework pulls these different parts of the analysis together to provide the basis for assessing a government's financial strengths and weaknesses and its overall financial condition.

Benchmarks for establishing financial strengths and weaknesses of governments need to be developed. Although the for-profit sector has well-established measures of profitability, rate of return, risk levels, and so forth, appropriate benchmarks for governments have been more difficult to establish. Some measures of government financial condition have been developed, however, and they provide the basis for financial analysis. Once financial measures have been determined, financial analysis consists of securing the data to estimate these measures and then making comparisons. The measures can be compared with past levels, with the levels in similar governments (a "reference group"), or in some cases with legal restrictions and experts' "rules of thumb." The framework for the analysis serves to organize different measures and comparisons in a way that overall evaluations of strengths and weaknesses can be made.

Finally, financial analysis requires data. Government financial statements, budgets, and other financial reports provide many of the data needed, but the analysis would not be complete or informative without data on the community's resources, costs, and needs. Similar data may be needed for other governments being used for comparisons. The smaller the government, the harder it is to secure the financial data needed and the less likely that the data will be easily accessible and understandable. Once the data have been collected, and this is often the most difficult task, they can be organized around the different components of the financial analysis framework: revenue, expenditures, debt, pensions, and internal resources.

## IV. USERS OF FINANCIAL ANALYSIS

The analysis of government finances and financial condition is crucial to many different individuals, groups, and organizations.

First, there are those elected and appointed officials who manage governmental organizations: governors, mayors, city managers, budget directors, finance officers, department heads, supervisors, and other public managers and administrators. Managers are responsible for planning and carrying out government operations, for deciding how resources are raised and spent, and for evaluating government activities, as well as being publicly accountable for their actions. Although their interests and needs vary, they all have to understand some aspects of government finances and the financial health of the government, or part of government, for which they are responsible in order to carry out their management responsibilities.

Second, there are those who directly oversee governmental operations: government legislatures, city councils, public authority commissions, town trustees, school boards, and other groups to which governments are directly accountable. These elected or appointed groups determine the broad goals and policies of the governmental organizations they oversee, and they are ultimately responsible to the public for the activities of government. In this role it is essential to understand government finances, available resources, expenditure pressures, and overall financial health. This understanding is needed to set spending limits, to approve major new programs or expenditure increases, to seek new revenue sources or expand the use of existing sources, to review government financial reports and proposals, and to conduct other functions needed to shape and oversee government operations.

Third, there are those organizations that regulate or constrain governments, ranging from the courts to specific agencies. Court officials may need information about government financial operations and condition to judge whether governments are meeting constitutional or higher governmental requirements; state inspector general offices or financial agencies may need such information for financial audits or to see if restrictions, like the Massachusetts Proposition 2½, are being followed; wage arbitration boards may need to know the financial condition of a city in establishing a fair increase in the salaries of public employees. External organizations of this sort, while not serving as direct overseers of government operations, may oversee specific activities or perform occasional broad audits, all of which may require financial information and analysis.

Fourth, there are the recipients of government goods and services: households receiving police and fire protection, local businesses receiving water and sewer services, specific client groups receiving health care or education. While represented through elected officials, such groups may wish to monitor government activities and finances themselves to determine whether they are receiving the goods and services for which they are entitled, and at a reasonable cost if fees or user charges must be paid.

Fifth, there are those who provide funds and services to governments: taxpayers, suppliers, banks, employees, other governments, and public organizations. Those providing grants or transfers, such as federal and state governments providing aid to local governments, may need to determine if the government needs the grant and/or has the financial capacity to meet any terms set by the grant. Creditors such as insurance companies buying government bonds or local banks making loans to government need to identify and assess the risks that the government may not pay back the loan on time, or even at all. Government employees contributing to a pension plan, providing the government some of their time and effort in return for future pension benefits, also fall into the creditor category. Employee unions may also need financial information and analysis to determine whether their members are being paid fairly and/or whether the government can afford to pay them more.

Finally, there is a wide range of research and educational organizations that need financial information and analysis. These include credit-rating agencies and government bond insurance companies that need to assess the risks associated with the bonds or other borrowing of particular governments, the staffs of congressional committees studying the financial condition of different classes of government, and academics trying to advance knowledge about government finances and to improve teaching in administration, economics, and political science.

## V. STRUCTURE OF THE BOOK

Following this introduction, the book is divided into nine chapters. Chapter 2, "Financial Information," provides readers with a basic level of understanding of the financial information needed to analyze the financial condition of governments. This chapter presents an introduction to governmental accounting, financial statements, and budgets, all essential sources of information for the government financial analyst.

The next seven chapters of the book present the framework and major components of financial analysis. This section begins with a description of this framework and of the major methods used to analyze financial information (Chapter 3), and it then goes into detailed analyses of government revenues (Chapter 4), expenditures (Chapter 5), debt (Chapter 6), pensions (Chapter 7), and internal resources (Chapter 8). Each component of the analysis provides detailed information on a particular aspect of government finances and what can be determined about a government's financial condition from that perspective.

The final two chapters of the book combine the different perspectives of financial analysis and provide an overall assessment of the financial strength or condition of government. First the methods and findings of the preceding seven chapters are summarized, and final conclusions are reached about the financial health of the city we use as a case study throughout the book (Chapter 9). Then a complete analysis of a second illustrative city government is presented as a final integrated example of the analysis of governmental financial condition (Chapter 10).

## QUESTIONS

1. This book is concerned with the financial health of a wide range of governmental organizations. Identify all the governments that you know that are providing services to and/or raising revenues from the locality where you reside. Be sure to include any school or special district governments, and local or regional public authorities, along with general-purpose local and state governments. What do you know about the financial condition of any or all of these governments?

2. Consider a decision made by a government with which you are familiar. It may be a decision about a new tax, cutbacks in a program, borrowing to finance a major expenditure, and so forth. How might this decision have affected the government's goals of efficiency, equity, financial condition, and

accountability? Identify ways in which this decision may have helped achieve one goal but detracted from another.

3.  What major groups or individuals, inside or outside of government, have an interest in the financial condition of your local general-purpose government? What are the specific interests of each group? In what ways are these interests similar? In conflict?

# CHAPTER 2 / Financial Information

Financial information developed by governments is an essential ingredient in financial analysis. This chapter discusses the organization and presentation of financial information including governmental accounting, financial statements, and budgets. Only an overview of the issues that are particularly important in financial analysis are presented in this chapter; more-detailed treatments of these topics are available elsewhere.[1]

## I. THE NATURE OF FINANCIAL INFORMATION

*Accounting* has been formally defined as the "process of identifying, measuring, and communicating economic information to permit informed judgment and decisions by users of the information."[2] While this definition applies to all organizations, the unique goals and characteristics of governments, described in Chapter 1, have led to governmental accounting systems that are not identical with those found in "for-profit" organizations. Although the emphasis in this chapter is financial analysis, accounting information is generated for other reasons, including control, accountability, implementation, planning, and

---

[1] For more-detailed treatments of governmental accounting and budgeting, see Leon Hay, *Accounting for Governmental and Nonprofit Entities,* 6th ed. (Homewood, Ill.: Richard D. Irwin, 1980); Emerson O. Henke, *Introduction to Nonprofit Organization Accounting* (Boston: Kent, 1980); Edward S. Lynn and Robert J. Freeman, *Fund Accounting, Theory and Practice* (Englewood Cliffs, N.J.: Prentice-Hall, 1974); and Robert D. Lee, Jr., and Ronald W. Johnson, *Public Budgeting Systems,* 3rd ed. (Baltimore: University Park Press, 1983).

[2] American Accounting Association, *A Statement of Basic Accounting Theory* (Evanston, Ill., 1966), p. 1.

evaluation.[3] The basic elements of governmental accounting are presented in section II.

Accountants, as a profession, have developed standards to define, record, and communicate accounting information. For example, accounting information should be relevant, free from bias, verifiable, and quantifiable.[4] Accountants also follow certain guidelines for determining appropriate methods for communication of information, including appropriateness to expected use, disclosure of significant relationships, inclusion of environmental information, uniformity of practices within and among entities, and consistency of practices through time.[5]

The basic tool used by the accountant to communicate financial information is the *financial statement*. The most common financial statements are found in annual reports that are produced by governments to summarize their financial position and operations. However, other financial statements and reports may be generated on a one-time basis for a specific decision. Financial statements vary according to the level of detail reported, with statements prepared for public consumption usually being the most highly summarized. Certain statements, particularly the annual financial statements, may be audited by an independent accounting firm or agency, while the internal operating statements are seldom audited. The financial statements most common to governments are covered in section III.

Government accounting and financial reporting is guided by what are referred to as "generally accepted accounting principles" (GAAP). These standards were previously formulated through the voluntary action of several professional groups, but the Governmental Accounting Standards Board (GASB) has recently been formed as the single organization to establish GAAP for governments.[6] Although not every government follows all aspects of GAAP, the emphasis in this chapter is on the accepted principles and practices because most recommended practices are in widespread use.[7]

---

[3] For a discussion of users and user needs, see Robert N. Anthony, *Financial Accounting in Nonbusiness Organizations, An Exploratory Study of Conceptual Issues* (Stamford, Conn.: Financial Accounting Standards Board, 1978); and Allan R. Drebin, James L. Chan, and Lorna Ferguson, *Objectives of Accounting and Financial Reporting for Governmental Units: A Research Study* (Chicago: National Council on Governmental Accounting, 1981), Vol. 1.

[4] American Accounting Association, *Statement of Basic Accounting Theory*, Chap. 2, especially pp. 7–18.

[5] Ibid., p. 14.

[6] For the status of the Governmental Accounting Standards Board, see its statements and interpretations; for example, Statement No. 1, *Authoritative Status of NCGA Pronouncements and AICPA Industry Audit Guide*, 1984. Also see NCGA Statements 1 and 2, Municipal Finance Officers Association, *Governmental Accounting Auditing, and Financial Reporting* (Chicago, 1980) (this publication, known as *GAAFR*, includes NCGA Statements 1 and 2); and American Institute of Certified Public Accountants, *Audits of State and Local Governmental Units*, 3rd ed. (New York, 1981). For a brief history of governmental accounting standards, see Appendix A of "Accounting Practices and Financial Reporting," in *Staff Report on Transactions in Securities of the City of New York* (Washington, D.C.: Securities and Exchange Commission, 1977).

[7] For a review of the degree to which governments follow generally accepted accounting principles, see Coopers & Lybrand and the University of Michigan, "Financial Disclosure Practices of the

The accepted practices in governmental accounting and reporting are presented to enable the reader to understand the information contained in financial reports and use this information in financial analysis. This presentation is not intended as an endorsement of accepted principles and practices. There are substantial concerns about many of the current practices, and many of these concerns will be evaluated by the newly formed GASB.[8]

Useful information for financial analysis is also contained in *budgets.* While accounting is concerned with reporting the financial history of an entity, budgets are financial plans for future operations. Budgets are usually prepared in advance of the reporting period, whereas accounting data are available a short time after the end of the period. Of course, budgets do not disappear, so at the end of each period we have both accounting data (history) and a budget (a forecast of what has become history, made at the beginning of the period), allowing analysis of the two together. The key difference, then, is that budgets are anticipatory while accounting data are retrospective. For the most part, both contain the same sort of information, although the level of detail may vary. Budgets for governments are considered in section IV.

## II. ACCOUNTING SYSTEMS IN GOVERNMENTS

This section explains the basic aspects of governmental accounting systems, including fund accounting, stocks and flows of resources, the accounting equation, and the basis of accounting. The approach throughout the chapter is to use generic concepts as much as possible. We recognize that the actual practices for a specific government may differ from the generic concepts. But if the reader understands the generic concepts, then applications of these concepts by a particular government should be comprehensible as well.

### A First Look at Fund Accounting

Governments obtain resources, use these resources (inputs) to produce goods and services (outputs), and then distribute these goods and services to their constituencies. Unlike for-profit organizations, government revenues are usually not generated by the sale of goods and services, and capital is not obtained by selling shares of stock that promise future financial returns. Thus governments are concerned with "bringing in as much money as goes out" (balancing the budget)

---

American Cities, A Public Report,'' published by Coopers & Lybrand, 1976; Ernst & Whinney, *How Cities Can Improve Their Financial Reporting* (Cleveland, 1979); and Cornelius E. Tierney and Philip T. Calder, *Governmental Accounting, Procedures and Practices, 1983* (New York: Elsevier, 1983).

[8] For a discussion of some of the problems with accepted practices and principles in governmental accounting, see Sidney Davidson et al., *Financial Reporting by State and Local Governmental Units* (Chicago: Center for the Management of Public and Nonprofit Enterprise, Graduate School of Business, University of Chicago, 1977); and Coopers & Lybrand, *Financial Disclosure Practices of the American Cities, II, Closing the Communications Gap* (New York, 1978).

and being accountable for the use of resources, but not with maximizing financial profit. Accounting in governments, as a result, emphasizes the recording of dollars that flow into and out of the organization, but not the calculation of net income or profit so important to for-profit organizations. Furthermore, when there is no direct relationship between government outputs and revenues, calculation of profit is not possible or useful except when the outputs are actually sold. Certain components of governments, such as hospitals, water companies, and airports, do of course sell their outputs and can be treated in some ways as "for-profit" organizations. These organizations will be discussed after considering accounting for governments in general.

*Fund accounting* is the basic framework that has been developed and used by accountants to record financial transactions in governments. Fund accounting was developed primarily for control purposes and is designed to record where resources come from and what they are used for, and to help ensure that governments conform to the legal constraints placed upon them.

What distinguishes fund accounting from conventional for-profit accounting is that the government is divided for accounting purposes into separate accounting entities, or *funds,* whereas for-profit accounting makes no similar divisions. Each fund is usually set up to record and account for the uses of a specific group of assets or sources of revenue, reflecting the control orientation of fund accounting. A government may have one or more funds.

Funds in government often correspond to activities and objectives of the organization, but they do not necessarily correspond to operating divisions such as departments or programs within the government. These activities or objectives are often specified by external organizations, such as higher levels of government providing revenues with restrictions on their use, or by a government's legislative branch requiring that funds raised in a certain way be put to a specific use. In most instances resources that are not restricted in their use are grouped into one fund. Although funds are independent accounting entities, transactions between funds are permitted and occur frequently.

Before we specify the nature of funds more precisely, we need to explain the accounting information contained in these funds. Since this information plays a critical role in financial analysis, we look at the organization of this information in some depth.

### Stocks, Flows, and the Accounting Equation

At a very basic level there are only two kinds of things that the accounting system records: *stocks* of resources and *flows* of resources. Stocks of resources are resource levels at one point in time (e.g., July 1, 1986). Flows of resources are increases or decreases in resources between two points in time (e.g., July 1, 1986, to June 30, 1987). These stocks and flows sometimes have different definitions, but we begin our discussion by treating the general case. To distinguish these generic definitions from the more specific ones we discuss later, the generic terms are written in CAPITAL letters. Although the generic definitions will be modified shortly, it is important to understand the basic concept initially. First we will consider stocks of resources.

As resources flow into a government, they are used to secure ASSETS, which in turn are used to produce goods and services. ASSETS are basically "resources owned or held by a government which have monetary value."[9] ASSETS are a stock of resources at a point in time. Examples of ASSETS (remember we are referring to the generic concept) include cash, marketable investments, resources owed to the government (also known as receivables), land, buildings, and equipment. As a simple illustration, a government collects taxes (resources) from its taxpayers and deposits the cash (ASSETS) in a bank account for the provision of goods and services in the future.

ASSETS are stocks of resources that the government *owns* at one point in time. A second type of stock, LIABILITIES, is what the government *owes* at a single point in time. LIABILITY is defined as a "debt or other legal obligation arising out of transactions in the past which must be liquidated, renewed, or refunded at some future date."[10] A government, for example, may purchase goods or services on credit. After the bill is due to be paid but before it is paid, the government has a LIABILITY known in this case as a "payable."

ASSETS and LIABILITIES are divided among the funds of governments. Each ASSET and LIABILITY belongs to a specific fund. Since every fund has certain specific ASSETS and LIABILITIES and they are not likely to be equal in value, fund accounting defines a third type of stock that represents the difference between a fund's ASSETS and its LIABILITIES. This difference is called the FUND BALANCE.

The definition of the three stocks—ASSETS, LIABILITIES, and FUND BALANCE—leads directly to the "accounting equation." The accounting equation is a relationship that holds true for every fund at every point in time and is specified as

$$\text{ASSETS} = \text{LIABILITIES} + \text{FUND BALANCE}$$

With the accounting equation, the fund structure is illustrated in Figure 2-1. Note that the ASSETS, LIABILITIES, and FUND BALANCES of the government are grouped into funds and that the accounting equation governs each fund. Note also that a FUND BALANCE does not equal *cash.* It would only be a coincidence if the value of the FUND BALANCE equaled the value of cash or, for that matter, of any asset.

Aside from stocks of resources, the accounting system records information on the flows of resources. We will return to the accounting equation after we define flows in a generic manner. Again, since flows are defined in different ways

---

[9] Municipal Finance Officers Association, *GAAFR,* Appendix B, p. 55.

[10] Ibid., Appendix B, p. 67.

| Fund A |
|---|
| ASSETS = |
| LIABILITIES + |
| FUND BALANCE |

| Fund B |
|---|
| ASSETS = |
| LIABILITIES + |
| FUND BALANCE |

| Fund C |
|---|
| ASSETS = |
| LIABILITIES + |
| FUND BALANCE |

| Fund D |
|---|
| ASSETS = |
| LIABILITIES + |
| FUND BALANCE |

Figure 2-1.   **THE FUND STRUCTURE OF A GOVERNMENT**

in fund accounting, the generic flow introduced here will be represented by CAPITAL letters.

In any fund accounting system, two kinds of flows are defined in a specific manner. INFLOWS are the flows of resources that increase ASSETS (decrease LIABILITIES) without increasing LIABILITIES (decreasing ASSETS). (For most fund accounting systems, INFLOWS defined in this way are called revenues, and these are discussed in more detail shortly.) If a government levies and collects taxes in cash and then deposits this cash in the bank, ASSETS have increased, LIABILITIES have not changed, and this would be considered an IN-FLOW.

OUTFLOWS are flows of resources that decrease ASSETS (increase LIA-BILITIES) without decreasing LIABILITIES (increasing ASSETS). (OUT-FLOWS will be defined shortly as expenditures or expenses in most fund account-ing systems.) An example would be a payment for salaries when they are due with a withdrawal of cash from the government's bank account.

When you combine the above definitions of INFLOWS and OUTFLOWS with the accounting equation, alternative definitions for the flows emerge. *An IN-FLOW is defined as an increase in the FUND BALANCE, while an OUTFLOW is a decrease in the FUND BALANCE.* These relatively simple definitions of stocks and flows and the accounting equation form the basis for the presentation and organization of most of the accounting data in each fund of a government. While the exact values of these variables depend on more precise definitions, a simple numerical example may clarify the general concepts.

Assume that a government at time 1 has $1,000 in cash in the bank and materials on hand (inventories) valued at $500. Also assume that the government has an outstanding obligation (an account payable) of $600 in the form of a bill owed to a supplier. From the accounting equation we can see that at time 1 ASSETS ($A_1$) are $1,500 (cash + inventories), LIABILITIES ($L_1$) are $600 (account payable), and therefore the FUND BALANCE ($FB_1$) is $900 ($1,500 − 600) because $A_1 = L_1 + FB_1$.

Let us further assume that during the period from time 1 to time 2 the government collects taxes of $400 in cash which it deposits in the bank, pays out $450 in cash from the bank for salaries, and pays off the account payable of $600 in full with cash from the bank. What are the flows over time? The INFLOWS $(I_{1,2})$ consist of the taxes collected ($400) and the OUTFLOWS $(O_{1,2})$ consist of the salary payment. The payment of the account payable is neither an OUTFLOW nor an INFLOW, since it changes both ASSETS and LIABILITIES simultaneously, leaving the FUND BALANCE unchanged. (An ASSET, *cash,* and a LIABILITY, *account payable,* both decrease by $600).

Now, what is the position of the government at time 2? Since the account payable was paid in full and no other obligations were incurred, there are no LIABILITIES remaining at time 2 $(L_2 = 0)$. ASSETS at time 2 $(A_2)$ are $850 because inventories remain at $500 and cash in the bank has decreased to $350 (due to the increase of $400 from collections and the decrease of $1,050 from paying salaries and the account payable.) The reader should verify that the FUND BALANCE at time 2 $(FB_2)$ must equal $850.

Thus the stocks of resources from one point in time to another are tied together by the INFLOWS and OUTFLOWS over the period between those two points in time. We will see in the next section how these stocks and flows are presented in a more-detailed fashion in a government's financial statements.

Up to this point we have described the generic stocks and flows in a fund accounting system. Across fund accounting systems and within them, however, the particular definitions of stocks and flows may vary from the generic definitions presented thus far. We turn next to an examination of these variations.

### The Basis of Accounting

More than the generic definitions of stocks and flows are needed to fully specify the stocks and flows used in particular fund accounting systems. For example, at what point should an accounting system treat taxes as an INFLOW: When the tax rate is set? When the tax bills are mailed out? When the taxes are due? Or when the taxes are actually paid? Fund accounting systems recognize these various events but treat only one as an INFLOW—the particular flow that changes the FUND BALANCE. Similar questions arise for OUTFLOWS and, moreover, for the way fund accounting systems record ASSETS and LIABILITIES.

The determination of when flows are treated as INFLOWS and OUTFLOWS and which stocks are recorded is accomplished by specifying a "basis of accounting." Although the issues of when to count flows and record stocks are sometimes treated separately, since they are so closely interconnected we consider them as one. There are three primary bases of accounting and one of the three, or a combination of two, is employed by every fund in governments.

The three primary bases of accounting for funds in governments are (1) *cash,* (2) *accrual for expenditures,* and (3) *accrual for expenses.* There are two distinguishing features of each basis of accounting. First, each basis has a particular way of determining when a flow is counted and the FUND BALANCE changes. Second, each basis varies in the extent to which it includes all ASSETS and LIABILITIES. To explain the bases we first examine flows and then stocks.

There are several stages that describe OUTFLOWS, when resources flow *out* of a government to acquire the goods and services used to produce outputs:

1. The first stage is usually a *budget authorization* and/or *appropriation.* This normally takes place at the beginning of the period during which the goods or services are to be acquired.
2. At a later point, an order is placed or a contract is signed for the goods or services. This may consist of a conventional order or, in the case of personnel, may be an explicit or implicit contract for services. At this point the government is committed to acquiring the good or service, providing that it is delivered satisfactorily by the supplier or the employee. When the organization is committed in this way, it has incurred an *obligation* or an *encumbrance.* These obligations or encumbrances may be recorded in the accounting system, although they are never the OUTFLOW that changes the FUND BALANCE.
3. When the goods or services are delivered, the government *acquires* them, receives a bill, and legally owes the supplier for these items. In the case of salaried personnel, this is the point when the employees' responsibilities under the contract have been fulfilled.
4. At some later point in time, usually after the delivery of goods and services or after the performance of services by the employee, the government *pays* the supplier or the individual for the goods or services.
5. Throughout the above discussion of resource transactions, no mention has been made of the dollar value of the good or service actually *used* by the government in a given period, not necessarily the same period when the resource is acquired. Many items are acquired and used in the same period. For instance, teachers' salaries for a given fiscal year would be an OUTFLOW that would indicate that services of the teachers were acquired and used. Other items, however, particularly supplies or long-lived assets such as buildings and equipment, may not be totally used in the period when acquired. This last stage, the period in which the assets are used, must be taken into account to fully explain the three bases of accounting.

These five stages may be used to define when an OUTFLOW is recorded by the three bases of accounting. Recall that in our scheme, an OUTFLOW changes the FUND BALANCE. For a *cash* system, the outflow occurs when cash is paid out by the organization, stage 4 in the above description. This is the point when the cash accounting system records a reduction in the fund balance.

In an *expenditure accrual* system, an outflow is recognized when an organization has acquired the good or service and has a legal obligation to pay for it, stage 3 in the above description. Under this system, when the outflow is recognized, a liability of the fund is created, such as an account payable or wage payable. This outflow is known as an *expenditure.* Note that this point may be different from stage 2, when the good or service is ordered (and an accounting obligation or encumbrance may be recorded), stage 4, when it is paid for, or stage 5, when it is used.

Since it is important to distinguish between an expenditure (stage 3) and when the good or service is paid for (i.e., stage 4 when cash changes hands), the latter flow is called a *disbursement.* If a government pays cash when a good or service is received, the expenditure and the disbursement are the same. (Stages 3 and 4 are simultaneous.) Similarly, expenditures and disbursements are identical in a cash system that does not generally record stages 2 and 3.

Finally, in an *expense accrual* system, the outflow is recognized when the good or service is used, stage 5 in the above description. *Expenses* thus reflect the use of assets rather than their acquisition, and although these are the same for many transactions (e.g., salaries) in governments, differences arise for certain assets such as prepaid items, buildings, equipment, and land.

To illustrate an expense accrual system, consider the purchase of a piece of equipment that will last for ten years. Assume that a government purchases a garbage truck for cash. Under an expenditure accrual (and cash) system, the outflow that changes the fund balance, in this case an expenditure, occurs when the truck is purchased. If the truck was purchased with payment promised in thirty days, the expenditure accrual system would record the outflow on the date of purchase and the cash system would record it when the bill was paid. But under an expense accrual system, the outflow would be recorded when the truck is used, presumably over its ten-year life. In this case, when the truck is purchased it is *capitalized,* that is, recorded as an asset and not as an expense (outflow). The truck purchase decreases one asset (cash) and increases another (truck) by the same amount, leaving the fund balance unchanged. Thus, at the point of purchase or payment an outflow has not occurred under the expense accrual system.

As the truck is being used, an expense accrual system decreases the truck's value to reflect this use. The decrease in value is known as *depreciation* and represents the outflow of resources under an expense accrual system. Depreciation reduces the value of the asset recorded in the accounting system (sometimes called its ''book value'' because it is based on the value carried on the books rather than its market value or replacement cost) and reduces the fund balance accordingly. Depreciation is an outflow and an expense, but it is not a disbursement because no cash is paid out at the time the depreciation is recorded. Depreciation is simply a way to allocate the value of a long-lived asset over its useful life. Under a cash or expenditure accrual system, there is no depreciation because the truck was not capitalized initially.

To summarize, OUTFLOWS occur when cash payment is made in a cash system, when the asset is acquired in an expenditure accrual system, and when the asset is used in an expense system.

An INFLOW to a government can also occur at different points:

1. When resources such as taxes or a grant are *owed* to the government. On this date the organization has a valid claim on the resources.
2. When the government actually *receives* the resource, usually as cash, which may or may not be different from the date of the valid claim.

3.  When the government actually *uses* resources that were received well in advance of their specified use. Some prepayments to government may require certain conditions be fulfilled before they are legally available for use.

*Revenues* are INFLOWS that increase the organization's fund balance. Under a cash system, inflows are recorded as revenues when they are received as cash. Under an expense accrual system, inflows are recorded as revenues when they are earned and legally owed to the organization, not necessarily when they are received in cash. The term *receipts* is used to designate the inflow of cash which may not occur at the same time as the revenue is recorded.

Under an expenditure accrual system, inflows are supposed to be recorded as revenues when they are "available and measurable." For example, suppose sales taxes are due from merchants on the fifteenth of the month but collections take until the twenty-fifth. Since the exact amount of the sales tax due is not known, as is the case for the property tax, the amount of the sales tax is not measurable and thus may not be counted as a revenue until it is received in cash.[11] Unfortunately, there is considerable ambiguity over the revenue definition in an expenditure system, and this leads to a system in which some revenues are accrued (recorded when legally owed) and others are counted only when received in cash. This hybrid system is known as the *modified accrual system.*

For our purposes here, assume that in an expenditure accrual system, all revenues and expenditures (inflows and outflows that change the fund balance) are recorded on an accrual basis, and that in a modified accrual system, expenditures are accrued, but some inflows may be recorded on an accrual basis while others are counted on a cash basis. Since there is some ambiguity on this point, it is important to determine how a specific government defines its basis of accounting for each fund. Most governments will put a *note* in their financial statements that explains the basis of accounting and other specific features of the government's accounting system and financial statements. As a general rule, the notes to the financial statements should always be consulted when financial information is used in analysis.

Throughout this discussion of the bases of accounting we have emphasized the timing of the flows, and when inflows and outflows are recorded under different bases. Generally speaking, each of the bases of accounting includes certain stocks and flows in the accounting system and excludes others. In a "pure" cash system, there is only one asset, cash or near-cash items such as certificates of deposit. No liabilities are recorded, and therefore cash equals the fund balance. By now the reader should see that a cash accounting system is similar to record keeping in a checkbook.

In an expense accrual system, all assets and liabilities normally recorded in a conventional "for-profit" accounting system are included: current assets and liabilities, and long-term assets and liabilities. *Current assets* are assets that are nor-

---

[11] Ibid., pp. 14–15.

mally converted to cash within one year and include ''cash, temporary investments, and taxes receivable which will be collected within one year.''[12] *Current liabilities* are accounts payable, wages payable, notes payable, and other liabilities that are expected to be paid off within one year. *Long-term assets* include land, buildings, and equipment, while *long-term liabilities* normally include debt and lease obligations that extend beyond one year.

In an expenditure accrual system, usually only certain current assets and liabilities are recorded. Assets such as prepaid items, land, building, and equipment are not counted as assets within a fund. Long-term liabilities such as long-term debt are also not carried as liabilities. In a modified accrual system, long-term assets and long-term liabilities are similarly excluded. Also, in a modified accrual system, even fewer items are counted as current assets, since those revenues recorded on a cash basis do not have a corresponding receivable associated with them.

To illustrate how different bases of accounting differ in their treatment of both flows and stocks, consider government borrowing. When the proceeds from a bond or other forms of long term borrowing are received, a government using a cash system would increase its fund balance by the amount of the proceeds. The long-term liability created by the borrowing, the principal of the debt, would not be recorded in a cash system. Bond obligations would be recorded outside of the fund accounting system. In an expense system, the receipt of the bond proceeds does not increase the fund balance, since the long-term liability, long-term bonds payable, is recorded. Thus bond proceeds are a receipt but not a revenue in an expense accrual system, and long-term liabilities are recorded within the accounting system. Long-term liabilities, however, are generally not included in an expenditure accrual system (or modified accrual system), so that proceeds from the bonds are treated as inflows and increase the fund balance. Sometimes, however, bond proceeds are distinguished from revenues and called *other sources of financing,* but they are treated the same way as revenues.

Table 2-1 summarizes the major distinctions we have drawn among the bases of accounting. It is worth repeating that these definitions are likely to be altered to some degree in particular funds, and the reader is urged to examine the precise definition of the basis of accounting for each fund used by the government under analysis. Certain types of funds are more likely to use one basis of accounting rather than another.

### Fund Accounting Revisited

Thus far we have introduced the notion of funds, defined stocks and flows, presented the accounting equation, and explained alternative bases of accounting. We will now fill in more of the details on the funds of governments.

---

[12] Ibid., Appendix B, p. 60.

TABLE 2-1    **Usual Definitions of Flows and Stocks Under Different Bases of Accounting**

| | | BASIS OF ACCOUNTING | | |
| --- | --- | --- | --- | --- |
| | Cash | Modified Accrual | Accrual Expenditures | Accrual Expense |
| OUTFLOWS | When good or service (input) is paid for with cash | When good or service (input) is acquired and legal obligation to pay incurred | When good or service (input) is acquired and legal obligation to pay incurred | When good or service (input) is used to produce output |
| INFLOWS | When resources are received in cash | When resources are measurable and available; accrual for more predictable inflows, cash for others | When resources are legally owed to the organization | When resources are earned and legally owed to the organization |
| ASSETS | Only cash | Current assets; only cash when inflows recorded on a cash basis | Current assets | Current assets and long-term assets |
| LIABILI-TIES | None | Current liabilities | Current liabilities | Current liabilities and long-term liabilities |

As discussed earlier, fund accounting is the basic structure of accounting in governments. A more complete definition of *fund* follows:

> A fund is defined as a fiscal and accounting entity with a self-balancing set of accounts recording cash and other financial resources, together with all related liabilities and residual equities or balances, and changes therein, which are segregated for the purpose of carrying on specific activities or attaining certain objectives in accordance with special regulations, restrictions, or limitations.[13]

Thus funds are defined by their purposes and the specific assets (and associated liabilities and fund balance) assigned to them. Since a government's assets may be divided in many different ways, what will concern us here is *how* they are separated into different funds and *why*.

Every government designs its fund structure to meet its specific needs. While it is important to become familiar with the details of the funds in the particular government under study, we present here the commonalities among government fund structures.

---

[13] National Council on Governmental Accounting, *Statement 1,* reprinted in Municipal Finance Officers Association, *GAAFR,* Appendix A, pp. 5–6.

The accepted fund structure for governments is set forth in *Statement 1* and further explained in *GAAFR*.[14] There are three broad categories of funds—governmental funds, proprietary funds, and fiduciary funds—and there are specific types of funds in each broad category.

*Governmental funds* typically include most of the ordinary or routine activities of a government. They are primarily designed to keep track of the revenues and expenditures related to these activities—what comes in and what is spent by the government in the conduct of these activities. As a result, governmental funds usually employ either an accrual expenditure or a modified accrual basis of accounting. Governmental funds are sometimes referred to as *expenditure* funds.

*Proprietary funds* are designed to account for those specific governmental activities for which a profit orientation is appropriate. This does not mean that a profit should be realized but only that the measurement of profit is possible and desirable. (In fact, many activities that are run on a "break-even" basis or with operating subsidies are still set up as proprietary funds.) Activities set up as proprietary funds often involve an exchange of resources for a product or service similar to a commercial venture. The accrual expense basis of accounting, the same one used by for-profit organizations, is accepted practice in proprietary funds. Proprietary funds are also referred to as *self-sustaining, nonexpendable,* or *commercial-type, funds.*

*Fiduciary funds* are established when the government must hold assets for individuals (such as employees in a pension fund) or for other organizations (as when a county collects sales tax for a city). Fiduciary funds are set up either as governmental or proprietary funds, depending on their specific purpose.

Within these three broad categories, the following eight types of funds are recommended:

A. Governmental Funds
1. *The General Fund*—to account for all financial resources except those required to be accounted for in another fund.
2. *Special Revenue Funds*—to account for the proceeds of specific revenue sources (other than special assessments, expendable trusts, or for major capital projects) that are legally restricted to expenditure for specified purposes.
3. *Capital Projects Funds*—to account for financial resources to be used for the acquisition or construction of major capital facilities (other than those financed by proprietary funds, special assessment funds, and trust funds).
4. *Debt Service Funds*—to account for the accumulation of resources for, and the payment of, general long-term debt principal and interest.
5. *Special Assessment Funds*—to account for the financing of public improvements or services deemed to benefit the properties against which special assessments are levied.

---

[14] Ibid., Appendix A, pp. 6–9, and Chap. 2.

B.  Proprietary Funds
    1.  *Enterprise Funds*—to account for operations (a) that are financed and operated in a manner similar to private business enterprises—where the intent of the governing body is that the costs (expenses, including depreciation) of providing goods or services to the general public on a continuing basis be financed or recovered primarily through user charges; or (b) where the governing body has decided that periodic determination of revenues earned, expenses incurred and/or net income is appropriate for capital maintenance, public policy, management control, accountability, or other purposes.
    2.  *Internal Service Funds*—to account for the financing of goods or services provided by one department or agency to other departments or agencies of the government unit, or to other government units, on a cost-reimbursement basis.

C.  Fiduciary Funds
    1.  *Trust and Agency Funds*—to account for assets held by a government unit in a trustee capacity or as an agent for individuals, private organizations, other governmental units, and/or funds. These include (a) Expendable Trust Funds, (b) Nonexpendable Trust Funds, (c) Pension Trust Funds, and (d) Agency Funds.[15]

The number of funds in any single governmental unit may vary considerably. Small towns may use only a few of the above mentioned funds, whereas states and larger cities may break these funds down further into an even larger set. Although the *general fund* is defined in a residual manner to handle resources not restricted to other uses and funds, this fund is central in governments. For the most part, the general fund contains the resources that are used for the operational activities of the government.

Note that most long-term assets and liabilities are not accounted for within the fund structure. The only exceptions are those long-term assets and liabilities associated with enterprise, internal service, and certain trust funds. Although not part of a fund subject to the accounting equation, it is still recommended that governments keep a record of their long-term assets and liabilities. Governments are supposed to set up special listings, called *account groups,* that document long-term assets and liabilities (not included in proprietary funds) in the general fixed asset account group and general long-term debt account, respectively. Unfortunately, however, since these account groups are outside the fund structure and are not governed by the accounting equation, the quality of the data in the account groups is likely to be lower than that of the fund accounting system.

It is important to stress that a breakdown of activities by funds is only one of several ways in which a government can be divided for analysis or management. Activities may also be examined, for example, by departments or programs. Since fund accounting has been developed primarily for control purposes, funds in governments seldom exactly parallel organizational units or programs. More

---

[15] Ibid., Appendix A, p. 7.

often funds cross organizational or program lines or contain many units or programs depending on the restrictions or lack of restrictions placed on the assets used in programs or units. As a result, it is sometimes necessary to adjust and supplement accounting data from a fund structure for use in financial analysis.

Finally, before financial statements are discussed, we need to introduce several additional definitions. As we have seen, governments are divided, for accounting purposes, into separate funds. These funds may be further divided into *accounts*. Examples of accounts discussed thus far include revenue, expenditure, asset, liability, and fund balance. Accounts within funds may be further subdivided according to *account classifications*. The fund for general operations in a public school district may have the expenditure account divided into administration, instruction, transportation, and so forth, and the revenue account divided into revenues from local, intermediate, state, and federal sources. The expenditure account classifications are often subdivided by *objects of expenditure*. Objects of expenditure include such items as salaries, supplies, and travel. When all the expenditure account classifications are itemized by the same objects of expenditure, a certain degree of aggregation is possible. Finally, objects of expenditure are composed of individual *line items*. These line items usually specify the actual position in the case of personnel objects or the actual type of article or service for nonpersonnel items.

### The Use of a Continuing Example

Throughout the remainder of the book, we will be examining a fictitious city to illustrate many of the concepts discussed in each chapter. As a basis for this example, we need to know a few facts about the accounting system of this fictitious city, Dyer Straits.

The city of Dyer Straits uses five funds. In addition to a general fund, there is a debt service fund that is used to keep track of principal and interest payments for general obligation debt, a capital projects fund where capital projects under way are accounted for, and two enterprise funds. These two enterprise funds are used for the water and sewage system that is accounted for in the water and sewer fund, and the system of municipal parking lots and garages that is accounted for in the municipal parking fund. Dyer Straits also utilizes two account groups that are basically lists of assets or liabilities that are separate from the fund structure. One account group, the fixed assets account group, lists long-lived assets, and the other, the general obligation debt account group, lists the principal outstanding on general obligation debt.

Dyer Straits uses an accrual system for revenues and *expenses* for the two enterprise funds, and an accrual system for revenues and *expenditures* for the general fund, debt service fund, and capital projects fund. The financial statements for Dyer Straits are presented in the next section.

## III. FINANCIAL STATEMENTS
## FOR GOVERNMENTS

The basic structure and content of a government accounting system were described in the preceding section. How does a user discover what is in the accounting system? The answer is, by reading and understanding financial statements and reports, the topic of this section.

The Municipal Finance Officers Association (now the Government Finance Officers Association) broadly defines *financial reporting* as "the total process of communicating information concerning the financial condition and financial activities of an entity."[16] Governments produce financial reports to serve the needs of the different users who are concerned about the financial health of the government. As we discuss in this section, financial statements communicate precise accounting information on a fund or group of funds, and these statements constitute a significant part of financial reports. And as we will see throughout this book, the information contained in financial reports, including financial statements, is an essential component of the data needed to analyze a government's financial health.

This section focuses on the financial reports of governments prepared for external use. We begin this section with a brief overview of the annual financial report prepared by governments. The second part of this section presents the financial statements for governmental funds, those that commonly use expenditure accrual or modified accrual accounting. The financial statements for proprietary funds, those that employ expense accrual accounting, are examined in the third and final part of this section.

### Annual Financial Reports

The financial reports for governments are generally designed to demonstrate compliance with the many requirements that the government faces in its gathering and use of resources. Although each government may prepare a unique set of financial reports, virtually all governments prepare an annual financial report that covers a fiscal year.

The National Council on Governmental Accounting (NCGA) in *Statement 1* recommends that the annual financial reports of governments be presented in three sections.[17] The introductory section contains general information on the government, such as a transmittal letter from the chief financial officer, organizational charts, staff directories, and a statement by the auditor if one is required or

---

[16] Municipal Finance Officers Association, *GAAFR,* p. 22.

[17] National Council on Governmental Accounting, *Statement 1,* reprinted in Municipal Finance Officers Association, *GAAFR,* Appendix A, pp. 19–25.

available. The second section contains the financial statements, and these are discussed below.

The third section is labeled the statistical section and contains historical accounting data and nonaccounting data covering such areas as economics and demographics that are useful in financial analysis. Although the contents of this section vary considerably from government to government, the NCGA, in *Statement 1* recommends that the following tables be included in the statistical section:

1. General Governmental Expenditures by Function—Last Ten Fiscal Years
2. General Revenues by Source—Last Ten Fiscal Years
3. Property Tax Levies and Collections—Last Ten Fiscal Years
4. Assessed and Estimated Actual Value of Taxable Property—Last Ten Fiscal Years
5. Property Tax Rates—All Overlapping Governments—Last Ten Fiscal Years
6. Special Assessment Collections—Last Ten Fiscal Years
7. Ratio of Net General Bonded Debt to Assessed Value and Net Bonded Debt Per Capita—Last Ten Fiscal Years
8. Computation of Legal Debt Margin
9. Computation of Overlapping Debt
10. Ratio of Annual Debt Service for General Bonded Debt to Total General Expenditures—Last Ten Fiscal Years
11. Revenue Bond Coverage—Last Ten Fiscal Years
12. Demographic Statistics
13. Property Value, Construction, and Bank Deposits—Last Ten Fiscal Years
14. Principal Taxpayers
15. Miscellaneous Statistics[18]

The use of these measures and data is examined in Chapters 4 through 10.

### Financial Statements for Governmental Funds

Certain financial statements are commonly produced for governmental funds, and most of these are recommended for inclusion in the financial report by the NCGA. In this section we examine four of the most common types of statements. The first three are required by the NCGA for inclusion in annual financial reports: balance sheets, statements of revenues and expenditures, and statements of changes in the fund balance. The fourth, statements of receipts and disbursements, is not required by the NCGA but is often found in the financial statements of governments.

At the end of the preceding section we introduced the city of Dyer Straits by describing its fund structure and bases of accounting. In this section and the next we illustrate the financial statements with examples from Dyer Straits.

---

[18] Ibid., Appendix A, p. 24.

**Balance Sheets.** As discussed earlier, one basic purpose of accounting is to report on the stock of resources of a government. The primary document in this area is the *balance sheet*. The balance sheet lists the assets, liabilities, and fund balances at any single point in time for an individual fund or group of funds. These stocks are organized into assets (usually presented on one side of the balance sheet), and liabilities and fund balances (usually presented on the other side of the balance sheet). On a balance sheet, assets always equal liabilities plus fund balance, thus satisfying the accounting equation.

For governments, balance sheets are usually presented in the financial reports for all funds (governmental, proprietary, and fiduciary) for the beginning and end of the fiscal year, and often the balance sheets for all funds are presented in a single combined statement. A *combined balance sheet* contains the balance sheets of every individual fund and account group and sometimes displays a total of each account—asset, liability, and fund balance—for the organization as a whole.

A combined balance sheet for the five funds and two account groups of Dyer Straits as of January 1, 1983, is shown in Table 2-2. The data are presented together for the five funds and two account groups, although a balance sheet for each fund and a listing for each account group could be displayed separately. Table 2-2 includes the two proprietary funds, since a combined balance sheet typically includes all funds. We will discuss these briefly here and provide further information when we present the statements of proprietary funds in the next section.

Several items on the combined balance sheet should be highlighted. First, each fund has a somewhat different set of assets and liabilities. In particular, fixed assets and long-term debt are not accounted for in the general, debt service, and capital projects funds, but they are included in the two enterprise funds. Second, there are interfund claims and obligations among the funds. These arise from interfund transfers made during the course of government operations and will be discussed below. Third, the combined balance sheet shows that cash is listed under several different assets depending on the way in which the cash is held (on hand, demand deposit, or time deposit) or the intended purpose for the cash (for payment of bond interest and principal that is due).

The combined balance sheet for Dyer Straits (Table 2-2) has an account listed between liabilities and fund balance, entitled *reserves,* that we have not yet considered. Reserves are those portions of the fund balance that are segregated for a specific future use and not available for further expenditure. Two common examples of reserves are reserve for encumbrances and reserve for inventories. The *reserve for encumbrances* represents the portion of the fund balance that is set aside to meet certain types of financial obligations not yet fulfilled. If the government has encumbered funds for certain items that have been ordered but not yet delivered, then the reserve shows that these orders are outstanding. In a fund using expenditure accrual accounting, when these items are delivered the organization incurs a liability (accounts payable) and the reserved portion of the fund balance is

TABLE 2-2  City of Dyer Straits, Combined Balance Sheet—All Funds and Account Groups, January 1, 1983 (All Figures in Thousands of Dollars)

| | GENERAL FUND | DEBT SERVICE FUND | CAPITAL PROJECTS FUND | WATER AND SEWER FUND | MUNICIPAL PARKING FUND | FIXED ASSETS ACCOUNT GROUP | GENERAL OBLIGATION DEBT ACCOUNT GROUP |
|---|---|---|---|---|---|---|---|
| *Assets:* | | | | | | | |
| Cash on hand | $14 | | $26 | $78 | $63 | | |
| Cash in demand deposits | 107 | $69 | 230 | 417 | 138 | | |
| Cash in time deposits | 118 | | 4,360 | 886 | 259 | | |
| Cash for bond interest and matured bonds | | 82 | | 22 | 7 | | |
| Property taxes receivable | 714 | | | | | | |
| Sales taxes receivable | 42 | | | | | | |
| Accounts receivable | 29 | | | 123 | 16 | | |
| State aid receivable | 58 | | | | | | |
| Federal aid receivable | 28 | | | | | | |
| Due from other funds | 38 | 15 | 120 | 4 | 31 | | |
| Other assets | 40 | | 6 | | | | |
| Inventories: | | | | | | | |
| Materials | | | | 17 | 4 | | |
| Equipment (net of depreciation) | | | | 183 | 26 | | |
| Land | | | | 768 | 377 | $8,150 | |
| Buildings (net of depreciation for enterprise funds) | | | | 4,219 | 2,762 | 32,595 | |
| Total Assets | $1,188 | $166 | $4,742 | $6,717 | $3,683 | | |

*Liabilities, Reserves, and Fund Balances or Retained Earnings*:

| | | | | | | |
|---|---:|---:|---:|---:|---:|---:|
| Liabilities: | | | | | | |
| Vouchers payable | $283 | | $387 | $77 | $16 | |
| Bond interest and matured bonds payable | | $82 | | | | |
| Salaries payable | 238 | | 103 | 22 | 7 | |
| Due to other funds | 31 | | 4 | 82 | 27 | |
| Bond anticipation notes payable | | | | 161 | 12 | |
| Capital notes payable | | | 2,936 | 1,838 | 1,331 | |
| General obligation bonds payable | | | 200 | 175 | 100 | |
| Revenue bonds payable | | | | 2,585 | 1,653 | $6,695 |
| Total Liabilities | $552 | $82 | $3,630 | $4,940 | $3,146 | |
| Reserves: | | | | | | |
| Reserve for encumbrances | 277 | | 193 | | | |
| Total Reserves | 227 | | 193 | | | |
| Fund Balances | 409 | 84 | 919 | | | |
| Retained Earnings | | | | 1,777 | 537 | |
| Total Liabilities, Reserves, and Fund Balances or Retained Earnings | $1,188 | $166 | $4,742 | $6,717 | $3,683 | |

decreased accordingly. The *reserve for inventories* represents the amount of the fund balance that is reflected in inventory. Table 2-2 indicates that the city of Dyer Straits uses only one reserve account: a reserve for encumbrances. This discloses the quantity of goods and services that have been ordered but not yet delivered.

Finally, the enterprise or proprietary funds use retained earnings to describe the difference between assets and liabilities, while the governmental funds use a fund balance. The use of the two accounts is similar when viewed from the accounting equation perspective; however, the distinction is helpful because the governmental funds use expenditure accounting while the proprietary funds use expense accounting. Moreover, although not shown on the Dyer Straits balance sheets, there may be *contributed capital* in the proprietary fund that is also part of the difference between assets and liabilities along with retained earnings.

When all the balance sheets are presented in a combined form, the interfund claims and obligations are maintained as shown in Table 2-2. Interfund claims are usually represented by an asset, *due from other funds,* and interfund obligations are represented by a liability, *due to other funds.* These claims and obligations are detailed in Table 2-3 This table shows, for example, that the $38,000 owed to the general fund consists of a $26,000 claim against the water and sewer fund and a $12,000 claim against the municipal parking fund.

If an asset of one fund is a liability of another fund, then total assets and liabilities of the organization in a combined statement include both, and this results in a somewhat distorted picture of the organization as a whole. When a balance sheet is presented for the organization as a whole without interfund claims and obligations (in fact, without any fund structure visible at all), it is called a *con-*

TABLE 2-3    **Interfund Claims and Obligations, City of Dyer Straits, January 1, 1983 (All Figures in Thousands of Dollars)**

|  | DUE FROM | | | | | |
|  | General Fund | Debt Service Fund | Capital Projects Fund | Water and Sewer Fund | Municipal Parking Fund | Total |
|---|---|---|---|---|---|---|
| *DUE TO* | | | | | | |
| General fund | — | — | — | $26 | $12 | $38 |
| Debt service fund | $15 | — | — | — | — | 15 |
| Capital projects fund | — | — | — | 120 | — | 120 |
| Water and sewer fund | — | — | $4 | — | — | 4 |
| Municipal parking fund | 16 | — | — | 15 | — | 31 |
| Total | $31 | — | $4 | $161 | $12 | $208 |

*solidated balance sheet.* In a consolidated balance sheet the interfund claims and obligations are "netted out," that is, dropped from the balance sheets because they cancel out when funds are added up. When this is done, *total* assets and liabilities on the consolidated balance sheet more nearly reflect the stock of resources of the organization as a whole rather than each separate fund. In actual practice, consolidated balance sheets are not commonly presented for governments.

**Statements of Revenues and Expenditures.**    Another purpose of the financial report is to provide information on the flows, as well as the stocks, of resources. The *statements of revenues, estimated and actual,* and *expenditures, authorized and actual,* are the principal statements to accomplish this task for governmental funds. The annual report may contain a combined statement for all governmental funds in addition to separate statements for each fund that show more detail than the combined statement.

An example of a statement of revenues, estimated and actual, is shown in Table 2-4 for Dyer Straits for 1983. Recall that the funds listed on this statement use an accrual basis of accounting for revenues (and expenditures). That is, the revenues are recorded when they are legally owed to Dyer Straits. The statement shows the sources of revenues for each fund. Most of the revenues of the general fund are from taxes and intergovernmental transfers, almost all the revenue of the debt service fund is a transfer from the general fund, and the capital projects fund derives the bulk of its revenue through the sale of bonds. Although the interfund transfers and proceeds from bonds are listed as revenues in Table 2-4, since these items differ from revenues like property taxes that come from outside the government and do not have to be paid back, they could be listed as *other sources of financing.* Under this basis of accounting, these other sources of financing do, however, increase the fund balance in the same way that revenues increase the fund balance.

The statement of revenues, estimated and actual, shown in Table 2-4 provides information for two important comparisons. First, the beginning-of-year revenue estimates are presented along with the end-of-year actual revenues. By comparing estimated and actual revenues we can see how well the government forecasts revenues. For example, Dyer Straits' 1983 property tax revenues fell below the estimated revenues by $121,000, or 2.6 percent. Second, the actual revenues from the prior year are presented and can be compared with the revenues from the most current year to determine revenue changes and trends. For Dyer Straits, all sources of revenue in the general fund in 1983 increased compared with 1982. As we will see in Chapter 4, the statement of revenues, estimated and actual, provides an essential source of information for revenue analysis.

A statement of expenditures may show authorized expenditures, actual expenditures, and encumbrances, and the difference between authorizations on the one hand and actual expenditures plus encumbrances on the other. This difference is called the *unencumbered balance.*

An example of a statement of expenditures, authorized and actual, appears

TABLE 2-4    **City of Dyer Straits, Statement of Revenues, Estimated and Actual, General Fund, Debt Service Fund, and Capital Projects Fund, January 1, 1983 to December 31, 1983 (All Figures in Thousands of Dollars)**

| | 1983 | | | 1982 |
|---|---|---|---|---|
| | Estimated Revenues | Actual Revenues | Over (Under) Estimate | Actual Revenues |
| *General Fund:* | | | | |
| Property taxes | $4,642 | $4,521 | $(121) | $4,077 |
| Sales taxes | 1,374 | 1,312 | (62) | 1,235 |
| Nontax local revenues | 1,032* | 994* | (38) | 962 |
| State aid | 1,640 | 1,667 | 27 | 1,523 |
| Federal aid | 1,021 | 1,033 | 12 | 869 |
| Total | $9,709 | $9,527 | $(182) | $8,666 |
| *Debt Service Fund:* | | | | |
| Transfer from general fund | $1,080 | $1,091 | $10 | $1,090 |
| Interest on investments | 20 | 20 | | |
| Total | $1,100 | $1,111 | $10 | $1,090 |
| *Capital Projects Fund:* | | | | |
| Proceeds from general obligation bonds | $800 | $797.8 | $(2.2) | $663.5 |
| Interest on investments | 175 | 192 | 17 | 206 |
| Transfer from water and sewer fund | 108 | 120 | 12 | 83 |
| Total | $1,083 | $1,109.8 | $26.8 | $952.5 |

*Includes interest on investments and transfers from water and sewer fund ($80) and from municipal parking fund ($60).

in Table 2–5 for the general, debt service, and capital projects funds for Dyer Straits in 1983. This statement breaks down the general fund expenditures by department and shows budget figures, encumbrances, unencumbered balances and actual expenditures for the current year, and actual expenditures for the prior year. Note that for Dyer Straits most departments exceeded their budget authorizations. In fact, for the general fund as a whole, actual expenditures plus encumbrances exceeded the budgeted figures by $329,000, or 3.4 percent of the total budget.

The expenditures for the debt service fund are relatively straightforward, since the payment of principal on long-term general obligation debt and interest on long- and short-term general obligation debt are the only expenditures. The expenditures accounted for in the capital projects fund are grouped by the particular

TABLE 2-5   City of Dyer Straits, Statement of Expenditures, Authorized and Actual, General Fund, Debt Service Fund, and Capital Projects Fund, January 1, 1983 to December 31, 1983 (All Figures in Thousands of Dollars)

| | 1983 | | | | 1982 |
|---|---|---|---|---|---|
| | Budget Authorizations | Actual Expenditures | Encumbrances | Unencumbered Balance | Actual Expendi- tures |
| *General Fund:* | | | | | |
| Police | $1,650* | $1,691* | $37 | $(78) | $1,474 |
| Fire | 1,600 | 1,603 | 49 | (52) | 1,395 |
| Public works | 900 | 895 | 32 | (27) | 772 |
| Judicial and correc- tions | 430 | 442 | 15 | (27) | 404 |
| Recreation and cul- tural | 550 | 541 | 36 | (27) | 491 |
| Social services | 550 | 560 | 14 | (24) | 474 |
| Health | 69 | 49 | 0 | 20 | 53 |
| Administration | 775 | 855 | 7 | (87) | 746 |
| Fringe benefits | 1,800 | 1,829 | 0 | (29) | 1,605 |
| Engineering | 230 | 226 | 15 | (11) | 193 |
| Transfer to debt service | 1,080 | 1,091 | 0 | (11) | 1,090 |
| Other expenditures | 75 | 49 | 2 | 24 | 79 |
| Total | $9,709 | $9,831 | $207 | $(329) | $8,776 |
| *Debt Service Fund:* | | | | | |
| Principal | $545 | $545 | $0 | $0 | $552 |
| Interest | 535 | 546 | 0 | (11) | 538 |
| Total | $1,080 | $1,091 | $0 | $(11) | $1,090 |
| *Capital Projects Fund:* | | | | | |
| Project expendi- tures: | | | | | |
| Allan Bridge | | | | | |
| Salaries | $900 | $780 | $72 | $48 | $625 |
| Materials, sup- plies | 400 | 309 | 59 | 32 | 227 |
| Bus Terminal | | | | | |
| Payment to con- tractor | 550 | 435 | 52 | 63 | 0 |
| Transfer to water and sewer fund | 108 | 80 | 10 | 18 | 64 |
| Total | $1,958 | $1,604 | $193 | $161 | $916 |

*Includes transfer to municipal parking fund of $120.

project for which the expenditures are made. Taking capital project fund revenues (Table 2-4) and expenditures (Table 2-5) together, we can see that the proceeds from long-term debt are being used to acquire fixed, or long-term, assets.

Under an expenditure accrual system, the fund accounting treatment of government debt differs between short-term and long-term debt. Governments sometimes acquire short-term debt prior to the issuance of long-term debt. For example, the balance sheet in Table 2–2 shows that the capital projects fund has short-term debt outstanding in the form of bond anticipation notes at the beginning of 1983 (bond anticipation notes payable of $2,936,000). Basically, when the long-term debt is issued, part or all of the proceeds are used to pay off the short-term debt acquired earlier in anticipation of long-term borrowing. Note, however, that the short-term debt outstanding is treated as a liability of a fund that uses expenditure accounting in contrast to the treatment of long-term debt where no liability is established. Since a liability is established when the short-term debt is issued, the proceeds from the short-term debt are not treated as a revenue, and therefore the payment of the principal on this short-term debt is not treated as an expenditure. That is why the receipt of the proceeds and the payment of principal on short-term debt do not appear in Tables 2–4 and 2–5. As we will see, however, the cash flows that result from the issuance and payment of short-term debt do appear on the statement of cash receipts and disbursements, to be discussed shortly. Finally, note that the interest on short-term debt is treated as an expenditure of the debt service fund.

It should also be noted that the format of the expenditure and revenue statements may vary considerably among different governments. For example, some governments display their expenditures by objects of expenditures instead of, or in addition to, the breakdown by functional area. Table 2–6 shows a state-

TABLE 2-6  **City of Dyer Straits, Statement of Expenditures, Authorized and Actual, General Fund, January 1, 1983 to December 31, 1983 (All Figures in Thousands of Dollars)**

|  | 1983 | | | | 1982 |
|---|---|---|---|---|---|
|  | Budget Authorizations | Actual Expenditures | Encumbrances | Unencumbered Balance | Actual Expenditures |
| *Objects of Expenditure:* | | | | | |
| Salaries | $5,291 | $5,447 | $0 | $(156) | $4,724 |
| Materials and supplies | 1,433 | 1,344 | 207 | (118) | 1,252 |
| Transfer to debt service fund | 1,080 | 1,091 | 0 | (11) | 1,090 |
| Transfer to municipal parking fund | 105 | 120 | 0 | (15) | 105 |
| Fringe benefits | 1,800 | 1,829 | 0 | (29) | 1,605 |
| Total | $9,709 | $9,831 | $207 | $(329) | $8,776 |

ment of expenditures, authorized and actual, for Dyer Straits' general fund for 1983 by object of expenditure. The expenditure statements found in annual financial reports provide important information for financial analysis. Expenditure data are utilized in Chapter 5 where expenditures are analyzed.

**Statements of Changes in Fund Balance.**  One statement that relates data on both flows and stocks of resources is the *statement of changes in fund balance.* This statement indicates beginning-of-period and end-of-period fund balances in addition to a summary of the changes in the fund balance over the period. The fund balance changes as a result of a difference between revenues and expenditures, changes in reserves established before the beginning of the period or during the period, and accounting corrections made to the fund balance. Note that if certain inflows such as proceeds from bonds are treated as other sources of financing (and not included in revenues), these would change still the fund balance in the same manner as revenues.

In section II, revenues and expenditures were defined in terms of their effect on the fund balance. Since revenues increase the fund balance and expenditures decrease the fund balance, the difference between revenues and expenditures is translated directly to a change in the fund balance. Since reserves are actually segregated portions of the fund balance, changes in reserves are also reflected in the changes in fund balance statement. Also, accounting changes from prior periods are occasionally reflected in the changes in fund balance statement.

A changes in fund balance statement is usually shown for all funds except proprietary funds. A changes in fund balance statement for the three governmental funds of Dyer Straits is shown in Table 2-7. The format for this particular statement shows budgeted and actual figures, although the changes in fund balances statement for some governments may only contain actual figures. Note that the actual figures on the statement of changes in fund balance for Dyer Straits are drawn from the beginning-of-period balance sheet (Table 2-2), the statement of revenues (Table 2-4), and the statement of expenditures (Table 2-5).

The purpose of the changes in fund balances statement is to derive the end-of-period fund balance. This is accomplished most directly when there are no reserves, as in the Dyer Straits' debt service fund. Here, the change in the fund balance is determined by adding the difference between actual revenues and expenditures ($1,111,000 – $1,091,000) to the beginning fund balance. For the debt service fund, revenues exceeded expenditures by $20,000, and therefore the fund balance increased by $20,000 over the period (from $84,000 to $104,000).

The existence of reserve funds makes the calculation of the ending fund balance more complicated. Since reserves are actually a segregated portion of the fund balance, changes in reserves also affect the change in fund balance. Only when the total amount of the reserve does not change, as in the capital projects fund, is the change in fund balance derived from the difference between revenues and expenditures ($1,109,800 – $1,604,000). When the beginning-of-period and end-of-period reserves are different, the differences in reserves changes the fund

TABLE 2-7   City of Dyer Straits, Statement of Changes in Fund Balance, General Fund, Debt Service Fund, and Capital Projects Fund, January 1, 1983 to December 31, 1983 (All Figures in Thousands of Dollars)

| | BUDGETARY ESTIMATE | ACTUAL FOR YEAR | OVER (UNDER) ESTIMATE |
|---|---|---|---|
| *General Fund:* | | | |
| Fund balance, Jan. 1, 1983 | $519 | $409 | $(110) |
| Add: | | | |
| Revenues, 1983 | 9,709 | 9,527 | (182) |
| Reserves at Jan. 1, 1983 | | | |
| Reserve for encumbrances | — | 227 | 227 |
| Total | 9,709 | 9,754 | 45 |
| Deduct: | | | |
| Expenditures, 1983 | 9,709 | 9,831 | 122 |
| Reserves at Dec. 31, 1983 | | | |
| Reserve for encumbrances | — | 207 | 207 |
| Total | 9,709 | 10,038 | 329 |
| Fund Balance, Dec. 31, 1983 | $519 | $125 | $(394) |
| *Debt Service Fund:* | | | |
| Fund balance, Jan. 1, 1983 | $84 | $84 | — |
| Add: | | | |
| Revenues, 1983 | 1,100 | 1,111 | 11 |
| Deduct: | | | |
| Expenditures, 1983 | 1,080 | 1,091 | 11 |
| Fund Balance, Dec. 31, 1983 | $104 | $104 | — |
| *Capital Projects Fund:* | | | |
| Fund balance, Jan. 1, 1983 | $870 | $919 | $49 |
| Add: | | | |
| Revenues, 1983 | 1,083 | 1,109.8 | 26.8 |
| Reserves at Jan. 1, 1983 | | | |
| Reserve for encumbrances | — | 193 | 193 |
| Total | 1,083 | 1,302.8 | 219.8 |
| Deduct: | | | |
| Expenditures, 1983 | 1,958 | 1,604 | (354) |
| Reserves at Dec. 31, 1983 | | | |
| Reserve for encumbrances | — | 193 | 193 |
| Total | 1,958 | 1,797 | (161) |
| Fund balance, Dec. 31, 1983 | $(5) | $424.8 | $429.8 |

balance over the period. For the general fund in Table 2-7, expenditures exceeded revenues by $304,000, but the fund balance decreased by only $284,000 due to the decrease in the reserve for encumbrances of $20,000 (from $227,000 to $207,000).

The changes in fund balance statement links the beginning and end of an accounting period and provides the end-of-period fund balances, an important figure for the end-of-period balance sheet. Changes in fund balances are treated more extensively in Chapter 8 when we analyze the availability of resources within the government.

**Statement of Cash Receipts and Disbursements.**    Balance sheets, statements of revenues and expenditures, and statements of changes in fund balance are statements required by the National Council on Governmental Accounting (NCGA) for governmental funds in the annual financial report. A statement that is not required by the NCGA but is useful and often presented for governmental funds is the statement of cash receipts and disbursements. This statement always shows inflows and outflows of cash, and very often shows beginning and ending cash as well. Some statements of cash receipts and disbursements also show the form in which the cash is held (demand deposits, time deposits, etc.).

For governments on a cash basis of accounting, this statement is unnecessary because it would be identical with a statement of revenues and expenditures. For governments using an expenditure accrual or modified accrual basis of accounting, this is not the case. None of the other statements discussed thus far present a description of the cash flows of the government.

Statements of cash receipts and disbursements for the general fund, debt service fund, and capital projects fund of Dyer Straits are presented in Table 2-8. This statement shows that the cash in each fund decreased over 1983. For example, the cash balance in the general fund was $239,000 at the beginning of the year

TABLE 2-8    **City of Dyer Straits, Statement of Cash Receipts and Disbursements, General Fund, Debt Service Fund, and Capital Projects Fund, January 1, 1983 to December 31, 1983 (All Figures in Thousands of Dollars)**

| | |
|---|---:|
| *General Fund:* | |
| Opening Cash, Jan. 1, 1983 | |
| Cash on hand | $14 |
| Cash in demand deposits | 107 |
| Cash in time deposits | 118 |
| Total Opening Cash, Jan. 1, 1983 | $239 |
| Receipts: | |
| Property taxes | 4,147 |
| Sales taxes | 1,354 |
| Nontax local revenues* | 994 |
| State aid | 1,652 |
| Federal aid | 1,030 |
| Total Receipts | $9,177 |
| Disbursements: | |
| Salaries | 5,309 |
| Materials and supplies | 1,223 |
| Transfer to debt service fund | 1,010 |
| Transfer to municipal parking fund | 20 |
| Fringe benefits | 1,829 |
| Total Disbursements | $9,391 |
| Total Closing Cash, Dec. 31, 1983 | $25 |
| Cash on hand | 12 |
| Cash in demand deposits | 13 |
| Cash in time deposits | 0 |

*(Continued)*

TABLE 2-8   (*continued*)

*Debt Service Fund:*

Opening Cash, Jan. 1, 1983

| | |
|---|---:|
| Cash on hand | 0 |
| Cash in demand deposits | 69 |
| Cash in time deposits | 0 |
| Cash for bond interest and matured bonds payable | 82 |
| Total Opening Cash, Jan. 1, 1983 | $151 |

Receipts:

| | |
|---|---:|
| Transfer from general fund | 1,010 |
| Interest on investments | 20 |
| Total Receipts | $1,030 |

Disbursements:

| | |
|---|---:|
| Principal | 565 |
| Interest | 550 |
| Total Disbursements | $1,115 |
| Total Closing Cash, Dec. 31, 1983 | $66 |
| Cash on hand | 0 |
| Cash in demand deposits | 8 |
| Cash in time deposits | 0 |
| Cash for bond interest and matured bonds payable | 58 |

*Capital Projects Fund:*

Opening cash, Jan. 1, 1983

| | |
|---|---:|
| Cash on hand | 26 |
| Cash in time deposits | 230 |
| Cash in demand deposits | 4,360 |
| Total Opening Cash, Jan. 1, 1983 | $4,616 |

Receipts:

| | |
|---|---:|
| Proceeds from bond anticipation notes | 3,631 |
| Proceeds from general obligation bonds | 797.8 |
| Interest on investments | 192 |
| Transfer from water and sewer fund | 180 |
| Total Receipts | $4,800.8 |

Disbursements:

| | |
|---|---:|
| Salaries | 820 |
| Materials and supplies | 325 |
| Payment to contractor | 435 |
| Transfer to water and sewer fund | 84 |
| Repayment of capital notes | 200 |
| Repayment of bond anticipation notes | 3,145 |
| Total Disbursements | $5,009 |
| Total Closing Cash, Dec. 31, 1983 | $4,407.8 |
| Cash on hand | 11.8 |
| Cash in time deposits | 236 |
| Cash in demand deposits | 4,160 |

*Includes receipts from water and sewer fund ($80) and municipal parking fund ($60).

but decreased to $25,000 by the end of the year. This statement of cash receipts and disbursements shows the cash balance at the beginning of the period that appears on the beginning-of-period balance sheet (see Table 2–2), and the end-of-period cash balance that will appear on the end-of-period balance sheet (see Table 2–9). When the statements of revenues and expenditures are compared with the statements of receipts and disbursements, it shows very clearly that with an expenditure accrual basis of accounting, changes in the cash balance are not the same as the difference between revenues and expenditures. For example, cash balances in the general fund decreased by $214,000 ($239,000 – $25,000) while expenditures *exceeded* revenues by $304,000 ($9,831,000 – $9,527,000).

TABLE 2–9    **City of Dyer Straits, Combined Balance Sheet, General Fund, Debt Service Fund, and Capital Projects Fund, December 31, 1983 (All Figures in Thousands of Dollars)**

|  | GENERAL FUND | DEBT SERVICE FUND | CAPITAL PROJECTS FUND |
|---|---|---|---|
| *Assets:* | | | |
| Cash on hand | $12 | | $11.8 |
| Cash in demand deposits | 13 | $8 | 236 |
| Cash in time deposits | 0 | | 4,160 |
| Cash for bond interest and matured bonds | | 58 | |
| Property taxes receivable | 1,088 | | |
| Sales taxes receivable | 0 | | |
| Accounts receivable | 29 | | |
| State aid receivable | 73 | | |
| Federal aid receivable | 31 | | |
| Due from other funds | 38 | 96 | 60 |
| Other assets | 40 | | 6 |
| Total Assets | $1,324 | $162 | $4,473.8 |
| *Liabilities, Reserves, and Fund Balances:* | | | |
| Liabilities: | | | |
| Vouchers payable | $404 | | $371 |
| Bond interest and matured bonds payable | | $58 | |
| Salaries payable | 376 | | 63 |
| Due to other funds | 212 | | 0 |
| Bond anticipation notes payable | | | 3,422 |
| Capital notes payable | | | 0 |
| Total Liabilities | $992 | $58 | $3,856 |
| Reserves: | | | |
| Reserve for encumbrances | $207 | — | $193 |
| Total Reserves | $207 | — | $193 |
| Fund Balances | $125 | $104 | $424.8 |
| Total Liabilities, Reserves, and Fund Balances | $1,324 | $162 | $4,473.8 |

**Other Statements and Schedules.**    In addition to statements of cash receipts and disbursements, several other items may be shown in greater detail in a separate listing, or schedule. Governments may also report on their fixed assets and equipment not included in proprietary funds in the annual reports. This may appear as a statement or list with significant groups of assets itemized, such as sewer mains or buildings. The fixed assets are almost always recorded at historical cost without any allowance for depreciation. The fixed assets in the proprietary funds are recorded within the fund structure, usually at historical cost, but depreciation is included. We will discuss proprietary funds in more depth later in this chapter. A separate schedule of bond obligations and other long-term liabilities is often provided.

**The Links Among Financial Statements.**    Thus far, various financial statements have been presented to describe the stocks and flows of resources in the governmental funds of a government. With a beginning-of-period balance sheet and the other statements listed above, we can put together an *end-of-period balance sheet* using knowledge of the linkages among the financial statements.

Figure 2-2 shows the interrelationships among the financial statements displayed thus far for governmental funds and the end-of-period balance sheet. The stock of cash at the beginning of the period is an input to the statement of cash receipts and disbursements $(A_1)$. The cash flows are added to the cash at the beginning of the period to yield the stock of cash at the end of the period which appears on the end-of-period balance sheet $(A_2)$. The beginning-of-period reserves and fund balance are used as inputs to the statement of changes in fund balance $(B_1, B_2)$. The difference between revenues and expenditures $(B_3)$ is added to the beginning reserves and fund balance $(B_1, B_2)$ to yield the ending fund balance and reserves $(B_4, B_5)$. In some cases subsidiary information may be needed to determine the end-of-period reserves.

The links between the other assets, liabilities, and reserves at the beginning of the period and the end of the period are provided by the statements of revenues and expenditures and the statement of receipts and disbursements $(C_1, C_2, C_3, C_4, C_5, C_6)$. If every revenue equaled its comparable receipt, and every expenditure equaled its comparable disbursement, and there were no other transactions, then assets (other than cash) and liabilities would not change. However, when, for example, certain revenues are not received in cash, certain expenditures are not paid in cash, some revenues of the prior period are collected in this period, short-term borrowing takes place, and/or obligations from the prior period are paid in this period, then noncash assets, liabilities, and reserves will also change during the period. To a large extent, this change occurs due to the differences between revenues and receipts, and between expenditures and disbursements.

These links can be illustrated more concretely by examining the balance sheet of Dyer Straits for the *end* of 1983. The balance sheets for the general fund, debt service fund, and capital projects fund in combined form for the city of Dyer Straits as of December 31, 1983, are shown in Table 2-9. All the data in Table 2-9

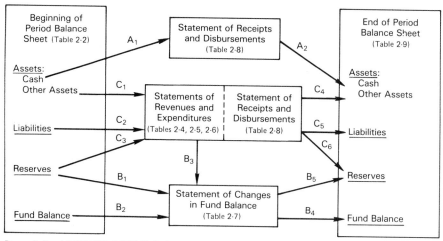

Figure 2-2.   **LINKAGES AMONG FINANCIAL STATEMENTS FOR GOVERNMENTAL FUNDS**

can be derived from the previous statements (plus the information in Table 2–3). Several entries for the general fund will be explained in detail; the reader should carry out a similar exercise for the remaining entries.

The cash amounts on the ending balance sheet are derived directly from the statement of receipts and disbursements, Table 2–8. In the general fund, for example, the cash on hand at the end of the period of $12,000 and the cash in demand deposits at the end of the period of $13,000 are derived from the beginning balances and cash flows. The end-of-period fund balance of $125,000 and reserve for encumbrances of $207,000 are taken from the statement of changes in fund balance, Table 2–7. Note that the ending reserves for encumbrances can be found on the statement of expenditures, Table 2–5.

The other individual asset entries and liability entries can be derived from the original balance sheet, the statement of receipts and disbursements, the statement of expenditures, and the statement of revenues. For example, there was $714,000 of taxes receivable due Dyer Straits at the beginning of the year in the general fund according to the balance sheet in Table 2–2. From the statement of revenues in the general fund, Table 2–4, we can see that $4,521,000 of property tax revenues accrued to Dyer Straits during 1983, but the statement of receipts and disbursements, Table 2–8, shows that only $4,147,000 was received as cash during the period. Therefore $374,000, or $4,521,000 less $4,147,000, was not collected, and the property tax receivable at the end of 1983 is the beginning-of-year property tax receivable of $714,000 plus $374,000, or $1,088,000. This is the amount that appears on the December 31, 1983, balance sheet for property tax receivable. These relationships among financial statements for Dyer Straits' property taxes are shown in Figure 2–3.

A similar set of calculations can be carried out to derive the liabilities on the

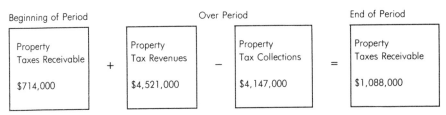

Figure 2-3.    CHANGE IN PROPERTY TAXES RECEIVABLE FOR DYER STRAITS, JANUARY 1, 1983 TO DECEMBER 31, 1983

December 31, 1983, balance sheet. For example, the salaries payable in the general fund at January 1, 1983, were $238,000, as shown in Table 2-2. From Table 2-6 we can see that $5,447,000 of salaries was expended by the general fund during 1983, but according to Table 2-8 only $5,309,000 was paid out. Therefore the total amount of salaries owed to employees from the general fund at the end of 1983 is the beginning payable, $238,000, plus the difference between the expenditure and the disbursement, $138,000 ($5,447,000 less $5,309,000), or $376,000 at December 31, 1983, and this appears in Table 2-9.

The primary financial statements for governmental funds have been explained and illustrated with examples from Dyer Straits. Next we examine the financial statements of proprietary funds.

### Financial Statements for Proprietary Funds

Enterprise funds, internal service funds, and certain trust funds are treated as proprietary funds in governments. Proprietary funds may record and report their financial information differently than governmental funds. We use the word *may* because even though a different set of accounting and reporting practices is recommended for proprietary funds, many governments do not always follow these recommendations and instead use practices similar to or the same as those recommended for governmental funds. In this section we describe the recommended practices for proprietary funds by presenting the principal financial statements utilized by these funds. It is recommended that proprietary funds use an expense accrual basis of accounting, rather than the modified accrual or expenditure accrual basis utilized in governmental funds.

**Balance Sheets.**    Proprietary fund balance sheets use the same format as governmental funds. In fact, proprietary fund balance sheets are often presented in a combined format with all other funds, as is done in Dyer Straits for the water and sewer fund and the municipal parking fund (Table 2-2). There are some differences in balance sheet categories, however.

First, note that the balance sheets for the two enterprise funds include inventories, land, and buildings as assets. These fixed, or long-term, assets are used for the operation of the water and sewer system and the municipal parking system only and are not the same fixed assets associated with the other funds. In addition, note that two of the fixed assets, equipment and buildings, are recorded net of depreciation, that is, original cost less the accumulated depreciation to the date of the balance sheet.

Second, on the liability side, the proprietary funds include long-term bonds payable, in this case revenue bonds, as a liability. This is in contrast to the governmental funds, which do not treat long-term borrowing as a liability. Both governmental and proprietary funds, however, treat short-term debt as a liability.

Third, note that the proprietary funds use a retained earnings account instead of a fund balance. Retained earnings should be interpreted somewhat differently than a fund balance due to the different definition of assets and liabilities in expense compared with expenditure accounting.

Finally, although it does not occur in the example in Table 2–2, proprietary funds sometimes place certain restrictions on their assets and liabilities, and these are often designated on the balance sheet. In the case of Dyer Straits, if a portion of the cash in the proprietary funds is for construction or acquisition of new facilities, this may be shown by restricting part of the cash and reporting this on the balance sheet as a separate cash item, "cash restricted for new facility." In some cases the restrictions may be so extensive that a (restricted) fund is set up within the proprietary fund.

**Statements of Revenues and Expenses.** In place of statements of revenues and expenditures used in governmental funds, a *statement of revenues and expenses* is usually presented for a proprietary fund. This statement is an operating statement, and because expense accounting is used, it more accurately reflects the use of resources in the operations of the enterprise compared with the statement of revenues and expenditures in a governmental fund. The statement of revenues and expenses is sometimes called an *income statement* and is analogous to the income statement used in for-profit organizations.

Two statements of revenues and expenses are shown in Tables 2–10 and 2–11 for the Dyer Straits water and sewer fund and the municipal parking fund for 1983. Both statements show the net operating income and the net income for the respective enterprise funds. Certain activities are considered "nonoperating," since they are not directly related to the production of the particular goods and services accounted for by the funds. The nonoperating items, however, affect the financial condition of the fund, so that they are included in the final net income figure. The interest earned by the funds on their investments and the interest paid by the funds on their debt are both treated here as nonoperating items. If the funds had received a grant from another organization or from the general fund to subsidize the operations of the fund, then these, too, would have been treated as nonoperating items.

The water and sewer fund in Dyer Straits has a loss from operations alone and suffers a larger loss when the nonoperating items are considered. The municipal parking fund shows a positive net income from operations, but it too

TABLE 2-10    **City of Dyer Straits, Statement of Revenues and Expenses, Water and Sewer Fund, January 1, 1983 to December 31, 1983 (All Figures in Thousands of Dollars)**

| | |
|---|---:|
| Operating Revenues: | |
| Sale of water | $1,711 |
| Sewer charges | 337 |
| Transfer from capital projects fund | 80 |
| Total Operating Revenues | $2,128 |
| Operating Expenses: | |
| Salaries | $729 |
| Materials and supplies | 448 |
| Repairs and maintenance | 257 |
| Utilities | 74 |
| Depreciation* | 352 |
| Other expenses† | 121 |
| Transfer to general fund | 80 |
| Transfer to capital projects fund | 120 |
| Transfer to municipal parking fund | 22 |
| Total Operating Expenses | $2,203 |
| Net Operating Income (Loss) | ($75) |
| Add: Nonoperating revenue | |
| Interest on investments | $63 |
| Total Nonoperating Revenue | $63 |
| Deduct: Nonoperating expense | |
| Interest expense | $258.1 |
| Total Nonoperating Expense | $258.1 |
| Net Income (Loss) | ($270.1) |

*Depreciation: $15 for equipment; $337 for buildings.
†Includes fringe benefits.

runs at a loss when nonoperating items are taken into account. Finally, note that depreciation is an expense in both proprietary funds.

**Statements of Changes in Retained Earnings.**    Proprietary funds are structured like entities in the for-profit sector. As a result, proprietary funds match liabilities, reserves, and *retained earnings* against assets. (Portions of retained earnings, like fund balances, may be reserved for specific purposes.) Thus the statement that relates the beginning-of-period balance sheet and the statement of revenues and expenses over the period to the balance sheet at the end of the period is the *statement of changes in retained earnings.* Changes in retained earnings from the beginning of the period may result from net income (or loss), accounting adjustments, and changes in reserves. The statement of changes in retained earnings serves the same purpose as the statement of changes in fund balance for the governmental funds.

Statements of changes in retained earnings for the water and sewer fund and the municipal parking fund for Dyer Straits for 1983 are shown in Tables 2–12 and 2–13, respectively. The framework is equivalent to the statement of changes in fund balance; the format is, however, somewhat different. The net income or

TABLE 2-11　City of Dyer Straits, Statement of Revenues and Expenses, Municipal Parking Fund, January 1, 1983 to December 31, 1983 (All Figures in Thousands of Dollars)

| | |
|---|---|
| Operating Revenues: | |
| Parking charges | $962 |
| Transfer from general fund | 120 |
| Transfer from water and sewer fund | 22 |
| Total Operating Revenues | $1,104 |
| Operating Expenses: | |
| Salaries | $491 |
| Materials and supplies | 32 |
| Repairs and maintenance | 63 |
| Utilities | 38 |
| Depreciation* | 240 |
| Other expenses† | 43 |
| Transfer to general fund | 60 |
| Total Operating Expenses | $967 |
| Net Operating Income (Loss) | $137 |
| Add: Nonoperating revenue | |
| Interest on investments | $18 |
| Total Nonoperating Revenue | $18 |
| Deduct: Nonoperating expense | |
| Interest expense | $173.1 |
| Total Nonoperating Expense | $173.1 |
| Net Income (Loss) | ($18.1) |

*Depreciation: $2 for equipment; $238 for buildings.
†Includes fringe benefits.

TABLE 2-12　City of Dyer Straits, Changes in Retained Earnings Statement, Water and Sewer Fund, January 1, 1983 to December 31, 1983 (All Figures in Thousands of Dollars)

| | |
|---|---|
| Retained earnings, Jan. 1, 1983 | $1,777 |
| Add: | |
| Net income (loss), 1983 | (270.1) |
| Retained earnings, Dec. 31, 1983 | $1,506.9 |

TABLE 2-13　City of Dyer Straits, Changes in Retained Earnings Statement, Municipal Parking Fund, January 1, 1983 to December 31, 1983 (All Figures in Thousands of Dollars)

| | |
|---|---|
| Retained earnings, Jan. 1, 1983 | $537 |
| Add: | |
| Net income (loss), 1983 | (18.1) |
| Retained earnings, Dec. 31, 1983 | $518.9 |

loss is added to the beginning-of-period retained earnings rather than separately adding the revenues and subtracting the expenses. For the two enterprise funds in Dyer Straits, retained earnings declined because of the net loss. As we will see below, the retained earnings on December 31, 1983, appears on the end-of-year balance sheet.

**Statements of Receipts and Disbursements.** Proprietary funds do not usually present statements of cash receipts and disbursements. Instead many financial reports for proprietary funds include a statement of changes in financial position, sometimes called a statement of sources and uses of cash, which discloses how cash changes over the period. For our purposes here, however, it is more useful to present the *statement of cash receipts and disbursements* and the *end-of-period balance sheet* prior to a discussion of the statement of changes in financial position.

Statements of cash receipts and disbursements for the water and sewer fund and the municipal parking fund for Dyer Straits for 1983 are shown in Tables 2–14 and 2–15. The basic format is identical with the one discussed earlier for the governmental funds (Table 2–8). The statements show that cash declined for both enterprise funds during 1983. Note that a number of items are receipts but not revenues. For example, for the water and sewer fund the proceeds from the revenue bonds, revenue bond anticipation notes, and capital notes are not revenues. Moreover, the payment of principal on the revenue bonds and the refunding of the bond anticipation and capital notes are disbursements but not expenses. Also observe that depreciation is an expense but not a disbursement. That is, depreciation is an accounting entry that reflects the fact that part of the physical plant is used up every period, although no cash is disbursed at that time due to depreciation. (The cash disbursement occurred when the plant was first built.)

**The Links Among Financial Statements.** The interrelationships among the beginning-of-period balance sheet, statement of revenues and expenses, statement of changes in retained earnings, statement of cash receipts and disbursements, and end-of-period balance sheet are basically the same as those displayed earlier in Figure 2–2. For the proprietary funds, the statement of revenues and expenses replaces the statement of revenues and expenditures, and retained earnings are used in place of fund balances. Using these interrelationships, the statements previously shown for the proprietary funds in Dyer Straits, and the added information that the materials inventory in both funds was the same at the end of the period as it was at the beginning, the end-of-period balance sheets for the two proprietary funds for Dyer Straits can be derived.

The balance sheets for the water and sewer fund and the municipal parking fund for Dyer Straits as of December 31, 1983, are shown in Table 2–16. Note that for proprietary funds, fixed assets and long-term liabilities are shown on the balance sheet.

The end-of-period balance sheets for the proprietary funds are derived from the previously shown statements for these funds. The cash entries are derived

TABLE 2-14    **City of Dyer Straits, Statement of Cash Receipts and Disbursements, Water and Sewer Fund, January 1, 1983 to December 31, 1983 (All Figures in Thousands of Dollars)**

| | |
|---|---:|
| Opening Cash, Jan. 1, 1983 | |
| Cash on hand | $78 |
| Cash in demand deposits | 417 |
| Cash in time deposits | 886 |
| Cash for bond interest and matured bonds | 22 |
| Total Opening Cash, Jan. 1, 1983 | $1,403 |
| Receipts: | |
| Sale of water | $1,687 |
| Sewer charges | 301 |
| Transfer from capital projects fund | 84 |
| Proceeds from revenue bonds | 345 |
| Proceeds from revenue bond anticipation notes | 2,227 |
| Proceeds from capital notes | 90 |
| Interest on investments | 63 |
| Total Receipts | $4,797 |
| Disbursements: | |
| Salaries | $684 |
| Materials and supplies | 433 |
| Repairs and maintenance | 257 |
| Utilities | 74 |
| Other expenses | 121 |
| Transfer to general fund | 80 |
| Transfer to capital projects fund | 180 |
| Transfer to municipal parking fund | 32 |
| Payment of principal—revenue bonds | 402 |
| Payment of interest | 258.1 |
| Payment of revenue anticipation notes | 1,932 |
| Payment of capital notes | 175 |
| Acquisition of fixed assets: Equipment | 35 |
| Buildings | 400 |
| Total Disbursements | $5,063.1 |
| Total Closing Cash, Dec. 31, 1983 | $1,136.9 |
| Cash on hand | $138 |
| Cash in demand deposits | 420 |
| Cash in time deposits | 556.9 |
| Cash for bond interest and matured bonds | 22 |

from the statements of cash receipts and disbursements (Tables 2–14 and 2–15). The retained earnings amounts are calculated on the statements of changes in retained earnings (Tables 2–12 and 2–13). The other assets and liabilities (and reserves if there are any) are derived from the statements of cash receipts and disbursements and the statements of revenues and expenses (Tables 2–10 and 2–11) in conjunction with the beginning-of-period balance sheet (Table 2–2).

For example, the municipal parking fund had $16,000 in parking charges receivable (labeled as accounts receivable in Table 2–2) at the beginning of 1983.

TABLE 2-15   **City of Dyer Straits, Statement of Cash Receipts and Disbursements, Municipal Parking Fund, January 1, 1983 to December 31, 1983 (All Figures in Thousands of Dollars)**

| | |
|---|---:|
| Opening Cash, Jan. 1, 1983 | |
| Cash on hand | $63 |
| Cash in demand deposits | 138 |
| Cash in time deposits | 259 |
| Cash for bond interest and matured bonds | 7 |
| Total Opening Cash, Jan. 1, 1983 | $467 |
| Receipts: | |
| Parking charges | $970 |
| Transfer from general fund | 20 |
| Transfer from water and sewer fund | 32 |
| Proceeds from revenue bonds | 221 |
| Proceeds from revenue bond anticipation notes | 1,424 |
| Proceeds from capital notes | 60 |
| Interest on investments | 18 |
| Total Receipts | $2,745 |
| Disbursements: | |
| Salaries | $460 |
| Materials and supplies | 30 |
| Repairs and maintenance | 63 |
| Utilities | 38 |
| Other expenses | 43 |
| Transfer to general fund | 60 |
| Payment of principal—revenue bonds | 188 |
| Payment of interest | 173.1 |
| Payment of revenue bond anticipation notes | 1,448 |
| Payment of capital notes | 100 |
| Acquisition of fixed assets: Equipment | 10 |
| Buildings | 250 |
| Total Disbursements | $2,863.1 |
| Total Closing Cash, Dec. 31, 1983 | $348.9 |
| Cash on hand | $58 |
| Cash in demand deposits | 83.9 |
| Cash in time deposits | 200 |
| Cash for bond interest and matured bonds | 7 |

During 1983, $962,000 in parking charges was due to the enterprise (Table 2-11), and during the year, $970,000 in parking charges was collected in cash (Table 2-15). Therefore $8,000 ($16,000 minus $8,000) was the outstanding accounts receivable on December 31, 1983, shown in Table 2-16. All the other assets and liabilities can be derived in a similar way.

**Statements of Changes in Financial Position or Statements of Sources and Uses of Cash.**   The final statement we will discuss for the proprietary funds is the *statement of changes in financial position.*

There are several varieties of the statement of change in financial position,

TABLE 2-16   City of Dyer Straits, Combined Balance Sheet, Water and Sewer Fund, and Municipal Parking Fund, December 31, 1983 (All Figures in Thousands of Dollars)

|  | WATER AND SEWER FUND | MUNICIPAL PARKING FUND |
|---|---|---|
| *Assets:* | | |
| Cash on hand | $138 | $58 |
| Cash in demand deposits | 420 | 83.9 |
| Cash in time deposits | 556.9 | 200 |
| Cash for bond interest and matured bonds | 22 | 7 |
| Accounts receivable | 183 | 8 |
| Due from other funds | 0 | 121 |
| Inventories: Materials | 17 | 4 |
| Equipment (net of depreciation) | 203 | 34 |
| Land | 768 | 377 |
| Buildings (net of depreciation) | 4,282 | 2,774 |
| Total Assets | $6,589.9 | $3,666.9 |
| *Liabilities, Reserves, and Retained Earnings:* | | |
| Liabilities: | | |
| Vouchers payable | $92 | $18 |
| Bond interest and matured bonds payable | 22 | 7 |
| Salaries payable | 127 | 58 |
| Due to other funds | 91 | 12 |
| Bond anticipation notes payable | 2,133 | 1,307 |
| Capital notes payable | 90 | 60 |
| Revenue bonds payable | 2,528 | 1,686 |
| Total Liabilities | $5,083 | $3,148 |
| Reserves | — | — |
| Retained Earnings | $1,506.9 | $518.9 |
| Total Liabilities, Reserves, and Retained Earnings | $6,589.9 | $3,666.9 |

but the one we discuss here, the statement of *sources and uses of cash,* is one of the most common. (An alternative statement is the sources and uses of working capital, which is quite similar.) This statement must be viewed as a whole; that is, a single entry in the statement must be read in the context of the entire statement. As we indicated earlier, many proprietary funds present this statement in place of the statement of cash receipts and disbursements. Instead of showing all cash flows, this statement shows how the change in cash is affected by the stock of current assets and liabilities, and it shows where the cash comes from and how it is used. In particular, the statement distinguishes among changes in cash resulting from different events.

There are several major sources of cash. The first item normally included as a source of cash is net income (the bottom line on the statement of revenues and expenses). This is a negative source if it is a net loss. (In all cases in this statement, a negative source has the same effect as a use, and a negative use has the same effect as a source.) Because net income includes certain items that do not involve cash, net income is generally adjusted by adding back noncash expenses and subtracting noncash revenues. Noncash expenses such as depreciation are added to net income as a source of cash because they were subtracted from revenues to obtain net income in the first place but did not represent a use of cash. Noncash revenues, such as the value of services in kind, are subtracted because they were included in revenues in computing net income but did not represent a source of cash.

Other sources of cash include proceeds from the sale of noncurrent assets and proceeds from the receipt of long-term financing. Also, if there are any other inflows that generate cash and are, for some reason, excluded from the revenue and expense statement, then they would be listed separately as a source of cash. An example might be a capital contribution.

Uses of cash include the acquisition of noncurrent assets and the retirement of debt through the payment of principal.

One final type of change may be a source or use of cash depending on the direction of the change. If we consider the sources and uses defined thus far, we have ignored sources and uses of cash that result from changes in current assets (other than cash) and current liabilities. For example, what if we have a receivable that is paid to the fund? This certainly is a source of cash but would not be captured by the sources and uses discussed up to this point. Or what if the fund buys items for its inventory with cash? This is a use of cash that would not show up in the sources and uses delineated above. Therefore the final item that must be included in the sources and uses statement is the changes in current assets (other than cash) and current liabilities. Recall that current assets and current liabilities are those that are expected to be utilized or liquidated during one fiscal year.

There are several different ways in which current assets (other than cash) and current liability changes may be included on the sources and uses statement. One method is to include each individual change on the sources and uses statement. Decreases in noncash current assets such as accounts receivable or inventories, and increases in current liabilities such as accounts payable or short-term debt payable, would be listed as sources. Increases in noncash current assets, and decreases in current liabilities, would be listed as uses. An alternative method is to list the net effect of all the changes in noncash current assets and current liabilities on the sources and uses statement.[19]

The statement of sources and uses of cash for the water and sewer fund for Dyer Straits is presented in Table 2–17. In this statement, each of the noncash current assets and current liabilities that changed is listed as a separate source or

---

[19] In this alternative method, *noncash working capital* is defined as the difference between current assets (other than cash) and current liabilities. The increases in noncash working capital over the period are listed as a source (positive or negative) of cash, and this captures all the increases and decreases in cash due to the changes in current assets (other than cash) and current liabilities.

TABLE 2-17   **City of Dyer Straits, Statement of Sources and Uses of Cash, Water and Sewer Fund, January 1, 1983 to December 31, 1983 (All figures in thousands of dollars)**

| | |
|---|---|
| *Sources of Cash:* | |
| Net income | $(270.1) |
| Add expenses not requiring cash outlays | |
| Depreciation: Equipment | 15 |
| Buildings | 337 |
| Proceeds from revenue bonds | 345 |
| Proceeds from revenue bond anticipation notes | 2,227 |
| Proceeds from capital notes | 90 |
| Increases in current liabilities | |
| Vouchers payable | 15 |
| Salaries payable | 45 |
| Decreases in current assets | |
| Due from other funds | 4 |
| Total Sources of Cash | $2,807.9 |
| *Uses of Cash:* | |
| Payment of principal—revenue bonds | $402 |
| Payment of revenue bond anticipation notes | 1,932 |
| Payment of capital notes | 175 |
| Acquisition of fixed assets: Equipment | 35 |
| Buildings | 400 |
| Increases in current assets | |
| Accounts receivable | 60 |
| Decreases in current liabilities | |
| Due to other funds | 70 |
| Total Uses of Cash | $3,074 |
| *Net Increase (Decrease) in Cash* | $(266.1) |

use. For example, since salaries payable increase, this is listed as a source of cash while the increase in accounts receivable is included as a use of cash. The other sources of cash include net income adjusted for depreciation and the proceeds from various forms of financing. The other uses are the payment of principal on various forms of debt and the acquisition of fixed assets. Similarly, the statement of sources and uses of cash for the municipal parking fund is presented in Table 2-18.

With the financial statements provided for the proprietary funds in Dyer Straits, the reader should be able to see that the statements of sources and uses of cash and the statements of receipts and disbursements convey similar information. The major difference between them is that in the statement of sources and uses of cash, net income adjusted for depreciation is used as a source, and the differences in stocks of current assets (other than cash) and current liabilities are used as a source and/or use, while the statement of receipts and disbursements reports only cash flows.

TABLE 2-18    City of Dyer Straits, Statement of Sources and Uses of Cash, Municipal Parking Fund, January 1, 1983 to December 31, 1983 (All figures in thousands of dollars)

| | |
|---|---:|
| *Sources of Cash:* | |
| Net income | $(18.1) |
| Add expenses not requiring cash outlays | |
| Depreciation: Equipment | 2 |
| Buildings | 238 |
| Proceeds from revenue bonds | 221 |
| Proceeds from revenue bond anticipation notes | 1,424 |
| Proceeds from capital notes | 60 |
| Increases in current liabilities | |
| Vouchers payable | 2 |
| Salaries payable | 31 |
| Decreases in current assets | |
| Accounts receivable | 8 |
| Total Sources of Cash | $1,967.9 |
| *Uses of Cash:* | |
| Payment of principal—revenue bonds | $188 |
| Payment of revenue bond anticipation notes | 1,448 |
| Payment of capital notes | 100 |
| Acquisition of fixed assets: Equipment | 10 |
| Buildings | 250 |
| Increases in current assets | |
| Due from other funds | 90 |
| Total Uses of Cash | $2,086 |
| *Net Increase (Decrease) in Cash* | $(118.1) |

## IV. BUDGETS FOR GOVERNMENTS

For financial analysis, it is desirable to have the most up-to-date information that is available, and budgets provide information that is more current than financial statements. *Budgets* are documents that categorize, organize, and present financial information for purposes of planning, evaluation, implementation, and/or control of financial resources. Budgets estimate or specify different types of resource flows to or from the government over different periods in the future and forecast future resource levels. A key difference between budgets and financial statements is the prospective, or future-oriented, nature of budgets compared with financial statements that provide a record of past financial activities. Some budgets are *projected* financial statements, specifying anticipated resource inflows and outflows and the financial position of the organization at some time in the future.

In this section we review the governmental budgets that are commonly available for financial analysis, including operating, capital, and cash budgets. Although other budgetary information, such as performance measurement, is becoming more prevalent, coverage in this section is limited to budgets that are available for most governmental units.[20]

### Operating Budgets

In most governments, particularly for funds that use expenditure accounting, operating budgets are synonymous with *revenue* and *expenditure* budgets. Expenditure budgets usually contain expected expenditures classified by organizational subunit (e.g., department) or by object of expenditure, or both, covering the upcoming fiscal year. Revenue budgets typically present the sources and expected levels of revenues, normally for the upcoming fiscal year.

Expenditure and revenue budgets vary in the level of aggregation. The most-aggregated budgets are generally known as *summary* budgets, while the most-detailed budgets that specify individual revenue and expenditure items are often called *line item* budgets. Other budgets, such as those that disclose objects of expenditure by department, fall in between summary and line item budgets. Typically every fund in a government has a revenue and expenditure (or expense) budget, and some governments present a budget for a group of funds, such as the general, special revenue, and debt service funds.

Table 2-19 shows a budget summary for the city of Dyer Straits. Note that Dyer Straits presents its budget by funds, indicating the appropriations and revenues for the general, debt service, capital projects, water and sewer, and municipal parking funds. *Appropriation* can be defined as ''[a] legal authorization granted by a legislative body to make expenditures and to incur obligations for specific purposes. An appropriation is usually limited in amount and as to the time when it may be expended.''[21] In the budget for Dyer Straits shown in Table 2-19, broad categories of appropriations are presented, aggregating appropriations roughly according to different departments in the city government. As an alternative, the city could have indicated its appropriations by object of expenditure for each fund. Revenues are broken down by source, and the projected or planned decrease in the fund balance (or retained earnings) is listed as a revenue source. Governments generally present a budget similar to the one shown in Table 2-19, along with detailed breakdowns of all items.

Due to the accounting and financial reporting practices adopted by governments, the entries in the budget summary must be interpreted carefully. For example, in Table 2-19 the total revenue and appropriation figures for each fund and the city as a whole are inflated because the interfund transfers are included. Also, since Dyer Straits accounts for revenues and *expenditures* in the general, debt

---

[20]For a review of performance measurement techniques in government, see Theodore H. Poister and Robert P. McGowan, ''The Use of Management Tools in Municipal Government: A National Survey,'' *Public Administration Review,* 44, No. 3 (May–June 1984), 215-23.

[21]National Council on Governmental Accounting, *Statement 1,* reprinted in Municipal Finance Officers Association, *GAAFR,* Appendix B, p. 55.

TABLE 2-19  City of Dyer Straits, Budget Summary—All Funds, January 1, 1983 to December 31, 1983 (All figures in thousands of dollars)

| | TOTAL | GENERAL | DEBT SERVICE | CAPITAL PROJECTS | WATER AND SEWER | MUNICIPAL PARKING |
|---|---|---|---|---|---|---|
| *Appropriations:* | | | | | | |
| Police | $1,530 | $1,530 | | | | |
| Fire | 1,600 | 1,600 | | | | |
| Public works | 900 | 900 | | | | |
| Judicial/correctional | 430 | 430 | | | | |
| Recreational/cultural | 550 | 550 | | | | |
| Social services | 550 | 550 | | | | |
| Health | 69 | 69 | | | | |
| Administration | 775 | 775 | | | | |
| Fringe benefits | 1,800 | 1,800 | | | | |
| Engineering | 230 | 230 | | | | |
| Principal | 545 | | $545 | | | |
| Interest | 950 | | 535 | | $250 | $165 |
| Allan Bridge | 1,300 | | | $1,300 | | |
| Bus terminal | 550 | | | 550 | | |
| Water/sewer | 1,878 | | | | 1,878 | |
| Municipal parking | 910 | | | | | 910 |
| Other expenditures | 75 | 75 | | | | |
| Transfers to: | | | | | | |
| General fund | 140 | | | | 80 | 60 |
| Debt service fund | 1,080 | 1,080 | | | | |
| Capital projects fund | 120 | | | | 120 | |
| Water and sewer fund | 108 | | | 108 | | |
| Municipal parking fund | 142 | 120 | | | 22 | |
| Total Appropriations | $16,232 | $9,709 | $1,080 | $1,958 | $2,350 | $1,135 |

*Revenues:*

| | Total | | | | | |
|---|---|---|---|---|---|---|
| Property tax | $4,642 | $4,642 | | | | |
| Sales taxes | 1,374 | 1,374 | | | | |
| Nontax local revenue | 852 | 852 | | | | |
| State aid | 1,640 | 1,640 | | | | |
| Federal aid | 1,021 | 1,021 | | | | |
| Interest on investments | 235 | 40 | $20 | $175 | | |
| Proceeds from GO bonds | 800 | | | 800 | | |
| Sale of water | 1,650 | | | | $1,650 | |
| Sewer charges | 320 | | | | 320 | |
| Parking charges | 993 | | | | | $993 |
| Transfers from: | | | | | | |
| General fund | 120 | | | | | 120 |
| Debt service fund | 1,080 | | 1,080 | | | |
| Capital projects fund | 120 | | | | 120 | |
| Water/sewer fund | 210 | 80 | | 108 | | 22 |
| Municipal parking fund | 60 | 60 | | | | |
| Decrease (increase) in fund balance or retained earnings | 1,115 | 0 | (20) | 875 | 260 | 0 |
| Total Revenues | $16,232 | $9,709 | $1,080 | $1,958 | $2,350 | $1,135 |

service, and capital projects funds, and revenues and *expenses* in the water and sewer and municipal parking funds, the appropriations in Table 2-19 are actually a mixture of expenditures and expenses.

Finally, note that Dyer Straits is forecasting that the general fund and the municipal parking fund will "break even," with revenues equaling appropriations without a change in the fund balance; the capital projects fund and the water and sewer fund will have deficits and draw down the fund balance; and the debt service fund will have a surplus and increase the fund balance. The capital projects fund is budgeted so that the large fund balance that existed at the beginning of 1983 (see Table 2-2) is reduced. Capital projects funds often run a relatively large deficit or surplus due to the difference in timing between the receipt of funds for construction, which are generally received toward the beginning of the project, and construction itself, which may take several years to complete. In the case of the water and sewer fund in Dyer Straits, the budget resulted from a policy decision made by the city to reduce the retained earnings that had accumulated.

Revenue and expenditure budgets are very helpful in evaluating the government's financial condition. These budgets often provide the most reliable forecast of revenues and expenditures for the current or upcoming year.

### Capital Budgets

Almost all governments prepare an operating budget, and in addition, many governments prepare a separate *capital budget.* Capital, or capital improvement, budgets provide financial information for planned capital expenditures —those expenditures made currently that yield significant benefits in the future, such as school buildings, hospital buildings and equipment, dams, bridges, and roads.

Conceptually, capital and operating expenditures differ in several ways, although in practice the specific definitions of *capital* and *operating* vary widely across governments. Besides having a useful life that extends beyond an operating cycle (usually one year), capital items are often nonrecurring or one-time expenditures, usually involve significant planning and construction that take more than one operating cycle to complete, are frequently large relative to the typical operating expenditures associated with the program, and, in many cases, are financed to a significant degree through borrowing. These differences lead to the preparation of a separate capital budget. Also, recall from section II that capital expenditures in governments are often accounted for in separate funds.

An example of a simplified capital budget is shown in Table 2-20 for the city of Dyer Straits (exclusive of the enterprise funds) for the years 1983 through 1987. Table 2-20, part A, shows the particular projects under construction or planned for construction during the five-year period. The total projected cost, authorizations prior to 1983, and the yearly authorizations from 1983 through 1987 are indicated for each project. The capital expenditures programmed for 1983 cor-

TABLE 2-20  City of Dyer Straits, Capital Budget—Five-Year Plan
A. Capital Project Expenditure Estimates, 1983–87 (All Figures in Thousands of Dollars)

| PROJECT TITLE | ESTIMATED TOTAL COST | PRIOR AUTHORIZATIONS | BUDGET YEAR 1983 | FUTURE YEARS | | | |
|---|---|---|---|---|---|---|---|
| | | | | 1984 | 1985 | 1986 | 1987 |
| 1. Holmes Courthouse Renovation | $3,200 | $3,092 | $108 | — | — | — | — |
| 2. Allan Bridge | 5,100 | 300 | 1,300 | $3,100 | $ 400 | — | — |
| 3. Bus Terminal | 900 | — | 550 | 350 | — | — | — |
| 4. Recreation Complex | 1,300 | — | — | 700 | 600 | — | — |
| 5. Downtown Repaving | 1,000 | — | — | 100 | 200 | $600 | $100 |
| 6. Firehouse Renovation | 2,100 | — | — | — | — | 400 | 1,700 |
| Total | $13,600 | $3,392 | $1,958 | $4,250 | $1,200 | $1,000 | $1,800 |

B. Methods of Financing, 1983–87 (All Figures in Thousands of Dollars)

| YEAR | TOTAL FINANCING | FROM GENERAL FUND | FROM GENERAL OBLIGATION BONDS | INTEREST ON INVESTMENTS | FROM ENTERPRISE FUNDS |
|---|---|---|---|---|---|
| 1983 | $1,083 | $0 | $800 | $175 | $108 |
| 1984 | 3,980 | 500 | 3,360 | 120 | 0 |
| 1985 | 1,200 | 400 | 410 | 190 | 200 |
| 1986 | 1,000 | 400 | 170 | 130 | 300 |
| 1987 | 1,800 | 300 | 1,440 | 60 | 0 |
| Total | $9,063 | $1,600 | $6,180 | $675 | $608 |

respond to those shown on the expenditure budget in Table 2-19, but more detail is shown in Table 2-20.

The second part of the capital budget for Dyer Straits, part B, summarizes the way in which the proposed capital improvements will be financed each year. The financing methods include funds from the general fund (the operating budget), general obligation bonds, earned interest, and transfers from the enterprise funds. Note that in all years except 1983, Dyer Straits is financing part of its capital expenditures through a capital appropriation in the general fund. Also, recall from Table 2-19 that part of the 1983 capital expenditures are being financed by a reduction in the capital projects fund balance.

Although the capital and operating budgets are often shown separately, there is a need to link the two together because many of the items in the capital budget have direct impact on the operating budget. Some governments are explicitly taking these links into account by showing the operating budget expenditures that will probably follow the capital expenditures, information that is very useful in financial analysis.

### Cash Budgets

Operating and capital budgets often employ some type of accrual basis of accounting. Governments that budget on an accrual or modified accrual basis need a different document to plan for their cash needs. The *cash budget* focuses on receipts and disbursements and identifies anticipated cash flows into and out of the government each period. Cash budgets are crucial when governments receive their revenues infrequently and in large amounts, such as the receipt of taxes or state aid one to four times per year. Cash budgets are also useful when reimbursements cause lags in payments to the government.

A cash budget for the general fund of Dyer Straits that was formulated prior to the start of 1983 appears in Table 2-21. This budget is divided by months and shows the cash inflows and outflows, and the beginning and ending cash balances, for each month. Note that the receipts are anticipated to be uneven due to the quarterly payment of property taxes and federal aid and the semiannual state aid payments. The disbursements, by comparison, are projected to be quite even over the twelve-month period.

The bottom three lines in the table show the projected beginning-of-month cash balance, the anticipated changes resulting from the inflows and outflows, and the projected end-of-month cash balance. The cash budget projects a negative cash balance for April and October, indicating that Dyer Straits may have to borrow money for short periods. The cash budget also indicates that the cash balances over the year are projected to decrease from $239,000 on January 1, 1983, to $21,000 on January 1, 1984. The cash budget is an important data source for the analysis of internal resources (see Chapter 8).

TABLE 2-21 City of Dyer Straits, Cash Budget—General Fund, 1983 (All Figures in Thousands of Dollars)

| | JAN. | FEB. | MAR. | APR. | MAY | JUNE | JULY | AUG. | SEPT. | OCT. | NOV. | DEC. | YEARLY TOTAL |
|---|---|---|---|---|---|---|---|---|---|---|---|---|---|
| *Cash Inflows:* | | | | | | | | | | | | | |
| Property taxes | $842 | $130 | $93 | $986 | $38 | $30 | $953 | $61 | $38 | $895 | $121 | $69 | $4,256 |
| Sales taxes | 102 | 102 | 109 | 116 | 116 | 102 | 102 | 109 | 122 | 116 | 129 | 136 | 1,361 |
| Nontax local revenues | 363 | 21 | 20 | 18 | 21 | 20 | 344 | 27 | 26 | 27 | 23 | 22 | 932 |
| State aid | | | | 820 | | | | | | 820 | | | 1,640 |
| Federal aid | 255 | | | 255 | | | 255 | | | 255 | | | 1,020 |
| Total | $1,562 | $253 | $222 | $2,195 | $175 | $152 | $1,654 | $197 | $186 | $2,113 | $273 | $227 | $9,209 |
| *Cash Outflows:* | | | | | | | | | | | | | |
| Salaries | $479 | $452 | $426 | $426 | $399 | $399 | $452 | $479 | $479 | $452 | $452 | $426 | $5,321 |
| Material, supplies | 112 | 105 | 99 | 99 | 93 | 93 | 105 | 112 | 112 | 105 | 105 | 99 | 1,239 |
| To debt service | 84 | 84 | 84 | 84 | 84 | 84 | 84 | 84 | 84 | 84 | 84 | 84 | 1,008 |
| To municipal parking | | | | | | | 20 | | | | | | 20 |
| Fringe benefits | 166 | 156 | 147 | 147 | 138 | 138 | 156 | 166 | 166 | 156 | 156 | 147 | 1,839 |
| Total | $841 | $797 | $756 | $756 | $714 | $714 | $817 | $841 | $841 | $797 | $797 | $756 | $9,427 |
| *Changes in Cash Balance:* | | | | | | | | | | | | | |
| Opening Cash | $239 | $960 | $416 | $(118) | $1,321 | $782 | $220 | $1,057 | $413 | $(242) | $1,074 | $550 | $239 |
| Net Cash Flow (Inflow-Outflow) | $721 | $(544) | $(534) | $1,439 | $(539) | $(562) | $837 | $(644) | $(655) | $1,316 | $(524) | $(529) | $(218) |
| Closing Cash | $960 | $416 | $(118) | $1,321 | $782 | $220 | $1,057 | $413 | $(242) | $1,074 | $550 | $21 | $21 |

Negative numbers are in parentheses.

61

## V. USEFULNESS OF FINANCIAL STATEMENTS
## AND BUDGETS IN FINANCIAL ANALYSIS

The various types of financial statements and budgets discussed in this chapter are essential input to the task of financial analysis, our concern in the remainder of the book. Of course, the economic, social, and demographic data that are not included in financial statements and budgets are also critical for financial analysis, but the structure and terminology used in the organization and presentation of financial information warrant the separate explanation given in this chapter.

One way to summarize the information contained in financial statements and budgets is to consider some of the questions that they are designed to answer. Table 2–22 contains questions that are related to financial analysis. This is not an

TABLE 2–22   Major Questions Addressed by Financial Statements and Budgets

| QUESTIONS* | FINANCIAL STATEMENTS | BUDGETS |
|---|---|---|
| 1. How much revenues are raised by the government, from what sources, and how much from each source? | Estimated and Actual Revenues Statement | Operating Revenues Budget |
| 2. When are these revenues received by the government as cash? | Cash Receipts and Disbursements Statement | Cash Budget |
| 3. How much does the government spend, what subunits are responsible for making these expenditures, and what are the expenditures for? | Authorized and Actual Operating Expenditures Statement | Operating Expenditures Budget |
| 4. When are these expenditures made as cash payments by the government? | Cash Receipts and Disbursements Statement | Cash Budget |
| 5. What expenditures are made for capital purposes, by what subunits, and how are they financed? | Authorized and Actual Capital Expenditures Statement | Capital Budget |
| 6. At a given point in time, what financial claims does the government have on others, and others have on the government? | Balance Sheet, Statement of Bonds Payable, Notes to Financial Statements | *Pro Forma* Balance Sheet† |
| 7. How are the financial claims on the government changing over time? | Balance Sheet, Change in Fund Balance Statement | *Pro Forma* Balance Sheet†, Projected Change in Fund Balance Statement |

*Although the questions are stated in the present tense, answers to the questions in the past tense are provided by financial statements, and in the future tense by budgets. A further breakdown of the financial statements and budgets by funds could also be made for all the questions listed.

†This is a forecast of the balance sheet at the end of the given period. Operating budgets are essentially *pro forma* revenue and expenditure statements.

exhaustive list, but the questions illustrate some of the main connections between the concerns of financial analysis and the information found in financial statements and budgets.

The questions listed in Table 2-22 are primarily descriptive, asking, for example: How much revenues have been raised? What expenditures have been made? and What are the financial claims on the government? Good financial analysis requires a clear understanding of what actually has been, is, or will be going on in the government. But financial analysis goes beyond description, using the information contained in financial statements and budgets as an important ingredient for the analysis and evaluation of government finances presented in the following chapters.

## QUESTIONS

1. How is accounting information organized in governments?
2. Differentiate between stocks and flows of resources. In a governmental accounting system, what are the primary stocks and flows?
3. Describe the principal bases of accounting and discuss the differences among the bases.
4. ''A fund balance is equivalent to cash.'' Discuss this statement. Under what conditions would it be true? False?
5. What major types of funds are recommended for governments? Describe the major purpose of each of the funds.
6. What is the distinguishing feature of the general fund?
7. What are the key accounting differences between funds that use expenditure and expense bases of accounting?
8. What are the major types of financial statements for funds that use expenditure accounting? Expense accounting?
9. Differentiate between financial statements and budgets.
10. What information is contained in the following types of budgets: (a) operating, (b) capital, and (c) cash?

─────────────────────────── **PROBLEMS** ───────────────────────────

1. This problem presents information on the fictitious city of Eliotville. First, analyze each piece of information and determine whether it is a *stock* or a *flow*. Second, for stocks, determine whether the information depicts an asset or a liability; for flows, whether it depicts a revenue, a receipt, an expenditure, or a disbursement. Finally, indicate the appropriate fund (or funds) in which the information should be recorded.

   Information on the financial events for Eliotville for a fiscal year is presented below. The city of Eliotville uses an accrual basis of accounting for revenues and expenditures. Also, Eliotville uses three funds: general fund, debt service fund, and capital projects fund.

### Information on the Financial Events for Eliotville

a. At the beginning of the fiscal year, there was $50,000 in cash in the general fund, $150,000 in cash in the debt service fund, and $300,000 in cash in the capital projects fund.

b. At the beginning of the fiscal year, there was $100,000 outstanding in property taxes due to Eliotville from taxpayers from the previous fiscal years. During the fiscal year, Eliotville levied $2,600,000 in property taxes. During the fiscal year, $2,500,000 was collected in property taxes for this year and the previous years.

c. At the beginning of the fiscal year, the state owed Eliotville $80,000 in state aid from the previous year. During the fiscal year, the state legally owed $1,100,000 to Eliotville but paid only $900,000 in cash to Eliotville during the year.

d. During the fiscal year, salaries due to employees were $2,000,000, and all of this was paid in cash.

e. At the beginning of the fiscal year, Eliotville owed $110,000 to the firms that provided its materials and supplies. During the fiscal year, Eliotville purchased $600,000 in materials and supplies (all of which were delivered) and paid out $520,000 in cash to these firms.

f. At the beginning of the fiscal year, the general fund owed $40,000 to the debt service fund. During the fiscal year, the general fund was legally bound, in an accounting sense, to transfer $800,000 to the debt service fund. However, only $750,000 was transferred from the general fund to the debt service fund during the year.

g. The interest and principal on outstanding debt that was due during the fiscal year were $430,000 and $460,000, respectively, and these amounts were paid in full in cash during the year.

h. At the beginning of the fiscal year, the general fund owed $30,000 to the capital projects fund. During the fiscal year, no new accounting transfers took place between the general fund and the capital projects fund. However, $10,000 was paid to the capital projects fund for preceding years' commitments.

i. During the year, a building was purchased by Eliotville for $1,500,000, and this amount was paid in full to the owner of the building. During the year, prior to the purchase of the building, Eliotville issued a bond to help finance the purchase of the building. The bonds were issued for $1,300,000, and all of this was received in cash. (No principal and interest payments were due on this particular bond during the fiscal year.)

2. After accounting for a series of events using expenditure accrual accounting, now examine a second problem in which the basis of accounting is accrual for expenses. The second example consists of a series of events for the municipal hospital, Clearview Hospital. To facilitate a comparison between the expenditure accrual basis of accounting used in Eliotville and the expense accrual basis of accounting used for Clearview Hospital, the transactions for Clearview will essentially be the same as the transactions for Eliotville. Clearview is accounted for in a single enterprise fund. Analyze each event to determine (1) whether it is a stock or a flow and (2) which particular type of stock or flow the event represents.

### Information on the Financial Events for Clearview

a. At the beginning of the fiscal year, there was $500,000 in cash in the enterprise fund.

b. At the beginning of the year, there was $100,000 outstanding in third-party payments owed by health insurance organizations to Clearview Hospital for services provided in the previous years. During the fiscal year, Clearview was entitled to receive $2,600,000 from the third parties. During the fiscal year, $2,500,000 was received in cash by Clearview from the third parties.

c.  At the beginning of the fiscal year, the state owed $80,000 in state aid to Clearview from the previous year. During the fiscal year, the state legally owed $1,100,000 to Clearview in state aid for the fiscal year but paid only $900,000 to Clearview.

d.  During the fiscal year, the salaries due to employees were $2,000,000, and all of this was paid in cash.

e.  At the beginning of the fiscal year, Clearview owed the firms that provided its materials and supplies $110,000. During the fiscal year, Clearview purchased $600,000 of materials and supplies (all of which were delivered) and paid $520,000 to these firms. The beginning-of-fiscal-year materials and supplies inventory, valued at cost, was $55,000. Clearview used $565,000 of materials and supplies during the fiscal year.

f.  (There is no comparable transaction for Clearview Hospital, since interfund transactions are not used.)

g.  At the beginning of the fiscal year, Clearview had $3,900,000 in bonds outstanding. The interest and principal on this outstanding debt that was due during the fiscal year were $430,000 and $460,000, respectively, and this was paid in full during the fiscal year.

h.  (There is no comparable transaction for Clearview Hospital, since interfund transfers are not used.)

i.  At the beginning of the fiscal year, Clearview owned $9,000,000 of buildings against which $4,500,000 of depreciation had been charged. Depreciation during the fiscal year was $600,000. During the fiscal year, a building was purchased for $1,500,000 by Clearview, and this amount was paid in full to the owner of the building. During the fiscal year, Clearview issued a bond to finance the purchase of the building. The bonds were issued for $1,300,000, and all of this was received in cash. (No principal or interest payments were due on this particular bond during the fiscal year.)

3.  Using the transactions presented for the city of Eliotville in problem 1 above, construct the following financial statements for each fund: (a) beginning-of-period balance sheet, (b) statement of revenues and expenditures, (c) statement of receipts and disbursements, (d) statement of changes in fund balance, and (e) end-of-period balance sheet. Recall that there are three funds, and all funds use an expenditure accrual basis of accounting.

4.  Using the transactions presented for Clearview Hospital in problem 2 above, construct the following financial statements for the enterprise fund that accounts for Clearview Hospital using an expense accrual basis of accounting: (a) beginning-of-period balance sheet, (b) statement of revenues and expenses, (c) statement of receipts and disbursements, (d) statement of changes in fund balance, (e) end-of-period balance sheet, and (f) statement of sources and uses of cash.

# CHAPTER
# 3 / Framework and Methods for Financial Analysis

In Chapter 1 we explained that strong financial condition is an essential concern of governments striving to provide needed public goods efficiently and equitably, and to be politically responsive and accountable. We stressed that financial strength cannot be the only or the dominant goal of government but must be sought in conjunction with other goals.

Without adequate financial strength, the ability of governments to perform their essential functions is severely limited and may create costs for a large number of individuals and groups. The government may have to default on its debt obligations, generating costs for those individuals, banks, insurance companies, and pension funds holding the government's debt; real capital needs may go unmet and cutbacks in services may occur, adversely affecting the community relying on those services; taxpayers may have to incur costly and inequitable taxes or pay high costs for emergency borrowing as the government struggles to meet its cash needs; and the community may lose some of its local autonomy if financial control is shifted in part or in total to another organization.

In recent years, scores of governments have faced financial difficulties that have detracted significantly from the performance of their functions. These difficulties have included defaults, inaccessibility to capital markets, high interest rates, lowered credit ratings, service cutbacks, employee layoffs, and interventions by state and federal governments.

Fortunately for most governments, the problem is not struggling with financial insolvency directly, but rather determining the likelihood that financial difficulties will occur in the future, and identifying what can be done to correct or avoid financial problems. To accomplish this, governments must be able to measure and evaluate their financial strengths and weaknesses. Learning how to perform this analysis of government finances is the purpose of this book.

A complete assessment of a government's financial condition requires analysis of the financial reports and budgets examined in the preceding chapter, along with other information, using reasonable measures of the components of financial condition. This chapter provides a framework for this analysis and presents several methods of analysis that will be used in the chapters that follow. Each of the next five chapters focuses on one part of the framework for evaluating a government's financial condition.

This framework is essential for effective financial analysis. Measuring and evaluating the financial condition or health of a government is still at a primitive stage, despite the recent attention it has received. Individual measures of financial condition, such as credit ratings, operating deficits, or short- and long-term debt, suffer from one or more failings that make them of limited usefulness, or sometimes even misleading, when used by themselves. Most measures capture at best only one dimension of financial condition and may be a crude measure of even that piece of the puzzle. Some are reasonable indicators conceptually but are difficult to measure with enough precision to be of value. Others are measurable but do not provide sufficient advanced warning of financial emergencies to allow governments to respond soon enough to avoid severe decline in their financial condition. The purpose of the framework developed in this chapter is to provide a basis for understanding and critiquing existing measures of financial condition and for developing a consistent set of measures that, taken together, result in a comprehensive view of a government's financial condition.

Developing a consistent set of measures of financial condition, however, requires an understanding of the relationships between a government's finances and the environment in which it operates. A government's financial condition reflects changes in the demand for government services; the costs of personnel, equipment, materials, and supplies to provide these services; and the revenues available to pay these costs. But these pressures on government finances result from other factors in the government's environment, such as movements of population and changes in the composition of population, changes in the industrial structure and employment patterns, changes in the power of public employees and client groups, and changes in the national and regional economy and capital market conditions, as well as changes arising from past and current governmental decisions and policies. Thus both internal and external factors and their relationships to financial condition need to be understood and incorporated into a framework for measuring, predicting, and responding to financial problems faced by governments.

Even if measures of financial condition are developed that reflect critical relationships between a government and its environment, this information about financial condition does not lend itself to a simple, back-of-the-envelope type of analysis. There are no simple formulas or rules of thumb for determining financial well-being. And yet more complex forms of analysis, such as multiple-equation econometric models of local economies and fiscal impacts, are often primitive, scarce, costly, and intimidating to government officials. At this point in time, to be both useful and reliable from the perspective of most of those who need to understand government finances, approaches to financial condition must steer their way carefully between oversimplified rules of thumb and over-complicated multiple-equation models. This is the approach we take in this book and in the framework and techniques developed in this chapter.

Finally, our approach emphasizes the financial condition of the government organization as a whole, and the factors that underlie its financial condition. We ask how strong the government is financially and determine what are the sources of its financial strength and weakness through the analysis of its revenues, expenditures, debt, pensions, and internal resources. While we may refer to specific governmental programs, projects, activities, or departments in conducting our analysis, our goal is to determine the financial condition of the governmental organization itself and not of any specific project or program.

To understand financial condition and to develop an approach to its analysis, we proceed in several steps. First, we define and discuss the characteristics of financial condition. Second, we develop a framework for the conduct of financial analysis which recognizes these different characteristics. We then briefly review existing measures of financial condition and relate them to our framework. Next we discuss the empirical determinants of financial condition to identify the external and internal factors that need to be incorporated into different components of financial analysis. Finally, we introduce a few basic analytical techniques that will be employed in later chapters to assess financial condition.

## I. CHARACTERISTICS
## OF FINANCIAL CONDITION

Financial condition goes by many names—financial health, solvency, strength, stress—all of which can be defined as the probability that a government will meet its financial obligations to creditors, consumers, employees, taxpayers, suppliers, constituents, and others as these obligations come due. And this probability depends, in turn, on the likelihood that the sources of cash available to the government and the required uses for cash at any point in time can be brought into equilibrium. Table 3-1, which lists major sources and uses of cash for governments, can be used to clarify the definition of financial condition and highlight its major characteristics.

First, financial condition has a *time dimension*. As shown in Table 3-1, available sources of cash and required uses for cash depend on the time horizon involved, with more sources and uses of cash possible as the time horizon lengthens. Consequently, how easily a government can meet its cash needs depends on *when* these cash needs must be met—next week, next year, or five years from now. Short-term financial condition depends on a government's "liquidity," or ability to raise cash quickly to meet immediate needs; long-term financial condition

TABLE 3-1   **Sources and Uses of Cash in Governments**

| TIME HORIZON | SOURCES OF CASH | USES OF CASH |
|---|---|---|
| Short Term | Draw down cash balances | Build up cash balances |
| | Convert short-term assets into cash (sell securities, speed up collections, reduce inventories) | Convert cash into other short-term assets (buy securities, build up inventories) |
| | Incur short-term liabilities to gain cash (borrow short term, slow down payments of accounts payable) | Use cash to lower short-term liabilities (retire short-term debt, speed up payment of accounts payable) |
| | Increase operating revenues, (property taxes, sales taxes, departmental income, intergovernmental transfers) or decrease operating expenditures | Increase operating expenditures or decrease operating revenues |
| | Increase long-term borrowing or cut back capital expenditures | Increase capital expenditures or repay long-term borrowing |
| Long Term | Secure new revenue sources | Expend funds on new projects and programs |

depends on a government's ability to secure resources and manage expenditures over the long term. Although the short-term and long-term financial condition of a government may be similar, this is not always the case.

Second, financial condition is rooted in the government's *economic environment*. Ultimately the likelihood that a government can secure cash to meet its cash needs depends on that government's ability to gain or earn resources (revenues) equal to or greater than its use of revenues (expenditures). All the short-term cash generation methods in the world (delaying payments, leasing instead of buying, emergency borrowing, etc.) cannot compensate indefinitely for a government's failure to generate resources to cover its use of resources. As the time horizon lengthens in Table 3-1, the sources and uses of *cash* depend more and more on the sources and uses of *economic resources* (revenues and expenditures), which, in turn, reflect in large part the resources and needs of the community served by the government. Consequently, financial condition, the ability to balance sources and uses of cash to meet financial obligations, has an underlying economic dimension: the ability to balance revenues and expenditures.

Third, financial condition is a *multidimensional* or *multiconstituency* concept. Financial condition depends on all sources and uses of cash that reflect the government's relationship with a wide variety of individuals and groups. Cash receipts come from taxpayers, users of services, other governments, creditors; cash payments go to consumer groups, suppliers, employees, bondholders, banks, and so forth. Thus financial condition cannot be measured solely with respect to a government's financial obligations to any one group, such as creditors, but has to be viewed as the net result of obligations to all governmental clientele receiving or providing resources. It requires analysis of all major sources and uses of resources (revenues, expenditures, borrowing, etc.) and not just one aspect (such as debt or internal resources).

Fourth, financial condition involves *implicit* as well as *explicit* financial obligations, where implicit obligations are changes in resource and service flows or requirements that do not reveal themselves explicitly in cash flows or financial contracts. For example, a government with cash reserves and untapped resources in a community that has substantial unmet needs for governmental services is, in an overall sense, less financially healthy than it appears from a strict cash flow analysis. And so is the government that has little debt but has let its physical capital deteriorate, reducing services to the community in the process. While these financial obligations to the community are frequently not in specific financial contracts, such as a lease or a pension plan, they must still be considered in the analysis of a government's financial condition.

Finally, financial condition is a *composite variable,* encompassing financial strengths and weaknesses, not a simple, one-dimensional measure of well-being. Furthermore, financial condition can vary greatly and is not just a matter of being solvent or insolvent. Consequently, financial analysis must recognize these different dimensions and distinguish different levels of financial well-being.

All of these characteristics should be kept in mind as we discuss the measurement of financial condition. To be useful, any measures should recognize the continuous nature of financial condition (the spectrum between excellent financial condition and financial insolvency), the time dimension and economic roots of financial condition, and the full financial implications of the responsibilities of government toward consumers, employees, taxpayers, lenders, and other clientele. With these characteristics in mind, we can now develop a framework for financial analysis.

## II. A FRAMEWORK FOR MEASURING
## FINANCIAL CONDITION

To develop our framework, we start with several general considerations, then present the framework and its components, and end with a discussion of the basic assumptions needed to make the framework operational.

### General Considerations

First, the system of financial condition measurement we present here does not consist of a single measure or formula of financial condition. Instead it is a framework for organizing and interpreting a wide range of measures related to financial condition which need to be viewed together to give a complete picture of the organization's financial condition. We view financial analysis as a way to learn about the various dimensions of financial condition for a government or set of governments. Our aim is to develop a way of thinking about financial condition, a way of organizing otherwise disparate information to provide a useful overview of financial condition and its different dimensions. This framework enables the analyst to clarify an organization's different financial strengths and weaknesses, not just determine whether the organization is in "good" or "bad" financial health.

Second, this framework combines a set of measures that recognizes the different dimensions of financial condition and the wide range of factors that influence financial condition. These measures include the following:

1. Both short-term and long-term factors of financial condition, such as liquidity measures that reflect the immediate ability to meet cash needs, and revenue capacity measures that are related to a government's long-term ability to meet expenditures. The particular measures used, however, depend on whether the analyst is concerned with short- or long-term financial condition or both.

2. Nonfinancial as well as financial variables. Governments operate within larger communities that both provide resources to and receive goods and services from the government. Consequently, some of the measures of financial condition, especially longer-term measures, must incorporate characteristics of this larger community.

3. Factors that represent all major constituencies of government, regardless of whether they take the form of financial obligations "on the books." As a result, we include measures of community need that represent obligations that are not explicitly contractual, as well as measures of explicit financial obligations to other groups, such as investors in government bonds.

Third, the measures of financial condition included in the framework must be compared with different standards in order to provide useful results. Expenditure pressures, available resources, and financial condition are all relative concepts—they need to be compared with some base line; their changes or differences are generally more important than their absolute level, although this is not always the case. While the standard or base-line measures will vary with different circumstances, we will use several types of standards in our analysis (to be discussed in section V).

Finally, the usefulness of this framework depends on a clear understanding of the limitations and qualifications of the financial condition measures included in the framework. It is often difficult to measure a specific aspect of financial condition accurately. Sometimes it is hard to formulate a measure that captures exactly what the analyst wants. A measure may reflect one dimension, not others, or many dimensions when only one is sought. Data may be inaccurate or inadequate; less satisfactory proxy measures may be necessary. And throughout the analysis, special features of individual communities may limit the usefulness of standard financial condition measures. Recognition of these limitations and qualifications must be an integral part of the analysis, not just something tacked on at the end.

### The Framework

We stated earlier that *financial condition* can be defined as the probability that a government will meet its financial obligations. Conceptually, as shown in Figure 3–1, this probability depends on the level of expenditure demands on the government (expenditure pressures) relative to the total resources available to meet those

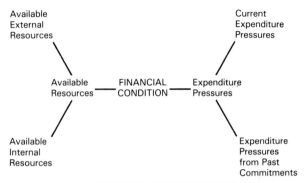

Figure 3-1.    **THE INGREDIENTS OF FINANCIAL CONDITION**

demands (available resources). Measures of operating and capital expenditure levels and debt and pension obligations are included in the expenditure pressures on a government; measures of external and internal resources are included in available resources.

In this context, the slack or gap between expenditure pressures and available resources becomes a measure of financial condition. A government that faces little pressure for additional expenditures and has substantial capacity to raise additional revenues is in good financial condition; a government with considerable pressures to increase its budget, but very little unused revenue capacity, is in poor financial condition.

Figure 3-1 displays our representation of financial condition and the internal and external factors related to a government's well-being. Expenditure pressures result both from demands for a greater quantity (or better quality) of services and from increases in costs just to provide the current levels of outputs. Thus the factors increasing the quantity, quality, and/or per unit cost of outputs will adversely affect financial condition. Expenditure pressures also come from past decisions to meet needs that resulted in liabilities faced currently by the government. These are primarily debt and pension liabilities.

Available resources can be either external or internal. A government will have, at any point in time, an external resource base (both local and nonlocal) that it can draw upon. The availability of this external base depends on, for example, the level of unused tax and other revenue capacity. Internal resources depend on the levels of different assets, relative to liabilities, and the ease with which these resources can be converted to cash.

Thus our conceptual framework is quite straightforward. A government's financial condition reflects the difference between available resources and expenditure pressures. To make this approach workable, we now need to develop the individual components of the framework.

### Components of the Financial Condition Framework

To use this framework for financial analysis, we need to relate the basic ingredients of Figure 3-1 to the different types of financial data presented in

Chapter 2. We will add non-financial data as we develop our framework further and will treat each of the financial analysis components in depth in later chapters.

The ingredients of financial condition from Figure 3–1 can be analyzed in the following separate components (and then combined for an overall analysis):

1. Available external revenues can be examined through *revenue analysis* to determine the government's ability to raise additional revenues from external sources (local economy, other governments). Revenue analysis examines the basic economic strength of the government, the resources that can be tapped, the capacity of the government to generate revenues, and the actual revenues raised.

2. Current expenditure pressures can be studied through *expenditure analysis* to determine the pressures on the government for additional expenditures. Expenditure analysis examines the needs of the community for government goods and services, the production and service conditions faced by the government, the price of physical resources needed to provide these goods and services, the resulting levels of expenditures required, and the actual expenditures made by the government.

3. Expenditure pressures from past commitments can be evaluated by *debt and pension analyses* to determine the pressures on government expenditures and available resources from past debt and pension decisions and the resulting ability of the government to incur additional debt and fund its pensions. Debt analysis examines the effects of borrowing, repayment, and existing levels of debt obligations; pension analysis examines the effects of the pension system's assets, liabilities, cash flow, and funding; both analyses evaluate the extent to which projected resources can carry debt and meet pension payments. (This component of financial analysis is broken into debt analysis and pension analysis in later chapters.)

4. Available internal resources can be studied by *internal resource analysis* to determine the government's ability to draw on internal financial resources to meet financial obligations. This analysis compares existing levels and liquidity of internal resources (based on actual fund balances and reserves, surpluses and deficits, and the levels of different short-term assets and liabilities) with estimates of the government's need for internal resources and liquidity.

Each of these components of financial analysis shown in Figure 3–2 reflects a government's financial relationships with different constituencies; each component is subject to a wide range of factors, many of which are unique to that component; and each component is analyzed separately and all the components are then viewed together to get a complete picture of a government's financial condition.

A government that cannot raise additional revenues, is not meeting its current expenditure needs, cannot incur additional debt and fund its pensions, and is faced with a cash flow problem is obviously in very poor financial condition. A government that has the ability to raise additional revenues, is meeting its current and future expenditure needs, has the ability to borrow additional funds, is funding its pensions satisfactorily, and has adequate cash on hand is in very good financial condition. In reality, however, most governments will fall somewhere between these two extremes, and the analysis of these components gives us a better understanding of a government's financial condition.

In each of the next five chapters, we examine these components of financial analysis, recognizing that all components fit together in the available resource-expenditure pressure framework of Figures 3–1 and 3–2.

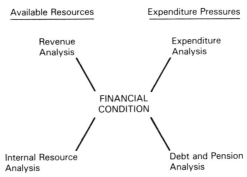

Figure 3-2.    **FRAMEWORK FOR THE ANALYSIS OF GOVERNMENT FINANCIAL CONDITION**

### Basic Assumptions

We make four basic assumptions in order to implement our framework and the basic components of financial analysis. We will utilize these assumptions in the chapters that follow. To make the framework operational, all of these assumptions have to be examined, and where the assumptions are not met, the framework and/or the analysis may have to be modified or qualifications placed on the results. Although the assumptions are important to the logic of our presentation, we believe that all of them are reasonable; if they cannot be met, the reader should be able to make the necessary modifications to the analysis.

First, we assume that the appropriate financial, economic, and social data are available over time for the government in question and its particular reference group. The nature of this reference group (one or two other governments, a sample of governments in the state or region, a national sample of governments, the rest of the county or state, etc.) will affect the conclusions that can be drawn from the analysis. If such data are not available for a particular government, the methods we present can still be applied to analyzing trends in financial condition using time series data for the government. Although we do not believe our data requirements are unrealistic, the analysis of some governments may have to rely on only a subset of the measures or be forced to use proxies for some of the measures we suggest. For most governments, however, analysts should have access to the data needed for the components of financial condition analysis that we develop.

Second, while we do not advocate a specific set of accounting definitions, we do assume that the accounting definitions and fund structure of all governments under study will permit the collapsing of the financial transactions into three groups: operating funds, capital funds, and special funds. *Operating funds* include general and debt service funds; *capital funds* include capital projects funds; and *special funds* include enterprise funds, intragovernmental service funds, and trust and agency funds. Special revenue funds and special assessment funds are included in the operating, capital, and/or special category depending on their nature. Thus the operating category includes the ongoing, ''normal'' operations of the government, including debt repayment; the capital category includes activities with a useful life extending beyond one year, such as construction projects and major equipment purchases; and the special category includes proprietary activities and any other "unusual" operations, where unusual is defined in the context of a particular analysis.

The specific set of conventions adopted to organize the accounting data and funds is not as important for an analysis of financial condition as is the consistency in the use of the adopted conventions across governments and over time. In the remainder of the book, we only specify if we are referring to capital or special funds; otherwise it can be assumed that we are referring to operating funds.

Third, we assume that the approach to the measurement of financial condition can be applied to governments alone or to governments combined with other overlapping jurisdictions, such as all municipalities and school districts together, or all local governments up to the county level. Although most of the discussion in the remainder of the book is simplified by referring to governments generally, or municipalities by themselves, the approach is generalizable, with some modifications, to any unit or combination of units of government. Again, as with the second assumption, the consistency in the choice of jurisdictions, both over time and compared with the reference group, is critical. In the chapters that follow, it can be assumed, unless otherwise indicated, that we are discussing one specific government.

Finally, we exclude from our analysis of financial condition political, interest group, and bureaucratic influences. We are trying to estimate the ability to raise resources from external and internal sources, and the levels of obligations and needs that underlie expenditure pressures; we are *not* trying to estimate the *political pressures* on the government or the *willingness* of a government to raise revenues, meet obligations, satisfy needs, and so forth. Analysts of financial condition can best gauge these political and bureaucratic possibilities and constraints in a case-by-case, subjective manner; incorporation of these factors into the analysis in a more formal way can in itself pose some extremely difficult problems. For example, should an organization's financial condition depend on the party in control, whether or not there is a city manager form of government, and the composition or organization of interest groups in the community? Until we are convinced that these other, more political factors should be included in the analysis and can present systematic ways to incorporate them, we will only include measures of factors such as community needs and resources, production and service conditions, and resource costs in our analysis.

## III. MEASURES OF FINANCIAL CONDITION

With the above framework for the analysis of financial condition in mind, we turn now to existing efforts to measure financial condition. Many of the measures presented can be useful in financial analysis once their differences and shortcomings are known and they are used within a framework that guides the selection and interpretation of such measures. Many of the measures listed will be defined and discussed more completely in later chapters as part of that framework. They are presented now to illustrate their diversity, special purposes, and limitations, and not to be studied in depth at this point.

Existing measures of financial condition depend on the questions being asked about governments and who is asking the questions. An investor may wish to measure financial condition to assess the chances a bond will be repaid; a public employee union to gauge the prospects for securing a wage increase; a researcher to rank cities according to financial stress; the federal government to allocate grants. The measure or measures of financial condition they use will reflect their particular concerns and interest, and it is unlikely that they will use the same measures. There are consequently a wide variety of measures of financial condition.

The best-known measures are probably credit ratings, such as those developed by Moody's and Standard and Poor's, which provide ratings of government bond issues.[1] These are single measures of financial condition derived from a wide range of data and are used to assist investors in their evaluation of governmental borrowings. Credit ratings, however, have been criticized as being subjective,[2] related to factors that are inappropriate measures of financial condition,[3] and not especially good predictors of financial emergencies.[4] Experience with credit ratings in New York City (and more recently the Washington Public Power Supply System) reinforces the view that credit ratings are far from precise measures of financial condition.[5]

The interest rate paid by a government on a bond of specific type and maturity, corrected for overall interest rates, has been put forth as a measure of financial condition.[6] To a certain extent, this is true. Studies explaining differences in government interest rates show that certain financial characteristics,

[1] See, for example, *Standard & Poor's Ratings Guide* (New York: McGraw-Hill, 1979); Wade S. Smith, *The Appraisal of Municipal Risk* (New York: Moody's Investors Service, 1979); and Hugh C. Sherwood, *How Corporate and Municipal Debt Is Rated* (New York: John Wiley, 1976).

[2] See John Petersen, *The Rating Game* (New York: Twentieth Century Fund, 1974).

[3] See Daniel Rubinfeld, "Credit Ratings and the Market for General Obligation Municipal Bonds," *National Tax Journal,* 26 (March 1973), 17–27.

[4] See Daniel Rubinfeld, "Credit Ratings, Bond Defaults, and Municipal Borrowing Costs: A New England Study," *National Tax Association Proceedings* (Washington, D.C.: 65th Annual Conference, October 8–12, 1972).

[5] See Edward Gramlich, "The New York Fiscal Crisis," *American Economic Review,* 66 (May 1976), 415–29; George E. Peterson, "Finance," in *The Urban Predicament,* ed. William Gorham and Nathan Glazer (Washington, D.C.: Urban Institute, 1976), pp. 64–67; and the Securities and Exchange Commission, *Report on Transactions in Securities of the City of New York* (Washington, D.C.: Committee on Banking, Finance and Urban Affairs, August 1977).

[6] See Lenox L. Moak and Albert M. Hillhouse, *Concepts and Practices in Local Government Finance* (Chicago: Municipal Finance Officers Association, 1975).

such as debt level, do affect the specific interest rates paid by governments.[7] But so do a variety of other factors, such as supply factors in the bond market, credit ratings, and the nature of the bond issued.[8] Consequently, interest rate differences are very crude measures of differences in the financial condition of the government under consideration.

In contrast to these measures based on some form of external evaluation, a wide variety of internal financial condition measures attempt to capture one or more of its dimensions. Some of these measures are evidently related to credit ratings and interest rates; all are believed by their proponents to be useful measures of, or proxies for, financial condition.

Most internal measures of financial condition reflect the different dimensions of financial condition developed in the preceding section. Resource-related measures include fiscal capacity and its utilization,[9] tax effort or burden,[10] and revenues divided by income.[11] Measures stressing ability to meet debt obligations include debt divided by full assessed value of property,[12] per capita long- and short-term debt,[13] and debt service related to revenues.[14] Expenditure-related measures include per capita expenditures,[15] expenditures relative to needs,[16] and

[7] See, for example, Lawrence Hastie, "Determinants of Municipal Bond Yields," *Journal of Financial and Quantitative Analysis,* June 1972, pp. 1729-47; and Rubinfeld, "Credit Ratings, Bond Defaults."

[8] For recent evidence, see David S. Kidwell and Patrick H. Hendershott, "The Impact of Advanced Refunding Bond Issues on State and Local Borrowing Costs," *National Tax Journal,* 31 (March 1978), 93-100; and Timothy Q. Cook, "Determinants of Individual Tax-Exempt Bond Yields: A Survey of the Evidence," *Economic Review,* 63, No. 3 (May/June 1982), 14-39.

[9] See, for example, the Advisory Commission on Intergovernmental Relations publications: *Measures of State and Local Fiscal Capacity and Tax Effort* (Washington, D.C.: ACIR, 1971); *Measuring the Fiscal "Blood Pressure" of the States—1964-1975* (Washington, D.C.: ACIR, February, 1977); "Measuring Metropolitan Fiscal Capacity and Effort: 1967-1980" (Working Paper 1, Washington, D.C., ACIR, July 1983); *1981 Tax Capacity of the Fifty States* (Washington, D.C.: ACIR, September 1983). See also John S. Akin, "Fiscal Capacity and the Estimation Method of ACIR," *National Tax Journal,* 26 (June 1973), 275-91; W. Douglas Morgan, "An Alternative Measure of Fiscal Capacity," *National Tax Journal,* 27 (June 1974), 361-65; and D. Kent Halsted, *Tax Wealth in Fifty States* (Washington, D.C.: National Institute of Education, 1978).

[10] See Touche Ross & Co. and the First National Bank of Boston, *Urban Fiscal Stress* (New York: Touche Ross & Co., 1979).

[11] See Colin Campbell and Rosemary Campbell, *A Comparative Study of the Fiscal Systems of New Hampshire and Vermont, 1970-1974* (Hampton, N.H.: Wheelabrator Foundation, 1976).

[12] See Moak and Hillhouse, *Concepts and Practices;* and J. Richard Aronson and Eli Schwartz, *Determining Debt's Danger Signals* (Washington, D.C.: International City Management Association, 1976).

[13] See Touche Ross and First National Bank of Boston, *Urban Fiscal Stress;* and Terry Nichols Clark and Lorna Crowley Ferguson, *City Money* (New York: Columbia University Press, 1983).

[14] See J. Richard Aaronson and Arthur E. King, "Is There a Fiscal Crisis Outside of New York?" *National Tax Journal,* 31 (June 1978), 158-64.

[15] See Touche Ross and First National Bank of Boston, *Urban Fiscal Stress;* and Clark and Ferguson, *City Money.*

[16] See Gramlich, "New York City Fiscal Crisis."

per unit costs of governmental services.[17] Internal resource and liquidity measures include ratios of current assets to current liabilities,[18] operating deficits,[19] change in unencumbered fund balance,[20] and deficit cash position and deficiency of revenues compared with expenditures.[21] The main limitation of these types of measures in general is that they measure only one dimension of financial condition and are presented without a framework showing their connections to measures of other dimensions. The framework developed in section III can be used to integrate different single dimension measures.

Another way to overcome the problem of single, one-dimension measures is to combine several measures into one.[22] Some researchers have constructed "composite" measures, or indexes of financial condition. These indexes usually incorporate measures from the revenue, borrowing, and expenditure dimensions of financial condition. For example, an analysis of federal economic stimulus programs combined population change, change in city income relative to change in national income, change in own source revenue divided by change in income, change in debt divided by change in income, and change in full market value of property to construct their fiscal strain index.[23] Other multiple-measure studies have been carried out, and these are included among the footnoted references.

Existing measures of financial condition represent either single dimensions of financial condition (such as revenue base or debt obligations or expenditure levels), combinations of these dimensions in simple forms such as ratios (debt divided by full assessed value of property for example), or more complex combinations such as fiscal strain indexes. Single variable or simple ratio measures, while useful in capturing one aspect or another of financial condition, are generally of limited value when viewed in isolation from other measures. And indexes combining different measures often lack any coherent framework that rationalizes the

---

[17] See D. F. Bradford, R. A. Malt, and W. E. Oates, "The Rising Cost of Local Public Services: Some Evidence and Reflections," *National Tax Journal,* 22, No. 2 (June 1969), 185–202.

[18] U.S. Congress Joint Economic Committee, *Trends in the Fiscal Condition of Cities: 1978–1980* (Washington, D.C.: Government Printing Office, April 20, 1980).

[19] See U.S. Congress Joint Economic Committee, *The Current Fiscal Position of State and Local Governments* (Washington, D.C.: Government Printing Office, 1975); U.S. Congress Joint Economic Committee, *Trends in the Fiscal Condition of Cities: 1980–82* (Washington, D.C.: Government Printing Office, 1982); and Jean Greenblatt, "The Determinants of Urban Operating Deficits" (master's thesis, Department of City and Regional Planning, Cornell University, Ithaca, N.Y., 1976).

[20] See U.S. Congress Joint Economic Committee, *Current Fiscal Position of State and Local Governments.*

[21] See the District of Columbia Municipal Research Bureau, *The Financial Health of Washington Area Governments* (Washington, D.C., 1978).

[22] See Advisory Commission on Intergovernmental Relations, *City Financial Emergencies* (Washington, D.C.: ACIR, 1973); and the District of Columbia Municipal Research Bureau, *Financial Health of Washington Area Governments.*

[23] See U.S. Government of the Treasury Office of State and Local Finance, *Report on the Fiscal Impact of the Economic Stimulus Package on 48 Large Urban Governments* (Washington, D.C.: Government Printing Office, January 1978).

particular measures being combined and the relative importance to be placed on each component. Whichever approach to measuring financial condition is used, there is a need for a single conceptual framework such as that of Figures 3-1 and 3-2 to guide the definition and measurement of financial condition.[24] Such a framework will use many of these existing measures, but in a way that provides a multidimensional view of financial condition.

## IV. THE DETERMINANTS OF FINANCIAL CONDITION

To expand and develop our framework for measuring and analyzing financial condition, we need to understand the major factors that affect the financial condition of a government and incorporate these factors into measures of different components of financial condition. Critical elements in the environment of governments—be they economic, political, or demographic—need to be identified and, whenever possible and appropriate, introduced into the measurement and analysis of financial condition. This is necessary in order to not only measure and predict changes in a government's financial condition but also develop appropriate governmental policies to avoid or respond to financial problems.[25]

The major determinants of government financial condition are listed in Table 3-2. These factors are drawn, for the most part, from empirical studies of the determinants of government expenditures and revenues[26] and studies of the

---

[24] Some studies of financial condition are based on more complete and explicit conceptual frameworks. See, for example, Stephen M. Barro, *The Urban Impacts of Federal Policies: Volume 3, Fiscal Conditions* (Santa Monica, Calif.: Rand Corporation, April 1978); and Roy Bahl, Edward M. Cupoli, and Joseph Liro, "Forecasting the Local Government Budget," in *Proceedings of the Seventieth Annual Conference, 1977,* National Tax Association and Tax Institute of America, pp. 278-87. Recent handbooks also present measures of financial condition within an overall framework. See Sanford Groves and W. Maureen Goodsey, *Evaluating Local Government Financial Condition* (Washington, D.C.: International City Management Association, 1980), Handbooks 1 through 5; Philip Rosenberg and C. Wayne Stallings, *Is Your Government Heading for Financial Difficulty?: A Guidebook for Small Cities and Other Governmental Units* (Washington, D.C.: Municipal Finance Officers Association, 1978); and New York State Office of the State Comptroller, *Financial Tracking System* (Albany, N.Y., June 1983).

[25] Studies of the determinants of the financial condition of non-governmental organizations include Edward I. Altman, "Financial Ratios, Discriminant Analysis, and the Prediction of Corporate Bankruptcy," *Journal of Finance,* 23 (September 1968), 589-606; Edward I. Altman, *Corporate Bankruptcy in America* (Lexington, Mass.: Heath-Lexington, 1971); Edward I. Altman, R. G. Haldeman, and P. Narayanan, "Zeta Analysis: A New Model to Identify Bankruptcy Risk of Corporations," *Journal of Banking and Finance* (June 1977), 29-54; John Craig and Michael Koleda, *The Future of the Municipal Hospital* (Washington, D.C.: National Planning Association, 1976); Jack Hadley, Ross Mullner, and Judith Feder, "Toward Understanding the Financially Distressed Hospital Problem" (Washington, D.C.: Urban Institute, June 1982); Susan Nesbitt, "The Financial Condition of New York Voluntary Hospitals" (Ph.D. dissertation, New York University, February 1985); and Andrew Lupton et al., "The Financial State of Higher Education," *Change,* September 1976, pp. 20-38.

[26] For a review of the literature on government expenditures, see Georges Vernez, *Delivery of Urban Public Services: Production, Cost and Demand Functions and Determinants of Public Expenditures for Fire, Police and Sanitation Services* (Santa Monica, Calif.: Rand Corporation, September 1976); John E.

TABLE 3-2    **Examples of Major Determinants of Financial Condition**

| DETERMINANTS | PROBABLE EFFECT ON FINANCIAL CONDITION* | OPERATES THROUGH: |
|---|---|---|
| Community Tastes and Needs: | | Level of current and future |
| Median family income† | − | needs; level and type of liabilities |
| Percent of population with family income below $3,000/year | − | |
| Percent of population with less than 5 years of schooling | − | |
| Percent of population under 21 years of age and/or over 65 | − | |
| Percent of residences that are owner-occupied | + | |
| Unemployment rate | − | |
| Production and Service Conditions: | | Costs of providing services |
| Population density | +/− | |
| Population size | +/− | |
| Population growth rate | + | |
| Housing conditions (age, percent substandard) | − | |
| Favorability of climate (mean January temperature) | + | |
| Capital, Labor, and Other Resource Markets: | | Costs of providing services |
| Wage rates of public employees | − | |
| Interest rates on municipal bonds | − | |
| Community Resources: | | Ability to increase revenues and |
| Personal income per capita† | + | to draw on internal resources |
| Employment rate | + | |
| Percent of employment in manufacturing | + | |
| Value of property per capita | + | |
| Retail sales per capita | + | |
| Political and Governmental Structure: | | Willingness to meet needs, incur |
| Metropolitan political fragmentation (central city population over urbanized population) | + | costs, pay liabilities, increase revenues, and/or draw on internal resources |
| Party in control | +/− | |
| Index of government reform (city manager, at-large elections, nonpartisan elections) | + | |

Mulford, Jr., "A Public Choice Model of the Revenue-Expenditure Process in Local Government" (Ph.D. dissertation, Department of City and Regional Planning Department, Cornell University, Ithaca, N.Y., 1978); Robert P. Inman, "The Fiscal Performance of Local Governments: An Interpretive Review," in *Current Issues in Urban Economics,* ed. Peter Mieszkowski and Mahlon Straszheim (Baltimore: Johns Hopkins University Press, 1979); and Normal Walzer and David Chicione, *Governmental Structure and Local Public Finance* (Cambridge, Mass.: Oelgeschlager, Gunn & Hain, 1985).

TABLE 3-2  *(continued)*

| DETERMINANTS | PROBABLE EFFECT ON FINANCIAL CONDITION* | OPERATES THROUGH: |
|---|---|---|
| Strength of interest groups (elderly, low income, owner-occupied housing, etc.) | $+/-$ | |
| Bureaucratic pressures (government size, existing budget level) | $+/-$ | |
| Federal and State Policies: | | All aspects of process |
| Intergovernmental transfers | $+$ | |
| Local Government Financial Policies and Practices: | | Level and type of liabilities, abil- |
| Debt and debt burden measures | $-$ | ity to increase revenues, draw on |
| Percent of taxes uncollected | $-$ | internal resources |
| Tax burden measures | $-$ | |
| Pension liabilities | $-$ | |

*"+" indicates that an increase in this factor probably improves financial condition; "−" indicates that an increase probably worsens financial condition; "+/−" indicates that the effect is uncertain, either because of the way *variable* is defined or because the factor has both positive and negative effects.

†Income measures operate both to increase public expenditures (−) and to provide community resources to increase revenues (+).

determinants of different measures of financial condition.[27] The latter studies helped identify the role of government practices on financial condition that were not included in expenditure studies.[28]

Table 3-2 indicates that a government's financial condition will depend on (1) community tastes and needs (poverty, education, unemployment, etc.), (2) the local conditions affecting production and distribution of public goods and services (population density, size, climate, etc.), (3) the costs of labor, capital, and other productive resources (wage rates, interest rates, etc.), (4) the wealth of the community (income, property values, retail sales, etc.), (5) the political and governmental structure in the locality and surrounding area (dominance of local govern-

---

[27] See Roy Bahl, "Measuring the Credit Worthiness of State and Local Governments: Municipal Bond Ratings," in *Proceedings of the National Tax Association, 1971,* pp. 600–619; Lawrence Hastie, "Determinants of Municipal Bond Yields"; Advisory Commission on Intergovernmental Relations, *City Financial Emergencies;* George W. Hempel, *The Postwar Quality of State and Local Debt* (New York: National Bureau of Economic Research, 1971); Rubinfeld, "Credit Ratings, Bond Defaults"; Clark and Ferguson, *City Money;* and Greenblatt, "Determinants of Urban Operating Deficits."

[28] For discussions of the general causes of municipal financial problems, see William Baumol, "Microeconomics of Unbalanced Growth: The Anatomy of Urban Crisis," *American Economic Review,* 57 (June 1967), 415–26; Gerald J. Boyle, "The Anatomy of Urban Fiscal Imbalance," *National Tax Journal,* 21 (December 1968), 412–24; William Neenan, *The Political Economy of Urban Areas* (Chicago: Markham, 1972); James O'Connor, *The Fiscal Crisis of the State* (New York: St. Martin's Press, 1973); Peterson, "Finance"; Roy Bahl, ed., *The Fiscal Outlook for Cities* (Syracuse, N.Y.: Syracuse University Press, 1978); Roy Bahl, *Financing State and Local Government in the 1980s* (New York: Oxford University Press, 1984); and Katherine Bradbury, Anthony Downs, and Kenneth Small, *Urban Decline and the Future of American Cities* (Washington, D.C.: Brookings Institution, 1982).

ment, city manager form, etc.), (6) federal and state policies affecting local resources, constraints, and responsibilities, and (7) government financial policies and practices (tax rates, debt, etc.). Differences in these factors are expected to have an influence on government financial well-being.

The determinants of financial condition in Table 3-2 are derived from numerous empirical studies of government finances. Measures of community tastes and needs, production and service conditions, and community resources have dominated empirical studies of government expenditures and need not be reviewed here. These factors will play a prominent role in Chapters 4 through 8 where we discuss the measurement of financial condition in some detail. Not surprisingly, higher levels of needs and the factors that make it costly to produce and distribute governments' goods and services lead to higher per capita expenditure levels; lower levels of community resources and lower intergovernmental expenditures usually mean lower per capita revenues and expenditures. Also, input prices have been included in expenditure studies, revealing a positive effect on expenditures of wage rates.[29] The effect of interest rates on expenditures, however, has not received much attention.[30] Increases in other prices, like energy costs, would certainly serve to put pressure on expenditures and worsen financial condition. Many of these need, cost, and resource factors, such as income, unemployment, price changes, and population shifts, reflect forces outside the community and, for the most part, outside the control of government officials.

Empirical evidence of the effect of measures of political and governmental structure on expenditures and revenues is mixed. Measures of metropolitan political fragmentation, indicating the extent to which central cities provide services to those in the metropolitan area outside their political jurisdiction, have been found to influence expenditures—the lower the concentration of the population in the central cities, the higher the central city per capita expenditures.[31] And there is some evidence that manager cities may spend less per capita than non-manager cities, although the reasons are not entirely clear.[32] But the role of political variables *per se* is ambiguous. As Richard I. Hofferbert states:

---

[29] See James C. Ohls and Terence J. Wales, "Supply and Demand for State and Local Services," *Review of Economics and Statistics,* 54 (November 1972), 424–30; Thomas E. Borcherding and Robert T. Deacon, "The Demand for Services for Non-Federal Governments," *American Economic Review,* 62 (December 1972), 891–901; Thomas C. Bergstrom and Robert P. Goodman, "Private Demands for Public Goods," *American Economic Review,* 63 (June 1966), 187–99; and Mulford, "Public Choice Model."

[30] For an exception where interest rates are considered, see Mulford, *"Public Choice Model."*

[31] See, for example, Harvey E. Brazer, "City Expenditures in the United States" (New York: National Bureau of Economic Research, 1959), Occasional Paper 76; Roy Bahl, *Metropolitan City Expenditures: A Comparative Analysis* (Lexington: University of Kentucky Press, 1969); and John C. Weicher, "Determinants of Central City Expenditures: Some Overlooked Factors and Problems," *National Tax Journal,* 23 (December 1970), 379–96.

[32] See Bernard Booms, "City Governmental Form and Public Expenditure Levels," *National Tax Journal,* 19 (June 1966), 187–99; and Robert L. Lineberry and Edmund P. Fowler, "Reformism and Public Policies in Cities," *American Political Science Review,* 61 (September 1967), 701–16.

The most controversial finding of the comparative state and local policy studies has been the repeated demonstration that nearly all the effects on policy that have often been attributed to variations in the political context—for example apportionment or party competitiveness—are in fact caused by differences in the socio-economic context [our community taste, need, cost, and revenue variables].[33]

The relative importance of political versus socioeconomic influences on government expenditures is far from resolved, but studies at the local government level have shown that political party control, as well as socioeconomic variables, influence expenditure levels.[34]

Interest groups, when represented in terms of groups in the community with special needs, have been shown to influence expenditures. It has been found that the percentage of the population above 65 and the percentage in poverty positively influence expenditures; the percentage of owner-occupied housing negatively influences expenditures.[35] Bureaucracy may represent another interest group with evidence that current expenditure levels and simple budgetary rules of thumb may explain future expenditures better than many more-complex models.[36] The effects of other interest groups, such as public employee unions, banks, and business groups, have not received much attention in empirical studies, although conceptual linkages can be hypothesized for these groups.

The influence of federal and state public policies on government financial condition is extremely complex, and only its transfer-of-funds effect has received much attention. Intergovernmental transfers of different types have been found by most researchers to be positively related to government expenditures, although the connection between grant levels (and provisions) and the response of local governments is not entirely clear.[37] The effects of other policies on financial condition, such as mandated programs, accounting and reporting regulations, and tax-exempt provisions for government debt, have yet to be subjected to thorough empirical analysis.

Finally, there are the effects on financial condition of government financial

---

[33] Hofferbert, *The Study of Public Policy,* (Indianapolis: Bobbs-Merrill, 1974), p. 203.

[34] See, for example, John E. Jackson, "Politics and the Budgetary Process," *Social Science Research,* 1 (April 1972), 35–60; and Douglas Ashford, Robert Berne, and Richard Schramm, "The Expenditure-Financing Decision in British Local Government," *Policy and Politics,* 5 (September 1976), 5–24.

[35] See Mulford, "Public Choice Model."

[36] See, for example, John P. Crecine, *Governmental Problem Solving: A Computer Simulation of Municipal Budgeting* (Chicago: Rand McNally, 1969); and Otto A. Davis, Michael Dempster, and Aaron Wildavsky, "Towards a Predictive Theory of Government Expenditures: U.S. Domestic Appropriations," *British Journal of Political Science,* 4 (October 1974), 419–52.

[37] See, for example, Inman, "Fiscal Performance of Local Governments"; Henry M. Levin and Mun C. Tsang, "Federal Grants and National Educational Policy," Institute for Research on Education Finance and Governance, Stanford University, July 1982; and Rolla Edward Park and Stephen J. Carroll, *The Search for Equity in School Finance: Michigan School District Response to a Guaranteed Tax Base* (Santa Monica, Calif.: Rand Corporation, March 1979).

management practices. There is less empirical evidence of specific financial management effects, largely because variables related to financial management have seldom been included in government expenditure studies. Some evidence can be gleaned, however, from studies of the determinants of different single measures of financial condition: credit ratings, interest rates, operating deficits, and actual municipal defaults.

Daniel Rubinfeld found that direct debt divided by assessed value of property, total overlapping debt, and percentage of taxes uncollected in previous years all had a negative influence on credit ratings[38] and, in another article, found an independent effect of credit ratings on interest costs.[39] Roy Bahl found that overlapping debt divided by personal income, and overlapping debt divided by true value of property, negatively influence credit ratings.[40] Lawrence Hastie found that outstanding debt divided by full value of property, and total outstanding debt, were positively related to municipal bond yields.[41] Jean Greenblatt found that total outstanding debt had a significant positive effect on urban operating deficits.[42] And, finally, George Hempel found that the amount of debt outstanding increased rapidly before each of the major default periods in U.S. history and prior to many individual default situations. At the same time, community resources appeared to grow at slower rates than debt service charges.[43] Also, evidence indicates that debt variables, tax burdens, and tax collection rates were associated with local government default during the thirties.[44]

Some factors, such as population density, can be put in more than one category; and many, such as income or education, are related to one another or reflect different aspects of the same thing. The effects of different factors have usually been studied in subsets, not all at once, and there is controversy over the relative importance of different factors. But in spite of these qualifications, Table 3-2 lists the major factors that increase expenditures or decrease revenues and ultimately affect the financial condition of governments. A framework for financial analysis needs to draw on these internal and environmental factors in forming appropriate measures for analysis.

While the empirical evidence of the factors creating expenditure pressures or reducing available resources continues to accumulate, the factors listed in Table 3-2 offer a sound conceptual and empirical basis for organizing the measurement and analysis of financial condition. The major factors in Table 3-2 will enter our

---

[38] See Rubinfeld, "Credit Ratings, Bond Defaults."

[39] See Rubinfeld, "Credit Ratings and the Market for General Obligation Municipal Bonds."

[40] See Bahl, "Measuring the Credit Worthiness."

[41] See Hastie, "Determinants of Municipal Bond Yields."

[42] See Greenblatt, "Determinants of Urban Operating Deficits."

[43] See George W. Hempel, "Discussion of Papers on 'The Markets for Municipals' " (New York: New York University Conference on Financial Crisis, May 20–21, 1976).

[44] See Advisory Commission on Intergovernmental Relations, *City Financial Emergencies.*

analysis of revenues, expenditures, debt, pensions, and internal resources in the chapters that follow.

## V. TECHNIQUES OF FINANCIAL ANALYSIS

The primary methodology of financial analysis is to extract relevant information about an organization from financial and nonfinancial documents and sources, put critical types of information in a form that allows analysis, and develop a set of comparative measures that both help describe and help analyze the government's financial performance, which in our case is limited to its financial condition. In this section we discuss the comparative techniques used frequently in financial analysis and consider some of the problems of measurement and comparisons commonly encountered, including the selection of a reference group.

### Methods of Comparison

Almost all of financial analysis involves comparisons of one sort or another. Measures of a government's financial condition are compared with experts' standards, legal ceilings or floors, measures for the same organization at different points in time, and measures for a set of similar organizations. More specifically, these bases of comparison are the following:

1. "Rules of thumb" or "expert guidelines" based on practitioner, analytic, and/or theoretical considerations are sometimes available. If their derivation and limitations are understood, they can then provide useful benchmarks for certain financial condition measures, allowing a comparison between particular measures for a government and these measures.

2. Legal ceilings or floors, or other types of legal standards, may impose themselves on a government's financial operations. While legal standards obviously cannot be ignored, they may not necessarily be the only appropriate guidelines for the financial condition measures to which they apply. These standards may not recognize a government's special circumstances and may have been developed with considerations other than financial condition in mind.[45] Moreover, the recent activity in the tax and expenditure limitation area has shown, quite dramatically, that legal limits are subject to change, sometimes in a rapid and drastic fashion.[46]

---

[45] See, for example, Dale Hickam, Robert Berne, and Leanna Stiefel, "Taxing Over Tax Limits: Evidence from the Past and Policy Lessons for the Future," *Public Administration Review*, 41, No. 4 (July–August 1981), 445–53.

[46] See, for example, Advisory Commission on Intergovernmental Relations, *State Limitations on Local Taxes and Expenditures* (Washington, D.C.: ACIR, February 1977); "Proceedings of a Conference on Tax and Expenditure Limitations," *National Tax Journal*, Vol. 32, No. 2, Supplement, June 1979; and James N. Danziger and Peter Smith Ring, "Recent Research on Fiscal Limitation Measures: A Selective Survey" (Irvine: Public Policy Research Organization, University of California, Irvine, 1980).

3.  The organization's own past (or forecasted) levels of variables can be used for comparison. Thus an organization's past liquidity or fiscal capacity may be used as a standard for comparison with today's level of these measures. This is the most common source of standards, although if used alone it never deals with the question of whether past values were really "good" or "bad."
4.  Similar organizations, or some other appropriate "reference group," can be used as a basis for comparison. Past, present, or forecasted average values for the reference group can be compared with past, present, or forecasted values of a specific government's financial condition measures to get a better picture of changes and differences in the various components of financial condition. While a very useful approach, it requires more data collection and extreme care in identifying a reference group of organizations operating under conditions similar to those of the organization under study (we discuss this further below).

In the face of these alternative methods of comparison, the analyst must strive to organize the comparative analysis carefully and know the limitations of the analysis and the conclusions reached. The discussion in this part and the next is designed to facilitate this process.

Time series analysis plays an integral part in financial condition analysis, and several techniques can be useful in presenting changes over time in a wide range of variables of interest. These techniques are the *percentage change, index number,* and *common size* techniques. The last technique is also useful for comparisons between organizations at a point in time.

Consider a numerical series over time, such as the expenditure data presented in panel A of Table 3-3. The series could be revenues, employment, income, population, or whatever, as long as it is in numerical form for a sequence of periods of equal length, such as years or months.

To study changes in the data in part A, Table 3-3, the series may be put in percentage change form as in panel B. The percentage change is the absolute numerical change in a series between two periods, divided by its value in the

TABLE 3-3    **Illustration of Percentage Change, Index Number, and Common Size Methods**

A. Expenditure Data—City of Upson Downs (in thousands of dollars)

| FUNCTION | 1978 | 1979 | 1980 | 1981 | 1982 | 1983 |
|---|---|---|---|---|---|---|
| General government | 9,327 | 9,862 | 11,456 | 11,939 | 12,665 | 12,092 |
| Protection of life and property | 33,438 | 36,880 | 41,216 | 41,909 | 50,991 | 50,979 |
| Health and sanitation | 20,055 | 21,392 | 24,748 | 24,467 | 25,352 | 24,549 |
| Public works | 14,338 | 15,671 | 16,885 | 16,331 | 17,645 | 18,179 |
| Education | 5,026 | 5,446 | 6,323 | 6,394 | 6,068 | 6,099 |
| Utilities enterprise | 4,299 | 4,492 | 4,948 | 5,404 | 5,801 | 5,985 |
| Special-purpose accounts | 5,442 | 6,719 | 8,442 | 11,835 | 17,481 | 21,952 |
| Common council contingent | 444 | 874 | 601 | 1,559 | 589 | 748 |
| Total | 92,369 | 101,336 | 114,619 | 119,838 | 136,592 | 140,583 |

TABLE 3-3  *(continued)*

B. Expenditure Data in Percentage Change Form—City of Upson Downs

| FUNCTION | 1978–79 | 1979–80 | 1980–81 | 1981–82 | 1982–83 | 1978–83 |
|---|---|---|---|---|---|---|
| General government | 5.7 | 16.1 | 4.2 | 6.1 | (4.5) | 29.6 |
| Protection of life and property | 10.3 | 11.8 | 1.7 | 21.7 | (.02) | 52.5 |
| Health and sanitation | 6.7 | 15.7 | (.1) | 3.6 | (3.2) | 22.4 |
| Public works | 9.3 | 7.7 | (.3) | 8.0 | 2.9 | 26.8 |
| Education | 8.4 | 16.1 | 1.1 | (5.1) | .5 | 21.3 |
| Utilities enterprise | 4.5 | 10.2 | 9.2 | 7.3 | 3.1 | 39.2 |
| Special-purpose accounts | 23.5 | 25.6 | 40.2 | 47.7 | 25.6 | 303.4 |
| Common council contingent | 96.8 | (31.2) | 159.4 | (62.2) | 27.0 | 68.5 |
| Total | 9.7 | 13.1 | 4.6 | 14.0 | 2.9 | 52.2 |

C. Expenditure Data in Index Number Form—City of Upson Downs (1978 = 100)

| FUNCTION | 1978 | 1979 | 1980 | 1981 | 1982 | 1983 |
|---|---|---|---|---|---|---|
| General government | 100.0 | 105.7 | 122.8 | 128.0 | 135.8 | 129.6 |
| Protection of life and property | 100.0 | 110.3 | 123.3 | 125.3 | 152.8 | 152.5 |
| Health and sanitation | 100.0 | 106.7 | 123.4 | 122.0 | 126.4 | 122.4 |
| Public works | 100.0 | 109.3 | 117.8 | 113.9 | 123.0 | 126.8 |
| Education | 100.0 | 108.4 | 125.8 | 127.2 | 120.7 | 121.3 |
| Utilities enterprise | 100.0 | 104.5 | 115.1 | 125.7 | 134.9 | 139.2 |
| Special-purpose accounts | 100.0 | 123.5 | 155.1 | 217.5 | 321.2 | 403.4 |
| Common council contingent | 100.0 | 196.8 | 135.4 | 351.1 | 132.7 | 168.5 |
| Total | 100.0 | 109.7 | 124.1 | 129.7 | 147.9 | 152.2 |

D. Expenditure Data in Common Size Form—City of Upson Downs (percentage of total expenditures in same year)

| FUNCTION | 1978 | 1979 | 1980 | 1981 | 1982 | 1983 |
|---|---|---|---|---|---|---|
| General government | 10.1 | 9.7 | 10.0 | 10.0 | 9.3 | 8.6 |
| Protection of life and property | 36.2 | 36.4 | 36.0 | 35.0 | 37.3 | 36.3 |
| Health and sanitation | 21.7 | 21.1 | 21.6 | 20.4 | 18.6 | 17.5 |
| Public works | 15.5 | 15.5 | 14.7 | 13.6 | 12.9 | 12.9 |
| Education | 5.4 | 5.4 | 5.5 | 5.3 | 4.4 | 4.3 |
| Utilities enterprise | 4.7 | 4.4 | 4.3 | 4.5 | 4.2 | 4.3 |
| Special-purpose accounts | 5.9 | 6.6 | 7.4 | 9.9 | 12.8 | 15.6 |
| Common council contingent | .5 | .9 | .5 | 1.3 | .4 | .5 |
| Total | 100.0 | 100.0 | 100.0 | 100.0 | 99.9 | 100.0 |

(Totals do not always add to 100.0 because of rounding.)

earlier period, and multiplied by 100. Thus the percentage change in expenditures for general government in Upson Downs between 1978 and 1979 is 5.7 percent [(100 × (9,862 − 9,327))/9,327]. The percentage change for the entire period, for general government in Upson Downs, is 29.6 percent [(100 × (12,092 − 9,327))/9,327].

The percentage change technique highlights the *relative* changes for each item over a period of time. Note that the increase in total expenditures is comprised of different patterns of change of expenditure items, both annual changes and changes over the 1978–83 period. These changes are emphasized by using the percentages rather than the absolute amounts. When both absolute and percentage changes are examined together, as in Table 3–3, panels A and B, a fuller picture of the behavior of the expenditures is obtained.

The percentage change technique is useful for a few periods. If a longer time span is the subject for analysis, however, the index number technique may prove to be more valuable. One period, usually the earliest period that does not contain a significant single-period deviation, is selected as the base year. Each *item* in a series is then expressed as an index number compared with the base year of that item. The index number for periods other than the base year is calculated by dividing the amount for the period by the base year amount, and then multiplying that quotient by 100.

Table 3–3, panel C, presents expenditure data in index number form. Using 1978 as the base year, later expenditures for each function are divided by the expenditure level in the base year and multiplied by 100. Thus the index number for 1979 general government is 105.7 [(9,862/9,327) × 100]. As with percentage changes, the absolute numbers must also enter the analysis to properly interpret the significance of the index number changes.

A third technique that is valuable for comparisons over time as well as interorganizational comparisons is the *common size statement*. In this case a key total or summary number on a statement is set equal to 100 percent, and all other items on the statement for the same period are converted to a percentage of this key number. For a balance sheet, this key number may be total assets (which equals liabilities plus reserves plus fund balances), while a statement of revenues and expenditures may be broken down so that revenues and expenditures are examined separately or together, and total revenues or expenditures may be used as a base. Since the key number is translated to 100 percent, regardless of the size of the organization, common size statement analysis permits a comparison of one organization with another of different size as well as comparisons over time.

Table 3–3, panel D, presents our basic expenditure data in common size form. Total expenditures in each year are used as the base (100.0) and divided into the different categories of expenditures for the same year. Thus the general government expenditures in 1978 are 10.1 percent of total expenditures in 1978 [9,327/92,369].

The common size method can be used to highlight the importance in each year of different categories of expenditures (or other types of series) relative to a base number such as total expenditures. Changes in relative importance over time, or between organizations, or compared with some sort of organization-type composite, can all be made using this type of presentation.

A technique used extensively in assessing the financial performance and condition of organizations is *ratio analysis*. Ratios are defined, measured, and compared to assess a particular aspect or dimension of a characteristic of the organization under study.

Similar to common size statements, ratio analysis may be used to compare one organization with another, or with some standard, or to analyze the historical events of one organization. Ratio analysis has been developed for use in the analysis of corporate financial statements, and more recently for hospital financial statements.[47] Not all of the commonly used ratios for organizations in the profit and health sector are applicable to governments, however, except for those activities in governments whose prime purpose is to *sell* goods and services, often set up as enterprise funds. Even here, the setting of user charges in the government is often concerned with more than just profitability. Almost all standard figures used as "rules of thumb" or criteria for ratios in the profit sector must be discarded due to the differences in purpose, organization, and accounting practices in governments compared with profit organizations.

The set of ratios used in the profit sector, which are designed to provide information on the balance sheet items, probably have the most applicability to governments. To illustrate the use of ratios, consider the *liquidity* of a government, a concept we will discuss more fully in Chapter 8. Liquidity is a measure of how quickly or easily an organization can meet its needs for cash or, in other words, the ability to meet current obligations by converting its assets into cash. Cash is the most liquid asset, since it is used as the medium of exchange. A liquidity ratio gives some measure of the ability of the organization to generate cash to meet its current obligations. The current ratio (current assets divided by current liabilities) and the quick ratio (current assets less inventory divided by current liabilities) are useful liquidity ratios which attempt to encompass the relationship between sources of cash and uses of cash to meet short-run financial obligations.

Ratios are also used to analyze items that are not on the balance sheet or to analyze financial data in relation to other useful statistics. Examples of the former are the ratios calculated by dividing items on a statement of revenues and expenditures by the total revenues or expenditures, illustrated in Table 3-3, panel D. Examples of the latter are commonly found in the debt area where ratios of debt to population, income, or wealth are used, and these are explained in more depth in Chapter 6.

A specific use of ratios relates to the comparison of the government under

---

[47] See, for example, Leopold A. Bernstein, *Financial Statement Analysis: Theory, Application and Interpretation*, 3rd ed. (Homewood, Ill.: Richard D. Irwin, 1983); and William O. Cleverly, "Financial Ratios: Summary Indicators for Management Decision Making," *Hospital & Health Services Administration*, Special Edition I, 1981, pp. 26–47.

study with a reference group of similar (or comparable) organizations. When comparing a large number of measures, over time, with a reference group's, ratios can concisely present the relationship between the government and the reference group. When ratios are used this way, they are sometimes referred to as *location quotients.* For example, suppose we had data on per capita expenditures for ten functions for a government and a reference group over five years. By dividing the expenditure number by the comparable number for the reference group, it is easy to determine whether the government is spending more than the reference group on a particular function, and whether it is growing slower or faster than the reference group.

Although we will be using location quotients later in the book, an example here will help clarify their meaning. Table 3-4 shows expenditures per capita on common functions (the normal functions that all governments included in the reference group carry out) for a sample government and a reference group for four years. The location quotients are calculated by dividing the per capita expenditure number for the sample government by the comparable number for the reference group. Thus the location quotient for 1980, 1.105, equals 420 divided by 380. The location quotients clearly indicate that per capita expenditures in the sample government were higher than those in the reference group in all years because the ratios are all greater than one. The increasing location quotients from 1980 to 1982 indicate that the sample government grew faster than the reference group over that period; the decreasing location quotient from 1982 to 1983 shows that between the last two years the sample government grew more slowly than the reference group.

Once developed, financial ratios and location quotients can be used for a variety of comparisons. Ratios for an organization can be compared with earlier levels, with the levels of similar organizations, with legal requirements when they exist, or with the "desired" levels set forth by "experts." All of these comparisons, however, are subject to caveats, which we discuss next.

### Problems of Measurement and Comparison and the Selection of the Reference Group

Much of the analysis of financial condition relies on measures such as ratios, percentage changes, and dollar figures, which require a great deal of interpretation and caution in their use. These measures are often surrogates, and possibly

TABLE 3-4    **Example of Ratios Used as Location Quotients: Expenditures Per Capita on Common Government Functions**

|  | 1980 | 1981 | 1982 | 1983 |
|---|---|---|---|---|
| Sample local government | $420 | $458 | $495 | $520 |
| Reference group | $380 | $403 | $427 | $461 |
| Location quotient* | 1.105 | 1.136 | 1.159 | 1.127 |

*Location quotient equals value for the sample government divided by value for the reference group.

not very good surrogates, for what we would really like to measure but cannot. Other measures may only capture one dimension of what we want to measure, so that the use of this measure, by itself, runs the risk of being worse than no measure at all. And many measures may be inaccurate, based on low-quality data. What this requires is not discarding all measures, but rather extra effort to understand exactly what a measure reveals, the use of several measures to capture alternative dimensions of an element under study, and honesty in describing what we really know and when there are some genuine doubts.

Moreover, as we mentioned above, most of these measures will be used on a comparative basis, perhaps over time for a single government, or across governments at a point in time. Such comparisons, even with accurate measures, require care in design and caution in use. Comparisons over time may reflect changes in the organization and its clientele that have little to do with what we are measuring. Comparisons across organizations require similarity of the organizations chosen and their communities, at least along the dimensions we are trying to measure. Since comparisons across other organizations occupy an important part of financial analysis, a few words on the selection of a reference group are in order.

In financial analysis, comparisons of a government with other organizations, known as a reference group, are often employed, and a key question is, how should the reference group be chosen? The answer is a judgment that must be made by the analyst based on what determines an appropriate comparison. The end product of any financial analysis is a conclusion that government X's financial condition is good or bad, or somewhere in the middle compared with something else, and the something else is the reference group. If the organization is examined over time, then the reference group is the same organization at different points in time, and conclusions such as "financial condition is better or worse than it was" can be produced by the analysis. If the government is compared with a set of ten similar governments, then conclusions such as "financial condition in government X is better or worse than in the reference group" can be made from the analysis.

A shortcoming of financial analysis that relies on a reference group is that the analysis may overlook the level of the reference group itself or fail to detect movement in the entire reference group. For example, suppose we are comparing a county with other counties in a particular state and we find that the county of interest is in relatively good financial condition. What this analysis may fail to reveal is that the entire set of counties in the state, when compared with other counties in other states, is in relatively poor financial condition.

This shortcoming associated with the use of a specific reference group for comparison can be addressed (it can never be entirely overcome due to the nature of public-sector financial analysis) in several ways. First, some absolute standards can be applied without a reference group, although the meaning of such absolutes must still be interpreted in the context of the complete picture of the government's financial condition. A revenue-expenditure deficit and a cash deficit are two examples. Moreover, some standards, particularly legal standards, can be approached or exceeded by all organizations in the reference group. A debt limit and expenditure limit are examples. Second, the analyst can employ several reference groups that expand the scope of comparison. After comparing a city with other cities in the region, the analyst could conduct a regional analysis, in somewhat less detail, to determine the region's financial condition.

To some degree, however, a local reference group is appropriate. In some ways, local governments in the same area compete for people, firms, and economic activity in general. Furthermore, many of the expectations about financial behavior are regional. If expectations about the level of taxation are different across regions, then a government in the low-tax region that is taxing high relative to other governments in the region may be unable to raise additional taxes even though it is taxing low relative to all governments in the high-tax region. Thus, in some ways, the choice of the reference group can take into account some of the political factors that we are not measuring directly in the analysis.

In addition to the context in which the financial analysis is taking place, there are a few variables that analysts should consider in choosing a reference group. Although the precise patterns of behavior are not known, it is generally believed that size, measured by population, differentiates between governments.[48] The social, political, economic, physical, and fiscal behavior of governments appears to depend, to some degree, on size, and therefore an argument can be made for comparing organizations of similar size. In a sense, the selection of similarly sized governments is controlling for size in the analysis, and all that size represents.

The analysis is also easier to interpret if the reference group consists of similar types of organizations. A comparison of small cities with a reference group comprised of other small cities, counties, and a few water districts will be difficult to assess due to the different taxing structures, intergovernmental transfer systems, legal constraints, political structures, and service responsibilities.

Similarity of service responsibilities is especially important in making comparisons. If some cities provide public education while others have an independent school district, comparisons will be affected. If comparisons of governments with different service responsibilities must be made, the data can be adjusted to account for the differences in service responsibilities.

A key consideration in the selection of a reference group that incorporates some of the items just discussed is the state boundary. Governments within a state tend to resemble other governments in the state, more so than governments in other states. Therefore comparisons will always be easier to interpret when comparing governments within one state, and usually regional comparisons are more straightforward than national ones. But these factors may be in conflict with the need to expand the reference group beyond a small area in order to assess the relative financial condition of the entire reference group. This is one of the many

[48] See William F. Fox, "Size Economies in Local Government Services: A Review," U.S. Department of Agriculture, Economics, Statistics, and Cooperatives Services, Rural Development Research Report No. 22, August 1980.

reasons that the judgment factor will never be replaced entirely by cookbook formulas.

Frequently comparisons will be made with industry or organizational averages or with prevailing market prices (such as interest rates on bonds) or with a given legislative floor or ceiling rather than with other specific organizations. It is worth emphasizing that these types of comparisons require examination of the relevance of the benchmark being used and the situation faced by the government under study. Is this government typical of the organizations to which the benchmark is supposed to apply? Are there special features affecting this organization's bond interest rate, such as insurance or a letter of credit, that explain the differences from the average? Does the legal limit, in and of itself, really suggest anything about good or bad financial condition? If so, what and why? Questions such as these must be asked continually.

There are times, due to either poor data availability or the need to enlarge the reference group discussed above, that the analyst can use aggregate figures from a larger jurisdiction, such as a state, for comparison, rather than the sum total of individual local governments. Suppose, for example, a large city in a state is being analyzed to determine how its financial condition compares with that of other cities in the state. But in this case, data on the economic base of other cities are not available, but state-level data on the economic base are available. These state-level, aggregated data may replace the individual city data as long as the shift in the reference group is recognized.

A brief hypothetical example of the use of an entire state as a reference group is given in Table 3–5. Population in the sample city was 13.1 percent of the state's population in 1980, but only 12.3 percent of the state's population in 1983. Population declined absolutely in the sample city, and relative to the state as a whole. At the same time, employment in the sample city in 1980 was 12.9 percent of employment in the state. Thus there were fewer jobs, per capita, in the sample city than in the state, since the sample city's share of jobs was lower than its share of population. The sample city's share of employment in 1983 was only 11.5 percent of the state's, indicating that employment per capita in the sample city had fallen further below employment per capita in the state. Finally, although the sam-

TABLE 3–5  **Sample City Compared with State as Reference Group**

|  | SAMPLE CITY | | STATE | | CITY AS SHARE OF STATE | |
|---|---|---|---|---|---|---|
|  | 1980 | 1983 | 1980 | 1983 | 1980 | 1983 |
| Population | 850,000 | 835,000 | 6,500,000 | 6,800,000 | 13.1% | 12.3% |
| Employment | 420,000 | 380,000 | 3,250,000 | 3,300,000 | 12.9% | 11.5% |
| Manufac- turing em- ployment | 176,000 | 152,000 | 1,235,000 | 1,320,000 | 14.3% | 11.5% |

ple city's share of manufacturing jobs exceeded its share of population and employment in 1980, its share of manufacturing jobs in 1983 fell below its share of population and equaled its share of employment. Thus, relative to the state, between 1980 and 1983 the city lost ground in terms of population, jobs, and manufacturing jobs; and by 1983 the sample city's ratio of employment per capita and manufacturing employment per capita was below the state's level. The selection and use of appropriate reference groups are some of the more challenging tasks in financial analysis.

Another caveat is the reliance on current and past data and measures to predict what the future will bring. Obviously, much of what the future holds depends on factors not reflected in current or historical financial or environmental data. The future of the U.S. economy will have much to do with the financial health of governments, and this may not be easily predicted from past data.[49] And even what was useful for prediction in the past may no longer be an effective predictor of the future. Again, our advice is to broaden the analysis as much as possible, using a set of measures or a "model" for guidance rather than a single measure or set of rules of thumb.

Finally, we will be relying significantly on either financial reports or budgets, used independently, to provide measures of financial condition. In some cases we will have a choice, so that it is important to remember that budget figures are estimates or forecasts, whereas financial statements rely on actual outcomes. Sometimes budgets include a systematic bias, and this can be determined by comparing past budgets with past financial reports. If a systematic bias is uncovered, such as overestimating revenues and/or overestimating expenditures, this bias should be taken into account when combining budgetary and financial statement information. It is complexities of this sort that necessitate extreme care in the use of information for financial analysis.

## QUESTIONS

1. Consider a common definition of *financial well-being:* "The ability to pay your bills." Is this an adequate definition of the financial well-being of a government? What important aspects of financial condition does this definition capture? What important aspects does it overlook?

2. Suppose you were asked to evaluate the financial condition of a government but were only allowed to use a single measure, such as debt per capita or total taxes divided by income. Which measure would you use and why? If you could add five other measures, which would you choose and why?

3. The purpose of financial condition measures is to evaluate different aspects of a government's financial well-being. What are the major characteristics

---

[49] See Bahl, *Financing State and Local Government in the 1980s.*

of financial condition? For each major characteristic, indicate a measure that you feel would be useful in evaluating this aspect of financial condition. Explain why you chose the measures you did.

4. The complexity of governmental financial analysis requires that a framework or model be used to organize the analysis. Yet the use of the difference between available resources and expenditure needs (or pressures) may seem overly simplistic. What is the purpose of a model of this sort? How can it be used in financial analysis? What alternative frameworks or models might be used for this analysis?

5. Suppose financial condition was determined by the difference between the value of all governmental assets and the value of all governmental liabilities at a given point in time, with the greater the difference, the better the government's financial health. How does this definition relate, if at all, to the available resource-expenditure pressure definition? In organizing the evaluation of financial condition, in what ways might the asset-liability definition be more useful than the framework developed in this chapter? In what ways might it be less useful?

6. Differentiate between single measures and composite indexes. Give examples of each type of measure used for evaluating financial condition. What are the advantages and disadvantages of each type of measure?

7. The financial condition of a government depends to a large extent on factors that may be largely out of the government's control. Drawing on the discussion of the determinants of financial condition, identify several important factors that are and are not subject to substantial governmental control. How would your lists differ if you were looking at a state rather than a local government? A general-purpose rather than a limited-purpose government? The long run rather than the short run?

8. In financial analysis, why is it important to understand the nonfinancial factors that affect financial condition? How can they be used in financial analysis? For purposes of analysis, does it matter whether or not these factors can be influenced by government actions?

9. Referring to Table 3-2, how in general does each major determinant of financial condition relate to the components of financial analysis: revenue, expenditure, debt, pension, and internal resource analysis?

10. Evaluate the following statement: ''All financial analysis is based on comparisons.'' Are there no absolutes in financial analysis? Why are comparisons needed?

11. Discuss the different types of comparisons used in financial analysis. What are some of the advantages and disadvantages of each method of comparison? Which method is the easiest to use? Which do you think is the most reliable?

12. What are ''reference groups'' and how are they used in financial analysis? What might be an appropriate reference group for a city government? A

state government? A local school district? A regional transportation authority? Explain your answers.

13.  Give an example of when you might use each of the following techniques for
financial analysis: percentage change, index number, and common size.
What do percentage changes show, if anything, that is different from that
shown by changes in an index number? What does a five-year series of common size statements show, if anything, that is different from five-year
percentage changes and index number changes?

─────────────────────── **PROBLEMS** ───────────────────────

1.  Examine the levels, percentages, and changes over time in the following three-year
time series using the percentage change, index number, and common size methods.

|                | 1960     | 1970     | 1980     |
|----------------|----------|----------|----------|
| Current assets | $2,500   | $3,000   | $4,500   |
| Fixed assets   | 7,500    | 8,000    | 7,500    |
| Total assets   | $10,000  | $11,000  | $12,000  |

Explain what each method reveals about these data. To what extent do the methods
show similar patterns? To what extent do they reveal different patterns or different
"pictures" of the data?

2.  In conducting a financial analysis of the midwestern city of Plainsville, you wish to
construct an appropriate reference group for comparative purposes. You have
gathered the following data on Plainsville and ten other cities in the Midwest:

| City        | Population | Per Capita Annual Income | Population Density (popul./sq. miles) |
|-------------|------------|--------------------------|----------------------------------------|
| Plainsville | 100,000    | $7,000                   | 5,000                                  |
| Prairieland | 50,000     | 8,500                    | 4,000                                  |
| Cedarbluff  | 60,000     | 7,000                    | 5,000                                  |
| Rollington  | 125,000    | 7,500                    | 9,000                                  |
| Cornville   | 100,000    | 6,500                    | 6,000                                  |
| Havenhills  | 120,000    | 5,000                    | 10,500                                 |
| Riverside   | 80,000     | 8,000                    | 4,000                                  |
| Watercreek  | 95,000     | 6,500                    | 9,500                                  |
| Ruralton    | 60,000     | 7,500                    | 3,500                                  |
| Opensky     | 130,000    | 8,000                    | 7,000                                  |
| Bluehaze    | 100,000    | 8,000                    | 4,500                                  |

With just these limited data, construct a reference group for your study. Explain how
you arrived at your choice of cities to include in the reference group, and indicate
what additional data you would like to have to develop a better reference group.

# CHAPTER
# 4 / Revenue Analysis

The financial analysis of governments requires examination of the complete process by which the organization raises financial resources and expends these resources in meeting particular needs of the community and clientele it serves. In this chapter we begin our analysis by studying the methods of raising revenues, the sources of these revenues, and the organization's performance in raising revenues to conduct its activities. This analysis of revenues, while helpful in and of itself, must be combined with the analysis of expenditures, debt and pensions, and internal financial resources, discussed in the following four chapters, to provide a complete picture of the government's financial condition.

This chapter is concerned with payments made to governments, either directly or indirectly, in return for the provision of public goods and services. These include such payments as property, sales, and income taxes; direct charges or fees for health, education, water, or other departmental services; and transfers from other levels of government. Some of these payments are linked directly to the supply of particular government services (user charges for water); others are linked only indirectly to any particular services (property taxes); but all the revenues considered in this chapter are made to governments for the provision of goods and services.

These revenues, however, are only one type of resource flow called "revenues" under most government accounting systems. Other payments called revenues include, for example, borrowed funds, contributions to pension funds, and funds from the sale of assets. These are considered revenues even though they are payments to governments that are not made in return for goods or services. Bond revenues are provided in return for future interest payments and return of principal; contributions to government pension plans by government employees are in return for future retirement income; and revenues from the sale of government assets, such as a surplus school or an unneeded police station, are received in exchange for these assets, not to pay for public goods or services.

This chapter examines the first type of accounting revenues, analyzing the flows of resources to governments from taxes, current charges, intergovernmental transfers, and other payments for services. Debt and pensions will be considered in Chapters 6 and 7. Other sources of funds, such as the use of an accumulated surplus or the sale of assets, will be considered when we discuss internal financial resources in Chapter 8.

## I. THE NATURE OF REVENUE ANALYSIS

The purpose of revenue analysis is to determine the current level, growth potential, and stability of revenues available to a government; the amount of current revenues compared with their theoretical maximum (that is, how much revenue reserves exist, if needed); and, if possible, the extent to which revenues have been raised efficiently and equitably. This information about revenues is needed to measure the probability that a government can increase revenues if needed, both now and in the future. This is one part of the overall analysis of the financial condition of governments.

Our analysis of revenues proceeds in four main steps. We begin with an analysis of the *economic base* of a particular community. Here we ask, what is the resource or economic base from which a government draws its revenues? We are concerned with the level of economic resources and their changes over time in order to assess the basic financial strength of a political jurisdiction, independent of the revenue options and actual revenues raised by a government.

We then examine the *revenue base* of the government, which is defined by the actual methods it can use to raise revenues. How does a government tap its economic base and what are the levels and changes in the particular tax and nontax bases used by the organization? This analysis allows us to determine the growth potential and stability of the actual revenue methods used by a government. It also allows an assessment of the efficiency and equity of the government's revenue-raising methods.

Our third step is to examine the *actual revenues* of an organization, the levels and changes of different types of tax and nontax revenues that finance the activities of the government. Here we look at the revenue data provided by financial statements and budgets and evaluate the government's reliance on different revenue sources.

Finally, we look at the *revenue capacity* and *reserves* of a government, combining the first three steps of our analysis to assess the organization's financial condition from the revenue standpoint. What is the capacity of this organization to raise revenues and to what extent has this capacity been used? What fiscal reserves does the organization have at its command and are these increasing or decreasing?

The relationships among these different revenue measures are summarized

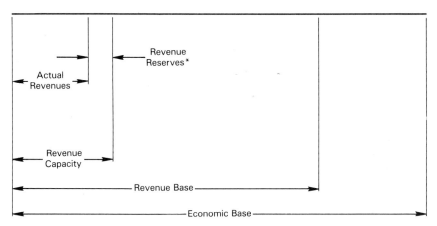

*Negative If Actual Revenues Are Greater Than Revenue Capacity

Figure 4-1.    **REVENUE RELATIONSHIPS**

in Figure 4-1. A government's *economic base* is dependent on the economic wealth of the community. It can only tap this wealth through specific revenue-raising methods, such as taxes and fees, which determine its *revenue base.* If the government were to tap this base to the maximum possible (set tax rates, current charges, and fees at the level that would generate the maximum revenue), it would generate a level of annual revenues that we call its *revenue* (or *fiscal*) *capacity. Actual revenues* are the dollars currently raised through taxation and other methods, and the difference between actual revenues and revenue capacity is the annual *revenue reserve,* or untapped revenue capacity. This reserve is a measure of the ease with which the government could increase revenues if needed.

All of these steps in revenue analysis are needed to evaluate the revenue-raising behavior and potential of a particular government as one component of financial condition analysis. In each section of this chapter we provide a general discussion of the concepts involved and then apply these concepts to our example city of Dyer Straits. We examine Dyer Straits along with a reference group of similar cities in the state and compare Dyer Straits with the average of the reference group.

Remember that the data we have assembled for the city of Dyer Straits to illustrate concepts and methods in this and the following chapters are not necessarily appropriate for all governments in all situations. The particular data chosen for any analysis—their level of aggregation, the number of years they cover, the reference group with which they are compared, etc.—all depend on a myriad of factors such as the questions to be asked, the importance of accuracy, the availability of data and resources, and the length of time required to complete the analysis. We have chosen our data to illustrate revenue analysis, not necessarily to provide a model or operating handbook appropriate for all circumstances.

## II. ECONOMIC BASE

We begin our analysis by examining the economic condition of the individuals and organizations that make up the community or clientele group ultimately providing the revenues used by a government. This is the resource base that affects the government's financial condition because most revenues raised locally are rooted, ultimately, in local economic activity. We refer to this resource base as the economic base of the organization. Actual revenues depend on both this economic base and the methods available to tap this potential.

For the most part those providing revenues to a government can be identified by a particular geographical area, usually the government's political jurisdiction. Thus, for example, property taxes apply to property located within a specified jurisdiction or district; individual income taxes and sales taxes apply to those residing, working, or shopping within a designated area; and most current charges apply to those living in a special district or the geographical area of the government providing the service. Even transfers to governments, such as state aid, may be traced to characteristics of individuals or organizations located within a specific geographical area, in this case the state's. While there are providers of local revenues who may not be easily defined in geographical terms, such as commuters or tourists paying sales taxes, we will emphasize local geographical characteristics and make the connections to these other cases as needed.

Because of this link between the providers of revenues and a specific geographical area, most of the analysis of the economic condition of revenue providers is, in fact, an analysis of the economic condition of a state, region, Standard Metropolitan Statistical Area (SMSA), city, county, school district, or otherwise identifiable area.[1] Most governments today are geographically anchored with little opportunity to alter their boundaries except through longer-term changes, such as annexation or merger, if these options are available to them.[2]

While the economic condition of a geographical area can be described in a variety of ways, we will look primarily at the economic performance of the area (employment, income, etc.) and at the economic structure and locational characteristics (export and local industries, labor force, infrastructure, etc.) that underlie the local economy's performance. Studies of the economies of regions, metropolitan areas, and other subnational units are very complex and may not be available for particular communities. All we intend to do here is indicate the general approach taken in such studies and identify some of the key data that are

---

[1] Another geographical area used by the U.S. Bureau of the Census is the Standard Consolidated Statistical Area (SCSA), which usually encompasses several SMSAs.

[2] Tax base sharing is another way of expanding the geographical area included in the economic base. See Roy Bahl and David Puryear, "Regional Tax Base Sharing: Possibilities and Implications," *National Tax Journal,* 29 (September 1976), 328–35.

useful as part of the financial analysis of governments operating in those economies.[3]

### Economic Performance

The performance of an economy is reflected in the magnitude and value of the goods and services it produces, the level and distribution of the returns it provides to the capital, labor, and other resources used in production, and the extent to which it employs local resources. While complete data to measure these different aspects of economic performance may be difficult if not impossible to assemble, it is usually possible to secure some data that measure the overall strength of a local economy.

**Measures of Performance.**    Information on the output, sales, and value added (sales less the cost of intermediate goods and services used in production) can be used to measure the level and changes in an economy's production. Data on sales may be available for most industries, but output and value-added information is usually only available for certain manufacturing industries where output may be easier to measure.

Data on unemployment of the labor force and unused industrial capacity can be applied to determine the extent to which a local economy is putting its labor force and productive capital to work. High unemployment and unused industrial capacity means that the economy is operating at an inefficient level, as well as having members of its labor force and their families in need of community support (see Chapter 5). Unemployment data are usually available from state labor departments; measures of unused capacity are more difficult to obtain and may require periodic surveys of local industry.

Finally, employment and income data measure the extent to which an economy is providing returns to labor, capital, and other resources used in production. To the extent that local residents own and/or work in local businesses, these returns from the local economy, along with employment data, measure both the performance of the economy and the economic well-being of the community. Since such data directly relate to this chapter's concern with the ability of govern-

---

[3] For a review of the general methods of regional and local economic analysis, see Walter Isard, *Methods of Regional Analysis: An Introduction to Regional Science* (Cambridge, Mass.: MIT Press, 1960); Avrom Bendavid-Val, *Regional and Local Economic Analysis for Practitioners* (New York: Praeger, 1983); Anthony H. Pascal and Aaron S. Gurwitz, *Picking Winners: Industrial Strategies for Local Economic Development* (Santa Monica, Calif.: Rand Corporation, March 1983); and Eva C. Galambos and Arthur F. Schreiber, *Making Sense out of Dollars: Economic Analysis for Local Governments* (Washington, D.C.: National League of Cities, 1978), Chaps. 1–3. For examples of economic analyses of urban areas, see Aaron S. Gurwitz and G. Thomas Kingsley, *The Cleveland Metropolitan Economy* (Santa Monica, Calif.: Rand Corporation, March 1982); and Mathew Drennan, "The Local Economy and Local Revenues," in *Setting Municipal Priorities, 1984,* ed. Charles Brecher and Raymond D. Horton (New York: New York University Press, 1983).

ments to raise revenues, most of the remaining discussion in this section will be about income data.

**Income Characteristics and Data.**    The income of individuals and organizations is probably the most important measure of their ability to provide revenues to a government, regardless of the particular revenue methods used. Income is obviously related directly to the provision of income tax revenues. It is also an important determinant of consumption, and thus sales tax revenues, and it influences a community's wealth, some of which may be subject to property taxes. Income levels may determine how much state or federal aid is provided to a local government. Furthermore, consumption of specific public services such as water, mass transit, parks, educational programs, and health facilities is often linked to the income levels of the groups using these services.

There are three main income characteristics of importance for revenue analysis: total income, income stability, and income distribution. We are interested in the levels of each of these income characteristics and their changes over time.

Conceptually, for revenue analysis, the *total income* of a geographical area of interest is the total income accruing to individuals and businesses located in the geographical area under study. This is comprised of wages and salaries, dividends, interest, rent, and unincorporated business income, all received by individuals, plus the income of incorporated businesses. If many nonresidents work and/or shop in the area, their income may have to be included or the boundaries modified for the analysis. Income to corporations in the area, whether ultimately accruing to individuals inside or outside the area, is still included because it may be taxed in addition to taxes on those individuals receiving income from these businesses.

Although this income breakdown is desirable conceptually, in most cases income data are only available for individuals or families at the local level (some data on wages by occupation groups may also be available). Total income may be presented in terms of average income per capita or per family, or as median income (the level of income earned by the middle individual or family when incomes are ranked from highest to lowest). In the case of income, several definitions are commonly used that differ in what they include, so that care should be exercised when analyzing these data.[4]

A second income characteristic of relevance to revenue analysis is *income stability*, or the fluctuation in income over time. Not only does the level and growth of an area's income ultimately impact on the revenues of a government, but so may the fluctuations in income over time. And for certain revenue sources, these

---

[4]For a review of the data used in the analysis of urban areas, see Government Finance Research Center, *Indicators of Urban Condition* (Washington, D.C.: Municipal Finance Officers Association, March 1982). To illustrate the sources of data used in a specific urban study, see Gurwitz and Kingsley, *Cleveland Metropolitan Economy,* Appendix B, pp. 218–20.

fluctuations may cause more problems from a fiscal point of view than the absolute level or average growth rate of income. Revenue analysis is concerned with the extent of these changes and ultimately how they affect the revenues of governments.

Finally, knowledge of the *distribution of income* among different individuals or families in an area under study is important for revenue analysis, since this distribution can influence the area's ability to provide revenues to government. Two regions with the same average income, but with one region's income divided sharply between rich and poor and the other's more equally distributed, may have different resource bases available to tap by their governments. The ability to provide revenues to governments differs markedly between income levels, and individuals with half the income of others may have less than half the ability to support public services. This suggests that income inequality may affect a government's economic base; it is clearly a measure of expenditure needs, as we will see in the next chatper.

### Economic Structure

What characteristics of a geographical area determine the area's economic performance? There has been extensive work done by economists to identify the factors that determine the output, employment, and income of a particular geographical area—nation, region, state, county, or city. We can only present a summary of their findings and provide references for those readers who are seeking a more complete treatment of the subject.[5]

Most studies have related the economic condition of an area either to the *demand* for products exported from the area or to the human and nonhuman resources available in the area to *supply* products for internal and external use. The first approach stresses conditions outside the area and the links of the area to its external economic or market environment; the second approach emphasizes the resources and productive capacity within the area itself. The appropriate approach depends a great deal on the size of the area under consideration, but in most cases an area's income depends on both supply and demand characteristics.

**Export Demand, Multipliers, and Industrial Structure.**     Demand-type studies, or economic base or export base studies, relate an area's employment and income to exports from the area and to the industrial structure that produces those exports.[6] Production from local businesses is classified as either export-oriented,

---

[5] See, for example, Katherine Bradbury, Anthony Downs, and Kenneth Small, *Urban Decline and the Future of American Cities* (Washington, D.C.: Brookings Institution, 1982); Wilbur R. Thompson, *A Preface to Urban Economics* (Baltimore: Johns Hopkins Press, 1965); Michael Conroy, *The Challenge of Urban Economic Development* (Lexington, Mass.: Lexington Books, 1975); and Isard, *Methods of Regional Analysis.*

[6] A well-known treatment of export demand studies is Charles M. Tiebout, *The Community Economic Base Study* (New York: Committee for Economic Development, 1962). Also see Edward Ullman, Michael Dacey, and Harold Brodsky, *The Economic Base of American Cities* (Seattle: University of Washington Press, 1971).

that is, produced for sale outside the area and thus bringing revenues into the area, or local production for consumption by businesses producing in the area or by local residents. The demand approach looks closely at the industrial structure of the area—the levels and types of industries—and how the output of each type of industry is divided between export and local consumption. Exports are seen as the driving force of the local economy.

For example, Table 4-1 shows the total employment and export employment in Cleveland SMSA industries in 1978.[7] This analysis examines employment in manufacturing (both durable and non-durable goods), retail and wholesale sales, services, and other industries, and it estimates the extent to which employment in each industry contributes directly to the production of exported goods and services. In the Cleveland area, industries as diverse as instruments, textiles, and hotels export much of their output, whereas other industries, such as food processing, eating and drinking establishments, and printing, sell mostly to local residents and businesses.

Knowledge of this industrial structure, the demand outside the area for different types of production (exports), and the links between export and local industry employment and income is used in the export base approach to predict levels and changes in the income of an area. Thus employment and income in local industries is derived from employment and income in export industries, with the quantitative relationships varying across different types of export industries. These relationships are often expressed as "income or earnings multipliers," or the ratio of local income to the income (or output) of different export industries operating within the area. "Employment multipliers" are derived in a similar fashion.

Table 4-2 shows earnings multipliers for the Cleveland SMSA industries listed in Table 4-1. For example, a multiplier of 2.55 in primary metals means that for every dollar of export sales of primary metals products, the total revenues of all Cleveland firms are increased by 2.55 dollars. High multipliers indicate industries that buy a large amount of locally produced inputs; low multipliers indicate industries that purchase less of their inputs from local producers.

The full impact of an industry's sales depends on the industry's size and the extent to which it exports its output (Table 4-1) and on its ties to other local industries, its multiplier effects (Table 4-2). Thus, from Tables 4-1 and 4-2, in 1978 nonelectrical machinery manufacturing in the Cleveland SMSA employed 45,116, produced mostly for export (80 percent), and had a high multiplier effect on other local industries (2.70). Conversely, the apparel industry hired only 8,091, produced primarily for local consumption, and when it did export its output, it had a low multiplier effect (1.94).

According to the export demand/multiplier approach to understanding the local economy, a strong economy will have a substantial export sector with high

---

[7] Gurwitz and Kingsley, *Cleveland Metropolitan Economy.*

TABLE 4-1 **Total Employment and Export Employment in Cleveland SMSA Industries, 1978**

| Industry | Total Employment | Percent Export Employment |
|---|---|---|
| *Durable Goods Manufacturing* | | |
| Primary Metals | 30,661 | 9 |
| Fabricated Metals | 43,832 | 78 |
| Nonelectrical Machinery | 45,116 | 80 |
| Electrical Equipment | 22,065 | 83 |
| Motor Vehicles | 22,088 | 41 |
| Other Transport Equipment | 5,875 | 87 |
| Instruments | 6,562 | 92 |
| Miscellaneous Manufactures | 4,166 | 94 |
| *Nondurable Goods Manufacturing* | | |
| Stone Products | 4,295 | 42 |
| Textiles | 1,970 | 90 |
| Apparel | 8,091 | — |
| Paper Products | 4,692 | 30 |
| Printing | 13,927 | — |
| Chemicals | 11,209 | — |
| Rubber Products | 11,224 | 68 |
| Lumber Products | 3,745 | 90 |
| Food Processing | 8,909 | — |
| *Sales* | | |
| Retail Sales | 106,930 | 17 |
| Eating and Drinking Est. | 40,424 | 8 |
| Wholesale Sales | 60,748 | 18 |
| *Services* | | |
| Finance | 14,882 | 37 |
| Insurance | 15,650 | * |
| Leasing | 10,531 | — |
| Hotels | 7,594 | 77 |
| Personal Services | 9,505 | — |
| Business Services | 47,247 | 36 |
| Health Services | 52,170 | 24 |
| Other Services | 41,512 | — |
| *Other* | | |
| Transportation | 26,782 | — |
| Communications | 12,808 | — |
| Utilities | 8,372 | — |
| Construction | 33,738 | 56 |
| Agriculture | 1,516 | 91 |

*Probable error in data.
—indicates no export employment.
SOURCE: Aaron Gurwitz and G. Thomas Kingsley, *The Cleveland Metropolitan Economy* (Santa Monica, Calif.: Rand Corporation, March 1982), Table 3.2, p. 41 (abridged).

TABLE 4-2    **Earnings Multipliers for Cleveland SMSA Industries, 1978**

| Industry | Earnings Multiplier |
| --- | --- |
| *Durable Goods Manufacturing* | |
| Primary Metals | 2.55 |
| Fabricated Metals | 2.74 |
| Nonelectrical Machinery | 2.70 |
| Electrical Machinery | 2.49 |
| Motor Vehicles | 2.71 |
| Other Transport Equipment | 2.88 |
| Instruments | 2.55 |
| Miscellaneous Manufactures | 2.61 |
| *Nondurable Goods Manufacturing* | |
| Stone Products | 2.13 |
| Textiles | 2.07 |
| Apparel | 1.94 |
| Paper Products | 2.11 |
| Printing | 2.51 |
| Chemicals | 2.41 |
| Rubber Products | 2.46 |
| Lumber Products | 2.60 |
| Food Processing | 2.42 |
| *Sales* | |
| Retail Sales | 2.33 |
| Eating and Drinking Est. | 2.42 |
| Wholesale Sales | 2.43 |
| *Services* | |
| Finance | 2.61 |
| Insurance | 2.89 |
| Leasing | 1.50 |
| Hotels | 2.40 |
| Personal Services | 2.76 |
| Business Services | 2.44 |
| Health Services | 2.31 |
| *Other* | |
| Transportation | 2.51 |
| Communications | 2.01 |
| Utilities | 1.92 |
| Construction | 2.69 |
| Agriculture | 2.18 |

SOURCE:    Aaron Gurwitz and G. Thomas Kingsley, *The Cleveland Metropolitan Economy* (Santa Monica, Calif.: Rand Corporation, March 1982), Table 3.1, p. 39.

export sales, and the export sector will purchase many inputs locally, generating additional sales for other local businesses. These local purchases, in turn, contribute to local incomes the more the local industries employ local residents (wages and salaries) and are owned by local residents (dividends, unincorporated profits).

Multiplier effects on income and income stability can be illustrated with a simple model. Suppose that

$$Y_{total} = Y_{local} + Y_{export} \tag{4-1}$$

and

$$Y_{local} = a_0 + a_1 Y_{export} \tag{4-2}$$

where $Y$ is sales; *local* and *export* refer to industries selling locally and those selling outside the area; and $a_0$ and $a_1$ are constants. In effect, $a_1$ is a multiplier. Then,

$$Y_{total} = a_0 + (1 + a_1) Y_{export} \tag{4-3}$$

and

$$\Delta\ Y_{total} = (1 + a_1)\ \Delta\ Y_{export} \tag{4-4}$$

where $\Delta$ means "change in." Thus changes in the sales of the export industries lead to smaller or larger changes in total sales (and thus in local incomes) depending on the magnitude of $a_1$.[8] The larger the value of $a_1$, the more the export industries buy from local businesses.

Thus income changes and stability depend on the relative importance of export industries in the local industrial mix and on the value of the multiplier. Fluctuations of demand for exports will make local sales and income fluctuate. The extent of fluctuations, however, depends on the particular export products involved. For example, since the demand for durable goods is generally volatile, the percentage of total industry in an area that produces durable goods for export is often used as a rough measure of the income stability of the area.

To illustrate this additional linkage, suppose income in export industries fluctuates with changes in national income or gross national product ($Y_{national}$). Thus let

$$Y_{export} = b_0 + b_1 Y_{national} \tag{4-5}$$

where $b_0$ and $b_1$ are constants.

Combining (4-3) and (4-5), we see that

$$Y_{total} = [a_0 + (1 + a_1)b_0] + (1 + a_1)b_1 Y_{national} \tag{4-6}$$

and

$$\Delta\ Y_{total} = (1 + a_1)b_1\ \Delta\ Y_{national} \tag{4-7}$$

Thus the changes or fluctuations in the total income of an area will depend on the extent to which the local economy responds to its export industries ($a_1$) and the extent to which the production of export industries fluctuates with national income ($b_1$). The more the cyclical industries, such as durable goods, make up an area's export industries, the larger the value for $b_1$ and the greater the fluctuations in total income.

---

[8]The importance of the income multiplier coefficient for income stability is discussed in Michael Conroy, "Alternative Strategies for Regional Industrial Diversification," *Journal of Regional Science,* 14 (1974), 31–46.

Besides total export levels and multiplier values, the extent to which the industrial structure is specialized or diversified may also affect income levels and stability. Industrial diversification measures include industrial concentration ratios (such as the percentage of output or value added produced by the top four or five industry groups in the local economy), and deviations of percentages of types of local industry from either national averages, equal percentages, or "minimum required" percentages (that percentage needed to just satisfy local needs).[9]

The industrial diversification of a local economy and the size of its business establishments are seen by some as measures of that economy's ability to respond to change. An economy that produces many different goods and services with smaller businesses may, in the short run, not be as "efficient" as "one-company" or "one-industry" towns, but it may be better able to respond to the changes that have turned many specialized economies, such as "mill towns," into disaster areas. Furthermore, a diversified economy may offer advantages to new industries that need to be close to the supply of certain goods and services.[10]

The theoretical rationale for industrial diversification measures as indexes of income stability is essentially that the wider the variety of output from an area's economy, the less susceptible the area is to changes in the demand for any single product. Michael Conroy, however, points out that it is not the variety of industries but the particular combination or "portfolio" of industries that creates stability or instability. Thus a city with one export industry that has stable demand such as a "university" town, or has two export industries that have demand cycles that are exactly opposite, may have much more stability than more-diversified cities. Conroy presents measures of "portfolio variance" as more accurate indexes of income stability.[11]

**Supply-Side Effects and Locational Characteristics.**    The supply-side, or resource-base, approach to determining the performance of an economy requires knowledge of the labor force (total size and distribution by education, skill levels, occupations, etc.), the productive capital (total value of equipment, age and condition of plant, etc.), and supporting institutions (transportation, social overhead capital, etc.) in the area. In its simplest form, this approach relates total income to the supply of labor in different occupations and the average wage rates in these occupations (or the capital-labor ratio in that occupation, which is used as a proxy for the wage rate). While this approach does not consider the effects of ex-

---

[9] The "minimum requirements" approach is presented in Edward Ullman and Michael Dacey, "The Minimum Requirements Approach to Urban Economic Base," *Papers and Proceedings of the Regional Science Association,* 6 (1960), 175–94. Alternative diversification measures are discussed in Roy Bahl, Robert Firestine, and Donald Phares, "Industrial Diversity in Urban Areas: Alternative Measures and Intermetropolitan Comparisons," *Economic Geography,* July 1971, pp. 414–21.

[10] This argument is developed in Jane Jacobs, *The Economy of Cities* (New York: Random House, 1970).

[11] Conroy, *Challenge of Urban Economic Development.*

ternal demand, migration, and the sources of nonwage income, it does indicate the role of the internal resources of an area in determining the area's total income.

This concern with the nature of an area's labor force and capital base is reflected in a similar approach to assessing an economy's vitality, an approach that focuses on the characteristics that lead businesses and households to "locate" in that area. Often referred to as "location theory," this approach asks what businesses need to operate profitably and what individuals need to keep them attracted to a particular area, and it then tries to determine to what extent these factors exist in a particular locality. Some of these factors are in conflict, attractive to businesses but not to households (such as low wage rates); others are attractive to both (such as a favorable climate); the ideal area balances these factors in a way that attracts both. An examination of the location characteristics of an area, then, contributes to an understanding of the long-term prospects for economic growth and vitality.

Most attention in the literature has been given to the factors that businesses find attractive. Most of these factors influence, directly or indirectly, the costs and revenues of different types of businesses, and thus their profits. On the revenue side, proximity to competitors and customers is often important. On the cost side, proximity to suppliers, access to transportation networks and low transportation costs, availability of needed labor skills, low wages and the absence of unions, low costs of energy, capital, and land, good infrastructure and public services, low taxes, and available public subsidies are among the factors that receive considerable attention. Table 4–3 lists the factors that may influence industrial location. Although subjective factors may play a role (the boss grew up in the area), more often it is these cost and revenue elements that need to be identified, and their relative importance determined, in deciding how attractive a local economy is to business. A similar analysis of the factors attracting and keeping households (and thus the labor force), such as wage rates, climate, crime rates, and schools, also contributes to an assessment of the long-term economic viability of an area, and its long-term ability to provide revenues to its governments.[12]

**Empirical Studies of Income Determinants.**     Drawing on both demand and supply factors, theoretical and empirical studies have identified some of the more important variables affecting the income characteristics of a local economy. For example, there is evidence that an area has higher per capita income:

—the higher the percentage of manufacturing and services in the industrial structure and the lower the percentage of agriculture;

---

[12] Factors influencing business location decisions are reviewed in Roger J. Vaughn, *The Urban Impacts of Federal Policies: Vol. 2, Economic Development* (Santa Monica, Calif.: Rand Corporation, June 1977); and Roger Schmenner, *Making Business Location Decisions* (Englewood Cliffs, N.J.: Prentice-Hall, 1982). For an application of business and household location factors to the study of a metropolitan economy, see Gurwitz and Kingsley, *Cleveland Metropolitan Economy,* Chap. 4.

TABLE 4-3    **Some Potential Factors Influencing Industrial Location**

## MARKETS AND RAW MATERIALS

Location of Markets and Raw Material Supplies
Transportation Costs and Facilities for Products and Raw Materials
 Railroads
 Motor trucking
 Waterways
 Air service

## LOCAL RESOURCE AVAILABILITY AND COSTS

Labor Supply
 Number of persons in labor force with appropriate skills
 Supply of unskilled labor
 Prevailing wage scales for all classes of employment
 Labor turnover
 Labor relations—strike frequency and duration
 Labor training facilities and programs
Availability of Land and Buildings
 Inventory of potential and existing sites
 Construction costs
Quantity and Quality of Public Services Supportive of Industrial Development
 Police
 Fire (fire insurance)
 Water and sewer system (year-round availability of water without shortages)
 Electric and gas utilities (capacity, history of shortages, rates, etc.)
 Refuse collection and disposal (private and public, rates, etc.)
 Streets and highways
Municipal Government
 Tax rates and assessments as percentage of market value
 Business license fees and other costs of doing business
 Political "environment"

## LOCAL COMMUNITY ENVIRONMENT

Quantity and Quality of Educational, Recreational and Community Services
 School systems (achievement test score levels, expenditure per pupil, etc.)
 Libraries
 Parks, tennis courts, golf courses, playgrounds, etc.
 Fine arts—theaters, symphonies, ballet, museums, etc.
 Newspapers, radio, television
 Hotels, motels, convention centers
 People transportation (bus systems, cabs, etc.)
 Hospitals and other health service facilities
Climate (temperature, precipitation, humidity, days with sunshine, etc.)
Cost of Living
Public Attitudes

SOURCE:  Eva Galambos and Arthur Schreiber, *Making Sense out of Dollars: Economic Analysis for Local Governments* (Washington, D.C.: National League of Cities, 1978), Table 2, p. 33.

—the higher the percentage of fabrication within its manufacturing sector and the lower the percentage of manufacturing raw materials;

—the higher its percentage of business services within its service sector;

—the higher its percentage of durable goods industries within its manufacturing sector;

—the higher the capital intensity (capital to labor ratio) of its industry (which usually means higher wage rates);

—the higher the percent employed and the lower the percent of the labor force that is self-employed; and

—the higher the proportion of its population that is 21 years or older, participating in the labor force, and educated.[13]

Evidence on cyclical stability is reported by Anthony Pascal and Aaron Gurwitz, where cyclical stability is measured in terms of changes in local employment associated with changes in national employment.[14] They report that an area's relative stability increases as its share of employment in services increases, particularly administrative employment, and decreases as its share of employment in manufacturing increases.

Finally, the determinants of an area's income distribution are quite complex, and the best way to understand them is to examine different sources and types of income (wages and salaries, rents, interest, capital gains, etc.) and the distribution of wealth and ownership of corporate stock of those in the area under study. The few empirical studies of determinants of income distribution in an area have been of a partial nature. For example, J. M. Matilla and W. R. Thompson found income inequality high in those SMSAs with higher percentages of non-white residents, larger differences in education levels of the population, and lower levels of median family income, percentage employed in manufacturing, and female participation in the labor force.[15] Conroy reports that inequality is also associated with larger cities, low growth, and high income stability.[16] The most accessible data revealing an area's income inequality consist of the percentage of families or individuals in different income classes or below a poverty level.

---

[13] For a discussion of the factors influencing urban growth and decline, see Bradbury, Downs, and Small, *Urban Decline and the Future of American Cities;* John Kordalewski, *An Initial Exploration of the Relationship between Industrial Composition and Urban Economic Distress* (Washington, D.C.: Urban Institute, February 1981); and Conroy, *Challenge of Urban Economic Development.* Also see Sheldon Danziger, "Determinants of the Level and Distribution of Family Income in Metropolitan Areas, 1969," *Land Economics,* 52 (November 1976), 467–78; and J. M. Matilla and Walter R. Thompson, "Toward an Econometric Model of Urban Economic Development," in *Issues in Urban Economics,* ed. H. S. Perlow and L. Wingo, Jr. (Baltimore: Johns Hopkins Press, 1968), pp. 63–78).

[14] Pascal and Gurwitz, *Picking Winners: Industrial Strategies for Local Economic Development.*

[15] Matilla and Thompson, "Toward an Econometric Model of Urban Economic Development."

[16] Conroy, *Challenge of Urban Economic Development.* Also see Danziger, "Determinants of the Level and Distribution of Family Income in Metropolitan Areas, 1969"; Barbara B. Murray, "Metropolitan Interpersonal Income Inequality," *Land Economics,* 45 (February 1969), 121–25; and H. E. Frech and L. S. Burns, "Metropolitan Interpersonal Income Equality: A Comment," *Land Economics,* 47 (February 1971), 104–8.

This section has reviewed some of the characteristics of an area that are believed to influence its income levels, stability, and distribution. The relative importance of these factors, however, will depend on the particular economy being studied.[17]

### Economic Base Data

Basic data on economic performance and structure can be used in financial analysis to measure the well-being of the economy providing most of the revenues to the government under study. Direct knowledge of income levels and trends provides a measure of the economic health of an area. Given the controversy over definitions of income stability and the difficulties in securing the data needed for their measurement, the pattern of income changes over time can be used to evaluate the income stability of an area and its effect on revenue streams. Income distribution concerns will be measured primarily by unemployment and poverty statistics.

To understand income levels and changes, or to provide measures in the absence of adequate income data, information on industrial structure, labor force characteristics, employment patterns, and demographic factors needs to be assembled and examined. This additional information reveals changes in the economic structure of an area and the characteristics of its population, providing a basis for longer-run predictions of economic health and the design of appropriate government revenue policies.

Typical data needed to examine the economic base of a geographical area are listed in Table 4–4. Both the levels of these variables and the changes in these variables are important for the assessment of an area's economic base. Many of the data listed can be disaggregated into specific occupation groups, age cohorts, different levels of education, and so forth, for more-detailed analysis if needed. This depends, however, on data availability. Certain types of geographical areas such as SMSAs have more readily available economic base data than cities, towns, villages, and school districts.

### An Application

While elaborate econometric models have been developed to estimate industry interactions and multipliers, the procedure most commonly used in financial analysis is to examine the levels and changes over time of a set of key variables related to the well-being of the local economy. There is considerable information

---

[17] For examples of the economic base in empirical financial condition studies, see Peggy L. Cuciti, *City Need and the Responsiveness of Federal Grant Programs* (Washington, D.C.: Congressional Budget Office, August 1978), Chap. 4; U.S. Department of the Treasury, Office of State and Local Finance, "Report on the Fiscal Impact of the Economic Stimulus Package on 48 Large Urban Governments," January 23, 1978; Touche Ross & Co. and the First National Bank of Boston, *Urban Fiscal Stress* (New York: Touche Ross & Co., 1979); and Bradbury, Downs, and Small, *Urban Decline and the Future of American Cities.*

TABLE 4-4    **Typical Data Used in Analysis of an Area's
Economic Performance and Structure**

1. **Population**
   Total
   Race, age, sex, education levels
   Percent in poverty
2. **Income**
   Average per capita or per family
   Median income of individuals, families, or households
3. **Labor Force and Employment**
   Total employment
   Labor force size and participation rates
   Unemployment rates
   Employment by industry and occupation
   Employment and unemployment by race, sex, age group
   Average wages by industry and occupation
4. **Productivity and Investment (Manufacturing)**
   Value added per production worker
   Value added less wages per production worker
   Investment per production worker
5. **Industrial Structure**
   Export employment by industry
   Earnings multipliers by industry

available about the income, demographic, employment, wage, productivity, and industrial characteristics of most areas which can be used for this analysis. To illustrate the assessment of the strength of a government's economic base, we use a small set of these variables in the example that follows.

Note that we are using this example to illustrate some of the analytical techniques described in Chapter 3. Our emphasis is on the use of data commonly available in published form. As a result, this illustration differs from an actual analysis where certain information on the local economy and the government will be available to the analyst, even though it is not in published form. The status of the government's economic development program, a recent plant closing or opening, or a natural disaster such as a flood are examples of factors that affect the economic base of an area and should be known by the analyst who is researching a particular location but may not be known by the analyst who relies primarily on published data. This type of information differs considerably between locations, so we do not discuss it in our applications. But its absence from the application is not a signal that it should be absent from an actual analysis.

Table 4–5 presents selected economic and demographic data for our example city of Dyer Straits and for a reference group of forty-nine cities in the same state that have populations between 10,000 and 100,000. For each series presented for 1960, 1970, and 1980, a location quotient (the Dyer Straits' value of the variable divided by the reference group's value) is computed. Although the

TABLE 4-5  Selected Economic and Demographic Data, City of Dyer Straits and Reference Group

| | DYER STRAITS | | | REFERENCE GROUP | | | LOCATION QUOTIENTS* | | |
|---|---|---|---|---|---|---|---|---|---|
| | 1960 | 1970 | 1980 | 1960 | 1970 | 1980 | 1960 | 1970 | 1980 |
| Population† | 32,840 | 34,262 | 32,705 | 1,409,443 | 1,502,719 | 1,515,011 | .0233 | .0228 | .0216 |
| Median age† | 33.6 | 30.9 | 33.3 | 33.1 | 30.3 | 31.8 | 1.015 | 1.020 | 1.047 |
| Persons 25 and over—median years of school completed† | 10.7 | 11.9 | 12.2 | 10.7 | 12.1 | 12.5 | 1.000 | .983 | .976 |
| Mean family income ($)† | $5,308 | $8,758 | $14,012 | $4,616 | $7,969 | $14,030 | 1.150 | 1.099 | .999 |
| Percent employed (total population)† | 43.1 | 42.6 | 42.9 | 41.6 | 40.1 | 45.8 | 1.036 | 1.062 | .937 |
| Percent unemployed† | 4.8 | 6.0 | 9.3 | 5.3 | 5.6 | 7.8 | 0.906 | 1.071 | 1.192 |
| Percent of employed working in manufacturing† | 30.8 | 25.6 | 21.3 | 28.6 | 24.2 | 20.9 | 1.077 | 1.058 | 1.019 |
| Wages of production workers ($ per hour)‡ | $2.35 | $4.14 | $7.16 | $2.15 | $3.95 | $7.03 | 1.093 | 1.048 | 1.018 |
| Value added per employee‡ | $8,590 | $15,694 | $34,097 | $8,405 | $15,569 | $34,200 | 1.022 | 1.008 | .997 |

†These items are collected by the U.S. Bureau of the Census, Census of Population.
‡These items are collected by the U.S. Bureau of the Census, Census of Manufacturers. Linear interpolation is used to derive data for years shown.
*Dyer Straits/Reference Group.

data selected are only representative of those listed in Table 4–4, a number of worrisome trends are apparent:

—Dyer Straits has been losing population since 1970 while the reference group's population has increased slightly since 1970.

—Median age declined and then increased, but in 1980 the median age is higher in Dyer Straits than in the reference group.

—Education levels are lower than those in the reference group in 1970 and 1980 and are growing more slowly.

—Mean family income is growing more slowly than the reference group's and by 1980 is slightly below the reference group's.

—The percentage of the total population that is employed is lower than the reference group's in 1980 and has been declining faster since 1970.

—The percentage of unemployed is lower in Dyer Straits in 1960 but has risen faster than the reference group's and by 1980 is 19 percent higher than that of the reference group.

—The percentage of employed who work in manufacturing is higher but declining faster than that of the reference group.

—Wages of production workers are higher but are growing more slowly than the reference group's.

—Value added per production worker is higher than the reference group's in 1960 and 1970 but not in 1980 and is rising more slowly.

From these data in Table 4–5 and our earlier discussion of the determinants of income, Dyer Straits' revenue potential appears to be declining relative to that of a set of similar cities in the state. Although the city appeared to be in reasonable economic condition in 1960, it has declined in absolute terms for some measures (such as population and percentage employed, and when these two variables are combined it is clear that the total number employed has declined as well from 1970 to 1980), and in relative terms for most others. Regardless of how these data are examined, a declining economic base is the bottom line. To determine how Dyer Straits has fared on a regional or national basis would require the addition of regional and national reference group data, which we do not include here.

Although the general economic situation in Dyer Straits seems to be apparent from Table 4–5, an actual economic base study would employ a much wider range of data, describe economic performance and structure in detail, compare data with a variety of reference groups, and identify economic strengths and weaknesses by industry, occupation, and so forth.[18] For our purposes, Table 4–5 provides enough information to highlight the economic problems that underlie the fiscal situation in Dyer Straits. How these forces manifest themselves in actual revenue behavior will be seen in the following sections.

---

[18] See references in footnotes 3 and 6 above.

## III. REVENUE BASE

How the economic well-being of a community affects the financial condition of its government depends on the particular methods used by the government to tap the community's income and wealth. In this section we examine the primary methods used by governments to raise revenues and the way in which these methods are linked to the government's jurisdiction. These methods determine the government's revenue base, which consists of both the legally defined base for levying taxes (for example, the value of property used for the property tax base) and, when appropriate, the empirically determined "base" for nontax revenues (for example, department charges may be closely related to income levels, so that income becomes the "base" for this revenue method). Thus the revenue base ultimately links government revenues to the economic base of the community, providing the financial base for government.

### Revenue Methods and Sources

A necessary beginning point for determining the revenue base is the identification of the major methods used by governments to raise revenues and the source of these payments to the organization. Knowledge of the methods used allows the analyst to compare a particular government's methods over time and with the methods used in other governments. In addition, the particular methods used define the government's sources of revenues and ultimately the organization's ability to raise the revenues needed to conduct its activities. In presenting revenue methods and sources, all we can hope to provide is an overview of the major types and their essential characteristics. Each revenue method has received extensive treatment elsewhere and, as we discuss each revenue source, we will provide references for those readers seeking additional information.[19]

The financial statements and budgets presented in Chapter 2 included some examples of the ways in which governments raise revenues. The major methods and sources to be discussed in this chapter are listed in Table 4–6 and include intergovernmental revenues (transfers from other governments) and "own source" revenues (those from taxes and charges raised from within the government's jurisdiction). The general revenue categories shown in Table 4–6 include many specific revenue methods, such as inventory and utility taxes, which are individually less important but may, for some governments, add up to a substantial amount. Although we will only discuss the general revenue methods here, the con-

---

[19] For general information on governmental revenue sources, see Richard A. Musgrave and Peggy B. Musgrave, *Public Finance in Theory and Practice* (New York: McGraw-Hill, 1984) or other public finance texts. For information on actual revenue-raising practices in government, see Lennox L. Moak and Albert M. Hillhouse, *Concepts and Practices in Local Government Finance* (Chicago: Municipal Finance Officers Association, 1975); and Richard J. Aronson and Eli Schwartz, eds., *Management Policies in Local Government Finance* (Washington, D.C.: International City Management Association, 1975).

TABLE 4-6 **Governmental Revenue by Source and Level of Government, 1982–83 (millions of dollars)**

| SOURCES | ALL GOVERN- MENTS | FEDERAL GOVERN- MENT | STATE GOVERN- MENTS | LOCAL GOVERN- MENTS |
|---|---|---|---|---|
| Total Revenue | *$1,181,420 | 679,663 | 357,637 | *338,070 |
| Total General Revenue | *878,782 | 483,733 | 290,456 | *298,542 |
| Intergovernmental Revenue | — | 1,846 | 72,704 | 119,399 |
| From federal government | — | — | 68,962 | 21,021 |
| From state governments | — | 1,846 | * | 98,378 |
| From local governments | — | — | 3,742 | * |
| Revenue From Own Sources | 1,181,420 | 677,817 | 284,933 | 218,670 |
| General revenue from own sources | 878,782 | 481,887 | 217,752 | 179,143 |
| Taxes | 665,764 | 381,179 | 171,440 | 113,145 |
| Property | 89,253 | — | 3,281 | 85,973 |
| Individual income | 344,067 | 288,938 | 49,789 | 5,340 |
| Corporation income | 51,280 | 37,022 | 13,153 | 1,105 |
| Sales and gross receipts | 144,718 | 44,471 | 83,895 | 16,352 |
| Customs duties | 8,727 | 8,727 | — | — |
| General sales & gross receipts | 64,890 | — | 53,639 | 11,250 |
| Selective sales & gross receipts | 71,101 | 35,744 | 30,255 | 5,102 |
| Motor fuel | 16,726 | 5,784 | 10,793 | 149 |
| Alcoholic beverages | 8,591 | 5,613 | 2,743 | 235 |
| Tobacco products | 8,322 | 4,140 | 4,001 | 181 |
| Public utilities | 11,818 | 2,947 | 5,621 | 3,250 |
| Other | 25,643 | 17,260 | 7,097 | 1,286 |
| Motor vehicle & operators licenses | 6,732 | — | 6,289 | 443 |
| Death and gift tax | 8,598 | 6,053 | 2,545 | — |
| All other | 21,117 | 4,695 | 12,490 | 3,932 |
| Charges and miscellaneous general revenue | 213,018 | 100,708 | 46,312 | 65,998 |
| Current charges | 113,172 | 50,547 | 23,182 | 39,443 |
| National defense & international relations | 7,122 | 7,122 | — | — |
| Postal service | 22,679 | 22,679 | — | — |
| Education | 18,829 | — | 13,126 | 5,703 |
| Hospitals | 19,320 | 76 | 5,309 | 13,935 |
| Sewerage | 5,816 | — | 7 | 5,809 |
| Sanitation other than sewerage | 1,644 | — | — | 1,644 |

(*Continued*)

TABLE 4-6    *(continued)*

| SOURCES | ALL GOVERN-MENTS | FEDERAL GOVERN-MENT | STATE GOVERN-MENTS | LOCAL GOVERN-MENTS |
|---|---|---|---|---|
| Parks and recreation | 1,778 | 67 | 403 | 1,308 |
| Natural resources | 13,227 | 12,326 | 637 | 264 |
| Housing & urban renewal | 3,116 | 1,473 | 147 | 1,496 |
| Air transportation | 2,559 | 24 | 235 | 2,300 |
| Water transport & terminals | 1,468 | 482 | 284 | 702 |
| Parking facilities | 435 | — | — | 453 |
| Other | 15,161 | 6,298 | 3,035 | 5,827 |
| Miscellaneous general revenue | 99,846 | 50,161 | 23,130 | 26,555 |
| Special assessments | 1,625 | — | 56 | 1,569 |
| Sale of property | 1,910 | 877 | 82 | 952 |
| Interest earnings | 47,465 | 21,363 | 12,185 | 13,917 |
| Other | 48,846 | 27,921 | 10,808 | 10,117 |
| Utility Revenue | 34,033 | — | 2,390 | 31,643 |
| Liquor Stores Revenue | 3,311 | — | 2,819 | 492 |
| Insurance Trust Revenue | 265,294 | 195,930 | 61,971 | 7,393 |

Note: (*) Net of duplicative intergovernmental transactions.
SOURCE:   Data from U.S. Department of Commerce, Bureau of the Census, *Government Finances in 1982–83* (Washington, D.C.: Government Printing Office, October 1984), Table 4, p. 5.

cepts and methods of analysis we present are equally useful for analysis of more specific types of revenues. We will discuss ''own source'' revenues first and then examine revenues transferred from other governments.

**Tax Revenues.**    Virtually all governments have taxing powers or receive much of their funding from organizations that have taxing powers. Taxation methods consist of the application of a tax *rate* to some measurable tax *base* with the product of the two yielding the tax *revenue* from that particular method and source. The tax rate may be fixed (like a 5 percent sales tax rate) or may vary according to a formula linking the rate to changes in the base's level or to some other characteristic (like an income tax with higher rates for higher income levels, or different rates for different types of businesses).

Tax bases for all levels of government include various forms of wealth (property and estate taxes), income and consumption (income and sales taxes), and transfers (gift taxes) with considerable variation across governments in what exactly is included in each of these bases and how they are measured. Both tax rates and tax bases are subject to a wide variety of legislation and regulation from different governmental bodies which both define and restrict their use by governments.

For local governments, including special districts and public school systems, taxes are a major source of revenues, especially when intergovernmental revenues are excluded. The relative importance of tax revenues can be seen in Table 4-6. In 1982-83, taxes were 52 percent of revenues from own sources. Although important, taxes as a percentage of revenue from own sources for local governments have declined since 1974-75 when they were 63 percent.[20] Taxes represent 60 percent of the own source revenues of state governments and 56 percent of those of the federal government.

The *property tax* is a major source of revenues for local governments, as shown in Table 4-6. In 1982-83 the property tax provided local governments with 39 percent of their total revenues from their own revenue sources and 76 percent of their total tax revenues, down from 50 percent and 82 percent, respectively, in 1974-75. The property tax is a minor source of revenues for state and federal governments.

The property tax is usually applied to the assessed value of nonexempt land and structures within a community or district. The rate may be fixed or may vary across different types of property (residential, commercial, industrial, farm, etc.) or between land and structures. The base may sometimes include other forms of property (household goods, automobiles, inventories) or financial assets (stocks, bonds, mortgages), or it may be limited solely to land (site value tax). The value of these properties is normally assessed to some fraction of market value, where the fraction need not be 100 percent. Many jurisdictions do, however, assess their property at its full market value. Governments, charitable, educational and religious organizations, and sometimes older or low-income residents are exempted from payment of the tax.

Property tax revenues depend on the value of all taxable property within the governmental jurisdiction or district levying the tax. Property values, in turn, depend on the type of property involved and the economic activity (including the taxation policies) and condition of the jurisdiction or district. Housing and commercial values also reflect the size and income of the population relative to the supply of housing and number of commercial establishments; industrial property market values also depend on the strength of both local and outside markets and the resulting profitability of the industrial establishment. Thus the size of the property tax base and the economic activity and viability of the local jurisdiction or district (examined in the preceding section) are closely linked. Note also that property taxes levied on certain property such as vacation property and industrial property may be "exported" to individuals and organizations residing in other jurisdictions.[21]

---

[20] Data for 1974-75 comparisons are from Bureau of the Census, *Government Finances in 1974-75* (Washington, D.C.: Government Printing Office, 1976).

[21] For a review of the property tax, see Aronson and Schwartz, *Management Policies in Local Government Finance,* Chap. 6; and Musgrave and Musgrave, *Public Finance in Theory and Practice,* Chap. 21. For more theoretical discussions of the property tax, see Dick Netzer, *Economics of the Property Tax*

*Sales and gross receipts taxes* are an important source of revenues for local governments, although nowhere near as important as they are for state governments. From Table 4-6 sales taxes were 7.5 percent of local government revenues from own sources in 1982–83 (up from 6.6 percent in 1974–75) and 14 percent of total tax revenues (up from 10.5 percent in 1974–75). In contrast the comparable percentages for state governments were 29 and 49 percent. While many local governments are authorized to impose sales taxes, some states levy the tax at the state level and transfer part of the proceeds to local governments.

Sales taxes are normally a fixed percentage of the sales tax base: the dollar value of the sales or gross receipts subject to taxation. A *general sales tax* is applied to most types of purchases for consumption, although certain items, such as food and sometimes clothing, may be exempted from the tax. A *selective sales tax* is limited to a few items or a single item, such as a tax on tobacco products, and is similar to an *excise tax* except that it is collected at the point of purchase rather than at the point of production.

The potential of the sales tax as a revenue source depends on the income levels and consumption patterns of those individuals and organizations in the jurisdiction levying the tax, and in the larger area that surrounds the jurisdiction. Depending on the shopping patterns that exist, some of the sales tax may be exported to residents of other jurisdictions.[22]

The *income tax* plays a major role at the federal and state levels, and a minor but increasing role at the local level. As of December 31, 1982, local governments in eleven states and the District of Columbia levied income taxes.[23] At the federal and state levels the tax is applied to individuals and corporations, while at the local level it is almost entirely a tax on individual income. From Table 4-6, in 1982–83 local government income taxes were 2.9 percent of total revenues from own sources (2.7 percent in 1974–75) and 5.7 percent of total tax revenues (4.3 percent in 1974–75). Income taxes represented 22 percent and 48 percent of state and federal own source revenues, and 37 and 86 percent of their total tax revenues.

The tax rate on individual income usually varies with income level and between ordinary income and capital gains, although a fixed or flat rate is often used at the local level. The income tax base is most comprehensive at the federal and state levels (for those states that have an income tax) and includes wages and salaries, interest, dividends, rents, and capital gains. At the local level, however, sometimes only wages and salaries are subject to income taxation; in most cases, at a minimum, dividends and capital gains are excluded from taxation. A variety

(Washington, D.C.: Brookings Institution, 1966); Henry Aaron, *Who Pays the Property Tax? A New View* (Washington, D.C.: Brookings Institution, 1974); and George E. Peterson, ed., *Property Tax Reform* (Washington, D.C.: Urban Institute, 1973).

[22] See Aronson and Schwartz, *Management Policies in Local Government Finance,* Chap. 7; John F. Due, *State and Local Sales Taxation* (Chicago: Public Administration Service, 1971); and Musgrave and Musgrave, *Public Finance in Theory and Practice,* Chap. 20.

[23] Advisory Commission on Intergovernmental Relations, *Significant Features of Fiscal Federalism, 1981–82* (Washington, D.C.: ACIR, 1983), Table 31.

of exemptions and deductions from income for tax purposes are allowed, although again these are less frequent at the local government level.[24]

The income tax links governments directly to the income levels of individuals and corporations residing in their jurisdictions and sometimes to nonresident individuals and corporations that earn some or all of their income within their jurisdictions.

**Current Charges and Special Assessments.**  *Current charges,* or *user charges* as they are sometimes called, are an important and growing source of revenues for local governments. From Table 4–6, current charges constituted 18 percent of total local government revenues from local sources in 1982–83, up from 15.5 percent in 1974–75. Current charges were only 8 percent of state own source revenues in 1982–83. If utility and liquor revenues are also included, the local and state percentages are significantly higher. In principle, current charges can be made for those services or commodities provided by a government that are like private goods: where those receiving the service can clearly be defined and charged for the service without major benefits accruing to those who do not pay, the so-called "free riders." Thus those who use water in their homes, swim in public pools, receive hospital treatment, or attend classes at a community college can be identified and may be charged for the good or service received in a fashion that excludes those who do not pay from receiving the direct benefits of these items.

As shown in Table 4–6, current charges are used in a wide variety of areas that lend themselves to this method of collection by governments. The list is led by hospital charges, education fees and tuition, and sewerage and other sanitation charges. Revenues from commercial type activities such as parking lots are included in current charges, but the Census Bureau lists revenues from the sale of liquor and the provision of public utility services as separate categories.

Since many services offered by governments provide both specific and generalized benefits, such services are often paid for by a combination of users and the general public. Current charges may be paid by those receiving specific benefits, and other revenue methods may be used to pay for the more broadly distributed benefits. Thus sewage treatment plants may finance construction costs through bonds repaid from property tax revenues and pay for operating costs by charges to those generating the sewage. *Special assessments,* or taxes to pay for specific projects such as sewer lines or sidewalk construction, play this dual role, as they combine characteristics of both current charges and general taxation. They are compulsory, yet they may vary within the taxing jurisdiction according to the benefits received. From Table 4–6, special assessments in 1982–83 were less than

---

[24] See Aronson and Schwartz, *Management Policies in Local Government Finance;* Musgrave and Musgrave, *Public Finance in Theory and Practice,* Chaps. 16–19; Richard Goode, *The Individual Income Tax* (Washington, D.C.: Brookings Institution, 1964); and Joseph Pechman, *Federal Tax Policy,* (Washington, D.C.: Brookings Institution, 1971).

1 percent of total revenues to local governments from all sources, about the same share as in 1974–75. They were a minor state and federal government revenue.

Current charges may be based on the amounts of the good or service consumed or simply be a flat fee for users regardless of their level of consumption. When the charge varies with the amount used, the current charge serves the role of a price for that service. Thus a water fee based on metered water usage charges heavy users more than light users and can serve to discourage excessive water use. Fixed charges, such as a single solid waste disposal fee per household, require that beneficiaries pay for the service but do not distinguish between households generating different amounts of solid waste. Fixed current charges are frequently used where it is difficult or costly to measure the amount of usage of a service by different beneficiaries.

Finally, those individuals or organizations paying current charges can usually be identified by the type of service or commodity they receive or by their geographical location. In the first case we can group individuals as consumers and study their economic behavior; in the second case we can group individuals by their location in the special districts frequently set up to provide these services or commodities, and we can study the characteristics of those within this geographical area to assess the potential revenue base provided by a particular current charge.[25]

**Intergovernmental Revenues.**    *Intergovernmental transfers,* sometimes referred to as *grants* or *aid,* are a major nontax revenue source for state and local governments. Table 4–6 indicates that in 1982–83 intergovernmental revenues from the federal government constituted 6.2 percent of total revenues for local governments, and intergovernmental revenues from state governments constituted 29 percent of total revenues for local governments. The comparable figures in 1974–75 were 6.8 percent for federal revenues and 32 percent for state revenues. States received about 23 percent of their total revenue from intergovernmental transfers in 1982–83.

Although state government grants to local governments averaged around 30 percent of total revenues in 1982–83, there was considerable variation among states with some over 40 percent and others under 20 percent.[26] A large part of this aid is for education and is received by school districts, but other purposes such as social services, public welfare, public works, and general revenue are important in some states.

While intergovernmental transfers come from outside the local gov-

---

[25] Current charges and special assessments are reviewed in Aronson and Schwartz, *Management Policies in Local Government Finance,* Chap. 8. For a more-detailed discussion of current charges, see Selma Mushkin, *Public Prices for Public Products* (Washington, D.C.: Urban Institute, 1972). See also Paul Downing, "User Charges and Service Fees," Urban Consortium, Public Technologies, Inc., 1981.

[26] Advisory Commission on Intergovernmental Relations, *Significant Features of Fiscal Federalism, 1981–82,* state profiles.

ernment's jurisdiction, these transfers still depend in large part on the economic and social conditions of the community served by the local government. Thus this revenue source, like taxes and current charges, has links with local characteristics that are subject to study as part of revenue analysis.

The revenue base for intergovernmental aid is not as explicitly defined as it is for tax bases, yet it should be assessed nonetheless. The important question to ask for each type of intergovernmental aid is, how is the amount of aid for the government determined? The answer to this question will help define the revenue base for the intergovernmental aid items. It must be kept in mind, however, that intergovernmental aid is subject to changes by the governments providing it. Consequently, the aid is less under the control of the local government than are the local taxes and charges.

A significant amount of intergovernmental aid to local governments is distributed on a formula basis. The aid may be a certain amount per capita or per student, and not vary based on other characteristics of the local government. Sometimes other characteristics enter into the formula to direct the aid to those who are in greater "need." For example, more per capita or per student aid may be allocated to local governments that have a lower ability to pay for services measured by low per capita (or per student) equalized property value or income. Furthermore, the aid may be a matching grant, determined by the amount of revenues raised by the local government, with, for example, twenty-five cents of aid for each dollar of revenues raised locally. Finally, the aid may be earmarked for a specific spending category such as highways, special education, or health care, or the aid may be available for the local government to spend in any way it sees fit.

Because of the diversity in distribution methods for intergovernmental transfers, the revenue base for intergovernmental aid must be developed by carefully identifying and assessing the factors that determine the way in which the aid is distributed, including formulas, matching rates, and restrictions on use. Moreover, the political climate and process surrounding the aid distribution should be analyzed as well. Sometimes trends in intergovernmental aid are suggested by political changes, as we saw when the Reagan administration replaced the Carter administration in Washington. Similar, but probably less dramatic, changes may take place at the state level. The financial condition of the state as a whole may influence how much aid is available for local governments. Also, the interaction of state and federal aid cannot be ignored, since actions at the federal level affect state aid programs, and vice versa. Although the analysis of intergovernmental aid is not straightforward, its importance as a revenue source requires that some attention be given it as part of revenue analysis.[27]

[27] See George F. Break, *Intergovernmental Fiscal Relations in the United States* (Washington, D.C.: Brookings Institution, 1980); and James A. Maxwell and J. Richard Aronson, *Financing State and Local Governments* (Washington, D.C.: Brookings Institution, 1977). For data on intergovernmental finance, see the annual issues of the Advisory Commission on Intergovernmental Relations, *Significant Features of Fiscal Federalism,* (Washington, D.C.: ACIR), and other ACIR publications.

### Revenue Elasticities

The particular revenue methods used by an organization determine the organization's revenue base. Thus a local government that relies largely on property and sales tax revenues will have the full value of taxable property and taxable retail sales in its revenue base. A local water district that sells water to residential, commercial, and industrial users will have the factors that influence the demand for water, such as residential income and industrial output, in its revenue base.

Besides the level of the revenue base, its growth potential and stability are also important in revenue analysis. Obviously an organization would like to draw its revenues from a revenue base that is growing rapidly (or at least as fast as expenditure needs) and evenly. Not surprisingly, this is seldom the case. Those revenue base items with the highest growth potential are frequently the least stable. Thus a tax based on income will grow with income growth and will rise and fall with business cycles.

Essentially, there are two ways in which the revenue from a tax may change: a change in the tax rate or a change in the tax base. Tax rate changes are generally government decisions, while changes in the tax base (other than definitional changes which are viewed here as a change in the tax itself) are seldom under local control. Changes in the tax base are often related to the changes in the economic base that we discussed in the preceding section.

One way of examining the linkages between the economic base and the tax base is to assess the *elasticity* of a particular tax. (Elasticities can be developed for any revenue source, including user charges and intergovernmental transfers, but we will focus on tax elasticities to illustrate their use in revenue analysis.) An elasticity is a measure of the relationship between two variables—more specifically it is a measure of the responsiveness of changes in one variable to changes in the other. This elasticity or responsiveness is usually expressed as the ratio of a percentage change in one variable to a percentage change in a second variable.

The most common way to calculate a tax revenue elasticity is to measure the percentage change in the particular tax revenue associated with a percentage change in a second variable of interest, usually a measure of income, holding other factors like the tax rate constant. This is called the "income elasticity" of that tax revenue. When an elasticity is calculated in this manner, the responsiveness of the tax revenue to changes in income can be assessed independently of any changes in the tax rate. Note that the condition that the tax rate and other factors affecting tax revenues be constant may present measurement difficulties that may require the use of statistical techniques such as regression analysis to overcome.

To illustrate the calculation of income elasticity and some problems of interpretation, suppose that over a period of time the total income (in $1,000s) in a jurisdiction grew from 1,200 to 1,500 while the total revenues from the tax grew from 35 to 50. Also assume that the tax rate stayed constant during the period. The tax revenue elasticity in this case is defined by the percentage change in tax revenues divided by the percentage change in income. The percentage change in tax revenue is [(50 − 35)/35] × 100, or 42.86 percent. The percentage change in income is [(1,500 − 1,200)/1,200] × 100, or 25 percent. Therefore the income elasticity in this case is 42.86 divided by 25, or 1.714. This means that for every 1 percent change in income, this tax revenue changes by 1.714 percent. It is common to refer to elasticities greater than one as elastic, and elasticities less than one as inelastic; thus this tax would be "income elastic."

Note that in this case we could calculate the elasticity of the tax directly from the data, since the tax rate has not changed. Although the rate has not changed, the rate structure itself may affect the elasticity in important ways. For example, suppose the tax above was a local income tax. Part of the observed elasticity may have been due to the particular type of income included in the definition of taxable income, and the way in which changes in this type of income (such as wages) compared with changes in the total income used to measure elasticity. A second part of the observed elasticity in this case may be due to the way in which the increase in the taxable income base interacts with the rate structure. If there is a progressive tax structure, with higher taxable incomes taxed at a higher rate, then as the taxable income base increases more taxpayers fall into higher tax brackets, causing the tax revenues to rise faster than the tax base.

When carrying out revenue analyses, a calculation of a tax revenue elasticity is sometimes beyond the scope of the analysis because of the difficulty in separating the tax revenue changes due to tax rate increases from those due to changes in the tax base. Because of this, calculation of elasticities of the revenue *base* rather than of the tax revenues themselves is more reliable and can be just as useful. Revenue base elasticities can be used to estimate revenue elasticities when combined with knowledge of the structure of the tax rate. Revenue base income elasticity measures will help answer such questions as the following: Will the growth in the revenue base be faster or slower than the growth in local economic conditions, as measured by income? Will the revenue base fluctuate more or fluctuate less than local economic conditions? Different revenue bases will have different growth potential and stability, concerns that enter into an assessment of the revenue methods used by governments.

Table 4-7 presents a range of estimates for the income elasticities of major state and local tax revenues. In each of these estimates, the tax rate or fee has been held constant. Note that income elasticities for various fees, such as charges for motor vehicle licenses and for hospital and education services, are included in Table 4-7. These can be estimated from knowledge of how the demand for these services changes with income. Other types of revenue elasticities, however, such as those for general intergovernmental transfers, cannot be estimated, since distribution formulas for different types of aid vary considerably. One could, however, estimate the income elasticity for a specific type of assistance if the distribution formula were known.

Although income elasticity estimates vary considerably for each tax, in general personal and corporate income taxes tend to be the most elastic, then sales taxes, property taxes, and finally more specific sales taxes like motor fuels and

TABLE 4-7    Income Elasticities of Major State and Local Taxes

| | |
|---|---|
| Individual income taxes | 1.3–2.4 |
| Corporate income taxes | 0.7–1.4 |
| Property taxes | 0.3–1.4 |
| General sales taxes | 0.8–1.3 |
| Motor fuel taxes | 0.4–0.8 |
| Alcoholic beverage taxes | 0.4–0.6 |
| Tobacco taxes | 0.0–0.5 |
| Other selective sales taxes | 0.9–1.1 |
| Motor vehicle licenses | 0.2–0.4 |
| Hospital and higher-education fees | 1.3–1.8 |

SOURCES: **Advisory Commission on Intergovernmental Relations, *Federal-State Coordination of Personal Income Taxes*, 1965, p. 42; Advisory Commission on Intergovernmental Relations, *Significant Features of Fiscal Federalism 1976–77*, II, Table 139, p. 254; and Tax Foundation, Inc., *Fiscal Outlook for State and Local Government to 1975*, 1966, p. 106.**

tobacco. The importance of each type of tax in an organization's revenue base will determine the overall growth potential and stability of the government's tax revenue. A government relying heavily on less-elastic taxes such as the property tax will probably experience slower growth of tax revenues relative to community income than a government relying on more-elastic taxes such as personal or corporate income. At the same time, however, when income declines, the government relying on taxes with lower elasticities may have lower fluctuations in tax revenues; the low-elasticity tax base serves as a cushion against fluctuations in income, usually resulting in more stability in its tax revenues.[28]

### Revenue Efficiency and Equity

While the main concern of this chapter is determining the availability, growth, and stability of government revenues, we also need to recognize the important concerns of revenue efficiency and equity. Different revenue methods can be more or less costly to use (efficiency) and more or less fair in terms of who ultimately provides the revenues (equity). This section briefly reviews these concerns, which are treated in considerable depth in books on public finance.[29]

**Efficiency.**    Different revenue methods have different effects on the allocation of resources. Suppose a million dollars of revenues can be raised by a variety of tax methods and current charges. In addition to the cost of $1 million imposed

[28] For examples of measures of revenue bases in empirical financial condition studies, see U.S. Department of the Treasury, "Report on the Fiscal Impact of the Economic Stimulus Package on 48 Large Urban Governments"; and Bureau of Governmental Research, University of Oregon, "Oregon Municipal Fiscal Indicators, an Exploratory Study," October 1983.

[29] See the references in footnote 19.

on those providing the revenues, there may be other costs as well, the so-called excess burden or efficiency costs of different revenue methods. These additional costs arise from the effect of the revenue method on the myriad of economic decisions made by those paying the tax or charge: decisions about income and leisure, present and future consumption, and types of goods and services consumed. Particular revenue methods may change these decisions from what they would have been; and the more these decisions are changed (and individual satisfaction is lost in the process), the less efficient is the revenue method. The "neutrality" of a particular tax is the extent to which changes in this tax leave patterns of economic behavior unchanged.

Different types of taxes affect different types of decisions, and to varying degrees. A lump sum tax, or "head tax," the same amount charged to every individual regardless of his or her economic condition or behavior, is considered an efficient tax. Since it cannot be avoided, individuals are less likely to decide to work less, change consumption patterns, and so forth, so that the costs of distorting economic behavior are not incurred. A general sales tax with no exemptions may affect decisions about how much one saves or spends, but it does not affect choices among relative amounts of goods and services consumed. A selective sales tax and a property tax affect the cost of consuming a particular good or service and may therefore cause individuals to shift their consumption to try to reduce or avoid the tax. Each type of tax, and the precise form of its rates and bases, has to be considered in detail to determine the net effects of the tax on economic behavior, and its resulting efficiency as a revenue-raising method.

Current charges may also be efficient or inefficient. Assuming charges are made for goods or services where benefits to specific individuals occur and where these individuals pay in proportion to the benefits received, then a current charge equal to the marginal cost of producing that good or service is considered efficient. Current charges in this form are essentially prices, and the conditions for efficient allocation of resources require that the price or value placed on a commodity equal the marginal or incremental cost of producing that commodity. Current charges or prices that deviate from marginal cost will result in overproduction or underproduction of the good or service and will result in inefficiencies in the allocation of resources. In somewhat oversimplified terms, current charges will be an efficient way of raising revenues to the extent that they act like prices (that is, are a charge per unit of the product consumed) and approach the marginal cost of producing the product.

The efficiency of revenue transfers to an organization depends on how these revenues were raised by the transferring organization and how the aid is distributed by the transferring organization. As an example on the revenue-raising side, state aid to a local government paid out of a state general sales tax would be more efficient than if these funds had been raised by a gasoline tax. On the aid distribution side, different distribution mechanisms create different incentives for the behavior of the government receiving the transfer. For example, a grant that is a fixed amount, even though it is intended to be devoted to a specific function, may act as an increase in income that the local government can use for a variety of purposes. A matching grant, on the other hand, may be more efficient in directing additional local government resources to a specific function.

Besides the economic costs of the revenue method itself, there may also be different costs of compliance and administration. Income taxes and sales taxes may require considerable time and paperwork for compliance, and property taxes may require elaborate property assessment procedures; these characteristics of revenue methods generate additional costs to the government and the revenue providers.

**Equity.**    Different revenue sources can be evaluated in terms of their equity as well as their efficiency, where revenue equity depends on the ability to pay of those ultimately providing the revenues to the government.[30] In general, if a particular revenue method results in individuals with higher-income levels paying a larger percentage of their income to the government (compared with lower-income individuals), then this revenue method will be considered more equitable than methods having the opposite result. Thus a progressive income tax, with rates increasing with income levels, is considered more equitable than, say, a lump sum tax independent of income, or a sales tax on essential commodities such as food or clothing.

To determine the equity of a particular revenue method requires knowledge of who actually pays the tax. This is not a simple question, since the individual or organization making the cash payment for the taxes may be able to shift the tax cost on to another individual or organization. Thus landlords may shift the property tax on to renters through higher rents, and retail stores may shift a cigarette tax on to smokers through higher prices. Many factors determine the ability to shift a particular tax on to others, and there is considerable controversy among economists over the extent to which different taxes can be shifted.

The determination of equity for current charges usually assumes that the demand for goods and services provided by the government is relatively income inelastic, with the demand for such goods and services not affected to a large extent by changes in income. Goods and services like water, sewer, electricity, and mass transit satisfy this condition for the most part. Expenditures for these services represent a smaller percentage of the total budget of higher-income groups. Consequently, charges for these services represent more of a "burden" (a higher percentage of income) on low-income people.

Estimation of the relative efficiency and equity of different revenue methods is a difficult and controversial exercise. The particular mix of revenue methods,

---

[30] We are using the "ability-to-pay" principle for determining the "fairness" or equity of different revenue sources and not the "benefit principle," which defines "fairness" as those receiving public benefits being the ones to pay for them regardless of their ability to pay. See Musgrave and Musgrave, *Public Finance in Theory and Practice,* Chaps. 5 and 11, for a discussion of tax equity. For a comprehensive study of state and local tax equity, see Donald Phares, *Who Pays State and Local Taxes* (Cambridge, Mass.: Oelgeschlager, Gunn and Hain, 1980).

and their relative importance in raising revenues, will determine the extent to which a particular government is raising funds in a low-cost and fair manner. Individuals conducting such an evaluation should, however, refer to the public finance literature for more precise guidance on revenue efficiency and equity.

### An Application

To illustrate the analysis of a particular revenue base, we return to our example of the city of Dyer Straits. Our concern in this application is the local or "own" sources of revenue of the city, and the associated local revenue base from which these tax and nontax revenues are drawn. Nonlocal sources of revenue, intergovernmental transfers, are discussed in the next section with actual revenues.

Table 4–8 presents the main elements in Dyer Straits' local revenue base in total and per capita terms for 1979–83. Dyer Straits relies primarily on property and sales taxes, so that the full value of taxable property and taxable retail sales is included in the local revenue base. Nontax local revenues are either related to the community's income levels or are composed of intergovernmental aid, so that mean family income is also included in the local revenue base. These elements in the local revenue base represent indexes of the ability of Dyer Straits to tap its local resources for the revenues needed to conduct its activities. The extent to which the revenue base has actually been drawn upon will be considered in the next section.

To understand the levels and changes in the local revenue base, we again compare Dyer Straits with the reference group introduced earlier. Table 4–8 indicates the following:

—Dyer Straits' property tax base is growing but more slowly than that of the reference group.

—The per capita property tax base is about 4 percent higher than the reference group's in 1983 but has been growing more slowly than the reference group's.

—The sales tax base total dollar value is growing but the growth has been slightly slower than the reference group's over the five-year period. It also reveals some fluctuations relative to the reference group.

—The per capita sales tax base is 4 percent higher than the reference group's in 1983 but is growing more slowly and with more fluctuations than the reference group's.

—In 1983 mean family income is 1 percent higher than the average for the reference group, but mean family income is growing more slowly than the reference group's over the period and with more fluctuations.

These changes can be seen more clearly in Table 4–9, which shows the percentage changes and estimated income elasticities of the revenue base components for 1979–83. The sales tax base has evidently grown more than the property tax base, but its changes over time are somewhat more erratic. The estimated income elasticities reveal that neither the property tax base nor the sales tax base grew as fast as income over this period. The higher income elasticity of the sales tax base is consistent with its growth patterns and its fluctuations, which more closely mirrored the changes in income in each period.

TABLE 4-8  Local Revenue Base, City of Dyer Straits and Reference Group, 1979–83

| | DYER STRAITS | | | | | REFERENCE GROUP | | | | | LOCATION QUOTIENTS* | | | | |
|---|---|---|---|---|---|---|---|---|---|---|---|---|---|---|---|
| | 1979 | 1980 | 1981 | 1982 | 1983 | 1979 | 1980 | 1981 | 1982 | 1983 | 1979 | 1980 | 1981 | 1982 | 1983 |
| Property Tax Base | | | | | | | | | | | | | | | |
| $ Millions | 165.3 | 169.5 | 177.4 | 187.0 | 192.4 | 7,091.3 | 7,369.8 | 7,757.7 | 8,160.0 | 8,596.0 | .0236 | .0230 | .0229 | .0229 | .0224 |
| $ Per capita | 5,026 | 5,183 | 5,475 | 5,825 | 6,031 | 4,591 | 4,864 | 5,155 | 5,462 | 5,786 | 1.095 | 1.066 | 1.062 | 1.066 | 1.042 |
| Sales Tax Base | | | | | | | | | | | | | | | |
| $ Millions | 80.2 | 83.7 | 91.2 | 95.0 | 100.9 | 3,447.0 | 3,686.6 | 3,942.9 | 4,217.0 | 4,510.2 | .0233 | .0227 | .0231 | .0225 | .0224 |
| $ Per capita | 2,438 | 2,560 | 2,815 | 2,960 | 3,163 | 2,260 | 2,434 | 2,620 | 2,821 | 3,036 | 1.079 | 1.052 | 1.074 | 1.049 | 1.042 |
| Income (Mean) | | | | | | | | | | | | | | | |
| $ Per family | 13,450 | 14,012 | 15,500 | 16,401 | 17,631 | 13,048 | 14,030 | 15,086 | 16,221 | 17,442 | 1.031 | .999 | 1.027 | 1.011 | 1.010 |
| Population (Thousands) | 32.89 | 32.7 | 32.4 | 32.1 | 31.9 | 1,525 | 1,515 | 1,505 | 1,495 | 1,485 | .0216 | .0216 | .0215 | .0215 | .0215 |

*Dyer Straits/Reference Group.

TABLE 4-9   **Dyer Straits' Local Revenue Base Percentage Changes and Income Elasticities**

| | 1979–80 | 1980–81 | 1981–82 | 1982–83 | 1979–83 Percentage Change | Income Elasticity* |
|---|---|---|---|---|---|---|
| | | Yearly Percentage Changes | | | | |
| **Property Tax Base** | | | | | | |
| $ Per capita | 3.1 | 5.6 | 6.4 | 3.5 | 20.0 | .65 |
| **Sales Tax Base** | | | | | | |
| $ Per capita | 5.0 | 10.0 | 5.2 | 6.9 | 30.0 | .96 |
| **Income (Mean)** | | | | | | |
| $ Per family | 4.2 | 10.6 | 5.8 | 7.5 | 31.0 | 1.00 |

*Income elasticity = Percentage change in revenue base ÷ Percentage change in income
Since income figures are per family, per capita (rather than total dollar) figures for property and sales tax base have been used to estimate elasticities.

## IV. ACTUAL REVENUES

With an understanding of the economic base of a government and the particular revenue methods and revenue base used by the organization, we are now in a position to ask how much revenues have actually been raised from each major revenue source. Conceptually, this step comes after our examination of the economic and revenue bases, but in practice this is often the first step.

The analysis of actual revenues consists of an examination of each revenue source over time and compared with a reference group. Since the levels and changes of revenue items depend on population levels and changes, it is useful to compute per capita revenue as well as total revenues. The simplest way to illustrate the analysis of actual revenues is to return to the Dyer Straits example.

Information on the actual revenues of Dyer Straits and the reference group is given in Table 4-10. For comparability, only the general and debt service fund revenues are shown for each city, but note that in this example the cities have structured their funds in a similar fashion and each has the same enterprise funds for water and sewer systems and for parking facilities. Furthermore, all cities use a debt service fund, but virtually all the revenue of the debt service fund is accounted for by fund transfers from the general fund. In actual practice, developing reference group data usually requires adjustments in individual jurisdiction data to make them comparable.

An examination of Table 4-10 reveals the following:

—Dyer Straits is increasing its use of all revenue methods, with total revenues growing slightly more rapidly than those of the reference group. Per capita total revenues are higher than the reference group's over the period, reaching 25 percent higher in 1983.

—Compared with the reference group, Dyer Straits' reliance on different revenue methods has changed over this period. While the use of the property tax, relative to the reference group's, has remained about the same in total dollar terms, Dyer Straits

TABLE 4-10 Actual Revenues, City of Dyer Straits and Reference Group, 1979–83

| | DYER STRAITS | | | | | REFERENCE GROUP | | | | | LOCATION QUOTIENTS* | | | | |
|---|---|---|---|---|---|---|---|---|---|---|---|---|---|---|---|
| | 1979 | 1980 | 1981 | 1982 | 1983 | 1979 | 1980 | 1981 | 1982 | 1983 | 1979 | 1980 | 1981 | 1982 | 1983 |
| **Property taxes** | | | | | | | | | | | | | | | |
| $ Millions | 3.587 | 3.814 | 3.903 | 4.077 | 4.521 | 117.83 | 125.14 | 133.04 | 140.46 | 149.13 | .0304 | .0305 | .0293 | .0290 | .0303 |
| Per capita | 109.06 | 116.63 | 120.44 | 127.01 | 141.72 | 77.27 | 82.60 | 88.40 | 93.95 | 100.42 | 1.411 | 1.412 | 1.362 | 1.352 | 1.411 |
| **Sales taxes** | | | | | | | | | | | | | | | |
| $ Millions | .642 | .670 | 1.186 | 1.235 | 1.312 | 27.58 | 31.34 | 33.51 | 40.49 | 43.09 | .0233 | .0214 | .0354 | .0305 | .0305 |
| Per capita | 19.51 | 20.49 | 36.60 | 38.47 | 41.13 | 18.09 | 20.69 | 22.27 | 27.08 | 29.02 | 1.078 | .990 | 1.643 | 1.421 | 1.417 |
| **Nontax Local Revenues** | | | | | | | | | | | | | | | |
| $ Millions | .816 | .868 | .902 | .962 | .994 | 37.09 | 39.14 | 40.60 | 41.20 | 42.73 | .0220 | .0222 | .0222 | .0233 | .0233 |
| Per capita | 24.81 | 26.53 | 27.84 | 29.97 | 31.16 | 24.32 | 25.83 | 26.98 | 27.56 | 28.77 | 1.020 | 1.027 | 1.031 | 1.087 | 1.083 |
| **State Aid** | | | | | | | | | | | | | | | |
| $ Millions | 1.011 | 1.142 | 1.305 | 1.523 | 1.667 | 48.55 | 53.86 | 60.32 | 67.89 | 72.82 | .0208 | .0212 | .0216 | .0224 | .0229 |
| Per capita | 30.73 | 34.91 | 40.27 | 47.45 | 52.26 | 31.84 | 35.55 | 40.08 | 45.41 | 49.04 | .965 | .982 | 1.005 | 1.045 | 1.066 |
| **Federal Aid** | | | | | | | | | | | | | | | |
| $ Millions | .583 | .636 | .739 | .869 | 1.033 | 26.94 | 30.30 | 34.09 | 38.94 | 45.79 | .0216 | .0210 | .0217 | .0223 | .0226 |
| Per capita | 17.73 | 19.46 | 22.81 | 27.07 | 32.38 | 17.67 | 20.00 | 22.65 | 26.05 | 30.84 | 1.003 | .973 | 1.007 | 1.039 | 1.050 |
| **Total Revenues** | | | | | | | | | | | | | | | |
| $ Millions | 6.639 | 7.13 | 8.035 | 8.666 | 9.527 | 257.99 | 279.78 | 301.56 | 328.98 | 353.56 | .0257 | .0255 | .0266 | .0263 | .0269 |
| Per capita | 201.84 | 218.04 | 247.96 | 269.97 | 298.65 | 169.17 | 184.67 | 200.37 | 220.05 | 238.09 | 1.193 | 1.181 | 1.238 | 1.227 | 1.254 |

*Dyer Straits/Reference Group.

132

is increasing its use of the sales tax and state and federal aid in total terms when compared with the reference group cities.

—In per capita terms, Dyer Straits is using the property tax much more heavily than the reference group and, by 1983, the same is true of the sales tax. State aid per capita has risen from about 4 percent below the reference group's to about 7 percent above by 1983.

Putting the data for Dyer Straits in the form of a common size statement helps highlight the changes in the city's revenue structure even more. Table 4–11 shows that property taxes, as a percentage of total revenues, have declined from 54.0 to 47.5 percent while sales taxes have risen from 9.7 to 13.8 percent over the 1979–83 period. Nontax local revenues have declined slightly in relative importance, but state and federal aid have both increased in relative importance over this period.

From these figures, the picture of heavy reliance on the property tax and less but growing reliance on the sales tax and intergovernmental transfers is quite clear. Moreover, per capita tax revenues for the two major local sources, the property and sales taxes, are over 40 percent higher than the reference group's in 1983. Since we determined in the preceding section that the property and sales tax bases are not that different from the bases in the reference group, the tax rates for the property and sales taxes must be significantly higher in Dyer Straits compared with the reference group. This will be our focus of attention in the next section.

These general conclusions are based on very aggregate data and, in an actual analysis, would have to be weighed against the specifics of revenue collection for Dyer Straits. For example, what methods are used in the category "nontax local revenues"? What procedures are used to assess property and sales tax bases? How exactly is state aid and federal aid allocated? Answers to questions of this sort are needed to analyze the actual revenues for Dyer Straits.

## V. REVENUE CAPACITY AND RESERVES

Economic base measures the ability of individuals and organizations in a geographical area to provide revenues to government. Revenue base measures the

TABLE 4-11   Common Size Statement—Dyer Straits' Revenues as Percentage of Total Revenues, 1979–83

|                      | 1979  | 1980  | 1981  | 1982  | 1983  |
|----------------------|-------|-------|-------|-------|-------|
| Property taxes       | 54.0  | 53.5  | 48.6  | 47.0  | 47.5  |
| Sales tax            | 9.7   | 9.4   | 14.8  | 14.3  | 13.8  |
| Nontax local revenues| 12.3  | 12.2  | 11.2  | 11.1  | 10.4  |
| State aid            | 15.2  | 16.0  | 16.2  | 17.6  | 17.5  |
| Federal aid          | 8.8   | 8.9   | 9.2   | 10.0  | 10.8  |
| Total Revenues       | 100.0 | 100.0 | 100.0 | 100.0 | 100.0 |

specific resources that can be tapped by government. But neither type of base measures the limits of revenue-raising power of the organization—the capacity or ability of a government to tap this revenue potential and revenue base.

All governments face political, legal, and economic realities which constrain their efforts to draw resources from their communities. The extent to which the economic base can be tapped by a government within these constraints is the organization's *revenue capacity,* often referred to as *fiscal capacity.* This limit or capacity, less the actual revenues raised, is the local government's *revenue reserves.* (See Figure 4-1.)

While the changes in income levels and other measures of the resources of a community will ultimately influence a government's capacity to raise revenues, it is the revenue capacity itself that forms the reality with which most governments must deal. Regardless of income levels, the government only has available a limited set of methods of raising revenues, as we discussed in section III. And these methods themselves cannot be applied without limit. They are subject to definitions and legal restrictions on tax rates and bases, competitive forces from other areas or governments eager to draw away suppliers of revenues, and a myriad of other forces that limit and shape the maximum feasible or allowable rate at which an organization can raise revenues without significant long-run disruption of its activities or diminution of its tax base. Organizations may go beyond this capacity, but not without the expectation of economic or fiscal repercussions.

Revenue capacity is an important factor in financial analysis for several reasons. First, the relationship between revenue capacity and economic base is of interest as an indicator of the extent to which different governments have the ability to raise revenues. The constraints on governments may differ greatly, and the economic impact of these constraints can be seen through the comparison of revenue capacity and economic base.

Second, the relationship of actual revenues collected to the revenue capacity of a government (revenue reserves) is an indicator of financial condition, as we will see later in this section. The extent to which actual revenues fall above or below revenue capacity is an important measure of the financial pressures faced by government.

Finally, revenue capacity measures are frequently included in formulas for the transfer of resources from the state and federal levels to local governments. Intergovernmental transfers, aimed at relieving fiscal pressures, may depend on revenue capacity, with increasing per capita grants for those governments with less capacity to raise revenues locally.

### Measures of Fiscal Capacity

The determination of fiscal capacity relies primarily on legal, judgmental, and comparative measurements. There is no single "correct" measure of fiscal capacity, so that it is important to be aware of the strengths and weaknesses of alternative measures.

TABLE 4-12  **Comparison of Cities Using Legal Tax Capacity**

| CITY | Tax Bases (in thousands of dollars) | | |
|---|---|---|---|
| | PROPERTY | SALES | INCOME |
| A | 1,000 | 2,000 | |
| B | 800 | 2,500 | |
| C | 1,000 | | 2,500 |

| CITY | Maximum Legal Tax Rates | | | LEGAL TAX REVENUE CAPACITY ($1,000/YEAR) |
|---|---|---|---|---|
| | PROPERTY | SALES | INCOME | |
| A | .02 | .03 | 0 | 80 |
| B | .02 | .03 | 0 | 91 |
| C | .02 | 0 | .03 | 95 |

*Legal restrictions* are the most obvious delineators of revenue capacity. Laws determine the revenue methods available to government, the definitions and restrictions on their use, and often the maximum rates that can be charged. Legal revenue capacity limits can be determined in a straightforward fashion and can be used to compare the extent to which different governments are legally constrained from drawing on local revenues. The recent movement toward restriction on the taxing and spending of state and local governments is, in part, an attempt to alter the legal restrictions on revenue capacity.[31]

Table 4-12 illustrates how legal tax revenue capacity, in this case in the form of a variety of tax rate limits, might be used to compare the revenue capacity of different cities. Cities A and B have access to property and sales taxes and rate limits on both; city C has access to property and income taxes and has a rate limit on both. For simplicity we will assume that all cities have the same population; otherwise we would use per capita values.

If we compare the *bases* of the different cities, it is difficult to determine which city has the highest legal tax revenue capacity. Even if we compare cities A and B, which have access to the same tax bases, it is not easy to determine which has the stronger overall tax base or the higher legal tax revenue capacity. One of the three cities does not dominate all others on all tax bases, and their access to different tax bases varies.

If we compare the maximum legal revenues possible for each city (legal tax revenue capacity), however, then differences between the cities become apparent. The different tax bases are "weighted" by their maximum tax rates to provide

[31] For a recent summary of the restrictions on state and local government tax and expenditure powers, see Advisory Commission on Intergovernmental Relations, *Significant Features of Fiscal Federalism, 1981–82* (Washington, D.C.: ACIR, April 1983), Table 43, p. 70; and "Proceedings of a Conference on Tax and Expenditure Limitations," *National Tax Journal Supplement,* 37 (June 1979).

capacity estimates for these comparisons. Using this procedure, city C has the highest legal tax revenue capacity, and city A has the lowest.

A point that applies to all measures of fiscal capacity can be raised in the context of this legal tax capacity example. This measure implicitly assumes that if a city is below its capacity, it can raise its tax rate and generate additional revenues, estimated by the increase in the tax rate times the tax base. Tax bases, however, which generally depend on individuals and businesses, can move between jurisdictions. People and firms can move, and if economic activity moves out as well, the value of the property and buildings that remain can decline. Therefore, if a government raises its tax rate, the value of the tax base may decline to the extent that economic activity is sensitive to the increase in the tax rate. Under these conditions, governments not currently at their maximum may have an effective maximum less than is indicated by the legal maximum.

Returning specifically to legal capacities as measures for revenue capacity, several limitations should be noted. Legal constraints are not absolute by any means. As we have seen in the recent changes in tax limits, regulations can be redrawn, laws changed, and even constitutions amended so that legal limits are not necessarily revenue limits. Furthermore, legal limits may not reflect economic realities or desirable financial practices. Other forces, such as the effects of the taxes on economic behavior, may set revenue limits. And a given tax limit, such as the limit on property taxes to a certain percentage of the full value of taxable property, may have little correspondence with the maximum level that might be carried "safely" by the taxing agency. These considerations require that economic and political realities be examined along with legal restrictions in developing estimates of revenue capacity.

Another basis for measuring revenue capacity is the use of *expert guidelines* and "rules of thumb." Academic and practitioner experience has produced judgments about maximum acceptable limits on the use of various financing methods, although these are used primarily in the area of borrowing (see Chapter 6). These limits often represent "conventional wisdom," and they may carry some weight in public financial management. To the extent that they actually reflect limits on disruptive or financially unwise behavior, rather than just "we've always done it that way," such guidelines may legitimately set limits on the use of some revenue sources and should be considered in estimating revenue capacity.

In the area of revenue capacity, we found no common or generally accepted judgmentally based *absolute* limits on the behavior of governments; no maximum safe own revenues or taxes per capita or per dollar of income, or other prescribed ceilings on revenue-raising ability. Most limits, as we discuss next, are of a *relative* rather than absolute nature and are based on comparisons of the government with appropriate reference groups.

While legal and judgmental limits tend to take a fixed character based on law or conventional wisdom, the most common method of estimating revenue capacity is based entirely on comparisons of one organization with a reference group of similar organizations. This method uses average behavior of the reference group as a basis for determining the capacity of the individual organizations in the group. (This approach is illustrated below.)

The estimation of revenue capacity using a *reference group basis* assumes in essence that the revenue capacity of a government can only be judged relative to those other entities with which it is most similar and with which it may be in long-run competition for resources. In this sense, the concept "capacity" takes on an average or typical or representative character, but it still provides a standard for comparisons with economic base and actual revenue collections. The empirical finding that governments with above-average tax rates are more likely to be subjected to tax and spending limits provides some. justification for the reference group approach.[32]

This comparative concept of fiscal capacity is discussed by Akin and Auten (pp. 453-54):

> Fiscal capacity, either for the nation or for local jurisdictions, could be defined as the maximum amount of revenue attainable by governments. Fiscal capacity would then be reached when further increases in tax rates give rise to sufficient evasion, avoidance, and emigration of people, wealth, and economic activity so that the reduction in tax bases would offset or more than offset rate increases. Conceptually this definition may have some appeal, but it is not empirically measurable.
>
> Rather than a maximum level, however, what is wanted is a measure of sustainable fiscal capacity under normal fiscal effort. Thus, fiscal capacity can be defined as the revenue that the jurisdiction could be expected to raise, given its relevant fiscal and economic resources, if it behaves with respect to these resources in a manner given by a norm such as the average behavior of like jurisdictions.[33]

Comparative measures of fiscal capacity can be divided into single and multifactor measures. Single-factor measures relate local tax and, in some cases, nontax revenue-raising ability to a single factor, such as population or income or wealth, and compare one organization with the average of a reference group of similar organizations. Thus the average per capita tax revenues of a reference group can provide a measure of the "capacity" of a similar organization to raise revenues through taxation. So, too, can average per capita income, taxable property, or taxable retail sales provide a measure of fiscal capacity. All these measures are indicators of the ability of similar organizations to raise revenues and could be used as capacity measures for individual organizations.

Perhaps the most commonly used single-factor fiscal capacity index is a measure of per capita income.[34] For example, per capita income is used in a

---

[32] Helen Ladd, "An Economic Evaluation of State Limitations on Local Taxing and Spending Powers," *National Tax Journal,* 31 (March 1978), 1-18.

[33] John Akin and Gerald E. Auten, "City Schools and Suburban Schools: A Fiscal Comparison," *Land Economics,* 52 (November 1976), 452-66.

[34] One exception to this statement is state aid for education, where equalized property value per capita is more commonly used than per capita income to measure local school district fiscal capacity (although some states use both).

number of federal aid programs to adjust for fiscal capacity. There are, however, several weaknesses with a single-factor, income-based measure.[35] First, the measurement of income often omits important income and wealth sources that could be available to pay taxes. For example, business income and the wealth generated by certain assets are excluded from available income statistics. Second, some measures of income may not accurately capture the income available to pay a jurisdiction's taxes, given the interjurisdictional complications caused by different residences and workplaces. Finally, through the use of various tax bases, jurisdictions have the opportunity to "export" some of their taxes to residents of other jurisdictions and this enhances a jurisdiction's tax capacity, although it does not show up in its local income. Taxes on vacation property, restaurant and hotel business, and some industrial and commercial property are taxes that are often considered as exported.[36]

A multifactor measure of revenue capacity is a measure that incorporates several factors, not just one, into the indicator of revenue-raising ability. The best-known example of this approach is the fiscal capacity measures of the Advisory Commission on Intergovernmental Relations (ACIR).[37]

To derive revenue capacity measures for states and local areas using a reference group approach, the ACIR computes average tax rates for all state and local governments combined, and it then applies these rates to the tax bases of specific states (where each state includes the local governments in that state) to estimate the state and local government tax capacity of each state. Twenty-six direct or indirect measures of different tax bases are used.[38] The ACIR tax rate for each base is the total revenue collected nationally for each tax, divided by the total value of the base. In some cases a proxy is used to estimate the tax base, so that the rate is not always an exact average of actual rates. To compute the tax revenue capacity of an individual state, the ACIR applies the average tax rates to the tax bases (or appropriate proxies) of that state.

A simple example of the ACIR approach applied to a local government may be helpful at this point. Suppose a particular government typically draws on some or all of three tax bases—property, sales, and income—and we have information

---

[35] These are discussed in Stephen M. Barro, *The Urban Impacts of Federal Policies: Vol. 3, Fiscal Conditions* (Santa Monica, Calif.: Rand Corporation, April 1978), p. 34; and Advisory Commission on Intergovernmental Relations, *Tax Capacity of the States: Methodology and Estimates* (Washington, D.C.: ACIR, March 1982), pp. 5–10.

[36] Helen Ladd and Katherine Bradbury, "Changes in the Fiscal Capacity of U.S. Cities, 1970–1982" (Paper prepared for the National Tax Association—Tax Institute Annual Conference, Nashville, Tenn., November 1984).

[37] Advisory Commission on Intergovernmental Relations, *Measuring the Fiscal Capacity and Effort of State and Local Areas* (Washington, D.C.: ACIR, March 1971), Report M-58; and "Metropolitan Fiscal Disparities," *Fiscal Balance in the American Federal System* (Washington, D.C.: ACIR, October, 1967).

[38] Advisory Commission on Intergovernmental Relations, *1981 Tax Capacity of the 50 States* (Washington, D.C.: ACIR, September 1983), Table 2, pp. 4–5.

about that government (Metroville) and the totals for all similar governments (see Table 4–13). Applying the average tax rates for the reference group to Metroville's base we have:

Tax revenue capacity of Metroville = (.0125)($500) + (.0075)($250)
$$+ (.01)($300) = $11.125 \text{ million}$$

Thus Metroville's capacity to raise revenues through taxation is estimated at $11.125 million using the ACIR approach. (Note that Metroville is only raising $10 million in actual collections, less than the ACIR measure of its capacity. We discuss this revenue "reserve" in the next section.)

ACIR's approach can also be used to measure nontax revenue capacity, although this is less commonly seen in practice. ACIR estimates the average ratio of the revenues from a particular source (such as user charges) to the operating expenditures on that function. For example, suppose government expenditures for a particular activity, say parking facilities, are $500 million and revenues for parking facilities are $300 million, or 60 percent of the expenditure level. The financing or revenue capacity for parking services is estimated to be 60 cents per dollar of that government's parking expenditures. Although this approach to nontax revenues has been implemented by the ACIR for state and local governments, the ACIR approach is employed primarily as a measure of tax capacity only.

The effect of using a multifactor capacity measure rather than a single-factor measure can be seen in Table 4–14. This table presents the ACIR estimates of tax capacity for 1981 for all states and the District of Columbia based on the representative tax approach and the income per capita approach which is a single-factor index. Both indexes are converted to a percentage of the U.S. average in order to compare the differences between the two measures. The differences in the indexes

TABLE 4–13 **Basic Data for Illustration of Calculation of ACIR Measure of Fiscal Capacity**

| | | Metroville | |
|---|---|---|---|
| TAX | TAX BASE* | TAX COLLECTION* | TAX RATE |
| Property | $500 | $7.5 | .015 |
| Sales | 250 | 2.5 | .01 |
| Income | 300 | 0 | 0 |

| | | Reference Group (All Similar Governments) | |
|---|---|---|---|
| TAX | TAX BASE† | TAX COLLECTION† | TAX RATE |
| Property | $10,000 | $125 | .0125 |
| Sales | 5,000 | 37.5 | .0075 |
| Income | 6,000 | 60 | .01 |

*$ millions
†$ billions

TABLE 4-14    **Comparison of Two Revenue Capacity Measures for State and Local Governments**

| STATE | ACIR ESTIMATES OF PER CAPITA REVENUE CAPACITY (1981) $ | % of U.S. Average | RESIDENTS' PER CAPITA PERSONAL INCOME (1981) $ | % of U.S. Average | PERCENT DEPARTURE OF INCOME INDEX FROM REVENUE CAPACITY INDEX* |
|---|---|---|---|---|---|
| United States, Total | 1,029 | 100.0 | 10,491 | 100.0 | 0 |
| Alabama | 766 | 74.5 | 8,219 | 78.3 | +5 |
| Alaska | 3,333 | 323.8 | 13,763 | 131.2 | −59 |
| Arizona | 913 | 88.7 | 9,754 | 93.0 | +5 |
| Arkansas | 839 | 81.6 | 8,044 | 76.7 | −6 |
| California | 1,186 | 115.2 | 11,923 | 113.6 | −1 |
| Colorado | 1,160 | 112.8 | 11,215 | 106.9 | −5 |
| Connecticut | 1,131 | 109.9 | 12,816 | 122.2 | +11 |
| Delaware | 1,143 | 111.1 | 11,095 | 105.8 | −5 |
| District of Columbia | 1,142 | 111.0 | 13,539 | 129.1 | +16 |
| Florida | 1,040 | 101.1 | 10,165 | 96.9 | −4 |
| Georgia | 838 | 81.4 | 8,934 | 85.2 | +5 |
| Hawaii | 1,076 | 104.6 | 11,036 | 105.2 | +1 |
| Idaho | 891 | 86.6 | 8,937 | 85.2 | −2 |
| Illinois | 1,070 | 103.9 | 11,576 | 110.3 | +6 |
| Indiana | 932 | 90.6 | 9,720 | 92.7 | +2 |
| Iowa | 1,053 | 102.3 | 10,474 | 99.8 | −2 |
| Kansas | 1,125 | 109.3 | 10,813 | 103.1 | −6 |
| Kentucky | 843 | 82.0 | 8,420 | 80.3 | −2 |
| Louisiana | 1,200 | 116.6 | 9,518 | 90.7 | −22 |
| Maine | 815 | 79.2 | 8,535 | 81.4 | +3 |
| Maryland | 1,009 | 98.0 | 11,477 | 109.4 | +12 |
| Massachusetts | 988 | 96.0 | 11,128 | 106.1 | +11 |
| Michigan | 990 | 96.2 | 10,790 | 102.9 | +7 |
| Minnesota | 1,030 | 100.1 | 10,768 | 102.6 | +2 |
| Mississippi | 737 | 71.6 | 7,408 | 70.6 | −1 |
| Missouri | 947 | 92.1 | 9,651 | 92.0 | 0 |
| Montana | 1,168 | 113.5 | 9,410 | 89.7 | −21 |
| Nebraska | 996 | 96.8 | 10,366 | 98.8 | +2 |
| Nevada | 1,523 | 148.0 | 11,576 | 110.3 | −25 |
| New Hampshire | 982 | 95.5 | 9,994 | 95.3 | 0 |
| New Jersey | 1,077 | 104.7 | 12,127 | 115.6 | +10 |
| New Mexico | 1,170 | 113.6 | 8,529 | 81.3 | −28 |
| New York | 916 | 89.0 | 11,466 | 109.3 | +23 |
| North Carolina | 818 | 79.5 | 8,649 | 82.4 | +4 |
| North Dakota | 1,271 | 123.5 | 10,213 | 97.4 | −21 |
| Ohio | 971 | 94.4 | 10,313 | 98.3 | +4 |
| Oklahoma | 1,310 | 127.3 | 10,247 | 97.7 | −23 |
| Oregon | 1,019 | 99.0 | 10,008 | 95.4 | −4 |
| Pennsylvania | 931 | 90.4 | 10,370 | 98.8 | −4 |
| Rhode Island | 827 | 80.4 | 10,153 | 96.8 | +9 |
| South Carolina | 774 | 75.2 | 8,039 | 76.6 | +2 |
| South Dakota | 888 | 86.3 | 8,833 | 84.2 | −2 |
| Tennessee | 812 | 79.0 | 8,447 | 80.5 | +2 |

TABLE 4-14   (continued)

| STATE | ACIR ESTIMATES OF PER CAPITA REVENUE CAPACITY (1981) $ | % of U.S. Average | RESIDENTS' PER CAPITA PERSONAL INCOME (1981) $ | % of U.S. Average | PERCENT DEPARTURE OF INCOME INDEX FROM REVENUE CAPACITY INDEX* |
|---|---|---|---|---|---|
| Texas | 1,359 | 132.1 | 10,729 | 102.3 | −23 |
| Utah | 890 | 86.5 | 8,313 | 79.2 | −8 |
| Vermont | 864 | 84.0 | 8,723 | 83.1 | −1 |
| Virginia | 969 | 94.1 | 10,349 | 98.6 | +5 |
| Washington | 1,020 | 99.1 | 11,277 | 107.5 | +8 |
| West Virginia | 926 | 90.0 | 8,377 | 79.8 | −11 |
| Wisconsin | 935 | 90.9 | 10,035 | 95.7 | +5 |
| Wyoming | 2,227 | 216.4 | 11,665 | 111.2 | −49 |

SOURCE:  ACIR, *1981 Tax Capacity of the Fifty States* (Washington, D.C.: ACIR, 1983), Table 4, pp. 8–9.
*(Percent income index minus percent ACIR capacity index)/Percent ACIR capacity index

can be seen in the extremes (Wyoming, Alaska, New Mexico, Texas, New York, etc.) and by the fact that the Pearson correlation between the two indexes is only 0.5835 (where 1.0 indicates a perfect correlation; 0.0 indicates no correlation).

The ACIR approach has been the subject of some controversy.[39] John Akin points out that each individual base only contributes to the tax capacity according to its share of taxes. Certain bases, however, most notably income, probably contribute more to tax capacity than just through their direct use as a tax base. Income levels, for example, affect sales, property values, and so forth, and this influences tax revenues beyond the tax revenues directly from the income tax itself. This is probably truer of local government fiscal capacity; at the local government level the income tax is a relatively minor tax source. A second problem with the ACIR method is that it computes an average effect; by taking the tax revenue and dividing by the tax base, an average tax rate is derived. In certain cases the marginal contribution of a particular tax base to fiscal capacity may not equal the average effect, and the ACIR method will not pick this up. Finally, the use of one tax base quite heavily may preclude the use of other bases, but the ACIR method does not take interactions among the bases into account.[40]

Of course, the problem we discussed earlier, the fact that when a local

[39] John Akin, "Fiscal Capacity and the Estimation Method of the Advisory Commission on Intergovernmental Relations," *National Tax Journal,* 26 (June 1973), 275–91; Allen D. Manvel, "Tax Capacity versus Tax Performance: A Comment," *National Tax Journal,* 26 (June 1973), 293–94; and W. Douglas Morgan, "An Alternative Measure of Fiscal Capacity," *National Tax Journal,* 27 (June 1974), 361–65.

[40] Akin, "Fiscal Capacity and the Measurement Method of the Advisory Commission on Intergovernmental Relations."

jurisdiction raises tax rates the tax base itself may decline, holds for the ACIR method applied to local governments just as it does for most fiscal capacity measures. Although the ACIR has applied its representative tax base approach to Standard Metropolitan Statistical Areas (SMSAs), it has some reservations about applying the methodology to local governments because of this problem.[41] Since, however, the problem that has prevented the ACIR from applying its methodology to local governments exists for all other approaches, we believe the advantages of the ACIR approach make it a valid alternative for calculating local government fiscal capacity. Despite its limitations, the ACIR method goes a long way toward meeting the need to develop measures that capture in an appropriate and empirically measurable way the relative capacities of different governments to raise revenues.

Some of the problems of the ACIR approach, discussed above, have led to the development of a multifactor fiscal capacity measure based on multivariate regression. Akin presented a regression-based fiscal capacity measure relating state tax revenues to resident income, wealth, and ability to tax nonresidents, and he also chose to include other variables representing the cost of providing services and the tastes and needs of the residents in the regression estimate.[42] While these latter factors are important for expenditure analysis (see Chapter 5) and clearly affect revenue needs and collections, their inclusion in a measure of revenue capacity is questionable because the revenue capacity measure should depend solely on the supply of resources and available methods of tapping these resources.

In more recent work, however, Akin and Auten chose to develop a multifactor regression-based fiscal capacity measure without including costs, tastes, and needs in the regression estimate.[43] They developed a regression equation that relates local government revenues to income and different types of taxable property. Using linear regression analysis, they found the following relationship for local government revenues in 104 New York State school districts in 1967–68:

$$R_i = -29.241 + .027\, MFI_i + .028\, RP_i + .412\, CP_i + .248\, IP_i + .159\, SP_i + 1.734\, OP_i$$

where

$R_i$ = per capita local government revenues in district $i$

$MFI_i$ = median family income in district $i$

$RP_i$ = per capita full value of residential property in district $i$

$CP_i$ = per capita full value of commercial property in district $i$

---

[41] Advisory Commission on Intergovernmental Relations, *Measuring Metropolitan Fiscal Capacity and Effort, 1967–1980* (Washington, D.C.: ACIR, July 1983).

[42] Akin, "Fiscal Capacity and the Measurement Method of the Advisory Commission on Intergovernmental Relations."

[43] Akin and Auten, "City Schools and Suburban Schools: A Fiscal Comparison."

$IP_i$ = per capita full value of industrial property in district $i$

$SP_i$ = per capita full value of seasonal property in district $i$

$OP_i$ = per capita full value of other types of property in district $i$

Eighty-nine percent of the variance in local government revenues was explained by the model, and all factors except residential property were highly statistically significant.

But how is this revenue equation related to fiscal capacity? For Akin and Auten, "capacity is the amount that would be raised by a local unit if that unit responds to the resource variables in accordance with the average response of all units subject to the analysis."[44] In other words, if a local government in 1967–68 had a median family income of $8,000 and per capita property values of $1,000 (residential), $500 (commercial), $500 (industrial), $100 (seasonal), and $50 (other), then substituting these values in the above equation, the local government's per capita revenue capacity, $RC_i$, would have been

$$RC_i = -29.241 + .027(\$8,000) + .028(\$1,000) + .412(\$500) \\ + .248(\$500) + .159(\$100) + 1.734(\$50) = \$647.359$$

Thus, if this local government extracted revenues from its tax bases at the same rates as the average of all local governments in the sample, this government would have raised $647.36 per capita. This would be the revenue capacity using this approach.

Clearly, more experimentation is needed to fully understand the regression-based multifactor fiscal capacity measures. Experimentation with various sets of independent variables and specifications is necessary. Yet the fact remains that at the local government level, income probably contributes more to fiscal capacity than its share of taxes. This is confirmed by multiple regression, making this a promising approach to measuring fiscal capacity.

Other conceptual and estimation developments in the fiscal capacity area are worth mentioning. First, Akin has used the concept of the utility function to relate fiscal capacity to the resources available in the tax bases and the resources available for private consumption.[45] His empirical estimates suggest that this new formulation differs from previously utilized definitions of fiscal capacity. Second, Aaron Gurwitz has begun to formulate a notion of fiscal capacity that is based on the "maximum net present value of a city's revenue stream," and this leads to an analysis over time of the way in which the tax base is altered by changes in the tax rate.[46] Thus Gurwitz has tried to incorporate explicitly the fact that increases in

---

[44] Ibid., p. 456.

[45] John Akin, "Estimates of State Resource Constraints Derived from a Specific Utility Function: An Alternative Measure of Fiscal Capacity," *National Tax Journal* 32 (March 1979) 61–71.

[46] Aaron Gurwitz, "The Fiscal Capacity of Major U.S. Cities", unpublished paper (Santa Monica, Calif.: Rand Corporation, no date), p. 2.

the tax rate are likely to generate decreases in the tax base, all other things being equal. Gurwitz uses a sample of cities to explore the estimation possibilities. Finally, Helen Ladd and Katherine Bradbury, and Stephen Barro, have refined the measurement of fiscal capacity to include the ability to export taxes.[47]

### Revenue Reserves

The primary reason for estimating revenue capacity is to assess the extent to which a government's actual revenues are over or under its capacity. Capacity measures are revenue benchmarks that allow organizations to be evaluated in terms of their relative "using up" or "drawing down" of their revenue base. If revenue capacity is greater than actual revenues, the difference represents the revenue reserves of the organization; if capacity is less than actual revenues, the difference is a measure of how overextended the organization is with respect to its resource base.

To use the concept of revenue reserves, or unutilized capacity, for analyzing financial performance, we need to remember its limitations. The existence of unused taxing power, whether based on legal limitations, averages of similar organizations, or some other method, does not mean that this reserve can necessarily be drawn upon easily. Political realities will clearly play a role in determining the ease with which these reserves can be put to use, as well as whether the need for resources can be met in some other fashion. Moreover, as we have indicated, raising (lowering) the tax rate beyond some point is likely to lower (raise) the absolute size of the tax base.

Regardless of these caveats, it is still important to know to what extent financial pressures can be relieved by raising additional revenues, as compared with, say, cutting the growth rate or absolute level of expenditures, or borrowing. In this sense, revenue or fiscal reserves shape the possibilities open to a particular government, with large reserves providing options unavailable to organizations facing limited reserves.

The analysis of revenue reserves also requires examination of the mix of financing reserves available to an organization. For example, an organization with considerable taxing reserves, providing a strong basis for financing in the long run, may still face short-run cash needs. Here, as we will see in Chapters 6 and 8, the ability to borrow in the short term may become critical, and although borrowing capacity depends to a large extent on taxing power, it is possible to have overborrowed to a point where short-run cash demands raise severe problems, even though the local government has long-run financing strengths. Thus the pat-

---

[47] Ladd and Bradbury, "Measuring the Fiscal Capacity of U.S. Cities, 1970–1982"; and Stephen Barro, "State Fiscal Capacity Measures: A Theoretical Critique" (Paper presented at the Tax Policy Roundtable, Lincoln Institute of Land Policy, Cambridge, Mass., April 27, 1984). For another example of a measure of fiscal capacity in an empirical financial condition study, see Katherine L. Bradbury, "Structural Fiscal Distress in Cities—Causes and Consequences," *New England Economic Review*, January–February 1983, pp. 32–43.

tern or mix of financial reserves must be studied as well as the total level of reserves.

Finally, revenue reserves must be examined along with unmet expenditure needs to determine the adequacy of these reserves. A government facing clientele groups with very real and apparent needs for more services may find even its large revenue reserves inadequate; a similar organization with less demands for services may be financially secure with smaller revenue reserves. Expenditure considerations will be examined in the next chapter.

Revenue reserves (or lack of reserves) attempt to measure the same thing as what are called tax or revenue *efforts* or *burdens.* The same measure is called revenue effort from the government's standpoint and revenue burden from the standpoint of those providing the revenues; therefore we will use both terms interchangeably.

Effort or burden measures are usually derived from single-factor capacity measures and relate actual local revenues raised (or specific types of revenues) to single factors such as population or income. Thus per capita tax and nontax revenues are one type of revenue burden measure, indicating the average payments made by a member of the community for each major local revenue method (or all local revenue methods together). This is a very crude measure, since it relies solely on the level of population and not its wealth or income.

A second burden measure is a community's actual tax rate for each major tax, which indicates how much each tax base has been "burdened" (is being drawn upon) to raise revenues. An advantage of tax rates as measures of tax burden is their availability and simplicity. At the same time, comparisons using tax rates are difficult for several reasons. First, it is difficult to compare burdens for combinations of taxes. A tax rate expressed as a percentage of full value of property is not easily combined with a tax rate expressed as a percentage of retail sales. Second, tax rates sometimes have multiple values, such as income taxes for different income ranges or property taxes that vary for different classes of property, which makes comparisons across time or jurisdictions more difficult. And last, if the tax bases are defined differently, then the comparisons of tax rates may not be appropriate.

The most common and frequently used measure of tax burden is total (or selected) taxes divided by total income, or the average percentage of income of a community that is being paid to a particular government or set of governments. Since taxes are known to vary according to level of income, sometimes this tax burden measure is presented for a specific income level. Table 4–15 shows state and local taxes as a percentage of personal income for selected years from 1953 to 1982. While the average burden peaked in the mid-Seventies, the considerable variation among the states still persists. Other examples are available where selected state and local taxes as a percentage of income are compared for a median income family of four in the largest city in each state in 1980.[48]

---

[48] See Advisory Commission on Intergovernmental Relations, *Significant Features of Fiscal Federalism, 1981–82* (Washington, D.C.: ACIR, April 1983), Table 33, p. 56. For examples of tax

TABLE 4-15 State and Local Tax Revenue in Relation To State Personal Income, by State and Region, Selected Years, 1953–1982

| STATE AND REGION | TAX REVENUE AS A PERCENT OF PERSONAL INCOME | | | | | | | |
|---|---|---|---|---|---|---|---|---|
| | 1982 | 1981 | 1980 | 1978 | 1975 | 1965 | 1953 | |
| United States* | 10.96% | 11.29% | 11.57% | 12.75% | 12.29% | 10.45% | 7.58% | |
| New England | 11.27 | 11.82 | 12.35 | 13.49 | 12.79 | 9.97 | 7.90 | |
| Connecticut | 10.22 | 10.20 | 10.55 | 11.64 | 10.82 | 9.08 | 6.06 | |
| Maine | 11.98 | 11.89 | 12.50 | 13.29 | 12.59 | 10.98 | 8.95 | |
| Massachusetts | 11.95 | 13.28 | 13.90 | 15.11 | 14.20 | 10.21 | 8.77 | |
| New Hampshire | 9.05 | 8.68 | 9.20 | 10.51 | 10.75 | 9.51 | 8.28 | |
| Rhode Island | 11.97 | 11.53 | 11.89 | 12.52 | 11.94 | 10.19 | 7.02 | |
| Vermont | 12.36 | 12.58 | 12.73 | 14.48 | 15.46 | 12.72 | 9.62 | |
| Mideast* | 12.86 | 13.11 | 13.68 | 14.50 | 13.94 | 10.54 | 7.46 | |
| Delaware | 10.97 | 10.84 | 11.60 | 12.28 | 11.66 | 8.98 | 4.21 | |
| Dist. of Col. | 14.17 | 14.69 | 13.57 | 13.63 | 10.67 | 8.09 | 5.90 | |
| Maryland | 10.94 | 11.24 | 12.03 | 13.02 | 12.26 | 9.34 | 6.33 | |
| New Jersey | 10.98 | 11.21 | 11.72 | 12.42 | 11.59 | 9.07 | 6.59 | |
| New York | 15.57 | 15.84 | 16.34 | 17.19 | 16.65 | 11.87 | 8.79 | |
| Pennsylvania | 10.70 | 10.92 | 11.56 | 12.25 | 11.68 | 9.47 | 6.17 | |
| Great Lakes | 10.44 | 10.59 | 10.66 | 11.60 | 11.35 | 9.73 | 6.78 | |
| Illinois | 10.29 | 11.05 | 11.25 | 11.80 | 11.73 | 8.89 | 6.37 | |
| Indiana | 9.00 | 9.23 | 8.82 | 10.29 | 11.15 | 10.24 | 7.08 | |
| Michigan | 11.64 | 11.57 | 11.50 | 12.67 | 11.66 | 10.67 | 7.31 | |
| Ohio | 9.47 | 9.20 | 9.35 | 9.93 | 9.69 | 8.64 | 5.87 | |
| Wisconsin | 12.23 | 12.24 | 12.47 | 14.16 | 13.83 | 12.55 | 8.91 | |

| Plains | 10.12 | 10.45 | 10.80 | 11.77 | 11.73 | 10.83 | 8.25 |
|---|---|---|---|---|---|---|---|
| Iowa | 10.51 | 11.08 | 11.07 | 11.62 | 12.14 | 11.63 | 9.22 |
| Kansas | 9.44 | 10.03 | 10.00 | 11.29 | 10.86 | 11.70 | 8.71 |
| Minnesota | 11.96 | 12.00 | 12.74 | 14.16 | 13.94 | 12.72 | 9.38 |
| Missouri | 8.59 | 8.77 | 9.30 | 9.94 | 10.35 | 8.74 | 6.14 |
| Nebraska | 10.10 | 10.37 | 11.06 | 12.15 | 10.96 | 9.34 | 7.69 |
| North Dakota | 10.25 | 11.24 | 10.22 | 11.63 | 10.95 | 11.77 | 11.27 |
| South Dakota | 9.93 | 10.85 | 10.59 | 11.48 | 11.60 | 12.60 | 10.79 |
| Southeast | 9.70 | 10.12 | 10.31 | 11.01 | 10.70 | 10.04 | 7.86 |
| Alabama | 9.16 | 9.85 | 9.64 | 10.21 | 9.94 | 9.74 | 7.00 |
| Arkansas | 8.90 | 9.32 | 9.87 | 10.18 | 9.90 | 9.77 | 7.92 |
| Florida | 8.71 | 9.34 | 9.75 | 10.64 | 9.94 | 10.53 | 9.20 |
| Georgia | 10.30 | 10.55 | 10.78 | 11.26 | 10.79 | 9.96 | 7.67 |
| Kentucky | 9.97 | 10.32 | 10.39 | 11.26 | 11.32 | 9.62 | 6.47 |
| Louisiana | 11.03 | 11.54 | 11.60 | 12.25 | 12.99 | 12.05 | 10.43 |
| Mississippi | 10.07 | 10.78 | 10.86 | 11.77 | 11.84 | 11.85 | 9.37 |
| North Carolina | 10.11 | 10.29 | 10.62 | 10.93 | 10.58 | 9.97 | 8.25 |
| South Carolina | 10.20 | 10.66 | 10.68 | 11.09 | 10.46 | 9.67 | 8.61 |
| Tennessee | 9.00 | 9.56 | 9.37 | 10.74 | 10.04 | 9.71 | 7.32 |
| Virginia | 9.72 | 10.05 | 10.25 | 11.05 | 10.67 | 8.55 | 6.09 |
| West Virginia | 11.47 | 10.71 | 11.21 | 11.29 | 12.27 | 9.85 | 6.81 |
| Southwest | 10.02 | 10.56 | 10.36 | 11.15 | 11.06 | 10.16 | 7.34 |
| Arizona | 10.45 | 11.49 | 13.27 | 14.28 | 13.26 | 12.15 | 8.50 |
| New Mexico | 12.82 | 14.02 | 12.18 | 13.26 | 13.54 | 12.16 | 8.66 |
| Oklahoma | 11.12 | 11.05 | 10.16 | 10.66 | 10.53 | 10.44 | 9.07 |
| Texas | 9.52 | 10.04 | 9.75 | 10.55 | 10.56 | 9.60 | 6.68 |

(Continued)

TABLE 4–15  (continued)

|  | | TAX REVENUE AS A PERCENT OF PERSONAL INCOME | | | | | |
| STATE AND REGION | 1982 | 1981 | 1980 | 1978 | 1975 | 1965 | 1953 |
| --- | --- | --- | --- | --- | --- | --- | --- |
| Rocky Mountain | 11.49 | 11.25 | 11.90 | 12.91 | 11.78 | 11.61 | 8.60 |
| Colorado | 10.13 | 10.20 | 11.31 | 12.55 | 11.61 | 11.40 | 8.93 |
| Idaho | 9.53 | 10.01 | 10.39 | 12.00 | 11.02 | 12.14 | 9.00 |
| Montana | 13.12 | 12.87 | 13.03 | 13.76 | 12.57 | 11.78 | 7.62 |
| Utah | 11.50 | 11.89 | 12.47 | 12.66 | 11.63 | 11.78 | 8.44 |
| Wyoming | 19.98 | 15.53 | 14.76 | 15.95 | 13.43 | 11.28 | 8.73 |
| Far West† | 10.99 | 11.30 | 11.91 | 15.13 | 14.07 | 11.79 | 8.34 |
| California | 11.12 | 11.49 | 12.17 | 15.80 | 14.59 | 11.98 | 8.41 |
| Nevada | 10.14 | 10.26 | 10.52 | 13.10 | 13.23 | 10.69 | 7.93 |
| Oregon | 11.08 | 11.85 | 11.41 | 12.80 | 12.13 | 10.94 | 8.24 |
| Washington | 10.28 | 10.04 | 10.88 | 12.73 | 12.06 | 11.18 | 8.07 |
| Alaska‡ | 45.42 | 50.02 | 36.78 | 17.49 | 21.45 | 8.11 | 5.03§ |
| Hawaii | 12.75 | 13.75 | 14.75 | 14.02 | 14.44 | 11.72 | 8.23§ |

*Excluding the District of Columbia.

†Excluding Alaska and Hawaii.

‡Because most of Alaska's revenue is derived from the taxation of oil production and the income of oil companies, the recent figures for the state of Alaska greatly overstate the actual tax burden borne by the residents of Alaska.

§Estimated, based on the U.S. average change between 1953 and 1957 (the earliest year readily available).

SOURCE: Advisory Commission on Intergovernmental Relations, Significant Features of Fiscal Federalism, 1982–83 (Washington, D.C.: ACIR, June 1984), Table 29.1, p. 41.

Burden or reserve measures may also be based on multifactor measures of capacity, such as ACIR estimates. The reserves are simply the difference between actual revenues and revenue capacity. Revenue burden measures are the ratio of actual revenues to income adjusted for revenue capacity. This adjustment may take several forms, but multiplication of income by the ratio of the revenue capacity index to the income index is the simplest method.

To illustrate the use of the ACIR capacity measures in estimating revenue reserves and burden, we will use the data in Table 4–14. Per capita state and local government revenues for Wyoming in 1981 were $1,615.[49] The ACIR revenue capacity estimate for Wyoming from Table 4–14 was $2,227. Thus per capita revenue reserves were $2,227—$1,615, or $612. Revenue burden was $1,615 divided by ($11,665 × 216.4/111.2), or 7.1 percent, where 216.4/111.2 is the ratio of Wyoming's revenue capacity to its personal income with each expressed as a percentage of the U.S. average from Table 4–14. Without the adjustment, the revenue burden would have been $1,615 divided by $11,665, or 13.8 percent, so the use of a multifactor capacity measure makes a difference in this case.

Revenue or fiscal capacity measures continue to be used to estimate the fiscal stress on different local and state governments. The ACIR attempts to incorporate a time dimension into the tax effort estimates by computing a ratio of the tax effort index to the change in the tax effort index over a period of time. The ratio, labeled "fiscal blood pressure" by the ACIR, thus indicates whether tax effort is high and rising (presumably the worst case), high and falling, low and rising, or low and falling. Table 4–16 presents the fiscal blood pressure measures for the fifty states for three different time periods. Although there are exceptions, these data suggest a regional pattern. For example, based on the ACIR tax capacity measures, New England's tax effort was 22 percent above the U.S. average tax effort in 1979, and the 1979 tax effort was 107 percent of New England's 1975 tax effort. Thus, New England's fiscal blood pressure for 1979/1975 is 122/107, placing New England in the high and rising group.

Reserve and burden measures can be estimated for the Akin and Auten revenue model approach. In our earlier example, the revenue capacity of a local government was calculated by putting that government's income and property value data into an equation that Akin and Auten fit for 104 local governments. The resulting revenue capacity ($647.36 per capita) can be compared with actual revenues in the same fashion as described above where the ACIR approach was used.

Finally, it is worth noting that the revenue burden measures developed

---

burden measures in empirical financial condition studies, see Touche Ross and First National Bank of Boston, *Urban Fiscal Stress,* p. 31; and U.S. Department of the Treasury, "Report on the Fiscal Impact of the Economic Stimulus Package on 48 Large Urban Governments," p. 57.

[49] Advisory Commission on Intergovernmental Relations, *1981 Tax Capacity of the 50 States,* Table A-51, p. 70.

TABLE 4-16    State Fiscal Blood Pressure Indices for 1979/1975, 1975/1967, and 1979/1967

| STATE | FISCAL BLOOD PRESSURE INDEX* | | |
|---|---|---|---|
| | 1979/1975 | 1975/1967 | 1979/1967 |
| New England | 122/107 | 114/105 | 122/112 |
| Connecticut | 102/103 | 99/106 | 102/110 |
| Maine | 111/107 | 104/99 | 111/106 |
| Massachusetts | 145/115 | 130/107 | 145/120 |
| New Hampshire | 78/103 | 76/94 | 78/96 |
| Rhode Island | 123/109 | 113/108 | 123/117 |
| Vermont | 110/101 | 109/92 | 110/92 |
| Mideast | 134/108 | 124/107 | 134/116 |
| Delaware | 95/113 | 84/93 | 95/106 |
| District of Columbia | 133/141 | 94/104 | 133/148 |
| Maryland | 110/104 | 106/103 | 110/107 |
| New Jersey | 117/114 | 103/106 | 117/121 |
| New York | 172/108 | 160/116 | 172/125 |
| Pennsylvania | 105/113 | 93/94 | 105/106 |
| Great Lakes | 99/102 | 97/104 | 99/106 |
| Illinois | 99/100 | 99/118 | 99/118 |
| Indiana | 84/91 | 92/97 | 84/88 |
| Michigan | 114/107 | 107/107 | 114/114 |
| Ohio | 86/108 | 80/98 | 86/105 |
| Wisconsin | 119/103 | 116/94 | 119/96 |
| Plains | 95/101 | 94/95 | 95/96 |
| Iowa | 93/99 | 94/90 | 93/89 |
| Kansas | 86/102 | 84/88 | 86/90 |
| Minnesota | 116/98 | 118/99 | 116/97 |
| Missouri | 83/99 | 84/98 | 83/97 |
| Nebraska | 98/115 | 85/109 | 98/126 |
| North Dakota | 77/84 | 92/95 | 77/79 |
| South Dakota | 84/95 | 88/82 | 84/79 |
| Southeast | 86/104 | 83/92 | 86/96 |
| Alabama | 87/109 | 80/90 | 87/98 |
| Arkansas | 82/104 | 79/95 | 82/100 |
| Florida | 79/107 | 74/88 | 79/94 |
| Georgia | 97/109 | 89/97 | 97/105 |
| Kentucky | 86/101 | 85/100 | 86/101 |
| Louisiana | 79/94 | 84/93 | 79/88 |
| Mississippi | 96/101 | 95/97 | 96/98 |
| North Carolina | 92/106 | 87/93 | 92/98 |
| South Carolina | 92/107 | 86/89 | 92/95 |
| Tennessee | 87/110 | 79/96 | 87/100 |
| Virginia | 89/101 | 88/98 | 89/99 |
| West Virginia | 81/94 | 86/90 | 81/84 |
| Southwest | 71/97 | 73/91 | 71/89 |
| Arizona | 116/107 | 108/99 | 116/106 |
| New Mexico | 84/95 | 88/96 | 84/91 |
| Oklahoma | 71/101 | 70/88 | 71/89 |
| Texas | 63/95 | 66/88 | 63/84 |

TABLE 4-16   *(continued)*

| STATE | FISCAL BLOOD PRESSURE INDEX* | | |
|---|---|---|---|
| | 1979/1975 | 1975/1967 | 1979/1967 |
| Rocky Mountain | 93/106 | 88/85 | 93/90 |
| Colorado | 96/107 | 90/85 | 96/91 |
| Idaho | 92/102 | 90/86 | 92/88 |
| Montana | 88/97 | 91/98 | 88/95 |
| Utah | 99/111 | 89/80 | 99/89 |
| Wyoming | 79/120 | 66/84 | 79/100 |
| Far West | 96/84 | 114/107 | 96/90 |
| California | 95/80 | 119/110 | 95/88 |
| Nevada | 65/93 | 70/99 | 65/92 |
| Oregon | 94/97 | 97/96 | 94/93 |
| Washington | 97/95 | 102/96 | 97/92 |
| Alaska | 126/168 | 75/72 | 126/121 |
| Hawaii | 128/107 | 120/89 | 128/95 |
| U.S. Average | 100/100 | 100/100 | 100/100 |

*Fiscal Blood Pressure = Tax Effort Index/Change in Tax Effort Index.
SOURCES:   Data from ACIR staff estimates. Table from ACIR, *Tax Capacity of the Fifty States: Methodology and Estimates* (Washington, D.C.: ACIR, March 1982), Table 8, pp. 46–47.

above do not include the additional burden or cost imposed on a locality due to inefficiencies in the revenue methods used, nor do they indicate how this burden is distributed across groups with different incomes or ability to pay. Tax revenues raised using inefficient and inequitable tax methods will generate greater tax burden than the standard burden measures reveal. Consequently, the revenue efficiency and equity considerations discussed in section III need to be considered along with the analysis of revenue reserves and burden.

### Price Effects

An important factor to consider as we complete our discussion of revenue analysis is the impact of price changes over time on measures of revenues, revenue base, and revenue capacity and reserves. Increases of the prices paid for goods and services over time (inflation) means that the value of the dollar in real purchasing power decreases over time. Consequently, during periods of inflation, the same dollar value of revenues collected by government in two different years means that the real value of revenues collected is less in the later year. A government with increasing revenues in current dollars may in fact be receiving fewer dollars each year in terms of their actual purchasing power. This holds true for measures of revenue base, capacity, and reserves as well.

Two approaches can be used to gain a more precise estimate of the real value of these revenue concepts. First, express these concepts as ratios as often as possible. The ratio of actual revenues collected to revenue capacity will remain a reliable measure of revenue reserves over time as long as inflation affects the numerator and denominator of this ratio equally. However, since some tax bases respond more quickly to inflation (e.g., sales) and others respond more slowly (e.g., property values), the reliability of the use of ratios to correct for inflation depends on the particular mix of revenues sources in the revenue base.

Second, divide the revenue measures by an appropriate price index to put all the measures in constant dollar terms. This requires a price index appropriate to the revenues of a particular government and its reference group. While some general price indexes are available, they may not be appropriate for a particular revenue analysis. The use of price indexes is examined in the next chapter.

### An Application

To illustrate the concepts of revenue capacity and reserves further, let us return to our example of Dyer Straits. Table 4–17 presents per capita tax revenue capacity information, 1979–83, for Dyer Straits and the reference group of forty-nine cities.

Table 4–17 has several single-factor tax and revenue capacity measures. Per capita property and sales tax bases are measures of tax capacity; total tax capacity is also estimated with an income base approach by multiplying the reference group's percentage of income that is paid as taxes (.0292 in 1979, .0294 in 1980, etc.) times Dyer Straits' income in that year. (Note that this income could have been adjusted with the ACIR tax capacity estimates as discussed earlier but was not adjusted in this example.) All of these single-factor capacity estimates for Dyer Straits are growing, but more slowly than for the reference group.

Table 4–17 also presents a variety of single-factor tax effort or burden estimates—per capita property, sales, and total tax revenues; actual property and sales tax rates; and tax revenues as a percentage of income. All of these measures are indicators of the extent to which Dyer Straits and the reference group have extracted revenues from their respective political jurisdictions. By all measures, the tax burden of Dyer Straits has risen, and risen more rapidly than the reference group's. The single exception is per capita property tax revenues, which grew at about the same rate as the reference group's, perhaps because Dyer Straits was constrained by some form of legal limit.

Finally, Table 4–17 presents ACIR-type tax capacity estimates, applying the reference group's average tax rates to Dyer Straits' property and sales tax bases. This measure of tax capacity is rising, but more slowly than the reference group's. Measures of tax reserves are also shown in Table 4–17 based on the ACIR-type measure and on a single-factor index based on income. Both measures show that Dyer Straits' reserves are negative (capacity is less than actual revenues) and are becoming more negative relative to the reference group over the period. No adjustment for inflation was made for these revenue measures. Ratios such as tax revenues/tax capacity are probably not influenced greatly by inflation over a five-year period.

At the local government level compared with the total state and local levels, it is more difficult to apply the ACIR approach to determine total revenue capacity rather than just tax revenue capacity. The Akin and Auten approach, however, provides a method that can, in principle, be applied to both tax and non-tax revenue capacity. Using data on all reference group cities, we used multiple-regression analysis to estimate the relationship between per capita (tax and non-tax) revenues (dependent variable) and per capita property values and retail sales, and family income in 1983. We found the following relationship:

Local revenues = 61.4 + .011(property value) + .0066(retail sales)
                  + .00015(family income)

Substituting in Dyer Straits' per capita property value and retail sales, and family income, we have:

Dyer Straits' per capita local revenue capacity = 61.4 + .011($6,031)
                  + .0066($3,163) + .00015($17,671) = $151

From Table 4-10, Dyer Straits' actual per capita local revenues, both tax and nontax, came to $214 in 1983, or $63 above its local revenue capacity ($151) using this multiple-regression approach.

Finally, an important caveat is that all of these estimates of fiscal capacity, revenue reserves, tax burden, and so forth, have been derived solely from actual revenues, revenue base, and revenue potential information. The analysis is entirely from the standpoint of resources and how much they have been drawn upon by the government. While these estimates are an integral ingredient of financial condition analysis, they are only one part of the story. They say nothing about the extent of liabilities such as debt and pensions, which may or may not create additional needs for revenues in the future; nor do they address the needs of the community for government services and how well they are being met, which also affects the need for revenues; nor do they consider the adequacy of cash balances to meet cash needs, which also affects the need for resources. All of these factors must be examined along with revenue analysis to get a complete picture of a local government's financial condition. We will consider these other factors in the following chapters.

## VI. SUMMARY

The final task in revenue analysis is to combine the four individual components of the analysis: economic base, revenue base, actual revenues, and revenue capacity and reserves. Moreover, in an actual analysis, relevant contextual factors, such as the fact that a new housing development will soon be completed or that a plant has closed in the jurisdiction, that are not reflected in the most up-to-date data, should be combined with the assessment of the four components. In addition, if regional or even local government-based econometric forecasts are available, these should

TABLE 4-17 Tax Revenue Capacity (Per Capita), City of Dyer Straits and Reference Group, 1979-83

| | DYER STRAITS | | | | | REFERENCE GROUP | | | | | LOCATION QUOTIENTS* | | | | |
|---|---|---|---|---|---|---|---|---|---|---|---|---|---|---|---|
| | 1979 | 1980 | 1981 | 1982 | 1983 | 1979 | 1980 | 1981 | 1982 | 1983 | 1979 | 1980 | 1981 | 1982 | 1983 |
| *Tax Revenues (per capita):* | | | | | | | | | | | | | | | |
| Property tax revenues | $109.06 | 116.63 | 120.44 | 127.01 | 141.72 | $77.27 | 82.60 | 88.40 | 93.95 | 100.42 | 1.411 | 1.412 | 1.362 | 1.352 | 1.411 |
| Property tax base | $5,026 | 5,183 | 5,475 | 5,825 | 6,031 | $4,591 | 4,864 | 5,155 | 5,462 | 5,786 | 1.095 | 1.066 | 1.062 | 1.066 | 1.042 |
| Property tax rate | .0217 | .0218 | .0220 | .0218 | .0235 | .01683 | .01698 | .01715 | .01720 | .01735 | 1.289 | 1.284 | 1.283 | 1.268 | 1.354 |
| Sales tax revenues | $19.51 | 20.49 | 36.60 | 38.47 | 41.13 | $18.08 | 20.69 | 22.27 | 27.08 | 29.02 | 1.078 | .990 | 1.643 | 1.421 | 1.417 |
| Sales tax base | $2,438 | 2,560 | 2,815 | 2,960 | 3,163 | $2,260 | 2,434 | 2,620 | 2,821 | 3,036 | 1.079 | 1.052 | 1.074 | 1.049 | 1.042 |
| Sales tax rate | .008 | .008 | .013 | .013 | .013 | .008 | .0085 | .0085 | .0096 | .0096 | 1.000 | .941 | 1.529 | 1.354 | 1.354 |
| Total tax revenues | $128.57 | 137.12 | 157.04 | 165.48 | 182.85 | $95.35 | 103.29 | 110.67 | 121.03 | 129.44 | 1.348 | 1.328 | 1.419 | 1.367 | 1.413 |
| *ACIR Capacity Measures†:* | | | | | | | | | | | | | | | |
| Property tax capacity | $84.59 | 88.01 | 93.90 | 100.19 | 104.64 | $77.27 | 82.60 | 88.40 | 93.95 | 100.42 | 1.095 | 1.066 | 1.062 | 1.066 | 1.109 |

| | | | | | | | | | | | | | | |
|---|---|---|---|---|---|---|---|---|---|---|---|---|---|---|
| Sales tax capacity | $19.50 | 21.76 | 23.93 | 28.42 | 30.36 | $18.08 | 20.69 | 22.27 | 27.08 | 29.02 | 1.079 | 1.052 | 1.074 | 1.049 1.046 |
| Total tax capacity | $104.09 | 109.77 | 117.83 | 128.61 | 135.00 | $95.35 | 103.29 | 110.67 | 121.03 | 129.44 | 1.092 | 1.063 | 1.065 | 1.063 1.043 |
| Tax revenue reserves‡ | $(24.48) | (27.35) | (39.21) | (36.87) | (47.85) | $0 | 0 | 0 | 0 | 0 | — | — | — | — — |
| *Income-Based Capacity Measures:* | | | | | | | | | | | | | | |
| Per cap tax revenues/per cap income§ | .0382 | .0391 | .0405 | .0404 | .0415 | .0292 | .0294 | .0293 | .0298 | .0297 | 1.308 | 1.330 | 1.382 | 1.356 1.397 |
| Total tax capacity‖ | $98.19 | 102.99 | 113.54 | 122.18 | 130.91 | $95.35 | 103.29 | 110.67 | 121.03 | 129.44 | 1.030 | .997 | 1.026 | 1.010 1.011 |
| Tax revenue reserves‡ | $(30.38) | (34.13) | (43.50) | (43.29) | (51.39) | $0 | 0 | 0 | 0 | 0 | — | — | — | — — |
| Tax revenues/tax capacity | 1.31 | 1.33 | 1.38 | 1.35 | 1.40 | | | | | | — | — | — | — — |

**Negative numbers are in parentheses.**

*Dyer Straits/Reference Group.

†Reference group average tax rates multiplied times each tax base of individual city.

‡Total tax capacity less total tax revenues.

§Per capita income = mean family income/4.

‖Per capita tax revenues/per capita income for reference group, multiplied times per capita income of individual city.

also be scrutinized and used where appropriate. But most importantly, the results of the analyses of the four components should be integrated, and we illustrate this briefly with the findings from Dyer Straits.

First, Dyer Straits, which over two decades ago had a relatively strong economic base when measured in terms of income, employment, unemployment, and so forth, has suffered decline over the past twenty years. Income levels are now close to the average of the reference group, and if the trend of slower growth than the reference group continues in the future, Dyer Straits could have a lower level of income than the reference group in a few years. Other troubling signs are a higher level of unemployment and a worsening situation vis-à-vis the reference group, and lower and declining levels of education, employment, and value added per employee relative to the reference group. Finally, although the reference group has been losing manufacturing jobs as a share of the total, Dyer Straits' loss in this area has been more severe. Thus all signs point to an economic base that is about equal to (or somewhat lower than) the reference group's but is not growing at the same rate as the reference group's.

The primary measures of Dyer Straits' revenue bases show the same trends as the measures of the economic base. From 1979 to 1983 the per capita property and sales tax bases have been growing more slowly than those of the reference group, and by 1983 both per capita bases are about 4 percent above the average for the reference group. Mean income per family is also slightly higher than the reference group's in 1983 and has grown more slowly than the reference group's over the period. When revenue base income elasticities are computed, the inelasticity of the property tax base, and to a lesser extent the sales tax base, becomes apparent. The fact that the tax bases have not declined as far as the economic base relative to the reference group could also be a reflection of these low elasticities.

The analysis of the actual revenues in Dyer Straits shows that per capita revenues in Dyer Straits have grown faster than their reference group's since 1979. Moreover, on a per capita basis, all major revenue categories are higher than the reference group's in 1983, with per capita property and sales taxes more than 40 percent above the reference group's in 1983. Both state and federal aid to Dyer Straits have grown slightly faster than the aid to the reference group and, by 1983, per capita aid in both categories is somewhat higher in Dyer Straits than in the reference group. Thus Dyer Straits has increased its revenues primarily, but not exclusively, by increasing its own taxes on property and sales.

Since Dyer Straits' revenues have increased faster than the reference group's but its tax bases have not, this suggests that Dyer Straits has been drawing more heavily on its revenue bases than have the comparable cities. This is precisely what the analysis of fiscal capacity and reserves indicates. Regardless of which fiscal capacity and reserve measures are calculated, the results show that Dyer Straits is tapping its revenue bases more heavily than the reference group and that the situation is worse in 1983 than it was in 1979. For example, the tax capacity measure computed using the ACIR approach resulted in a tax capacity of $135 per capita in 1983 at a time when the actual per capita revenues were $183, indicating that Dyer Straits was taxing over the average levels of the reference group by $48 per capita.

Thus increases in the economic and revenue bases do not appear to be forthcoming unless recent trends show a significant reversal. Revenues are high on a per capita basis, primarily because Dyer Straits is putting considerable pressure on its revenue base. Taking all things into account, the prospects for short- or medium-term revenue increases do not appear promising unless they are to come from state and federal sources. For our hypothetical city, these are not promising prospects.

## QUESTIONS

1.  What major questions are addressed in revenue analysis? How are these questions related to the other parts of financial analysis (expenditures, debt, pensions, and internal resources)?

2.  Can you determine how close a government is to its revenue-raising limit by examining only its actual revenues? What if you had comparable data on actual revenues for a set of similar governments? What questions can such data answer, and what additional data would you need to determine the government's ability to raise additional revenues?

3.  Why is it useful to begin revenue analysis by looking at the economy of the area served by the government under study? How is this economy linked to the government's revenues? Name some revenue methods that are closely linked to the local economy. Name some methods that are not.

4.  How do you measure the performance of a state, regional, or urban economy? If you could only obtain data on five measures, which would you choose and why?

5.  Suppose you were studying an economy and found that most local residents were employed in a single large business that produced automobile parts for export from the area and imported most of its supplies and materials from outside the area. From this information alone, what would you suspect were some of the strengths and weaknesses of this economy? How might these strengths and weaknesses affect the level, growth, and stability of the local government's revenue base?

6.  What are the principal ways that governments raise revenues? How do they vary across federal, state, and local governments? What are the major concerns of governments in deciding what revenue sources to use? If a government could establish any revenue source it wanted, what do you think this method would be? Why would it be "ideal"?

7.  Suppose a government secures most of its revenues through fees for water and sewer, a property tax, a payroll tax, a tax on the income of local utilities, a portion of the state sales tax, and state aid based on the locality's fiscal con-

dition. What is this government's "revenue base" and what, in general, are the revenue "rates" and "bases" for each of these revenue sources?

8.  Select two taxes or other revenue sources commonly used by a state or local government. Compare these two methods in terms of how income elastic, efficient, and equitable they are as revenue sources. Based on this, discuss the advantages and disadvantages of these two methods for raising revenues.

9.  There are constitutional and other legal limits on the types of revenue-raising methods a government can use. What are some of the legal, political, and economic limits on the extent to which any individual type of revenue method might be used? Give an example of each type of limit using a specific revenue method and type of government. Are there limits that apply to total revenues but do not limit the use of any individual method?

10. Limits on the use of different revenue sources, or on the total revenues raised, form the basis for the concept of "revenue capacity." What is revenue capacity and what alternative ways have been developed to measure it?

11. Why is total or per capita income often used as a measure of a jurisdiction's revenue capacity? Would this be true of a government that did not have an income tax? Why or why not?

12. How can you measure the extent to which a government has used up its revenue capacity (or has "revenue reserves")? List three measures of revenue reserves and discuss their advantages and disadvantages.

13. Tax effort or burden measures are often used as measures of revenue reserves. What are the advantages and disadvantages of using per capita taxes, actual tax rates, taxes divided by income, or taxes divided by "fiscal capacity" as measures of revenue reserves?

---

## PROBLEMS

Information presented here for the following two problems will be used in problems in later chapters.

1.  The city of Medville has had the following revenues and operating expenditures over the past three years:*

| Revenues ($ millions) | 1982 | 1983 | 1984 |
|---|---|---|---|
| Property tax | 15.0 | 16.0 | 17.0 |
| Sales tax | 5.0 | 5.5 | 6.0 |
| Water charges | 3.5 | 3.75 | 4.0 |
| Sewer charges | 2.5 | 2.75 | 3.0 |
| Public transportation charges | 2.0 | 2.5 | 2.75 |
| State aid | 6.0 | 7.0 | 8.0 |
| Federal aid | 3.0 | 4.0 | 5.0 |
| Other revenue | 1.0 | 1.5 | 1.75 |
| Total Revenues | 38.0 | 43.0 | 47.5 |

| Expenditures ($ millions) | 1982 | 1983 | 1984 |
|---|---|---|---|
| Police | 6.0 | 7.0 | 8.0 |
| Fire | 6.0 | 7.0 | 8.0 |
| Streets | 7.0 | 8.0 | 9.0 |
| Public transportation | 2.0 | 2.5 | 3.0 |
| Recreation | 3.0 | 3.2 | 3.25 |
| Health | 2.0 | 2.15 | 2.25 |
| Refuse | 2.0 | 2.0 | 2.25 |
| Sewer | 2.0 | 2.15 | 2.25 |
| Water | 3.0 | 3.25 | 3.5 |
| Administration | 2.0 | 2.5 | 3.0 |
| Debt service | 4.0 | 4.25 | 4.5 |
| Total Expenditures | 39.0 | 44.0 | 49.0 |

*Consolidation of all revenues and expenditures for all funds except the capital projects fund.

a. Using the percentage change, index number, and/or common size methods, what were the major changes in the city's pattern of revenues over the 1982–84 period?

b. The city's property and sales tax bases and rates, and personal income levels over the 1982–84 period, were:

| | 1982 | 1983 | 1984 |
|---|---|---|---|
| Full value of property ($ millions) | 750 | 800 | 850 |
| Property tax rate (%) | 2 | 2 | 2 |
| Taxable retail sales ($ millions) | 100 | 110 | 120 |
| Sales tax rate (%) | 5 | 5 | 5 |
| Personal income ($ millions) | 150 | 150 | 150 |

Using these data, discuss the income elasticities of the property and sales tax bases between 1982 and 1984. Which tax appears to be more "income elastic"? What are the advantages and disadvantages of highly income elastic tax bases?

c. Suppose you have the following ACIR-type estimates of average tax rates and current charges (based on the specific expenditures for which the charges are made) for cities in the same population range as Medville:

| | | |
|---|---|---|
| Average property tax rate | = | 1.9% of full assessed value |
| Average sales tax rate | = | 5.7% of taxable sales |
| Average water charges | = | 110% of water expenditures |
| Average sewer charges | = | 125% of sewer expenditures |
| Average public transportation charges | = | 90% of public transportation expenditures |

Using the revenue data for Medville, compute the city's capacity as of 1984 to raise revenues from local taxes and current charges using the ACIR approach. How much of this capacity is being used? (That is, what are the city's local fiscal reserves, if any?) Where is the city overutilizing or underutilizing local fiscal resources compared with the average of similar cities?

TABLE A    **Nonfinancial Information for City of Red Lion and Ten Other Cities in State**

|  | RED LION | | AVERAGE FOR TEN OTHER CITIES IN STATE | |
| --- | --- | --- | --- | --- |
|  | 1977 | 1983 | 1977 | 1983 |
| Population | 200,000 | 195,000 | 200,000 | 208,000 |
| Employment | 60,000 | 57,000 | 60,000 | 63,000 |
| Unemployment rate | 8.0 | 7.4 | 6.0 | 6.0 |
| Density (pop. sq. mile) | 3,000 | 3,000 | 3,000 | 3,100 |
| % Population below poverty line | 12.2 | 16.0 | 11.5 | 11.9 |
| % Housing over 30 years old | 35.0 | 39.0 | 29.0 | 32.0 |
| Municipal employees | 1,610 | 1,950 | 1,550 | 1,810 |
| Average municipal salary | $15,800 | $18,500 | $15,500 | $17,900 |
| Average years education of municipal employees | 13.1 | 14.0 | 13.2 | 14.3 |
| % Population over 65 | 12.2 | 15.2 | 10.1 | 12.1 |
| % Population under 18 | 21.3 | 20.3 | 23.3 | 25.3 |
| % Employed in manufacturing | 25.0 | 19.0 | 36.0 | 32.0 |
| %Employed in services (real estate, finance, wholesale, and retail trade) | 48.0 | 51.0 | 36.0 | 42.0 |
| Price index | 112 | 139 | 100 | 128 |

2.  As a financial analyst, you have gathered the information in Tables A, B, and C about the city of Red Lion, and a reference group of ten other cities in the state. You are to use these data in this and following chapters to analyze the financial condition of Red Lion from different perspectives.

   a .  Using information on income, population, employment, etc., evaluate the relative strengths and weaknesses of Red Lion's economic or resource base compared with the average of similar cities.

   b .  Using information on local tax methods, what is Red Lion's local revenue base? Is this revenue base growing or declining? How do the level and changes in Red Lion's different revenue bases compare with those in its reference group? Estimate income elasticities for major revenue sources. What are the strengths and weaknesses in Red Lion's revenue base?

   c .  What is Red Lion's "fiscal capacity" and how has it changed between 1977 and 1983? How does this capacity compare with the fiscal capacity of its reference group?

   d .  Using information on actual revenues, determine the relative importance of different revenue methods in Red Lion. How has the relative importance of different revenue methods changed over time? Compare the levels and changes in actual revenues of Red Lion and in the reference group and discuss your findings.

TABLE B  Financial Information for City of Red Lion and Ten Other Cities in State ($ millions)

| | RED LION | | AVERAGE FOR TEN OTHER CITIES IN STATE | |
|---|---|---|---|---|
| a. During Fiscal Year | 1977 | 1983 | 1977 | 1983 |
| Operating expenditures* | 35.9 | 50.2 | 40.5 | 51.1 |
| Debt service | 6.2 | 8.6 | 5.6 | 6.2 |
| Revenues | | | | |
|   Property tax | 20.5 | 28.0 | 26.9 | 32.0 |
|   Sales tax | 4.7 | 9.2 | 4.3 | 10.1 |
|   Income tax | 2.9 | 3.0 | 2.7 | 3.2 |
|   State and federal aid | 8.0 | 7.9 | 6.5 | 6.4 |
|   Other revenues | 5.0 | 7.6 | 6.8 | 6.5 |
| Borrowing (during fiscal year) | | | | |
|   Short-term notes | 2.0 | 4.0 | 1.5 | 1.0 |
|   Long-term bonds | 1.0 | 5.0 | 3.0 | 3.0 |
| *Includes the following government contributions to the pension system | 2.9 | 5.5 | 2.4 | 3.6 |

| | RED LION | | AVERAGE FOR TEN OTHER CITIES IN STATE | |
|---|---|---|---|---|
| b. End of Fiscal Year | 1977 | 1983 | 1977 | 1983 |
| General Fund | | | | |
|   Assets | | | | |
|     Cash | 7.0 | 2.0 | 8.0 | 8.0 |
|     Taxes receivable | 3.0 | 4.0 | 2.0 | 2.5 |
|     Due from other governments | 1.0 | 2.0 | 1.0 | 1.0 |
|   Total Assets | 11.0 | 8.0 | 11.0 | 11.5 |
| Liabilities and Fund Balance | | | | |
|   Accounts payable | 1.0 | 2.0 | 3.5 | 3.5 |
|   Notes payable | 2.0 | 4.0 | 1.5 | 1.0 |
|   Fund balance | 8.0 | 2.0 | 6.0 | 7.0 |
| Total Liabilities and Fund Balance | 11.0 | 8.0 | 11.0 | 11.5 |
| Fixed Asset Account (excluding enterprise fund fixed assets) at Cost | 70.0 | 75.0 | 92.0 | 101.0 |
| Long-Term Debt Outstanding | | | | |
|   Bonds, total | 62.5 | 71.5 | 58.0 | 63.0 |
|   Payable in next fiscal year | 3.0 | 4.0 | 2.0 | 2.2 |
| Assets in pension funds | 30.4 | 34.0 | 40.8 | 56.4 |
| Pension benefits paid out | 3.8 | 6.2 | 3.4 | 5.1 |
| Total pension fund receipts (government contributions plus investment earnings) | 4.1 | 6.4 | 5.7 | 9.2 |

TABLE C   **Data on Tax Bases for Red Lion and Reference Group ($ millions)**

|  | RED LION | | AVERAGE FOR TEN OTHER CITIES IN STATE | |
|---|---|---|---|---|
|  | 1977 | 1983 | 1977 | 1983 |
| Property tax base | 600 | 600 | 700 | 750 |
| Income tax base | 1,000 | 1,200 | 950 | 1,280 |
| Sales tax base | 220 | 250 | 210 | 270 |

e .  Calculate Red Lion's local ''revenue reserves'' in 1977 and 1983, and discuss your findings.

f .  From the perspective of revenue analysis alone, list your major (tentative) conclusions about Red Lion's financial strengths and weaknesses.

# CHAPTER

# 5 Expenditure Analysis

The analysis of the financial condition of a government cannot stop with the examination of the revenues presented in Chapter 4. To add to our understanding of an organization's financial condition, we need to study how resources are used as well as how they are raised. Recall that in Chapter 3 we stated that the major goal of expenditure analysis is to determine the pressures on the government for additional expenditures. If we can ascertain that a government has pressure to spend more (less) than it is now spending to meet the needs of its community, this may represent a negative (positive) factor in the assessment of financial condition.

Of course, the most critical word in the preceding sentence is the word *if*. It is important to admit at the outset that the measurement and analysis of expenditure pressures, compared with other components of financial analysis presented in this book, are the most difficult, subjective, and, in some ways, underdeveloped. Given this situation, we could have decided to exclude the analysis of expenditure pressures from our presentation. However, even though some measurement and conceptual problems have not yet been solved, the questions asked by expenditure analysis are so crucial to our overall conception of financial condition that we believe it is preferable to assess expenditure pressures to the limited extent now possible, even if our analysis does not provide all the answers we would like.

This chapter analyzes the capital and operating expenditures of governments. Expenditures for debt service, pension payments, and public enterprise activities will receive special attention in Chapters 6, 7, and 8, respectively. We begin with a discussion of what we mean by *expenditure analysis*. Second, we summarize the types and levels of expenditures encountered in governments and examine basic expenditure data. Third, we consider the effects of different input prices, across time and location, on expenditures. In the fourth and fifth sections we analyze two sets of factors that help determine expenditure pressures: production and service conditions, and community and clientele needs. In section VI we demonstrate how the concepts analyzed in this chapter are related to expenditure pressures, the expenditure component of financial condition. Finally, we look briefly at the treatment of expenditure types that differ across governments.


## I. THE NATURE OF EXPENDITURE ANALYSIS

Traditional economic analysis of public expenditures focuses on the efficiency and equity of resource use. Have government expenditures maximized public benefits for the costs of the resources used? And has the resulting distribution of benefits and costs been equitable, based on economic need (ability to pay)?

In financial analysis we are still concerned with efficiency and equity, but we emphasize their connection to the financial strength of government. Inefficiencies and inequities, besides being undesirable for their own sake, may increase the expenditure pressures on government and adversely affect its financial condition. In the following analysis we will consider efficiency and equity as they relate to expenditure pressures on government.

### From Expenditures to the Satisfaction
### of Community Needs

Expenditure pressures arise ultimately from how well community and clientele needs are being met. Thus to understand expenditure analysis we need to begin by reviewing the connection between government expenditures and the satisfaction of community and clientele needs.

First, governments spend money on the personnel, materials and supplies, equipment, land, and so forth, needed to conduct government activities. These dollar expenditures are recorded in various financial statements, reports, and budgets.

Second, these dollar expenditures represent the product of the amounts of specific goods and services received (inputs) and the price or unit cost of these inputs (input prices). Thus personnel expenditures represent hours of work provided times the wage rate for different types of personnel; material expenditures represent the amount of different materials times their prices; and so forth.

Third, it is the productive inputs, not dollar expenditures, that are used to provide public goods and services (outputs) to the community. Thus individuals, equipment, materials, and so forth, are used in government departments to provide specific public services like fire inspections, police patrols, health clinics, and other outputs needed by the community.

Fourth, the conversion of physical resources (inputs) into goods and services provided by governments (outputs) depends on the productivity of the inputs, the way in which government activities are managed, and the production and service conditions faced by a particular government. Thus the quality of equipment and materials, level of employee and management skills, severity of weather, density of housing, and so forth, determine the level of public outputs that results from a particular mix of productive inputs.

Finally, the public outputs emerging from this process are ultimately aimed at meeting community and clientele needs for public goods and services. The impact of outputs on outcomes (satisfaction of public needs) is the final link in the chain between expenditures and meeting community needs. This final link, however, is not always direct, and increases in government outputs do not always help meet local needs.

This complex linkage between government expenditures and the meeting of community needs is what makes expenditure analysis so difficult. Expenditures alone, without knowledge of input prices, production and service conditions, and community and clientele needs, provide a very limited basis to determine whether a government faces growing or declining pressures to provide public services, and it is these expenditure pressures that play a major role in public financial analysis. To estimate these pressures, we need to try to go beyond actual expenditures to examine these other elements.

### The Stages of Expenditure Analysis

We begin with expenditures. Expenditures, particularly as we saw in Chapter 2, have many labels—operating, capital, line item, program, departmental, etc.—but whatever their labels, they all represent the use of financial resources, the spending or "expending" of monies by a government on different items and for different purposes. The past, present, and proposed use of these resources, as documented in financial statements and budgets, provides the raw material for expenditure analysis.

But how should our analysis of this "raw material" proceed and what questions should be asked of this expenditure data? Our first step in expenditure analysis is to separate and reorganize our expenditure data so that we have a much clearer picture of actual expenditures over time, both for the government under study and for its reference group, in the categories best suited for our analysis. This reorganization and examination can teach us a great deal by highlighting changes and differences in expenditure levels and in the circumstances that may have led to these changes.

The second step of expenditure analysis is to determine the effects of input prices (wage rates, prices of materials, etc.) on expenditure levels. Input prices typically vary over time due to inflation and across locations due to differences in the "cost of living." Knowledge of input prices over time is useful in determining, for example, how much input costs have risen for an organization and whether they are rising faster or slower than for similar organizations. With detailed input prices over time, we can attempt to separate changes in expenditures due to *price changes* from changes due to the *quantity* of inputs used by the organization.

Knowledge of input prices for different localities at the same point in time can also be helpful. When comparing governments, input prices may vary due to locational factors that are beyond the government's control. As a result, a dollar in one jurisdiction may not purchase the same quantity (and quality) of inputs; governments in relatively higher priced areas will not be able to provide the same level of outputs for a given dollar of expenditure. All else being equal, higher input prices over time or across locations increase expenditure pressures.

It is the outputs that result from expenditures, however, that ultimately meet the needs of the community. Thus our third step in expenditure analysis is to explore government productive activities—the relationships among inputs and outputs. This is a difficult step in expenditure analysis because measures of public outputs are inadequate and data are hard to obtain. A full understanding of the relationship between inputs and outputs in governments may require an assessment of production and service conditions at a level of government so disaggregated—the individual activities within departments—that data are almost always unavailable to the public. Using individual activities as a conceptual starting point, however, we can ask what more readily available aggregate expenditure data can or cannot tell us about levels of government outputs. This approach will reveal the potential shortcomings of assuming expenditures measure outputs and may, under some circumstances, provide estimates of government outputs themselves.

In addition to an attempt to assess government production and service requirements and to link expenditures to outputs, we also discuss how outputs are related to the satisfaction of community or clientele needs (the outcomes of government activities). We examine several single and composite indexes that have been developed to approximate community and clientele needs. Our concern is to estimate changes in community needs and compare them with changes in government expenditures. For example, if community needs for public services are growing, and all else is equal, expenditure pressures on government will rise. Again, we may have to be satisfied with using very approximate need measures and relying on comparisons of aggregate expenditures.

Finally, we pull the steps of the analysis together and look at the relationship of expenditure levels to financial condition. Our approach builds on the premise that governments have financial obligations to all the groups they serve, which must be weighed along with financial obligations to employees, taxpayers, and creditors in determining overall financial condition. Thus the adequacy of expenditures in meeting community or clientele needs—expenditure "pressures" or "reserves"—must be seen as part of an analysis of financial condition. A government may have some revenue reserves but may face such extensive unmet needs in its community that its long-run financial condition is clearly in question. Expenditure analysis, therefore, must include an examination of expenditures relative to need to provide additional information on a government's ability to meet financial demands in the future.

All of these steps in expenditure analysis should make it clear that data on expenditures alone, the "raw material" of expenditure analysis, are not sufficient to answer questions about how well resources are being used by an organization. Expenditure data are, however, a necessary element in expenditure analysis, and we begin our analysis with an examination of them.

## II. PRESENTATION AND ASSESSMENT OF BASIC EXPENDITURE DATA

### *Categories of Expenditures*

In the conduct of their activities, governments continually put their financial resources to use in the form of payments to individuals, groups, or other organizations either in exchange for the goods and services they provide to the government or for their benefit as clients or constituents of the government. These are the government's expenditures, which were defined in Chapter 2.

Government expenditures clearly encompass a wide variety of uses of financial resources. Thus, to begin our expenditure analysis, we review in this section the major categories of government expenditures and present some data on actual expenditures as well. We then analyze basic expenditure data for our illustrative city of Dyer Straits.

**Direct and Intergovernmental Expenditures.** The first major distinction among expenditures is between those resources used directly by the government to benefit its clientele (direct expenditures) and those transferred to other governments for their use (intergovernmental expenditures or transfers). Table 5-1 lists the direct and intergovernmental expenditures for 1982-83. The federal government transferred about $88.5 billion to state and local governments in 1983, or about 10 percent of its total expenditures, down from about 15 percent in 1974. Of these transfers, 76 percent went to state governments and 24 percent to local governments. Of state government expenditures, 30.3 percent were intergovernmental, down from 33 percent in 1974, with virtually all the transfers going to local governments. Local governments, in turn, made almost no transfers to other levels of governments.[1]

Direct expenditures are largely the general fund expenditures of an organization. There are, however, special activities that sometimes fall into the jurisdiction of an organization, such as public enterprises or major trust fund responsibility, which are also included in the direct expenditures of the organization. Table 5-2 presents the breakdown of direct expenditures among general expenditures, public utility and liquor store expenditures, and insurance trust expenditures for different levels of government. Note that the percentage of direct

---

[1] For data on government expenditures, see U.S. Bureau of the Census, *Governmental Finances in 1982-83* (Washington, D.C.: Government Printing Office, October 1984).

TABLE 5-1   **Direct and Intergovernmental Expenditures by Level of Government, 1982–83 (millions of dollars)**

|  | FEDERAL GOVERNMENT | | STATE GOVERNMENTS | | LOCAL GOVERNMENTS | |
|---|---|---|---|---|---|---|
|  | Total | % of Total Expenditures | Total | % of Total Expenditures | Total | % of Total Expenditures |
| Total Expenditures | 874,264 | 100.0 | 334,019 | 100.0 | 335,098* | 100.0 |
| Intergovernmental Expenditures | 88,539 | 10.1 | 101,309 | 30.3 | 3,005* | .9 |
| To Federal Government | — | | 1,765 | | — | |
| To State Government | 67,384 | | — | | 3,005 | |
| To Local Government | 21,155 | | 99,544 | | — | |
| Direct Expenditures | 785,725 | 89.9 | 232,710 | 69.7 | 332,093 | 99.1 |

*Net of duplicative intergovernmental transactions. See source.
SOURCE:   U.S. Bureau of the Census, *Governmental Finances in 1982–83* (Washington, D.C.: Government Printing Office, October 1984), Table 9, p. 17.

expenditures classified as general expenditures is highest at the local government level and lowest at the federal government level.

**Function of Expenditure.**   Another important type of classification of expenditures is by the "function" or set of activities that these expenditures serve. The classification of expenditures by function provides useful information about

TABLE 5-2   **Governmental Direct Expenditure, by Type, by Level of Government, 1982–83**

|  | AMOUNT (MILLIONS OF DOLLARS) | | | |
|---|---|---|---|---|
| ITEM | All Governments | Federal Government | State Governments | Local Governments |
| Direct Expenditure | 1,350,527 | 785,725 | 232,710 | 332,093 |
| By Type: | | | | |
| General Expenditure | 1,000,287 | 535,631 | 183,732 | 280,924 |
| Utility Expenditure | 49,995 | — | 4,417 | 45,579 |
| Liquor Stores Expenditure | 2,816 | — | 2,381 | 436 |
| Insurance Trust Expenditure | 297,429 | 250,094 | 42,180 | 5,154 |

SOURCE:   U.S. Bureau of the Census, *Government Finances in 1982–83* (Washington, D.C.: Government Printing Office, October 1984), Table 9, p. 17.

the major expenditure priorities of governments. For many governments, these functions are defined by specific departments or sets of departments performing related tasks, although in some cases the functions may not correspond to the departmental structure of the organization.

Table 5-3 lists governmental general expenditures by function for various levels of government in 1982-83. The table includes the direct expenditures devoted to these functions, along with the funds passed to lower levels of government that are spent on these functions (intergovernmental expenditures). The difference in the responsibilities of different levels of government is evident in this table. The federal concern with national defense and international relations, the states with public welfare, and the localities with education can be seen by comparing percentages of direct expenditures devoted to different functions.

**Character or Object of Expenditure.**     As discussed in Chapter 2, expenditures may also be classified according to the resources secured by the expenditure, that is, the "object" of the expenditure. This usually includes expenditures for personal services, contract services, materials and supplies, and other sources that are used by the government in producing goods and services. Table 5-4 shows some direct expenditures broken down by object. For example, capital outlays are divided into construction, and equipment, land, and existing structures. These represent the purchase of particular inputs of use by the government making the capital outlay. The direct expenditures for salaries and wages, shown at the bottom of Table 5-4, are another example of a classification of direct expenditures by the object of expenditure. Capital and operating (line-item) budgets normally present expenditures classified by object of expenditure.

The distinction between capital and current expenditures is important for financial analysis, since capital outlays (streets, firehouses, schools, etc.) last for many years, whereas current expenditures (salaries, materials and supplies, etc.) provide services, for the most part, only in the current fiscal year. A change in the proportion of expenditures devoted to these two purposes reflects a change in the emphasis being placed by the government on meeting future versus present needs. For example, a declining percentage of expenditures devoted to capital goods suggests a growing interest in meeting present needs and deferring expenditures benefiting future generations.

Between 1960 and 1980, capital investment by state and local governments as a percentage of total outlays declined from 25 to 15 percent (Figure 5-1). Not only did the percentage fall, but state and local government dollar outlays for capital goods corrected for inflation fell by almost 50 percent from 1968 to 1981.[2]

---

[2] For further discussion of capital investment needs, see the sources for Figures 5-1 and 5-2 and Roy Bahl, *Financing State and Local Government in the 1980s* (New York: Oxford University Press, 1984), Chap. 3; George Peterson, "Capital Spending and Capital Obsolescence: The Outlook for Cities," in *The Fiscal Outlook for Cities*, ed. Roy Bahl (Syracuse, N.Y.: Syracuse University Press, 1979); and National Infrastructure Advisory Committee, *Hard Choices: A Report on the Increasing Gap between America's Infrastructure Needs and Our Ability to Pay for Them* (Washington, D.C.: Joint Economic Committee of Congress, February 1984).

TABLE 5-3 Governmental General Expenditure (Direct and Intergovernmental) by Function and Level of Government, 1982-83

| | AMOUNT (MILLIONS OF DOLLARS) | | | | PERCENT | | | |
|---|---|---|---|---|---|---|---|---|
| FUNCTION | All Governments | Federal Government | State Governments | Local Governments | All Governments | Federal Government | State Governments | Local Governments |
| *All functions* | 1,000,287 | 624,170 | 285,042 | 283,929 | 100.0 | 100.0 | 100.0 | 100.0 |
| *Direct* | 1,000,287 | 535,631 | 183,732 | 280,924 | 100.0 | 85.8 | 64.5 | 98.9 |
| *Intergovernmental* | (¹) | 88,539 | 101,309 | ¹3,005 | — | 14.2 | 35.5 | 1.1 |
| National defense and international relations | 228,763 | 228,763 | — | — | 22.9 | 36.7 | — | — |
| Postal service | 23,561 | 23,561 | — | — | 2.4 | 3.8 | — | — |
| General revenue sharing | 4,620 | ²4,620 | — | — | .5 | .7 | — | — |
| Space research and technology | 6,816 | 6,816 | — | — | .7 | 1.1 | — | — |
| Education | 176,649 | 25,301 | 107,703 | 119,599 | 17.7 | 4.1 | 37.8 | 42.1 |
| Direct | 176,649 | 12,773 | 44,584 | 119,291 | 17.7 | 2.0 | 15.6 | 42.0 |
| Intergovernmental | (¹) | 12,528 | 63,118 | 307 | — | 2.0 | 22.1 | .1 |
| Highways | 37,215 | 9,411 | 26,431 | 15,536 | 3.7 | 1.5 | 9.3 | 5.5 |
| Direct | 37,215 | 560 | 21,153 | 15,502 | 3.7 | .1 | 7.4 | 5.5 |
| Intergovernmental | (¹) | 8,851 | 5,277 | 35 | — | 1.4 | 1.9 | — |
| Public Welfare | 83,484 | 61,031 | 57,544 | 15,327 | 8.3 | 9.8 | 20.2 | 5.4 |
| Direct | 83,484 | 24,749 | 44,454 | 14,281 | 8.3 | 4.0 | 15.6 | 5.0 |
| Intergovernmental | (¹) | 36,282 | 13,091 | 1,046 | — | 5.8 | 4.6 | .4 |
| Health and Hospitals | 56,495 | 16,059 | 23,926 | 23,653 | 5.6 | 2.6 | 8.4 | 8.3 |
| Direct | 56,495 | 12,377 | 20,834 | 23,284 | 5.6 | 2.0 | 7.3 | 8.2 |
| Intergovernmental | (¹) | 3,682 | 3,092 | 369 | — | .6 | 1.1 | .1 |

| | | | | | | | | |
|---|---|---|---|---|---|---|---|---|
| Natural Resources | 54,757 | 49,768 | 5,834 | 1,555 | 5.5 | 8.0 | 2.0 | .5 |
| Direct | 54,757 | 47,675 | 5,545 | 1,537 | 5.5 | 7.6 | 1.9 | .5 |
| Intergovernmental | (¹) | 2,093 | 289 | 18 | — | .3 | .1 | — |
| Housing and urban renewal | | | | | | | | |
| Direct | 18,522 | 15,600 | 1,003 | 7,872 | 1.9 | 2.5 | .4 | 2.8 |
| Direct | 18,522 | 10,017 | 655 | 7,850 | 1.9 | 1.6 | .2 | 2.8 |
| Intergovernmental | (¹) | 5,583 | 348 | 22 | — | .9 | .1 | — |
| Airports | 5,385 | 2,830 | 431 | 2,681 | .5 | .5 | .2 | .9 |
| Direct | 5,385 | 2,371 | 333 | 2,681 | .5 | .4 | .1 | .9 |
| Intergovernmental | (¹) | 459 | 98 | 1 | — | .1 | — | — |
| Social insurance administration | 5,897 | 5,876 | 2,464 | 10 | .6 | .9 | .9 | — |
| Direct | 5,897 | 3,424 | 2,464 | 10 | .6 | .5 | .9 | — |
| Intergovernmental | (¹) | 2,452 | — | — | — | .4 | — | — |
| Interest on general debt | 132,871 | 108,735 | 11,252 | 12,885 | 13.3 | 17.4 | 3.9 | 4.5 |
| Other and combined | 169,866 | 65,799 | 48,455 | 84,811 | 17.0 | 10.5 | 17.0 | 29.9 |
| Direct | 169,866 | 53,804 | 32,459 | 83,604 | 17.0 | 8.6 | 11.4 | 29.4 |
| Intergovernmental | (¹) | 11,995 | 15,996 | 1,208 | — | 1.9 | 5.6 | .4 |

Note: Because of rounding, detail may not add to totals. Local government amounts are estimates subject to sampling variation;

— Represents zero or rounds to zero.

¹Duplicative transactions between levels of governments are excluded;

²Federal General Revenue Sharing payments to local governments amount to $4,568 million. Special distribution of State reserve funds totaled $46 million and administration expense was $6 million.

SOURCE: U.S. Bureau of the Census, *Governmental Finances in 1982–83* (Washington, D.C.: Government Printing Office, October 1984), Table 10, p. 18.

171

TABLE 5-4     Governmental Direct Expenditure by Character and Object,
by Level of Government, 1982-83

|  | AMOUNT (MILLIONS OF DOLLARS) | | | |
| ITEM | All Governments | Federal Government | State Governments | Local Governments |
| --- | --- | --- | --- | --- |
| Direct Expenditure | 1,350,527 | 785,725 | 232,710 | 332,093 |
| By Character and Object: | | | | |
| Current Operation | 692,826 | 290,781 | 144,018 | 258,026 |
| Capital Outlay | 148,728 | 80,744 | 23,357 | 44,633 |
| Construction | 62,062 | 8,796 | 18,616 | 34,650 |
| Equipment, Land, and | | | | |
| Existing Structures | 86,666 | 71,948 | 4,735 | 9,983 |
| Assistance and Subsidies | 73,633 | 55,371 | 11,452 | 6,809 |
| Interest on Debt | 137,913 | 108,735 | 11,708 | 17,470 |
| Insurance Benefits and | | | | |
| Repayments | 297,429 | 250,094 | 42,180 | 5,154 |
| Direct Expenditures for | | | | |
| Salaries and Wages | 314,019 | 109,641* | 60,348 | 144,031 |

*Includes pay and allowances for military personnel, amounting to $61,785 million.
SOURCE:  U.S. Bureau of the Census, *Government Finances in 1982-83* (Washington, D.C.: Government
Printing Office, October 1984), Table 9, p. 17.

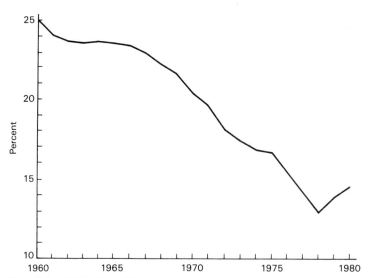

Figure 5-1.    STATE AND LOCAL CAPITAL INVESTMENT AS A PERCENT OF TOTAL
OUTLAYS. SOURCE:    U.S. General Accounting Office, *Effective Planning
and Budgeting Practices Can Help Arrest the Nation's Deteriorating Public
Infrastructure* (Washington, D.C.: GAO/PAD-83-2, November 18, 1982), Fig.
1, p. 14.

This decline is mirrored in changes in total government capital investment over time, as shown in Figure 5-2.

Besides capital and current expenditures, the direct expenditures in Table 5-4 also include assistance and subsidies, interest on debt, and insurance benefits and repayments, all of which have increased in dollar amounts and in their relative importance over the past decade.

**Other Expenditure Categories.** There are other categories of expenditures, such as transfer payments to specific clientele groups and expenditures related to specific work activities and/or programs. The availability of these data, however, varies considerably across governments.

Extreme care should be exercised when comparing different categories of expenditures across different governments. Definitions and data collection techniques may affect the comparability of different items. Although this is true when assessing any aspect of governments, the expenditure data are very prone to comparability problems. Also, changes in a government's accounting system can affect comparisons over time.

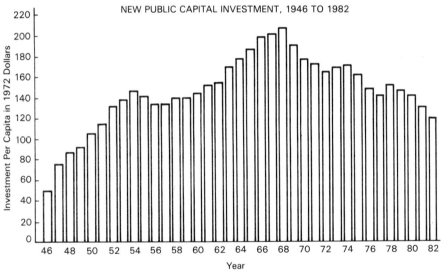

Figure 5-2.   NEW PUBLIC CAPITAL INVESTMENT, 1946 TO 1982. Note: The capital investment data exclude the costs of operation, supplies, maintenance and routine short-term repairs—current, rather than capital spending—which are unavailable in a comparable time series. A year's capital spending includes new, additional and replacement infrastructure investment; unfortunately, we cannot separate these components. SOURCES:   ACIR staff computations, based on unpublished estimates from the U.S. Bureau of Economic Analysis (BEA), using the GNP implicit price deflator. Population figures were obtained from the U.S. Department of Commerce, Bureau of the Census, *Current Population Reports,* Series P-25, No. 939 and No. 802. Population estimates in all figures include armed forces overseas and Alaska and Hawaii for 1959 to 1982. Military infrastructure is excluded in all figures. Figures shown are for calendar years unless otherwise indicated. Graph from Advisory Commission on Intergovernmental Relations, *Financing Public Physical Infrastructure* (Washington, D.C.: Government Printing Office, June 1984), Graph 1, p. 8.

**An Application.**   To illustrate the various categories of expenditures, we return to our example, the city of Dyer Straits. To be consistent with our revenue analysis, we will concentrate on the five-year period 1979–83. Since Dyer Straits does not transfer any of its resources to other levels of governments, our comparisons are for direct expenditures only.

We begin with capital expenditures. Table 5-5 presents actual expenditures for capital projects for 1979–83, with project expenditures broken down by object of expenditure. This information is from annual statements of Authorized and Actual Expenditures—Capital Projects Fund, such as that shown in Chapter 2, Table 2-5. In the case of Dyer Straits, all the capital expenditures are accounted for in the capital projects fund, although this need not be the case for all governments. It is not unusual for some capital expenditures to be accounted for in the

TABLE 5-5   **Capital Expenditures, City of Dyer Straits, 1979–83 ($ Thousands)**

| PROJECT TITLE | 1979 | 1980 | 1981 | 1982 | 1983 |
|---|---|---|---|---|---|
| 1. City Jail | | | | | |
|    Personnel | 38 | 12 | | | |
|    Materials and supplies | 6 | 3 | | | |
|    Contractual services | 455 | 57 | | | |
| 2. Downtown Overpass | | | | | |
|    Personnel | 634 | 513 | 362 | | |
|    Materials and supplies | 289 | 103 | 94 | | |
|    Contractual services | 62 | 89 | 49 | | |
| 3. Olympic Park | | | | | |
|    Personnel | 74 | 192 | 252 | | |
|    Materials and supplies | 8 | 14 | 77 | | |
|    Contractual services | — | — | 719 | | |
| 4. Allan Bridge | | | | | |
|    Personnel | | | | 625 | 780 |
|    Materials and supplies | | | | 227 | 309 |
|    Contractual services | | | | — | — |
| 5. Bus Terminal | | | | | |
|    Personnel | | | | | — |
|    Materials and supplies | | | | | — |
|    Contractual services | | | | | 435 |
| 6. Downtown Repaving | | | | | |
|    Personnel | | | | | |
|    Materials and supplies | | | | | |
|    Contractual services | | | | | |
| 7. City Office Building Renovations | | | | | |
|    Personnel | | | | | |
|    Materials and supplies | | | | | |
|    Contractual services | | | | | |
| 8. Transfer to water and sewer fund | 58 | 49 | 70 | 64 | 80 |
| Total Capital Expenditures | $1,624 | $1,032 | $1,483 | $916 | $1,604 |

general fund or in special assessment funds. The capital expenditures for the enterprises are accounted for in their respective enterprise funds.

When assessing data on current expenditures, the question of which current expenditures to include must be addressed. For the analysis of Dyer Straits, we have chosen to analyze the enterprise activities separately, and they are not included in this assessment. Therefore the general fund includes all the relevant current expenditures with the exception of the expenditures for debt service. The general fund transfers funds to the debt service fund to pay for the debt service, so that, in effect, the general fund with the transfers includes all the relevant expenditures for Dyer Straits.

Table 5-6 presents actual expenditure data for each functional area for Dyer Straits, 1979–83, from annual statements of Authorized and Actual Expenditures —General Fund (Chapter 2, Table 2-5). Table 5-7 presents actual expenditure data categorized by object of expenditure for the same period. Note that debt service and fringe benefits are identical in the two tables. Tables 5-5 through 5-7 represent the type of expenditure data that is likely to be available for governments, and we will now analyze these data.

### Analyzing Basic Expenditure Data

**Objectives.**   We begin our analysis of expenditures by examining the basic expenditure data discussed above. This initial step represents only a partial evaluation of expenditures, yet it is critical because it provides some preliminary insights into expenditure trends and priorities, lays the groundwork for later steps in the analysis, and given the frequent unavailability of data and the relative

TABLE 5-6   **General Fund Expenditures, City of Dyer Straits, 1979–83 ($ Thousands)**

|  | 1979 | 1980 | 1981 | 1982 | 1983 |
|---|---|---|---|---|---|
| Police | 1,083 | 1,197 | 1,315 | 1,474 | 1,691 |
| Fire | 1,023 | 1,131 | 1,244 | 1,395 | 1,603 |
| Public works | 735 | 715 | 702 | 772 | 895 |
| Judicial and corrections | 281 | 314 | 351 | 404 | 442 |
| Recreation and cultural | 388 | 416 | 454 | 491 | 541 |
| Social services | 341 | 379 | 430 | 474 | 560 |
| Health | 33 | 36 | 48 | 53 | 49 |
| Administration | 535 | 598 | 662 | 746 | 855 |
| Engineering | 201 | 204 | 215 | 193 | 226 |
| Other expenditures | 60 | 51 | 48 | 79 | 49 |
| Debt service* |  |  |  |  |  |
| Principal | 411 | 496 | 552 | 552 | 545 |
| Interest | 409 | 457 | 552 | 538 | 546 |
| Fringe benefits | 1,183 | 1,299 | 1,427 | 1,605 | 1,829 |
| Total Expenditures | 6,683 | 7,293 | 8,000 | 8,776 | 9,831 |

*Transfer to debt service fund.

TABLE 5-7   General Fund Expenditures, by Objects of Expenditure, City of Dyer Straits, 1979–83 ($ Thousands)

| OBJECTS OF EXPENDITURE | 1979 | 1980 | 1981 | 1982 | 1983 |
|---|---|---|---|---|---|
| Salaries | 3,529 | 3,855 | 4,216 | 4,724 | 5,447 |
| Materials and supplies | 691 | 683 | 695 | 742 | 793 |
| Contractual services* | 460 | 503 | 558 | 615 | 671 |
| Fringe benefits | 1,183 | 1,299 | 1,427 | 1,605 | 1,829 |
| Debt service | 820 | 953 | 1,104 | 1,090 | 1,091 |
| Total Expenditures | 6,683 | 7,293 | 8,000 | 8,776 | 9,831 |

*Includes transfer to municipal parking fund.

underdevelopment of later steps in the analysis, it is sometimes the only step that can be completed in the expenditure analysis of governments.

The objective of this initial stage of the analysis is limited. As will become clear, we can make only approximate first judgments about the expenditure component of financial condition from expenditure data in isolation from other information about prices, service conditions, and needs. Consequently, our initial focus will be on answers to a few simple questions about the government—questions that can be answered by looking solely at the levels of different types of expenditures compared with the past and with the expenditures of similar organizations.

First, we can ask, what are the "expenditure priorities" of the government? Into what types of functions and types of resources is the organization putting its money? And how do these priorities compare with similar organizations and with the past?[3] This may provide us with some sense of what the organization is trying to accomplish and highlight areas where additional questions need to be raised.

Second, we can use the level and growth rate of expenditures to develop first approximations of the extent to which an organization's expenditures are "too high" or "too low" from a financial condition standpoint, an approach that will be refined as the chapter unfolds.

The techniques of this initial stage of expenditure analysis are exactly those that we have already used. We need to identify an appropriate reference group and time period for our analysis. We need to make adjustments in accounting measures, expenditure categories, and so forth, to ensure comparability with the reference group and with the same organization at earlier points in time. If the governments in the reference group expend their resources on different sets of activities, we must decide whether to include those different functions or to limit the expenditure analysis to a set of "common" functions, the normal expenditures of all governments in the reference group. Usually the latter decision is made, and

[3]For an example of this form of analysis applied to New York City, see Charles Brecher and Raymond D. Horton, "Expenditures," in *Setting Municipal Priorities, 1984,* eds. Charles Brecher and Raymond D. Horton (New York: New York University Press, 1983), Chap. 3.

the expenditures for the "noncommon" functions are analyzed separately. (In our framework, we follow this practice and analyze the noncommon functions separately in section VII. Since these functions in this application are financed by user charges and set up as enterprises, we examine the revenues and expenses together in Chapter 8 where we focus on internal resources.) A decision must be made on whether to include debt service in the expenditure analysis or to limit the debt service analysis to the debt analysis component. (We include it in both places.) Pension expenditures are discussed in Chapter 7.

Finally, the analysis should be carried out using per capita expenditures, as well as absolute levels, to help compare governments of different size. And we need to employ methods like location quotients, common size statements, and index numbers to highlight important differences or changes. Applications of these techniques to this initial stage of expenditure analysis are best illustrated by returning to the continuing saga of Dyer Straits.[4]

**An Application.**     We will examine the expenditure data of Dyer Straits (Tables 5-5 through 5-7) in two stages. First, we will look at capital expenditures, the way in which they have changed over time, and their relationship to total expenditures (capital and current). Second, we will examine general fund expenditures by object of expenditure and by function. In each case, where appropriate, we will attempt to identify Dyer Straits' expenditure priorities and develop our first estimate of how its expenditures affect its financial condition. We will apply the analysis to expenditures on functions that are common to Dyer Straits and the reference group, which in the case of Dyer Straits coincides with the expenditures in the general fund.

*Capital and Current Expenditures.*     Table 5-8 shows the capital fund expenditures for Dyer Straits (from Table 5-5) and its reference group, in dollars and as a percentage of total capital and general fund expenditures. Dyer Straits' capital outlays over 1979-83 show fluctuations but no clear trend. The fluctuations are not surprising, as capital outlays often come in large "lumps" with (for example) an unexpected major bridge repair perhaps doubling capital outlays from the previous year.

Comparisons of Dyer Straits' capital outlays with its total capital and general fund expenditures show that capital expenditures have declined slightly as a percentage of total outlays, but again it is the fluctuations over time that are most apparent. Comparisons with its reference group, however, suggest that Dyer Straits has emphasized capital expenditures more than similar cities. Capital ex-

---

[4] For examples of per capita expenditures in empirical financial condition studies, see Touche Ross & Co. and the First National Bank of Boston, *Urban Fiscal Stress* (New York: Touche Ross, 1979); Bureau of Governmental Research and Service, University of Oregon, "Oregon Municipal Fiscal Indicators, an Exploratory Study," October 1983; and Joint Economic Committee, "Trends in the Fiscal Condition of Cities: 1980-1982" (Washington, D.C., 1982).

TABLE 5-8    **Capital Projects Fund Expenditures—Level and Percentage of Capital Projects and General Fund Expenditures, City of Dyer Straits and Reference Group, 1979–83**

|  | 1979 | 1980 | 1981 | 1982 | 1983 |
|---|---|---|---|---|---|
| *Dyer Straits:* | | | | | |
| Capital projects fund expenditures ($ millions) | 1.624 | 1.032 | 1.483 | .916 | 1.604 |
| Capital projects fund expenditures/capital projects and general fund expenditures (%) | 19.5 | 12.4 | 15.6 | 9.5 | 14.0 |
| *Reference Group:* | | | | | |
| Capital projects fund expenditures ($ millions) | 41.8 | 49.5 | 56.1 | 30.9 | 29.8 |
| Capital projects fund expenditures/capital projects and general fund expenditures (%) | 14.0 | 15.0 | 15.7 | 8.6 | 7.8 |

penditures as a percentage of total outlays were higher in Dyer Straits than in its reference group or were about the same in four out of five years, and significantly higher in 1983. This is a generally positive finding, suggesting that Dyer Straits has continued to maintain its capital stock in spite of other financial pressures. This finding, however, must be viewed along with observations from other components of financial analysis.

*Objects of Expenditure.*    Table 5-9 compares object-of-expenditure data for Dyer Straits (developed from Tables 5-6 and 5-7) with those of the forty-nine-city reference group for 1979–83. These data are presented on a per capita basis and in index number and common size form in Tables 5-10, 5-11, and 5-12, respectively. These tables reveal the following patterns:

- *Salaries* per capita are high in Dyer Straits compared with those in the reference group (Table 5-10), and they are rising more rapidly than the average for the reference group cities (Table 5-11). By 1983, salaries per capita are 33 percent higher in Dyer Straits compared with the reference group's (Table 5-11). In Dyer Straits, salaries represent a higher proportion of total expenditures than for comparable cities, and they are increasing in importance for Dyer Straits and at a faster rate than for the reference group (Table 5-12). Based on these observations, expenditures on salaries appear to merit closer examination.
- *Materials and supplies* expenditures per capita in Dyer Straits in 1979 were slightly higher on average than in the reference group (Table 5-10), but over the period they have grown more slowly than total expenditures in Dyer Straits and more slowly than per capita materials and supplies expenditures in the reference group (Table 5-11). Recent levels of materials and supplies expenditures per capita in Dyer Straits are actually lower than the reference group's (Table 5-10). The relative importance of materials and supplies in total expenditures is declining for both Dyer Straits and its

TABLE 5-9  General Fund Expenditures on Different Types of Inputs, City of Dyer Straits and Reference Group, 1979–83 ($ Millions)

| OBJECTS OF EXPENDITURE | DYER STRAITS | | | | | REFERENCE GROUP | | | | | LOCATION QUOTIENTS* | | | | |
|---|---|---|---|---|---|---|---|---|---|---|---|---|---|---|---|
| | 1979 | 1980 | 1981 | 1982 | 1983 | 1979 | 1980 | 1981 | 1982 | 1983 | 1979 | 1980 | 1981 | 1982 | 1983 |
| Salaries | 3.529 | 3.855 | 4.216 | 4.724 | 5.447 | 133.53 | 145.81 | 156.85 | 174.31 | 190.41 | .0264 | .0264 | .0269 | .0271 | .0286 |
| Materials and supplies | .691 | .683 | .695 | .742 | .793 | 30.90 | 32.54 | 33.90 | 35.95 | 37.68 | .0224 | .0210 | .0206 | .0206 | .0210 |
| Contractual services† | .460 | .503 | .558 | .615 | .671 | 20.94 | 22.62 | 24.54 | 26.50 | 28.59 | .0220 | .0222 | .0227 | .0232 | .0236 |
| Fringe benefits | 1.183 | 1.299 | 1.427 | 1.605 | 1.829 | 41.65 | 46.12 | 50.05 | 54.92 | 59.39 | .0284 | .0282 | .0285 | .0292 | .0308 |
| Debt service | .820 | .953 | 1.104 | 1.090 | 1.091 | 30.04 | 32.40 | 35.95 | 37.15 | 37.35 | .0273 | .0294 | .0307 | .0293 | .0292 |
| Total Expenditures | 6.683 | 7.293 | 8.000 | 8.776 | 9.831 | 257.06 | 279.49 | 301.29 | 328.83 | 353.42 | .0260 | .0261 | .0266 | .0267 | .0278 |

*Dyer Straits/Reference Group.
†Includes transfer to municipal parking fund.

TABLE 5-10  General Fund Per Capita Expenditures on Different Types of Inputs, City of Dyer Straits and Reference Group, 1979–83 ($)

| OBJECTS OF EXPENDITURE | DYER STRAITS | | | | | REFERENCE GROUP | | | | | LOCATION QUOTIENTS* | | | | |
|---|---|---|---|---|---|---|---|---|---|---|---|---|---|---|---|
| | 1979 | 1980 | 1981 | 1982 | 1983 | 1979 | 1980 | 1981 | 1982 | 1983 | 1979 | 1980 | 1981 | 1982 | 1983 |
| Salaries | 107.30 | 117.89 | 130.12 | 147.17 | 170.75 | 87.56 | 96.24 | 104.22 | 116.60 | 128.22 | 1.225 | 1.225 | 1.249 | 1.262 | 1.332 |
| Materials and supplies | 21.01 | 20.89 | 21.45 | 23.12 | 24.85 | 20.26 | 21.48 | 22.52 | 24.05 | 25.37 | 1.037 | 1.028 | .952 | .961 | .980 |
| Contractual services | 13.99 | 15.38 | 17.22 | 19.16 | 21.03 | 13.73 | 14.93 | 16.31 | 17.73 | 19.25 | 1.019 | 1.030 | 1.056 | 1.081 | 1.092 |
| Fringe benefits | 35.97 | 39.72 | 44.04 | 50.00 | 57.34 | 27.31 | 30.44 | 33.26 | 36.74 | 39.99 | 1.317 | 1.305 | 1.324 | 1.361 | 1.434 |
| Debt service | 24.93 | 29.14 | 34.07 | 33.96 | 34.20 | 19.70 | 21.39 | 23.89 | 24.85 | 25.15 | 1.265 | 1.362 | 1.426 | 1.367 | 1.360 |
| Total Expenditures† | 203.19 | 223.02 | 246.91 | 273.40 | 308.18 | 168.56 | 184.48 | 200.19 | 219.95 | 237.99 | 1.205 | 1.209 | 1.233 | 1.243 | 1.295 |

*Dyer Straits/Reference Group.
†Totals may not add due to rounding.

TABLE 5–11  General Fund Per Capita Expenditures on Different Types of Inputs, City of Dyer Straits and Reference Group, 1979–83, Index Number Form (1979 = 100.00)

| OBJECTS OF EXPENDITURE | DYER STRAITS | | | | | REFERENCE GROUP | | | | | LOCATION QUOTIENTS* | | | | |
|---|---|---|---|---|---|---|---|---|---|---|---|---|---|---|---|
| | 1979 | 1980 | 1981 | 1982 | 1983 | 1979 | 1980 | 1981 | 1982 | 1983 | 1979 | 1980 | 1981 | 1982 | 1983 |
| Salaries | 100.0 | 109.9 | 121.3 | 137.2 | 159.1 | 100.0 | 109.9 | 119.0 | 133.2 | 146.4 | 1.000 | 1.000 | 1.019 | 1.030 | 1.087 |
| Materials and supplies | 100.0 | 99.4 | 102.1 | 110.0 | 118.3 | 100.0 | 106.0 | 111.2 | 118.7 | 125.2 | 1.000 | .938 | .963 | .989 | .945 |
| Contractual services | 100.0 | 109.9 | 123.1 | 137.0 | 150.3 | 100.0 | 108.7 | 118.8 | 129.1 | 140.2 | 1.000 | 1.011 | 1.036 | 1.061 | 1.072 |
| Fringe benefits | 100.0 | 110.4 | 122.4 | 139.0 | 159.4 | 100.0 | 111.5 | 121.8 | 134.5 | 146.4 | 1.000 | .990 | 1.005 | 1.033 | 1.089 |
| Debt service | 100.0 | 116.9 | 136.7 | 136.2 | 137.2 | 100.0 | 108.6 | 121.3 | 126.1 | 127.7 | 1.000 | 1.076 | 1.127 | 1.080 | 1.074 |
| Total Expenditures | 100.0 | 109.8 | 121.5 | 134.6 | 151.7 | 100.0 | 109.4 | 118.8 | 130.5 | 141.2 | 1.000 | 1.004 | 1.023 | 1.031 | 1.074 |

*Dyer Straits/Reference Group.

TABLE 5–12  General Fund Per Capita Expenditures on Different Types of Inputs, City of Dyer Straits and Reference Group, 1979–83, Common Size Statement Form (Percentages)

| OBJECTS OF EXPENDITURE | DYER STRAITS | | | | | REFERENCE GROUP | | | | | LOCATION QUOTIENTS* | | | | |
|---|---|---|---|---|---|---|---|---|---|---|---|---|---|---|---|
| | 1979 | 1980 | 1981 | 1982 | 1983 | 1979 | 1980 | 1981 | 1982 | 1983 | 1979 | 1980 | 1981 | 1982 | 1983 |
| Salaries | 52.8 | 52.9 | 52.7 | 53.8 | 55.4 | 51.9 | 52.2 | 52.1 | 53.0 | 53.9 | 1.017 | 1.013 | 1.012 | 1.015 | 1.028 |
| Materials and supplies | 10.3 | 9.4 | 8.7 | 8.5 | 8.1 | 12.0 | 11.6 | 11.2 | 10.9 | 10.7 | .858 | .810 | .777 | .780 | .757 |
| Contractual services | 6.9 | 6.9 | 7.0 | 7.0 | 6.8 | 8.1 | 8.1 | 8.1 | 8.1 | 8.1 | .852 | .852 | .864 | .864 | .840 |
| Fringe benefits | 17.7 | 17.8 | 17.8 | 18.3 | 18.6 | 16.2 | 16.5 | 16.6 | 16.7 | 16.8 | 1.093 | 1.079 | 1.072 | 1.096 | 1.107 |
| Debt service | 12.3 | 13.1 | 13.8 | 12.4 | 11.1 | 11.7 | 11.6 | 11.9 | 11.3 | 10.6 | 1.051 | 1.129 | 1.160 | 1.097 | 1.047 |
| Total Expenditures† | 100.0 | 100.0 | 100.0 | 100.0 | 100.0 | 100.0 | 100.0 | 100.0 | 100.0 | 100.1 | — | — | — | — | — |

*Dyer Straits/Reference Group.
†Totals may not add due to rounding.

reference group, and the share of total expenditures is lower for Dyer Straits than for the reference group (Table 5-12).

- *Contractual services* expenditures per capita in Dyer Straits appear to be in line with these expenditures in comparable cities, although slightly higher on average and growing slightly faster in Dyer Straits compared with the reference group's (Tables 5-10 and 5-11). The share of expenditures devoted to contractual services is relatively constant in Dyer Straits absolutely and relative to the reference group, and its share is lower relative to the reference group throughout the period (Table 5-12).

- *Fringe benefits* per capita, like salaries, appear to merit attention. They are substantially higher, on average, than those in the reference group (Table 5-10), growing faster than the total expenditures or the salary expenditures in Dyer Straits, and faster than fringe benefit expenditures by the reference group cities (Table 5-11). The relative importance of fringe benefits in Dyer Straits is growing, and growing faster than in comparable cities (Table 5-11). Although part of the problem may be explained by the high salary expenditures (fringe benefits are often related to salaries), further investigation is warranted. (Pension obligations are assessed in Chapter 7.)

- *Debt service* per capita is 26 to 36 percent higher, on average, in Dyer Straits than in the reference group (Table 5-10), but its growth in Dyer Straits seems to have slowed toward the end of the period, with debt service expenditures becoming stable for Dyer Straits while continuing to rise in the reference group (Table 5-11). Debt service as a share of total expenditures in Dyer Straits varies between 11 and 14 percent, but it ends the period at its lowest level. Throughout the period, however, Dyer Straits devotes a larger share of its expenditures to debt service compared with the reference group (Table 5-12). Despite the stabilization in recent years, this is definitely an area that needs further attention (see Chapter 6).

*"Fixity" of Expenditures.* Object-of-expenditure data can provide some clues about financial condition. Since financial condition depends in part on the "fixity" of expenditures—how easily and quickly expenditure levels can be changed in the face of revenue declines or unplanned needs for resources—shifts in the pattern of expenditures toward more or less "fixed" expenditures can affect the government's financial strength.

Dyer Straits' relatively high debt service represents fixed obligations that may lower financial flexibility. How fixed this debt service requirement is, however, depends in part on the specific forms of the outstanding debt, the conditions of repayment, and the ability of the organization to alter these conditions (see Chapter 6).

The fringe benefits in Dyer Straits are likely to be relatively fixed. The fringes that are being used to satisfy pension obligations may be fixed, since prior commitments are not likely to be changed. But depending on funding policies, inflation, and investment performance, pension expenditures can change without a simultaneous change in the benefits (see Chapter 7). Fringes that are part of a collective bargaining agreement will be relatively fixed until the next contract negotiations.

The fixity of the salary expenditures is determined by the number of people employed, their salaries, and existing contracts. Individual governments usually have some flexibility in determining the level of employment, but less for salaries because they are usually set in a bargaining situation and require negotiations to be changed.

Slower growth in materials and supplies expenditures may mean a reduction in inventories of these items and less of a reserve for emergencies, suggesting reduced flexibility for the city to cut expenditures in this area. On the other hand, the reduced expenditures may mean greater efficiency and a reduction in the need for these expenditures. Contractual services are difficult to assess without knowing the essentiality of services performed under contract, but they may include some nonessential services (like ''special studies'') that may be delayed or not renewed the next year.

Overall the analysis raises the possibility that Dyer Straits' expenditures are becoming harder to change, although there are certain offsetting trends. The fixity of salary expenditures is obviously a key item. But the ability of Dyer Straits to cut city employees depends in part on the city's service conditions and needs, topics that we introduce later in the chapter.

*Expenditure Functions.*    Dyer Straits' expenditures on different functions can be examined using the same approach applied earlier to objects of expenditures. Table 5–13 shows the annual total expenditures by function for Dyer Straits and its reference group. As before, only the expenditures for the common functions are compared in this analysis. In some cases where the governments spend money on a wide variety of activities, the task of separating the expenditures for a common set of functions creates a difficult, but necessary, task in assembling data, since cities may define their functions in different ways. For cities within the same state, this task may be easier if consistent accounting procedures are required for state audits; for cities in different states, it is a much more difficult task.[5] Table 5–13 also shows the location quotients relating Dyer Straits' expenditures to the reference group's.

Table 5–14 puts the expenditure data in per capita terms to adjust for the population differences between Dyer Straits and the reference group. The per capita figures are also compared using location quotients. Tables 5–15 and 5–16 put these data in index number and common size forms, respectively, to highlight changes over time in different expenditure categories and the importance of each type of expenditure relative to total expenditures.

Using these tables, we can make the following general observations about functional expenditures of Dyer Straits:

- *Police* expenditures represent the single largest category of expenditures for the city and are higher in per capita terms than the police expenditures in the reference

---

[5] As examples, see Roy Bahl, Allan Campbell, and David Greytak, *Taxes, Expenditures and the Economic Base: Case Study of New York City* (New York: Praeger, 1974); Edward Gramlich, ''The New York City Fiscal Crisis,'' *American Economic Review,* 66 (May 1976), 415–29; and Katherine L. Bradbury, ''Structural Fiscal Distress in Cities—Causes and Consequences,'' *New England Economic Review,* January–February 1983, pp. 32–43.

TABLE 5-13 General Fund Expenditures by Function, City of Dyer Straits and Reference Group, 1979–83 ($ Millions)

| | DYER STRAITS | | | | | REFERENCE GROUP | | | | | LOCATION QUOTIENTS* | | | | |
|---|---|---|---|---|---|---|---|---|---|---|---|---|---|---|---|
| | 1979 | 1980 | 1981 | 1982 | 1983 | 1979 | 1980 | 1981 | 1982 | 1983 | 1979 | 1980 | 1981 | 1982 | 1983 |
| Police | 1.083 | 1.197 | 1.315 | 1.474 | 1.691 | 43.45 | 46.96 | 50.66 | 55.25 | 59.75 | .0249 | .0255 | .0260 | .0267 | .0283 |
| Fire | 1.023 | 1.131 | 1.244 | 1.395 | 1.603 | 42.93 | 46.68 | 49.75 | 54.59 | 59.39 | .0238 | .0242 | .0250 | .0256 | .0270 |
| Public works | .735 | .715 | .702 | .772 | .895 | 23.91 | 26.28 | 28.04 | 30.58 | 34.29 | .0307 | .0272 | .0250 | .0252 | .0261 |
| Judicial and corrections | .281 | .314 | .351 | .404 | .442 | 10.54 | 11.46 | 11.76 | 13.15 | 14.50 | .0267 | .0274 | .0298 | .0307 | .0305 |
| Recreation and cultural | .388 | .416 | .454 | .491 | .541 | 18.00 | 20.13 | 21.41 | 24.34 | 26.87 | .0216 | .0207 | .0212 | .0202 | .0201 |
| Social services | .341 | .379 | .430 | .474 | .560 | 11.83 | 13.14 | 14.77 | 16.11 | 17.68 | .0288 | .0288 | .0291 | .0294 | .0317 |
| Health | .033 | .036 | .048 | .053 | .049 | 3.09 | 3.63 | 4.52 | 5.59 | 6.72 | .0107 | .0099 | .0106 | .0095 | .0073 |
| Administration | .535 | .598 | .662 | .746 | .855 | 19.54 | 20.96 | 23.22 | 24.99 | 27.22 | .0274 | .0285 | .0285 | .0299 | .0314 |
| Fringe benefits | 1.183 | 1.299 | 1.427 | 1.605 | 1.829 | 41.65 | 46.12 | 50.05 | 54.92 | 59.39 | .0284 | .0282 | .0285 | .0292 | .0308 |
| Engineering | .201 | .204 | .215 | .193 | .226 | 6.94 | 7.54 | 7.54 | 7.56 | 6.72 | .0290 | .0271 | .0285 | .0255 | .0287 |
| Debt service | | | | | | | | | | | | | | | |
| Principal | .411 | .496 | .522 | .552 | .545 | 22.60 | 23.21 | 24.89 | 24.88 | 25.14 | .0182 | .0214 | .0210 | .0222 | .0217 |
| Interest | .409 | .457 | .552 | .538 | .546 | 7.44 | 9.19 | 11.06 | 12.27 | 12.21 | .0550 | .0497 | .0499 | .0438 | .0447 |
| Other expenditures | .060 | .051 | .048 | .079 | .049 | 5.14 | 4.19 | 3.62 | 4.60 | 3.54 | .0117 | .0122 | .0133 | .0172 | .0138 |
| Total Expenditures for Common Functions | 6.683 | 7.293 | 7.970 | 8.776 | 9.831 | 257.06 | 279.49 | 301.29 | 328.83 | 353.42 | .0260 | .0261 | .0265 | .0267 | .0278 |

*Dyer Straits/Reference Group.

183

TABLE 5-14 General Fund Per Capita Expenditures by Function, City of Dyer Straits and Reference Group, 1979-83 ($)

| | DYER STRAITS | | | | | REFERENCE GROUP | | | | | LOCATION QUOTIENTS* | | | | |
|---|---|---|---|---|---|---|---|---|---|---|---|---|---|---|---|
| | 1979 | 1980 | 1981 | 1982 | 1983 | 1979 | 1980 | 1981 | 1982 | 1983 | 1979 | 1980 | 1981 | 1982 | 1983 |
| Police | 32.93 | 36.61 | 40.59 | 45.92 | 53.01 | 28.49 | 31.00 | 33.66 | 36.96 | 40.24 | 1.156 | 1.181 | 1.206 | 1.242 | 1.317 |
| Fire | 31.10 | 34.59 | 38.40 | 43.46 | 50.25 | 28.15 | 30.81 | 33.06 | 36.52 | 39.99 | 1.105 | 1.123 | 1.162 | 1.190 | 1.263 |
| Public works | 22.35 | 21.87 | 21.67 | 24.05 | 28.06 | 15.68 | 17.35 | 18.63 | 20.45 | 23.09 | 1.425 | 1.261 | 1.163 | 1.176 | 1.215 |
| Judicial and corrections | 8.54 | 9.60 | 10.83 | 12.59 | 13.86 | 6.91 | 7.56 | 7.81 | 8.80 | 9.76 | 1.236 | 1.270 | 1.387 | 1.431 | 1.420 |
| Recreation and cultural | 11.80 | 12.72 | 14.01 | 15.30 | 16.96 | 11.80 | 13.29 | 14.23 | 16.28 | 18.09 | 1.000 | .957 | .985 | .939 | .938 |
| Social services | 10.37 | 11.59 | 13.27 | 14.77 | 17.55 | 7.76 | 8.67 | 9.81 | 10.78 | 11.91 | 1.336 | 1.337 | 1.353 | 1.370 | 1.474 |
| Health | 1.00 | 1.10 | 1.48 | 1.65 | 1.54 | 2.03 | 2.40 | 3.00 | 3.74 | 4.53 | .493 | .458 | .493 | .441 | .400 |
| Administration | 16.27 | 18.29 | 20.43 | 23.24 | 26.80 | 12.81 | 13.83 | 15.43 | 16.72 | 18.33 | 1.271 | 1.322 | 1.324 | 1.390 | 1.462 |
| Fringe benefits | 35.97 | 39.72 | 44.04 | 50.00 | 57.34 | 27.31 | 30.44 | 33.26 | 36.74 | 39.99 | 1.317 | 1.305 | 1.324 | 1.361 | 1.434 |
| Engineering | 6.11 | 6.24 | 6.64 | 6.01 | 7.08 | 4.55 | 4.98 | 5.01 | 5.06 | 4.53 | 1.343 | 1.253 | 1.325 | 1.188 | 1.563 |
| Debt service | | | | | | | | | | | | | | | |
| Principal | 12.50 | 15.17 | 16.11 | 17.20 | 17.08 | 14.82 | 15.32 | 16.54 | 16.64 | 16.93 | .843 | .990 | .974 | 1.034 | 1.009 |
| Interest | 12.44 | 13.98 | 17.04 | 16.76 | 17.12 | 4.88 | 6.07 | 7.35 | 8.21 | 8.22 | 2.549 | 2.303 | 2.318 | 2.041 | 2.083 |
| Other expenditures | 1.82 | 1.56 | 1.48 | 2.46 | 1.54 | 3.37 | 2.77 | 2.41 | 3.08 | 2.38 | .540 | .563 | .614 | .799 | .647 |
| Total Expenditures for Common Functions | 203.19 | 223.03 | 245.99 | 273.40 | 308.18 | 168.56 | 184.48 | 200.19 | 219.95 | 237.99 | 1.205 | 1.209 | 1.229 | 1.243 | 1.295 |

*Dyer Straits/Reference Group.
†Totals may not add due to rounding.

TABLE 5-15  General Fund Per Capita Expenditures by Function, City of Dyer Straits and Reference Group, 1979–83, Index Number Form (1979 = 100.0)

| | DYER STRAITS | | | | | REFERENCE GROUP | | | | | LOCATION QUOTIENTS* | | | |
|---|---|---|---|---|---|---|---|---|---|---|---|---|---|---|
| | 1979 | 1980 | 1981 | 1982 | 1983 | 1979 | 1980 | 1981 | 1982 | 1983 | 1980 | 1981 | 1982 | 1983 |
| Police | 100.0 | 111.2 | 123.3 | 139.4 | 161.0 | 100.0 | 108.8 | 118.1 | 129.7 | 141.2 | 1.022 | 1.044 | 1.075 | 1.140 |
| Fire | 100.0 | 111.2 | 123.5 | 139.7 | 161.6 | 100.0 | 109.4 | 117.4 | 129.7 | 142.1 | 1.016 | 1.052 | 1.077 | 1.137 |
| Public works | 100.0 | 97.9 | 97.0 | 107.6 | 125.5 | 100.0 | 110.7 | 118.8 | 130.4 | 147.3 | .884 | .816 | .825 | .852 |
| Judicial and corrections | 100.0 | 112.4 | 126.8 | 147.4 | 162.3 | 100.0 | 109.4 | 113.0 | 127.4 | 141.2 | 1.027 | 1.122 | 1.157 | 1.149 |
| Recreation and cultural | 100.0 | 107.8 | 118.7 | 129.7 | 143.7 | 100.0 | 112.6 | 120.6 | 138.0 | 153.3 | .957 | .984 | .940 | .937 |
| Social services | 100.0 | 111.8 | 128.0 | 142.4 | 169.2 | 100.0 | 111.7 | 126.4 | 138.9 | 153.5 | 1.001 | 1.013 | 1.025 | 1.102 |
| Health | 100.0 | 110.0 | 148.0 | 165.0 | 154.0 | 100.0 | 118.2 | 147.8 | 184.2 | 223.2 | .931 | 1.001 | .896 | .690 |
| Administration | 100.0 | 112.4 | 125.6 | 142.8 | 164.7 | 100.0 | 108.0 | 120.5 | 130.5 | 143.1 | 1.041 | 1.042 | 1.094 | 1.151 |
| Engineering | 100.0 | 102.1 | 108.7 | 98.4 | 115.9 | 100.0 | 109.5 | 110.1 | 111.2 | 99.6 | .932 | .987 | .885 | 1.164 |
| Other expenditures | 100.0 | 85.7 | 81.3 | 135.2 | 84.6 | 100.0 | 82.2 | 71.5 | 91.4 | 70.6 | 1.043 | 1.137 | 1.479 | 1.198 |
| Debt service | | | | | | | | | | | | | | |
| Principal | 100.0 | 121.4 | 136.3 | 137.6 | 136.7 | 100.0 | 103.4 | 111.6 | 112.3 | 114.2 | 1.174 | 1.221 | 1.225 | 1.197 |
| Interest | 100.0 | 112.4 | 137.0 | 134.7 | 137.6 | 100.0 | 124.4 | 150.6 | 168.2 | 168.4 | .904 | .910 | .801 | .817 |
| Fringe benefits | 100.0 | 110.4 | 122.4 | 139.0 | 159.4 | 100.0 | 111.5 | 121.8 | 134.5 | 146.4 | .990 | 1.005 | 1.033 | 1.089 |
| Total Expenditures for Common Functions | 100.0 | 109.8 | 121.5 | 134.6 | 151.7 | 100.0 | 109.4 | 118.8 | 130.5 | 141.2 | 1.004 | 1.023 | 1.031 | 1.072 |

*Dyer Straits/Reference Group.

TABLE 5-16  General Fund Per Capita Expenditures by Function, City of Dyer Straits and Reference Group, 1979-83, Common Size Form (Percentages)

| | DYER STRAITS | | | | | REFERENCE GROUP | | | | | LOCATION QUOTIENTS* | | | | |
|---|---|---|---|---|---|---|---|---|---|---|---|---|---|---|---|
| | 1979 | 1980 | 1981 | 1982 | 1983 | 1979 | 1980 | 1981 | 1982 | 1983 | 1979 | 1980 | 1981 | 1982 | 1983 |
| Police | 16.2 | 16.4 | 16.5 | 16.8 | 17.2 | 16.9 | 16.8 | 16.8 | 16.8 | 16.9 | .959 | .976 | .982 | 1.000 | 1.018 |
| Fire | 15.3 | 15.5 | 15.6 | 15.9 | 16.3 | 16.7 | 16.7 | 16.5 | 16.6 | 16.8 | .916 | .928 | .945 | .958 | .970 |
| Public works | 11.0 | 9.8 | 8.8 | 8.8 | 9.1 | 9.3 | 9.4 | 9.3 | 9.3 | 9.7 | 1.183 | 1.043 | .946 | .946 | .938 |
| Judicial and corrections | 4.2 | 4.3 | 4.4 | 4.6 | 4.5 | 4.1 | 4.1 | 3.9 | 4.0 | 4.1 | 1.024 | 1.049 | 1.128 | 1.150 | 1.098 |
| Recreation and cultural | 5.8 | 5.7 | 5.7 | 5.6 | 5.5 | 7.0 | 7.2 | 7.1 | 7.4 | 7.6 | .829 | .792 | .803 | .757 | .724 |
| Social services | 5.1 | 5.2 | 5.4 | 5.4 | 5.7 | 4.6 | 4.7 | 4.9 | 4.9 | 5.0 | 1.109 | 1.106 | 1.102 | 1.102 | 1.140 |
| Health | .5 | .5 | .6 | .6 | .5 | 1.2 | 1.3 | 1.5 | 1.7 | 1.9 | .417 | .385 | .400 | .353 | .263 |
| Administration | 8.0 | 8.2 | 8.3 | 8.5 | 8.7 | 7.6 | 7.5 | 7.7 | 7.6 | 7.7 | 1.053 | 1.093 | 1.078 | 1.118 | 1.130 |
| Engineering | 3.0 | 2.8 | 2.7 | 2.2 | 2.3 | 2.7 | 2.7 | 2.5 | 2.3 | 1.9 | 1.111 | 1.037 | 1.080 | .957 | 1.211 |
| Other expenditures | .9 | .7 | .6 | .9 | .5 | 2.0 | 1.5 | 1.2 | 1.4 | 1.0 | .450 | .467 | .500 | .643 | .500 |
| Debt service | | | | | | | | | | | | | | | |
| Principal | 6.2 | 6.8 | 6.9 | 6.3 | 5.5 | 8.8 | 8.3 | 8.3 | 7.6 | 7.1 | .705 | .819 | .831 | .829 | .775 |
| Interest | 6.1 | 6.3 | 6.9 | 6.1 | 5.6 | 2.9 | 3.3 | 3.7 | 3.7 | 3.5 | 2.103 | 1.909 | 1.865 | 1.649 | 1.600 |
| Fringe benefits | 17.7 | 17.8 | 17.8 | 18.3 | 18.6 | 16.2 | 16.5 | 16.6 | 16.7 | 16.8 | 1.093 | 1.079 | 1.072 | 1.096 | 1.107 |
| Total Expenditures for Common Functions† | 100.0 | 100.0 | 100.0 | 100.0 | 100.0 | 100.0 | 100.0 | 100.0 | 100.0 | 100.0 | — | — | — | — | — |

*Dyer Straits/Reference Group.
†Totals may not add due to rounding.

group. They are also growing faster than most other expenditures in Dyer Straits at a rate that is higher than the rate for police expenditures in the reference group.

- *Fire* expenditures are one of the highest expenditure categories in per capita terms for Dyer Straits and higher than the reference group's expenditures on this function. They are also growing at a higher rate compared with other expenditures in Dyer Straits and faster than the reference group's expenditures on fire protection.

- *Public works* expenditures are one of the highest expenditure categories for Dyer Straits and higher than the reference group's. They are, however, growing much more slowly than most other expenditure categories in Dyer Straits and more slowly than the reference group's outlays for public works.

- *Judicial and corrections* expenditures in per capita terms are about average for all functions but are substantially higher than the reference group's expenditures in this area. The growth rate in this functional area is high relative to other functions in Dyer Straits and high relative to comparable reference group expenditures.

- *Recreation and cultural* expenditures in per capita terms are lower than the reference group's expenditures in this area. They are also growing somewhat more slowly than other expenditures in Dyer Straits and the reference group's expenditures on recreation and cultural activities.

- *Social service* per capita expenditures are about the same magnitude as the prior two categories in Dyer Straits, but they are substantially higher, on average, than reference group social service expenditures. This functional area has the highest growth rate of all Dyer Straits' functional areas and is growing faster than the reference group's expenditures in this area as well.

- *Health* per capita expenditures are receiving the lowest dollar allocation of any function in Dyer Straits, and much lower than per capita expenditures on health by the reference group cities. They are growing around the average for Dyer Straits' expenditures, but much more slowly than reference group health expenditures.

- *Administration* per capita expenditures are much higher than the average per capita allocation of the reference group on administration. They are growing at a high rate relative to both other city expenditures and the reference group's administration outlays.

- *Engineering* expenditures, per capita, are low relative to other functions but are much higher than the average for the reference group. Even though they are the slowest-growing functional expenditure for Dyer Straits, reference group expenditures in this area are growing at a much slower rate.

Before we use these observations to answer questions about expenditure priorities and financial condition, there are several items we should mention. The data in Tables 5-13 through 5-16 are summarized in Table 5-17. Note, first, the large differences in the relative importance and growth rates of different functional areas. This suggests that an examination of any one measure alone, such as the percentage of total expenditures, gives only a partial picture of the behavior of that expenditure category. Second, even the four measures in Table 5-17 do not capture all the characteristics of expenditures. Year-to-year changes in expenditures vary considerably across expenditure categories, as seen in Table 5-15. Some expenditures, such as police, grow smoothly but at an increasing rate; others, such as public works, have periods of ups and downs. Fluctuations or accelerating or decelerating growth patterns may reflect some internal changes that

TABLE 5-17    **Summary of Functional Expenditure Patterns, City of Dyer Straits, 1979–83**

| | IMPORTANCE OF FUNCTION FROM STANDPOINT OF | | | |
| Expenditure Category | Per Capita Expenditures: | | Growth Rate of Expenditures:* | |
| | Relative to Other Expenditures by Dyer Straits | Relative to Reference Group | Relative to Other Expenditures by Dyer Straits | Relative to Reference Group |
|---|---|---|---|---|
| Police | Highest | Higher | High | Higher |
| Fire | High | Higher | High | Higher |
| Public works | High | Higher | Low | Lower |
| Judicial and corrections | Average | Much higher | High | Higher |
| Recreation and cultural | Average | Lower | Below average | Lower |
| Social services | Average | Much higher | Highest | Higher |
| Health | Lowest | Much lower | Average | Much lower |
| Engineering | Low | Much higher | Lowest | Highest |
| Administration | Above average | Much higher | High | Higher |
| Total | — | Higher | — | Higher |
| Main Reference Table | 5-16 | 5-14 | 5-15 | 5-13, 5-14 |

*Percentage Increase in Expenditures, 1979–83

the analyst may want to investigate further. If so, these changes can be seen more clearly if the data are put in percentage change form.

*Expenditure Priorities.*    Drawing on observations from Tables 5–13 through 5–17, we can now address the issue of expenditure priorities. Later in the chapter when we assess service conditions and needs, we will be able to determine whether the priorities are, in part, in response to these conditions and needs. Although expenditures do not inform us directly about the results of a government's activities, we can discuss the expenditure priorities in terms of what functions are receiving the most money:

—Police and fire expenditures are high-priority items and are becoming more important over time.

—Social services, judicial and corrections, and administrative expenditures are somewhat lower priority items but are becoming more important over time.

—Public works and, to a lesser extent, recreation and cultural expenditures have been high-priority items but are receiving less weight over time.

—Engineering is a low-priority expenditure and has declined in importance (although the decline in the reference group has been greater).

—Health is a low-priority expenditure and constant as a share of Dyer Straits' expenditures.

*Needs, Revenues, and Elasticities.* While functional expenditures will be useful in our examination of service conditions and needs, data on total expenditures can be used to draw some preliminary inferences about financial condition. First, total per capita expenditures in Dyer Straits are higher than those in the reference group (almost 30 percent higher in 1983) and are consistently growing more rapidly than those in the reference group. If we can view population as the simplest measure of need, Dyer Straits may be able to cut back its expenditures and still meet those needs. Of course, its actual ability to cut back expenditures is open to question.

Next, we can examine the growth in expenditures compared with the growth in revenues. As we will see in Chapter 8, this is a significant contributing factor in the organization's ability to build internal reserves. Table 5–15 indicates that per capita expenditures in Dyer Straits have grown by 51.7 percent over the 1979–83 period. During this same period, however, total revenues grew by only 48 percent, indicating a potential problem. Moreover, own source revenue in Dyer Straits, revenue from property and sales taxes and other local sources, grew only by 39 percent over the period. Because external aid accounted for a significant part of the revenue growth in Dyer Straits and because the distribution of this aid is largely out of Dyer Straits' control, this could make it vulnerable in the future.

Finally, although the comparison with the reference group is one way to assess the growth in expenditures in Dyer Straits, a second way is to compare the growth in per capita expenditures with the growth in per capita income. If expenditures are growing more rapidly than income, then an increasingly larger share of income is being devoted to government expenditures. We will define *income elasticity of expenditures* as the ratio of the percentage change in per capita expenditures to the percentage change in per capita income. In our case, since we only have data on income per family we will use it in place of per capita income and will assume that family size is relatively constant over the five years. In Chapter 4 we indicated that per family income increased by 31.1 percent over the period. With per capita expenditures growing at 51.7 percent, the expenditure elasticity is 51.7 divided by 31.1, or 1.66. Thus expenditures are growing much faster than income and, since the revenue base elasticities calculated in Chapter 4 were equal to or less than one, much faster than the revenue bases that support expenditures. This is a further sign of potential trouble. The expenditure elasticity in the reference group is 41.2 divided by 33.7, or 1.22, still greater than one but considerably less than the expenditure elasticity in Dyer Straits.

Thus expenditure growth is exceeding the growth rate in income, revenues, and revenue bases, adversely affecting Dyer Straits' financial condition. At the same time, however, if our earlier tentative conclusion that Dyer Straits' higher per capita expenditures means it may be more than meeting its expenditure needs is true, then Dyer Straits may be able to reduce its expenditures while still meeting its needs adequately. In the next two sections we undertake the difficult task of trying to determine the validity of this tentative conclusion.

## III. EXPENDITURE LEVELS AND INPUT PRICES

In section II we looked at expenditure patterns to get an approximate idea of what needs the government was attempting to meet, where it was putting its efforts, and how its priorities and efforts were changing over time. Since we looked only at expenditures, we assumed as a first approximation that expenditures were proxies for the inputs used by the government and, in turn, that these inputs were proxies for outputs and even outcomes of government activities. These assumptions allowed us to link dollar expenditures to the meeting of community needs. We now need to examine these assumptions. In this section we study the relationships between expenditures and inputs. In later sections we will examine the links to outputs and needs.

The examination of dollar levels of expenditures is an important first step in expenditure analysis, but refinements of these data are needed to provide more precise and reliable answers to our questions about financial condition from the expenditure perspective. Our first refinement will be to isolate the effects on expenditures of the levels and changes in input prices. While precise price adjustments for the government sector are often difficult if not impossible, understanding the need for price adjustments and ways to approximate price effects represents a contribution to the analysis of financial condition.

Expenditures on employees, materials and supplies, and other inputs of governments represent *levels* of physical inputs—number of person-hours, physical amounts of supplies, number of pieces of equipment, etc.—multiplied by the *prices* paid for each of these inputs. Thus different expenditure levels or changes in expenditures may reflect changes in both input levels and input prices. For example:

> Two cities with different expenditures on employees may have the same number of employees and pay them different wages, or pay the same wages to different numbers of employees, or have both different wage scales and different numbers of employees.
>
> The causes of increases in a city's expenditures on supplies over time may be the result of increases in the quantity of supplies purchased, or increases in the prices of the supplies, or increases in both the quantity and the price of the supplies.

Since expenditure data incorporate both input *levels* and *prices,* if we are using expenditure data to measure and compare the levels of inputs used in government, then we have to correct the expenditure data for price effects. If part of the differences in expenditures that we observe over time, or at one point in time across locations, is due to differences in the prices that are paid for the inputs, and if we assume that price differences, *per se,* have no effect on the outputs or outcomes produced by a unit of input, then we should try to remove these price effects to identify the effects solely from input quantities.

To sort out the price and quantity effects so that we can better understand the expenditure data presented above, we need to use price indexes. In the next part we briefly explain the structure of a price index, and then we discuss the problems encountered when estimating these price indexes for government inputs.

### The Structure of Price Indexes

Governments purchase or hire a multitude of inputs—employees performing a wide variety of tasks, supplies of all different kinds, different types of energy, a variety of equipment—and to derive a price index based on each individual input is a mammoth task. Consequently, price indexes, based on a representative sample of inputs (a "market basket") and their prices, are being developed and used as a proxy for the full range of prices paid by the particular government under study.

Before we consider the application of price indexes to governments, a few comments on the structure of a price index will be helpful.[6] The usual formula for a price index, $I$, in period $t$, based on inputs $X_1, X_2, \ldots, X_n$ and their prices, $P_1$, $P_2, \ldots, P_n$, is the following:

$$I_t = (P_{1t}X_{1b} + P_{2t}X_{2b} + \ldots + P_{nt}X_{nb}) / (P_{1b}X_{1b} + P_{2b}X_{2b} + \ldots + P_{nb}X_{nb})$$

where $b$ refers to the base year of the index. Thus $P_{1t}X_{1b}$ is the price of the first input in period $t$ times the quantity of that input used in the base period $b$, and so on. The resulting price index is an average of input prices in time $t$, "weighted" by the quantity of that input used in the base period.

This equation can be restated in a form that is easier to apply:

$$I_t = [(P_{1t}/P_{1b})P_{1b}X_{1b} + (P_{2t}/P_{2b})P_{2b}X_{2b} + \ldots$$
$$+ (P_{nt}/P_{nb})P_{nb}X_{nb}]/(P_{1b}X_{1b} + P_{2b}X_{2b} + \ldots + P_{nb}X_{nb})$$
$$= [(P_{1t}/P_{1b})E_{1b} + (P_{2t}/P_{2b})E_{2b} + \ldots + (P_{nt}/P_{nb})E_{nb}]/ (E_{1b} + E_{2b} + \ldots + E_{nb})$$
$$= [(P_{1t}/P_{1b}) (E_{1b}/E_b)] + [(P_{2t}/P_{2b}) (E_{2b}/E_b)] + \ldots + [(P_{nt}/P_{nb}) (E_{nb}/E_b)]$$

where $E_{ib}$ refers to the dollar value of expenditures on input $i$ in the base period, $P_{ib}X_{ib}$ (where $i = 1, 2, \ldots n$), and $E_b = E_{1b} + E_{2b} + \ldots + E_{nb}$ (the dollar value of expenditures in the base year on all the inputs in the index). In this form the price index in any year is the sum of the "price relatives" for each input in the index, e.g., $(P_{1t}/P_{1b})$, each weighted by the proportion of total expenditures spent on that particular input in the base year, e.g., $E_{1b}/E_b$).

To illustrate, suppose an organization hires or purchases two classes of inputs—labor and nonlabor—and in the base year (1971), expenditures on these two types of inputs are $2 million and $1 million, respectively. Now suppose that the price of labor in 1983 is 1.6 times what it was in 1971 and the price of nonlabor input is 1.5 times its 1971 price, then,

---

[6] For a more complete discussion of price indexes in general, see Edwin Mansfield, *Microeconomics, Theory and Application*, 4th ed. (New York: W. W. Norton and Co., 1982), pp. 98–105.

$$I_{1983} = [(1.6)2 + (1.5)1]/[2 + 1] = 1.57,$$

or input prices, in index form, have risen to 1.57 times their 1971 level.

While this illustrates the mechanics of calculating a price index, the actual problems of grouping expenditures and estimating the price relatives for each group are substantial.[7] Furthermore, the weights in the index from the base year may not accurately reflect the relative importance of expenditures on different inputs many years later, creating errors in the estimates of price changes. And finally, there may be quality changes in the inputs—the equipment input in the base year may be very different ten years later—that are difficult to capture.

The actual estimation of price indexes for governments has developed along two fronts. First, there have been estimates of indexes of changes in prices over time for individual governments and for groups of governments. These price indexes are aimed at measuring the inflation component in price differences. Second, over the past ten years, researchers have been estimating the differences in prices across geographical locations for inputs, particularly inputs of school districts. We will briefly review both of these next.

### Estimates of Price Indexes

The estimation of price indexes is not yet to a point where price indexes for specific governmental units are readily available for financial analysis. However, several price indexes for governments have been developed, and we can use them to illustrate and discuss the use of price indexes in financial analysis.

First, price indexes such as the consumer price index and the wholesale price index are regularly produced and widely utilized. Their validity for measuring price changes for government expenditures is questionable, however, for several reasons. For one thing, the items that compose the "market basket" for these indexes are not the same as the items that are used as inputs for governments. Moreover, these indexes are not for specific locations, but rather for the entire nation.

The first objection is met by an index produced by the Department of Commerce, called the "implicit price deflator for state and local government purchases of goods and services." This index, with a base year of 1972 (equal to 100), was at 222.9 in 1982, indicating that prices for state and local governments had increased by 122.9 percent in a decade.[8] The implicit price deflator for state and local government purchases of goods and services is constructed by using payroll data and data on full-time equivalent employees, adjusted to reflect the changing composition of the government work force. The problem still remains, however, that it is one index for the nation, and this limits its utility for financial analysis of individual governments.

---

[7] See David Greytak, Richard Gusteley, and Robert J. Dinkelmeyer, "The Effects of Inflation on Local Government Expenditures," *National Tax Journal,* 27, No. 4 (December 1974), 583–93.

[8] See U.S. Department of Commerce, *Survey of Current Business,* various issues.

When constructing a price index over time for a single government or a group of governments, there is one conceptual problem that is difficult to overcome and is often dealt with by using one or more assumptions. The problem stems from the fact that a large part of government expenditures is for labor inputs, and any increase in the price of a labor input may represent either a pure price increase (a higher price for the exact same input) or an increase in price that partially reflects the increase in quality of the input (increased productivity). With consumer goods, there are ways of measuring the input quality (grades of food, etc.) to ensure that the price increase is a pure price increase. This type of control is lacking for labor inputs, so that part of the observed price increase may represent an increase in the quality of the inputs. If the input quality does increase as a result of the price increase, then only part of the price increase is a pure price effect, and as a result, only part of the price increase should be included in the price index. The difficulty is in sorting out the quality effect from the price effect.

Note that the quality increase can occur for at least two reasons. First, the labor inputs may gain experience on the job or from additional training, on or off the job, and increase in quality as a result. Second, the price change, relative to price changes in other occupations or organizations, may influence who actually works for the government, and job turnover could potentially increase or decrease quality.

In spite of the difficulties involved, price indexes have been constructed that can serve as examples of the type of indexes that are useful in financial analysis. Norman Walzer has been developing and refining price indexes for municipalities in Illinois for over a decade.[9] Walzer recognizes the quality problem discussed above but basically assumes that for labor inputs, wage increases only include a pure price effect.[10] With this assumption, Walzer examines over forty different input categories on a department-by-department basis to develop a carefully constructed index for twenty-four Illinois municipalities.

Table 5–18 shows the municipal price index developed by Walzer for 1970 through 1976 compared with the consumer price index, the wholesale price index, and the implicit price deflator for purchases of state and local governments. Note how the different indexes vary over the period compared with one another, suggesting that the municipal price index is measuring something different from that measured by the other indexes. Walzer also estimated price indexes on a department-by-department basis, and these are shown in Table 5–19. Note again

[9] See Norman Walzer, "A Price Index for Municipal Purchases," *National Tax Journal*, 23, No. 4 (December 1970), 441–47; Walzer, "Measuring Inflation and Municipal Expenditures," *Governmental Finance*, 4, No. 3 (August 1975), 14–17; Walzer and Peter J. Stratton, "Inflation and Municipal Expenditure Increases in Illinois" (Springfield: Illinois Cities and Villages Municipal Problems Commission, October 1977); and Walzer, "1983 Municipal Price Index," *Illinois Municipal Review*, April 1984, 9–12.

[10] See Walzer and Stratton, "Inflation and Municipal Expenditure Increases," pp. 36–38. They also present arguments why the quality differences are likely to be small.

TABLE 5-18    **Alternative Price Indices (1970 = 100.0)**

| PRICE INDEX | 1970 | 1971 | 1972 | 1973 | 1974 | 1975 | 1976 |
|---|---|---|---|---|---|---|---|
| Consumer Price Index | 100.0 | 104.3 | 107.7 | 114.4 | 127.0 | 138.0 | 146.6 |
| Wholesale Price Index | 100.0 | 103.2 | 107.9 | 122.0 | 145.0 | 164.2 | 171.7 |
| Implicit Price Deflator (State and Local Gov't.) | 100.0 | 107.0 | 113.3 | 121.5 | 134.8 | 146.9 | 157.1 |
| Illinois Municipal Index | 100.0 | 106.7 | 115.3 | 121.2 | 133.3 | 142.8 | 151.1 |

SOURCE:    **Norman Walzer and Peter J. Stratton, "Inflation and Municipal Expenditure Increases in Illinois"** (Springfield: Illinois Cities and Villages Municipal Problems Commission, October 1977).

that there is considerable variation in the indexes by 1976, ranging from 136 for building and health inspections to 156.2 for streets.

A price index for New York City using a similar methodology was developed by David Greytak, Richard Gustely, and Robert J. Dinkelmeyer. To deal with the quality problem posed above, these authors used externally generated indexes for each input to identify the pure price effect.[11] Examples of the price indexes for the period 1965-72 are shown in Table 5-20. Note the differences between payroll contributions and retirement contributions and across different input types.

Although price indexes such as the ones just reviewed are useful in helping separate price increases from real expenditure growth (an example of this will be given shortly), these indexes are not designed to compare price differences across

TABLE 5-19    **Department Price Indices for Illinois Municipalities (1970 = 100.0)**

| FUNCTION | 1970 | 1971 | 1972 | 1973 | 1974 | 1975 | 1976 |
|---|---|---|---|---|---|---|---|
| Police Protection | 100.0 | 108.8 | 116.2 | 123.5 | 136.0 | 144.9 | 155.4 |
| Fire Protection | 100.0 | 104.9 | 117.2 | 124.3 | 136.4 | 144.1 | 155.5 |
| Streets | 100.0 | 106.6 | 113.7 | 119.5 | 134.4 | 149.2 | 156.2 |
| Water-Sewer | 100.0 | 105.9 | 113.2 | 117.8 | 130.3 | 141.0 | 147.0 |
| General Control | 100.0 | 106.5 | 114.2 | 119.8 | 129.8 | 140.7 | 152.0 |
| Other Sanitation | 100.0 | 105.5 | 113.2 | 120.3 | 135.8 | 145.5 | 150.3 |
| Parks & Recreation | 100.0 | 106.5 | 115.3 | 120.6 | 131.7 | 144.8 | 150.4 |
| Libraries | 100.0 | 108.6 | 117.7 | 122.0 | 133.1 | 140.2 | 143.7 |
| Building & Health Inspections | 100.0 | 106.6 | 116.1 | 119.2 | 128.3 | 133.6 | 136.0 |
| Civil Defense | 100.0 | 106.0 | 113.4 | 118.3 | 129.6 | 138.9 | 146.6 |
| Miscellaneous | 100.0 | 107.2 | 117.4 | 121.8 | 132.5 | 138.5 | 144.4 |

SOURCE:    **Normal Walzer and Peter J. Stratton, "Inflation and Municipal Expenditure Increases in Illinois"** (Springfield: Illinois Cities and Villages Municipal Problems Commission, October 1977).

---

[11] See Greytak, Gusteley, and Dinkelmeyer, "The Effects of Inflation on Local Government Expenditures."

TABLE 5-20   **Input Price Changes for New York City Government Expenditures, 1965–72\***

| INPUT | PRICE INDEX IN 1972 (1965 = 100.0) | | |
|---|---|---|---|
| | Payroll | Other | Retirement |
| *Employees Payroll and Retirement Costs* | | | |
| *(by employment category):* | | | |
| Executive | 141.8 | | 270.4 |
| Delivery | 167.1 | | 98.9 |
| Laborer | 151.6 | | 289.1 |
| Clerical | 146.6 | | 279.6 |
| Other | 158.0 | | 301.3 |
| *Non-Labor Inputs:* | | | |
| Supplies | | 117.2 | |
| Materials | | 128.2 | |
| Equipment | | 126.4 | |
| Contractual Services | | 137.3 | |

\*Composite of six departments: Police, Fire, Environmental Protection, Public Schools, Higher Education, and Social Services.
SOURCE:   David Greytak, Richard Gusteley, and Robert J. Dinkelmeyer, "The Effects of Inflation on Local Government Expenditures," *National Tax Journal*, 27, No. 4 (December 1974), 597–98.

localities. Interjurisdictional comparisons of price levels with these indexes are impossible because the indexes typically begin in a base year at a fixed point such as 100, and there is no reason to believe that prices were the same in different jurisdictions at that point in time.[12] A different research approach has been developing, however, that is designed to compare prices across governments, and although it has been limited to school districts, the methodology is applicable to all governments.

The quality problem is still present when price indexes are developed for a single point in time to compare price differences across jurisdictions. To illustrate, suppose we are comparing the salary levels of two teachers in different school districts. If all the observed salary differences are due to price differences, then an index could be constructed quite simply using a consumer price index-type methodology. The difference is not, however, likely to be solely a price difference because, even if we control for factors such as experience and education, the school district that offers a higher salary is likely to employ a teacher of higher quality. Thus the quality problem complicates the calculation of interjurisdictional price indexes.

To overcome this problem, researchers have estimated econometric models that try to isolate the price effects from the quality effects. Two different econometric techniques have been developed, one based on individual data and

---

[12] Note, however, that the price indexes developed above are suitable for comparisons of price *changes.*

TABLE 5-21    Price Index Values for Major Central Cities Across Various States

| CITY | TEACHER PRICE INDEX | STATE MINIMUM[e] | STATE MAXIMUM[e] |
|------|------|------|------|
| Albany, New York[a] | 0.970 | 0.730 | 1.220 |
| Buffalo, New York[a] | 1.020 | 0.730 | 1.220 |
| Chicago, Illinois[b] | 1.077 | 0.843 | 1.077 |
| Kansas City, Missouri[c] | 1.084 | 0.906 | 1.138 |
| Los Angeles, California[d] | 1.107 | 0.858 | 1.118 |
| New York, New York[a] | 1.130 | 0.730 | 1.220 |
| St. Louis, Missouri[c] | 1.108 | 0.906 | 1.138 |
| San Francisco, California[d] | 1.102 | 0.858 | 1.118 |

SOURCES:

[a]Data from: Wayne Wendling, "The Cost of Education Index: Measurement of Price Differences of Education Personnel among New York State School Districts" (*Working Paper No. 26*, Education Finance Center, Education Commission of the States, April 1980).

[b]Associates for Education Finance and Planning, *The Development of a Resource Cost Model Funding Base for Education Finance in Illinois* (Prepared for the Illinois State Board of Education, December 1982).

[c]Jay Chambers, "An Analysis of Education Costs Across Local School Districts in the State of Missouri, 1975–1976" (*Working Paper No. 7*, Education Finance Center, Education Commission of the States, January 1978).

[d]Jay Chambers, *Educational Cost Differentials Across School Districts in California* (Prepared for the California State Department of Education, September 1978).

[e]The state minimum (maximum) indicates the lowest (highest) value of the teacher price index in the state in which the city is located.

Table from E. Kathleen Adams, Robert Berne, and Wayne Wendling, "The Illinois Cost of Education Index" (Report to the Director, Public School Finance Project, Illinois State Board of Education, October 31, 1983).

the other based on school district data, and the reader is referred elsewhere for a detailed comparison of the two methods.[13] Table 5–21 presents selected data from individual-level price indexes, and these show that the variation in prices, in this case for teachers, can be considerable in one state at one point in time. Even if these types of price indexes are not available for financial analysis, this research at least provides an initial estimate of the magnitude of the price variation we may find in a state-level reference group.

### A Proxy for Real Inputs

The existing research on price indexes is still in its developmental stages. Moreover, a substantial effort is required to estimate a price index, either over

---

[13]For a comparison of individual- and district-level studies, see Stephen M. Barro, "Educational Price Indices: A State-of-the-Art Review" (Washington, D.C.: AUI Policy Research, March 1981). For individual-level studies, see the references in Table 5–21 and Alvin S. Rosenthal, Jay H. Moskowitz, and Stephen M. Barro, "Developing a Maryland Cost of Education Index" (Washington, D.C.: AUI Policy Research, July 1981); for district-level studies, see Rosenthal, Moskowitz, and Barro, "Developing a Maryland Cost of Education Index," and Leanna Stiefel and Robert Berne, "Price Indexes for Teachers in Michigan: A Replication and Extension," in *Selected Papers in School Finance, 1981,* ed. Esther Tron (Washington, D.C.: U.S. Department of Education, March 1981), pp. 159–211.

time or across jurisdictions. For these reasons, it is useful to ask whether there is a more readily available proxy to separate the price effects in government expenditures. While one of the readily available indexes discussed earlier could be used if a site specific index is not required, when an index for a specific government is needed, the number of employees can be used as an approximate index of real expenditures.

Recall that price indexes attempt to separate the effects of price differences from other causes of changes or differences in expenditures, such as increases in the quantity and quality of inputs. Since employees are the primary input of governments, real inputs may be assumed to change as the number of employees changes. Thus employees per unit of population (normally employees per 10,000 population) is a proxy for real expenditures per capita because a count of employees includes no price effects. Using this approach, if total dollar expenditures triple over a given period while the number of employees only doubles, we can assume that one-third of the increase in dollar expenditures is due to price increases, and two-thirds represents the increase in real inputs.

An advantage of using employees per capita as a measure of real expenditures per capita is that, compared with price indexes, data on employees are usually available and simple to compile. Moreover, employees per unit of population can be compared across time and across jurisdictions. There are, however, several significant disadvantages as well. First, employee inputs represent only a portion of all inputs of governments. For example, Table 5-4 indicated that in 1982–83, direct expenditures for salaries and wages at the local level were about 56 percent of direct expenditures for current operations. Thus other inputs (44 percent) are not included in the personnel category. Second, there are various types of employees, and simply adding them up is only a rough approximation of their ability to contribute as inputs to the production process of the government. And third, even if it is legitimate to add up the numbers of employees, the quality differences among the employees that are bound to exist over time and between governments are totally ignored. Only when additional research is carried out that compares price indexes with employees per capita will we be able to know the reliability of this proxy measure of real inputs.[14]

### An Application

Despite the limited availability of price indexes, it is useful to see how they might be incorporated into financial analysis. To show this, we return to our city of Dyer Straits. Suppose that Dyer Straits commissioned the construction of price indexes for major objects of expenditures and major functions between 1979 and 1983, like the Illinois municipalities in Walzer's research. These appear in Table 5-22. How can these indexes be used in expenditure analysis?

---

[14] For an example of the use of real inputs in an empirical financial condition study, see Touche Ross and First National Bank, *Urban Fiscal Stress.*

TABLE 5-22  Price Effects on Expenditures, City of Dyer Straits, 1979-83

| | DOLLAR EXPENDITURES IN INDEX NUMBER FORM* | | PRICE INDEX | | "REAL" EXPENDITURES IN INDEX NUMBER FORM† | | PER CAPITA EXPENDITURES IN "REAL DOLLARS"‡ | | % Change |
|---|---|---|---|---|---|---|---|---|---|
| | 1979 | 1983 | 1979 | 1983 | 1979 | 1983 | 1979 | 1983 | |
| *Objects of Expenditure:* | | | | | | | | | |
| Personal services | | | | | | | | | |
| Salaries | 100.0 | 154.3 | 100.0 | 142.1 | 100.0 | 108.6 | 107.30 | 120.16 | 12.0 |
| Fringe benefits | 100.0 | 154.6 | 100.0 | 143.7 | 100.0 | 107.6 | 35.97 | 39.90 | 10.9 |
| Materials and supplies | 100.0 | 114.8 | 100.0 | 121.5 | 100.0 | 94.5 | 21.01 | 20.45 | (2.7) |
| Contractual services | 100.0 | 145.9 | 100.0 | 147.3 | 100.0 | 99.0 | 13.99 | 14.27 | 2.0 |
| *Major Functional Expenditures:* | | | | | | | | | |
| Police | 100.0 | 156.1 | 100.0 | 144.1 | 100.0 | 108.3 | 32.93 | 36.79 | 11.7 |
| Fire | 100.0 | 156.7 | 100.0 | 145.2 | 100.0 | 107.9 | 31.10 | 36.79 | 11.3 |
| Public works | 100.0 | 121.8 | 100.0 | 130.8 | 100.0 | 93.1 | 22.35 | 21.45 | (4.0) |
| Judicial and corrections | 100.0 | 157.3 | 100.0 | 137.2 | 100.0 | 114.7 | 8.54 | 10.10 | 18.3 |
| Recreational and cultural | 100.0 | 139.4 | 100.0 | 138.5 | 100.0 | 100.6 | 11.80 | 12.24 | 3.7 |
| Social services | 100.0 | 164.2 | 100.0 | 135.3 | 100.0 | 121.4 | 10.37 | 12.97 | 25.1 |
| Health | 100.0 | 148.5 | 100.0 | 151.0 | 100.0 | 98.3 | 1.00 | 1.02 | 2.0 |
| Engineering | 100.0 | 112.4 | 100.0 | 137.8 | 100.0 | 81.6 | 6.11 | 5.14 | (15.9) |
| Administration | 100.0 | 159.8 | 100.0 | 139.1 | 100.0 | 114.9 | 16.27 | 19.27 | 18.4 |
| Total Expenditures | 100.0 | 147.1 | 100.0 | 140.8 | 100.0 | 104.5 | 203.19 | 218.87 | 7.7 |

*Developed from Tables 5-9 and 5-13.

†Dollar expenditures ÷ price index.

‡Per capita dollar expenditures (from Tables 5-10 and 5-14) ÷ price index.

We begin by applying the price indexes to "deflate" the dollar expenditures between 1979 and 1983 for each expenditure category to indicate what the expenditures would have been if all input prices had remained constant over this period. For example, total expenditures on police were $1.083 million in 1979 and $1.691 million in 1983 (from Table 5-13) for an increase in dollar outlays of 56.1 percent over this period (see Table 5-22). To estimate the change in "real" expenditures—the amount that actually went to increase the levels of physical inputs and not for higher prices for the same inputs—we divide dollar expenditures by the price index. Thus real expenditures for police are $1.083 million in 1979 and $1.173 million in 1983 ($1.691 million divided by 1.441), or an increase of only 8.3 percent for the 1979–83 period. This real expenditure increase was only 18.8 percent of the dollar expenditure increase (8.3 divided by .441) over the period. In per capita terms, using 1979 as the base year, real expenditures for police rose from $32.93 to $36.79, or 11.7 percent from 1979 to 1983. Most of the increase in dollar expenditures was due to price effects and not increases in the inputs devoted to police services.

The price index thus allows us to separate the effects on expenditures of price changes from input quantity and quality changes, with only the latter two influencing the production of goods and services by Dyer Straits. These price adjustments can be used to put the earlier data in a clearer perspective:

- Expenditures for *salaries and fringe benefits,* which increased more than 50 percent between 1979 and 1983, resulted largely from increases in salary and fringe levels and not increases in the quantity and quality of inputs (e.g., the number employed). Real expenditures on personal services increased only about 8 percent during the period.
- *Material and supply* expenditures actually dropped in real terms between 1979 and 1983 (fewer materials and supplies purchased) because prices rose faster than actual dollar expenditures. And this occurred with only a moderate increase in material and supply prices compared with other expenditure categories.
- The increase in dollar expenditures for *contractual services* was due to price increases, not increases in services, as the level of total real expenditures on contractual services dropped slightly.
- The increase in *police* and *fire* expenditures was due largely to increases in prices; the increase in real per capita police and fire expenditures from 1979 to 1983 was between 11 and 12 percent.
- Increases in dollar expenditures on *public works, recreational and cultural,* and *health* were essentially all due to changes in the prices paid for personal services, materials and supplies, and contractual services for these functions, and not to an increase in the inputs. The city actually made considerably less use of *engineering* in real per capita terms even though dollar expenditures were growing; the price index grew faster than dollar expenditures.
- *Social services, judicial and corrections,* and *administrative* expenditures represented very substantial increases in real per capita terms compared with other functions even though they faced price increases for the inputs they used.

Knowledge of price changes and their differences across objects of expenditures and functional areas can reveal a great deal about a government's actual priorities. Dyer Straits' expenditure increases were strongly influenced by price changes. Only a few functions expanded their use of inputs over the five-year period. With the effects of the price changes removed, the actual patterns of government priorities in providing different functions become much clearer.

Besides the direct use of price indexes, we can also use the number of employees to estimate price effects. Although we do not go into the detail provided for price-adjusted expenditures, Table 5–23 shows the total employees and employees per 10,000 population in Dyer Straits and the reference group, along with average salary information. While only an example, this table supports the findings from the use of the price index. For example, Table 5–10 indicated that per capita dollar expenditures increased by 52 percent in Dyer Straits over the five-year period. Table 5–23 indicates, however, that employees per 10,000 population increased by 21 percent over the period. This figure is closer to the 7.7 percent increase in real per capita expenditures derived with the price adjustment than it is to the increase in dollar expenditures.

The data on employees per capita can also be used to compare the ''real'' expenditures in Dyer Straits with those in the reference group. Table 5–10 indicated that per capita expenditures were 29.5 percent higher in Dyer Straits than in the reference group in 1983. Since employees per 10,000 population, a proxy for real expenditures per capita, is only 20.7 percent higher in Dyer Straits compared with the reference group in the same year, part, but not all, of the difference in expenditures can be explained by interjurisdictional price differences. Thus the levels of goods and services delivered by Dyer Straits may not be as high relative to the reference group as the dollar-expenditure-per-capita figures would lead us to believe. Furthermore, when we combine the findings from employees and price indexes, this suggests that over the five years real inputs per capita have only increased in the 7 to 21 percent range, much lower than the 50 percent increase indicated without considering price increases.

This analysis sheds some additional light on the financial condition of Dyer Straits. The growth in dollar expenditures may be a source of financial pressure on Dyer Straits, and if this pressure stems primarily from price changes and not expanding inputs, the increase in financial pressure may not be accompanied by increased services to the community. This suggests that the city may be increasing its financial obligations without fulfilling its social obligations to community and clientele groups that need more services. While the identification of price effects can help reveal these sorts of problems, until we address the needs of a community directly we will only be seeing part of the picture.

## IV. OUTPUTS: PRODUCTION AND EFFICIENCY

In the preceding section we discussed how to use input prices to evaluate the real, physical inputs or resources used by government. We now look at how inputs are combined through a production process to provide government outputs, and how

TABLE 5-23  City Employees and Salaries for Dyer Straits and Reference Group, 1979–83

| | DYER STRAITS | | | | | REFERENCE GROUP | | | | | LOCATION QUOTIENTS* | | | | |
|---|---|---|---|---|---|---|---|---|---|---|---|---|---|---|---|
| | 1979 | 1980 | 1981 | 1982 | 1983 | 1979 | 1980 | 1981 | 1982 | 1983 | 1979 | 1980 | 1981 | 1982 | 1983 |
| Total salaries ($ millions) | 3.529 | 3.855 | 4.216 | 4.724 | 5.447 | 133.53 | 145.81 | 156.85 | 174.31 | 190.41 | .0264 | .0264 | .0269 | .0271 | .0286 |
| Average salary per employee ($) | 11,640 | 12,441 | 13,245 | 14,238 | 15,450 | 10,352 | 11,210 | 11,961 | 12,927 | 13,880 | 1.124 | 1.110 | 1.107 | 1.101 | 1.113 |
| Total city employees | 303 | 310 | 318 | 332 | 353 | 12,887 | 13,007 | 13,113 | 13,484 | 13,718 | .0235 | .0238 | .0243 | .0246 | .0257 |
| City employees per 10,000 population | 92 | 95 | 98 | 103 | 111 | 85 | 86 | 87 | 90 | 92 | 1.082 | 1.105 | 1.126 | 1.144 | 1.207 |

*Dyer Straits/Reference Group

the efficiency of converting inputs into outputs can affect expenditure pressure and ultimately the financial condition of government.

Government efficiency is difficult to measure, especially at the aggregate level. In those cases, however, where we can identify the extent to which outputs are being produced efficiently from given inputs (technical efficiency) or at a given cost (cost efficiency), then we may be in a position to judge whether a government can increase its efficiency and reduce expenditure pressures in the process.

However, as in other parts of expenditure analysis, conceptual development and data availability may be such that for most government financial analyses, the methods we present in this section may not all be applicable at the current time. But we believe that the current financial pressures on governments will encourage the additional conceptual development and increased data availability required to carry out expenditure analysis along the lines suggested in this section.

### Measuring Outputs

We begin our examination of input-output relationships and efficiency by discussing some of the problems that surround output measurement for governments, where outputs are the specific products, or goods and services, produced and distributed by governments. Our concern here is the definition and availability of *output data* and how they can be used as part of expenditure analysis.

As we have seen, government outputs are the specific goods and services produced by activities that combine and utilize various inputs. Properly defined, outputs can be measured in terms of the number of units of specified quality characteristics provided per unit of time.[15] Goods, such as the supply of water, are relatively easy to quantify; most services, such as police protection and education, however, are more difficult to put in quantitative terms. For example, in a field such as mental health, even though the number of visits can be measured, the differences in patient treatments are difficult to quantify.

These problems of measurement have limited the success of widescale use of an output orientation in public expenditure analysis. As Werner Hirsch writes:

> Attempts at identifying output units and valuing them in terms of quality characteristics have proved most successful in cases where there are few externalities, and where basic service units can be defined and quantified; where relatively few important quality dimensions exist and where to some extent these services are devoid of vertical integration (control of a series of steps in the production and supply of the service). Refuse collection and water services are such examples.[16]

For the purposes of aggregate expenditure analysis, where we normally do not have access to reliable expenditure data below the department level, the measure-

---

[15] See Werner Hirsch, *The Economics of State and Local Government* (New York: McGraw-Hill, 1970), p. 148.

[16] See Werner Hirsch, *Urban Economic Analysis* (New York: McGraw-Hill, 1973), p. 316.

ment problems are even more difficult. Even at the department level, a variety of outputs are produced which may or may not be similar. Consequently, in many cases it may be impossible to develop a single departmental output measure.

If the organization has performance or program budgets or produces output data on a regular basis, we may be able to use this information for our analysis.[17] If we are to link inputs and outputs in a way that is representative of the actual production process, we will need output measures (or proxies for outputs) at the function or department level. Without reliable output measures (the more typical case), we are forced in expenditure analysis to rely on input and expenditure data alone, or to use very approximate relationships between expenditures, production and service conditions, and community and clientele needs. (See section V below.)

### Technical and Cost Efficiency

The relationship between inputs and outputs is commonly depicted in the form of a "production function," written symbolically as

$$Q = f(I, S)$$

where $Q$ is the maximum quantity of output of given quality attainable per unit of time from given inputs, $I$ represents the quantities of various resource inputs used, and $S$ represents the production and service conditions affecting input requirements.[18] In this production function, $Q$ is the *maximum* level of output attainable with a given level of inputs. For a particular local government, how much of a specific good or service results from the employment of physical inputs depends on the technology used by the organization and the conditions faced by that organization that facilitate or complicate the production and distribution of that good or service (production and service conditions). The government that produces the maximum output, given these production and service conditions, is *technically efficient*. A government that is far from technical efficiency could presumably reduce expenditure pressures by producing more efficiently, getting more outputs from its current input levels.

If we could develop and estimate production functions for all the goods and services produced by governments, we would be able to use these functions to evaluate the efficiency of specific governments. Unfortunately, relatively few em-

---

[17] For an example of a report that produces output data on a regular basis, see New York City's *Mayor's Management Report,* various years.

[18] See Georges Vernez, "Delivery of Urban Public Services: Production, Cost and Demand Functions, and Determinants of Public Expenditures for Fire, Police and Sanitation Services" (Santa Monica, Calif.: Rand Corporation, September 1976), Paper Series P-5659; Werner Hirsch, "Cost Functions of an Urban Government Service: Refuse Collection," *Review of Economics and Statistics,* 54 (November 1972), 431–38; and Arora Mehar, "Survey of Literature Regarding Production Functions of Education and the Applications Specially in Education," *Socio-Economic Planning Sciences,* 6 (December 1972), pp. 507–22.

pirical production functions have been estimated for government services, and most of these suffer from major statistical and measurement problems.[19] More attention has been given to estimating education production functions, but these are also subject to criticism.[20] Regardless of the validity of these studies, most are not of the form and level of aggregation that would enable them to be used to incorporate technical efficiency into financial analysis.

The question, then, is, are there ways to employ the concept of technical efficiency in financial analysis without exact knowledge of production functions? If we examine one government over time, and assume that the service conditions and production technology remain relatively constant, then changes in the ratio of a major output to a major input may approximate changes in technical efficiency. For example, changes in the ratio of cubic feet of solid waste collected to the number of public employees in a sanitation department may approximate changes in technical efficiency—output per employee—over a period of several years. A worsening of technical efficiency over time indicates that there may be an opportunity to ease expenditure pressures if the trend in technical efficiency can be reversed.

It is also possible to compute output to input ratios for a set of governments at one point in time to suggest the relative efficiency of different organizations.[21] Comparability in terms of services performed, output quality, financial data, and organization structure is likely to be less when more than one city is examined, and therefore the data must be interpreted carefully. If the comparisons are appropriate, intercity analyses may point out areas where technical efficiency can be increased and, as a result, expenditure pressures reduced.

Besides technical efficiency, a second type of efficiency, commonly labeled *cost efficiency,* can be utilized in expenditure analysis. While technical efficiency compares outputs with inputs, cost efficiency relates the dollar value of inputs to the physical level of outputs. These are average costs of producing outputs.[22]

---

[19] See Vernez, "Delivery of Urban Public Services."

[20] See Mehar, "Survey of Literature Regarding Production Functions"; Vernez, "Delivery of Urban Public Services"; Lawrence J. Lau, "Educational Production Functions," in *Economic Dimensions of Education* (Washington, D.C.: National Academy of Education, May 1979); and Eric A. Hanushek, "A Reader's Guide to Educational Production Functions" (Paper prepared for NIE Conference of School Organization and Effects, January 1978).

[21] See Frank Levy, Arnold Meltsner, and Aaron Wildavsky, *Urban Outcomes* (Berkeley: University of California Press, 1975), p. 177, who use measures such as books circulated per staff member in comparing different library systems.

[22] Cost functions may also reveal the impacts on average costs of different external factors. For example, one production and service condition that has been extensively examined through cost functions is the size of government itself, measured in population. William Fox, "Size Economies in Government Services: A Review," U.S. Department of Agriculture, Economics Statistics and Cooperative Services, Rural Development Research Report No. 22, August 1980, reviewed around eighty cost function studies for local government and found that average costs decrease with size (economies of scale) to some degree for education, fire protection, police services, refuse collection, roads and highways, and water and sewer utilities. The size of population providing minimum average costs, however, varied across functional areas, and there was some evidence of diseconomies of scale beyond a certain population level.

To understand cost efficiency, we need to understand the relationships between costs and output. Cost functions relate input *costs* (the dollar value of inputs, not the physical levels of inputs) to output levels and other factors and can provide the basis for developing estimates of cost efficiency, or costs per unit of output. Cost functions take the following general form:

$$\text{ATC} = f(Q, I, S, P),$$

where ATC is the average total cost of output (total cost divided by output level), $Q$, $I$, and $S$ are the quantity of output, input levels, and production and service conditions as discussed earlier, and $P$ represents the prices for the different resource inputs used.[23] Thus cost functions represent the relationship between the average costs of providing a government service or product and the level of that service, various service conditions, and input levels and prices.

If cost functions for different government goods or services were available, we could use them to determine how cost efficient a particular government is in producing a particular output. By plugging actual values of $I$, $S$, $P$, and $Q$ into the equation, we could estimate what the average cost should be and compare it with what it actually is. Needless to say, the estimation of cost efficiency is nowhere near this point. Some cost functions have been developed, but they cannot be used directly for financial analysis.[24]

Due to the paucity of cost function studies, the difficulties of measurement (of costs, outputs, etc.), and the level of aggregation of readily available data, it is necessary to use more approximate methods to incorporate the notion of cost efficiency into expenditure analysis. If data are available, one approach is to examine the costs for particular functions for one government over time. Anytime costs per unit of output are reduced, expenditure pressures will be reduced.

If we can correct a government's expenditure data for changes in input prices as we discussed in the preceding section, the ratio of "real" expenditures for a particular service to a measure of output for that service may be instructive. Assuming production and service conditions remain constant, a decline in real costs per unit of output suggests improvements in production technology and/or increases in the productivity of the inputs used that have more than compensated for increases in the prices for different inputs. This reduction in real unit costs reduces expenditure pressures because lower expenditures are necessary to meet a given level of need.

Consider, for example, the information in Table 5-24. Using *dollar* costs (actually expenditures in place of costs in this example), the average cost per unit of output rose from $100 ($10,000 divided by 100 units) to $114 ($20,000 divided by 175 units), suggesting a decrease in cost efficiency. This, however, is an incor-

---

[23] See Hirsch, *Urban Economic Analysis;* and Vernez, "Delivery of Urban Public Services."

[24] According to Vernez, however, "few bona fide empirical estimates of cost functions for urban public service have been attempted. Most attempts have been for services having outputs that are relatively easy to identify and measure, such as for hospitals and water and electricity services." See Vernez, "Delivery of Urban Public Services," p. 123.

TABLE 5-24    **Changes in Costs and Output for a Government Department**

| YEAR | DOLLAR EX-PENDITURES FOR DEPART-MENT | REAL (PRICE-ADJUSTED) EXPENDI-TURES FOR DEPARTMENT | INDEX OF OUTPUT FOR DEPARTMENT | AVERAGE DOLLAR EX-PENDITURES PER UNIT OF OUTPUT FOR DEPARTMENT | AVERAGE REAL EX-PENDITURES PER UNIT OF OUTPUT FOR DEPARTMENT |
|------|------|------|------|------|------|
| 1973 | $10,000 | $10,000 | 100 units | $100 | $100 |
| 1983 | $20,000 | $15,000 | 175 units | $114 | $86 |

rect interpretation, since it fails to correct for input price increases.[25] Using a price index to yield real expenditures, we find average costs per unit of output have fallen from $100 to $86 over the ten-year period, indicating an increase in cost efficiency that should reduce expenditure pressure, all else being equal.

Comparisons of unit costs across governments at a single point in time avoid the inflation problem but still require some stringent conditions to allow reasonable interpretations. To be an appropriate estimate of relative cost efficiency, the production and service conditions, technology, and input prices have to be similar across the organizations. Only then does this comparison tell us anything about the relative cost efficiency of the functional area under study.[26] As was the case for technical efficiency, when comparing cost efficiency both over time and across different governments, external factors may cause changes that are beyond the government's control. Regardless of the cause, however, decreases in per unit costs will decrease expenditure pressure.

Our review of production and cost relationships suggests that *if we can develop output measures* at the function or department level, then we may be able to develop useful approximations to efficiency measures by calculating (1) the output level divided by the level of the major input involved in producing that output and (2) the average "real" expenditures per unit of output. This type of analysis assumes that the expenditures and the inputs associated with each output can be identified and measured. Moreover, efficiency comparisons of this sort build in the assumption that we have controlled for changes or differences in production and service conditions.[27]

While it is important to understand the relationship of technical and cost ef-

---

[25] Either input costs have to be deflated (the price effect removed from input expenditures) or the output units have to be put in dollar terms (to reflect their growth in dollar values as other commodities rise in price).

[26] For cost comparisons between Oakland and other California cities, see Frank Levy, Meltsner, and Wildavsky, *Urban Outcomes.*

[27] *If we cannot develop output measures,* then we can still gain useful information about expenditures by comparing input levels, expenditures, and measures of production and service conditions faced by a reference group of similar governments. We illustrate this approach in the next section.

ficiency to expenditure pressures and financial condition, it is unlikely that governmental efficiency can be directly measured. If we are performing a financial analysis of a specific government, the chances of knowing the production or cost functions for that organization are very slim, as is the likelihood of having the data needed to apply them. The best we can hope for is probably information on the number and types of employees by department or function, expenditures on employees and other inputs by department or function (corrected, it is hoped, for input price changes), and possibly some proxy measures for major activities or outputs that may be associated with these inputs and expenditures. At best, we may be able to examine a few output-input ratios or real expenditures per unit of output over time to get a rough idea of whether technical or cost efficiency is high or low, or rising or falling, and come to very approximate or qualified conclusions. With all these measurement difficulties for individual governments, comparisons across organizations may not be possible or appropriate.

Because of these measurement difficulties, we need to move on to methods that may theoretically be less precise but lend themselves more readily to aggregate expenditure analysis. These are methods that measure governmental efficiency indirectly and do not require the specification and measurement of outputs, the most difficult problem faced in directly estimating technical and cost efficiency. We turn to these methods in the next two sections.

## V. PRODUCTION AND SERVICE CONDITIONS

In section III we showed why, all else being equal, a government that faces higher input prices, either over time or compared with a reference group, will have greater expenditure pressures. In the preceding section we studied how, when government outputs are known, we can estimate the impacts of technical and cost inefficiencies on expenditure pressure. We now consider additional factors that create expenditure pressures on governments which can be studied without data on outputs.

First, as discussed above, every government produces outputs from a set of inputs, and this input-output process is governed by a production process in which the inputs are combined and are used to produce outputs. If there are factors that cause the government to use more inputs or more costly inputs to produce outputs, either over time or compared with a reference group, then, all else being equal, expenditure pressures will be greater. These factors that affect the input-output process are the *production and service conditions,* mentioned in section IV but treated as fixed in studying efficiency.

Second, because of the characteristics of the clientele or community, governments may have to produce different levels of outputs to meet the needs of those affected by the government's output. Governments that must produce more outputs because of these characteristics, all else being equal, face greater expenditure pressures. We refer to the characteristics that affect the level of outputs as *community and clientele needs.*

In some cases it may be possible to separate production and service conditions from needs. Take snow removal as an example. If community A is hilly and windy and community B is flat and calm, then for every inch of snow that falls and must be removed, community A will have to use more inputs because of the difficulty of removing snow on hills and the problems caused by drifting snow. This is an example of production and service conditions increasing expenditure pressures on community A. If, however, community B receives more inches of snow that must be removed, then this greater *need* to remove snow increases the expenditure pressures on community B. In this example the distinction between production and service conditions on the one hand and needs on the other is straightforward.

In other cases the separation is not that simple. Consider the example of housing inspections. An older housing stock in one community compared with another may cause that community to use more inputs for each inspection (because of the complicated nature of the potential problems) and to carry out more inspections per capita or per square foot (because of the higher incidence of the problems). In this case one factor, an older housing stock, is both a production and service condition and a need, and a distinction between the two is not possible.

Although there are problems in separating production and service conditions from needs, we examine them separately with the knowledge that the distinction between them may sometimes be somewhat artificial.

### Production and Service Conditions

Our concern here is how production and service conditions can be combined with expenditure data to analyze the expenditure pressures on governments, without any data on government outputs, production, or cost functions. In section VI we examine the role of community and clientele needs in financial analysis under similar data restrictions.

The specific factors affecting the production and service conditions of governments have received attention in empirical studies of government expenditures. In these studies, population size is often included to measure the effect of size or scale (and associated technology) on production, and population density is included to measure the effect of clientele location on delivery conditions. The distribution of population within and outside the jurisdiction may also affect service requirements. More specific factors such as population growth rates, housing density and conditions, intensity of housing use, number of employees per manufacturing establishment, or weather conditions may affect production and delivery conditions for particular types of governmental functions.[28]

---

[28] See, for example, John Weicher, "Determinants of Central City Expenditures: Some Overlooked Factors and Problems," *National Tax Journal,* 23, No. 4 (December 1970), 379–96; and the reviews of the literature in Vernez, "Delivery of Urban Public Service."

For example, George Pidot combined population density, population growth rate, and age of housing into an index of "metropolitanism" that he found to be an important determinant of government expenditures. This index captures some of the factors that influence production and service conditions.[29] In a different study, Edward Gramlich examined the factors that explained government expenditures in order to see if the high levels of expenditures in New York City could be accounted for by adjusting for factors such as production and service conditions. Among other variables, Gramlich included population, population density, city-county structure, and regional variables that contain elements of production and service conditions.[30]

As the measurement of these factors improves, we can develop indexes of production and service conditions faced by governments and use them to help answer such questions as how do the production and service conditions compare with other governments? And are the real expenditures of this government high or low when compared with the real expenditures of other organizations facing similar production and service conditions? All else being equal, production and service conditions that require higher government expenditures will increase the expenditure pressures on that government. A government with more severe production and service conditions will have to spend more to provide the same outputs.[31]

At the same time, higher expenditures *not* due to production and service conditions may offer opportunities for that government to reduce expenditure pressures. If a particular government is spending significantly more than other governments facing similar production and service conditions, we would expect that government was providing more outputs to its clientele, thus reducing the pressure to spend more. We should try to look for evidence that this is actually occurring. If it is not producing more, then relative inefficiency in production and distribution by the government may be the explanation. In this case, increases in efficiency reduce expenditure pressure. We illustrate this approach below.

### An Application

Returning to the Dyer Straits example, we can ask whether Dyer Straits' expenditures appear to be in line with the conditions Dyer Straits faces in producing and delivering services and goods when compared with cities in the reference group. When compared with cities facing similar production and service conditions, are Dyer Straits' expenditures exceptionally high or low? If so, can we ex-

---

[29]George B. Pidot, Jr., "A Principal Components Analysis of the Determinants of Local Government Fiscal Patterns," *Review of Economics and Statistics,* 51 (May 1969), 176–88.

[30]See Gramlich, "New York City Fiscal Crisis."

[31]For examples of the incorporation of production and service conditions into empirical financial condition studies, see Katherine L. Bradbury, Helen F. Ladd, Mark Perrault, Andrew Reschovsky, and John Yinger, "State Aid to Offset Fiscal Disparities across Communities," *National Tax Journal,* 37, No. 2 (June 1984), 151–70; and Katherine L. Bradbury, "Structural Fiscal Distress in Cities—Causes and Consequences."

TABLE 5-25    **Expenditure and Production and Service Conditions, City of Dyer Straits and Reference Group, 1983**

| | INDEX OF PRO-DUCTION AND SERVICE CONDI-TIONS* | PER CAPITA EXPENDITURES | |
| --- | --- | --- | --- |
| | | Dollar† | Real‡ |
| Average for 10 cities with highest index | .466 | 294.5 | 210.4 |
| Average for all cities | .217 | 238.0 | 172.5 |
| Average for 10 cities with lowest index | .103 | 155.4 | 115.1 |
| *Dyer Straits* | *.250* | *308.2* | *218.9* |

*Index is a composite of land area, population density, and housing density. Each variable is normalized by the formula $(X_i - X_{min})/X_{max} - X_{min})$, where $X_i$ is the value for city $i$ and $X_{min}$ and $X_{max}$ are the minimum and maximum for all cities in the reference group. The index is the sum of the normalized values for all three variables divided by 3. This methodology is used by Richard P. Nathan and Charles Adams, "Understanding Central City Hardship," *Political Science Quarterly*, 91, No. 1, (Spring 1976), 47–62.

†From Table 5–10 and other reference group data not presented.

‡From Table 5–22 and data not previously presented. The price index combines intertemporal and intercity differences, with Dyer Straits' index equaling 100 in 1979.

plain the differences? And, finally, do the explanations offer possibilities for reducing expenditure pressure?

To illustrate this approach, Table 5-25 compares per capita expenditures for Dyer Straits and its reference group along with information on the production and service conditions faced by these cities. Using an index of three factors (land area, population density, and housing density), which are often considered important environmental factors that affect the production and delivery of government services, Table 5-25 shows that per capita expenditures for reference group cities tend to be higher for cities facing more demanding production and service conditions (higher indexes). Dyer Straits, however, with production and service conditions only slightly more demanding than the average conditions faced by the reference group, has per capita expenditures that are higher than the average for the ten reference group cities with the highest production and service indexes, even when corrected for input price differences. What are the possible explanations for these higher than expected per capita expenditures?

There are many possible explanations: The index does not capture important factors that make the production and delivery of services more difficult in Dyer Straits than in the reference group; Dyer Straits has more abundant resources than other cities, resulting in fewer financial constraints on its expenditures; Dyer Straits has greater needs for government goods and services, and this generates increased expenditures; and finally, Dyer Straits is just plain inefficient in using its resources. An alternative explanation, that of higher input costs, has already been treated through the use of "real" per capita expenditures in Table 5-25.

Assuming the production and service index is satisfactory (a fuller analysis would employ a more complex index than we have used for illustrative purposes),[32] and the different costs of inputs have been accounted for through the use of real expenditures, we come down to a different resource base, varying needs, and inefficiencies as remaining explanations. Based on our analysis in Chapter 4, it is unlikely that Dyer Straits' higher spending is due to abundant resources, so that explanation is ruled out. We will examine needs in the next section, but if we assume for now that needs are not exceptionally high relative to those of other cities, then the needs explanation is ruled out. This then suggests that the findings shown in Table 5–25 may best be explained by technical and/or cost inefficiencies. Dyer Straits' very high per capita expenditures appear to be the result of using more resources than necessary to provide goods and services, given the production and service conditions it faces and the other factors we have discussed.

If this analysis and its underlying assumptions are correct, Dyer Straits may have the potential to improve its financial condition from the expenditure perspective by improving its technical and/or cost efficiency, where apparently there is some slack. This is a long way around to test for inefficiencies and identify ways to improve financial condition, but in the absence of reliable data on outputs, it may be the only way to conduct this aggregate analysis.

We mentioned differences in needs as another factor in expenditure analysis. We now turn to this factor.

## VI. COMMUNITY AND CLIENTELE NEEDS

Although we have covered expenditure levels and priorities, real expenditures and inputs, technical and cost efficiency, and production and service conditions, we have not examined how all these steps are related to meeting the needs of those served by the government. This is the important and difficult final link of expenditures to community and clientele needs. To be complete, an analysis of governmental expenditures should include an understanding of *why* the organization exists—why the expenditures made by a particular government are needed by the community or clientele it serves—and *how* expenditures ultimately do or do not satisfy these needs.

The connection between the satisfaction of community or clientele needs and the spending of money by governments, however, is long and complex. "Needs" are hard to define and measure; which needs should be met by the government, rather than some other level of government or the private sector, may not be clear; even when a certain need may be met by a government, the types of goods and services to provide to meet this need may be difficult to determine; the government then has to decide how to produce and distribute its goods

---

[32] For example, see the indexes developed by Pidot, "Principal Components Analysis of the Determinants of Local Government Fiscal Patterns."

and services and what resources (inputs) are needed; and finally, the level and types of expenditures must be set.

Besides being long and complex, the connection between needs and expenditures runs both ways and is probably best viewed as a simultaneous process. We have just described needs as leading to outputs that require inputs and ultimately government expenditures. In earlier sections of this chapter we implied a process that proceeds from expenditures to inputs to outputs and, finally, to the satisfaction of needs. Whichever way we proceed, the important point is that all the components are, or should be, connected and the process viewed in its entirety.

The purpose of this section is to complete our examination of these connections and to ask how an understanding of community or clientele needs can be used in expenditure analysis. We first discuss the problems and possibilities for developing measures of needs that can be used in our analysis. We then discuss how these need measures can be related to expenditures to gain insight into financial condition from the expenditure perspective.

### Identifying and Measuring Needs

There are a variety of ways, none totally successful, to identify and measure the broad range of social and economic needs of those groups actually or potentially served by governments. We discuss several of these approaches to better understand the full nature and breadth of the needs of these groups and to provide a basis for needs measurement that can be used for an aggregate expenditure analysis.

Needs are not static. They change continually in response to a variety of forces, both within and outside the control of a particular government. Changes in macroeconomic conditions, institutional arrangements, activities of other organizations, individual life styles and values, all affect the nature and intensity of community and clientele needs. This dynamic and multidimensional character of needs means that any single set of measures is bound to be limited in its use.

The degree to which needs actually receive attention from governments is, of course, an important issue. We try to present methods to measure what we believe "should" represent the focus of government activities, and this must be based to some degree on value judgments. Ultimately, the decisions of governments are made through a complex political process, and this analysis can be viewed as one way of assessing that process.

**Demand and Expenditure Models.**    The entire concept of "needs" is vague and illusory. Economists frequently argue that individual utility functions reflect individual "needs" and reveal themselves in the demand for goods and services in markets. Thus markets, and the resulting prices and quantities of marketable goods and services, are supposedly instruments to measure individual needs (among other things) aggregated to the market level.

However, demand functions, which relate quantities demanded of particular goods or services to their prices and other factors, are not independent of institutional forces, such as advertising or government regulation, which shape needs. They also depend on the "ability to pay" of individuals, which reflects the existing distribution of income. If ability to pay is very low for those with the greatest needs, market demand may not measure important needs in a community. Consequently, demand functions, even when markets exist for private goods and services, are not always a reliable method to arrive at estimates of the "needs" of individuals and groups.

The use of demand functions to identify needs is even more difficult in the public sector. Governments frequently provide goods and services where markets do not exist and where, if markets did exist, they might not provide prices that reflect the "true" value people place on these goods because of the "free rider" effect (see Chapter 4). Moreover, the question of estimating group or collective needs, introducing interpersonal comparisons of different distributions of income, health, well-being, and so forth, makes demand functions a less than perfect means of estimating the full range of community needs.

Although imperfect, demand studies, or studies incorporating demand considerations, can still help us identify some of the main types of needs, or proxies for needs, that influence expenditures. Demand functions relate the quantity of a particular good or service demanded to its price, the prices of other products that complement or substitute for this good or service, income or ability to pay, and other factors that are often labeled as "tastes."[33] For our purposes, we are interested in what demand studies tell us about the role of consumer "tastes," which are the economists' proxy for needs; the other factors in demand functions have been considered, at least partially, in our earlier discussions of revenues and costs.

Our first problem is that there have not been that many studies conducted of the demand for public goods and services. As Vernez writes:

> The estimate of a demand function for a specific good or service necessitates the availability of a reliable price attached to the consumption of that good or service. Unfortunately, direct money prices are not widely used for many urban public service outputs. As a result, there have been relatively few bona fide attempts at estimating demand functions for urban public services. Most of these attempts have been made for services that have a private substitute, such as higher education and hospitals, or for services that even though zero-priced had some other rationing devices [such as travel distance or time that could be used like prices].[34]

---

[33]This is discussed in most standard price theory texts. See, for example, Jack Hirschleifer, *Price Theory and Applications* (Englewood Cliffs, N.J.: Prentice-Hall, 1983). For an application to the issue of financial condition, see Stephen M. Barro, *The Urban Impacts of Federal Policies: Vol. 3, Fiscal Conditions* (Santa Monica, Calif.: Rand Corporation, April 1978), especially Chap. 3.

[34]Vernez, "Delivery of Urban Public Services," p. 134. A selective review of estimated demand functions for public services can be found in Werner Hirsch, *Urban Economic Analysis.* See also Robert Inman, "The Fiscal Performance of Local Governments: An Interpretive Review," in *Current Issues in Urban Economics,* eds. Peter Mieszkowski and Mahlon Straszheim (Baltimore: Johns Hopkins University Press, 1979).

While there are very few demand studies to draw on to identify needs, demand-related factors have been incorporated into "expenditure determinant" studies. These studies relate total per capita expenditures or per capita expenditures on major functions (not output *quantities* as in demand studies) to a wide variety of factors affecting expenditures, such as ability to pay, outside aid, and needs. These studies have been criticized for their lack of an adequate theoretical basis, but they can still be used to suggest important needs-related factors that influence expenditures.[35] Note that in these types of studies, the needs factors identified are those that have been found to actually influence output and expenditure levels; whether they "should" influence these decisions is still a matter of judgment that must be brought in as part of the analysis.

The expenditure analysis cited earlier by Gramlich that included certain production and service conditions can also be cited as an example of a study that examined needs. One variable in particular, the percentage of the households in the city with low incomes, could be viewed as a need variable.[36] Vernez has reviewed demand and determinant studies to identify need variables. Table 5-26 lists some of these variables related to community or clientele needs that have been found to play a major role in either demand or expenditure determinant studies. There is continuing controversy over the relative importance of different factors, but this list includes many of the need factors that have received at least some empirical support in the literature.

TABLE 5-26    **Examples of Community Taste or Need Factors
from Demand and Expenditure Studies**

---

Percent population of foreign stock
Percent population non-white
Percent population under 21
Percent population over 65
Median years of schooling of those 25 or older
Percent population over 25 years old with less than five years of schooling
Percent population over 25 who are college graduates
Percent of city employment in manufacturing
Number of employees per manufacturing establishment
Dollar value of retail sales per store

---

SOURCE:  Georges Vernez, "Delivery of Urban Public Services: Production, Cost and Demand Functions, and Determinants of Public Expenditures for Fire, Police and Sanitation Services" (Santa Monica, Calif.: Rand Corporation, September 1976), Rand Paper Series P-5659, pp. 43–44.

---

[35] John E. Mulford, Jr., "A Public Choice Model of the Revenue-Expenditure Process in Local Government" (Ph.D. dissertation, Cornell University, Ithaca, N.Y., 1978); and Inman, "The Fiscal Performance of Governments."

[36] Gramlich, "New York City Fiscal Crisis." See also John Akin and Gerald E. Auten, "City Schools and Suburban Schools: A Fiscal Comparison," *Land Economics*, 52, No. 4 (November 1976), 452–66, for a determinants approach to needs in an empirical financial condition study.

**Social Indicators and Indexes.** Demand and expenditure studies highlight a range of need factors that affect expenditures in total and for different functions. However, a second approach, the use of social indicators and indexes, can both identify those factors that can be measured readily for a particular government and its reference group and put these factors in a simple usable form. Social indicators and indexes are constructed from economic and social variables that are felt to be direct or indirect measures of different types of needs. This method is of particular relevance to financial analysis, since needs indexes can be developed, compared over time and across organizations, and related to government expenditures.

Social indicators can be illustrated by examining measures of the conditions prevailing in an urban area using the approach and methods developed by Michael Flax.[37] Table 5-27 presents a representative list of categories of the "quality" of urban life, all of which reflect broad goals or desired conditions. The list includes such concerns as income, housing, health, racial equality, educational attainment, and air quality, all of which reflect different dimensions of what many

TABLE 5-27 **Quality Categories and Selected Indicators**

| QUALITY CATEGORIES | INDICATORS USED |
| --- | --- |
| Unemployment | % of labor force unemployed |
| Poverty | % of households with incomes less than $3,000 per year |
| Income | *Per capita money income adjusted for cost-of-living differences |
| Housing | Cost of housing a moderate income family of four |
| Health | Infant (under 1 year) deaths per 1,000 live births |
| Mental Health | Reported suicides per 100,000 population |
| Public Order | Reported robberies per 100,000 population |
| Racial Equality | Ratio between white and non-white unemployment rates |
| Community Concern | *Per capita contributions to United Fund appeals |
| Citizen Participation | *% of voting age population that voted in recent presidential elections |
| Educational Attainment | *Median school years completed by adults |
| Transportation | Cost of transportation for a moderate income family of four |
| Air Quality | Average yearly concentration of three air pollution components, and change in the concentration of suspended particulates |
| Social Disintegration | Estimates of number of narcotics addicts per 10,000 population |

*An increase in the absolute value of these indicators is assumed to represent an improvement in the quality of life. The reverse is true of all the others.
SOURCE: Michael Flax, *A Study in Comparative Urban Indicators*, (Washington, DC: Urban Institute, 1972), p. 9, with modifications.

[37] Michael Flax, *A Study in Comparative Urban Indicators* (Washington, D.C.: Urban Institute, 1972).

people might include in the quality of life. Each quality-of-life category in turn has associated with it an indicator or measure of this quality. Some qualities may require several measures rather than one, and others may not be measurable at all. The list, however, provides individual measures to illustrate how representative qualities might be measured and compared over time and/or across communities.

Community needs include capital "infrastructure," which is not included explicitly in Table 5-27. The condition of streets, bridges, water and sewer systems, schools, public transportation, and government buildings influence the mobility, education, health, and well-being of local residents. Deterioration of this physical capital has become a major concern,[38] with clear implications for the expenditure needs for localities that have not kept their infrastructure in good condition. Inclusion in community needs indexes of measures of infrastructure condition (for example, age of water treatment plant, number of complaints about road conditions) may help determine the pressures on a government for additional capital expenditures. Such information can be used in conjunction with the analysis of actual capital fund expenditures presented in section II.

Social indicators of this sort can be used to present, in an oversimplified but still useful fashion, the major social and economic needs of a particular community. These indicators provide rough benchmarks for evaluating change and identifying major problem areas and may be compared with expenditures as part of expenditure analysis. Where desirable, the need categories may be broken down to provide a more-detailed and comprehensive picture of needs.

Social indicators can be combined to provide composite indexes of economic and social needs. As we will demonstrate, these indexes, representing a measure of the overall needs of a community, can be compared with the total per capita expenditures of a government.

A major advantage of the social indicator approach to need measurement is that it is feasible. Michael Flax reviewed urban indicator research conducted during the 1970–77 period and found fifty-eight studies that examined a single location such as a city or county and twenty-five studies that compared two or more communities.[39] Principal disadvantages, however, are the somewhat arbitrary choice of the elements included in the index, the difficulties in measuring these elements, and the lack of an empirical test of the relationships between social indicators and a fiscal variable such as expenditures.

An actual study can serve to illustrate the social indicator approach. Nathan and Adams combined the following variables into an index of "intercity hardship":

---

[38] See references in footnote 2, and Harry B. Hatry and George Peterson, *Guides to Managing Urban Capital* (Washington, D.C.: Urban Institute Press, 1985).

[39] Michael Flax, "Survey of Urban Indicator Data, 1970–77" (Washington, D.C., Urban Institute, February 1978).

1.  Unemployment (percent of civilian labor force unemployed)
2.  Dependency (persons less than eighteen or over sixty-four years of age as a percent of total population)
3.  Education (percent of persons twenty-five years of age or more with less than twelfth grade education)
4.  Income level (per capita income)
5.  Crowded housing (percent of occupied housing units with more than one person per room)
6.  Poverty (percent of families below 125 percent of low-income level)[40]

In addition to comparing various cities, Nathan and Adams used the index to compare suburban areas and central cities with the rest of the metropolitan area. In the intercity index, Newark, St. Louis, and New Orleans are the highest in terms of hardship; and Fort Lauderdale, Greensboro, N.C., and Seattle are the best off among the fifty-five cities examined.[41] While expenditure levels depend on a variety of factors besides the six combined in the hardship index, data in this form can be of value in comparing expenditures of different governments with indexes of the relative needs of the communities they serve.[42]

**Government Information Systems.**     Another method of assessing the needs of groups served by governments is through regular and systematic information gathering by the government itself, such as (1) an established information system that continually monitors attitudes of relevant groups, their assessment of problems, and their reactions to governmental actions; (2) surveys of public needs and attitudes; and (3) direct participation of clientele in the decisions of the government, beyond the electoral process. These methods may provide detailed information that is useful for management and decision making at the program level but may not be in a form that is appropriate for aggregate expenditure analysis.

### An Application

Of the three methods we have identified, expenditure determinants and social indicator approaches have the most potential for use in financial analysis. In this part we illustrate the use of a social needs index based on social indicators.

---

[40]Richard P. Nathan and Charles Adams, ''Understanding Central City Hardship,'' *Political Science Quarterly,* 91, No. 1 (Spring 1976), 47–62. For a second example of a needs index in an empirical financial condition study, see Peggy L. Cuciti, *City Need and the Responsiveness of Federal Grants Programs* (Washington, D.C.: Congressional Budget Office, August 1978).

[41]Nathan and Adams, ''Understanding Central City Hardship,'' pp. 55–56.

[42]For another example using census tract data rather than city data, see D. G. Colley, ''A Social Change Index—An Objective Means to Discern and Measure the Relative Current Social Condition of Cities, Towns, and their Sub-Communities,'' *Social Indicators Research,* 2 (1975), 93–118.

As Nathan and Adams's social needs index indicates, these indexes can be developed for a particular jurisdiction and a reference group from census data and other standard data sources. Comparisons of expenditures with need indexes can highlight whether a government is spending more or less relative to its needs.

Table 5–28 shows the results of computing an index of social needs for Dyer Straits and the reference group cities. In general, cities with higher needs indexes have higher dollar and real expenditures per capita. Dyer Straits' needs index is very high, but its per capita expenditures are disproportionately higher. In other words, Dyer Straits spends more on a per capita basis than do reference group cities facing similar local needs.

Comparisons of per capita expenditures and indexes of needs can draw attention to a city whose expenditures are considerably out of line with those of similar cities. Again we find Dyer Straits spending more than we would expect from the behavior of cities with similar needs. From what we have learned earlier about Dyer Straits, its high levels of expenditures can only be partially explained by high needs and input costs, and somewhat above-average production and service conditions, especially in the face of a lower-than-average resource base. Either Dyer Straits is providing more outputs relative to its needs than comparable cities or Dyer Straits is operating inefficiently. If the former is true, then Dyer Straits may be able to cut back its expenditures and at least remain comparable with the reference group. (Of course, the possibility exists that none of the cities are actually meeting the needs in an absolute sense.) If the latter is true, Dyer Straits may be able to increase its efficiency and either produce more outputs at the current level of expenditures or decrease expenditures while holding outputs constant. In either case, there appear to be options open for the reduction in expenditures. This is certainly a more positive conclusion than if, with Dyer Straits' already high expenditures, the analysis of prices, production and service conditions, and needs indicated that expenditures should be even higher.

TABLE 5–28    **Expenditures and Community and Clientele Needs, City of Dyer Straits and Reference Group, 1983**

| | INDEX OF COMMUNITY NEEDS* | PER CAPITA EXPENDITURES† Dollar | Real |
|---|---|---|---|
| Average for 10 cities with highest index | .605 | 261.0 | 194.9 |
| Average for all cities | .502 | 238.0 | 172.5 |
| Average for 10 cities with lowest index | .361 | 182.2 | 161.2 |
| *Dyer Straits* | *.602* | *308.2* | *218.9* |

*Index is a composite of measures of poverty, unemployment, education levels attained, housing without plumbing, and elderly population. General method of index construction is explained in the first footnote in Table 5–25.

†See the second and third footnotes in Table 5–25.

## VII. EXPENDITURES
## AND FINANCIAL CONDITION

### *Measuring Expenditure Pressure*

The various components of expenditure analysis include examinations of input levels and prices, outputs, production and service conditions, needs, and the expenditures themselves. The issue we address in this final section is how to bring these findings together to draw conclusions about financial condition from the expenditure perspective.

In considering financial condition from the revenue side, we compared a government's revenues with its capacity to raise revenues. The resulting revenue reserves (or lack of reserves) provided us with one measure of the organization's financial condition. But available resources from revenues are only one of the five ingredients of financial condition; the adequacy of expenditures relative to the needs, prices, and production and service conditions faced by the organization is another.

Substantial unmet needs in a community, regardless of the level of available resources, create ''pressures'' for additional expenditures that impair the government's financial condition. This ingredient of financial condition is not shown in any financial reports but is every bit as important as revenue or debt capacity or internal reserves. If the expenditures of a government fail to satisfy the needs of its clientele adequately, pressures to increase expenditures will take their place along with pressures to lower taxes, repay loans, fund pensions, raise wages, and so forth.

The purpose of expenditure analysis as we have defined it is to determine the pressure on the government for additional expenditures. High expenditure pressures worsen the organization's financial condition in our framework. In this chapter we have identified a number of factors that, when everything else is held constant, increase expenditure pressures and worsen financial condition as a result.

First, governments face an array of prices for the inputs they use in their production processes. These input prices may vary over time, and governments in different locations may face different prices at one point in time. All else being equal, an increase in input prices increases the expenditure pressures for a government because it takes more dollars to purchase a given set of inputs.

Second, governments convert inputs into goods and services through a production process, and they can do this with varying levels of technical and cost efficiency. Although it is not a simple task, if we can measure levels or changes in efficiency, this can help us evaluate expenditure pressure. Suppose, for example, we find that efficiency in a particular government is low relative to a comparable reference group. This increases expenditure pressure because if production is done more efficiently, higher levels of output can be produced at the same level of input or costs.

Third, because of the various production and service conditions they face, governments incur different levels of costs in converting inputs into outputs. All else being equal, more severe production and service conditions will increase expenditure pressures and worsen financial condition from the expenditure perspective.

Finally, governments produce outputs to meet needs, and the needs that governments face can vary over time and compared with a reference group's. Again, assuming that nothing else varies, the higher the level of needs, the higher the expenditure pressures and the poorer the financial condition from the expenditure perspective.

Without even examining actual expenditures, we can assess some of the underlying factors that contribute to expenditure pressures by analyzing input prices, production and service conditions, and needs. Combinations of variables that measure these concepts can be utilized to gauge expenditure pressures, but it is only a partial view until actual expenditures are included in the analysis.

The question we must now address is how to combine the information on these factors with information on actual expenditures. A commonly used method to estimate whether a government is spending too little or too much is simply to compare expenditures per capita over time or across organizations.[43] As we have seen, this is a rough measure that fails to take into consideration the effects of input prices, production and service conditions, and needs of the groups served by the government. Expenditures per capita may be identical for two cities, yet one city may pay much higher wages to its employees, have more-demanding production and service conditions, and have greater community needs, all of which are not reflected in per capita expenditure comparisons. In the absence of any of this additional information, expenditures per capita may have to suffice as a measure of expenditure pressure, but it is a very limited measure.

We can, however, develop much better estimates of the expenditure pressures that affect financial condition if we develop estimates of input prices, production and service conditions, and needs. If a government's real expenditures are high relative to comparable governments with similar needs and service conditions, we can presume either that the government's expenditures are more than adequate, in which case there is little pressure for additional expenditures, or that the government is operating inefficiently, in which case the expenditure pressures can be reduced by improving efficiency. On the other hand, if the government's real expenditures are low relative to comparable jurisdictions, we can presume either that the expenditures are less than adequate and that there is pressure for additional expenditures or that the government's efficiency allows it to produce sufficient outputs to meet its needs at a lower level of expenditures.

If, for the moment, we ignore the difficult task of measuring efficiency, the key to estimating expenditure pressures lies in comparing real (price-level-

---

[43] See Lennox L. Moak and Albert M. Hillhouse, *Concepts and Practices in Local Government Finance* (Chicago: Municipal Finance Officers Association, 1975).

adjusted) expenditures with the levels of productions and service conditions and needs that generate those expenditures. Although this task is admittedly difficult, there are several ways in which we can attempt to estimate the necessary relationships.

First, we can construct an index that combines community needs and production and service conditions and compare this index with real expenditures per capita for different governments or, in the absence of an input price index, with dollar expenditures per capita.

The comparison may take many forms. It may be a simple two-dimensional division into high, medium, and low levels of the index and of expenditures per capita, as shown in Table 5-29. This can be accomplished by dividing the distribution into thirds, either by using standard deviations or by taking advantage of natural breaks in the distribution. Then the combination of the real expenditures and the index of needs and production and service conditions will place each government in one of the nine categories corresponding to levels of expenditure pressure. If this methodology is used, we can identify governments with little or no expenditure pressure (the six categories on or above the diagonal) and governments experiencing expenditure pressure (the three categories below the diagonal). Note that governments in the three categories above the diagonal are spending more than their indexes indicate, and they may be able to lower their expenditures without creating expenditure pressures. This can be viewed as a form of "expenditure reserve."

A second way of presenting this information is to compute the ratio of real expenditures per capita to our index of needs and production and service conditions for the government and its reference group. This ratio indicates the relative expenditure pressure for the government, with lower (higher) values of this ratio signifying greater (less) expenditure pressure. It also measures how expenditure

TABLE 5-29  **Measurement of Expenditure Pressure**

| | REAL EXPENDITURES PER CAPITA | | |
| | Low | Middle | High |
|---|---|---|---|
| Low index* | No expenditure pressure | No expenditure pressure; expenditures might even be reduced | No expenditure pressure; expenditures might even be reduced |
| Middle index* | Some expenditure pressure | No expenditure pressure | No expenditure pressure; expenditures might even be reduced |
| High index* | High expenditure pressure | Some expenditure pressure | No expenditure pressure |

*Index combining need and production service conditions.

pressure is changing over time or compared with that of other organizations, important information for the analysis of financial condition.

A third approach is to plot expenditures per capita and the index of needs and production and service conditions, as shown in Figure 5-3. This allows us to estimate expenditure pressure in real dollars per capita. In this figure we show a line fitted to the data (either by regression analysis or by "eye balling"). Governments falling above the line have real expenditures that are high relative to the need and cost factors they face and, therefore, have no expenditure pressure and may even have a reserve if they are far above the line; those below the line have expenditures that are low relative to need and cost factors, and they face expenditure pressures with those farthest below the line having the greatest expenditure pressure. The vertical distance between the actual real expenditures per capita and the estimated line (in Figure 5-3, *AB* is an example of this distance) is an estimate of the real dollar value of expenditure pressure.

A somewhat different method of estimating expenditure pressure is to compare actual expenditures with the level of expenditures predicted from a regression model relating expenditures to measures of needs and production and service conditions. This approach is analogous to the regression-based fiscal capacity method developed in Chapter 4 and can also be viewed as a refinement of the method shown in Figure 5-3. Once a regression estimate of per capita (real) expenditures as a function of needs and production and service conditions is available, the expenditure pressures for a particular government can be determined by (1) inserting that organization's values for the need and production and service condition variables into the equation, (2) computing the *predicted* value for expenditures as if this organization behaved like the average of the organizations in the reference group, and (3) comparing the organization's *actual* expenditures with its predicted expenditures. If predicted expenditures are greater than actual expenditures, the government is "underspending" and has expenditure pressures; if actual expenditures are greater than predicted expenditures, then the local government is "overspending" and, theoretically, has no pressures for additional expenditures. We illustrated this approach for computing revenue reserves in Chapter 4, and we will apply it to Dyer Straits below.[44]

When data are unavailable on needs and/or production and service conditions, then expenditure pressures can be estimated from per capita real expenditures *if* we can realistically assume that these environmental factors are similar across organizations and over time. With this assumption, a government with low per capita expenditures would have high expenditure pressures and vice versa, but it is unlikely that these differences in environmental factors can be ignored. The analysis of expenditure pressures can also be carried out using dollar rather

---

[44]Variations of this method are used in Akin and Auten, "City Schools and Suburban Schools"; Gramlich, "New York City Fiscal Crisis"; and Bradbury et al., "State Aid to Offset Fiscal Disparities across Communities."

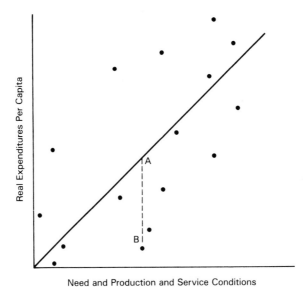

Figure 5-3. **GRAPHICAL ESTIMATE OF EXPENDITURE PRESSURE**

than real expenditures if price differences across jurisdictions and across time are not significant.

### An Application

In this part we summarize what we have found in the various expenditure components for Dyer Straits and reach a conclusion on the extent to which it faces pressures for more expenditures.

The key to measuring the expenditure pressure component of financial condition is to relate real expenditures in Dyer Straits to measures of its needs and production and service conditions, and then compare this relationship with Dyer Straits' past or with its reference group. For example, drawing on the preceding two sections, we could compute the sum of the needs index and the production and service condition index for Dyer Straits and the reference group and then compare how Dyer Straits ranks on its real expenditures with how it ranks on the combined index. This comparison would show that Dyer Straits ranks considerably higher on its real expenditures than on its combined index, indicating that Dyer Straits is overspending compared with other cities facing similar conditions.

To estimate the dollar value of Dyer Straits' overspending, we could plot real expenditures against the combined index or we could use a regression approach. Since we illustrated the graphical approach in Figure 5-3, we will use the regression method here.

For Dyer Straits and its reference group cities, we used multiple-regression analysis to estimate the following relationship between real expenditures per capita and various measures of needs and production and service conditions in 1983:

$$EXP_i = -54.3 + 20.6\,POV_i - 1.86\,EDUC_i + 5.63\,HOUS_i \\ + .061\,LAND_i + .012\,POP\,DENS_i + .005\,HOUS\,DENS_i,$$

where

$EXP_i$ = real expenditures per capita for city $i$

$POV_i$ = percentage of population below poverty level in city $i$

$EDUC_i$ = percentage of population in city $i$ who have completed at least four years of high school

$HOUS_i$ = percentage of housing in city $i$ without complete plumbing

$LAND_i$ = area of city $i$ in square miles

$POP\,DENS_i$ = residents per square mile in city $i$

$HOUS\,DENS_i$ = housing units per square mile in city $i$

Now if we substitute Dyer Straits' levels of poverty, education, and so forth, into this equation, we find that the *predicted* level of real expenditures per capita is *$187* in 1983. Since *actual* real expenditures per capita in 1983 in Dyer Straits are *$219*, we estimate that Dyer Straits is overspending by *$32* per capita. This suggests that there are no expenditure pressures for Dyer Straits and it may even be possible for Dyer Straits to cut back on its expenditures, either by improving efficiency or by reducing the level of outputs or both, and still meet its needs. The political possibilities of such a cutback are, however, another matter.

Recall that in our analysis of Dyer Straits' revenues in Chapter 4, using a similar regression approach we found that Dyer Straits was raising local revenues beyond its local revenue capacity. More specifically, Dyer Straits was raising more per capita in local revenues than were cities with property values, retail sales, and family income similar to Dyer Straits. Now we find that this overraising of revenues, which adversely affects financial condition, is somewhat offset by the fact that Dyer Straits seems to be spending more than its needs, prices, and production and service conditions require.[45] This overspending can be viewed as a source of financial strength (or a positive aspect of financial condition) that will permit Dyer Straits, at least conceptually, to slow its growth of expenditures in the future.

Our final conclusion that Dyer Straits may not face high expenditure pressures is only one of many findings related to expenditures that we have uncovered in this analysis. It is useful to summarize these other findings.

---

[45] For a more precise comparison, both revenue reserves and expenditure pressure estimates should be put into real dollars.

First, we examined Dyer Straits' per capita expenditures over time and compared with a reference group's by object of expenditure and function. We found expenditures on almost all objects of expenditures to be higher in Dyer Straits compared with the reference group's, particularly salaries, fringe benefits, and debt service. These latter two items will be examined more closely in the next two chapters. The functional analysis of expenditures also showed that expenditures on most functions were higher in Dyer Straits than in the reference group, and some functions were growing more rapidly in Dyer Straits as well. The results of this initial analysis raised the possibility that Dyer Straits was overspending, and they pointed out the potentially dangerous trend of expenditure growth far exceeding revenue growth. If, to improve its financial condition, Dyer Straits is to take advantage of the fact that it is overspending, it will have to reduce its growth in expenditures relative to its own revenues and income, and to those of its reference group.

Second, we examined the input prices in Dyer Straits. Here we found that prices had been rising in Dyer Straits and that "real" expenditures had increased only 4.5 percent from 1979 to 1983. This suggested that the increased expenditures had not been matched by the same growth in physical inputs. By examining a proxy for prices, employees per 10,000 population, we confirmed the finding that real expenditures had probably grown much less than expenditures measured in dollars. Moreover, we found that employees per 10,000 population were higher in Dyer Straits than in the reference group in 1983, suggesting that some of the overspending may have been due to high personnel costs.

Next, we investigated the production and service conditions in Dyer Straits and concluded that these conditions in Dyer Straits were only slightly more demanding than those faced by comparable cities. Thus production and service conditions did not explain the high levels of expenditures in Dyer Straits compared with the reference group. This analysis raised the possibility that there was room for efficiency improvements in Dyer Straits. Confirmation of this hypothesis would require more-detailed analysis at the function or activity level.

Finally, we determined that Dyer Straits has substantially higher needs than the other cities in the reference group. Moreover, if these needs become greater, all else being equal, this will worsen Dyer Straits' financial condition. Even with these needs and somewhat higher production and service conditions, Dyer Straits' real expenditures still appear to be more than adequate.

## VIII. HANDLING "NONCOMMON" GOVERNMENT EXPENDITURES

The final issue of concern in this chapter is the issue of service responsibilities of government. Up to this point, the analysis has examined "common functions," the services and goods normally delivered by all governments under investigation. In some cases, however, governments assume or are required to assume responsibility for other "noncommon" functions, and the expenditures for these activities should also be examined.

Some noncommon functions are structured as enterprises where the revenues are intended to cover the expenditures or expenses of the activity. Airports and utilities are examples. The analysis of these enterprise-like activities is discussed in Chapter 8. Education is another special case. In some localities it is provided through an independent school district; in others it is included among the local government's responsibilities. In general, regardless of whether a particular government has or does not have the responsibility for K–12 education, the analysis should be carried out consistently (with or without education) for the entire sample of governments.

The final group of noncommon activities is services other than enterprises or education that are performed by some, but not all, governments, such as expenditures on welfare or Medicaid. Also included in this final group are enterprises like a municipal hospital system, which are run with significant governmental subsidies.

Whenever a government provides one of these noncommon functions, it is either meeting a need that in most other governments is being met through another mechanism (for example, by the state government, an enterprise run on a "break-even" basis, or a private organization) or meeting a need that is somehow unique to this government. Both of these cases require a separate analysis of the expenditures in question.

In the former case, the added service responsibility increases expenditure pressure and thus worsens financial condition unless new revenue sources are shifted along with the responsibility. Examples include the city's providing welfare benefits or extensive free health care that is normally provided by the federal government, state, or county.

In the latter case, a unique need, it is more difficult to assess the impact on financial condition. In some situations, if the "need" is one that the government no longer has to meet because of changed circumstances, the government may be able to eliminate this noncommon function and thus relieve expenditure pressures and improve financial condition as a result. A city college that becomes part of the state system is an example. In other situations, performing this noncommon function may be meeting a need that other governments have not identified as a need. This uniquely defined need and the associated expenditures will increase expenditure pressures, but because of the different nature of the function, the expenditures should be analyzed separately. An example of this separate analysis can be found in Gramlich's assessment of New York City's financial problems in which he traced a substantial portion of New York City's problems to noncommon functions.[46]

---

[46]Gramlich, "New York City Fiscal Crisis." Also see other references in footnote 5.

## QUESTIONS

1. What basic questions are addressed in the analysis of government expenditures? How are these questions related to the other components of financial analysis?

2. What can be learned about a government's financial condition by examining actual expenditures by themselves? What categories of expenditures should be analyzed for a complete treatment of government expenditures? What are "expenditure priorities," and how can they be revealed through expenditure analysis? What do comparisons of expenditures per capita (total, by objects of expenditure, and by function) reveal about a government's financial condition? What don't they reveal? What are the major limitations of an analysis that looks only at actual expenditures?

3. How do actual governmental expenditures ultimately result in the satisfaction of community and clientele needs? What are the stages of this process? What might happen at each stage to reduce the ultimate impact on needs of the initial expenditures?

4. What is the impact, taken by itself, of each of the following on a government's financial condition:

   —An increase in the prices paid for government inputs?

   —A decrease in the efficiency of transforming government inputs into public goods and services (outputs)?

   —A decrease in the costs of producing a given level of government outputs?

   —Severe production and service conditions faced by a government?

   —Improving economic conditions, reducing the need for certain government services?

5. How can the income elasticity of expenditures be estimated? What can a comparison of the income elasticities of revenues and expenditures reveal about the potential for future financial problems?

6. Why is it important to estimate "real" expenditures rather than rely solely on actual expenditures unadjusted for input price changes? What does a comparison of adjusted and unadjusted expenditures reveal about expenditure pressures on government? What are price indexes? What are some of the problems involved in their construction and use in financial analysis?

7. In the absence of a price index, a government official has decided to use the change in the number of municipal employees to measure changes in "real" expenditures. To what extent is this change a "proxy" for price changes? How might it be used? What does it show that can be of use in financial analysis? What are some of the limitations of its use?

8. How do production and cost functions relate government inputs, and input costs, to outputs? What is meant by technical and cost efficiency in the transformation of inputs to outputs? How does each type of efficiency affect the financial condition of a government? Why is it difficult to determine government efficiency directly?

9. How can an analysis of the production and service conditions faced by a government and the needs of a government's clientele and community be used to evaluate government efficiency and expenditure pressures? What does it mean if a government's expenditures are high or low relative to these conditions and needs? How can government "overspending" or "underspending" be estimated? What are the technical and political limitations of such estimates?

10. How can the various factors affecting expenditure levels be combined to estimate the pressures on a government to increase expenditures?

─────────────────────**PROBLEMS**─────────────────────

1. Returning to problem 1 in Chapter 4:

   a. Using percentage change, index number, and/or common size methods, identify the major changes in the pattern of Medville's expenditures over 1982–84.

   b. Suppose a price index for total governmental expenditures rises from 100 in 1982 to 105 in 1983, and to 110 in 1984. Using this index, distinguish between increases in total expenditures in Medville due to increases in input *prices* and due to increases in the *quantity* of inputs purchased by the government.

   c. Using data from Medville and a reference group of similar cities, the following expenditure, production and service conditions, and community needs information has been assembled for 1984:

   | | |
   |---|---|
   | Total Expenditures ($ per capita): | |
   | Medville | 550 |
   | Similar cities (average) | 400 |
   | Production and Service Condition Index: | |
   | Medville | 110 |
   | Similar cities (average) | 100 |
   | Community Needs Index: | |
   | Medville | 120 |
   | Similar cities (average) | 100 |

   Although Medville is spending more on a per capita basis than the average of similar cities, can this extra spending be explained by more severe production and service conditions? By greater community needs? By both together? Based on the information given, do you think Medville is "overspending" or "underspending"? What other information would you like to have to help explain these differences in expenditure levels?

2. Returning to the data in Chapter 4 (problem 2) on the city of Red Lion:

   a. Using data on expenditures, population, municipal employees, salary and non-salary costs, and fixed assets, evaluate Red Lion's expenditures between 1977 and 1983 compared with the average of similar cities.

   b. Estimate, compare, and discuss the income elasticity of total expenditures in Red Lion and similar cities. How does this elasticity compare with the elasticities of the city's major revenue sources? What is the significance of any differences between expenditure and revenue income elasticities?

   c. Using price indexes, estimate, compare, and discuss Red Lion's and the reference group's real expenditures over the period 1977–83. How have price changes, taken alone, affected Red Lion's financial condition?

   d. From the data provided, discuss the differences in production and service conditions, and community needs, between Red Lion and its reference group. Relate these differences to differences in real expenditure levels.

   e. Looking at actual expenditures, price changes, production and service conditions, and community needs, do you think Red Lion is "overspending" or "underspending" compared with similar cities? Explain how you reached your conclusions.

   f. From your expenditure analysis alone, list your major conclusions about Red Lion's financial strengths and weaknesses.

# CHAPTER
# 6 / Debt Analysis

For the most part, the expenditures analyzed in the preceding chapter are devoted to the provision of services and goods in the same period in which the expenditures are made. There are, however, two important types of current expenditures that are exceptions: expenditures to secure debt and meet pension obligations.

These debt and pension expenditures are different from other current expenditures because they are the result of past rather than current expenditure commitments. When a government (or any entity for that matter) borrows funds for capital needs, it receives a sum of money when the debt is issued, the *principal* of the debt. The government is obligated to pay back to the lender over a set period of time this principal plus an additional payment for the use of the funds, the *interest* on the debt. Thus the repayment of principal and interest, commonly known as *debt service*, is the result of a borrowing and expenditure decision made sometime in the past. Current pension expenditures, discussed in the next chapter, are similarly the result of commitments made in the past.

Because of the long-term nature of both debt and pension commitments, we single them out for special attention in this and the next chapter. They are, however, still interconnected with other forms of analysis. For example, the revenues used to pay debt service and pension contributions are included in the total revenues analyzed in Chapter 4. Moreover, the expenditures for pension contributions, often grouped in the fringe benefit object of expenditure, and debt service are included in total expenditures assessed in Chapter 5.

This chapter is concerned with the nature of government debt and the analysis of the impact of debt on the government's financial condition. We begin by discussing debt analysis in general terms, then look at the characteristics of debt, and finally examine how to assemble and analyze debt information.

## I. THE NATURE OF DEBT ANALYSIS

In Chapter 4, when revenues were analyzed, we presented a technique to measure the *revenue capacity* of a particular government and determine how much of this capacity is available for future use (*revenue reserves*). Similarly, in Chapter 5, we developed methods to measure an organization's expenditure *needs* and the extent to which these needs were unmet (*expenditure pressures*). In this chapter we present various ways to analyze a government's financial condition from the debt perspective that parallel and rely on the revenue and expenditure analyses presented in the preceding two chapters.

An analysis of financial condition from the debt perspective seeks to answer the following two questions:

1. What is the *debt capacity* of a government? That is, how much total debt can an organization carry?
2. How much of the government's debt capacity is being utilized, and how much debt capacity is available for future borrowing? How much additional borrowing (*debt reserves*) can the government undertake?

If there were a government with unlimited resources at its disposal to meet any financial obligation, and there existed an unlimited supply of potential lenders, then the government would have an unlimited debt capacity and an unlimited ability to borrow. Obviously these conditions are not realistic for state and local governments. These governments have a finite capacity to borrow, and this borrowing capacity depends on the ability of the government to pay for its debt, the availability of willing lenders, and the amount of outstanding debt it is currently carrying.

In this section we examine the questions of determining a government's debt capacity and debt reserves and use this discussion to review traditional debt "burden" measures. We then develop the general steps to be followed in debt analysis, and we show how traditional and newer debt measures can be used in a complete analysis of the impacts of debt and borrowing on financial condition.

### Debt Capacity

Debt capacity is not a simple identifiable figure that is constant for all governments. It should vary according to certain characteristics of the government, and although it is difficult to measure debt capacity precisely, we can identify the characteristics that determine it and try to incorporate those factors into measures of debt capacity.

First, the level of resources available to the government should influence its debt capacity. All else being equal, the greater the resources available to pay back debt, the greater the debt capacity. The measures of local fiscal capacity and reserves discussed in Chapter 4 represent partial measures of the organization's available resources. In addition, intergovernmental transfers that constitute a significant portion of the revenues of many governments also contribute to available resources. Current levels, stability, and growth potential of the government's resources are an essential factor in determining debt capacity.

These resources, however, are used for many other expenditures than debt service. Consequently, the need faced by a government to provide goods and services through current and capital expenditures is a second factor that affects a government's debt capacity. All else being equal, the larger the share of the government's available resources that must be devoted to expenditures other than debt service, the lower the capacity to carry debt.

While revenue availability and expenditure needs are two important determinants of the government's debt capacity, another important factor deserves mention even though it is somewhat "external" to the government. This is the ability and willingness of individuals and institutions to lend money to the government. To the degree that this supply of loanable funds is based on certain debt management decisions, the government has some control over the lenders' willingness to invest. For example, the security behind particular debt issues should influence the decision of lenders. A government can also increase the supply of funds from lenders by increasing the interest rate it proposes to pay on its debt. But as the interest rate increases this raises the cost of the debt, so that more resources will be needed to pay debt service. There is usually some interest rate above which governments are unwilling to borrow.[1]

There are, however, additional external and largely uncontrollable influences on the supply of funds that can influence a government's debt capacity. First, the overall money supply influences the funds that potential lenders have at their disposal. When the supply of money decreases, there are fewer funds available to state and local lenders.

Second, an investor's willingness to purchase state debt and local government debt depends on the return and riskiness they offer compared with alternatives. If lenders have an opportunity to obtain a more favorable return on their investments with comparable risks, they will not be willing to lend to state and local governments.

Finally, since state and local government debt is primarily purchased by households, commercial banks, and fire and casualty insurance companies, the overall savings or profitability of these sectors, their needs for liquidity, their potential income tax liabilities, and so forth, are likely to influence their willingness to invest in state and local government debt.[2]

---

[1] For evidence on debt postponements due to high interest rates, see Joint Economic Committee, *Trends in the Fiscal Condition of Cities: 1980–1982* (Washington, D.C.: Congress of the United States, September 30, 1982).

[2] See, for example, Ronald W. Forbes and John E. Petersen, "Background Paper," in Twentieth Century Fund, *Building a Broader Market* (New York: McGraw-Hill, 1976), Chap. 6; U.S. General Accounting Office, *Trends and Changes in the Municipal Bond Market as They Relate to Financing State and Local Public Infrastructure* (Washington, D.C., September 12, 1983); and M. Arak and K. Guentner, "The Market for Tax-Exempt Issues: Why Are the Yields so High?" *National Tax Journal*, 36, No. 2 (June 1983), 145–61.

Our conceptual arguments yield three broad factors that influence a government's debt capacity: resource availability, expenditure needs, and willingness of lenders to purchase the debt. Later in this chapter we will attempt to incorporate these factors into our analysis of debt capacity, although a methodology is not currently available to translate these concepts into a single precise empirical measure.

### Debt Reserves

If we could come up with a measure of a government's debt capacity, we could compare it with the government's use of debt to answer our second question, how much of the debt capacity is currently being utilized? In other words, how much additional borrowing (debt reserves) can the organization do? We can draw on our discussion of debt capacity to address the second question of available borrowing or debt reserve. We begin by developing conceptual or "ideal" measures and then look at current practice in measuring debt reserves.

Suppose we have carried out a revenue analysis along the lines suggested in Chapter 4 and estimated a government's fiscal capacity as well as its revenue reserves. Included in revenue reserves would be unused local revenue capacity as well as prospects for increased outside aid. Suppose also that we have carried out an expenditure analysis following the methods presented in Chapter 5, which gave us an estimate of the needs for additional expenditures by the government.

Once we measure revenue reserves and expenditure pressures, they can be used to estimate how much additional borrowing the government can undertake. A government with no revenue reserves and considerable pressure for additional expenditures will be hard pressed to borrow additional funds. Conversely, a government with ample revenue reserves and little expenditure pressure will be in a good position to borrow additional funds.

Although this conceptual approach is not simple to implement, it is worth illustrating with an example. Suppose we have a city with a revenue capacity of $100 million per year, of which $80 million is being used for expenditures for items other than debt service. Current debt service is $5 million per year, making the city's revenue reserves $15 million per year. In addition, the city faces $10 million per year of unmet expenditure needs (high expenditure pressures) which have been estimated, say, using a regression approach with the reference group. This reduces the revenue reserves available to cover new debt service to $5 million per year. This estimate may be quite different from estimates provided by the traditional debt measures which we will examine next.

### Debt Burden

Our conceptual examination of debt capacity reveals that revenue-raising ability, expenditure needs, and willingness of lenders to supply funds influence debt capacity. Debt reserves, in turn, depend conceptually on the revenue reserves available to government and the expenditure pressures faced by government, with the difference available for carrying more debt.

The traditional measures of debt capacity, "debt burden" measures, do not fully incorporate all the factors treated in our discussion of debt analysis. If used judiciously, however, they can provide helpful estimates of debt usage and reserves.

Debt burden measures relate the level of government debt or debt service to population, income, tax base, revenues, and similar variables. The measures usually incorporate debt and one of the other variables into a simple ratio, such as debt per capita or debt service divided by local revenues. They may include *stock* variables like total debt and total value of taxable property and *flow* variables like annual debt service and annual revenues.

Traditional debt burden measures are consistent with some aspects of our conceptual discussion in that they include a measure of outstanding debt and a measure of the revenues or revenue base of the organization. The debt burden measures do not, however, normally include expenditures other than debt service, nor do they actually measure debt capacity or reserves. Debt burden measures quantify the usage of debt by the government; however, evaluation of whether the government can borrow additional funds goes beyond the measurement of debt usage.

Similarly, measures of the lending community's willingness to purchase a government's debt are not included in the debt burden measures but may influence the way in which the debt burden measures are interpreted. For example, the assessment of a debt burden measure in terms of its being "high" or "low" may depend, to some degree, on the money supply; a moderate debt burden in times of "easy money" may be perceived as high during a "credit crunch"—a period when money is very tight. Consequently, debt burden measures require additional interpretation to assess a government's ability to increase its debt. Evaluation and use of these measures is presented in more detail in section IV.

### Steps in the Analysis

The purpose of debt analysis is to determine the impact of a government's current debt holdings on its financial condition and the extent to which it could engage in additional borrowing without significant adverse effects on its financial well-being.

In conducting this analysis we begin by assembling information on what levels and types of debt are carried by the government, how this debt has changed over time, and how it compares with similar governments or other reference groups (section III). Other information about the debt such as interest rate, conditions, and maturities is assembled as part of this stage of the analysis. Comparative measures such as location quotients, index numbers, and percentage changes may be useful at this point.

The second stage of analysis (section IV) focuses on the development of indicators of the extent of debt usage by the government, whether this is excessive or not, and to what extent the government has room to add more debt. In this stage we develop and interpret traditional measures of debt burden, and we supplement these measures with additional indicators of debt capacity, usage, and reserves.

Before we begin debt analysis and its application, we need a general understanding of state and local government debt. This is presented in the next section.


## II. CHARACTERISTICS OF GOVERNMENT DEBT

It is important that the reader understand certain basic aspects of government debt, and to accomplish this, we briefly answer the following nine questions about state and local government debt:[3]


1.  Why issue debt?
2.  Who lends the funds to governments?
3.  Who issues debt?
4.  What are the uses of the debt?
5.  For what period of time is debt issued?
6.  What is the security behind the debt?
7.  How is debt repaid?
8.  What determines the cost of the debt?
9.  How has government debt changed recently?


Prior to answering these questions, however, one important characteristic of state and local government debt should be mentioned: the exemption from certain income taxes of interest paid on this debt. The interest received as a result of lending money to corporations is included in taxable income and subject to income taxes. This is not the case with state and local government debt. The interest earned on the debt issued by these governments is generally exempt from federal income taxes and is often exempt from income taxes in the state and locality in which the issuer of the debt is located. As a result, the interest paid by governments is generally lower than debt of comparable risk issued by organizations that are not tax-exempt. This tax exemption influences who lends to governments, the cost of the debt, and several other of the questions we discuss below.

---

[3] We present only a brief overview of the issues that affect the analysis of debt from a financial condition perspective. For a more complete assessment of tax-exempt debt, see Lennox L. Moak, *Municipal Bonds; Planning, Sale, and Administration* (Chicago: Municipal Finance Officers Association, 1982); Public Securities Association, *Fundamentals of Municipal Bonds* (New York, 1981); and Robert Lamb and Stephen P. Rappaport, *Municipal Bonds* (New York: McGraw-Hill, 1980).

### Purpose of Debt

Governments issue debt for several reasons, most of which involve the financing of expenditures in the current period with revenues from future periods. First, debt is often used to finance capital expenditures such as land, building, and equipment acquisition, which provide benefits in the future. Used in this way, debt tends to link future benefits with future costs, and it reduces the reliance on current revenues to pay for future benefits. Capital expenditures tend to be large relative to the current operating budget and may vary substantially from year to year. Thus the existing revenue structure could be overburdened if capital expenditures were funded completely from current revenues. The General Accounting Office (GAO) estimates, for example, that in the eleven years from 1971 to 1981, long-term debt financed 42 percent of the investment in infrastructure by state and local governments, federal grants financed 34 percent, and current revenues financed only 24 percent.[4]

Second, debt may be used to finance revenue-producing activities of government. The revenues of a government may not be measurably affected as a result of some capital expenditures, for example, when a city builds a courthouse, paves a street, or purchases a fire engine. Certain operations, however, generate their own revenues often through user charges, and borrowing for these revenue-producing activities can be considered a second purpose of debt. Examples include parking lots, housing projects, swimming pools, convention centers, and industrial parks. Many of the revenue-producing projects are undertaken by special authorities or districts rather than municipalities or states.

Although there is not always a clear division between capital for "normal" operations and capital for revenue-producing projects, at times the link between the project to be financed and the debt is explicit. In these cases the debt is used to finance the capital expenditures for a project or enterprise, and the revenues from the project or enterprise are used to pay back the debt. This type of debt, often called "self-supporting" or "revenue" debt, is sometimes treated differently from other debt in the analysis of financial condition from a debt perspective.[5] We will discuss this distinction in greater depth when we consider the security behind the debt.

The third purpose of borrowing falls into the category of financing expenditures that result from emergencies, such as the damage caused by natural disasters such as floods or hurricanes or unusual workloads caused by a heavy snowfall. This type of borrowing is justified either because current revenues cannot provide the funds for rebuilding after the disaster or because the disaster causes the government to replace and partially upgrade worn-out buildings and

---

[4] General Accounting Office, *Trends and Changes in the Municipal Bond Market*, pp. 35–38.

[5] For a more-detailed treatment of revenue debt, see the references cited in footnote 3.

equipment.[6] The use of emergency borrowing is not restricted to natural emergencies but may include "man-made" emergencies such as poor revenue estimation or a sudden decline in the tax base.[7] While borrowing as a result of a natural disaster is considered a legitimate use of debt, borrowing to meet other revenue shortfalls is more questionable and is more easily justified when it can be shown that the revenue shortfall is a one-time or temporary phenomenon.

A fourth purpose of debt is deficit borrowing where governments issue debt to finance a recurring deficit. This practice, since it is done on a continuing basis rather than for an occasional emergency, is viewed as an improper use of debt from a financial management standpoint because future revenues are being used to finance current expenditures. Despite the inadvisability of deficit borrowing, it still occurs. A most notable case was the city of New York, where from the early 1960s to the mid-1970s debt was issued regularly to meet operating deficits.[8]

A fifth purpose of debt is "anticipation" borrowing. A characteristic of government finances is the unevenness of revenues over the fiscal year compared with expenditures. For example, a government that collects taxes once or twice a year but has to make expenditures prior to when the taxes are received may face a cash-timing problem. Thus, faced with a temporary cash shortage, a government can issue debt in anticipation of the revenues coming in, use the proceeds from the debt for the expenditures, and then pay back the principal and interest on the debt when the revenues are actually received. This revenue anticipation debt is usually paid back in less than a fiscal year.

Anticipation borrowing is not restricted to one type of revenues. Governments borrow in anticipation of taxes, revenues from other organizations or other levels of government, and receipt of principal from longer-term bonds. Bond anticipation borrowing, usually in the form of bond anticipation notes (BANs), is an example of the last use. Such borrowing allows a project to begin while long-term borrowing is being arranged. Although there is risk involved in this type of borrowing (for example, the anticipated revenues may not all be forthcoming), properly used, BANs can be an efficient financing mechanism.

Another purpose of debt is the issuance of debt to refund previously outstanding debt.[9] In a refunding, new debt is issued and the receipts from the new issue are used to "pay back" the outstanding principal of the original debt, in many cases to reduce interest costs. A *call* feature in the original debt enables the government to "call," or pay off, the debt prior to its original repayment date.

---

[6] Lennox I. Moak and Albert M. Hillhouse, *Concepts and Practices in Local Government Finance* (Chicago: Municipal Finance Officers Association, 1975), p. 259.

[7] See Alan Walter Steiss, *Local Government Finance, Capital Facilities Planning and Debt Administration* (Lexington, Mass.: Lexington, 1975), p. 76.

[8] See, for example, U.S. General Accounting Office, *The Long Term Fiscal Outlook for New York City* (Washington, D.C., April 1977).

[9] For more on refundings, see Moak, *Municipal Bonds*, Chap. 21.

Governments may also use refunding to change other features of outstanding debt, such as the principal repayment schedule.

Governments may issue new debt to replace outstanding debt if their revenues are not sufficient to pay the principal and interest on outstanding obligations. This type of refunding to lengthen the payback of debt and ease cash problems may raise questions about the government's financial viability.

A final purpose of debt is to borrow in order to relend for particular public purposes. Since the economic base of a government determines much of its revenue potential, governments often search for mechanisms to improve their economic base. Some of the debt included in the first two purposes, capital projects and revenue projects, is used for economic development. But some governments and public authorities have been permitted to issue tax-exempt debt to finance capital projects undertaken by private enterprises. A government could issue debt to build a manufacturing plant that is then leased to a private company, and the debt service is paid by the lease payments from the private company to the local government.[10] Other examples of borrowing to relend include government mortgages for housing loans and pollution control investments.

### Debtholders

The individuals and organizations that lend funds to governments—the holders of government debt—have a direct interest in the government's financial condition, in general, and its use of debt, in particular. The lenders and potential lenders act, in part, on their assessment of financial condition, and their willingness to lend affects the interest rate that the government must pay on its debt.[11]

Table 6-1 shows the absolute dollar amounts and the percentage of total state and local government debt held by the different types of investors.[12] Until 1981, commercial banks had been the primary investors in state and local government debt. The holdings of commercial banks are influenced by the money supply, regulations and structure of the banking industry, tax regulations facing the banking industry, and alternative investments. Since 1969 a series of changes in these factors has reduced the relative attractiveness of tax-exempt debt for commercial banks.[13]

---

[10] For more details on this type of financing, see Moak, *Municipal Bonds,* Chap. 16; and Randy Hamilton, ''The World Turned Upside Down: The Contemporary Revolution in State and Local Government Capital Financing,'' *Public Administration Review,* 43, No. 1 (January–February 1983), 22–31. States now face limits for local governments established by the federal government for certain ''private purpose'' financing.

[11] For a full discussion of the determination of interest rates, see James C. Van Horne, *Financial Market Rates and Flows,* 2nd ed. (Englewood Cliffs, N.J.: Prentice-Hall, 1984).

[12] For an analysis of the principal holders of state and local government debt, see Forbes and Petersen, *Building a Broader Market,* Chap. 6.

[13] See General Accounting Office, *Trends and Changes in the Municipal Bond Market,* pp. 20–25.

TABLE 6-1    Composition of Holdings of Outstanding State and Local Debt by Major Investor Groups, 1970–82, Year-End Outstanding

| | | | ($ IN BILLIONS) | | |
| --- | --- | --- | --- | --- | --- |
| YEAR | Households | Commercial Banks | Non-Life Ins. Co. | Other | Total |
| 1970 | $46.0 | $70.2 | $17.0 | $11.2 | $144.4 |
| 1971 | 46.1 | 82.8 | 20.5 | 12.4 | 161.8 |
| 1972 | 48.4 | 90.0 | 24.8 | 13.3 | 176.5 |
| 1973 | 53.7 | 95.7 | 28.5 | 13.6 | 191.5 |
| 1974 | 61.9 | 101.1 | 30.7 | 14.0 | 207.7 |
| 1975 | 68.1 | 102.9 | 33.3 | 19.5 | 223.8 |
| 1976 | 70.1 | 106.0 | 38.7 | 24.7 | 239.5 |
| 1977 | 70.1 | 115.2 | 49.4 | 28.2 | 262.9 |
| 1978 | 72.7 | 126.2 | 62.9 | 29.5 | 291.3 |
| 1979 | 82.7 | 135.6 | 72.8 | 30.0 | 321.1 |
| 1980 | 94.6 | 149.2 | 80.5 | 32.6 | 356.9 |
| 1981 | 115.0 | 154.2 | 84.5 | 36.1 | 389.8 |
| 1982 | 161.8 | 153.9 | 86.8 | 48.0 | 450.5 |

| | | | (IN PERCENT)* | |
| --- | --- | --- | --- | --- |
| YEAR | Households | Commercial Banks | Non-Life Insurance Companies | Other |
| 1970 | 32 | 49 | 12 | 8 |
| 1971 | 28 | 51 | 13 | 8 |
| 1972 | 27 | 51 | 14 | 8 |
| 1973 | 28 | 50 | 15 | 7 |
| 1974 | 30 | 49 | 15 | 7 |
| 1975 | 30 | 46 | 15 | 9 |
| 1976 | 29 | 44 | 16 | 10 |
| 1977 | 27 | 44 | 19 | 11 |
| 1978 | 25 | 43 | 22 | 10 |
| 1979 | 26 | 42 | 23 | 9 |
| 1980 | 27 | 42 | 23 | 9 |
| 1981 | 30 | 40 | 22 | 9 |
| 1982 | 36 | 34 | 19 | 11 |

*Totals may not add to 100% due to rounding.
SOURCES:    Data from Federal Reserve Board, *Flow of Funds Accounts*, various years. Table from U.S. General Accounting Office, "Trends and Changes in the Municipal Bond Market as They Relate to Financing State and Local Public Infrastructure," GAO Report PAD-83-46, September 12, 1983, p. 52.

In 1982 commercial banks were bypassed as the largest single holder of state and local government debt by the household sector. The household sector has been attracted to tax-exempt debt in part because of higher interest rates and the rise in tax-exempt rates relative to taxable debt, and in part because households can buy and sell these bonds more easily due to the growth in funds that hold tax-exempt bonds. Bond fund holdings of state and local government debt are included in the "other" category in Table 6-1, although these funds are purchased mostly by households. In 1982 the household sector and bond funds together purchased 87 percent of the new debt that was issued.[14] Recent changes in tax laws that lower marginal income tax rates and thus reduce the advantage of holding tax-exempt bonds, and the increased availability of other tax shelters such as individual retirement accounts (IRAs), may moderate or reduce the growth of holdings by the household sector in the future.[15]

The final significant type of holder of state and local government debt is the fire and casualty insurance company. Life insurance companies and corporations have not shown much interest in state and local government debt, in part because of income tax regulations.

### Debt Issuers

As the right-hand column on the upper part of Table 6-1 indicates, total outstanding state and local government debt more than tripled between 1970 and 1982. During this period, the composition of the issuers of government debt changed considerably.

From 1970 to 1982 the share of the volume of tax-exempt debt issued by states declined from 23 to 11 percent; the share issued by municipalities, townships, counties, and school districts declined from 46 to 32 percent; and the share issued by special districts and statutory authorities increased from 31 to 57 percent. Much of the debt issued by the special districts and statutory authorities is paid back from revenues of the particular activities of the entities or through revenues from leasing arrangements, since most of these entities do not have general taxing power.

The multilayered nature of general-purpose governments and the existence of school districts, special districts, and statutory authorities have created the need to look beyond the debt of a single organization in debt analysis. Besides examining the debt of the particular government under study, we must also examine the debt held by other governmental bodies that serve the residents within the political boundary or jurisdiction of the government under study and allocate a portion of this debt to these residents. The term used to describe debt measured using the jurisdictional approach, rather than the organizational approach, is *overlapping* debt. Thus, if we are examining the public debt carried by the residents of a particular city, we have to add overlapping debt (a portion of county, school district, local special district, and local statutory authority debt) to the debt of the city.[16]

---

[14] Ibid., p. 22.

[15] For evidence on this point, see Arak and Guentner, "Market for Tax-Exempt Issues."

[16] The allocation of overlapping debt to the underlying entities is discussed further in section III.

### Uses of Debt

The way in which state and local government debt is used has changed considerably in recent years. Table 6–2 shows the functional uses of state and local government debt from 1970 to 1982. These data document that the traditional uses of long-term debt, such as education, transportation, and water and sewer, are growing much more slowly than the newer uses such as housing, industrial development, pollution control, and hospitals. This trend is what we would expect, given the increase in the role of special districts and statutory authorities. The large "other/unidentified" category prevents more-detailed analysis, but this category probably includes debt for other general-purpose activities, such as a police station or a new park, as well as some debt that was not allocated to the other listed functions. Recent federal legislation has imposed new restrictions on the uses of state and local government debt.

### Maturity of the Debt

Debt is generally classified as long term or short term depending on whether the period of final principal payback is greater or less than one year. There is some correspondence between the period of the debt and the purposes for which the debt is issued. Borrowing in anticipation of taxes, other revenues, or the issuance of long-term debt is almost always short-term debt. Debt that is issued to finance capital facilities, both revenue- and nonrevenue-producing activities, tends to be long-term debt. Debt issued to fund deficits, meet other emergency expenditures, and refund outstanding debt may be either long term or short term.

The relative importance of short-term borrowing has decreased in recent years. After growing in the early seventies to over half the dollar value of total borrowing, the annual volume of short-term borrowing has fallen to about a third (see Table 6–3). In 1982 roughly 1.7 times more long-term debt was issued than short-term debt.

Note that although the amount of short-term and long-term borrowing during any year is of the same order of magnitude, the amount of long-term debt outstanding at any one point in time is considerably greater than the amount of short-term debt outstanding. This is because short-term debt is retired or refinanced much more frequently than long-term debt.

Debt is generally issued in a form that corresponds to the period of the debt. Most long-term debt is issued in the form of a *bond,* which the Public Securities Association defines as "an interest-bearing promise to pay a specified sum of money—the principal amount—due on a specific date."[17] In general, bonds have a maturity date that is more than one year after the date of issue. There are a number of forms of short-term debt, although the most widely used is the *note.*[18] A

---

[17] Public Securities Association, *Fundamentals of Municipal Bonds,* p. 193.

[18] Other forms of short-term debt include negotiated loans, warrants, and scrip. For more details on short-term debt, see Moak, *Municipal Bonds,* Chap. 8 and pp. 298–300.

TABLE 6-2 Trends in the Volume of New Long-Term Tax-Exempt Bonds by Traditional and Non-Traditional Purposes, 1970–1982

($ IN BILLIONS)

| | 1970 | 1971 | 1972 | 1973 | 1974 | 1975 | 1976 | 1977 | 1978 | 1979 | 1980 | 1981 | 1982 |
|---|---|---|---|---|---|---|---|---|---|---|---|---|---|
| *Traditional Public Purposes:* | | | | | | | | | | | | | |
| Education | 5.0 | 5.7 | 5.0 | 4.8 | 4.7 | 4.4 | 4.9 | 5.0 | 4.7 | 4.6 | 4.1 | 3.4 | 4.7 |
| Transportation | 3.2 | 4.3 | 3.0 | 1.6 | 1.7 | 2.2 | 3.0 | 3.0 | 3.5 | 2.4 | 2.6 | 3.5 | 6.2 |
| Water & Sewer | 2.2 | 3.2 | 2.4 | 2.3 | 2.0 | 2.5 | 3.0 | 3.3 | 3.3 | 3.1 | 2.9 | 2.9 | 5.0 |
| Public Power | 1.1 | 1.3 | 1.2 | 1.6 | 1.5 | 2.2 | 2.7 | 3.4 | 4.5 | 3.5 | 3.4 | 6.3 | 7.1 |
| Other/Unidenti- fied | 5.7 | 7.3 | 6.8 | 3.6 | 7.6 | 11.6 | 10.5 | 11.4 | 11.4 | 8.2 | 9.5 | 10.1 | 16.8 |
| Sub-Total | 17.2 | 21.8 | 18.4 | 13.9 | 17.5 | 22.9 | 24.1 | 26.1 | 27.4 | 21.9 | 22.5 | 26.2 | 39.8 |
| *Non-Traditional Purposes:* | | | | | | | | | | | | | |
| Housing | 0.7 | 2.1 | 2.2 | 3.2 | 1.9 | 1.6 | 3.4 | 3.7 | 6.1 | 12.4 | 15.8 | 6.2 | 14.3 |
| Industrial Development | 0.1 | 0.1 | 0.3 | 2.7 | 0.5 | 1.3 | 1.5 | 2.2 | 3.4 | 7.1 | 9.2 | 12.6 | 12.7 |
| Pollution Control | — | — | 0.6 | 1.7 | 2.2 | 2.5 | 1.9 | 2.6 | 2.7 | 2.1 | 2.3 | 4.3 | 5.3 |
| Hospitals | — | 0.4 | 0.5 | 0.7 | 0.8 | 2.0 | 2.3 | 3.3 | 2.1 | 3.4 | 3.6 | 5.4 | 9.5 |
| Student Loans | — | — | — | — | — | — | 0.1 | 0.1 | 0.3 | 0.6 | 0.5 | 1.0 | 1.6 |
| Sub-Total | 0.8 | 2.6 | 3.6 | 8.3 | 5.4 | 7.4 | 9.2 | 11.9 | 14.6 | 25.6 | 31.4 | 29.5 | 43.4 |
| Refundings | 0.1 | 0.5 | 1.7 | 1.6 | 0.7 | 1.1 | 3.2 | 8.8 | 8.7 | 1.2 | 2.0 | 1.3 | 4.3 |
| Total | 18.1 | 24.9 | 23.7 | 23.8 | 23.6 | 31.4 | 36.5 | 46.8 | 50.7 | 48.7 | 55.9 | 57.0 | 87.5 |

—Figures not available.

Note: These figures are primarily based on PSA data. Other sources are used where PSA data are not available. CBO estimates are used for small issue IDBs beginning in 1975 and total volume figures are adjusted accordingly to compensate for their increase above PSA's publicly reported amount. IDB figures for 1982 are preliminary estimates.

SOURCES: Data from Public Securities Association, Municipal Finance Officers Association, Treasury, Congressional Budget Office and Federal Reserve Board. Methodology developed by the National League of Cities. Table from U.S. General Accounting Office, "Trends and Changes in the Municipal Bond Market as They Relate to Financing State and Local Public Infrastructure," GAO Report PAD-8-46, September 12, 1983, p. 48.

TABLE 6-3    Volume of Short-Term Borrowing As A Share of Total Volume, 1970-82

| | ($ IN BILLIONS) | | SHORT-TERM |
| YEAR | TOTAL BOND AND NOTE VOLUME | SHORT-TERM NOTE VOLUME | AS % OF TOTAL |
| --- | --- | --- | --- |
| 1970 | $35.6 | $17.9 | 50.3 |
| 1971 | 50.7 | 26.3 | 51.9 |
| 1972 | 49.2 | 25.2 | 51.2 |
| 1973 | 47.6 | 24.7 | 51.9 |
| 1974 | 51.9 | 29.0 | 55.9 |
| 1975 | 58.3 | 29.0 | 49.7 |
| 1976 | 55.4 | 20.1 | 36.3 |
| 1977 | 71.5 | 24.8 | 34.7 |
| 1978 | 69.7 | 21.4 | 30.7 |
| 1979 | 65.0 | 21.7 | 33.4 |
| 1980 | 76.2 | 27.7 | 36.4 |
| 1981 | 85.2 | 37.4 | 43.9 |
| 1982 | 122.0 | 44.7 | 36.6 |

SOURCES:    Data from Public Securities Association. Table from U.S. General Accounting Office, "Trends and Changes in the Municipal Bond Market as They Relate to Financing State and Local Public Infrastructure," GAO Report PAD-83-46, September 12, 1983, p. 41.

note is defined similarly to a bond except that the maturity date is usually no more than one year from the date of issue.

### Security Behind the Debt

An important consideration in debt analysis is the resources the government legally commits to the payment of principal and interest on the debt. This commitment is commonly referred to as the *security* pledged behind the debt by the issuer.

There are different ways in which state and local governments can back up their agreement to pay principal and interest on a debt obligation. Furthermore, different references may categorize the alternative types differently, so care should always be exercised when scrutinizing bonds classified by security type.

For our purposes here, we distinguish between two broad types of security, recognizing that some debt may not fall exactly into either type. The first type of security pledge is a *general obligation*. Most general obligation securities pledge the full faith and credit—the full taxing and revenue-generating capacity—of the issuer behind the debt. Historically, the full faith and credit pledge referred to the government's ability to levy property taxes. As we showed in Chapter 4, however, the property tax is no longer the dominant revenue source it once was, so that the full faith and credit pledge now normally includes the full range of taxes and revenues at the disposal of the issuer.

In some cases when a government issues debt with all its taxes and revenues as security, certain restrictions apply to the government's ability to repay the debt.

For example, if the government operates under a property tax rate limit and debt is not excluded from the limit, a government may be constrained in its use of the property tax as security for the debt. When a full faith and credit pledge is constrained by a factor such as a tax limit it is sometimes called ''limited tax'' debt as opposed to unlimited tax debt. Both (unlimited) full faith and credit and limited tax debt are considered general obligation debt.

The second broad type of security is all security less than that behind general obligation debt. Sometimes this less-secured debt is called nonguaranteed debt, limited obligation debt, or revenue debt. We will use the term *limited obligation* to distinguish this less-secured debt from *general obligation*. Limited obligation debt may be backed by a variety of different security pledges, including special assessments, special taxes, and revenues that are primarily from enterprises or self-supporting activities.

State and local governments sometimes undertake projects that only benefit a particular subset of the population and finance these projects with special assessments. In some cases when debt is issued to finance the projects initially, the revenues generated by the special assessment may constitute the security behind the debt.

When the proceeds from a special tax or other designated revenue source are used as the sole form of debt security, the debt is also considered a limited obligation. A common example in this case is the use of a gasoline tax as the security for debt that is issued to finance the construction of a highway.

Finally, certain capital projects financed by state and local governments generate their own revenues, sometimes by charging for goods and services, and these user charges may be designated the security behind the debt. This type of limited obligation debt is commonly referred to as *revenue* debt. In some cases the revenues to the entity issuing the debt consist of lease payments rather than user charges, and these lease payments may be pledged as security.

Although in theory these different security pledges are distinguishable, in practice there is some ambiguity. This exists in part because of the different terminology used by different organizations. The terms *limited obligation debt, nonguaranteed debt,* and *revenue debt* are sometimes used differently. Moreover, *self-supporting debt* is a term that is often used interchangeably with any or all of the above terms. However, almost all the classification systems, including the one used by the U.S. Bureau of the Census, distinguish between general obligation debt and other forms of debt.[19]

A second confusion arises due to the use of multiple-security pledges. That is, the full faith and credit of the state or local government may be the backup or secondary security for the debt in addition to the proceeds from a special tax, revenues from an enterprise, and so forth, which are the primary security. In most cases where there is a full faith and credit pledge either as primary or secondary security, the debt is classified as general obligation.

---

[19] For more details on the classification systems, see Moak, *Municipal Bonds,* pp. 41–43.

Since 1970 long-term state and local government debt has increasingly been issued as limited obligation debt. In 1970 limited obligation debt comprised 34.5 percent of the volume of long-term state and local government debt issued, while general obligation debt comprised the remaining 65.5 percent. By 1982 limited obligation debt comprised 73 percent of the volume of long-term state and local government debt issued, while general obligation debt comprised the remaining 27 percent.[20] This trend is consistent with the trends observed for the purpose of the debt and the entity issuing the debt.

### Repayment of Debt

Although almost all long-term debt involves the payment of principal and interest on the principal over time, there are a number of ways in which these debt service payments can be structured. The basic difference among these payment schemes is the timing of the principal payments. The two major types of bonds, classified according to their repayment schedules, are *term bonds* and *serial bonds.* A particular debt issue may consist of term bonds or serial bonds or both. Term bonds are issued such that the entire principal is to be repaid at the final date of the maturity of the issue, while interest is paid on the outstanding principal for the life of the bond. The issuer is not expected to ignore the principal over the life of the bond and may be required to accumulate funds to repay the principal when it becomes due. These funds are accumulated in what is called a *sinking fund.*

Serial bonds do not utilize sinking funds. Serial bonds are structured so that some principal is paid back every year, instead of waiting until the last year of the bond issue. This is usually accomplished by scheduling a certain portion of the debt to mature in each year. Thus a twenty-year serial bond could actually be comprised of a number of separate bonds with maturities ranging from one to twenty years. Serial bonds vary in terms of how much principal is paid back in each year, with a "straight serial bond" structured to pay back the same amount of principal in each year (leading to declining debt service) and an "annuity serial bond" structured so that debt service is equal in each year (with increasing principal payments).[21]

### Cost of Debt

The cost of state and local government debt, or any debt for that matter, is determined by comparing the amount that is initially borrowed (principal) with the amount that is repaid (principal plus interest) and the timing of the repayments. With these inflows and outflows the effective interest cost, or yield, of

---

[20] General Accounting Office, *Trends and Changes in the Municipal Bond Market,* p. 50.

[21] For a discussion of term versus serial bonds, see Moak and Hillhouse, *Concepts and Practices in Local Government Finance,* pp. 312–14.

a debt issue can be determined using present value methods.[22] Since the yield of a government's debt, compared to the yield on debt of similar governments, is sometimes used as a proxy for the government's financial condition, it is important to be aware of the array of factors that determine yields.

First, the yields on state and local government debt are significantly affected by the overall interest rate in the economy. As Table 6–4 shows, yields on tax-exempt issues parallels yields on corporate issues, and other data could be presented to show that it parallels treasury issues as well. Thus the factors that affect the supply of and demand for financial assets in general influence the interest rates paid by governments. A discussion of the factors that determine market interest rates is beyond the scope of this book. Instead we focus on the factors that influence the cost of government debt, given the market rate of interest.

Clearly, the tax-exemption feature affects local government debt costs. Table 6–4 shows the ratio of yields of tax-exempt to taxable bonds of comparable risk from 1950 to 1982. The ratio has varied from a low of 61.2 percent in 1951 to a high of 87.2 percent in 1969. The 1982 figure, 78.5 percent, represents a substantial rise since 1979. A factor that influences this ratio is income tax policy. As marginal income tax rates decrease, the value of the tax-exemption decreases, and this should lower the demand for tax-exempt debt and raise its yield relative to taxable debt. A series of tax changes that have lowered marginal rates and created new tax shelters, along with the increased volume of tax-exempt debt issued, may keep the ratio of tax-exempt to taxable yields high in the near-term future.[23]

Beyond factors that influence overall interest rates and the relative position of tax-exempt issues, there are other factors that influence the cost of a particular state and local government debt issue at a specific point in time. Many of these characteristics influence the cost of a debt issue by increasing the riskiness of the investment to the lender. By *riskiness* we mean the probability that the lender will not receive the promised principal or interest if the issue is held to maturity, or the principal and accumulated interest if sold prior to maturity. In general, debt characteristics that increase riskiness will increase cost, all else being equal.

A key factor that influences the riskiness of the debt is the overall financial condition of the issuer. Governments that are in worse financial condition are likely to pay a higher cost for their debt, all else being equal. A number of organizations such as Standard and Poor's and Moody's rate individual bond issues, and one of the key factors (but not the only factor) in their ratings is the

---

[22] Certain widespread measures of debt cost, such as net interest cost, add up interest payments in different periods without considering when they occur, resulting in less-accurate cost estimates than present value methods. For an analysis of alternative methodologies for estimating borrowing costs, see Michael Hopewell and George Kaufman, *Improving Bidding Rules to Reduce Interest Costs in the Competitive Sale of Municipal Bonds* (Eugene, Oreg.: Center for Capital Market Research, University of Oregon, 1977); and Moak, *Municipal Bonds,* Chap. 12. We discuss the present value approach in Chapter 7.

[23] General Accounting Office, *Trends and Changes in the Municipal Bond Market,* pp. 9–25.

TABLE 6-4   Average Annual Tax-Exempt/Taxable Yield Ratio, 1950–82
(Moody's Aa-Rated Issues) (Percentages)

| YEAR | AVERAGE ANNUAL MUNICIPAL BOND YIELDS | AVERAGE ANNUAL CORPORATE BOND YIELDS | TAX EXEMPT/ TAXABLE YIELD RATIO |
|---|---|---|---|
| 1950 | 1.76% | 2.69% | 65.4% |
| 1951 | 1.78 | 2.91 | 61.2 |
| 1952 | 2.00 | 3.04 | 65.8 |
| 1953 | 2.54 | 3.31 | 76.7 |
| 1954 | 2.16 | 3.06 | 70.6 |
| 1955 | 2.32 | 3.16 | 73.4 |
| 1956 | 2.72 | 3.45 | 78.8 |
| 1957 | 3.33 | 4.03 | 82.6 |
| 1958 | 3.17 | 3.94 | 80.5 |
| 1959 | 3.55 | 4.51 | 78.7 |
| 1960 | 3.51 | 4.56 | 77.0 |
| 1961 | 3.46 | 4.48 | 77.2 |
| 1962 | 3.17 | 4.47 | 70.9 |
| 1963 | 3.16 | 4.39 | 72.0 |
| 1964 | 3.19 | 4.49 | 71.0 |
| 1965 | 3.25 | 4.57 | 71.1 |
| 1966 | 3.76 | 5.23 | 71.9 |
| 1967 | 3.86 | 5.66 | 68.2 |
| 1968 | 4.31 | 6.38 | 67.6 |
| 1969 | 6.28 | 7.20 | 87.2 |
| 1970 | 6.28 | 8.32 | 75.5 |
| 1971 | 5.36 | 7.78 | 68.9 |
| 1972 | 5.19 | 7.48 | 69.4 |
| 1973 | 5.09 | 7.66 | 66.4 |
| 1974 | 6.04 | 8.84 | 68.3 |
| 1975 | 6.77 | 9.17 | 73.8 |
| 1976 | 6.12 | 8.75 | 69.9 |
| 1977 | 5.39 | 8.24 | 65.4 |
| 1978 | 5.68 | 8.92 | 63.7 |
| 1979 | 6.12 | 9.94 | 61.6 |
| 1980 | 8.06 | 12.50 | 64.5 |
| 1981 | 10.89 | 14.75 | 73.8 |
| 1982 | 11.31 | 14.41 | 78.5 |

SOURCES:   Data from Moody's Investor Service. Table from U.S. General Accounting Office, "Trends and Changes in the Municipal Bond Market as They Relate to Financing State and Local Public Infrastructure," GAO Report PAD-83-46, September 12, 1983, p. 39.

financial condition of the issuer. Although bond ratings themselves may have a small independent effect on bond yield, it is important to remember that the ratings are measuring an underlying condition and that the difference in yields between bonds with different ratings is not due largely to the rating *per se*.[24]

---

[24] For a description of bond ratings, see Moak, *Municipal Bonds,* Appendix D; and Hugh C. Sherwood, *How Corporate and Municipal Debt Is Rated* (New York: John Wiley, 1976). For an analysis of

Three other factors that influence the cost of debt by affecting the riskiness of the issue are the period of the debt, the security behind the debt, and the existence of a call provision. In general, longer-term issues are considered riskier than shorter-term issues because future interest rates cannot be predicted perfectly. As a result, if interest rates rise, the holder of a long-term issue may face a loss indirectly because of the lost opportunity or directly if the debt must be sold on the secondary market before maturity. Most of the time, issues with longer maturity are costlier, all else being equal.[25]

The security behind a debt issue can also affect its riskiness. For the most part, general obligation debt is considered less risky than limited obligation debt because of the larger revenue base that can be drawn upon for repayment of debt by the organization. All else being equal, limited obligation debt is more costly to the issuer than general obligation debt.[26]

Finally, the call feature of a debt instrument can also affect the cost of the debt. Since debt with a call provision can be refunded by the issuer when it faces favorable market conditions, a risk is added for the lender. To compensate for this risk, the lender requires a higher yield, so that debt is usually costlier to the issuer when it contains a call provision.[27]

A recent review of the determinants of tax-exempt bond yields by Timothy Cook identified a number of other factors that influence the cost of debt.[28] Certain marketing and structural variables such as the number of underwriters competing for the issue (more competition, lower costs), the coupon structure of the bond, and whether the issue is negotiated or bid competitively (negotiated is usually associated with higher costs) have been found to influence the cost of debt. Also factors in the regional market of the issue and the size of the issue may influence debt costs.

### Recent Trends in State and Local Government Debt

This review has identified a number of trends in the market for state and local government debt. Over the past twenty years, the volume of state and local government debt has increased significantly, a greater percentage of the debt is being issued as limited obligation rather than general obligation debt, and more of

---

the effects of ratings, see Daniel Rubinfeld, "Credit Ratings and the Market for General Obligation Bonds," *National Tax Journal,* 26, No. 1 (March 1973), 17–27; G. R. Jantscher, "The Effects of Changes in Credit Ratings on Municipal Borrowing Costs" (IBA Occasional Paper 11, Investment Bankers Association of America, 1970); and Timothy Q. Cook, "Determinants of Individual Tax-Exempt Bond Yields: A Survey of the Evidence," *Economic Review,* Federal Reserve Bank of Richmond, 68, No. 3 (May–June, 1982), 14–39.

[25] See Public Securities Association, *Fundamentals of Municipal Bonds,* pp. 142–45.

[26] See Cook, "Determinants of Individual Tax-Exempt Bond Yields."

[27] Ibid.

[28] Cook, in "Determinants of Individual Tax-Exempt Bond Yields," reviews twenty-five regression studies of the costs of tax-exempt debt.

the debt is being used for "nontraditional" purposes. This increased use of debt for nontraditional purposes, however, has led to increased congressional scrutiny of the laws and regulations that allow these uses.

In order to market the large increase in volume of state and local government debt, changes have also taken place in the way in which debt instruments are structured. Innovations such as zero coupon bonds, compound interest bonds, stepped coupon bonds, and floating rate bonds are now being tried.[29] New ways to combine lease and debt financing are also being designed to take advantage of tax laws and market conditions.[30] Another set of changes involves risk spreading using vehicles such as bond banks and insurance.[31] If the recently identified need to rebuild the nation's infrastructure is met and/or if the federal income tax is altered, the demands on the bond market are likely to require even more innovations in the future.

## III. DEBT INFORMATION
## AND INITIAL ANALYSIS

Up to this point we have discussed debt analysis and examined the characteristics of state and local government debt in a general way. To analyze the debt of a particular government, however, we need to accumulate data on that organization and its reference group. In this section we illustrate the collection of debt information and the use of comparisons over time and with a reference group to provide an initial analysis of the data. To do this, we examine the debt of our sample city, Dyer Straits, and the reference group of forty-nine cities. We examine the outstanding debt, borrowings during recent years, debt service payments, overlapping general obligation debt, and future debt service payments for Dyer Straits and the reference group. In the next section we conduct the second stage of the analysis, focusing on the evaluation of debt capacity and reserves.

First, the outstanding debt for the city of Dyer Straits and the cities that make up the reference group are shown in Table 6–5 for 1979 through 1983. Note that the table shows only the outstanding organizational debt and does not include the debt of the overlapping jurisdictions. The table also shows the *constitutional debt limit* for Dyer Straits and the reference group. This is the legal limit on the amount of general obligation debt that a local government can borrow, and for our cities, it is set by the state constitution at 6.4 percent of the full assessed value of the city.

In Table 6–5, total outstanding debt is shown according to the security

---

[29] For a description of these innovations, see Hamilton, "The World Turned Upside Down."

[30] Ibid.

[31] For more information on bond banks, see Martin Katzman, "Municipal Bond Banking: The Diffusion of a Public Finance Innovation," *National Tax Journal*, 33, No. 2 (June 1980), 149–60. For additional information on bond insurance, see Public Securities Association, *Fundamentals of Municipal Bonds*, p. 64.

TABLE 6-5  Outstanding Municipal Debt (End of Year), City of Dyer Straits and Reference Group, 1979–83 ($ Thousands)

| MUNICIPAL DEBT | DYER STRAITS | | | | | REFERENCE GROUP | | | | | LOCATION QUOTIENTS* | | | | |
|---|---|---|---|---|---|---|---|---|---|---|---|---|---|---|---|
| | 1979 | 1980 | 1981 | 1982 | 1983 | 1979 | 1980 | 1981 | 1982 | 1983 | 1979 | 1980 | 1981 | 1982 | 1983 |
| Constitutional debt limit | 10,594 | 10,863 | 11,369 | 11,984 | 12,330 | 454,460 | 472,308 | 497,168 | 522,950 | 550,892 | .0233 | .0230 | .0229 | .0229 | .0224 |
| *Outstanding Debt:* | | | | | | | | | | | | | | | |
| Total outstanding debt | 13,041 | 14,225 | 17,245 | 17,513 | 18,174 | 342,092 | 367,561 | 420,158 | 429,189 | 432,214 | .0381 | .0387 | .0410 | .0408 | .0420 |
| Total GO outstanding debt† | 8,265 | 8,325 | 9,685 | 9,831 | 10,370 | 205,857 | 214,000 | 240,353 | 242,362 | 248,567 | .0401 | .0389 | .0403 | .0406 | .0417 |
| Total LO outstanding debt‡ | 4,776 | 5,900 | 7,560 | 7,682 | 7,804 | 136,235 | 153,561 | 179,805 | 186,827 | 183,647 | .0350 | .0384 | .0420 | .0411 | .0425 |
| Long-term debt outstanding | 6,840 | 8,214 | 10,257 | 10,933 | 11,162 | 183,711 | 221,253 | 266,073 | 277,771 | 264,266 | .0372 | .0371 | .0396 | .0394 | .0422 |
| Long-term GO | 4,926 | 5,477 | 6,583 | 6,695 | 6,948 | 120,278 | 139,157 | 168,221 | 169,750 | 157,499 | .0410 | .0394 | .0391 | .0394 | .0441 |
| Long-term LO | 1,914 | 2,737 | 3,944 | 4,238 | 4,214 | 63,433 | 82,096 | 97,852 | 108,021 | 106,767 | .0302 | .0333 | .0403 | .0392 | .0395 |
| Short-term Debt outstanding | 6,201 | 6,011 | 6,718 | 6,580 | 7,012 | 158,381 | 146,308 | 154,085 | 151,418 | 167,948 | .0392 | .0411 | .0436 | .0435 | .0418 |
| Short-term debt GO | 3,339 | 2,848 | 3,102 | 3,136 | 3,422 | 85,579 | 74,843 | 72,132 | 72,612 | 91,068 | .0390 | .0381 | .0430 | .0432 | .0376 |
| Bond anticipation GO | 3,339 | 2,848 | 2,702 | 2,936 | 3,422 | 82,374 | 70,869 | 67,516 | 67,803 | 86,512 | .0405 | .0402 | .0400 | .0433 | .0396 |
| Capital notes GO | 0 | 0 | 400 | 200 | 0 | 3,205 | 3,974 | 4,616 | 4,809 | 4,556 | — | — | .0867 | .0416 | — |
| Short-term debt LO | 2,862 | 3,163 | 3,616 | 3,444 | 3,590 | 72,802 | 71,465 | 81,953 | 78,806 | 76,880 | .0393 | .0443 | .0441 | .0437 | .0467 |
| Bond anticipation LO | 2,762 | 3,163 | 3,241 | 3,169 | 3,440 | 62,241 | 61,173 | 72,200 | 69,665 | 66,192 | .0444 | .0517 | .0449 | .0455 | .0520 |
| Capital notes LO | 100 | 0 | 375 | 275 | 150 | 10,561 | 10,292 | 9,753 | 9,141 | 10,688 | .0095 | — | .0385 | .0301 | .0140 |

*Dyer Straits/Reference Group.
†GO = General obligation.
‡LO = Limited obligation.

pledged—general obligation and limited obligation. For our sample of cities, all debt either has a general obligation (full faith and credit) backing or is secured by enterprise revenues. Note that the total amount of outstanding limited obligation debt for 1983 is taken from the balance sheets of Dyer Straits' enterprise funds, shown in Chapter 2, Table 2-16.

From Table 6-5 we can see that both general obligation debt and limited obligation debt have increased for Dyer Straits and the reference group, although the percentage increase is higher for Dyer Straits for both types of debt. Also, the proportion of outstanding debt that is limited obligation has increased for both Dyer Straits and the reference group over the five-year period. Total outstanding debt, broken down by short-term and long-term maturities, is also shown in Table 6-5. Outstanding short-term debt has not increased as rapidly as long-term debt for Dyer Straits or the reference group from 1979 through 1983. During this period, general obligation short-term debt grew less rapidly in Dyer Straits relative to the reference group, while the reverse is true of limited obligation short-term debt. Finally, we can see from Table 6-5 that almost all the short-term debt is comprised of bond anticipation notes, although both Dyer Straits and the reference group do make some use of capital notes that are usually negotiated with a local bank.

Table 6-6 shows the amounts of new borrowing that took place during the five-year period 1970–83 for Dyer Straits and the reference group. This table includes the debt of the city alone and not of other overlapping jurisdictions. Again the debt is shown by type of security and length of term. Yearly amounts of long-term borrowing decreased for Dyer Straits and the reference group for both general and limited obligation debt from 1979 through 1983. Moreover, there are only relatively small changes in the amount of short-term borrowing between 1979 and 1983 for Dyer Straits and the reference group.

The debt service payments made by Dyer Straits and the reference group for 1979 through 1983 are shown in Table 6-7. Debt service consists of principal on long-term debt and interest on both long-term and short-term debt. The principal on short-term debt is not included in the debt service figures, since the principal will be paid within one year after the proceeds are received unless the debt is refinanced. (If new short-term debt is continually issued to repay existing short-term debt, then this short-term debt principal is effectively substituting for long-term debt and would be included in the debt service figures.) The data in Table 6-7 indicate that both total principal and interest payments increase somewhat more rapidly for Dyer Straits over the five-year period compared with the reference group, although there is considerable variation in the relative growth rates for the various components of debt service.

The outstanding long-term debt at year-end listed in Table 6-5 can be derived for a particular year by adding the preceding year's outstanding debt to the new borrowing during the year and subtracting the year's principal payments. For example, the outstanding general obligation long-term debt for Dyer Straits at the end of 1980 ($5,477,000) equals the outstanding long-term general obligation

TABLE 6-6  Long and Short Term Borrowing, City of Dyer Straits and Reference Group, 1979–83 ($ Thousands)

| | DYER STRAITS | | | | | REFERENCE GROUP | | | | | LOCATION QUOTIENTS* | | | | |
|---|---|---|---|---|---|---|---|---|---|---|---|---|---|---|---|
| | 1979 | 1980 | 1981 | 1982 | 1983 | 1979 | 1980 | 1981 | 1982 | 1983 | 1979 | 1980 | 1981 | 1982 | 1983 |
| Long-term—total | 2,311.8 | 2,360.6 | 3,452.9 | 1,593.2 | 1,363.8 | 48,947 | 80,420 | 92,114 | 59,554 | 34,539 | .0472 | .0294 | .0375 | .0267 | .0395 |
| Long-term GO† | 1,158.7 | 1,047.2 | 1,658.2 | 663.5 | 797.8 | 27,765 | 42,093 | 53,952 | 26,405 | 12,888 | .0417 | .0249 | .0307 | .0251 | .0619 |
| Long-term LO‡ | 1,153.1 | 1,313.4 | 1,794.7 | 929.7 | 566.0 | 21,182 | 38,327 | 38,162 | 33,149 | 21,651 | .0544 | .0343 | .0470 | .0280 | .0261 |
| Short-term—total | 6,736 | 6,366 | 7,206 | 7,195 | 7,432 | 165,692 | 155,386 | 162,081 | 159,249 | 178,250 | .0407 | .0410 | .0445 | .0452 | .0417 |
| Short-term GO | 3,568 | 3,035 | 3,352 | 3,498 | 3,631 | 89,688 | 78,602 | 76,824 | 76,027 | 97,536 | .0398 | .0386 | .0436 | .0460 | .0372 |
| Bond anticipation notes | 3,568 | 3,035 | 2,952 | 3,298 | 3,631 | 85,269 | 72,751 | 70,007 | 69,120 | 91,127 | .0418 | .0417 | .0422 | .0477 | .0398 |
| Capital notes | 0 | 0 | 400 | 200 | 0 | 4,419 | 5,851 | 6,817 | 6,907 | 6,409 | — | — | .0587 | .0290 | — |
| Short-term LO | 3,168 | 3,331 | 3,854 | 3,697 | 3,801 | 76,004 | 76,784 | 85,257 | 83,222 | 80,714 | .0417 | .0434 | .0452 | .0444 | .0471 |
| Bond anticipation notes | 3,068 | 3,331 | 3,479 | 3,422 | 3,651 | 64,113 | 63,312 | 75,150 | 71,717 | 68,614 | .0479 | .0526 | .0463 | .0477 | .0532 |
| Capital notes | 100 | 0 | 375 | 275 | 150 | 11,891 | 13,472 | 10,107 | 11,505 | 12,100 | .0084 | — | .0371 | .0239 | .0124 |

*Dyer Straits/Reference Group.

†GO = General obligation.

‡LO = Limited obligation.

251

TABLE 6-7 Debt Service—Municipal Debt, City of Dyer Straits and Reference Group, 1979-83 ($ Thousands)

| | DYER STRAITS | | | | | REFERENCE GROUP | | | | | LOCATION QUOTIENTS* | | | | |
|---|---|---|---|---|---|---|---|---|---|---|---|---|---|---|---|
| | 1979 | 1980 | 1981 | 1982 | 1983 | 1979 | 1980 | 1981 | 1982 | 1983 | 1979 | 1980 | 1981 | 1982 | 1983 |
| Principal repayments on long-term debt | 859.8 | 986.6 | 1,139.9 | 1,187.2 | 1,134.8 | 39,941 | 42,888 | 47,294 | 47,856 | 48,044 | .0215 | .0230 | .0241 | .0248 | .0236 |
| Principal—GO† | 410.7 | 496.2 | 552.2 | 551.5 | 544.8 | 22,602 | 23,214 | 24,888 | 24,876 | 25,139 | .0182 | .0214 | .0222 | .0222 | .0217 |
| Principal—LO‡ | 449.1 | 490.4 | 587.7 | 635.7 | 590.0 | 17,339 | 19,674 | 22,406 | 22,980 | 22,905 | .0259 | .0249 | .0262 | .0277 | .0258 |
| Interest on all debt— | | | | | | | | | | | | | | | |
| Total | 691.3 | 814.4 | 1,020.0 | 983.3 | 976.9 | 15,362 | 17,606 | 21,842 | 21,353 | 20,601 | .0450 | .0463 | .0467 | .0460 | .0474 |
| Long-term GO | 215.4 | 263.2 | 304.2 | 321.1 | 333.5 | 4,811 | 5,705 | 6,897 | 7,299 | 7,087 | .0448 | .0461 | .0441 | .0440 | .0471 |
| Short-term GO | 193.7 | 193.7 | 248.2 | 216.4 | 212.2 | 2,632 | 3,489 | 4,159 | 4,969 | 5,125 | .0736 | .0555 | .0597 | .0436 | .0414 |
| Long-term LO | 116.2 | 142.4 | 178.3 | 208.2 | 208.6 | 4,279 | 4,303 | 5,049 | 4,357 | 4,553 | .0272 | .0331 | .0353 | .0478 | .0458 |
| Short-term LO | 166.0 | 215.1 | 289.3 | 237.6 | 222.6 | 3,640 | 4,109 | 5,737 | 4,728 | 3,836 | .0456 | .0523 | .0504 | .0503 | .0580 |

*Dyer Straits/Reference Group.
†GO = General obligation.
‡LO = Limited obligation.

debt at the end of 1979 ($4,926,000) plus the new long-term general obligation borrowing during 1980 (1,047,200) less the principal paid during 1980 on long-term general obligation debt ($496,200).

The preceding three tables displayed the outstanding debt, new borrowings, and debt service payments for the cities of Dyer Straits and those that are included in the reference group. The residents of these cities, however, are also the residents of other entities that issue debt, specifically school districts and county governments. Since we will need to examine the overlapping debt of Dyer Straits and the reference group later in this chapter, these data are shown in Table 6-8. The outstanding overlapping general obligation debt and overlapping general obligation debt service are shown for 1979 through 1983 for Dyer Straits and the reference group. To obtain a total debt amount for each overlapping jurisdiction, debt has been allocated on the basis of full assessed value when overlapping jurisdictions are not coterminous. Table 6-8 shows that total outstanding overlapping general obligation debt and debt service increased over the period more rapidly for Dyer Straits than for the reference group.

The final data on the debt obligations for Dyer Straits and the reference group are the future principal payments that are currently obligated for the city and overlapping debt. These data are shown in Table 6-9. Note that the jurisdictions that contribute to the overlapping debt use debt obligations with longer maturities.

This concludes our presentation of debt-related data for Dyer Straits and the reference group and our preliminary descriptive analysis. Next we will discuss how to analyze the debt obligations of a government so that we can assess the financial condition from a debt perspective.

## IV. ANALYSIS OF DEBT CAPACITY AND RESERVES

After assembling the basic debt information on a government and making some initial comparisons over time and with a reference group, we can now turn to more direct analysis of the impact of debt on government financial condition. In this section we try to determine the extent to which a government has used up its debt capacity, or, in other words, whether it is carrying "too much" debt, threatening its financial health.

From our earlier discussion (section I), we saw that to answer the question of how much debt capacity had been used (or what is still available), ideally we would estimate the government's revenue reserves and expenditure pressures to determine how much revenue reserves were available to carry additional debt. This information, coupled with knowledge of the supply of funds from lenders, could be used to estimate how close the government was to its borrowing limit.

Because the "ideal" measures are difficult if not impossible to measure accurately and easily, we will rely primarily on traditional measures of debt burden

TABLE 6-8 Overlapping Debt and Debt Service—General Obligation, City of Dyer Straits and Reference Group, 1979–83 ($ Thousands)

| | DYER STRAITS | | | | | REFERENCE GROUP | | | | | LOCATION QUOTIENTS* | | | | |
|---|---|---|---|---|---|---|---|---|---|---|---|---|---|---|---|
| | 1979 | 1980 | 1981 | 1982 | 1983 | 1979 | 1980 | 1981 | 1982 | 1983 | 1979 | 1980 | 1981 | 1982 | 1983 |
| Outstanding Debt— | | | | | | | | | | | | | | | |
| Total | 23,959 | 25,807 | 29,615 | 30,655 | 31,629 | 686,250 | 695,385 | 707,350 | 714,610 | 724,680 | .0349 | .0371 | .0419 | .0429 | .0436 |
| Long term | 14,855 | 16,516 | 19,546 | 20,845 | 22,140 | 452,925 | 452,000 | 452,704 | 450,204 | 449,301 | .0328 | .0365 | .0430 | .0463 | .0493 |
| Short term | 9,104 | 9,291 | 10,069 | 9,810 | 9,489 | 233,325 | 243,385 | 254,646 | 264,406 | 275,379 | .0390 | .0382 | .0395 | .0371 | .0355 |
| Debt Service— | | | | | | | | | | | | | | | |
| Total | 2,424 | 2,737 | 3,310 | 3,400 | 3,477 | 68,735 | 71,851 | 75,772 | 74,166 | 72,852 | .0353 | .0381 | .0437 | .0458 | .0477 |
| Principal | 1,322 | 1,470 | 1,730 | 1,834 | 1,948 | 38,499 | 38,872 | 38,933 | 38,718 | 39,089 | .0343 | .0378 | .0444 | .0474 | .0498 |
| Interest | 1,102 | 1,267 | 1,580 | 1,566 | 1,529 | 30,236 | 32,979 | 36,839 | 35,448 | 33,763 | .0364 | .0384 | .0429 | .0442 | .0453 |

*Dyer Straits/Reference Group.

TABLE 6-9     **Future City and Overlapping General Obligation Principal Payments for City of Dyer Straits and Reference Group ($ Thousands)**

| | DYER STRAITS | | REFERENCE GROUP | |
| | City | Overlapping | City | Overlapping |
| YEAR | Debt | Debt | Debt | Debt |
|---|---|---|---|---|
| 1984 | $535.2 | $1,903 | $20,142 | $69,203 |
| 1985 | 480.6 | 1,873 | 18,193 | 51,035 |
| 1986 | 480.6 | 1,759 | 13,165 | 46,139 |
| 1987 | 430.2 | 1,515 | 11,004 | 39,059 |
| 1988 | 430.2 | 1,398 | 9,715 | 36,094 |
| 1989 | 407.9 | 1,243 | 9,103 | 23,029 |
| 1990 | 406.2 | 1,229 | 8,729 | 16,153 |
| 1991 | 400.1 | 1,007 | 7,729 | 15,068 |
| 1992 | 387.3 | 949 | 6,926 | 13,444 |
| 1993 | 367.1 | 929 | 5,938 | 12,903 |
| 1994 | 320.3 | 907 | 5,805 | 11,849 |
| 1995 | 300.0 | 894 | 5,712 | 10,105 |
| 1996 | 296.8 | 891 | 5,251 | 9,893 |
| 1997 | 284.7 | 883 | 5,023 | 9,321 |
| 1998 | 279.4 | 821 | 4,919 | 8,703 |
| 1999 | 270.2 | 702 | 4,826 | 8,519 |
| 2000 | 212.3 | 693 | 4,713 | 7,914 |
| 2001 | 197.4 | 521 | 4,462 | 7,322 |
| 2002 | 180.6 | 407 | 3,122 | 7,115 |
| 2003 | 180.6 | 382 | 2,019 | 6,989 |
| 2004 | 100.3 | 293 | 1,003 | 6,755 |
| 2005 | — | 276 | — | 6,328 |
| 2006 | — | 205 | — | 6,214 |
| 2007 | — | 183 | — | 6,214 |
| 2008 | — | 183 | — | 6,009 |
| 2009 | — | 47 | — | 5,919 |
| 2010 | — | 47 | — | 2,005 |
| Total | $6,948.0 | $22,140 | $157,499 | $449,301 |

that are much easier to assemble. Their interpretation, and in some cases their refinement and extension, will be guided by our "ideal" measures.

In this section we examine debt burden measures in detail, evaluate their use, and adapt them when necessary for improved debt analysis. We then apply these measures to information from Dyer Straits to illustrate in detail the use of debt analysis within the framework developed in this book.

### Data for Debt Burden Measures

Debt burden measures are designed to evaluate the government's use of debt compared with the government's ability to repay the debt. To make the measures appropriate and comparable over time and across governments, only certain types of outstanding debt are included in the calculation of the debt burden. (Decisions on the inclusion of debtlike obligations such as leases should be made on the same basis as decisions on which debt to include.) First we discuss the inclusion of long-term debt, then short-term debt.

Long-term debt can be classified according to the security behind the debt—general obligation debt and limited obligation debt. The outstanding debt used to calculate debt burden measures includes all general obligation debt that is repaid from the government's revenue base. If general obligation debt is issued for a revenue-generating enterprise and the debt is fully self-supporting, this debt may be excluded from the debt burden measures. Limited obligation debt that is repaid from project specific sources such as user charges or leases, and presumably does not draw on the revenue base in the same way as general revenues, is usually excluded from the calculation of the debt burden measures. These rules are not absolute. If, despite the security pledge, certain limited obligation debt issues are actually being repaid from general revenues, then this debt should be included in the debt burden measure.

Certain long-term debt is issued with multiple-security pledges, and a common form of this is a "primary" security from project revenues and a "secondary" general obligation pledge. The probability that this debt will draw on the general revenue base of the government can be used as the criterion to determine whether this debt is included in the debt burden measure. Although actual practice in this area varies, a possible approach would be to include any multiple security debt that has more than a 50 percent chance of drawing on general revenues. A more conservative approach would be to include debt that has more than a 25 percent chance.[32]

Because of the variation in repayment methods, not all outstanding general obligation long-term debt is included in the debt burden measures. The dollar value of outstanding serial bonds that meet the security criteria above should be included in the debt burden measures. However, the outstanding amount of term bonds included in the debt burden measures should be reduced by the amount held by the government in sinking funds for term bonds.

To summarize, the outstanding long-term debt included in the debt burden measures should include all debt with primary general obligation securities, secondary general obligation securities that are likely to draw on the general revenue base, less the amount of debt paid from self-supporting revenues and less the amount held in sinking funds for the retirement of long-term bonds. Also, limited obligation debt that is being paid with general revenues should be included. Finally, certain forms of debt such as zero coupon bonds may have to be converted to an equivalent amount of outstanding principal and interest using present value techniques in order to calculate the debt burden measures.

---

[32] Practices vary in the inclusion of multiple security debt in debt analysis, so individual debt measures should be examined carefully. Sometimes debt measures calculated by a government may exclude multiple-security debt, while debt analysis by a rating agency or bond insurance company may include it.

Some, but not all, short-term debt should be included in the outstanding debt for the debt burden measures. Many governments issue short-term debt (bond anticipation notes) prior to the issuance of long-term debt, and this type of short-term debt should be included in the outstanding debt for the debt burden measures if the type of anticipated long-term debt would normally be included. The other major type of short-term borrowing is tax or revenue anticipation borrowing. If this short-term debt is being used as intended, to smooth out uneven revenue flows, and is fully paid off when due, it should not be included in the debt burden measures. If, however, this debt is rolled over or reissued on a regular basis so that it is continuously rather than periodically outstanding, then a case can be made for its inclusion in the debt burden measures. Regardless of whether it is included in the debt burden measures, the use of short-term debt by the government should be examined separately, and this will be discussed below.

Finally, the complexities introduced by overlapping local jurisdictions must be taken into account in the debt burden measures. The debt burden measures that we will discuss below can and should be calculated using the outstanding debt, as defined above, for the government. In addition, due to the use of special districts, and the existence of school districts, villages, towns, cities, and counties, a geographical revenue base is often burdened with the debt of more than one local jurisdiction. Therefore, in order to provide a more comparable measure of outstanding debt, the debt burden measures should be computed using the overlapping debt that pertains to the jurisdiction of the government under study in addition to outstanding debt of the local government alone.

Traditionally, when jurisdictions are not coterminous, overlapping debt is allocated on the basis of equalized assessed value. As the revenue sources of governments and other local entities become more diversified, however, allocation on other bases such as population may be more appropriate.

Finally, we need to consider how to define *debt service.* The debt service measure should include the principal and interest paid on the types of long-term debt included in the measures of outstanding debt. Self-supporting debt where debt service is totally paid from project revenues should be excluded. Most limited obligation debt will fall into this group. In the case of term bonds with sinking funds, the debt service measure should include the amounts that are paid to sinking funds. The same is true of zero coupon bonds.

For most short-term debt, it is not appropriate to include the principal payment in the debt service amount. In the case of bond anticipation notes, the proceeds for the long-term bond issues, not the government's revenues, will repay the principal, and in the case of revenue anticipation notes, the timing of the revenues and not their use is affected. When the revenue anticipation notes are rolled over or refinanced, however, this indicates that they are being used as longer-term debt, so that the principal of these notes should be included in the debt service figure. Even though the principal on short-term debt is not a burden on current revenues if the debt is being used correctly, the interest on all short-term debt should be included in the debt burden measure except where interest is paid from specific project-related revenues.

### Debt Burden Measures

Before we discuss the actual debt burden measures, we need to raise a few points about their interpretation. In general, there are three ways in which each of the debt burden measures can be interpreted. First, as we saw in Chapters 4 and 5, each of the measures can be computed for the government to be analyzed and for a reference group and compared both cross-sectionally and over time. The government's position in the reference group and the changes in the position over time can be documented, but the assessment is relative; a high or low debt burden is in relation to the debt burden of a specific reference group.

Second, these measures can be compared with established standards. Debt analysis has been practiced for some time by municipal bond analysts, and they have developed rough standards for many of the measures. Since it is somewhat difficult to determine these standards objectively, they should be viewed as somewhere between expert judgments and rules of thumb. Note, however, that when the judgment of municipal analysts is heavily relied on, their standards become important by definition.

Finally, these measures can be compared with legal limits. Many governments face legal limitations on the amount of debt that can be issued. Some of these limits are set constitutionally; others, by statutes. In most cases the limits apply to organizational rather than overlapping debt.

In this discussion of the debt burden measures themselves, we assume that the debt that is included satisfies the conditions discussed above. We begin with measures that employ stocks of resources and then review measures that focus on flows.

### Outstanding Debt/Full Assessed Value of Taxable Property.    Historically, the most commonly used debt burden measure is the ratio of outstanding debt to the value of the property tax base in the jurisdiction, measured in full assessed value. Full assessed value, sometimes called full value or market value, is usually higher than assessed value, since many jurisdictions assess at a "percentage" of market value. For most jurisdictions, however, data are available to convert total assessed value to estimated full or market value. This ratio is usually computed for both organizational and overlapping debt.[33]

The rationale behind this measure is that the property tax base provides a major revenue source for debt payment and there is some percentage "limit" on the amount that can be borrowed relative to the property tax base. This measure of debt burden has been the most prevalent historically, since the property tax was the most important source of revenues for local governments in the past. As the

---

[33] For examples of the use of this measure in empirical financial conditions studies, see Bureau of Governmental Research, University of Oregon, "Oregon Municipal Fiscal Indicators, An Exploratory Study," October 1983, p. 23; and City of Seattle, Office of the Comptroller, "Financial Condition of Seattle," August 18, 1983, p. 62.

revenues of local governments have diversified and the role of the property tax has diminished, this measure can no longer claim to be the sole indicator of debt burden. Nevertheless, the property tax is still important as a revenue source for local government debt, and the measure is one of several that are appropriate.

Because fiscal and borrowing practices vary considerably by state, it is useful to compare ratios of outstanding debt with full assessed value of local governments within the same state. Table 6-10 presents such a comparison for different size municipalities in Massachusetts and shows, for example, that ratios of debt to full assessed value increase with size and are consistently lower than comparable national averages.

Interpretation of this ratio follows the methods described above. First, as in our usual approach, the values for the government under study can be compared over time and with a relevant reference group's to indicate the direction in which the organization is moving and the level of debt burden relative to similarly situated organizations. Since governments differ in terms of functions provided, revenue sources, size, and legal restrictions, these comparisons can be considered the most satisfactory way to interpret the ratio for both organizational and overlapping debt. Also, rating agencies such as Moody's Investors Service regularly compute median values of debt to full assessed valuation for different types of local governments, stratified by population size. Median values between 3 and 6 percent are quite common.[34]

TABLE 6-10    **Comparison of Debt Per Capita and Debt as a Percent of Equalized Valuation for Massachusetts Municipalities and Municipalities in the Nation, 1982**

| | MASSACHUSETTS | | U.S.A. | |
|---|---|---|---|---|
| SIZE OF MUNICIPALITY | Direct and Overlapping Debt Per Capita | Direct and Overlapping Debt as a Percent of Equalized Valuation | Median Overall Debt Per Capita | Median Overall Debt as a Percent of Equalized Valuation |
| 0–4,999 | $202 | 0.68% | $793* | 3.2%* |
| 5,000–9,999 | 258 | 1.01 | 793* | 3.2* |
| 10,000–24,999 | 317 | 1.38 | 584 | 2.9 |
| 25,000–49,999 | 415 | 1.84 | 589 | 2.9 |
| 50,000+ | 522 | 2.88 | 497–678† | 2.7–3.6† |

*Moody's median for cities under 10,000.

†Data not broken down by Moody's as one category for cities with over 50,000 population. Excluded is the "over a million" population category, which does not apply in Massachusetts.

SOURCES:  Massachusetts data from Massachusetts Municipal Data Base and Massachusetts Department of Revenue. U.S. data from Moody's Investors Service, Inc. Table from Neville Lee ed., *Debt Survey of Massachusetts Cities & Towns* (Bank of Boston, September 1983), Table 9, p. 18.

---

[34] Public Securities Association, *Fundamentals of Municipal Bonds,* p. 119.

Second, the ratio of debt to property value is the most prevalent form of legal debt limits imposed by states on local government units. These limits usually apply to the outstanding general obligation debt of a school district, municipality, or county and can be constitutional or statutory or both. Most states employ a debt limit of this form for some combination of school districts, municipalities, and/or counties.[35]

As Moak and Hillhouse pointed out, however, it may be difficult to attach significance to the government's position relative to the debt limit because these limits vary considerably across states, do not appear to take organizational differences into account within states, usually ignore overlapping debt, and are sometimes based on locally assessed property values, rather than some form of equalized or full value.[36]

Third, since the ratio of outstanding debt to full assessed value has been used for some time by municipal bond analysts and financial managers, certain benchmarks are often applied in the interpretation of this ratio. Again, it is difficult to assess the validity of these standards except to note that they seem to be widely used. For example, recently several authors suggested as a rule of thumb that a ratio of 10 percent or higher for the ratio of outstanding overlapping debt to full assessed value signifies some potential for trouble for municipal governments.[37]

**Outstanding Debt/Population.**    An alternative measure of the debt burden of a government is per capita organizational and/or overlapping outstanding debt. While a per capita debt burden measure is not subject to the problems inherent in the assessment of taxable property, it does have the serious shortcoming that population, *per se,* is not necessarily a good measure of ability to pay. The measure implies that each individual has some fixed capacity to pay for debt independent of his or her associated wealth or tax base. Nonetheless, the measure does show the value of outstanding debt attributable to the resident of a jurisdiction, and this can be compared with other jurisdictions.[38]

Again it is useful to interpret this measure over time and compared with a reference group. Moody's also presents median values for this ratio by size of city and, as shown in Table 6-10, values range from just under $500 per capita to

---

[35] See Advisory Commission on Intergovernmental Relations, *Understanding the Market for State and Local Government Debt* (Washington, D.C.: ACIR, May 1976), Exhibit B-5, pp. 46–53; and Moak, *Municipal Bonds,* pp. 152–53.

[36] Moak and Hillhouse, *Concepts and Practices in Local Government Finance,* pp. 275–78.

[37] See George C. Kaufman, "Debt Management," in *Management Policies in Local Government Finance,* ed. J. Richard Aronson and Eli Schwartz (Washington, D.C.: International City Management Association, 1981), p. 313; and Sherwood, *How Corporate and Municipal Debt Is Rated,* p. 117. For data on the debt burden of large cities, see Moody's Investors Service, *Moody's Analytical Overview of 25 Leading U.S. Cities* (New York, 1977).

[38] For examples of the use of this measure in empirical financial condition studies, see Joint Economic Committee, *Trends in the Fiscal Condition of Cities: 1980–1982,* p. 38; and Touche Ross & Co. and the First National Bank of Boston, *Urban Fiscal Stress, A Comparative Analysis of 66 U.S. Cities* (New York: Touche Ross & Co., 1979), p. 32.

almost $800 per capita. In the Massachusetts municipalities shown in Table 6-10, per capita debt ranges from $202 to $522 per capita, consistently below the national medians.

In addition, municipal bond analysts have established a benchmark or rule of thumb that they claim serves as a rough indicator of a high debt burden for a municipality. For overlapping debt, a per capita debt burden above $1,000 to $1,300 is cited as a critical value.[39] This must be viewed as a rough criterion because debt appears to vary by size of local government and because, unlike the debt to full assessed value of property ratio, inflation affects only the numerator of the debt per capita ratio. Moreover, the variation across population in the ability to pay makes it more difficult to agree on a single benchmark for this measure.

**Outstanding Debt/Personal Income.**   A third measure of outstanding debt burden is the ratio of outstanding debt to personal income. As we discussed in Chapter 4, there are conceptual and empirical reasons to argue that income is an important measure of revenue capacity, even though local governments do not rely heavily on the local income tax. Therefore the logic behind the measure is that a certain proportion of local wealth, measured in terms of personal income, can be devoted to local government debt. Like the preceding two measures, this measure should be examined for both organizational and overlapping debt.[40]

Although this measure has not been used extensively by bond analysts in the past, this is probably not the case today. For example, Hugh Sherwood reports that this ratio is used in the evaluation of municipal bonds performed by Standard & Poor's when it rates municipal bonds. Sherwood indicates that Standard & Poor's views debt as a percentage of personal income above 15 percent as a "little high."[41] Of course, comparisons over time and with a reference group are also appropriate for this measure. For example, the ratio of outstanding debt to personal income for all municipalities in Massachusetts is 7 percent for direct and overlapping debt.[42]

**Outstanding Debt/Fiscal Capacity.**   The denominators of the preceding three ratios can be viewed as attempts to measure the revenue capacity or tax base of a government. In Chapter 4 we presented measures of fiscal capacity, such as the ones developed by the ACIR, as alternative measures of revenue capacity. Thus fiscal capacity measures can also be used as denominators in debt burden

---

[39] For the $1,000 figure, see Public Securities Association, *Fundamentals of Municipal Bonds,* p. 119; for the $1,300 figure, see Kaufman, "Debt Management," *Management Policies in Local Government Finance,* p. 313.

[40] For an example of the use of this measure in an empirical financial condition study, see City of Seattle, "Financial Condition of Seattle," p. 62.

[41] Sherwood, *How Corporate and Municipal Debt Is Rated,* p. 117.

[42] Neville Lee, ed., *Massachusetts Municipal Data Base, Debt Survey of Massachusetts Cities and Towns* (Boston: Bank of Boston, 1983), p. 20.

ratios. To implement this approach, a measure of fiscal capacity has to be chosen, estimated for each government in the reference group, and then used to compute ratios of outstanding debt to fiscal capacity. Because this approach is not widely used by municipal analysts no benchmarks are available, so that comparisons over time and with a reference group must be used for interpretation.

Thus far we have introduced four measures of debt burden based on stocks of outstanding debt. However, the dollar value of outstanding debt may not necessarily be a good proxy for the actual yearly expenditures that the government makes to pay back the debt. The impact of debt obligations results from the fixed annual payments they impose, more than from the total value of the obligation. Consequently, measures of the debt burden that are based on financial flows (debt service and revenues) rather than financial stocks have been developed.

**Debt Service/Annual Revenues.**    The most widely used measure of debt burden, expressed in terms of flows, is the ratio of debt service to annual revenues. Sometimes the inverse of this ratio is used and is called the *coverage ratio* because it represents the ability of revenue flows to "cover" or pay back the debt service.[43]

This measure can be thought of as a set of measures, since alternative definitions of revenues are often employed. First, an argument can be made for a total revenue figure that includes taxes, user charges, and intergovernmental aid. For consistency, revenues from projects where the debt is excluded from the debt service measure should be excluded. Furthermore, it is not appropriate to include the proceeds from bonds as revenues even though the accounting system may do so.

An alternative measure of revenues excludes intergovernmental transfers. This revenue measure is often termed "own source revenues," and to the extent that intergovernmental aid is uncertain, this is a more conservative measure. Finally, measures of revenues (and debt service) can be defined for the government or the overlapping jurisdiction. In most instances, however, debt service ratios are calculated only with government (organizational) debt.

Total and own source revenues are the most widely used in debt service burden ratios. In addition to comparing these ratios over time and with a reference group, bond analysts have developed benchmarks, and a debt service to own source revenue ratio over 25 percent is considered a cause for concern.[44]

**Debt Service/Fiscal Capacity.**    The various measures of revenues typically included in debt service ratios measure the actual own source or total

---

[43] For examples of the use of debt burden measures that include debt service, see J. Richard Aronson and Arthur E. King, "Is There a Fiscal Crisis Outside of New York?" *National Tax Journal,* 31, No. 2 (June 1978), 153–63; Bureau of Governmental Research, University of Oregon, "Oregon Municipal Fiscal Indicators, An Exploratory Study," p. 23; and City of Seattle, "Financial Condition of Seattle," p. 62.

[44] See Kaufman, "Debt Management," *Management Policies in Local Government Finance,* p. 313.

revenues, but they do not incorporate the notion of the government's revenue capacity. In some cases it may be useful to know how debt service compares with a measure of the government's ability to raise revenues, not the actual revenues being raised. If, for example, a government has a relatively high debt service to own tax revenue ratio but has considerable revenue reserves, then the debt service to fiscal capacity ratio will be lower and will show that there *may* be more revenues available to pay the debt service. We must use *may* because the *willingness* of the government to raise its tax rates to cover additional debt service also has to be taken into account.

**Other Flow Measures of Debt Burden.** In addition to debt service to revenue and fiscal capacity ratios, the distribution of future principal payments can be examined to determine whether the government intends to repay the outstanding debt rapidly enough to issue new debt to meet its needs. For example, if debt has been issued somewhat evenly in the past with relatively comparable maturities, then the future principal commitments should decline evenly over the next twenty to thirty years. If, on the other hand, the principal payments are relatively heavy in the long term compared with the short term, then the ability to issue debt in the near term may be limited because the debt service will not decrease in the next few years. Moreover, lenders usually prefer to purchase the securities of governments that plan to pay back their debt more rapidly.

The repayment schedule can be examined to quantify how quickly the government plans to pay back its debt. One measure of this is the *average maturity of the outstanding long-term debt.* For this measure, a range of ten and one-half to fifteen years has been cited as a rough measure of acceptability.[45] Alternatively, the analyst can determine the percentage of the outstanding debt that is scheduled for repayment in the next year, five years, ten years, and so forth. Note that if the average maturity of the outstanding debt is ten years, then roughly 50 percent should be scheduled for repayment within ten years. These measures can also be computed over time and compared with a reference group's.

### Using and Supplementing Debt Burden Measures

The measures of debt burden that we have considered here represent accepted practice in municipal analysis, although they fall short of our conceptual definition of borrowing capacity. Instead of directly estimating a government's ability to borrow additional funds, we have defined ratios that help us assess the extent to which the government has incurred debt in the past, and we have viewed these ratios as proxies for its ability to borrow additional funds in the future.

The debt burden measures can be used to evaluate the government's use of debt over time compared with other governments and, to a limited degree, com-

---

[45] Moak and Hillhouse, *Concepts and Practices in Local Government Finance,* p. 276.

pared with rules of thumb, benchmarks, or legal limits. Each measure is only a partial measure, however, and therefore it is advisable to use several measures simultaneously when evaluating a government's financial condition from the debt perspective. Furthermore, the analysis of debt burdens by themselves is a partial view, so that the debt measures should be supplemented by the revenue, expenditure, pension, and internal resource analysis we present in other chapters. As we indicated in our conceptual discussion of borrowing capacity, certain conclusions reached from these other analyses could influence the interpretation of the debt burden measures. For example, a government with growing and stable economic and revenue bases, untapped fiscal capacity, and few unmet expenditure needs, and a management capability to plan and forecast its financial responsibilities, should be able to carry a heavier debt burden than it would in the absence of these factors. This kind of analysis is illustrated when we examine the debt burden of Dyer Straits in the next part.

In addition to these debt burden measures, several other questions about the government's borrowing activities should be investigated. To answer many of these questions, the analyst will probably have to go beyond the available information in published reports such as the bond prospectus and annual financial reports.

For long-term general obligation debt, the debt issued over the past five to ten years can be analyzed to determine whether the debt has been used according to its stated intentions. For example, have capital projects financed from debt been constructed as planned? If not, why? And what was done with the proceeds instead? If the project was overfunded (i.e., built to a smaller scale than planned), were the excess resources used to finance current operations? If the project was underfunded, was the construction plan altered or additional financing sought? Underfunding or overfunding may be a sign of poor management and may point to a misuse of debt financing.

At the organizational level, the amount of debt issued can be compared with the amount of capital spending over a several-year period. Both the construction time and the use of bond anticipation borrowing should be taken into account. If this comparison of borrowing and capital spending shows that the former exceeds the latter, then this may be an indication that the debt is being used for other purposes, but further investigation would be necessary to come to a more definite conclusion.

The government's debt repayment record can also be examined to determine whether any long-term debt has been refinanced, not only to improve the terms of the debt such as the interest cost but because the government was unable to pay back the original debt on time. This may signal that the government is near its borrowing limit.

Certain questions can also be asked about the government's use of short-term debt. Is any short-term debt being used as a substitute for long-term financing? If the borrowing is in anticipation of revenues, is it necessary to borrow due to problems of timing within one operating cycle, or are the revenues from the next year being used to finance operating activities in the current year? Is revenue anticipation borrowing growing or declining? Are the proceeds from bond anticipation borrowing being used as intended or are they serving as interim financing for operations? As we pointed out in Table 6–3, a significant amount of short-term debt is issued every year by governments, so that the use and misuse of short-term debt by the government warrants careful attention.

Finally, since a significant portion of government debt is limited obligation, that is, revenue or self-supporting debt, and this form of debt is usually excluded from the traditional measures of debt burden, limited obligation debt should be examined separately so that no debt of the government goes unscrutinized.

At a conceptual level, an analysis of the revenue debt of a government is comprised of analyses of the revenues and expenses of the enterprises for which the debt was issued. The basic question is whether the revenues (and to some degree internal resources) of the enterprise are sufficient to cover all the expenses of the enterprise including debt service. A useful measure to assess this is the coverage ratio, the ratio of revenues less expenses (excluding debt service) to debt service. All else being equal, the higher the ratio, the more secure the debt service payments are likely to be.

Clearly the coverage ratio should be greater than one. It is not possible, however, to specify a satisfactory coverage ratio for all enterprises. For example, an acceptable coverage ratio for an enterprise with a low price elasticity (water utility) may be considerably lower than one facing a high price elasticity (civic auditorium) because the former can increase revenues more easily by increasing its prices.

An analysis of the revenue debt of an organization should include an assessment of the coverage ratio and a determination of whether the enterprise requires subsidies from the government in order to cover all expenses including debt service. If a subsidy is required, then for purposes of the debt burden analysis, some portion of the debt should be reclassified as organizational debt rather than debt of the enterprise. We will discuss the analysis of enterprises in greater depth in Chapter 8.

### An Application

In this part we illustrate the various approaches to debt analysis with an application to Dyer Straits. First, the debt burden ratios are examined to assess the amount of Dyer Straits' debt compared with various measures of its revenue capacity and revenues. Second, the revenue and expenditure components of our financial condition analysis are combined to assess whether Dyer Straits appears to have the ability to issue additional debt. Finally, these two approaches are combined to draw conclusions on Dyer Straits' financial condition from a debt perspective.

Table 6–11 shows a number of the debt burden ratios for Dyer Straits and

TABLE 6-11  Debt Burden Measures—Part I, City of Dyer Straits and Reference Group, 1979–83

| DEBT LIMIT MEASURES | DYER STRAITS | | | | | REFERENCE GROUP | | | | | LOCATION QUOTIENTS* | | | | |
|---|---|---|---|---|---|---|---|---|---|---|---|---|---|---|---|
| | 1979 | 1980 | 1981 | 1982 | 1983 | 1979 | 1980 | 1981 | 1982 | 1983 | 1979 | 1980 | 1981 | 1982 | 1983 |
| Debt†/full assessed value | | | | | | | | | | | | | | | |
| Municipal debt only | .0500 | .0491 | .0546 | .0526 | .0539 | .0290 | .0290 | .0310 | .0297 | .0289 | 1.724 | 1.693 | 1.761 | 1.771 | 1.865 |
| Total overlapping debt | .1449 | .1523 | .1669 | .1639 | .1644 | .0968 | .0944 | .0912 | .0875 | .0843 | 1.497 | 1.613 | 1.830 | 1.873 | 1.950 |
| Debt†/population | | | | | | | | | | | | | | | |
| Municipal debt only | $251 | $255 | $299 | $306 | $325 | $135 | $141 | $160 | $162 | $167 | 1.859 | 1.809 | 1.869 | 1.889 | 1.947 |
| Overlapping debt | $728 | $789 | $914 | $955 | $992 | $450 | $459 | $470 | $478 | $488 | 1.618 | 1.719 | 1.945 | 1.998 | 2.032 |
| Debt†/income (Personal) | | | | | | | | | | | | | | | |
| Municipal debt only | .0747 | .0727 | .0771 | .0747 | .0737 | .0414 | .0402 | .0423 | .0399 | .0383 | 1.804 | 1.808 | 1.823 | 1.872 | 1.924 |
| Overlapping debt | .2164 | .2250 | .2357 | .2329 | .2251 | .1378 | .1306 | .1244 | .1179 | .1119 | 1.570 | 1.723 | 1.895 | 1.975 | 2.012 |
| Debt subject to limit/ constitutional debt limit | .780 | .766 | .852 | .820 | .841 | .453 | .453 | .483 | .463 | .451 | 1.722 | 1.691 | 1.764 | 1.771 | 1.865 |
| Debt†/fiscal capacity | | | | | | | | | | | | | | | |
| Municipal debt only | 2.414 | 2.319 | 2.537 | 2.381 | 2.408 | 1.416 | 1.368 | 1.443 | 1.339 | 1.293 | 1.705 | 1.695 | 1.758 | 1.778 | 1.862 |

*Dyer Straits/Reference Group.

†Debt defined as general obligation, long-term and short-term debt.

the reference group. The debt data are from Tables 6–5 and 6–8, and the measures of full assessed value, population, and so forth, have been taken from various tables in Chapter 4.

The first debt burden ratio listed in Table 6–11 is debt/full assessed value of property. For the debt of Dyer Straits alone, labeled "municipal debt only" in Table 6–11, this debt burden ratio ranges from 4.9 percent to 5.4 percent, with a slight but uneven increase over the period. Comparable ratios for the reference group are even more stable over the period, varying between 2.9 percent and 3.1 percent. Thus this debt burden ratio is substantially higher for Dyer Straits relative to the reference group, and by 1983 the debt/full assessed value of property in Dyer Straits is 1.865 times the value of the ratio in the reference group.

Similar findings emerge when we calculate debt/full assessed value of property for municipal and overlapping debt. The ratio in Dyer Straits increases from 14.5 to 16.4 percent over the five-year period while the ratio in the reference group actually decreases from 9.7 to 8.4 percent. By the end of the period, this ratio is nearly twice as high for Dyer Straits as it is for the reference group, indicating that each dollar of the property tax base in Dyer Straits has twice as much outstanding general obligation municipal and overlapping debt associated with it.

Finally, Dyer Straits' ratio of debt/full assessed value of property is not only high relative to the reference group, but it is also higher than the 15 percent benchmark used by municipal bond analysts. Thus both the reference group analysis and the industry rule of thumb indicate that outstanding debt in Dyer Straits is high compared with its full assessed value of property. Moreover, this ratio is increasing slightly in Dyer Straits, indicating that despite its high levels of debt, Dyer Straits is continuing to borrow.

Similar conclusions can be drawn when we examine the second debt burden ratio, per capita debt. Both per capita municipal and municipal plus overlapping debt increase in Dyer Straits compared with the reference group, and both measures of per capita debt are close to twice as high in Dyer Straits compared with the reference group by 1983. In addition, Dyer Straits is approaching $1,000 per capita in the latest year in which data are available.

The finding that outstanding debt is high is confirmed when the ratio of debt/personal income is examined. This ratio is about twice as high for Dyer Straits compared with the reference group in 1983 and is well above the danger signal of 15 percent suggested by municipal bond analysts.

When the three debt burden ratios are computed for municipal debt alone and compared with the ratios for municipal plus overlapping debt, it shows that a substantial part of Dyer Straits' high debt burden is the result of the outstanding debt of the overlapping units. For example, per capita municipal debt in Dyer Straits in 1983 is less than one-third as high as per capita municipal and overlapping debt in the same year. Thus, although all three ratios indicate that outstanding debt is high in Dyer Straits compared with the reference group and professional rules of thumb, Dyer Straits still has the legal capability to borrow additional funds under its constitutional debt limit of 6.4 percent of full assessed value. This is an illustration of why examining a debt limit on organizational debt, and not on overlapping debt, may not be a good way to evaluate the debt burden carried by residents.

The final debt burden ratio shown in Table 6–11 is the ratio of outstanding debt to fiscal capacity. This ratio compares the outstanding debt with the annual revenues that would be raised if the "average" tax rates of the reference group were levied against an individual government's actual tax bases. Note that the numerator of this ratio is a stock while the denominator, fiscal capacity, is a flow, and as a result the actual values of the ratios are quite different from the other debt burden ratios we have examined. Regardless of this difference in formulation, the outcome is the same. Compared with the reference group, outstanding debt to fiscal capacity in Dyer Straits is both high and rising. This ratio is only computed for municipal debt, since the fiscal capacity measures were not computed for the overlapping jurisdictions.

The second set of debt burden measures, based on flows, are shown in Table 6–12. The first ratio is debt service/total revenues, and this indicates that for municipal debt, Dyer Straits and the reference group are at comparable levels. In 1983 about 11 percent of Dyer Straits' and the reference group's total revenues were devoted to debt service. Moreover, this ratio for municipal debt has declined slightly in Dyer Straits and in the reference group over the five-year period. When this ratio is computed for municipal plus overlapping debt, however, the relative position of Dyer Straits changes. Although 11 percent of total revenues of Dyer Straits and its overlapping units is devoted to debt service in 1983, the ratio is only 6.2 percent for the reference group in the same year. This corroborates our earlier finding that overlapping debt is contributing significantly to Dyer Straits' high levels of debt. In addition, since outstanding municipal debt is higher in Dyer Straits than in the reference group, this suggests that the debt structure in Dyer Straits for municipal debt is somehow different from the debt structure of municipal debt in the reference group.

The second debt burden measure based on debt repayment shown in Table 6–12 is debt service/own source revenues. The patterns of this ratio for municipal debt and municipal plus overlapping debt parallel those for the prior ratio. Also note that neither of these two "flow" measures approaches the 25 percent figure that is cited by municipal bond analysts as a danger signal.

To further investigate our hypothesis that the debt service structure for municipal debt in Dyer Straits is different from the debt structure in the reference group, we can examine the debt structure that was shown in Table 6–9. A calculation of the percentage of the principal that is due in various years is one way to compare the structures. For example, by the end of the fifth year, 1988, 33.9 percent of Dyer Straits' current principal on municipal debt will be paid off, while the comparable figure for the reference group is 45.8 percent. At the end of ten years, Dyer Straits will have paid off 62.2 percent of its municipal debt, and the reference group will have paid off 70.3 percent. Thus one reason why Dyer Straits' debt burden ratios based on debt service are not as high as the ratios based on outstanding debt is that Dyer Straits has a less-rapid payment schedule.

TABLE 6-12 Debt Burden Measures—Part II, City of Dyer Straits and Reference Group, 1979–83

| | DYER STRAITS | | | | | REFERENCE GROUP | | | | | LOCATION QUOTIENTS* | | | | |
|---|---|---|---|---|---|---|---|---|---|---|---|---|---|---|---|
| | 1979 | 1980 | 1981 | 1982 | 1983 | 1979 | 1980 | 1981 | 1982 | 1983 | 1979 | 1980 | 1981 | 1982 | 1983 |
| Debt service†/total revenues‡ | | | | | | | | | | | | | | | |
| Municipal debt only | .123 | .134 | .137 | .126 | .114 | .116 | .116 | .119 | .113 | .106 | 1.060 | 1.155 | 1.151 | 1.115 | 1.075 |
| Overlapping debt | .114 | .120 | .127 | .119 | .109 | .081 | .078 | .076 | .067 | .062 | 1.407 | 1.538 | 1.671 | 1.776 | 1.758 |
| Debt service†/own revenues‡ | | | | | | | | | | | | | | | |
| Municipal debt only | .162 | .178 | .184 | .174 | .160 | .165 | .166 | .174 | .167 | .159 | .982 | 1.072 | 1.057 | 1.042 | 1.006 |
| Overlapping debt | .178 | .189 | .201 | .197 | .182 | .135 | .131 | .128 | .117 | .107 | 1.319 | 1.443 | 1.570 | 1.684 | 1.701 |
| Adjusted debt service§/total revenues‡ | | | | | | | | | | | | | | | |
| Municipal debt only | .099 | .107 | .112 | .102 | .094 | .069 | .071 | .077 | .074 | .070 | 1.435 | 1.507 | 1.455 | 1.378 | 1.343 |
| Overlapping debt | .087 | .092 | .098 | .091 | .083 | .062 | .060 | .060 | .053 | .047 | 1.403 | 1.533 | 1.633 | 1.717 | 1.766 |
| Adjusted debt service§/own revenues‡ | | | | | | | | | | | | | | | |
| Municipal debt only | .131 | .142 | .150 | .141 | .131 | .097 | .102 | .111 | .110 | .105 | 1.351 | 1.392 | 1.351 | 1.282 | 1.248 |
| Overlapping debt | .135 | .145 | .155 | .151 | .138 | .104 | .101 | .101 | .092 | .083 | 1.298 | 1.436 | 1.535 | 1.641 | 1.663 |
| Debt service/fiscal capacity | | | | | | | | | | | | | | | |
| Municipal debt only | .2395 | .2655 | .2893 | .2638 | .2532 | .2066 | .2071 | .2158 | .2053 | .1943 | 1.1592 | 1.2820 | 1.3406 | 1.2849 | 1.3031 |

*Dyer Straits/Reference Group.
†Debt service defined as principal on long-term general obligation debt plus interest on long-term and short-term general obligation debt.
‡Revenues and own revenues in ratios for overlapping jurisdictions include revenues of overlapping jurisdictions.
§Adjusted debt service defined as 5 percent of principal on general obligation long-term debt plus interest on long-term and short-term general obligation debt.

By stretching out these payments compared with the reference group, Dyer Straits is not placing as heavy a burden on its revenues. At the same time, however, if neither Dyer Straits nor the reference group issues new debt, after several years the debt service burden ratios in the reference group will be much lower than those in Dyer Straits.

Besides examining the debt service repayment schedule directly, we have computed "adjusted" debt service burden ratios. Instead of using the existing principal repayment schedule for the governments, we have assumed that the principal is being repaid in equal amounts at 5 percent of principal in each of twenty years. If we add this adjusted principal to the actual interest and use this as the numerator in the debt service ratios, we are partially controlling for the different debt service schedules. (To fully control for the different schedules we would have to recompute interest, but we have not done that here.)

Two ratios, adjusted debt service/total revenues and adjusted debt service/own revenues, are shown in Table 6–12. These ratios for municipal debt show a higher burden for Dyer Straits compared with the reference group. The location quotients are not as high as they were for outstanding debt—not only because we have not adjusted for interest payments but also because, as we noted in Chapter 4, Dyer Straits is raising more revenues than a comparable city in the reference group.

Thus a second reason why the debt service to own source revenue ratio may not tell the entire story, besides the differences in maturity structures, is the greater use of revenue capacity by Dyer Straits compared with the reference group. To confirm this, we compute the ratio of debt service to fiscal capacity, and this is the final ratio shown in Table 6–12. Since the ratios of debt service to fiscal capacity are from 15 to 30 percent higher in Dyer Straits, this indicates that Dyer Straits is tapping its revenue base to a higher degree in order to keep its ratio of debt service to own source revenues at the same level as the reference group's. Thus if Dyer Straits' debt maturity structure was similar to the reference group's, and if Dyer Straits were taxing *at* as opposed to *over* the average tax capacity level, Dyer Straits' ratio of debt service to own source revenues would be considerably higher than the reference group's.

Other aspects of Dyer Straits' debt practices are not problematic. For example, Dyer Straits has no short-term revenue anticipation debt outstanding at year-end. Dyer Straits does use bond anticipation notes, but these were factored into the debt burden ratios. In addition, Dyer Straits does have a capital program that is commensurate with its borrowing. Thus it appears that Dyer Straits has high levels of debt in order to rebuild its old and poorly maintained infrastructure. Note, however, that Dyer Straits has significant capital spending plans over the next two years. Dyer Straits' capital budget, shown in Chapter 2, Table 2–20, indicates that the "Allan Bridge" project will require a higher level of yearly general obligation borrowing in 1984 than in any of the preceding five years. Given Dyer Straits' repayment schedule, Dyer Straits' ability to borrow for the remainder of the Allan Bridge project is questionable. At this point we could also analyze Dyer

Straits' limited obligation debt, but we will do this in Chapter 8 when we examine the enterprises more carefully.

The conclusion based on traditional debt burden analysis plus the use of fiscal capacity measures is that Dyer Straits' level of outstanding debt is high for both municipal and municipal plus overlapping debt. Moreover, the debt service ratios indicate that the levels for municipal debt are comparable with the reference group's while the levels in Dyer Straits for municipal plus overlapping debt again exceed the levels in the reference group. When examined in total, the debt burden analysis suggests that Dyer Straits will not be able to borrow additional funds easily in the future. The final question we address in this part is whether an examination of the revenue and expenditure components of financial condition analysis leads to a similar conclusion.

One way for a government to have the ability to borrow additional funds (more than just the amount it is currently repaying) is to be able to raise additional revenues. But we concluded at the end of Chapter 4 that the prospects for increasing short- or medium-term revenues do not appear promising unless they are to come from state or federal sources. Knowing what we know about the hypothetical state in which Dyer Straits is located as well as our information on the not-so-hypothetical federal government, the likelihood of increased aid from these sources is low. Since we do not anticipate new growth in Dyer Straits' economic or revenue base, and because Dyer Straits is already tapping its local tax base to a significantly greater degree than the reference group, additional revenues to support additional debt are not likely to be forthcoming. This is consistent with the high debt burden ratios using fiscal capacity.

A second way for Dyer Straits to be able to borrow additional funds, however, is if slack exists on the expenditure side. That is, if Dyer Straits could somehow reduce its expenditures on common functions and still meet the needs of the community, the reduction in current expenditures could be used to support additional debt without changing the total amount of revenues. Based on the analysis presented in Chapter 5, this may be possible.

In Chapter 5 we found that Dyer Straits is spending considerably more than the reference group. Although some of the higher spending can be accounted for by higher prices, slightly more demanding production and service conditions, and greater needs, even after taking these factors into account, Dyer Straits is spending more than the reference group and more than it may need to spend. Therefore *if* Dyer Straits can reduce its expenditures by increasing its efficiency or reducing its levels of outputs in those areas where it is "overmeeting" its needs, then resources may be available to increase borrowing.

Thus, by approaching the question of Dyer Straits' ability to borrow additional funds using the framework we develop rather than the traditional perspective, the possibility of room for additional borrowing is raised. Note that if expenditures can be reduced in the manner we suggest, the debt burden ratios will remain just as high and some of them may even increase. This is precisely why we recommend this alternative approach. Although Dyer Straits' financial condition from the debt perspective is not very positive, there may be a few avenues open to borrow additional funds, particularly if the funds raised from borrowing are put to appropriate use such as capital projects that increase expenditure efficiency or projects that lead to revenue increases.

## QUESTIONS

1. What major questions are addressed in debt analysis? How is debt analysis dependent on and related to the other components of financial condition analysis?
2. Define a government's *debt capacity.* What factors influence debt capacity, and which of these factors can a government control?
3. What are the different ways to measure a government's debt reserves? How are debt reserves related to debt capacity?
4. Most state and local government debt is "tax exempt." What is meant by tax-exempt debt, and what are the effects of the tax exemption?
5. How are the different reasons for issuing debt related to an analysis of financial condition? Are some uses of debt signals of financial problems?
6. Discuss the difference between general and limited obligation debt. In a financial condition analysis, why is this difference important? Are there situations in a financial condition analysis where limited obligation debt is treated as general obligation debt? Explain.
7. What factors determine the cost of a government's debt? Explain why a government's financial condition both affects and is affected by the cost of a government's debt.
8. How is *overlapping debt* defined for a particular local government? Should overlapping debt be taken into account in financial condition analysis? If so, why and how?
9. Suppose you were analyzing the debt of a government. Which debt should be included in the analysis and which excluded? What are the reasons for excluding debt from the analysis?
10. How is short-term debt treated in debt analysis? Is a distinction drawn between bond and revenue anticipation debt? What are the financial implications of a government that uses increasing amounts of revenue anticipation borrowing year after year?
11. How important are constitutional debt limits in financial condition analysis?
12. How are debt burden measures related to the concepts of debt capacity and debt reserves? What are the most commonly employed debt burden measures and how are they interpreted? What are the shortcomings of different debt burden measures and how can these shortcomings be remedied?
13. True or false: "A government with low debt burden ratios can easily issue additional debt. It is inadvisable for a government with high debt burden ratios to issue additional debt." Explain.

## PROBLEMS

1. Listed below is a summary of the outstanding debt of a city government. Assume that you have been asked to analyze this city's debt from a financial condition perspective. Determine the city's current total outstanding debt and current year's debt service for use in debt analysis. Justify the choices you have made.

**Outstanding Debt**

a.  General obligation debt issued in 1962; serial bonds; final maturity in 1992; total amount outstanding at current time, $4.5 million; debt service in current year, $.5 million principal, $.2 million interest.

b.  General obligation debt issued in 1974; term bonds; final maturity in 1994; total amount outstanding at current time, $15 million; amount in sinking fund at current time, $6.8 million; current interest payment, $1.2 million; current payment to sinking fund, $.8 million.

c.  General obligation debt issued in 1984; serial bonds; final maturity in 1999; total amount outstanding at current time, $16 million; debt service in current year, $1.3 million principal, $1.8 million interest.

d.  Limited obligation debt secured by revenues of city airport issued in 1979; serial bonds; final maturity in 2009; total amount outstanding at current time, $17.9 million; debt service in current year, $.7 million principal, $1.9 million interest; airport has operated on a break-even basis since debt was issued without operating subsidies from the city.

e.  Limited obligation debt secured by revenues of the city's water and sewer system issued in 1981; serial bonds; final maturity in 2001; total amount outstanding at current time $12.0 million; debt service in current year, $.55 million principal, $1.4 million interest; city has provided subsidies to water and sewer fund every year except one since this debt was issued, subsidy in current year expected to be $1.1 million.

f.  Bond anticipation notes outstanding at current time, in anticipation of general obligation debt expected to be issued next year (in eleven months); total amount outstanding at current time, $15 million; interest payment in current year, $1.05 million.

g.  Tax anticipation notes outstanding at current time, in anticipation of property taxes due in seven months, notes are due in ten months; amount outstanding at current time, $4.5 million; interest payment in current year, $.4 million; last year tax anticipation notes of $3.1 million were issued and these were fully repaid when due, in part ($.9 million) with proceeds from the current issue.

2.  a.  The problems at the end of Chapters 4 and 5 required an analysis of the revenues and expenditures of the city of Red Lion. From these two analyses, what can be concluded about the ability of Red Lion to borrow additional funds?

b.  The data on Red Lion and a reference group presented at the end of Chapter 4 included information on outstanding debt and debt service. Using the appropriate data, calculate alternative measures of debt burden for Red Lion and the reference group. Do the conclusions from the measures based on stocks differ from those based on flows? How do the debt burden measures compare with the benchmarks discussed in this chapter? What is your conclusion about Red Lion's ability to borrow based solely on the debt burden measures?

c.  What are your overall conclusions on Red Lion's financial condition from a debt perspective based on the revenue, expenditure, and debt analyses? What other information would be useful for this analysis beyond that presented in the problem?

# CHAPTER
# 7 / Pension Analysis

It is now common practice for many public and private organizations, including governments, to provide *pensions* for employees so that they can have an adequate standard of living when they reach retirement age. Assets in pension funds for government employees approached $250 billion in 1982.[1] These retirement plans have become extremely important for employees; their financial implications for governments are equally important.

Like government debt, government pensions are also the result of commitments made in the past. Normally, government employees, while they are working, are promised certain current compensation (salaries, wages, etc.) for their efforts, plus future compensation (pensions) that they will begin to receive on a retirement date. A government need not wait until the employee retires to provide the funds for the employee's pension; the government may put some funds aside every year during the employee's career so that by the time the employee retires the funds will be on hand to meet the promises made earlier in the employee's career.

Pensions and debt are similar because both place demands on the government for expenditures in the future. When a government borrows, debt service must be paid for one or more years to come. When a government establishes a pension system (or joins an already established system), pension payments must be made in the future. One factor, however, differentiates future debt payments from future pension commitments, and that is uncertainty. At any point in time,

---

[1]U.S. Department of Commerce, Bureau of the Census, *Employee Retirement Systems of State and Local Governments,* 1982 Census of Governments (Washington, D.C.: Government Printing Office, August 1983), Table A, p. v.

the outstanding debt and future debt service of a government can be determined with certainty in most cases. The same is not true of future pension payments, and this uncertainty is a critical and complicating factor in pension fund financing and analysis.

The purpose of pension analysis is to assess the current and potential expenditure pressures placed on a government by the level of its pension obligations and the methods it employs to meet these obligations as they come due. This analysis is aggravated by the complexities and uncertainties that characterize pension plans that cover many employees, of many ages, over many years. The purpose of this chapter is to explain these complexities and provide a set of measures that can be used to evaluate the financial impacts of pensions.

This chapter analyzes the financial condition of a government from a pension perspective. First, we present a brief introduction to state and local pension systems, describe how pension liabilities are related to government financial strength, and discuss the basic approach to pension analysis. In section II we discuss various aspects of pension system financing that lie at the heart of pension analysis. Included are considerations of pay-as-you-go financing versus advance funding, the role of uncertainty in pension funding, alternative funding methods, and pension funding disclosure. Knowledge of these issues is a prerequisite to the measurement of financial condition from the pension perspective, which is the subject of section III. Finally, in the fourth and final section we analyze the pension obligations of Dyer Straits.

## I. THE NATURE OF PENSION ANALYSIS

Government pensions have the potential to seriously affect financial condition. To understand these effects and to determine how close a government is to having problems in the pension area, we need to develop a method of analyzing pensions and a set of measures to indicate the likelihood of pension problems. To do this, we begin with an introduction to government pensions, review pension problems faced by governments, and lay out an approach to pension analysis.

### An Introduction to Government Pensions

There is no single pension system for all state and local government employees; instead a multitude of pension systems are operated by both state and local governments. In 1981–82 there were 190 state-administered pension systems. There were 10,141,062 members in these state systems, including both employees of state governments and employees of local governments that participate in a state-administered plan. In addition, there were 2,369 locally administered plans (counties, municipalities, townships, special districts, etc.), but the membership of these plans was only 1,465,642, roughly 15 percent of the membership in state-administered plans.[2]

The funds that individuals receive as payments from the pension system when they retire may come from several sources. First, some pension systems require employees to contribute to the system during their working lives. This component of the contribution is known as the *employee's contribution.* These funds are then invested and are available at retirement. Second, the government may put dollars into the fund during the employee's working life and these, too, earn a return and are available at retirement. Third, a government may pay funds directly to the pension system for retirees' benefits, without having set aside funds for that purpose during their career. These latter two elements constitute the *employer's contribution.*

For the 2,559 pension plans covered by the census, data are available on the yearly contributions from employees, state and local governments, and earnings on the assets already contributed to the funds by both governments and employees. In 1981–82 the pension systems received $48,961 million distributed as follows: $8,123 million (17 percent) from employees, $21,808 million (45 percent) from governments, and $19,030 million (38 percent) from earnings on investments of funds previously contributed.[3] In 1981–82 there were 2,897,000 *beneficiaries,* people receiving benefits from the plans.[4] Moreover, the pension systems had $245.3 billion in total assets.[5]

State and local government pension systems are important not only because of the size of their membership, assets, and contributions but also because pension contributions constitute a significant portion of government expenditures. A recent study of state and local pensions estimates that employee and employer contributions to pensions are greater than 10 percent of payroll for close to three-quarters of the pension system. Furthermore, in 5 percent of the plans, pension payments are over 30 percent of payroll.[6]

How much will the employee receive when he or she retires? The answer depends on the way in which the pension system is designed. Most systems can be categorized into one of two major types. Some pension plans are designed to accumulate the employees' and employer's contributions and pay out an amount to the retirees every year based solely on how much has accumulated for each retiree when retirement begins. This type of system is known as a *defined contribution* plan, since the payments to the retiree are based entirely on previous contributions in his or her name to the system.

---

[2]Ibid., Table 5, p. 11.

[3]Ibid., Table A, p. v.

[4]Ibid., Table D, p. viii.

[5]Ibid., Table B, p. vii.

[6]Committee on Education and Labor, House of Representatives, *Pension Task Force Report on Public Employee Retirement Systems* (Washington, D.C.: Government Printing Office, March 15, 1978), Table F4, p. 137.

Other pension plans base pension payments on such variables as the employee's salary, years of service, and age at retirement. For example, a pension system may specify that an individual who retires at the age of 65 will receive 1.5 percent of his or her final year's salary for every year of service to the organization. Thus an individual who has worked thirty years would receive 45 percent of his or her last year's salary as the annual retirement pay. This type of system specifies the benefits that the retiree will receive in advance and is called a *defined benefit* plan. A Pension Task Force established by Congress accumulated extensive data on state and local pensions in 1975 and estimated that over 80 percent of all state and local employees covered by pension systems are members of defined benefit plans.[7] Some plans combine elements of both defined contribution and defined benefit plans.

Thus all pension plans involve a system of contributions to the fund, the management and investment of these funds, and the distribution (benefits) to participants upon retirement. The design and the management of these systems are extremely complex and have been studied from many different perspectives.[8] Our sole concern in this chapter, however, is the impact of the pension system and its financing on government financial condition.

### The Need for Pension Analysis

Pensions are singled out for particular consideration primarily because governments can postpone setting aside financial resources to meet pension obligations to the point where their ability to meet obligations comes into question. Although employees earn benefits during their working lives, they do not have to be paid benefits until they retire. Thus governments can postpone pension funding, which can lead to higher pension costs and increased risks of not being able to keep pension promises at some time in the future. Moreover, there are cities where the underfunding of the pension system contributed significantly to the decline in their financial condition.

An example is Hamtramck, Michigan, where, in 1970, Hamtramck "failed to pay its employees, its pensioners, and its creditors because it had literally run out of money."[9] A major reason cited by the ACIR for Hamtramck's problems was its pension funding:

> Chief among Hamtramck's problems is pension funding. Police and fire pension requirements for 1972 totalled 22 percent of the 1972 budget which sufficed to meet current payrolls only. The pension system lacks reserve funding thus pension costs will

---

[7] Ibid., p. 54.

[8] See, for example, Robert Tilove, *Public Employee Pension Funds,* a Twentieth Century Fund Report (New York: Twentieth Century Fund, © 1976); and the Urban Institute, *The Future of State and Local Pensions* (Washington, D.C., April 1981), Final Report.

[9] Advisory Commission on Intergovernmental Relations, *City Financial Emergencies: The Intergovernmental Dimension* (Washington, D.C., July 1973), p. 36.

continue to be a serious problem for the city. . . . Actuarial funding of the city's police and fire pension system would require approximately $1.8 million annually, or about 40 percent of the city budget. To provide such funding, the city would have to use practically the entire 20-mill property tax rate authorized under the State Constitution.[10]

Of course, most cities do not have the severe problems characterized by this example. But how widespread is the Hamtramck experience or the potential for such experience? We can use two recent studies that have examined a significant portion of the state and local pension systems to help answer this question.

First, the General Accounting Office has used the data gathered by the Pension Task Force to forecast the status of all state and local pension systems from 1980 through 2020.[11] This study, referred to in the rest of this chapter as the GAO study, reached the following conclusion:

> Our analysis of several measures of financial soundness showed evidence of an increasing financial burden on State and local Government pension plans in the aggregate. In our analysis this problem is caused largely by the increasing proportion of retirees in the population of State and local government employees. Varying the economic parameters does not change this fact but merely changes the year in which the problem is first evident. Furthermore, growth in employment above the levels shown does not seem likely, and the characteristics of the plans were purposely unchanged, since a basic tenet of the review was to see what could happen if current benefit and financing levels were continued. Therefore, under the assumptions of this report a worsening financial status for State and local plans in the aggregate is certain.[12]

These conclusions can be illustrated with a few of the specific findings from the GAO study. First, retired employees as a percentage of total employees are projected to increase from 15 percent in 1980 to 24 percent in 2020. Second, benefits as a percentage of payroll are projected to increase from 8 percent to 17 percent over the same period.[13] Finally, while contributions to the plans exceeded benefits paid out ($24 billion compared with $13 billion) in 1980, by 2020 benefits paid out will exceed contributions ($995 billion compared with $851 billion).[14] For most of the assumptions tested by the GAO, the most rapid decline in the pension system's financial condition will occur after the turn of the century.[15]

A second study, carried out by the Urban Institute, does not reach the pessimistic conclusions of the GAO study. The Urban Institute studied one hun-

---

[10] Ibid., p. 39.

[11] U.S. General Accounting Office, *An Actuarial and Economic Analysis of State and Local Government Pension Plans* (Washington, D.C., February 26, 1980).

[12] Ibid., pp. i–ii.

[13] Ibid., Table 2, p. 10.

[14] Ibid., Table 3, p. 13.

[15] Ibid., Fig. 2, p. 21.

dred of the largest state and local pension systems and estimated that if current funding practices continue, the contributions to the systems by governments will be able to ''drop from the current 12.7 percent of payroll to 8.6 percent of payroll in 2024.''[16] These more optimistic findings arise from the use of a different set of assumptions, including a higher proportion of advance funded plans in its sample, a lower rate of increase in pension benefits, a higher rate of return on investments, and a higher starting contribution rate.[17] All of these differences operate in the same direction—they tend to make the Urban Institute conclusions more favorable in terms of future funding prospects. This optimism has been reinforced by significant stock market gains since publication of both studies.

Because individual governments differ in their pension management, and because the results of two major studies of pensions are so dependent on their sample and specific assumptions about contributions, investment returns, benefit growth, and so forth, there is obviously a need for improved pension analysis of individual governments. While the aggregate financial impacts of pensions may be uncertain, there is no question that individual governments may face severe financial costs and risks due to poor pension management.

### Pension Analysis

How can we analyze a pension system—its contributions, investments, and benefits—to determine the extent to which the pension system is generating additional unmet expenditure pressures on governments? Every government with a pension system has obligations to provide a specific amount of retirement benefits to particular individuals. Some governments make extensive arrangements to meet these obligations (build up assets, establish adequate future contributions, etc.) while others make no arrangements whatsoever, planning to meet the obligations when they come due out of current revenues. The former governments set aside funds to meet these future pension obligations, keeping unmet expenditure pressures from pensions down; the latter governments have no such arrangements and unmet expenditure pressures grow along with the growth in pension obligations.

Since commitments made to current employees concerning their pension benefits need not be met until they retire, the analysis of a government's financial condition should include an assessment of the way in which pensions will influence future expenditures. Some pension systems will require increasing pension contributions by the government in the future, and this will increase the expenditure pressures on the government and worsen financial condition as a result. Other pension systems will not require increased funding levels, so the impact on financial condition will be neutral, and there may be cases where the pension contribu-

---

[16] Urban Institute, *Future of State and Local Government Pensions*, p. 18–13.

[17] See Ibid., pp. 18–14 to 18–17, for a comparison of these two studies.

tion will decrease, and this will reduce expenditure pressures and exert a positive influence on financial condition.

Thus pension analysis essentially involves comparing pension obligations with pension financing reserves to estimate current and future expenditure pressures. While conceptually straightforward, in practice this is difficult to do. Pension obligations and financing involve a wide range of *uncertainties* (benefit levels, contribution levels, return on pension investments, etc.) and differences in *timing* (years of contributions, retirement dates, years of benefits, etc.) that make it hard to specify and compare reserves and obligations of differing uncertainty and timing. How do you compare a pension obligation due in twenty years with current pension assets? And how do you compare relatively certain pension assets on hand with less-certain pension benefits that will be paid to retirees? All the measures used in pension analysis are aimed at clearing up the uncertainties and handling differences in timing in order to make consistent and accurate comparisons of pension finances and obligations.

To handle uncertainty, pension analysis emphasizes getting as much relevant information about the pension system as possible and using a variety of measures to assess pension impacts from different perspectives. Thus in the sections that follow we examine the major characteristics of pensions, discuss how these characteristics affect pension funding and obligations, and review the availability of government pension information for use in analysis. We also present three different sets of measures, derived from (1) pension assets and liabilities, (2) pension actuarial assumptions and funding methods, and (3) pension receipts and disbursements. Although not equally reliable, all of these measures can be useful in pension analysis. Since they use different data we can normally develop at least a few measures even when information is limited. Whenever possible we use several different methods to check on the accuracy of our conclusions.

In pension analysis, the concept of *present value* is used to take differences in timing into account, for example when contribution and benefit streams at different points in time need to be compared. The present value concept converts a future stream of benefits (or costs) into an equivalent value if those benefits (or costs) were to be available now (their present value). By converting future benefit streams into their present values, comparisons of different pension obligations can be made even though their diverse patterns of future contributions and benefits are not comparable.

To understand the use of the present value concept in pension analysis, consider a government that expects the following simplified flow of pension contributions and benefits over the next fifteen years:

| YEAR | CONTRIBUTIONS | BENEFITS |
|------|---------------|----------|
| 1 | $300,000 | $200,000 |
| 2 | 300,000 | 200,000 |
| 3 | 300,000 | 300,000 |

| YEAR | CONTRIBUTIONS | BENEFITS |
|------|---------------|----------|
| 4 | 300,000 | 400,000 |
| 5 | 300,000 | 400,000 |
| 6 | 400,000 | 400,000 |
| 7 | 400,000 | 400,000 |
| 8 | 400,000 | 400,000 |
| 9 | 400,000 | 500,000 |
| 10 | 400,000 | 500,000 |
| 11 | 500,000 | 500,000 |
| 12 | 500,000 | 500,000 |
| 13 | 500,000 | 700,000 |
| 14 | 500,000 | 700,000 |
| 15 | 500,000 | 800,000 |

Now suppose we asked whether this government's attempts to build up pension assets are adequate to meet its obligations over, for simplicity, this fifteen-year period (normally the analysis would use a longer time horizon). It is hard to judge by just looking at the patterns over time. In the earlier years contributions are greater than benefits paid out; in the later years it is the reverse. But if we can replace each of these streams by its present value, a comparison can be made.

The present value of a future stream of benefits over a given period is the amount of money that, if deposited in a bank now paying a known interest rate (compounded yearly in this case), would allow withdrawals each year equal to the yearly benefits over the given period.

Suppose the interest rate were 10 percent per year. Then it can be shown that if $3,054,000 is put in the bank now, the withdrawals will equal the benefits in the above example: $200,000 per year in the first two years, $300,000 in the third year, $400,000 in the next five years, and so forth, and after withdrawing $800,000 in year 15 the account would be empty. Thus, with a 10 percent interest rate, the present value of this fifteen-year stream of benefits is $3,054,000. A second way to view the present value of the benefits is to answer the question, how much do you have to invest now at 10 percent to get $200,000 in year 1, how much more now to get $200,000 in two years, . . . and, finally, how much more now to get $800,000 in fifteen years? Adding all the investments up, the answer is a total investment now of $3,054,000. By similar methods, the present value of the stream of contributions above is $2,810,000.

By converting funding and benefit streams into their present values, they can be compared to see if the funding is adequate to meet pension obligations, and if not, how much additional investment would be required to fully fund the pension obligations. In this example, the additional investment needed now would be $244,000 ($3,054,000 − $2,810,000). This additional investment to fully fund the pension obligations is one way to measure the expenditure pressures on the government caused by its pension system.

This above example illustrates how present values are used to compare different patterns of future pension contributions and benefits. It also illustrates one approach to measuring unmet expenditure pressures. Later in the chapter these concepts and others are used to form more precise measures of the pressures on a government that emanate from the pension system. In pension analysis of this kind, the goal is systematic comparison of the pension obligations with the assets and/or contributions the government makes to meet these obligations. Inadequate assets compared with obligations may indicate the need for additional expenditures in the future; these pressures may threaten the financial health of a government to the extent that other resources cannot be found or freed up to meet these needs.

## II. PENSION FINANCING

Before we present techniques for pension analysis, it is important to understand certain issues in pension financing. *Pension financing* deals with the level and timing of contributions of money into a pension system. Note that in a defined contribution plan, the accumulation of assets at the retirement date is the sole determinant of the payments to the retiree. There is never really a question of financing or a funding gap.[18] Therefore, in the remainder of this chapter, we are concerned only with defined benefit plans, which cover most government employees.

In a defined benefit plan, the amounts that are contributed to the pension system in the years when employees are working will in part determine how much will have to be contributed by the government when the employees retire. If there are no contributions until employees retire, the entire benefit will have to be paid beginning on the retirement date. If sufficient funds are contributed each year during the employees' working lives, the accumulated assets and earnings may be sufficient to pay the full payments of the retirees without additional contributions. Thus the analysis of pension fund financing focuses on the size and timing of these pre-retirement contributions relative to the benefits promised at retirement.

We begin our discussion of pension financing by summarizing the reasons why governments should not wait until an employee retires before beginning to contribute funds for his or her retirement. We then examine the uncertainties that characterize pension financing and create financial risks for governments. Finally we look at pension costs, alternative funding systems, and the availability of pension information.

### Pay-As-You-Go versus Advance Funding

Since a government is an ongoing entity, why should contributions be made to a pension system during the employees' working life? Instead, why shouldn't a

---

[18] In a defined contribution plan there may be a question of the adequacy of the benefits from the retiree's perspective, but this is not a financing question.

government wait until an employee retires and then raise the necessary resources to pay the benefits promised? These questions outline two approaches to pension system financing.

The first approach is to contribute to the pension system only the resources that are necessary to pay those who are currently retired. This approach, often called *pay-as-you-go* financing, requires no contribution on the part of the government during an employee's working life, although an employee may be required to contribute certain amounts every year he or she is working. When a pension system is financed on a pay-as-you-go basis, the government's contribution is likely to increase over time, with the extent of the increase depending on factors such as the age of the work force, the growth in the work force, and salary increases.

The second approach, often called *advance* funding, calls for contributions by the government (and sometimes the employees) over the employees' working lives so that funds and their investment earnings accumulate until the retirement dates. If the accumulated funds are sufficient to pay the defined benefit payments to the retirees, additional payments by the government are not required. There are several arguments in favor of advance funding versus pay-as-you-go.[19]

First, what happens to pension obligations if the government disappears either physically (e.g., a ghost town) or fiscally (e.g., bankruptcy)? These possibilities, however remote, argue for advance funding. Although governments are intended to be continuing entities, pension system members and beneficiaries should be protected against catastrophes. And even if the government does not completely disappear, in times of financial hardship payments to retirees may be temporarily threatened, a threat that can be avoided with advance funding.[20] This reasoning was probably a contributing factor to the federal government's 1974 decision to mandate advance funding of private-sector pension systems.

Second, with advance funding, the full costs of decisions involving personnel are taken into account. This should improve decision making about wages versus pension benefits, capital versus labor expenditures, public production versus contracting out and other choices involving labor costs.[21] Of course, the cost implications of the pensions could be recognized without advance funding, but this is less likely.

A third argument for advance funding focuses on equity between generations. In a pay-as-you-go system, one generation (retirees) receives the benefits

---

[19] These arguments are explained further in the Urban Institute, *Future of State and Local Government Pensions,* Chap. 4; Tilove, *Public Employee Pension Funds,* Chap. 8; and Committee on Education and Labor, *Pension Task Force Report,* p. 146.

[20] The Urban Institute specifically mentions "payless paydays" for pensions in *The Future of State and Local Government Pensions,* p. 4–7. See also Advisory Commission on Intergovernmental Relations, *City Financial Emergencies.*

[21] See, for example, the Urban Institute, *Future of State and Local Government Pensions,* p. 4–12; and Bernard Jump, Jr., "Compensating City Government Employees: Pension Benefit Objectives, Cost Measurement, and Financing," *National Tax Journal,* 29, No. 3 (September 1976), 251.

while the next generation pays the costs in terms of pension contributions to retirees. Once a pension system reaches a steady state where new employees are replacing retiring ones (sometimes called a *mature* pension system), this will no longer be a problem. However, due to the growth in public employees over the past years and the relative newness of many pension systems, this steady state will not be reached for some time for many state and local systems.

A fourth argument sometimes offered as an advantage of advance funding is that it avoids an escalation in costs. At the same time, however, advance funding requires higher initial costs compared with pay-as-you-go financing. Moreover, as pointed out in the Urban Institute study, once a steady state is reached, this argument is no longer valid.[22]

There are other less important arguments in favor of advance versus pay-as-you-go funding, including the tax advantages, the impact on borrowing costs due to "sounder" financial management practices, and the need for protection against drastic cuts in the tax base. It is also possible to use accountability as a reason to favor advance funding.[23] Although an argument in favor of pay-as-you-go financing can be mounted, the assumptions needed for this argument (such as the inflation rate exceeding the yield on investments) are not realistic over the long run.[24]

Because of these reasons, most pension analysts, managers, and scholars recommend advance funding over pay-as-you-go funding for state and local pension systems.[25] This preference is also apparent when the funding approaches of state and local pension systems are examined. The Pension Task Force in its survey of all state and local systems in 1975 reported that only 17 percent of all systems were funded on a pay-as-you-go basis.[26] The Urban Institute studied one hundred of the largest state and local pension systems and reported that only 10 percent were funded on a pay-as-you-go basis.[27]

### The Role of Uncertainty

After a decision to advance fund a pension system has been reached, uncertainty comes into play. Uncertainty is generated by the need to forecast several variables in order to determine the resources that should be contributed over the employees' working lives so that the necessary funds are accumulated when the

[22] Urban Institute, *Future of State and Local Government Pensions*, p. 4–11.

[23] Ibid., Chap. 4.

[24] Ibid., p. 4–17.

[25] See, for example, the Urban Institute, *Future of State and Local Government Pensions*, pp. 4–3 and 4–25; Jump, "Compensating City Government Employees," p. 251; Committee on Education and Labor, *Pension Task Force Report*, pp. 145–46; and Tilove, *Public Employee Pension Funds*, Chap. 8.

[26] Committee on Education and Labor, *Pension Task Force Report*, Table G1, p. 151.

[27] Urban Institute, *Future of State and Local Government Pensions*, p. 18–14.

employees retire. These variables include factors associated with the employee, government, and economy.

Since pension systems have many members and beneficiaries, forecasts for the employee-based variables are made on a group basis, rather than on an individual basis, in order to average out risks. Even so, there is still considerable uncertainty. First, the rate at which members retire must be forecast. With changing norms and laws concerning retirement ages, differences across individuals in terms of their age at retirement may be increasing. Second, since retirement benefits often depend on how long the employees worked for the government, the employees' length of service at the retirement date must also be estimated. Third, the length of time that people will live after they retire must be estimated to determine the period over which benefits must be paid. If the pension has a provision for survivors (e.g., spouse), then their mortality must also be estimated. Other variables such as the turnover of the work force and the age of new entrants must also be estimated because this affects the pool of active members (the work force) and beneficiaries. Next, since most pension systems allow for retirement on disability prior to normal retirement age, the disability rates must be forecast. Finally, if employees have the right to withdraw from the pension system and take with them their own contribution as well as part of the government's, then the frequency and timing of this occurrence must be estimated.

There are other difficult projections that arise from the organization's policies and economic environment. Perhaps the most important organizational factor is the rate at which salaries will increase. A component of this estimate is usually a forecast of future inflation. Once the rate of inflation has been estimated, the growth of salaries relative to the inflation rate can be forecast.

The most important economic estimate is the earning rate on the assets accumulated in the pension system. Again, this estimate is usually made in conjunction with the estimate of the inflation rate. Pension systems invest in a diverse set of instruments including stocks, corporate bonds, and real estate, and the estimation of the returns on the investments must take this "portfolio" into account.

The number and complexity of these variables makes estimating their values for a pension system a very difficult task. In fact there are professionals, known as *actuaries,* whose job it is to estimate these variables and determine funding policies for pensions and insurance systems.

Pension systems that are advance funded based on the estimation of the above variables by actuaries are known as *actuarially funded* systems. Systems that are advance funded without using actuarial estimations are known as *nonactuarially funded* systems. These latter systems are advance funded because the contributions exceed the payments to retirees and, therefore, assets are accumulating. But instead of basing the contributions on actuarial estimates and assumptions, the contributions are set by policies such as matching employees' contributions or at a fixed percentage of payroll. The Pension Task Force reported that 52 percent of all state and local pension systems are advance funded on some type of actuarial basis while 25 percent of all state and local pension systems are advance funded on a nonactuarial basis.[28]

### Normal and Supplemental Costs

One additional distinction in pension systems needs to be introduced before we can discuss alternative funding methods. Actuarially based contributions to pension systems are composed of two components. The first component covers the pensions being earned by current and future members of the system, and this is referred to as the normal cost. Robert Tilove defines *normal cost* as the actuarially determined answer to the following question:

> How much would have to be contributed each year for each covered employee as a level amount or percentage of pay, from the time he started creditable service, for the value of his pension to be accumulated at the time he is expected to retire?[29]

There are a number of reasons why the normal cost is not the only cost of a pension system. Sometimes pension benefits are liberalized, that is, increased beyond that specified in the existing plan. Since the normal contributions made prior to the liberalization were based on the earlier (preliberalization) benefit levels, a new higher normal cost is required. However, employees who were part way to retirement when the liberalization occurred will not accumulate sufficient assets by retirement by just increasing their contribution to the new normal cost level. Additional contributions for the liberalized benefits credited to the employees for their past service are needed, since the earlier normal contributions were too low.

A similar need for additional contributions arises when a pension system is initiated and current employees are given credit for some or all of their years of service prior to the beginning of the pension system. In this case there were no normal costs contributed for part of their working lives, and the normal cost contributions for the remainder of their working lives will not be sufficient to accumulate the required funds.

Finally, the normal cost contributions may be based on incorrect actuarial estimates, so the normal contributions based on these estimates may also be incorrect. As a result, even after revising the normal costs to reflect the new estimates, an additional adjustment (either positive or negative) must be made to cover the period during which the estimates were faulty.

These additional factors—liberalized benefits, prior service credit, and actuarial gains and losses—are often covered in a second contribution to the pensions called a *supplemental cost,* or sometimes the *accrued cost.*

---

[28] Committee on Education and Labor, *Pension Task Force Report,* Table G1, p. 151. Of the remaining systems, 17 percent are on a pay-as-you-go basis and the funding method is unknown for 6 percent.

[29] Tilove, *Public Employee Pension Funds,* p. 150.

Although it is somewhat of a simplification, alternative actuarially based advance funded systems are defined by the way in which they fund the normal cost and the supplemental cost.

### Alternative Funding Methods

In discussing alternative funding systems it is important to realize that *there is no one correct way to fund pension systems,* even for an actuarially based advance funded system.[30] Different circumstances, judgments, and goals lead to different funding systems. Equally important is that certain measures of the financial status of pension systems depend on the funding method. Consequently, the range of acceptable methods can at times yield different conclusions about the financial status of a pension system.

Even if one preferred funding method cannot be specified, it is possible to articulate a set of generally agreed-upon criteria to assess any funding method. Tilove has put forward the following as one set of criteria:

1. All elements of long-term cost should be taken into account.
2. Contributions should approximate a level percentage of the payroll.
3. Additional funding should be provided only to the extent that security is needed against the possibility of future incapacity of the government to pay.
4. The funding method should provide fair and realistic cost estimates for benefit proposals.
5. The funding method should be one that can be firmly maintained in the face of political pressure and debate.[31]

A number of funding methods can satisfy these criteria. Although a detailed description and comparison of all of these methods is beyond the scope of this book, the presentation of a few of the basic characteristics of the funding methods will improve our ability to assess a pension system's impact on financial condition.[32]

Many actuarial funding methods consist of a normal cost contribution and a supplemental cost contribution. We begin with a discussion of the normal cost contribution because certain elements of the normal cost are used to calculate the supplemental cost.

A key factor that results in different normal cost contributions is the specification of the way in which the assets in the fund are to accumulate. Assuming that we agree on an amount that should be in the system for each retiree when he or she retires (this assumes agreement on actuarial estimates), there are still an

---

[30] Ibid., p. 142.

[31] Ibid., p. 164. For a different set of criteria, see the Urban Institute, *Future of State and Local Government Pensions,* p. 7–8.

[32] For more details on funding methods, see Tilove, *Public Employee Pension Funds,* Chaps. 8 and 9; and the Urban Institute, *Future of State and Local Government Pensions,* Chaps. 7 through 11.

infinite number of contribution schemes that will lead to the ultimate accumulation. High contributions can be made early in the career, in which case less has to be put in the fund later in the career, or small early contributions can be followed by higher contributions later. For example, the Urban Institute study considered, among others, accumulation streams based on (1) a level (constant) percentage of the payroll contributed in each year and (2) a level (constant) percentage of the benefits earned in each year.[33] Since employees' accrued benefits in most defined benefit plans start relatively lower and grow more rapidly than their payroll (because they are earning benefits based on a greater percentage of pay and their final pay is increasing), the level percentage of benefit method has lower initial contributions and higher later contributions over an employee's career compared with the level percentage of payroll method.

One way to see the differences between these methods is to compare various aspects of a set of plans using alternative funding methods. The Urban Institute carried out such an analysis on its sample of the one hundred largest state and local pension systems. For example, using alternative normal cost funding methods for the one hundred sample plans, the Urban Institute estimated that in 1980 the level percentage of payroll method would require 12.6 percent of payroll, while the level percentage of benefit method would require 9.4 percent of payroll.[34] Translated to dollars, the contributions for the one hundred plans assuming a level percentage of payroll normal cost method for 1980 would be $15.9 billion, while the 1980 contributions for the level percentage of benefit normal funding method would be $11.9 billion.[35] Thus, with two different actuarially sound pension financing systems, the proper contribution to the pension system varies significantly. These differences will become important when we discuss measures of pension system financing. There are other normal cost funding methods, but the basic points raised for the two examples here hold for those as well.

Once a normal cost funding method has been chosen for an actuarially based advance funded pension system, the second choice in the determination of the funding method is the way in which the supplemental or accrued liability is funded. The supplemental liability would be zero if normal costs were paid from the inception and there were no start-up liabilities, benefit liberalizations, or actuarial losses. But since these conditions usually do not hold, there is often some supplemental liability.

The supplemental liability is based on the amount of funds that should be in the system at a particular point in time. Moreover, this amount is determined using the same assumptions built into the calculation of the normal cost regarding the rate of accumulation of assets. As a result, the amount of the supplemental liability also varies with the normal cost funding method. For example, normal

---

[33] Urban Institute, *Future of State and Local Government Pensions,* Chap. 8.

[34] Ibid., p. 8–14.

[35] Ibid., Table 8–5, p. 8–15.

cost methods that require higher contributions earlier in the employee's career will lead to a calculation of a supplemental liability that is higher than the supplemental liability under normal cost methods that have higher pension contributions later in an employee's career.

The supplemental liability may be thought of as an amount that can be repaid over time like a mortgage. If no additional supplemental liability is generated, then part of the supplemental liability plus interest could be paid every year until the supplemental liability is zero. Interest must be paid because if these funds were already in the pension system, they would be earning a return.

State and local government pension systems will usually have substantial assets accumulated at any point in time if they have been using a normal cost method, even if they also have a supplemental liability. If substantial assets are accumulated and are likely to exist for some time in the future (as is the case for many state and local pension systems), it is not imperative to pay off the supplemental liability immediately. One strategy is to totally ignore the supplemental liability, in which case it will grow because it would have earned a return if it had been funded. A second strategy is to pay only the interest on the supplemental liability, in which case the supplemental liability will remain constant. A third strategy is to pay the interest and part of the supplemental liability in each year, in which case it would eventually decline to zero.

This third strategy is like a mortgage, and the term *amortization,* repaying part of the principal each year over a set number of years, is used in pension funding as well. Pension systems that elect the third strategy to pay for supplemental liabilities must decide on the period over which the liability will be paid and the method of payments. Most pension systems electing this third strategy plan to amortize the full supplemental liability over twenty to forty years. One-half of the one hundred plans in the Urban Institute sample amortized the supplemental liability over a specified period, and forty-two of these fell between twenty and forty years.[36]

The Pension Task Force reported that 52 percent of all plans used an actuarially based advance funded system with a known funding method. This 52 percent is comprised of plans that fund the normal cost and no supplemental cost (17.4 percent), plans that fund the normal cost and amortize the supplemental liability over forty years or less (26.8 percent), and plans that fund less than the combination of normal cost and the amortization of the supplemental liability over forty years (7.8 percent).[37]

The decision of which supplemental funding strategy to use is a judgment that must be made based on the goals of the pension system, available resources, characteristics of the work force, and so forth. As with the normal cost funding method, there is no one best way to fund supplemental costs. It is possible to treat

[36] Ibid., Table 9–1, p. 9–11.

[37] Committee on Education and Labor, *Pension Task Force Report,* Table G1, p. 151.

the initial, start-up supplemental liability differently than supplemental liabilities that stem from benefit liberalization and actuarial gains and losses. For example, the Urban Institute study recommends a relatively short amortization period for the latter two components of the supplemental liability so that the costs are paid by the generation that imposed them.[38]

Thus, to fully determine the funding policies of many state and local systems, both the normal and supplemental cost funding methods have to be specified, with one major exception. One funding method, used by some state and local government pension systems, does not differentiate between normal and supplemental costs. This funding method, known as *aggregate funding,* basically subtracts the value of assets on hand from the present value of all future benefits, and divides this difference by the present value of the future salaries of current employees to determine the percentage of salary that should be contributed in the year. This calculation is then repeated every year. This method implicitly pays off what would be the supplemental liability (if one was calculated) over the remaining working lives of the employees. Since this is usually a shorter period of time than most amortization periods, this funding method yields relatively high contributions in the early years of an employee's career.

### The Disclosure of State and Local Pension Information

In an ideal world, every pension system would clearly specify its design and assumptions, provide all necessary pension data, and report measures of financial condition to the public so that interested parties could interpret the measures and reach conclusions. Unfortunately, the real world is a far cry from the ideal world in terms of the disclosure of pension information. Although data quality and availability are problems in many areas of government financial analysis, pension disclosure problems may be the most severe.

The reporting and disclosure of pension information is improving, but it still has a long way to go. The Pension Task Force summarized its conclusions on disclosure as follows:

> Serious deficiencies exist among public employee retirement systems at all levels of government regarding the extent to which important information is reported and disclosed to plan participants, public officials, and taxpayers. . . . Public employee retirement systems at all levels of government are not operated in accordance with the generally accepted financial and accounting procedures applicable to private pension plans and other important financial enterprises. The potential for abuse is great due to the lack of independent and external reviews of the operations of many plans. There is an incomplete assessment of true pension costs at all levels of government due to the lack of adequate actuarial valuations and standards. In general, the absence of uniform accounting, auditing, and actuarial standards impeaches the credibility of the current practices in these areas.[39]

---

[38] Urban Institute, *Future of State and Local Government Pensions,* pp. 9–25 to 9–26.

[39] Committee on Education and Labor, *Pension Task Force Report,* p. 3.

A study conducted by Ernst & Whinney examined the annual financial reports of one hundred cities that reported on 251 pension systems. Ernst & Whinney analyzed the reporting of funding policies (labeled "accounting" policies in the study), accrued liabilities, and amortization periods. Only 58 percent of the pension systems reported their funding policies—i.e., whether the pensions were funded on a pay-as-you-go, actuarially advance funded, nonactuarially advance funded, and so forth. Furthermore, while 43 percent of the systems disclosed the accrued liability of the plan (we will discuss this concept in greater depth in the next part of the chapter), 10 percent reported that the accrued liability was "unknown," and the remaining 47 percent disclosed nothing at all about their accrued liability. Finally, the amortization period of the accrued liability was "unknown" or not disclosed for 73 percent of the plans.[40]

Currently there is not a single accepted standard for state and local government pension system reporting practices. For example, the Urban Institute identified eight different sets of standards.[41] Yet when the Urban Institute assessed disclosure using all eight standards and eighty-six plans, it never found more than 57 percent of the recommended items disclosed for any specific standard. For six of the eight sets of standards, the average number of required items disclosed ranged between 40 and 50 percent in the eighty-six-plan sample.[42]

Thus, while the measurement of pension financing is difficult with adequate data, it is further complicated by poor reporting of financial information. The absence of systematic and consistent disclosure of data for different pension systems makes it essential to have a variety of alternative measures based on different types of data so that at least some analysis can be conducted of every pension system.

## III. PENSION ANALYSIS MEASURES

In this section we discuss three types of measures that are useful in assessing the degree to which pensions will place an increasing burden on the expenditures of governments. The first set of measures is primarily based on measures of the liabilities and assets of the pension systems. The second set is derived from the characteristics of the pension systems, while the third contains measures based, for the most part, on the current resource flows into and out of the pension systems. Due to the problems of disclosure discussed above, it is unlikely that all of these measures can be computed with readily available data for any particular plan. Therefore the analyst will be forced to use various combinations of the three sets of measures.

---

[40] Ernst & Whinney, *How Cities Can Improve Their Financial Reporting* (Cleveland, Ohio, 1979), Table 4–14, p. 118.

[41] Urban Institute, *Future of State and Local Government Pensions*, p. 16–8.

[42] Ibid., Table 16–1, p. 16–10.

### Measures Based on the Assets and Liabilities
### of the Pension Systems

The most widely cited and controversial measures of the financial condition of a pension system are those based on the assets and liabilities of the plans at a point in time. One aspect that is not widely recognized, however, is that these measures depend in part on the funding method used to measure the plan's liability.

The measure that is probably reported the most frequently is the *unfunded pension liability*. The unfunded liability is usually defined as the difference between the present value of all future benefits and the present value of all assets, including the assets expected as a result of the normal contributions.[43]

It is not unusual for a pension system to have unfunded liabilities—certain accrued benefits for which no assets are on hand or expected from normal cost contributions—due to benefit liberalizations, start-up benefits, and actuarial losses. The question becomes how should the magnitude of unfunded liabilities be interpreted?

Since the present value of future benefits and future normal contributions depends on the funding methods, particularly the differences in timing of contributions, different funding methods, consequently, lead to different levels of unfunded liabilities. For example, the Urban Institute estimated that using the level percentage of payroll method for normal costs, unfunded liabilities of all state and local pension systems with membership over one thousand are $154 billion. In contrast, the unfunded liabilities using the level percentage of benefits funding method were $76 billion.[44]

In addition to the funding method, the actuarial assumptions and estimations used for the pension plan also affect the calculation of the unfunded liability. Thus, to interpret the unfunded liability reported by a pension system, we need to know a series of assumptions and policies inherent in the pension system as well as the funding methods.

The unfunded liability is most often reported as an absolute dollar amount, and since virtually all systems will have a positive unfunded liability, what should be highlighted in an analysis of financial condition? We will assume for the moment that the funding and actuarial assumptions behind the calculation of the unfunded liability are within the bounds of acceptable pension system management. Due to the differences in the sizes of pension systems and governments they serve, the absolute dollar unfunded liability is difficult to interpret by itself. It is often compared with some other aspect of the pension system itself or with a characteristic of the government unit.

Instead of expressing the unfunded liability as an absolute dollar amount calculated as the difference between the present value of assets (including future

---

[43] Ibid., p. 7–11.
[44] Ibid., p. 8–16.

normal contributions) and the present value of benefits, it is simpler to determine the ratio of a measure of the value of assets to the present value of benefits. The value of this ratio, known as the *funded ratio,* varies from zero for a pension system with no assets (totally funded on a pay-as-you-go basis) to one for a system that is "said to be 'fully funded.' "[45]

The Pension Task Force calculated the funded ratios (defined as the ratio of assets on hand to the plan's accrued liability) for state and local pension systems in 1975 and found that 13.7 percent of the systems had ratios of 0 to .2, 16.8 percent had ratios of .2 to .4, 33 percent had ratios of .4 to .6, 27.2 percent had ratios of .6 to .8, and 9.3 percent had ratios of .8 to 1.0.[46] In the Urban Institute study, the ratio of assets on hand to the target assets (what assets should be in a fully funded system given the funding method) was 56 percent in 1980 and projected to be 82 percent in 2024 using the funding assumptions employed by the plans.[47]

The interpretation of the funded ratio depends to some degree on the plan's characteristics. A very new pension system, for example, may be expected to have a relatively low funded ratio due to the benefits for which no payment has been made.[48] If an older more "mature" system with a significant portion of its former members already receiving benefits has a low funded ratio, this may be a danger signal. According to Bernard Jump:

> Few other generalizations about a plan's condition can be made on the basis of no more than the funded ratio for a single year. The careful analyst will want to look at the ratio's trend. If the examination of the trend reveals a history of increasing ratios, and few instances of declines, the system is probably being soundly financed. Conversely, there would be grounds for concern if the ratio has deteriorated steadily during recent years. Obviously then, it must be recognized that retirement systems with identical funded ratios may not have equally favorable (or unfavorable) financial prospects. Furthermore, it is essential to understand that . . . this method . . . use[s] estimates of the liability measure that will vary according to which actuarial cost method is used in the plan valuation.[49]

Thus both the level and trends in the funded ratio provide information on whether the contributions to the pension system are likely to create an increased burden on the government.

A second way to assess the unfunded liability is to compare it with the yearly payroll of the governments in the system. For this ratio, *unfunded liability to annual payroll,* a value of zero signifies a fully funded system with no unfunded liability. The ratio increases with no upper limit as the unfunded liability increases. Again, it is not so much the value of this ratio, *per se,* that is important, but changes in the ratio over time, with decreasing values of this ratio implying improving funding.

---

[45] Committee on Education and Labor, *Pension Task Force Report,* p. 162.

[46] Ibid., Table G7, p. 164.

[47] Urban Institute, *Future of State and Local Government Pensions,* Table 18–6, p. 18–24.

[48] Jump, "Compensating City Government Employees," p. 253.

[49] Ibid.

The Urban Institute calculated the ratio of unfunded liability as a percentage of plan payroll for its one-hundred-plan sample and found that in 1980, twenty-seven had values of 0 to 50 percent (four had values of 0), twenty-seven had values of 50 to 100 percent, twenty-eight had values of 100 to 200 percent, nine had values of 200 to 300 percent, seven had values of 300 to 400 percent, and two had values over 400 percent. In addition, the Urban Institute estimated the value of this ratio for 2024 using the funding assumptions employed by the plans and found the following distribution: sixty-eight had values of 0 to 50 percent (fifty-two had values of zero), ten had values of 50 to 100 percent, eight had values of 100 to 200 percent, two had values of 200 to 300 percent, ten had values of 300 to 400 percent, and two had values over 400 percent.[50] The comparison of the early and later years indicates the progress that many of the systems are projected to show over the next forty years. It is also interesting that the Urban Institute notes that ''the plans shown with higher remaining unfunded liabilities are the legislated rate plans with rates that do not cover future costs and the pay-as-you-go plans.''[51]

A different approach is to compare the unfunded liability with certain characteristics of the governments in the pension system, such as population and property values. The logic behind these pension ratios is similar to the logic behind the ratios of outstanding debt that were discussed in the preceding chapter. Two commonly used ratios are the *per capita unfunded liability* and the *unfunded liability as a percentage of full assessed value of property*. A disadvantage of the first ratio, compared with the second, is that per capita unfunded liability ratios do not reflect the effects of inflation while the unfunded liability to the property value ratios do.[52]

When ratios such as these are calculated, they are sometimes evaluated in combination with similar debt ratios.[53] In any comparison of this kind, it is important to make sure that the unfunded liabilities are calculated consistently. Moreover, debt and pension liabilities should be added together with some caution because of the time frame over which they are due.

Recall that in the preceding chapter we reported values of debt burden measures for the municipalities in Massachusetts (see Chapter 6, Table 6-10). The Bank of Boston, which calculated those debt ratios, also computed similar ratios for the pension systems used by the Massachusetts municipalities. Table 7-1 shows the unfunded pension liabilities for municipal governments in Massa-

[50] Urban Institute, *Future of State and Local Government Pensions,* Fig. 18-2, p. 18-27.

[51] Ibid., p. 18-26. Note that incorporated into these projections are the assumptions that there will be no future benefit liberalizations and very limited inflation increases for benefits.

[52] For examples of pension measures based on unfunded liabilities in empirical financial condition studies, see City of Seattle, Office of the Comptroller, ''Financial Condition of Seattle,'' August 18, 1983, pp. 70-72. See also Richard B. Victor, *The Financial Condition of Teacher Retirement Systems* (Santa Monica, Calif.: Rand Corporation, December 1980).

[53] John Nuveen & Co., ''Public Employee Pension Funds'' (Chicago, July 1, 1976), pp. 13-15. This report indicates that for cities per capita unfunded accrued liabilities plus debt averaged about $800 nationally in 1976.

TABLE 7-1    Unfunded Pension Liabilities, Massachusetts Municipalities, 1982

| POPULATION OF MUNICIPALITIES | UNFUNDED PENSION LIABILITIES PER CAPITA | UNFUNDED PENSION LIABILITIES AS A PERCENTAGE OF EQUALIZED VALUE OF PROPERTY |
|---|---|---|
| 0–4,999 | $133.50 | 0.51% |
| 5,000–9,999 | 230.00 | 0.97 |
| 10,000–24,999 | 402.00 | 1.71 |
| 25,000–49,999 | 624.00 | 2.72 |
| 50,000+ | 853.00 | 5.71 |
| State Median | 313.00 | 1.26 |

Data are based on the 231 municipalities only. No data on unfunded pension liabilities are available for the remainder.

SOURCES:   Data from Massachusetts Municipal Data Base and Massachusetts Retirement Law Commission. Table from Neville Lee, ed., *Debt Survey of Massachusetts Cities and Towns*, Bank of Boston, September 1983, Table 14, p. 27.

chusetts on a per capita basis and as a percentage of equalized value of property. Except for the smallest two categories of municipalities, the ratios for unfunded liabilities are higher than the comparable ratios for outstanding overlapping debt. For the largest cities in Massachusetts (populations over 50,000), the sum of overlapping debt and unfunded pension liabilities is $1,375 per capita and 8.59 percent of equalized assessed value of property. Because most pension systems in Massachusetts are funded on a pay-as-you-go basis, according to the Bank of Boston:

> Funds to meet retirement obligations are appropriated as needed when the employees retire. Consequently, many cities and towns are building up large future pension liabilities for which funds are not being put aside. Although these liabilities are not "debt" in the formal sense, they are similar to debt in that they represent a long-term obligation which will eventually have to be paid through annual budget appropriations. The continuing increase in this liability, and the need to appropriate retirement funds when due, within the constraints of Proposition 2½, may create severe budgetary problems for many cities and towns.[54]

This assessment is confirmed by the analysis reported by John Nuveen & Co. which shows that Massachusetts and the city of Boston have relatively high ratios of both per capita unfunded pension liabilities and pension liabilities as a percentage of full value of property.[55]

Because the measures of unfunded liability are so dependent on the funding

---

[54] Neville Lee, ed., *Massachusetts Municipal Data Base, Debt Survey of Massachusetts Cities and Towns* (Boston: Bank of Boston, 1983), p. 26.

[55] John Nuveen & Co., "Public Employee Pension Funds," p. 14.

methods and actuarial estimates of the system, measures that assess pension system assets and liabilities without as heavy a reliance on funding and actuarial decisions have been developed. The *plan termination liability,* defined as the accrued liabilities that would be present if the plan terminated immediately minus the assets on hand, is less dependent on funding and actuarial decisions. If the plan terminates immediately, the employee cannot receive a higher salary or accumulate additional years of service. Since the benefits will be based on a known salary and a known term of service, both of which are likely to be less than the actual final values if the plan were to continue, plan termination liabilities will be less than unfunded liabilities. There is not complete agreement on definition of the plan termination liability; for example, nonvested benefits may or may not be included.[56] Therefore care should be exercised when reported plan termination liabilities are assessed. The same techniques that were discussed for unfunded liabilities can be used to interpret this measure.

A second measure that is also less dependent on funding and actuarial decisions is the *quick pension liability ratio.* (We refer to this measure as the quick pension liability ratio rather than the more common ''quick liability ratio'' to distinguish it from the ''quick ratio,'' used to assess liquidity and discussed in the next chapter.) The quick pension liability ratio is defined as the ratio of plan assets to the ''actuarial value of future benefits for those persons already receiving benefits'' and the ''accumulated value of [employee] contributions for present active members,'' often expressed as a percentage.[57] Thus, not included in the denominator are the benefits earned by employees who have not yet retired, beyond their own contributions.

While some actuaries consider quick pension liability ratios below 100 percent to be characteristic of poor funding, the Pension Task Force reports that for the systems for which this measure is available, 40 percent have values of less than 100 percent.[58] Again it should be pointed out that this measure will probably be very low for new plans, since they have relatively few retirees.

A measure that is related to the quick pension liability ratio is the *reserve ratio,* defined as the ratio of assets to the present value of future benefits for those persons already receiving benefits, again expressed as a percentage.[59] The Pension Task Force estimates that 24.9 percent of the plans for which this measure is available have a reserve ratio below 100 percent.[60]

A different approach to correct for the effects of funding and actuarial deci-

---

[56] Urban Institute, *Future of State and Local Government Pensions,* p. 8–39. An individual's pension benefits are ''vested'' when he or she has the right to receive a defined benefit at retirement. Vesting usually occurs after the individual has been a member of the system for a specified number of years. See Tilove, *Public Employee Pension Funds,* pp. 36–38.

[57] Committee on Education and Labor, *Pension Task Force Report,* p. 166.

[58] Ibid., pp. 166–67. This measure is available for 60 percent of all systems.

[59] Ibid., p. 168.

[60] Ibid., Table G9, p. 168.

sions on comparisons of pension assets and liabilities is to use one funding method and one set of actuarial assumptions and estimates to calculate the unfunded liability of different pension systems to be compared at one point and over time. This approach increases the comparability and utility of pension measures that use the unfunded liability. The Urban Institute study discusses such a measure, the *plan continuation liability.*[61] Until vastly increased uniformity of disclosure is achieved in state and local government pension system reporting, however, this type of measure is not likely to be provided by most plans.

### Measures Based on Actuarial Estimates and Funding Methods

Measures of pension systems that focus on assets and liabilities provide direct indicators of the funding status of a pension system. Because of the inconsistency in the disclosure of these measures as well as the variability in the way in which the measures are calculated, other, more indirect, measures of the financial status of pension systems are desirable. An assessment of certain characteristics of the pension system is one way to determine a pension system's funding status indirectly. We consider two of these characteristics in this part, the pension system's actuarial estimates and funding method.

Earlier in the chapter we described the many estimates that are normally made by actuaries to determine the employer's contributions to a pension system Included are estimates of the rate at which people retire, their longevity after retirement, disability rates and lifespans on disability, employee turnover, yields on the investments held by the pension system, and salary increases.

The importance of these estimates is described by the Pension Task Force as follows:

> It is well recognized in the public pension arena that the one who controls the actuarial assumptions also controls the level and timing of employer contributions. This has led to a struggle among actuaries, boards of trustees, state legislatures, elected officials and others over the ultimate control of such assumptions. For some plans, the use of particular actuarial assumptions is mandated by statute. For other plans the retirement board may accept or reject recommendations made by the plan actuary. Small plans, in particular, may rely solely on the plan actuary to recommend adequate assumptions and contribution levels.
>
> However, just because actuarial assumptions may be chosen by an ''actuary'' there can be no assurance that they meet any particular standard of reasonableness or adequacy. In the public pension area actuaries are not required to meet any minimum qualification standards (as they are in the private sector).[62]

---

[61] Urban Institute, *Future of State and Local Government Pensions,* pp. 8–42 to 8–43 and 18–28 to 18–29. The Government Accounting Standard Board has also recently proposed a comparable measure for all pension systems.

[62] Committee on Education and Labor, *Pension Task Force Report,* p. 159.

Thus the analysis of financial condition from the pension perspective should include an examination of the reasonableness of the actuarial estimates (assumptions) because some faulty estimates can lead to an employer contribution that is too low. Moreover, when this low contribution level is corrected, there will be an unfunded liability that could require increased contribution levels in the future, which increases expenditure pressures and worsens financial condition.

An example of the effects of poorly specified actuarial assumptions and estimates is the New York City pension systems prior to 1977. By using a particular set of assumptions that the Pension Task Force characterized as "gimmickery," New York City was able to keep its contributions to the pension systems lower than what they would have been with more reasonable assumptions. For example (excluding the pension system for the Board of Education, which used reasonable assumptions), the mortality rates (percentage of retirees expected to die each year) assumed by the plans ranged from 136.8 to 469.4 percent of the actual rates measured over the last few years. By assuming that retirees would die sooner, on average, the employer's contribution was lower. Similarly, the mortality rates for disability pensioners for the same retirement systems (city employees, teachers, police, and firefighters) ranged from 129.1 to 800.0 percent of recent experience. Finally, the estimated salary increases assumed by these pension systems ranged from 1.0 to 2.4 percent per year, while recent experience actually ranged from 6.1 to 9.1 percent per year.[63]

The New York City case provides evidence of how unrealistic actuarial estimates can translate into low contributions that, if continued, may eventually lead to a poorly funded system and financial problems. For fiscal year 1977, using the existing funding method and the then in-place actuarial estimates, the yearly employer contribution to the five pension systems was estimated to be $1.22 billion. With the same funding method and actuarial estimates "updated to more realistic levels, the estimated yearly employer contribution increased 38 percent to $1.68 billion."[64]

Although qualified actuaries may have certain available techniques that permit them to make valid estimates of variables such as retirement rates, turnover, and mortality rates, actuaries usually do not have special qualifications for estimating economic variables such as the yield on investments, future salary increases, and inflation rates. Furthermore, the Urban Institute reports that the economic assumptions can have a greater effect on contribution levels than can the other assumptions.[65]

By using simulations, the Urban Institute shows the substantial effects of different economic estimates. For example, in a representative plan for state and

---

[63] Data reported in Committee on Education and Labor, *Pension Task Force Report,* p. 160.

[64] Data reported in Sixth Interim Report to the Mayor by the Temporary Commission on City Finances in "The Fiscal Impact of Retirement Benefits: Some Proposals for Reform," May 27, 1976, Table XVII, p. 41.

[65] Urban Institute, *Future of State and Local Government Pensions,* pp. 6-1 to 6-2.

local government employees, changing the yield on investments from 7 to 11 percent and simultaneously changing the salary increase estimate from 6 to 7 percent lowers the employer's cost as a percentage of payroll from 14 to 6.[66] This is an example of how the difference between the yield on investment assumption and the salary increase assumption is important. By increasing this difference from one percentage point (7 percent less 6 percent) to four percentage points (11 percent less 7 percent), the employer contribution was reduced by 57 percent (from 14 to 6 percent of payroll).

Because the actuarial estimates can have such a profound effect on the proper level of the employer's contribution, the actuarial estimates of the pension systems serving the governments under study should be scrutinized carefully. Where possible, analyses of the actuarial estimates should be made to determine whether incorrect prior estimates will lead to increased or decreased contributions in the future. In addition, the frequency with which the actuarial estimates are changed should be determined. This is particularly important in today's world of changing inflation rates, yields on investments, and rates of salary increases.

The funding method employed by the pension system is the second characteristic that can be examined to help in an assessment of the financial soundness of a pension system. Of course, a key distinction is whether the pension system is funded on a pay-as-you-go basis or advance funded. In many cases, particularly with a pension system that is not relatively new and has a "maturing" work force, pay-as-you-go funding can lead to escalating pension contributions when measured as a percentage of salary.

For advance funded systems, pension contributions depend on whether or not they are actuarially funded. Earlier we pointed out that a significant portion of advance funded state and local government pension systems (roughly one out of three) are not actuarially funded. The contributions to these systems tend to be set by a legislature or other body at a fixed percentage of salary. Without actuarial estimates, systems funded in this way run the risk of underfunding. Unfortunately, if a system is funded without an actuarial methodology, many of the actuarially based measures of pension funding, such as the ones we considered in the preceding part, may not be reported. Based on evidence reported to date, a system that is advance funded on a nonactuarial basis merits considerable skepticism.

Finally, for actuarially based advance funded pension systems, the funding methods should be ascertained. When a separate funding method is used for the normal costs and the supplemental costs, these should be examined. Recall that the contributions under various normal and supplemental funding methods will vary. For normal funding, if the methodology calls for relatively lower payments earlier in the employee's career, and the system is not yet mature, this could signal that future normal contributions will increase as a percentage of payroll.

There is even more flexibility in the policies for supplemental costs. But recall that the supplemental liability need not be paid off immediately, and in

---

[66] Urban Institute, *Future of State and Local Government Pensions,* Table 6-1, p. 6-3.

some cases may remain forever. However, if the supplemental liability is totally ignored, it will grow because it would have earned a return if it had been funded. Thus the supplemental cost funding method can be examined to determine whether the interest is being paid on the liability and whether, in addition, some of the principal is being amortized. As part of the funding methodology, the amortization period is often reported.

Note that pension systems that report the use of an ''aggregate funding'' method will not indicate separate funding methodologies for the normal and supplemental costs. In aggregate funding, however, the contributions are usually higher than for most combinations of normal and supplemental cost-funding methodologies.[67]

Finally, for any funding methodology, even pay-as-you-go, it is important to determine whether the contributions that are specified under the funding method are actually paid to the pension system. Because assets are accumulated by most pension systems, it is possible for most systems to remain solvent for some time without any contribution. Therefore a temptation always exists for the government under financial stress to cut back on its pension contribution. Even if the actuarial estimates and the funding method are sound, if the government does not contribute what is required, future payments may have to be increased to make up the difference.

### Measures Based Primarily on Cash Flows

The final set of measures, based on the cash inflows and outflows of the pension system, have advantages and disadvantages compared with earlier measures. On the one hand, cash flows for pension systems are not dependent on any actuarial estimates, and are often readily available for many pension systems. Many of the measures we will be discussing in this part are actually available on a national and state level from the Bureau of the Census.[68] On the other hand, however, without an actuarial methodology, cash flow measures are only proxies for the actual funding status of state and local government pension systems. Ideally, these measures should be used in combination with the measures described in the preceding two parts. When used alone, they should be interpreted cautiously.

The first measure in this group we will consider is the *ratio of cash receipts to cash disbursements.* Cash receipts typically include contributions from the employee, contributions from the employer (state and local government), and earnings on the assets in the system. Cash disbursements usually include benefits to retirees, withdrawals by individuals prior to retirement, and other disbursements including administrative costs. (This last item is not always available.)

In most pension systems that use some form of actuarially advance funding,

---

[67] See Tilove, *Public Employee Pension Funds,* Table 8.1, pp. 144–45.
[68] See Bureau of the Census, *Employee Retirement Systems.*

assets will build up prior to when they are needed to pay retirees, and therefore the ratio of cash receipts to disbursements will exceed one. On the other hand, for a pay-as-you-go system, cash receipts will equal cash disbursements for a ratio value of one.

Of course, the desirable ratio value should be determined by the combined effects of the actuarial estimates and the funding methods. But without knowledge of this desirable value, the ratio for the government pension system in question can be compared with a reference group average. In many instances a ratio of cash receipts to disbursements that is relatively low compared with a relevant reference group's may be indicative of an inadequate funding status of the pension system. This is particularly true of pensions that are comparable in terms of size, date of inception, and maturity of the work force. In addition, trends in this ratio over time should indicate whether or not the system is improving its funding status.

The U.S. Bureau of the Census, in the Census of Governments, provides data on the cash receipts and disbursements of state and local government pension systems. Table 7-2 shows ratios of cash receipts to cash disbursements (along with two other ratios to be discussed shortly) for selected pension systems. The ratio of cash receipts to disbursements for all state and local systems is 2.68, somewhat higher than this ratio for the locally administered systems by themselves, which is 2.29. Although it is not true in every case, as a general rule locally administered systems tend to be less well funded compared with state systems.

The ratio of cash receipts to disbursements for the locally administered systems in selected states is also shown in Table 7-2. The states were selected to show a range in the values of the ratios. For example, Wisconsin is a state that is known for its well-funded pension systems while, as we saw earlier in the chapter, Massachusetts relies primarily on pay-as-you-go funding. The other states were selected to fall somewhere between Wisconsin and Massachusetts. The expectations concerning the states at the extremes are confirmed by the ratios of cash receipts to cash disbursements. Wisconsin's value of this ratio, 3.59, is much higher than the average for all systems and the average for locally administered systems. Massachusetts's low value of 1.36 indicates that there is now some attempt to at least partially advance fund the system, since this ratio is above one. The other four states fall between Wisconsin and Massachusetts; California is close to the national average of locally administered systems while New York and Pennsylvania have values close to two. West Virginia has a low value, 1.54, which is close to the value for Massachusetts.

It is worth repeating that these cash flow ratios must be interpreted with care because of their failure to include actuarial considerations. Yet it is difficult to imagine a set of circumstances where a well-funded, ongoing system would have a ratio of cash receipts to disbursements that is close to one.[69]

---

[69] For an example of the use of this ratio in empirical financial condition studies, see Terry Nichols Clark and Lorna Crowley Ferguson, *City Money* (New York: Columbia University Press, 1983), pp. 65-70. See also John Nuveen & Co., "Public Employee Pension Funds."

TABLE 7-2     **Pension System Cash Flow Ratios for Selected Systems, 1981-82**

| SYSTEM | RATIO OF CASH RECEIPTS TO CASH DISBURSEMENTS | INVESTMENT EARNINGS AS A PERCENTAGE OF BENEFITS | RATIO OF ASSETS TO BENEFITS |
|---|---|---|---|
| All state and local pension systems | 2.68 | 121 | 15.64 |
| All locally administered pension systems | 2.29 | .83 | 12.23 |
| Locally administered systems in: | | | |
| California | 2.26 | 99 | 14.16 |
| Massachusetts | 1.36 | 39 | 4.90 |
| New York | 2.09 | 46 | 11.99 |
| Pennsylvania | 1.95 | 70 | 8.00 |
| West Virginia | 1.54 | 38 | 4.50 |
| Wisconsin | 3.59 | 201 | 19.61 |

SOURCE:   **U.S. Department of Commerce, Bureau of the Census,** *Employee-Retirement Systems of State and Local Governments,* **1982 Census of Governments (Washington, D.C.: Government Printing Office, August 1983), Table 3, pp. 4-9.**

The second cash flow ratio we will discuss is *investment earnings as a percentage of benefits*. Systems that are more fully funded will have accumulated a significant stock of assets at a particular point in time, and the size of the earnings on these assets can be judged relative to the benefits that are paid by the system. This ratio captures not only the size of the benefits accumulated but also the earnings performance of the system's investments. For a pure pay-as-you-go system this ratio will be zero, since there are no assets accumulated and, therefore, there can be no earnings. The desirable value of this ratio again depends on actuarial estimates, funding methods, maturity of the work force, and so forth. An important caveat for this ratio is that for those systems with a relatively young work force and few retirees (a relatively immature system), ratios of investment earnings to benefits may be high simply due to the low level of benefits currently being paid by the system.

The values of earnings as a percentage of benefits for selected systems are shown in Table 7-2. As expected, the value of this measure for all state and local pension systems, 121 percent, is higher than the value for all locally administered pension systems, 83 percent. Thus, for all state and local pension systems as a group, investment earnings were greater than benefits paid to retirees, but this was not the case for locally administered systems.

The highest value for this measure for the selected states is 201 percent for Wisconsin, the same state that had the highest ratio for the preceding measure. Among the six states, earnings as a percentage of benefits is lowest for West Virginia, slightly below Massachusetts. New York has a relatively low value of earnings as a percentage of benefits, California is somewhat above the average for locally administered systems, and Pennsylvania is again below average.

The third ratio we examine in this section, the *ratio of assets to benefits,* is not strictly a cash flow ratio, since the numerator is a stock rather than a flow. Nevertheless, we discuss it in this section because its calculation does not require actuarial estimates. This ratio has been cited as a particularly useful measure when actuarial valuations are not disclosed because of the close correlation between this ratio and a system's funding methods. Systems that use advance funded actuarial methods are more likely to have higher ratios of assets to benefits.[70]

The ratio of assets to benefits for all state and local pension systems for 1981–82 was 15.64, as reported in Table 7–2, while the value for all locally administered pension systems was 12.23, lower than the value for all systems as expected. The Pension Task Force suggests that the ratio of assets to benefits should be at least between 10 and 15 if the system is to be "considered minimally funded."[71]

The ratio of assets to benefits for locally administered systems in Wisconsin, 19.61, again tops the list of six states shown in Table 7–2. The ratios of assets to benefits for West Virginia and Massachusetts are the lowest on the list, at 4.50 and 4.90, respectively. The value of assets to benefits for California is somewhat above average, New York is near the average on this ratio, while Pennsylvania is considerably below.

Before turning to the fourth and final cash flow ratio, it is useful to review our findings on the locally administered pension systems in the six states we examined in Table 7–2. A more complete analysis would be possible with values for these ratios over time, but we can still reach tentative conclusions based on Table 7–2.

First, the three measures confirm our prejudgment of the Wisconsin systems; they appear to be very well funded. Second, the values of the three measures raise serious questions about the systems in Massachusetts (which we already know rely heavily on pay-as-you-go financing) and West Virginia. Third, the systems in California, while not as well funded as those in Wisconsin, also appear to be in good shape, particularly relative to the average values for all the locally administered systems. Fourth, the New York systems (which consist primarily of New York City systems) are close to the average of locally administered systems in terms of the ratios of cash receipts to disbursements and assets to benefits. Clearly, additional information is needed to draw a firm conclusion, but the ratios raise the possibility that the assets in New York's locally administered systems are earning a relatively low rate of return. Pennsylvania, which has relatively low values of investment earnings as a percentage of benefits and assets to benefits, may be a case of a poorly funded system that is trying to improve its below-average funding status, since its ratio of cash receipts to disbursements is much closer to the average than the other two ratios. Based on

---

[70] See discussion in Committee on Education and Labor, *Pension Task Force Report,* pp. 171–72.

[71] Ibid., p. 170. For an example of the use of this ratio in an empirical financial condition study, see Clark and Ferguson, *City Money,* pp. 65–70.

the data in Table 7-2, the locally administered systems in Massachusetts, West Virginia, and, to some degree, Pennsylvania are likely candidates to place future expenditure pressures on the local governments because of the need to increase pension contributions.

The fourth and final cash flow measure is *contributions to pension systems as a percentage of total salaries.* Ideally, this measure should only include the government's contributions, but sometimes data do not permit a separation of the government's and the employees' contributions. Employee contributions may be zero or may be as high as the government's contributions.[72] This measure directly assesses the current burden that pensions are placing on government expenditures, but as with all cash flow ratios, it is difficult to interpret this measure taken by itself. For example, a pension system that is slightly below the average in terms of governmental pension contribution as a percentage of salary may be a system with an unusually high employee contribution, a well-funded system that has accur  ited a significant asset base, or a system whose funding and current contributions are below average. Low levels now may mean that higher levels will be needed later, and very high levels now may indicate that earlier underfunding has now come home to roost. Thus measures based on assets and liabilities, or even cash flow measures such as the asset to benefit ratio, should be examined together with this measure.

The Pension Task Force has computed the contribution to salary ratio for certain plans: "For the larger state and local defined benefit plans the total employer and employee contributions as a percentage of payroll averages about 16 percent. The average payroll contribution for smaller defined benefit plans is somewhat larger—18 percent".[73] When the Pension Task Force examined all state and local pension systems together, 26 percent of the systems had employer and employee contributions below 10 percent, and about 18 percent of the systems had employer and employee contributions above 25 percent.[74] Finally, John Nuveen & Co. examined this ratio and reported that the government contribution to pension systems averages about 17 percent.[75]

## IV.  OUR CONTINUING EXAMPLE

In this section we apply the pension analysis to our sample city of Dyer Straits. Dyer Straits, like all local governments in the reference group, covers virtually all of its employees in a locally administered pension system. The pension systems in both Dyer Straits and the reference group rely exclusively on government con-

---

[72] Committee on Education and Labor, *Pension Task Force Report,* pp. 135–36.

[73] Ibid., p. 136.

[74] Ibid., Table F4, p. 137.

[75] John Nuveen & Co., "Public Employee Pension Funds," p. 19.

tributions. Dyer Straits' pension system is undergoing changes in terms of its funding. As recently as 1960 all pension systems in the reference group were funded on the basis of a percentage of salary set by the city. In most cases this method led to some advance funding, but not at a level equal to normal and supplemental costs. Thus unfunded liabilities grew in all of the systems. In 1960 a state-level task force recommended that the pensions change to an actuarially based advance funded method, but its recommendations were not binding and only about half of the pension systems changed voluntarily. Due to a near default in a neighboring state, a blue-ribbon panel established in 1975 again recommended that actuarially based advance funding be used. The state legislature passed a law mandating this by 1989. Beginning in 1975, all pension systems in the state have been required to have an actuary calculate the unfunded liability using a similar set of estimates and funding methods, even if the system is not advance funded.

By 1983, all but five pension systems in the state had made the recommended change by completely switching to an actuarially based advance funded system. Dyer Straits had begun to make the change on a gradual basis in 1978; by 1983 it was funding normal costs plus interest on supplemental cost, and in some years it was able to amortize a part of supplemental cost. The goal in Dyer Straits was to meet the 1989 deadline for an actuarially based advance funded system.

Only six pension systems in the reference group, including Dyer Straits, automatically adjust the benefits of retirees for the cost of living. For Dyer Straits, the automatic adjustment is 80 percent of the consumer price index up to a maximum of 6 percent per year. Most of the other pension systems in the reference group provide cost-of-living adjustments on an *ad hoc* basis, but these are not normally as generous as the automatic increases. Except for moderate benefit liberalizations in 1981, there have been no significant changes in the structure of Dyer Straits' pension system since 1975.

Basic data on the pension systems in Dyer Straits and the reference group are listed in Table 7–3. Year-end assets have grown in both Dyer Straits and the reference group, although the increase in the reference group, 80.4 percent, exceeds the increase in Dyer Straits, 41.0 percent. Table 7–3 also includes the yearly government contribution and earnings on assets, as well as the benefits paid to retirees. Finally, the unfunded liabilities of the pension systems are estimated. The actuarial estimates and funding methods used in this latter calculation are similar in Dyer Straits and the reference group because of procedures set down by the 1975 blue-ribbon panel.

The first set of measures we will use to examine the funding status of Dyer Straits' pension system and the future impact that the pension system will have on Dyer Straits' expenditures is based on the assets and liabilities of the pension system. These measures are shown in Table 7–4. The unfunded accrued liability (present value of benefits less present value of assets) is listed first. In Dyer Straits the unfunded liability has increased slightly, while the unfunded liability in the reference group has actually declined by about 20 percent. This is the first sign

TABLE 7-3  Basic Data on Pension Systems, City of Dyer Straits, and Reference Group, 1979-83 ($ millions)

| | DYER STRAITS | | | | | REFERENCE GROUP | | | | |
|---|---|---|---|---|---|---|---|---|---|---|
| | 1979 | 1980 | 1981 | 1982 | 1983 | 1979 | 1980 | 1981 | 1982 | 1983 |
| Assets in pension system at year-end | 3.347 | 3.696 | 4.041 | 4.427 | 4.720 | 153.68 | 176.81 | 203.62 | 244.36 | 277.29 |
| Government contribution | .710 | .805 | .928 | 1.107 | 1.317 | 22.08 | 24.91 | 27.03 | 29.66 | 32.67 |
| Earnings on assets | .152 | .201 | .259 | .323 | .332 | 6.72 | 9.22 | 12.38 | 16.29 | 18.94 |
| Benefits paid to retirees | .546 | .657 | .842 | 1.044 | 1.356 | 9.60 | 10.99 | 12.59 | 15.21 | 18.68 |
| Unfunded liability | 27.90 | 27.70 | 27.39 | 27.67 | 28.46 | 570.7 | 550.4 | 526.3 | 488.2 | 457.8 |

TABLE 7-4  Measures of Pension Funding Status Based on Assets and Liabilities, City of Dyer Straits and Reference Group, 1979–83

| | DYER STRAITS | | | | | REFERENCE GROUP | | | | | LOCATION QUOTIENTS* | | | | |
|---|---|---|---|---|---|---|---|---|---|---|---|---|---|---|---|
| | 1979 | 1980 | 1981 | 1982 | 1983 | 1979 | 1980 | 1981 | 1982 | 1983 | 1979 | 1980 | 1981 | 1982 | 1983 |
| Unfunded liability ($ millions) | 27.90 | 27.70 | 27.39 | 27.67 | 28.46 | 570.7 | 550.4 | 526.3 | 488.2 | 457.8 | .049 | .050 | .052 | .057 | .062 |
| Funded ratio (assets as a percent of unfunded liabilities plus assets) (%) | 10.7 | 11.8 | 12.9 | 13.8 | 14.2 | 21.2 | 24.3 | 27.9 | 33.4 | 37.7 | .505 | .486 | .462 | .413 | .377 |
| Unfunded liability per capita ($) | 848 | 847 | 845 | 862 | 892 | 374 | 363 | 350 | 327 | 308 | 2.267 | 2.333 | 2.414 | 2.636 | 2.896 |
| Unfunded liability as a percent of full assessed value of property (%) | 16.9 | 16.3 | 15.4 | 14.8 | 14.8 | 8.0 | 7.5 | 6.8 | 6.0 | 5.3 | 2.113 | 2.173 | 2.265 | 2.467 | 2.792 |
| Unfunded liability plus outstanding overlapping GO debt per capita ($) | 1,577 | 1,636 | 1,759 | 1,817 | 1,883 | 824 | 822 | 820 | 805 | 796 | 1.914 | 1.990 | 2.145 | 2.257 | 2.366 |
| Unfunded liability plus outstanding overlapping GO debt as a percent of full assessed value of property (%) | 31.4 | 31.6 | 32.1 | 31.2 | 31.2 | 17.7 | 16.9 | 15.9 | 14.7 | 13.8 | 1.774 | 1.870 | 2.019 | 2.122 | 2.260 |

*Dyer Straits/Reference Group.

that the funding of Dyer Straits' pension system may be a problem relative to the pension systems in the reference group.

The unfunded liability, by itself, is difficult to interpret because the sizes of the pension systems and cities are not the same. The next three ratios correct for this in different ways. First, the funded ratio, the ratio of assets to unfunded accrued liabilities plus assets, is shown for Dyer Straits and the reference group. The funded ratio for Dyer Straits has increased over the five years from 10.7 to 14.2 percent. Although the fact that this ratio has increased is a good sign, the absolute level of the ratio is quite low. Recall that we reported earlier in the chapter that only 13.7 percent of state and local pension systems in 1975 had funded ratios below 20 percent. Moreover, the funded ratio in the reference group increased from 21.2 to 37.7 percent over the same period. Thus, although Dyer Straits' pension system is accumulating assets faster than it is accumulating liabilities, the absolute level of assets to liabilities suggests there may be problems.

In order to compare the unfunded liability, standardizing for the size of the city, per capita unfunded liabilities are computed. The relatively poor position of Dyer Straits' pension system relative to the reference group is indicated by two findings. First, the level of the per capita unfunded liabilities for Dyer Straits is nearly three times as high as the average for the reference group in 1983. Second, while the average per capita unfunded liabilities has declined in the reference group over the five-year period, it has grown in Dyer Straits, particularly from 1981 to 1983.

The unfunded liability is computed as a percentage of full assessed value of property in order to determine how the pension liabilities relate to one measure of ability to pay. In terms of levels, Dyer Straits' unfunded liability is, again, nearly 2.8 times as high as the average for the reference group in 1983. Primarily because of the growth in the full assessed value of property, this ratio has declined in both Dyer Straits and the reference group. The decline in the reference group is greater than the decline in Dyer Straits; this is indicated by the increase in the location quotients over the five-year period.

Since both outstanding debt and future pension obligations are long-term commitments of a city, measures of debt and pensions are combined in the final two ratios shown in Table 7-4. Outstanding overlapping general obligation debt plus unfunded pension liabilities are computed on a per capita basis and as a percentage of full assessed value of property. Both ratios confirm the high level of long-term obligations in Dyer Straits compared with the reference group. Moreover, the absolute values of these ratios are considerably greater than national averages, or even the averages for Massachusetts, a state that relies heavily on pay-as-you-go funding.

The second set of measures we recommend for pension analysis examines the characteristics of the pension systems directly. Only limited information is available in this category for Dyer Straits and the reference group, and we reviewed most of this at the beginning of the discussion of pensions in Dyer Straits. The most critical factor is that Dyer Straits has not yet switched to an actuarially based advance funded system, as recommended by most pension analysts. Although Dyer Straits faces a law that mandates this preferred funding method by 1989, as of 1983 it is still contributing only an amount that is equivalent to the normal cost, interest on the supplemental liability, and a small part of the supplemental liability itself. Because of the length of time that Dyer Straits' pension system has operated without actuarial funding, the maturity of the work force in Dyer Straits, and the large and growing unfunded liability, when Dyer Straits finally makes the switch to the preferred funding method, the burden on its expenditures may be enormous. The fact that Dyer Straits provides an automatic cost-of-living adjustment, compared with the *ad hoc* (and lower) adjustments provided by the pension systems in the reference group, is also a factor that is likely to increase Dyer Straits' future pension commitments compared with the reference group's.

Table 7-5 presents four measures based for the most part on the cash flows of the pension systems beginning with the ratio of cash receipts to disbursements. Recall that a ratio of cash receipts to disbursements that exceeds one is required to accumulate assets in the pension system. The ratio of cash receipts to disbursements declines from about 1.6 in 1979 to 1.2 in 1983 in Dyer Straits. This ratio also declines in the reference group, but its absolute level is over twice as large as the level in Dyer Straits in four of the five years, and the rate of decline is lower in the reference group compared with Dyer Straits. Since the data in Table 7-2 showed that the national average of cash receipts and disbursements for locally administered pension systems was about 2.3 in 1981–82, questions must be raised about the system in Dyer Straits.

The second ratio listed in Table 7-5 is earnings as a percentage of benefits. The national average for this figure for locally administered systems in 1981–82 was 83 percent while the values for Dyer Straits varied from 24 to 31 percent over the five years. This is in contrast to earnings as a percentage of benefits in the reference group, which generally increased over the period and ended the period over 100 percent. This is a further signal that Dyer Straits' pension system has accumulated a low level of assets compared with the reference group's or national averages.

The next measure in Table 7-5 is the ratio of pension assets to benefits. This ratio declines for both Dyer Straits and the reference group over the period, but the decline is greater in Dyer Straits. The value of the ratio of assets to benefits is 14.8 for the reference group in 1983, over four times as large as the value in Dyer Straits in that year. The questionable status of Dyer Straits' system is also highlighted by the national average of the assets to benefits ratio of 12.23 for locally administered pension systems in 1981–82, which is nearly three times the value for Dyer Straits, 4.240, in 1982. Thus the first three ratios shown in Table 7-5 raise questions about the funding status of Dyer Straits' pension system that are similar to the questions raised by the ratios of assets and liabilities. It appears that by contributing only a fraction of what is needed with an actuarially based advance funded system, Dyer Straits has built up significant pension commitments in the future that are likely to increase expenditure pressures.

TABLE 7-5    Measures of Pension Funding Status Based on Cash Flows, City of Dyer Straits and Reference Group, 1979-83

| | DYER STRAITS | | | | | REFERENCE GROUP | | | | | LOCATION QUOTIENTS* | | | | |
|---|---|---|---|---|---|---|---|---|---|---|---|---|---|---|---|
| | 1979 | 1980 | 1981 | 1982 | 1983 | 1979 | 1980 | 1981 | 1982 | 1983 | 1979 | 1980 | 1981 | 1982 | 1983 |
| Ratio of cash receipts to cash disbursements | 1.579 | 1.531 | 1.410 | 1.370 | 1.216 | 3.000 | 3.105 | 3.130 | 3.021 | 2.763 | .526 | .493 | .450 | .453 | .440 |
| Investment earnings as a percentage of benefits (%) | 27.8 | 30.6 | 30.8 | 30.9 | 24.5 | 70.0 | 83.9 | 98.3 | 107.1 | 101.4 | .397 | .365 | .313 | .289 | .242 |
| Ratio of assets to benefits | 6.130 | 5.626 | 4.799 | 4.240 | 3.481 | 16.008 | 16.088 | 16.173 | 16.065 | 14.844 | .383 | .350 | .297 | .262 | .235 |
| Government contributions as a percentage of payroll (%) | 20.1 | 20.9 | 22.0 | 23.4 | 24.2 | 16.5 | 17.1 | 17.2 | 17.0 | 17.2 | 1.218 | 1.222 | 1.279 | 1.376 | 1.407 |

*Dyer Straits/Reference Group.

The final ratio in Table 7–5 is government contributions as a percentage of payroll. When viewed in combination with the other ratios that indicate a large unfunded liability and low levels of accumulated assets, the relatively high level of government contributions as a percentage of payroll for Dyer Straits is very problematic. Even without funding the sum of normal costs, interest on the supplemental liability, and an amortized part of the supplemental liability, Dyer Straits is devoting a substantially larger portion of its payroll to pensions compared with the reference group. Since Dyer Straits is postponing a significantly greater part of its pension obligations compared with the reference group, the already high level of pension contributions as a percentage of payroll is likely to increase in the future and expenditure pressures will increase as a result.

Thus, from a pension point of view, the financial condition of Dyer Straits is not very positive. Currently, Dyer Straits has substantial long-term pension commitments, and when it eventually changes to an actuarially based advance funded system the share of payroll devoted to pensions is likely to increase considerably above the 1983 level of 24 percent. The reference group, on the other hand, by moving to an actuarially advance funded system sooner, on average, may have reached a peak in its pensions as a percentage of payroll well below 20 percent. When this is combined with the fact that prospects for Dyer Straits on the revenue side are rather bleak, the possibility of reducing the "unneeded" expenditures discussed in Chapter 5 becomes more urgent. Moreover, the finding from the debt analysis that the expenditure slack, if realized, may be used for increased borrowing must be called into question because of the likelihood that pension contributions will claim an increasing share of expenditures and an increasing amount of resources. The overall conclusion for pensions in Dyer Straits is that they are a current burden and that this burden will probably get worse in the future.

## QUESTIONS

1. Why is pension analysis an important component of financial condition analysis? How is pension analysis related to the other components of financial condition analysis?

2. For a government pension, what are the typical financial inflows and outflows? Financial stocks?

3. What uncertainties must be addressed to determine the future obligations of a pension system? How are these estimates obtained?

4. Why is the concept of *present value* important in pension analysis?

5. Differentiate between a defined contribution pension plan and a defined benefit pension plan. From a financial condition perspective, why is the distinction important?

6. Discuss the difference between a pay-as-you-go and an advance funded pension system. What are the arguments in favor of an advance funded versus pay-as-you-go system? What are the implications of this difference for financial condition analysis?

7. When a pension system is described as being an actuarially based advance funded

system, what does this mean? How does it differ from a non-actuarially based advance funded system?

8. Define *normal costs* and *supplemental costs*. In what alternative ways can normal and supplemental costs be funded in an actuarially based advance funded system?

9. Suppose you were asked to evaluate the financial condition of a pension system. What information would you need?

10. What are alternative measures of the financial status of a pension system based on the assets and liabilities of the system?

11. Sometimes measures of the unfunded liabilities of a government's pensions are added to the government's debt to compute pension plus debt burden measures. What are the strengths and weaknesses of such measures?

12. True or false: "A government pension system with an unfunded liability is in serious financial trouble." Explain.

13. Suppose you were evaluating a government's pension system that had no record of the actuarial estimates used in pension financing and management. If you had the opportunity to interview the system's actuary, what questions would you ask and why?

14. What *cash flow* measures are available to evaluate the financial condition of a pension system? What are the strengths and weaknesses of cash flow measures?

15. Based on the empirical information presented in the chapter, what is the financial condition of the locally administered pension systems in Massachusetts? What additional information on the locally administered systems in Massachusetts would you like to have before reaching a conclusion?

---
**PROBLEMS**
---

1. Information on the locally administered retirement systems in four states—Colorado, Florida, Michigan, and Texas—is given below for 1981–82. Using this information and the information given in the chapter, analyze the pension financing of the locally administered systems in these four states. In which states are the pensions likely to cause increased pressure on the local governments (in the aggregate)?

Financial Information on Locally Administered Pension Systems in Four States, 1981–82 ($ thousands)

| STATE | TOTAL RECEIPTS | EARNINGS ON INVESTMENTS | TOTAL DISBURSEMENTS | TOTAL BENEFITS | TOTAL ASSETS |
|---|---|---|---|---|---|
| Colorado | 105,161 | 51,513 | 26,355 | 20,915 | 560,538 |
| Florida | 238,386 | 87,544 | 87,460 | 73,333 | 1,072,440 |
| Michigan | 829,320 | 316,258 | 273,961 | 224,824 | 3,806,074 |
| Texas | 289,203 | 111,101 | 85,919 | 72,369 | 1,310,664 |

SOURCE:  U.S. Department of Commerce, Bureau of the Census, *Employee-Retirement Systems of State and Local Governments*, 1982 Census of Governments (Washington, D.C., August 1983), Table 3, pp. 4–9.

2. Information on the pension systems in the city of Red Lion and a reference group were presented in the problem at the end of Chapter 4. Use this information to analyze the financial status of the pensions in Red Lion.

   a. How likely are Red Lion's pensions to cause expenditure pressures in the future?

   b. Suppose the unfunded liabilities in Red Lion were $38 million and $51 million in 1977 and 1983, respectively, and the unfunded liabilities in the reference group were $27 million and $28 million in 1977 and 1983, respectively. How would this information affect the conclusions from part a?

c.  Suppose the funded ratios were .44 and .40 in Red Lion in 1977 and 1983, respectively, and the funded ratios were .60 and .67 in the reference group in 1977 and 1983, respectively. How would this information affect the conclusions from parts a and b?

# CHAPTER
# 8 / Internal Resource Analysis

At any point in time, a government controls a fixed amount of *internal financial resources*, funds that can be appropriated relatively quickly for use in meeting the government's goals without raising additional revenues or redirecting expenditures to new uses. The level of these internal resources will vary over time and between organizations, reflecting differences in past and current expenditures and revenues, organizational needs, and policies regarding the holding of resources. The ability of governments to put these resources to immediate use will also vary, depending on the form in which these resources are held.

The purpose of internal resource analysis, the last component of financial condition analysis, is to determine the government's ability to draw on these internal resources to meet financial obligations. This component of financial analysis is primarily directed at the question of *short-term* financial strength, the ability to meet cash demands today, next week, or within the year. While highly dependent on the longer-term financial condition questions raised in our earlier revenue, expenditure, debt, and pension analyses, short-term financial strength depends on current conditions and policies as well. The longer-term financial condition of a government usually affects the organization's ability to build up internal resources or, in the face of unexpected cash demands, provides a basis for securing needed cash from external sources. But it is still possible to be in good financial condition in the long run yet operate with inadequate levels of internal resources or have internal resources that cannot easily be converted into cash (i.e., not "liquid"), which may create serious short-term financial problems. This is why internal resource analysis, which has a shorter-term perspective compared with the other components, is necessary for a complete financial condition analysis.

This chapter examines both the level and the accessibility (or "liquidity") of the internal resources of a government. In the first section we discuss the nature of internal resource analysis, including a review of the sources and uses of cash and the distinction between the level and the liquidity of internal resources. In the second section we examine the information available for internal resource analysis, including balance sheet data, and illustrate these data with our continuing example. In the third section we describe how to assess internal resource levels in more detail and discuss the factors that increase or decrease these levels. A discussion of the liquidity of these internal resources and available measures to evaluate a government's liquidity is presented in the fourth section. In the final section we discuss the analysis of government enterprises and their impact on internal resources. Throughout the final three sections of the chapter we use our continuing example to illustrate internal resource analysis.

## I. THE NATURE OF INTERNAL RESOURCE ANALYSIS

To understand how internal resource analysis fits into our overall analysis of governments, we need to draw on and integrate some of the concepts discussed in earlier chapters.

### Time and the Sources and Uses of Cash

A government's internal resources determine its ability to generate cash to meet cash needs. As discussed in Chapter 3 (see Table 3–1), the sources of cash and needs for cash depend on the time available to raise cash and/or change cash needs. It is useful to reconsider some of these implications in this chapter and, therefore, that table is reproduced here as Table 8–1.

Table 8–1 presents the sources and uses (needs) of cash according to different time horizons to illustrate how an organization's options increase with the time horizon involved. In the very short term (say, less than day), cash needs can usually only be met from current cash holdings, and extra cash generated from operations can only be held as additional cash balances. With a somewhat longer time horizon (a day or so), the government can usually convert short-term assets into cash to meet cash needs or can invest extra cash in interest-earning accounts, marketable securities, or other short-term assets. Similarly, short-term liabilities such as short-term borrowings can be increased or decreased to gain or use cash. With more and more time to generate or use cash (weeks, months), operating budget revenues and expenditures can be modified, capital budgets and borrowing plans can be changed, and new methods of raising and using resources can be developed.

The time dimension illustrated in Table 8–1 is critical to our concept of internal resources. Up to this point, we have discussed revenue, expenditure, debt, and pension decisions that influence the long-term financial position of the government (the sources and uses of cash below the dashed line in Table 8–1).

TABLE 8-1    **Sources and Uses of Cash in Governments**

| TIME HORIZON | SOURCES OF CASH | USES OF CASH |
|---|---|---|
| Short Term | Draw down cash balances | Build up cash balances |
| | Convert short-term assets into cash (sell securities, speed up collections, reduce inventories) | Convert cash into other short-term assets (buy securities, build up inventories) |
| | Incur short-term liabilities to gain cash (borrow short term, slow down payments of accounts payable) | Use cash to lower short-term liabilities (retire short-term debt, speed up payment of accounts payable) |
| | Increase operating revenues (property taxes, sales taxes, departmental income, intergovernmental income, intergovernmental transfers) or decrease operating expenditures | Increase operating expenditures or decrease operating revenues |
| | Increase long-term borrowing or cut back capital expenditures | Increase capital expenditures or repay long-term borrowing |
| Long Term | Secure new revenue sources | Expend funds on new projects and programs |

Longer-term sources of cash depend on revenue reserves and expenditure pressures. Changes in external factors, such as economic base and expenditure needs, will influence a government's long-term financial condition without necessarily having an immediate impact on its short-term internal resources. Since we have examined these long-term factors in detail in previous chapters, the task that remains is to identify and assess the short-term factors associated with the levels and liquidity of internal resources (the sources and uses of cash above the dashed line in Table 8-1).

Even though the determinants of longer-term financial condition are not emphasized in this chapter, their influence on a government's internal financial resources and short-term financial position should be apparent. The level of internal resources depends to a large extent on longer-term forces operating on the government. And the ability to draw on external resources quickly, such as the use of short-term borrowing, also depends in part on the government's ability to generate revenues in excess of expenditures. These long-term factors serve as a backdrop for our examination of the level and liquidity of internal resources.

### Level and Liquidity of Internal Resources

Given our emphasis on short-term internal resources, it is important to understand the distinction between the level and the liquidity of internal resources. By *level of internal resources* we mean the dollar amount of resources held by the government at a given point in time, against which there are no existing claims by individuals or organizations such as suppliers, retirees, and bondholders. Thus internal resources represent the internal wealth or "net worth" of the government, the amount of the community's wealth held by the government. A primary (although limited) measure of these internal resources is the government's unreserved fund balances (assets less liabilities and reserves), but other measures can be used as well and these are discussed below.

But the level of internal resources and the liquidity of those internal resources are two different matters (as the wealthy property owner with inadequate cash to pay property taxes would argue). As we indicated in Chapter 2, fund balances are not the same as cash balances, and a government with substantial internal resources may find these resources inaccessible in the short run. Fund balances are a measure of the difference between levels of assets and liabilities; *liquidity of internal resources,* on the other hand, is a measure of the "nearness to cash" of these assets (the ease and speed with which existing assets can be converted into cash) and the "nearness to cash demands" of these liabilities (the ease and speed with which liabilities can turn into demands for cash, for example, as bills come due).

Taken together, the levels and liquidity of assets and liabilities determine the ability of a government at any point in time to generate cash to meet cash demands. While a government with high levels of internal resources will often enjoy high liquidity—the greater the wealth, the more easily the cash demands can be satisfied—this is not always the case, and therefore the analysis of both the levels and the liquidity of internal resources is important.

## II. INFORMATION FOR INTERNAL RESOURCE ANALYSIS

Unlike the earlier components of financial analysis, most of the data we use to study the levels and liquidity of internal resources can generally be found in financial statements. These statements are very useful, but their limitations should be kept in mind.

### Balance Sheets

A primary source of information is the balance sheet. As we noted in Chapter 2, the purpose of the balance sheet is to present a picture at a single point in time of the stocks of resources held by a fund and a fund's outstanding obligations. Thus balance sheets present data on assets, liabilities, reserves, and fund balances to convey information on the level, composition, and control of resources held by the government.

But balance sheets in governments suffer from many problems of estimation and organization that may sometimes limit their usefulness for internal resource analysis. First, balance sheets are developed for different funds and are seldom consolidated to establish appropriate estimates of the total resources and liquidity of the government. For example, a recent review of governmental accounting reports the following:

> Although governments have experimented with consolidated and condensed financial statements, such methods of presentation are not presently considered to be in accordance with generally accepted accounting principles. Combined statements merely sum the data of the fund types and account groups and do not conform with the corporate consolidated accounting practices, even if certain interfund eliminations were to be made.[1]

Until governments change their current practice and begin to provide consolidated statements, balance sheets from the individual funds must be analyzed separately and carefully to draw conclusions about the government's financial position.

A second problem, related to the first, is the inconsistent and sometimes insufficiently detailed categories of assets and liabilities used in the balance sheets. When one fund uses an account that combines cash and investments while another fund lists cash and investments separately, the level of analysis suffers. Similarly, when funds use different bases of accounting, the way in which certain assets such as receivables are recorded may make comparisons across funds difficult. These problems exist among funds in one government and are compounded when comparisons are attempted across organizations.

The different bases of accounting cause a third problem. As we noted in Chapter 2, some fund balance sheets in governments do not include certain assets and liabilities (such as capital equipment and long-term borrowing) while others include virtually all the assets and liabilities commonly recorded in private-sector accounting. Limited coverage of a fund's balance sheet means that certain assets and liabilities are presented in other documents or, in some cases, not recorded anywhere. This causes difficulties in assembling data and in making comparisons.

The use of *reserves* (and *designations*) is a fourth problem associated with balance sheets. As we noted in Chapter 2, *reserves* are designed to show that a particular part of the fund balance is segregated for a particular use as the result of transactions that limit the funds for general expenditures in the future. A reserve for encumbrances is the most common example.[2] A *designation* is similar to a reserve except that the segregation is usually the result of a policy instead of a transaction. A designation of funds as revenues for next year's budget is an example. The basic problem for internal resource analysis is to determine the limitations associated with the reserves and designations, often in the face of inadequate explanations. Moreover, in some cases the term *reserve* is misused and appears in the asset or liability section of the balance sheet.

---

[1] Cornelius E. Tierney and Philip T. Calder, *Governmental Accounting, Procedures and Practices, 1983* (New York: Arthur Young & Co., Elsevier, 1983), p. 150.

[2] Ibid., p. 120.

A final problem is not related to governmental accounting practices but to the fact that the balance sheet reports stocks of resources and obligations at a single point in time, usually at the end of the government's fiscal year. Many governments face substantial swings in their internal resource levels and composition over the course of the year, and the year-end statements may not reveal the full extent of liquidity problems that may exist at other times of the year. If available, interim financial statements can help solve this problem.

Thus, along with the usual caveats about comparability and consistency of data over time and across organizations, additional concerns with balance sheets must be addressed in internal resource analysis.

### Other Financial Statements

Since a government's internal resources change over time due to financial flows (revenues, expenditures, borrowing, etc.) into and out of the government, other financial data are needed for internal resource analysis. Differences in financial flows change the levels of financial stocks, so that statements that depict the flows are also useful. The difference between a government's revenues and its expenditures (yielding a surplus or deficit) changes the fund balance. Consequently, the statements of revenues and expenditures and the statements of changes in the fund balance provide information that is needed for internal resource analysis. The inflows and outflows of cash are particularly important to the government's liquidity, and therefore the statements of receipts and disbursements and the statements of sources and uses of cash are also very important. In short, the basic set of financial statements that are usually available for every fund are critical inputs to internal resource analysis.

### An Application

In this chapter we illustrate internal resource analysis using our example, the city of Dyer Straits. Although some of the data needed for this analysis appeared in the earlier chapters, most of the information needed for a thorough internal resource analysis has not been disclosed. Consequently, a series of financial statements that constitute the data base for internal resource analysis are presented in this section for Dyer Straits and its reference group.

When analyzing the internal resources of a government, a decision must be made about how the organization should be structured for the analysis. At a conceptual level, it is desirable to combine into one unit of analysis all the financial transactions and data that relate to the "basic" or "normal" activities of the government. For Dyer Straits and the reference group cities, these basic activities include the financial transactions recorded in the general fund and the debt service fund. Debt service is included with the general fund because (1) the revenues used for the payment of debt service draw on the exact same revenue sources as the activities accounted for in the general fund, and (2) the repayment of debt is a normal activity of the government that occurs regularly every year. (Only general obligation debt is repaid through the debt service fund in this example; limited obligation debt is paid in enterprise funds, which are examined separately.) Moreover, in many cases in the reference group, debt is repaid from the general fund rather than from a specific debt service fund.

In addition to grouping the basic or normal activities, it is useful to group separately the organization's financial activities devoted to capital projects. Since capital is often financed by sources such as debt and grants that are not available for operations, and because capital spending in a government is typically uneven in terms of amounts over time, this separation is warranted. Therefore the financial statements for the capital project funds in Dyer Straits and the reference group are reported separately.

Finally, many governments operate enterprises that are structured to operate more like ''break-even'' private businesses where revenues generated by the activities themselves are used to meet expenses. Sometimes, however, the financial activities of government enterprises spill over to the other parts of the government, either because the surpluses from the enterprise are being transferred to other parts of the government or because the government is subsidizing the operations of the enterprise. Because of the ''break-even'' business philosophy and self-sustaining linkages among revenues and expenses, it is appropriate to consider enterprises separately in internal resource analysis. At the same time, however, because of the possibility of various financial flows between the enterprises and the rest of the government, these linkages and flows should be examined as part of the analysis. For Dyer Straits and the reference group, there are two enterprises accounted for in two separate enterprise funds, a water and sewer fund and a municipal parking fund. The analysis of enterprises is discussed in section V.

Thus, for this analysis, the finances of Dyer Straits and the reference group are divided into four groupings: the general and debt service fund, the capital projects fund, the water and sewer fund, and the municipal parking fund. The balance sheets for Dyer Straits and the reference group for the general and debt service funds and the capital projects fund over the period 1979–83 are presented in Tables 8-2 and 8-3. (Data on the enterprise funds are presented in section V.) The balance sheets for Dyer Straits in 1982 and 1983 are consistent with those presented in Chapter 2. Note, however, that the interfund obligations between the general and debt service funds have been eliminated. In addition, note that the short-term general obligation debt reported in Table 8-3 for the capital projects fund is consistent with the data reported in Chapter 6.

Data on financial inflows and outflows are reported in the next two tables. Table 8-4 presents the revenues and expenditures of the general and debt service funds, combined, for Dyer Straits and the reference group for 1979–83. The data for Dyer Straits and the reference group in Table 8-4 appeared in Chapters 4 and 5 for all five years, and these data are also consistent with the 1982 and 1983 financial statements for Dyer Straits' general and debt service funds that were presented in Chapter 2.

TABLE 8-2  Balance Sheets—Combined for General and Debt Service Funds, City of Dyer Straits and Reference Group, End of Year, 1979-83 ($ Thousands)

| | DYER STRAITS | | | | | REFERENCE GROUP | | | | |
|---|---|---|---|---|---|---|---|---|---|---|
| | 1979 | 1980 | 1981 | 1982 | 1983 | 1979 | 1980 | 1981 | 1982 | 1983 |
| *Assets:* | | | | | | | | | | |
| Cash | 492 | 202 | 357 | 272 | 91 | 19,500 | 19,700 | 20,300 | 20,000 | 20,400 |
| Time deposits | 156 | 188 | 218 | 118 | 0 | 8,800 | 8,700 | 8,800 | 8,900 | 9,000 |
| Property taxes receivable | 279 | 388 | 484 | 714 | 1,088 | 13,600 | 16,500 | 21,300 | 24,700 | 23,800 |
| Sales taxes receivable | 22 | 32 | 27 | 42 | 0 | 2,200 | 1,900 | 3,700 | 3,900 | 4,100 |
| Accounts receivable | 19 | 51 | 32 | 29 | 29 | 2,900 | 3,200 | 2,700 | 2,600 | 2,700 |
| State aid receivable | 114 | 168 | 60 | 58 | 73 | 1,900 | 2,900 | 2,600 | 3,100 | 3,800 |
| Federal aid receivable | 108 | 142 | 47 | 28 | 31 | 1,700 | 3,100 | 2,000 | 1,900 | 2,200 |
| Due from other funds | 15 | 39 | 30 | 38 | 38 | 3,300 | 3,200 | 2,200 | 2,100 | 2,900 |
| Other Assets | 17 | 64 | 48 | 40 | 40 | 1,100 | 1,300 | 1,400 | 1,600 | 1,900 |
| Total Assets | 1,222 | 1,274 | 1,303 | 1,339 | 1,390 | 55,000 | 60,500 | 65,000 | 68,800 | 70,800 |
| *Liabilities:* | | | | | | | | | | |
| Vouchers payable | 117 | 187 | 195 | 283 | 404 | 6,750 | 8,560 | 9,090 | 11,940 | 13,300 |
| Bond interest and matured bonds payable | 41 | 65 | 52 | 82 | 58 | 1,400 | 1,000 | 1,100 | 2,300 | 2,600 |
| Salaries payable | 99 | 194 | 204 | 238 | 376 | 7,400 | 9,300 | 10,100 | 9,200 | 11,300 |
| Due to other funds | 27 | 53 | 22 | 16 | 116 | 2,200 | 4,100 | 6,900 | 7,400 | 5,500 |
| Total Liabilities | 284 | 499 | 473 | 619 | 954 | 17,750 | 22,960 | 27,190 | 30,840 | 32,700 |
| *Reserves:* | | | | | | | | | | |
| Reserve for encumbrances | 200 | 200 | 220 | 227 | 207 | 9,705 | 9,740 | 9,810 | 9,800 | 9,800 |
| Total Reserves | 200 | 200 | 220 | 227 | 207 | 9,705 | 9,740 | 9,810 | 9,800 | 9,800 |
| *Fund Balances* | 738 | 575 | 610 | 493 | 229 | 27,545 | 27,800 | 28,000 | 28,160 | 28,300 |

TABLE 8–3  Balance Sheets—Capital Projects Fund, City of Dyer Straits and Reference Group, End of Year, 1979–83 ($ thousands)

| | DYER STRAITS | | | | | REFERENCE GROUP | | | | |
|---|---|---|---|---|---|---|---|---|---|---|
| | 1979 | 1980 | 1981 | 1982 | 1983 | 1979 | 1980 | 1981 | 1982 | 1983 |
| *Assets:* | | | | | | | | | | |
| Cash | 258 | 283 | 311 | 256 | 247.8 | 12,500 | 13,000 | 13,900 | 14,900 | 15,300 |
| Time deposits | 4,126 | 4,223 | 4,501 | 4,360 | 4,160 | 167,800 | 172,400 | 178,400 | 185,900 | 191,200 |
| Due from other funds | 31 | 12 | 32 | 120 | 60 | 1,500 | 1,100 | 1,700 | 2,400 | 3,300 |
| Other assets | 5 | 4 | 4 | 6 | 6 | 500 | 600 | 400 | 300 | 400 |
| Total Assets | 4,420 | 4,522 | 4,848 | 4,742 | 4,473.8 | 182,300 | 187,100 | 194,400 | 203,500 | 210,200 |
| *Liabilities:* | | | | | | | | | | |
| Vouchers payable | 262.9 | 606.7 | 461.5 | 387 | 371 | 5,500 | 17,000 | 17,400 | 23,000 | 16,000 |
| Salaries payable | 94 | 214 | 89 | 103 | 63 | 22,627 | 23,063 | 21,429 | 11,944 | 7,000 |
| Due to other funds | 15 | 8 | 16 | 4 | 0 | 1,900 | 1,300 | 700 | 3,200 | 1,400 |
| Bond anticipation notes payable | 3,339 | 2,848 | 2,702 | 2,936 | 3,422 | 82,374 | 70,876 | 67,516 | 67,803 | 86,512 |
| Capital notes payable | 0 | 0 | 400 | 200 | 0 | 3,205 | 3,974 | 4,616 | 4,809 | 4,556 |
| Total Liabilities | 3,710.9 | 3,676.7 | 3,668.5 | 3,630 | 3,856 | 115,606 | 116,213 | 111,661 | 110,756 | 115,468 |
| *Reserves:* | | | | | | | | | | |
| Reserve for encumbrances | 202 | 189 | 204 | 193 | 193 | 8,700 | 8,700 | 8,800 | 9,000 | 9,000 |
| Total Reserves | 202 | 189 | 204 | 193 | 193 | 8,700 | 8,700 | 8,800 | 9,000 | 9,000 |
| *Fund Balances* | 507.1 | 656.3 | 975.5 | 919 | 424.8 | 57,994 | 62,187 | 73,939 | 83,744 | 85,732 |

TABLE 8-4  Statements of Revenues and Expenditures—Combined for General and Debt Service Funds, City of Dyer Straits and Reference Group, 1979–83 ($ thousands)

| | DYER STRAITS | | | | | REFERENCE GROUP | | | | |
|---|---|---|---|---|---|---|---|---|---|---|
| | 1979 | 1980 | 1981 | 1982 | 1983 | 1979 | 1980 | 1981 | 1982 | 1983 |
| *Revenues:* | | | | | | | | | | |
| Property taxes | 3,587 | 3,814 | 3,903 | 4,077 | 4,521 | 117,830 | 125,140 | 133,040 | 140,460 | 149,130 |
| Sales taxes | 642 | 670 | 1,186 | 1,235 | 1,312 | 27,580 | 31,340 | 33,510 | 40,490 | 43,090 |
| Nontax local revenues | 816 | 868 | 902 | 962 | 994 | 37,090 | 39,140 | 40,600 | 41,200 | 42,730 |
| State aid | 1,011 | 1,142 | 1,305 | 1,523 | 1,667 | 48,550 | 53,860 | 60,320 | 67,890 | 72,820 |
| Federal aid | 583 | 636 | 739 | 869 | 1,033 | 26,940 | 30,300 | 34,090 | 38,940 | 45,790 |
| Total Revenues | 6,639 | 7,130 | 8,035 | 8,666 | 9,527 | 257,990 | 279,780 | 301,560 | 328,980 | 353,560 |
| *Expenditures:* | | | | | | | | | | |
| Salaries | 3,529 | 3,855 | 4,216 | 4,724 | 5,447 | 133,530 | 145,810 | 156,850 | 174,310 | 190,410 |
| Fringe benefits | 1,183 | 1,299 | 1,427 | 1,605 | 1,829 | 41,650 | 46,120 | 50,050 | 54,920 | 59,390 |
| Materials and supplies | 691 | 683 | 695 | 742 | 793 | 30,900 | 32,540 | 33,900 | 35,950 | 37,680 |
| Contractual services | 460 | 503 | 558 | 615 | 671 | 20,940 | 22,620 | 24,540 | 26,500 | 28,590 |
| Debt service | 820 | 953 | 1,104 | 1,090 | 1,091 | 30,040 | 32,400 | 35,950 | 37,150 | 37,350 |
| Total Expenditures | 6,683 | 7,293 | 8,000 | 8,776 | 9,831 | 257,060 | 279,490 | 301,290 | 328,830 | 353,420 |

The revenues and expenditures for the capital projects fund for Dyer Straits and the reference group over the five-year period are presented in Table 8-5. The capital expenditures for Dyer Straits were presented in Chapter 5, and the proceeds from general obligation bonds were reported in Chapter 6. Data for 1982 and 1983 for Dyer Straits were also reported in Chapter 2.

Finally, the cash flows for the combined general and debt service funds and the capital projects fund are reported in Table 8-6. The receipts and disbursements for Dyer Straits during 1983 appeared in Chapter 2, but the remainder of the data in Table 8-6 is presented in this table for the first time.

## III. LEVELS OF INTERNAL RESOURCES

Everything else the same, a government with more internal resources at its command is in better financial condition than a government with less. However, if these resources are idle, or poorly employed, or drawn from those least able to provide them to government, the holding of these resources may involve certain inefficiencies and inequities.

We begin by developing alternative measures of the level of internal resources. Next, to gain a better understanding of these resource levels and why they change, we review the financial factors that affect these levels. Finally, we discuss how to use these measures to evaluate whether a government has too low (or, perhaps, too high) a level of internal resources, and we illustrate our approach by again using the city of Dyer Straits as an example.

### Measures of the Level of Internal Resources

The usual measure of internally held resources is the government's fund balances. Subject to the limitations of the government's accounting system, a fund balance is the difference between the value of resources that the government has a claim on or controls (assets) and the resources that it owes to others (liabilities) or are being held aside for specific purposes (reserves). The residual is the fund balance that can be appropriated for any purpose for which the fund was established. These are labeled *fund balances,* or *unappropriated fund balances,* or *unreserved fund balances.*

Since governments usually have many funds, and thus many fund balances, internal resources for several funds are typically included in the analysis. For a government, this would include an analysis of the fund balances of the general fund (combined, if possible, with the debt service fund), capital projects funds, and important enterprise funds. In addition, if there are significant special revenue funds that cannot be combined with the general fund (many special revenue funds are separate simply for external reporting purposes) or special assessment funds that cannot be combined with the capital projects fund, these too may have to examined by themselves. Finally, trust and agency funds, by their

TABLE 8-5 Statements of Revenues and Expenditures—Capital Projects Fund, City of Dyer Straits and Reference Group, 1979-83 ($ thousands)

| | DYER STRAITS | | | | | REFERENCE GROUP | | | | |
|---|---|---|---|---|---|---|---|---|---|---|
| | 1979 | 1980 | 1981 | 1982 | 1983 | 1979 | 1980 | 1981 | 1982 | 1983 |
| *Revenues:* | | | | | | | | | | |
| Proceeds from general obligation bonds | 1,158.7 | 1,047.2 | 1,658.2 | 663.5 | 797.8 | 27,765 | 42,093 | 53,952 | 26,405 | 12,888 |
| Interest on investments | 72 | 84 | 108 | 141 | 192 | 9,100 | 10,100 | 11,700 | 13,400 | 17,600 |
| Interfund transfers | 41 | 37 | 51 | 44 | 120 | 1,900 | 1,500 | 2,300 | 1,100 | 1,300 |
| Total Revenues | 1,271.7 | 1,168.2 | 1,817.2 | 848.5 | 1,109.8 | 38,765 | 53,693 | 67,952 | 40,905 | 31,788 |
| *Expenditures:* | | | | | | | | | | |
| Project expenditures | 1,566 | 983 | 1,553 | 852 | 1,524 | 40,800 | 47,300 | 55,000 | 31,500 | 27,600 |
| Interfund transfers | 58 | 49 | (70) | 64 | 80 | 1,000 | 2,200 | 1,100 | (600) | 2,200 |
| Total Expenditures | 1,624 | 1,032 | 1,483 | 916 | 1,604 | 41,800 | 49,500 | 56,100 | 30,900 | 29,800 |

Negative numbers in parentheses

TABLE 8-6 Statements of Receipts and Disbursements—Selected Funds, City of Dyer Straits and Reference Group, 1979-83 ($ thousands)

| | DYER STRAITS | | | | | REFERENCE GROUP | | | | |
|---|---|---|---|---|---|---|---|---|---|---|
| | 1979 | 1980 | 1981 | 1982 | 1983 | 1979 | 1980 | 1981 | 1982 | 1983 |
| *General and Debt Service Funds:* | | | | | | | | | | |
| Receipts | 6,593 | 7,027 | 7,985 | 8,504 | 9,197 | 257,100 | 279,100 | 300,800 | 327,100 | 351,200 |
| Disbursements | 6,617 | 7,285 | 7,800 | 8,689 | 9,496 | 256,300 | 279,000 | 300,100 | 327,300 | 350,700 |
| *Capital Projects Fund:* | | | | | | | | | | |
| Receipts | 3,852 | 4,138 | 5,104 | 4,407 | 4,800.8 | 122,000 | 127,700 | 136,300 | 105,000 | 115,000 |
| Disbursements | 3,994 | 4,016 | 4,798 | 4,603 | 5,009.0 | 127,800 | 122,600 | 129,400 | 96,500 | 109,300 |

very nature, do not include resources that are usable by the government, so that these should be excluded from the analysis of the level of internal resources.

A major limitation of the fund balance as a measure of internal resources is the often arbitrary definition and allocation of monies to reserve funds or the designation of part of the fund balance for a specific purpose. This suggests that in certain cases, the sum of fund balances and particular reserves or designations, and their levels and changes over time, may serve as a better estimate of internal resources than do fund balances alone. For example, if a government regularly designates part of its fund balance for the next year's expenditures, this designation should be viewed as a source of internal resources even if the designated amount is not included in the unappropriated fund balance.

The analysis of fund balances in a government is even more complex because of interfund transfers that are often counted as revenues and expenditures or other sources of financing, and change the fund balances of many funds. Thus interfund transfers may be used to create favorable balances in those funds, like the general fund, that are most subject to public scrutiny. Not all or even most interfund transfers are used to alter fund balances in this fashion, but explanations for major fund transfers should be sought to determine their financial legitimacy. Legitimate explanations for fund transfers include payment for services performed by one fund for another (such as when an engineer in the public works department does design work for an enterprise) or provision of resources from the general fund for the specified purpose of the other fund (such as a transfer of funds from the general fund to the capital projects fund).

Finally, internal resources may often be measured more precisely by *changes* rather than by levels. Internal resources rise or fall over time depending on the extent to which a government raises revenues and borrows compared with its current and capital expenditures and debt retirement. In the general fund, these differences in revenues and expenditures reveal themselves in *operating surpluses or deficits,* which change fund balances over time. Similar surpluses or deficits appear in the revenue and expenditure statements of the other funds.

Thus a fund's surplus or deficit, and its changes over time, should provide a useful measure of whether a government is increasing or decreasing its control over resources internal to the organization. Note that this analysis of surpluses and deficits pulls together the analysis of current expenditures and revenues from earlier chapters. Again, the levels of surpluses and deficits may depend on arbitrary interfund transfers and appropriations into or out of reserve funds, so that this measure will have to be scrutinized carefully and examined simultaneously with changes in the fund balances and reserves.

### Determinants of Internal Resource Levels

With these measures in mind, we now ask what determines how much resources a government controls internally. Since changes in the levels of fund balances are determined in an accounting sense by surpluses and deficits, it is the determinants of surpluses and deficits that are of primary interest.

Deficits and surpluses arise for many reasons. To begin with, there are long-term forces in the government's environment—such as levels of activity in the economic base, employment, condition of the housing stock, and income and poverty levels—that allow the organization to build up or draw down its internal resources. Jean Greenblatt studied the determinants of operating deficits and surpluses for fifty-four cities in New York State.[3] Her model included environmental factors such as the ones mentioned above, plus factors that influence the cost of service production and delivery (public-sector wages for example), factors related to the pressures created by previous borrowing and capital expenditure decisions, and factors related to intergovernmental aid. Greenblatt found that many of these factors were statistically related to the average level of deficit or surplus experienced by cities in New York State during the early 1970s.

While long-term environmental factors create the forces that make it harder or easier for a government to keep its revenues and expenditures in line, it is past and present expenditure and revenue decisions that produce actual surpluses or deficits. These may include conscious decisions to build up or reduce surpluses over time, although the creation or use of surpluses is often subject to legal conditions. These decisions or legal requirements may reveal themselves as appropriations of surplus funds or fund balances that enter as a revenue source in the following year's operating budgets.

Forecasting and budgeting biases may also enter in, and this can be confirmed for individual governments by examining past budgets compared with actual revenues and expenditures. It is not uncommon for a government, consciously or unconsciously, to overestimate budgeted expenditures and underestimate expected revenues. This practice creates a surplus at year-end and, if continued, will contribute to increased fund balances over time. Sometimes, however, these budgeting biases operate in the opposite direction where wishful thinking puts a budget in balance and actual revenues and expenditures create a deficit.

As we indicated earlier, operating deficits and surpluses in one particular fund may also arise from activities in other funds. Of particular importance are the activities of enterprise funds and other self-sustaining funds that may require transfers from the general fund, either lowering internal resources or requiring increases in taxes and other revenues. Deficits in the enterprise funds may be creating pressure on the rest of government, suggesting inadequate revenue-raising capacity or excessive expenditure pressures in conducting enterprise activities. As a result, financial analysis of these enterprise funds is often necessary, and this is discussed further in the last section of this chapter. As a general rule, examination of deficits and surpluses in *all* major funds, and a determination of their underlying causes, need to be included in internal resource analysis.

Other factors affecting internal resources can be identified by looking at

---

[3] Jean Greenblatt, "The Determinants of Urban Operating Deficits" (Unpublished Thesis, Department of City and Regional Planning, Cornell University, Ithaca, N.Y., 1976).

balance sheet information over time. Changes in encumbrances and in various other reserves will change fund balances independently of surpluses and deficits. Unusual changes in these accounts should be scrutinized more carefully. Certain extraordinary changes or adjustments to assets and liabilities may also affect the fund balance. An example is an adjustment to taxes receivable to reflect uncollectable taxes from prior years. These items, too, may influence the level of internal resources in a government.

### Analysis of Levels of Internal Resources

After identifying measures of internal resources and some of the factors that affect these levels, we can now turn to our major concern: estimating whether a government is carrying too little (or too much) internal resources. For many governments, the salient question is whether they have enough internal resources. The survey of 301 cities conducted in 1982 by the Joint Economic Committee of Congress concluded that because of a slower growth in revenues compared with expenditures,

> cities are increasingly subject to cash squeezes and current deficits. In fact, forty percent of the respondents in 1981 reported that current outlays, including debt service payments, exceeded current revenues. And, on the basis of their projections for 1982, 60 percent could be in such a condition unless expenditures are reduced or more revenues are raised than were projected. Meanwhile, the cushion provided by carry-over balances (amounts collected in the previous years available for future spending) continues to decrease. For cities, the margin for fiscal error grows thinner each year.[4]

To analyze the levels of internal resources in governments properly, we need to understand why organizations have to carry some internal resources at all times. There are three main explanations.

First, governments both give and receive short-term credit—these are the short-term assets and liabilities carried by the organization. Tax bills are sent out, but individuals and organizations have thirty days to pay; funds from other organizations are owed to the government but will not be received for a few months; the government receives supplies or a consulting report and has sixty days to pay, and so forth. One reason to carry internal resources is to have adequate funds to allow a government, in its normal operations, to provide credit in excess of the credit it receives from others.

Second, governments experience differences in the timing and level of cash inflows and outflows, so that some additional funds may be needed to help smooth out cash receipts and payments. In addition, internal resources provide a reserve for unanticipated cash demands that may arise from poorly estimated revenues or an unexpected expenditure.

---

[4]Joint Economic Committee, *Trends in the Fiscal Condition of Cities: 1980–1982* (Washington, D.C., Congress of the United States, 1982), pp. 1–2.

Third, governments may want to have a reserve to smooth out fluctuations in resource flows from year to year. There may be certain years when revenues are greater than normal or than expected, and the excess may be used in years when expenditures are unexpectedly or abnormally high. This is the notion of a "rainy day" fund. There is, however, a question of whether last year's or next year's taxpayers should pay for this year's services, so that the amount of internal resources used for this purpose is often relatively small by design.

For similar governments and for one government over time, these credit, cash flow, and resource needs probably rise with the level of transactions carried out by the government, measured by annual revenues or expenditures. This suggests that the *ratio of fund balances* (or other measures of the level of internal resources) *to total revenues or total expenditures* can provide a useful basis for comparisons. A high and rising fund balance to expenditures ratio compared with the past and with that of similar organizations may be indicative of excessive internal funds; a low and declining fund balance to expenditures ratio may be indicative of inadequate funds. There are, however, several important caveats to the use of the fund balance to expenditures ratio.

First, the relationship of internal funds to total transactions may not be linear—i.e., the required ratio may not be constant for different levels of transactions. Studies of optimal cash holdings (not the same as internal resources but related) suggest that the level of cash an organization should carry rises with the level of transactions engaged in by the organization, but less than proportionately.[5] Furthermore, the cash holdings needed rise with fluctuations in these transactions, but again less than proportionately.[6] If we assume that fluctuations are higher when transactions are higher, these studies support relating required internal resources to total expenditures but suggest that it is a much more complex relationship than a simple ratio. In other words, governments with twice the level of revenues or expenditures may not need twice the level of internal resources. Consequently, those making comparisons of internal resource to expenditure ratios should be alert to substantial differences in the size of the governments being compared.

Second, the credit, cash flow, and resource needs can be met in other ways than the use of internal resources held by the government. A government may be able to hold lower levels of internal resources if the resources are more easily converted into cash—i.e., highly liquid. Or a government may meet credit, cash flow, or resource needs from external sources, such as short-term borrowing, if it has not already exhausted its short-term borrowing capacity. Thus we see that the composition and liquidity of the internal reserves must be examined along with

---

[5] William J. Baumol, "The Transactions Demand for Cash: An Inventory Theoretic Approach," *Quarterly Journal of Economics,* 66, No. 4 (November 1952), 543–46.

[6] H. Miller and D. Orr, "A Model for the Demand for Money by Firms," *Quarterly Journal of Economics,* 80, No. 3 (August 1966), 413–35.

the level of internal resources to fully understand the government's internal resources.

### Summary of Internal Resource Level Analysis

The analysis of the level of internal resources in an organization is comprised of several approaches that can be applied to the general fund and other major governmental funds:[7]

1. *Fund balances* are a principal measure of the internal resources in a government. In certain cases where reserves represent prior commitments of internal resources, such as reserves for encumbrances, the *reserves* should be excluded from this measure of internal resources. Reserves that are not committed may be added to the fund balance to obtain a more comprehensive measure of available resources. *Ratios of fund balances to revenues or expenditures* should be computed to determine whether the level of internal resources is too low (or, perhaps, too high).

2. *Deficits and surpluses* are a primary measure of the changes in the level of internal resources. If the government uses part of the preceding year's fund balance as a revenue source, it is also advisable to calculate the surplus or deficit without this appropriation to determine the year-to-year revenue and expenditure imbalances and to examine the *appropriation of surplus* separately. *Ratios of surpluses or deficits to revenues or expenditures* are a useful measure that controls for size of the government. An examination of individual *revenue and expenditure* items may help explain the source of the deficit or surplus.

3. *Interfund transfers* often affect the surpluses and deficits and fund balances of individual funds, and they should therefore be scrutinized separately. Where possible, the purposes or policies behind the interfund transfers should be identified to determine whether the transaction involves a "payment" for services or a transfer of funds. The latter use is more likely to imply certain intraorganizational subsidies.

4. *Budgeting biases* from past budgets compared with actual revenues and expenditures should also be examined. Since the budget often contains the most up-to-date information, if consistent biases are present, such as overestimating or underestimating revenues and/or expenditures, the budget data and the estimates for the current year should be adjusted accordingly.

5. *Accounting adjustments* of various kinds often influence the reported levels of internal resources. Special attention should be paid to changes in the basis of accounting and the way in which specific assets and liabilities are valued. Receivables are commonly adjusted to take uncollectable revenues into account.

6. The longer-term financial condition of the government, measured by the analyses of *revenues, expenditures, debt,* and *pensions,* should also be examined simultaneously with the measures of internal resources. In many cases an organization that has better long-term prospects can operate with lower levels of internal resources and vice

[7] For examples of the measures of internal resources in empirical financial condition studies, see Joint Economic Committee, *Trends in the Financial Condition of Cities,* pp. 12 and 16; Edward M. Gramlich, "The New York City Fiscal Crisis: What Happened and What Is to Be Done?" *American Economic Review,* 66, No. 2 (May 1976), 415–29; Bureau of Governmental Research, University of Oregon, "Oregon Municipal Fiscal Indicators, An Exploratory Study," October 1983, p. 22; and City of Seattle, Office of the Comptroller, "Financial Condition of the City of Seattle," August 18, 1983, pp. 50 and 54.

versa. This is because the government that has a stronger longer-term financial condition has better access to resources in the short run, from short-term debt or by obtaining credit from suppliers, for example.

As in all our analyses, these measures should be assessed over time and compared with those of a reference group. Moreover, the levels of internal resources should be examined along with their liquidity, which we discuss later in this chapter.

### An Application

To illustrate the analysis of the levels of internal resources in a government, we continue with our example, Dyer Straits. The normal and recurring operations of the city are accounted for in the combined general and debt service funds, and we examine these first. We then examine the levels of internal resources in the capital projects fund.

**Combined General and Debt Service Fund.**   The primary measures of the level of internal resources, fund balances and surpluses and deficits, are presented in Table 8–7 for Dyer Straits and the reference group over a five-year period, 1979–83. The unappropriated fund balances show quite clearly that Dyer Straits' levels of internal resources in the general and debt service funds have declined consistently over the five-year period. In fact, by 1983 the unappropriated fund balance in Dyer Straits is only 31 percent of the fund balance in 1979. Moreover, the decline runs counter to the trends in the reference group where the unappropriated fund balances increased slightly over the same period.

Although the fund balances in Dyer Straits have clearly declined more than those in the reference group, this decline may not be a problem if, for example, the level of the fund balance is still high relative to the reference group's. By comparing the location quotients for the fund balances with similar location quotients for population, we can provide a measure of whether the fund balances in Dyer Straits are high or low relative to its population. (This method is an alternative to computing per capita fund balances.) In Chapter 4, Table 4–8, the location quotients for population in Dyer Straits compared with the reference group's were shown to be around 0.0216 over the five-year period. In other words, Dyer Straits' population is 2.16 percent of the reference group's. Since in 1979 the location quotient for fund balances is 0.0268, this indicates that Dyer Straits' fund balances are larger than the reference group's, relative to population. By 1983, however, the location quotient for fund balances had dropped to 0.0081, a level that indicates that based on population, Dyer Straits' fund balances are much lower than the reference group's.

The second item shown in Table 8–7, the ratio of fund balances to revenues, confirms the population-based analysis. The ratio of fund balances to revenues declined dramatically in Dyer Straits over the five-year period and, by 1983, is only 30 percent of the level in the reference group. Thus the level of internal

TABLE 8-7  Measures of Levels of Internal Resources, Combined General and Debt Service Funds, City of Dyer Straits and Reference Group, 1979–83

| | DYER STRAITS | | | | | REFERENCE GROUP | | | | | LOCATION QUOTIENTS* | | | | |
|---|---|---|---|---|---|---|---|---|---|---|---|---|---|---|---|
| | 1979 | 1980 | 1981 | 1982 | 1983 | 1979 | 1980 | 1981 | 1982 | 1983 | 1979 | 1980 | 1981 | 1982 | 1983 |
| Fund balances, unappropriated† | 738 | 575 | 610 | 493 | 229 | 27,545 | 27,800 | 28,000 | 28,160 | 28,300 | | | | | |
| Fund balances/revenues | .1112 | .0806 | .0759 | .0569 | .0240 | .1068 | .0994 | .0929 | .0856 | .0800 | .0268 | .0207 | .0218 | .0175 | .0081 |
| Surplus (deficit)† | (44) | (163) | 35 | (110) | (304) | 930 | 290 | 270 | 150 | 140 | 1.0412 | .8108 | .8170 | .6647 | .3000 |
| Surplus (deficit)/revenues | (.0066) | (.0229) | .0044 | (.0127) | (.0319) | .0036 | .0010 | .0009 | .0005 | .0004 | NC | NC | NC | NC | NC |

Negative numbers are in parentheses.

NC = Not calculated.

*Dyer Straits/Reference Group.

†Thousands of dollars.

resources in Dyer Straits is low and has declined substantially over the past five years.

The data on the surpluses and deficits in Table 8–7 show that the reduction in the fund balances in Dyer Straits is the result of deficits in four of the five years. This occurred when, in the aggregate, there were no deficits in the reference group. Although the size of the deficit in Dyer Straits has varied over the five years, the fact that the largest deficit, in absolute terms or as a percentage of revenues, occurs in 1983 may be a further negative sign.

Several other factors should be examined before we draw final conclusions about the levels of internal resources in the combined general and debt service fund. First, although not shown in Table 8–4, transfers between the combined general and debt service fund and other funds are not significant. The only time that interfund transfers are used between these combined funds and other funds is in exchange for particular services, such as when the police cars are stored in the municipal parking garage. Second, there is no need in this case to examine budgeting biases, since we do not have the budgeted data for the most recent year, which in this case would be 1984. If we did have the 1984 budget, we could use the budgeting biases to adjust the revenues and expenditures. Third, there are no accounting adjustments that could have influenced either the fund balances or the surpluses and deficits. Finally, both Dyer Straits and the reference group use only one reserve account, a reserve for encumbrances. The size of this reserve has remained quite stable over the five-year period in both Dyer Straits and the reference group. Dyer Straits' reserve for encumbrances is about 2 percent of the reference group's, indicating that the levels are comparable on a per capita basis.

The assessment of the level of internal resources in the combined general and debt service funds in Dyer Straits is rather negative. Moreover, when this assessment is combined with our findings regarding revenues, expenditures, debt, and pensions in Dyer Straits where we found several problem areas, it is possible that Dyer Straits will have to draw even more heavily on its internal resources in the future. It is not inconceivable that if the most recent trends continue, the level of internal resources in Dyer Straits in the combined general and debt service funds could become negative.

**Capital Projects Fund.**     Capital projects funds should always be examined separately from the general and debt service funds and the enterprise funds. Since the purpose of the capital projects fund is to accumulate funds for capital projects and to expend these funds on the acquisition or construction of the capital items, these funds are not generally available for normal operations. Although governments have in some instances utilized capital funds for operating purposes, this is not regarded as sound financial management practice. Thus the primary purpose of an examination of the level of internal resources in the capital projects funds is to ensure that the resources on hand are what is expected concerning future capital projects.

Note that because inflows and outflows are irregular, there can be large changes in internal resources in the capital projects fund from year to year. In addition, since policies on the level of resources that are accumulated in advance of construction or acquisition can vary, and since long-term debt is not treated as a liability, some capital projects funds may occasionally have significant levels of internal resources. Because of these characteristics of capital projects funds, comparisons with a reference group may yield dissimilar patterns that have little meaning.

Table 8–8 shows the data on fund balances and surpluses and deficits for the capital projects funds in Dyer Straits and the reference group for 1979–83. As expected, the data do not resemble the comparable figures for the combined general and debt service funds. As a result of surpluses in some years and deficits in others, the fund balance increases and decreases in both Dyer Straits and the reference group. In the capital projects fund, however, the fact that there is a deficit in any particular year may only indicate that the resource inflows for one set of capital projects are less than the dollars expended on what may be a somewhat different set of capital projects. Since resources often flow in long before they are expended, the deficit often results from expending the resources that have been accumulated in advance. This appears to be the case in Dyer Straits from 1981 to 1983.

What the data in Table 8–8 do not show is whether the resources on hand or expected are sufficient to fund the capital projects for which the government is committed. For example, if a government has planned to build new school facilities and has used bonds and grants to fund the construction, are the funds on hand, plus the interest they will earn, sufficient to complete the planned construction? If not, then additional funds will have to be raised from bonds or grants (this may be difficult), or the projects will have to be scaled back, or transfers from other government funds will have to be made. Regardless of which action is taken, it is likely to worsen the government's financial condition by increasing debt service, forgoing capital projects that are presumably needed, or reducing the levels of internal resources in other government funds. A project-by-project analysis is required to determine whether capital resources match capital plans.

Although we do not present a project-by-project analysis for Dyer Straits, the conclusions from such an analysis indicate that in virtually all cases, the revenues of the capital projects funds are sufficient to finance the projects as planned. Between 1979 and 1981, Dyer Straits was receiving revenues considerably in advance of construction and acquisition, and this accounts for the increasing (1979 to 1981) then decreasing (1981 to 1983) fund balances. Dyer Straits does not transfer significant resources between the general fund and the capital projects fund, so that the capital projects fund appears to be operating as expected without affecting the level of internal resources in the rest of the government. At the same time, however, the internal resources of the capital projects fund are committed to future capital projects and, as a result, are not available to offset declining resources in the general and debt service funds.

TABLE 8-8  Measures of Levels of Internal Resources, Capital Projects Funds, City of Dyer Straits and Reference Group, 1979–83

| | DYER STRAITS | | | | | REFERENCE GROUP | | | | | LOCATION QUOTIENTS* | | | | |
|---|---|---|---|---|---|---|---|---|---|---|---|---|---|---|---|
| | 1979 | 1980 | 1981 | 1982 | 1983 | 1979 | 1980 | 1981 | 1982 | 1983 | 1979 | 1980 | 1981 | 1982 | 1983 |
| Fund balances unappropriated† | 507.1 | 656.3 | 975.5 | 919 | 424.8 | 57,994 | 62,187 | 73,939 | 83,744 | 85,732 | .0087 | .0106 | .0132 | .0110 | .0050 |
| Fund balances/ revenues | .3988 | .5618 | .5368 | 1.0831 | .3328 | 1.4960 | 1.1582 | 1.0881 | 2.0473 | 2.6970 | .2666 | .4851 | .4933 | .5290 | .1419 |
| Surplus (deficit)† | (406.1) | 136.2 | 334.2 | (67.5) | (494.2) | (3,035) | 4,193 | 11,852 | 10,005 | 1,988 | NC | NC | NC | NC | NC |
| Surplus (deficit)/ revenues | (.3193) | .1166 | .1839 | (.0796) | (.4453) | (.0783) | .0781 | .1744 | .2446 | .0625 | NC | NC | NC | NC | NC |

Negative numbers are in parentheses.

NC = Not calculated.

*Dyer Straits/Reference Group.

†Thousands of dollars.

## IV. LIQUIDITY OF INTERNAL RESOURCES

We now can discuss the last and most "short-term" concern of financial analysis: the *liquidity* position of a government, that is, its ability to meet cash needs from its internal resources. This is appropriately last on our agenda because the assessment of an organization's liquidity depends on its longer-term fiscal strength and expenditure needs and on the level of internal resources carried by the government.

We begin by explaining more precisely what we mean by *liquidity position* and why this is of concern in financial analysis. We draw on our earlier discussion of a government's sources and uses of cash (and of cash budgets) to illustrate the relevance of longer-term considerations to an understanding of liquidity and to demonstrate the methods available to a government to meet its cash needs and put its excess cash to better use. Next, we develop measures of liquidity that can be used, along with the results of our earlier analyses, to complete our assessment of a government's internal resources. Finally, we apply these techniques to Dyer Straits.

### Cash Flows and Liquidity

To understand a government's liquidity position, we begin by clarifying the need for liquidity. We saw earlier (Table 8–1) that an organization has various sources and uses of cash and, depending on the time available for decision making, has different options for ensuring that sources of cash are adequate to meet cash needs. This can be seen more directly by looking at a government's cash budget.

Table 8–9 is the same cash budget we discussed in Chapter 2. This shows expected monthly cash inflows and outflows and the resulting net cash flow (inflows minus outflows) over a twelve-month period. The net cash flow figure for each month defines the government's cash problem. In some months the government has more cash coming in than going out; in others it is the other way around. The result is that the government has the problem of both putting excess cash to productive use and making sure that adequate cash is available when cash outflows exceed inflows.

Let us consider the various ways in which this cash problem could be handled. Note first that total cash inflows for the year ($9.209 million) are less than total cash outflows ($9.427 million). Total cash inflows and outflows for the year may be closely related to whether the government is running a surplus or a deficit, so that consideration of the factors affecting the level of internal resources discussed in the preceding section is necessary. Longer-term solutions, such as new revenue sources or additions to existing revenue sources or cuts in existing expenditures, might influence this annual cash imbalance.

Additionally, total cash inflows and outflows for the year may reflect short-term factors like delays in issuing tax bills or slower than normal collections of last

TABLE 8-9  City of Dyer Straits, Cash Budget—General Fund, 1983 ($ Thousands)

| | JAN. | FEB. | MARCH | APRIL | MAY | JUNE | JULY | AUG. | SEPT. | OCT. | NOV. | DEC. | YEARLY TOTAL |
|---|---|---|---|---|---|---|---|---|---|---|---|---|---|
| **Cash Inflows:** | | | | | | | | | | | | | |
| Property Taxes | $842 | 130 | 93 | 986 | 38 | 30 | 953 | 61 | 38 | 895 | 121 | 69 | $4,256 |
| Sales taxes | 102 | 102 | 109 | 116 | 116 | 102 | 102 | 109 | 122 | 116 | 129 | 136 | 1,361 |
| Nontax local revenues | 363 | 21 | 20 | 18 | 21 | 20 | 344 | 27 | 26 | 27 | 23 | 22 | 932 |
| State aid | | | | 820 | | | | | | 820 | | | 1,640 |
| Federal aid | 255 | | | 255 | | | 255 | | | 255 | | | 1,020 |
| Total Cash Inflow | $1,562 | 253 | 222 | 2,195 | 175 | 152 | 1,654 | 197 | 186 | 2,113 | 273 | 227 | $9,209 |
| **Cash Outflows:** | | | | | | | | | | | | | |
| Salaries | $479 | 452 | 426 | 426 | 399 | 399 | 452 | 479 | 479 | 452 | 452 | 426 | $5,321 |
| Materials and supplies | 112 | 105 | 99 | 99 | 93 | 93 | 105 | 112 | 112 | 105 | 105 | 99 | 1,239 |
| To debt service | 84 | 84 | 84 | 84 | 84 | 84 | 84 | 84 | 84 | 84 | 84 | 84 | 1,008 |
| To municipal parking | | | | | | | 20 | | | | | | 20 |
| Fringe benefits | 166 | 156 | 147 | 147 | 138 | 138 | 156 | 166 | 166 | 156 | 156 | 147 | 1,839 |
| Total Cash Outflow | $841 | 797 | 756 | 756 | 714 | 714 | 817 | 841 | 841 | 797 | 797 | 756 | $9,427 |
| Opening Cash | $239 | 960 | 416 | (118) | 1,321 | 782 | 220 | 1,057 | 413 | (242) | 1,074 | 550 | $239 |
| Net Cash Flow (inflow-outflow) | $721 | (544) | (534) | 1,439 | (539) | (562) | 837 | (644) | (655) | 1,316 | (524) | (529) | ($218) |
| Closing Cash | $960 | 416 | (118) | 1,321 | 782 | 220 | 1,057 | 413 | (242) | 1,074 | 550 | 21 | $21 |

Negative numbers are in parentheses.

year's tax receivables. In this case solutions like short-term borrowing may be more appropriate than changes in operating revenues and expenditures. Furthermore, longer-term solutions may not be feasible for a government facing negative cash flows in the current month. It is the ability of a government to handle its cash flow fluctuations in periods of less than a year that brings in considerations of liquidity.

Returning to Table 8-9, we see that this government has an initial cash balance that allows it to meet the problem of negative cash flows in all months except March and September. Thus the carrying of cash balances is obviously one method of meeting cash flow deficits. This is part of the government's liquidity position. But meeting cash needs goes beyond using available cash balances to include methods of changing both the levels and the timing of cash inflows and outflows.

Thus the government's internal liquidity position depends on the relationship of expected cash inflows to expected cash outflows over a given period, usually a year or less, and the ability of the government to respond to any cash flow problems that arise using cash balances and/or changing cash flows. If expected cash inflows are generally greater in magnitude than outflows and they arrive in advance of outflows *or* the government has high cash balances *or* can easily change its pattern of cash flows to achieve this relationship, then the government has adequate internal liquidity.

To ascertain whether a government's internal resources are sufficiently liquid, we need to develop measures that reflect the magnitude and timing of cash inflows relative to outflows and, if possible, the ability of the government to change the level and timing of cash flows to always ensure an adequate supply of cash to meet its cash needs. These measures can also be used to determine whether the government's liquidity is excessively high relative to its needs for liquidity.

### Measures of Liquidity

**Existing Liquidity.**    Now how can we use financial data of a government to estimate its needs for cash over a given period and its ability to meet that need from internal resources?

Obviously if we had access to a monthly cash budget for the coming year such as that in Table 8-9, we could see what the estimated cash inflows and outflows were for each period, when the cash needs were greatest, and whether or not the cash balances could meet the cash needs as they arise. This would tell us a great deal about the government's liquidity position and whether the organization may face problems of inadequate or excessive cash balances.

Unfortunately, many governments do not prepare cash budgets and reports regularly, or if they do, this information may not be available for financial analysis. Consequently, other financial data must be used to assess a government's liquidity position, and this information is of value whether or not cash budgets and reports are available.

The magnitude and timing of cash inflows and outflows are related to several factors that can be measured, at least approximately, from a government's financial data. As we have seen, the *magnitude* of total cash inflows less outflows for the general fund over the year will usually be related to whether the fund runs a surplus or a deficit. Even under different bases of accounting, the probability that cash inflows will be greater than cash outflows increases as the surplus (the difference between revenues and expenditures) increases. Surpluses in all funds, or an expected net surplus of all funds together, is a strong (but not absolute) indication that the magnitude of total cash inflows will equal or exceed that of cash outflows.

Examination of past annual (and quarterly if available) cash receipts and disbursements statements can also provide clues about the relative magnitudes of cash inflows and outflows. These statements are important because under some bases of accounting, a surplus of revenues over expenditures may not translate to a surplus of receipts over disbursements. The particular way in which receivables are accounted for often plays a major role in explaining the difference between a cash surplus (or deficit) and a revenue and expenditure surplus (or deficit).

Another important indicator is the level of short-term debt, other than bond anticipation debt. If this type of short-term debt is growing, this suggests that the government may have been facing greater cash outflows than cash inflows in the past.

This information helps establish whether annual (and sometimes quarterly) cash receipts have covered cash disbursements. But the *magnitude* of cash inflows and outflows is not the entire story. Even if revenues are expected to be greater than expenditures, the *timing* of revenues and expenditures, and the pattern of cash flows that results, can cause liquidity problems. High initial expenditures, even if followed by even higher revenues, can create short-term cash flow problems for a government. Here is where cash budgets are of greatest value. In their absence we need other measures that reflect the probable timing of cash flows, as well as their magnitudes.

Most conventional measures of a government's liquidity position are based on the level and composition of the organization's short-term (or current) assets and liabilities. Current assets are claims on resources that are cash, or are expected to become cash within a year; current liabilities are claims on the organization for which cash is expected to be needed within a year. Current assets include cash, time deposits of a year or less, marketable securities, taxes receivable, state or federal aid due to the government, and inventories that will be used during the year; current liabilities include wages owed to employees, accounts payable to suppliers, payments owed to other levels of government or other funds, and debt service due within a year on notes and bonds.

Liquidity measures based on current assets and liabilities assume that the relative magnitude and timing of cash inflows and cash outflows can be approximated by the dollar value of different types of assets and liabilities. Each asset and liability has associated with it a dollar amount and an approximate time by which the asset will be converted into cash or the liability into the need for cash. Cash is, obviously, already converted into cash. Time deposits will be converted into cash at a specific date, and some can be converted into cash sooner with a penalty. Marketable securities will (or could) be converted into cash very quickly. Taxes receivable (or some portion thereof) will be converted into cash in a period that can range from several weeks to several months. On the liability side, accounts payable will become a demand for cash within a specified period, usually thirty to sixty days. Short-term notes may require cash payment within six months or a year. Thus the dollar value of each type of asset or liability provides information about the approximate level and timing of cash inflows and cash outflows. Consequently, various combinations and ratios of short-term assets and liabilities are used as measures of liquidity.

The first liquidity measure is *net working capital,* which is current assets less current liabilities. This provides an estimate of the relative magnitude of existing cash balances and cash inflows relative to cash outflows. In essence, if net working capital is positive, it indicates that the dollar value of cash and cash inflows from current assets in the next, say, thirty to sixty days is expected to be larger than the dollar value of cash requirements from current liabilities coming due over the same period.

A second measure, the *current ratio,* is defined as current assets divided by current liabilities and puts the same information contained in the net working capital measure in ratio form. The current ratio provides somewhat different information than net working capital, since the latter provides information about the difference between current assets and liabilities while the former reveals their relative magnitudes. A small and a large government with the same net working capital would probably have very different current ratios.

Both these measures suffer from a major problem. Neither indicates the timing of cash flows, since current assets or current liabilities may include many different types of assets and liabilities, which become cash or cash demands at very different times. Thus even though cash inflows are expected to be greater than cash outflows, if the cash outflows come first the government may face a liquidity crisis. Measures presented below attempt to deal with this problem.

A different liquidity measure based on the balance sheet attempts to recognize the cash flow timing element more directly. The *quick ratio* is defined as quick assets—those current assets expected to be converted into cash quickly (usually cash, marketable securities like treasury notes, and receivables that are due very shortly)—divided by current liabilities. This ratio recognizes that some current assets, such as various types of inventories or intergovernmental transfers not to be received for, say, several months, may not be converted into cash quickly enough to meet current liabilities coming due. Sometimes, to be conservative, even receivables are not considered quick assets. Unlike the current ratio, the quick ratio takes into account the timing of the cash flows from current assets and provides a safer estimate of whether or not the government has the liquidity to meet cash demands (Like the current ratio however, the quick ratio does not consider the timing of current liabilities which may be critical.)

An important problem common to all of the above liquidity measures is that the balance sheet records the level of assets and liabilities at a single point in time. These levels may not be indicative of the levels that exist at other times in the fiscal year (or even between quarterly balance sheets, if these are prepared). In fact, for many governments, certain own-source revenues may be raised in large amounts only at a few relatively short periods during the year. Moreover, intergovernmental transfers may not be received evenly throughout the year. These cash flows may or may not be reflected in the revenue receivable levels at the point in time represented by the balance sheet.

**Ability to Create Liquidity.**     While the above liquidity measures attempt to capture the magnitude and timing of cash flows and indicate whether a government may or may not be subjected to liquidity pressures, they do not tell us much about the government's ability to change these cash flows to avoid cash problems. In other words, these measures may identify the possibility of cash flow problems arising but do not fully measure the organization's ability to respond to these problems. We have already discussed the government's ability to borrow to meet cash needs, and the role of longer-term financial considerations in determining borrowing capacity. But there are other ways to create liquidity by changing the magnitude and timing of cash flows that we would like to measure as well.

First, we can measure the government's ability to change the *magnitude* of its cash inflows and outflows in the short run in order to meet cash problems. This involves close examination of expenditure and revenue items to see which expenditures can be reduced and which revenues can be increased to meet liquidity problems in the short run, without inordinate costs that may come back to haunt the government in the future.

To estimate this ability to change expenditures and revenues quickly, we need measures of the relative "fixity" of revenues and expenditures within the fiscal year or during a shorter time period. Examination of specific revenue and expenditure items is a good place to begin, trying to identify which revenue sources generate cash flows that might be increased quickly or, more likely, which expenditure items (perhaps nonpersonnel items) might be cut in a relatively short time period to reduce cash outflows.

Dividing the government's revenue sources into those that can be varied within a year and those that cannot may provide an estimate of "revenue fixity." For each revenue source, can the government vary the tax rate, user charges, grant provisions, and so forth, needed to raise that revenue level during the year or is that revenue level fixed until the next fiscal year? Dividing revenues into these categories may be difficult and, in any case, would probably reveal that most revenues (other than borrowing possibilities) are relatively fixed. "Expenditure fixity," however, may offer a more promising approach for measurement.

The ability to vary expenditures is not the same for all expenditure items. A ratio of *nonpersonnel to personnel expenditures* may be an index of the government's short-term flexibility to lower cash outflows. A government may have more discretion in varying nonpersonnel expenditures between budget periods than personnel expenditures.

Another way to estimate "expenditure fixity" is to ask what percentage of expenditures goes to pay long-term financial obligations. This suggests several measures we have seen earlier in a different context. First, the ratio of *debt service payments* (principal and interest) *to total revenues* (or *total expenditures*) *plus any reserves for debt service payments* is similar to the debt service ratios we discussed in Chapter 6. The higher the percentage of total revenues or expenditures needed to meet fixed debt payments, the more constrained a government may be in meeting unanticipated cash needs. It is often difficult to avoid these expenditures, thus limiting the government's flexibility.

Another measure related to debt service coverage is the ratio of *short-term debt to total debt* (short and long term). This measure indicates the percentage of debt principal that has to be repaid (or refinanced by additional borrowing) in the short run. While this percentage is reflected in required interest and principal payments, governments may carry high short-term debt, planning to refinance or "roll over" this debt (replace an expiring loan with a new loan) when long-term debt is issued or other sources of cash are available. The higher the percentage of short-term debt, the more vulnerable a government may be to changes in borrowing conditions that make refinancing of current-term debt difficult and costly. If a government relies heavily on short-term debt to solve a liquidity problem, and then the debt cannot be refinanced, the government may be forced to default on some or all of its short-term debt.

Debt obligations are, however, but one form of fixed cash flows affecting a government's ability to meet short-term cash needs. Longer-term contracts of all forms, such as *leases* and *required payments to pension systems,* impose constraints on short-term decision making. Such payments can be added to debt payments in the ratio of total fixed payments to total revenues or expenditures used to measure the extent of expenditure fixity.

Second, we can measure a government's ability to change the *timing* of its cash flows to meet cash flow problems. For given revenue and expenditure levels, and assets and liabilities, cash needs can be met by changing the timing of cash flows. Thus a government may speed up its billings, arrange earlier due dates on tax revenues or intergovernmental transfers, or provide incentives to speed up collections of water bills, and so forth, to receive cash owed to the government sooner, to help offset demands for cash made on the government. Similarly, a government may want to delay expenditures or payments or rearrange contracts, and so forth, to shift the timing of cash outflows by weeks or months, to decrease current cash demands on the organization. These measures tend to have once-and-for-all (or one-shot) effects on cash flow patterns but are worth examining, often for reasons of efficiency as well as decreasing the needs for cash faced by the government. Having access to cash sooner, a government can put these resources to use sooner, speeding up expenditures or gaining interest from investments. Thus opportunities for speeding up cash inflows and slowing down cash outflows need to be assessed on both liquidity and efficiency grounds.

This ability to change the timing of cash flows is not measured by the liquidity measures presented above. For example, current levels of taxes receivable may be an estimate of cash inflows expected from tax payments over the next one or two months, but this does not, in and of itself, tell us whether the government can speed up these cash payments. Nor does the dollar value of total expenditures or revenues indicate whether these cash flows can easily be speeded up or slowed down as a means of meeting cash problems. Other measures are needed.

Measures of a government's ability to change the timing of cash flows are difficult to develop, but several steps might be taken to get a sense of the organization's additional flexibility in meeting cash needs by changing the timing of cash flows.

A closer look at different assets and liabilities in conjunction with revenue and expenditure information indicates areas where cash flows might be varied. Different ratios of assets or liabilities to specific revenues or expenditures can be used in certain circumstances to indicate possibilities for speeding up cash inflows (or slowing down cash inflows). *Collection rates* for certain assets and *payment rates* for certain liabilities may reveal such possibilities. For example, if a department sends out water bills at an average of $10,000 per day and has an average of $200,000 of water charges outstanding (unpaid water bills owed to the department) at any one time, the approximate collection period of its water bills is $200,000 divided by $10,000, or 20 days. This is also referred to as 20 *days outstanding.* In other words, if it takes an average of twenty days for water bills to be paid, then there will be an average of twenty days' worth of bills (20 times $10,000 equals $200,000) outstanding at any given point. Similarly, if tax bills are sent out uniformly over the entire year, tax collection rates can be estimated by dividing taxes receivable by the average daily billings.

Estimation of a collection rate in this fashion allows comparisons with past years and other organizations to determine whether or not a particular government's collection rate is abnormally high. If this is the case, reduction in this rate is a potential source of additional liquidity for the organization. For example, a reduction in the average collection period from twenty to fifteen days would lower the water accounts receivable to 15 times $10,000, or $150,000, freeing up $50,000 ($200,000 less $150,000) which could be held as a reserve to meet cash needs.

Calculation of average collection or payment rates for other current assets and liabilities can be made using the general formula:

Average collection (payment) period = [Current asset (or liability) level]/
[Annual revenue (or expenditure) flow/Days in the year]

Use of this formula is subject to one caveat. The computation of the average collection period for water bills assumed a constant daily billing rate. If the billing rate, or rate at which an obligation to or by the government is incurred, is not constant over the year, then the ratio of the asset or liability to the average revenue or expenditure item involved is only a rough index at best of the collection or payment rate. For example, suppose property tax bills are all mailed out on September 1 and we know the amount of property taxes due (receivable) as of December 31. The ratio of property taxes receivable to the annual property tax billings divided by the number of days in the year does not provide an average collection rate that has any absolute meaning, since the tax billings are not uniform over the year. The ratio, however, can provide an index of collection time for comparison with the past or with other organizations issuing property tax bills under similar situations.

A similar measure is the ratio of the *amount of bills outstanding (receivable) to the annual billing.* This ratio indicates the fraction of total revenues from a particular source that are still owed to the government. Like collection rates, this ratio can be used in comparisons over time and with a reference group to assess whether there is the potential to speed up collection from a particular source. In our earlier example from the water department, the receivable is $200,000 and the yearly revenues are $3,650,000. Thus the fraction of the revenue outstanding is $200,000 divided by $3,650,000 or 0.05. A common measure of this sort is the percent of property taxes outstanding at the end of the fiscal year.

### Summary of Liquidity Analysis Methods

In summary, our assessment of the liquidity of internal resources proceeded in two steps:[8]

1. We estimated the expected magnitude and timing of cash flows, and the probability of cash flow problems, by examining surplus and deficit information, past cash receipts and disbursements, cash budgets (if available), and liquidity measures such as net working capital, the current ratio, and the quick ratio. This analysis should indicate whether the internal resources are liquid enough to meet cash flow problems.

2. Given that an internal liquidity problem may exist, we tried to estimate how much flexibility the government has in meeting this problem. Besides the borrowing capacity discussed earlier, we examined the government's ability to change the magnitude of cash flows, increasing revenues and decreasing expenditures during the fiscal year. We also estimated the possibilities for speeding up cash inflows and slowing down cash outflows by computing, where appropriate, the government's collection and payment rates.

As a supplement to the various liquidity measures, the presentation of the balance sheet for the general fund in common size format helps to highlight changes in the mix of specific assets and liabilities over time and differences com-

---

[8] For an example of liquidity measures in empirical financial condition studies, see City of Seattle, ''Financial Condition of the City of Seattle,'' pp. 57–58.

pared with the reference group's so that items for more intensive investigation can be identified. Taken together, the various measures presented in this section can help us evaluate the liquidity of a government's internal resources.

### An Application

To illustrate the various approaches to the measurement of liquidity, we examine the liquidity of Dyer Straits. The liquidity of the combined general and debt service funds is analyzed first, followed by a few comments on the liquidity of the capital projects fund. In all cases the assessment of liquidity is closely related to the levels of internal resources measured earlier in this chapter.

**Combined General and Debt Service Funds.**   We begin our analysis of the liquidity of the combined general and debt service funds by examining the cash flows over the five-year period 1979–83. Table 8–10 shows the opening cash, cash receipts, cash disbursements, net cash change, and closing cash for Dyer Straits and the reference group over the five years. These data indicate that in four of the five years the net cash flow (receipts minus disbursements) in Dyer Straits was negative, causing the level of cash over the period to drop from $672,000 at the beginning of 1979 to $91,000 by the end of 1983. This decrease in cash parallels the negative findings on the levels of internal resources in the combined general and debt service funds. This is evident from the data on the revenue and expenditure surplus or deficit presented in Table 8–10.

The significant negative cash flow in Dyer Straits over the period stands in contrast to the performance in the reference group. In four of the five years in the reference group, cash receipts exceeded cash disbursements, and the level of cash at the end of the five-year period was higher than the level at the beginning.

Thus the negative cash flows in four of five years, the low absolute level of cash in Dyer Straits at the end of 1983, and the fact that the largest cash deficit occurred in the most recent year, strongly suggest that Dyer Straits may be facing a liquidity crisis in the combined general and debt service funds. An examination of the liquidity ratios for Dyer Straits can determine whether current assets other than cash are available to modify this conclusion.

Three liquidity ratios for Dyer Straits and the reference group are presented in Table 8–11. Net working capital has declined by over $500,000 in Dyer Straits over the five-year period while it has increased slightly in the reference group. The location quotients suggest that after 1981, the levels of net working capital in Dyer Straits were lower than those in the reference group, since the location quotient for population was about .0216. Despite the decline in net working capital in Dyer Straits, it is still positive in 1983, signaling that current assets exceed current liabilities.

The decreasing level of liquidity in Dyer Straits is confirmed by the declining current ratio. Since the current ratio in Dyer Straits is still greater than one at the end of the period, the total current assets in Dyer Straits are sufficient in dollar

TABLE 8-10  Cash, Cash Flows, and Surplus, Combined General and Debt Service Funds, City of Dyer Straits and Reference Group, 1979–83 ($ thousands)

| | DYER STRAITS | | | | | REFERENCE GROUP | | | | |
|---|---|---|---|---|---|---|---|---|---|---|
| | 1979 | 1980 | 1981 | 1982 | 1983 | 1979 | 1980 | 1981 | 1982 | 1983 |
| Opening cash | 672 | 648 | 390 | 575 | 390 | 27,500 | 28,300 | 28,400 | 29,100 | 28,900 |
| Receipts | 6,593 | 7,027 | 7,985 | 8,504 | 9,197 | 257,100 | 279,100 | 300,800 | 327,100 | 351,200 |
| Disbursements | 6,617 | 7,285 | 7,800 | 8,689 | 9,496 | 256,300 | 279,000 | 300,100 | 327,300 | 350,700 |
| Net cash change | (24) | (258) | 185 | (185) | (299) | 800 | 100 | 700 | (200) | 500 |
| Closing cash | 648 | 390 | 575 | 390 | 91 | 28,300 | 28,400 | 29,100 | 28,900 | 29,400 |
| Revenue and expenditure surplus (deficit) | (44) | (163) | 35 | (110) | (304) | 930 | 290 | 270 | 150 | 140 |

Negative numbers in parentheses.

TABLE 8-11  Liquidity Measures, Combined General and Debt Service Funds, City of Dyer Straits and Reference Group, End of Year 1979–83

| | DYER STRAITS | | | | | REFERENCE GROUP | | | | | LOCATION QUOTIENTS* | | | | |
|---|---|---|---|---|---|---|---|---|---|---|---|---|---|---|---|
| | 1979 | 1980 | 1981 | 1982 | 1983 | 1979 | 1980 | 1981 | 1982 | 1983 | 1979 | 1980 | 1981 | 1982 | 1983 |
| Net working capital† | 738 | 575 | 610 | 493 | 229 | 27,500 | 27,800 | 28,000 | 28,160 | 28,300 | .0268 | .0207 | .0218 | .0175 | .0081 |
| Current ratio‡ | 2.525 | 1.823 | 1.880 | 1.583 | 1.197 | 2.564 | 1.850 | 1.757 | 1.693 | 1.666 | .9848 | .9854 | 1.0700 | .9350 | .7185 |
| Quick ratio§ | 1.339 | .558 | .830 | .461 | .078 | 1.031 | .869 | .786 | .711 | .692 | 1.2987 | .6421 | 1.0560 | .6484 | .1127 |

*Dyer Straits/Reference Group.
†Current assets less current liabilities (including reserve for encumbrances) in thousands of dollars.
‡Current assets divided by current liabilities (including reserve for encumbrances).
§Cash plus time deposits divided by current liabilities (including reserve for encumbrances).

terms to meet all the current liabilities. (If the liabilities need payment sooner than the assets become cash, a current ratio considerably above one may be needed.) The trend in the current ratio indicates, however, that it may not be above one for long.

A more conservative liquidity ratio that only compares the most liquid current assets with the current liabilities is the quick ratio, and this is also shown in Table 8-11. The quick ratios have declined in both Dyer Straits and the reference group, but the decline in Dyer Straits has been more precipitous. In fact, by the end of the period, the quick ratio in the reference group is almost nine times higher than in Dyer Straits. The comparison of the quick ratio with the current ratio in Dyer Straits indicates that most of Dyer Straits' current assets are not cash or "near-cash" assets. If the current liabilities must be paid soon, Dyer Straits may have problems if it cannot convert other current assets into cash quickly.

The common-size balance sheets for the combined general and debt service funds in Dyer Straits shown in Table 8-12 confirm the dramatic decline in cash over the five-year period. They also document the dramatic rise in property taxes receivable over the period, another cause for concern for Dyer Straits. The rate of payment of property taxes in Dyer Straits has slowed down, so that a major source of current assets in Dyer Straits has become less liquid. The order of magnitude of these receivables is shown in Table 8-2; property taxes receivable are over $1 million in 1983 and annual property tax revenues are $4.5 million in 1983 (see Table 8-4). This high level of property taxes receivable suggests that unless Dyer Straits expects to collect a substantial portion of taxes soon, the quick ratio may be more indicative of the actual status of liquidity in Dyer Straits than the current ratio which includes taxes receivable.

Table 8-12 shows that two current liabilities, vouchers payable and salaries payable, have increased over the five-year period and constitute a larger share of total liabilities in Dyer Straits compared with the reference group. This suggests that the lagging collection of property taxes has caused Dyer Straits to slow down its payables to employees and suppliers. However, this practice can only go so far.

More details on the days outstanding for the major receivables and payables are contained in Table 8-13. The days outstanding for the property taxes of 87.8 days in 1983, compared with 49.9 days in the reference group that is on the same payment schedule, indicates that Dyer Straits has a serious property tax collection problem. The days outstanding for vouchers payable, over 100, indicates that suppliers may be reluctant to extend additional credit to Dyer Straits and may even charge higher prices to compensate for the delayed payment. The salaries payable account has also grown significantly in Dyer Straits, perhaps because the city has switched from biweekly to monthly paychecks for more of its employees.

When all the findings on liquidity for Dyer Straits are pulled together, the outlook is rather negative. Over the past five years, cash outflows have exceeded cash inflows, in part because Dyer Straits has had deficits in the combined general and debt service funds, and in part because property tax collections have slowed down considerably. If the collection of state aid had not improved and the

TABLE 8-12  Common Size Balance Sheets, Combined General and Debt Service Funds, City of Dyer Straits and Reference Group, 1979-83 (total assets equal 100 percent)

| | DYER STRAITS | | | | | REFERENCE GROUP | | | | | LOCATION QUOTIENTS* | | | | |
|---|---|---|---|---|---|---|---|---|---|---|---|---|---|---|---|
| | 1979 | 1980 | 1981 | 1982 | 1983 | 1979 | 1980 | 1981 | 1982 | 1983 | 1979 | 1980 | 1981 | 1982 | 1983 |
| *Assets:* | | | | | | | | | | | | | | | |
| Cash | 40 | 16 | 27 | 20 | 7 | 35 | 33 | 31 | 29 | 29 | 1.1429 | .4848 | .8710 | .6897 | .2414 |
| Time deposits | 13 | 15 | 17 | 9 | 0 | 16 | 14 | 14 | 13 | 13 | .8125 | 1.0714 | 1.2143 | .6923 | 0 |
| Property taxes receivable | 23 | 30 | 37 | 53 | 78 | 25 | 27 | 33 | 36 | 34 | .9200 | 1.1111 | 1.1212 | 1.4722 | 2.2941 |
| Sales taxes receivable | 2 | 3 | 2 | 3 | 0 | 4 | 3 | 6 | 6 | 6 | .5000 | 1.0000 | .3333 | .5000 | 0 |
| Accounts receivable | 2 | 4 | 2 | 2 | 2 | 5 | 5 | 4 | 4 | 4 | .4000 | .8000 | .5000 | .5000 | .5000 |
| State aid receivable | 9 | 13 | 5 | 4 | 5 | 3 | 5 | 4 | 5 | 5 | 3.0000 | 2.6000 | 1.2000 | .8000 | 1.0000 |
| Federal aid receivable | 9 | 11 | 4 | 2 | 2 | 3 | 5 | 3 | 3 | 3 | 3.0000 | 2.2000 | 1.3333 | .6667 | .6667 |
| Due from other funds | 1 | 3 | 2 | 3 | 3 | 6 | 5 | 3 | 3 | 4 | .1167 | .6000 | .6667 | 1.0000 | .7500 |
| Other assets | 1 | 5 | 4 | 3 | 3 | 2 | 2 | 2 | 2 | 3 | .5000 | 2.5000 | 2.0000 | 1.5000 | 1.0000 |
| Total Assets† | 100 | 100 | 100 | 100 | 100 | 100 | 100 | 100 | 100 | 100 | 1.0000 | 1.0000 | 1.0000 | 1.0000 | 1.0000 |
| *Liabilities:* | | | | | | | | | | | | | | | |
| Vouchers payable | 10 | 15 | 15 | 21 | 29 | 12 | 14 | 14 | 17 | 19 | .8333 | 1.0714 | 1.0714 | 1.2353 | 1.5263 |
| Bond interest and matured bonds payable | 3 | 5 | 4 | 6 | 4 | 3 | 2 | 2 | 3 | 4 | 1.0000 | 2.5000 | 2.0000 | 2.0000 | 1.0000 |
| Salaries payable | 8 | 15 | 16 | 18 | 27 | 13 | 15 | 16 | 13 | 16 | .6514 | 1.0000 | 1.0000 | 1.3846 | 1.6875 |
| Due to other funds | 2 | 4 | 2 | 1 | 8 | 4 | 7 | 11 | 11 | 8 | .5000 | .5714 | .1818 | .0909 | 1.0000 |
| Total Liabilities† | 23 | 39 | 36 | 46 | 69 | 32 | 38 | 42 | 45 | 46 | .7188 | 1.0263 | .8517 | 1.0222 | 1.5000 |
| *Reserves* | 16 | 16 | 17 | 17 | 15 | 18 | 16 | 15 | 14 | 14 | .8889 | 1.0000 | 1.1333 | 1.2143 | 1.0714 |
| *Fund Balances* | 60 | 45 | 47 | 37 | 16 | 50 | 46 | 43 | 41 | 40 | 1.2000 | .9783 | 1.0930 | .9024 | .4000 |

*Dyer Straits/Reference Group.

†Totals may not add due to rounding.

348

TABLE 8-13 Other Measures of Liquidity, Combined General and Debt Service Funds, City of Dyer Straits and Reference Group, 1979-83

| MUNICIPAL DEBT | DYER STRAITS | | | | | REFERENCE GROUP | | | | | LOCATION QUOTIENTS* | | | | |
|---|---|---|---|---|---|---|---|---|---|---|---|---|---|---|---|
| | 1979 | 1980 | 1981 | 1982 | 1983 | 1979 | 1980 | 1981 | 1982 | 1983 | 1979 | 1980 | 1981 | 1982 | 1983 |
| *Expenditure Fixity:* | | | | | | | | | | | | | | | |
| Ratio of materials and supplies plus contractual services to total expenditures | .1722 | .1626 | .1566 | .1546 | .1489 | .2017 | .1974 | .1940 | .1899 | .1875 | .854 | .824 | .807 | .814 | .794 |
| *Days Outstanding:* | | | | | | | | | | | | | | | |
| Property taxes receivable | 28.4 | 37.1 | 45.3 | 63.9 | 87.8 | 60.4 | 57.5 | 55.7 | 52.0 | 49.9 | .470 | .645 | .813 | 1.229 | 1.760 |
| State aid receivable | 41.2 | 53.7 | 16.8 | 13.9 | 16.0 | 14.3 | 19.7 | 15.7 | 16.7 | 19.0 | 2.881 | 2.726 | 1.070 | .832 | .842 |
| Vouchers payable | 37.1 | 57.6 | 56.8 | 76.1 | 100.7 | 47.5 | 56.6 | 56.8 | 69.8 | 73.3 | .781 | 1.018 | 1.000 | 1.090 | 1.374 |
| Salaries payable | 10.2 | 18.4 | 17.7 | 15.8 | 25.2 | 20.2 | 23.3 | 23.5 | 19.3 | 21.7 | .505 | .790 | .753 | .819 | 1.161 |

*Dyer Straits/Reference Group.

payables to employees and suppliers had not slowed down, it is highly likely that Dyer Straits would not have had a positive cash balance in 1983.

Two other factors reinforce these negative findings. First, the measure of expenditure fixity shown in Table 8-13 indicates that Dyer Straits has few expenditures it can reduce readily to lower its cash outflows. Moreover, the share of these "flexible" expenditures has been decreasing over the past five years. Finally, recall that Table 8-9 indicated that the year-end (December) is not necessarily the worst time in terms of levels of cash. Thus the low levels of cash shown in Table 8-10 may be even lower, and even negative, at other times of the year. This means that Dyer Straits must resort to short-term borrowing to have positive levels of cash, and given Dyer Straits' overall financial condition, these may be expensive (and even unavailable) sources of short-term cash. At least Dyer Straits has been able to fully pay off these short-term obligations in the past. But if the trends that have led to the current situation continue, a severe liquidity crisis for the combined general and debt service funds will probably occur in the near future.

**Capital Projects Fund.**    The capital projects fund is designed to account for the accumulation of assets that will be spent on capital projects. As we pointed out earlier in the chapter, the cash flows of the capital project fund tend to be rather uneven because of the "lumpy" nature of capital expenditures and financing. The liquidity of the capital projects fund should depend on the relationship between the inflows of sources of financing and the outflows of expenditures for the capital projects. Since sources of financing typically flow into the capital projects fund prior to the completion of the construction or acquisition of the capital item, a capital projects fund usually has significant liquid assets. These liquid assets, however, are often committed to particular capital projects and are not available for general use by the government.

Two issues should be addressed when examining the liquidity of the capital projects fund. First, are the assets in the fund in such a form that they can be used to acquire the capital in a timely fashion? Second, if the answer to the first question is no, how can the government make the needed adjustments? In particular, can the capital projects fund turn to other government funds, particularly the general fund for resources? Because of these concerns, and the nature of the cash flows of the capital projects fund, the liquidity measures used for the general fund are not appropriate for the capital projects fund. Instead the liquidity of the capital projects fund must be determined on a case-by-case basis.

The balance sheet shown for Dyer Straits and the reference group in Table 8-3 contains important information for the liquidity analysis of the capital projects fund. Both Dyer Straits and the reference group have significant liquid assets in the form of time deposits and cash. The other current assets are primarily amounts due from other funds, but these are relatively small.

Both Dyer Straits and the reference group have substantial current liabilities in the form of short-term financing, bond anticipation notes, and capital notes.

Many governments will borrow short term in the early stages of a capital project with the expectation that they will pay off the short-term debt when they raise long-term debt. If interest rates do not rise substantially while the short-term debt is outstanding, the issuance of short-term debt prior to the issuance of long-term debt may be cost effective for the government. The other current liabilities that appear in Table 8–3 are payables that are typical of funds with ongoing construction projects.

Thus it appears that the assets in the capital projects funds of Dyer Straits and the reference group are liquid. Moreover, in the earlier assessment of the levels of internal resources we learned that the funds on hand are sufficient to complete the planned capital projects. Finally, the use of interfund transfers is limited to the payment for services (such as engineering or construction) performed by one fund for another. As it stands now, therefore, the liquidity position of the capital project fund is satisfactory. Given the liquidity problems of Dyer Straits' combined general and debt service funds, the possibility in the future of the diversion of capital funds for operating purposes should not be overlooked. With the high degree of debt financing of Dyer Straits' current capital projects, this would amount to borrowing for operating purposes.

## V. FINANCIAL ANALYSIS OF GOVERNMENT ENTERPRISES

Throughout the analysis of revenues, expenditures, debt, and pensions, we have essentially ignored the finances of governmental enterprises, those activities that involve the sale of services or goods and are normally designed to operate in a fiscally independent, "self-sustaining" manner. We have not treated the enterprise revenues, expenditures, and debt in the respective analyses because, for enterprises, it is more appropriate to treat the enterprise's finances in an integrated way, more closely approximating private-sector financial analysis. The nature of the enterprise is such that it does not usually rely on taxation, its expenses (not expenditures) are usually matched against revenues, and its debt is usually not secured against the taxing power (i.e., full faith and credit) of the government. Although a financial analysis of an enterprise is considerably more than an analysis of the levels of its internal resources, the orientation of enterprise fund analysis is such that it is usefully examined as a component of internal resource analysis.

We assume that the purpose of a governmental enterprise is to provide a public good or service in exchange for payments from the users of that good or service. Utilities, airports, transportation systems, convention centers, and recreational facilities are examples of activities organized on an enterprise basis.

It is impossible in the limited space we have available to explain comprehensively how to analyze a "for-profit" enterprise; entire books are devoted to the topic.[9] What we can do in this section, however, is to suggest how to examine enterprises in the context of an analysis of a government's financial condition. Part of this analysis will be similar to the internal resource analysis we have just presented, but the assessment of enterprises must go much further.

The major question we address in this analysis is, how do government enterprises affect the financial condition of a government? If an enterprise operates on a break-even basis without subsidies from other parts of the government, the enterprise should have no adverse affect on the financial condition of the government. Moreover, by providing a valued good or service to the community and thereby meeting a need that might not be met without the enterprise, the operation of the enterprise should result in an improvement in the financial condition of the government. Finally, a government enterprise may produce a surplus ("profit") which may be available for use elsewhere in the government.

If an enterprise fails to operate at least on a break-even basis, it may weaken the financial condition of the government by requiring subsidies from other funds in the form of money or services. But just because the enterprise puts a financial burden on the government does not mean that the goods or services from the enterprise are not "worth" the cost. Subsidies for certain public enterprises may be socially desirable. What it does mean is that the enterprise has an effect on the financial condition of the government, and that this financial effect should be recognized.

Our analysis of the influence of enterprises on the financial condition of a government consists of four components: (1) assessments of demand and supply, (2) operational performance, (3) capital structure, and (4) liquidity.

### Demand and Supply

A distinguishing feature of enterprises, compared with the other activities of governments, is that they operate in markets where resources are exchanged for goods and services. Thus it is important to examine the enterprise's role in the supply of and demand for the services in question.

An important aspect of the market is the degree of competition. In some respects the financial riskiness of the enterprise increases with the competition in the market. For example, if as is often the case the enterprise is in a monopoly position, then there will be no actions by direct competitors, such as price cutting or product enhancement, that could affect the financial condition of the enterprise in a negative way. While many public enterprises approximate monopoly suppliers, such as airports and water systems, others face direct competition, such as recreation facilities. Thus an examination of the enterprise should include an investigation of the nature of the direct competition. The public enterprise's market

---

[9] For example, see Leopold A. Bernstein, *Financial Statement Analysis: Theory, Application, and Interpretation,* 3rd ed. (Homewood, Ill.: Richard D. Irwin, 1983).

share should be examined over time to determine whether its position in the market is growing or declining.

The market should also be examined to understand the nature of indirect competition. For example, a city may operate the only commuter rail line, but the railway may face competition from automobiles and private express buses. Similarly, a municipally owned cable television system may face competition from satellite systems and home video recorders. Again, competing products and prices may lower the revenues to a public enterprise.

In addition to a general market analysis, many enterprises operate in industries that are faced with special regulations, and these affect the supply of and demand for products. Regulations may improve or worsen the finances of an enterprise, and as a result, they must be assessed on a case-by-case basis. Examples include the environmental regulations that affect sewer systems, nuclear regulatory effects on electric utilities, and the move away from cost reimbursement toward prospective reimbursement in the health industry.

Finally, the market analysis should include an estimate of the relationship of the quantity of the product demanded to the price charged for the product. This relationship can be represented by the specification of a demand curve and/or estimation of the elasticity of demand with respect to price. This elasticity is specified as the percentage change in the quantity of the product demanded that is associated with a percentage change in price. If the percentage change in the product demanded is less (more) than the associated percentage change in price, the demand is called inelastic (elastic) with respect to price. Enterprises that face an inelastic demand are in a better position from a financial perspective because they will receive more revenues for a given price increase than they would if their demand were more elastic.

### Operational Performance

The analysis of the operational performance of an enterprise is most analogous to internal resource analysis, since it involves the assessment of revenues and expenses. In general, the better the operational performance of the enterprise, the less likely it is that the government will become involved in subsidizing the enterprise. Since the financial goal of enterprises is assumed to be break-even operations, this can be used as a benchmark in the analysis of operational performance.

Although break-even performance may be the financial goal, there are several reasons why a positive *net income* (revenues less expenses) may be appropriate. Most of the reasons stem from the notion that break-even performance is the long-run goal rather than the objective for any particular year. The excess of revenues over expenses may be needed for capital purposes, either for capital expansion or for replacement, or to pay back contributed capital that is sometimes used to start up a public enterprise. In growing enterprises there may be a need for additional working capital, which can be generated by operating with a positive net income. Or the enterprise may wish to operate with a positive net income in some years as a contingency for those years in which unexpected events have a negative effect on its earnings. For this reason, it is better to examine the enterprise's revenues and expenses over several years rather than for a single year. The ability of an enterprise to raise its rates or prices to improve its operational performance should also be examined.

There are a number of measures available to assess an enterprise's operational performance. Most enterprises report their income in at least two parts. The first part is typically labeled *operating income,* or *net income from operations.* This is the difference between operating revenues and operating expenses where *operating* refers to those flows "which are directly related to the fund's [enterprise's] primary service activities."[10] The second part is *net income,* or *total net income,* and includes nonoperating revenues and expenses as well as operating income. Sometimes, in order to compare the income data for enterprises of various sizes, operating income and net income are divided by revenues. This ratio is called the *operating margin* in some industries.[11]

Another measure of the enterprise's operational performance is the *return on investment.* This ratio assesses the earnings of the enterprise compared with the asset base generating the earnings. The numerator of this ratio may be based on operating income or total income. Usually interest expense is added to the income figure in the numerator because interest is part of the total return on assets, the part paid to the debtholders.[12] The denominator is the total assets of the enterprise. Thus the return on investment from operations equals [net income from operations plus interest expense] divided by [total assets]; the total return on investment equals [total net income plus interest expense] divided by [total assets]. Since assets are typically measured by historical cost less depreciation, asset valuations are affected by inflation. Financial ratios that use assets measured in this way are less reliable than those that use more current data, so they have to be interpreted more cautiously.[13]

A final type of ratio that is useful in the evaluation of operational performance is the *activity ratio,* although it, too, often uses a measure of enterprise assets measured in historical terms. Activity ratios usually compare a measure of the enterprise's input with its output. For example, the *total asset turnover* ratio is computed by dividing total annual operating revenues by total assets.[14] If this ratio is

---

[10]Municipal Finance Officers Association, *Governmental Accounting, Auditing, and Financial Reporting* (Chicago, 1980), Appendix B, p. 69.

[11]William O. Cleverly, "Financial Ratios: Summary Indicators for Management Decision-Making," *Hospital & Health Services Administration,* Special Edition I, 1981, p. 37.

[12]Bernstein, *Financial Statement Analysis,* p. 603.

[13]For a discussion and illustration of the problems with historical costs in financial ratios, see Steven A. Finkler, "Ratio Analysis: Use with Caution," *Health Care Management Review,* 7, No. 2, Spring, 1982, pp. 65–72.

[14]Cleverly, "Financial Ratios," pp. 35–36.

high, it suggests that every dollar of assets is generating a high value of revenues, implying efficient use of these assets.

### Capital Structure

The ability of the enterprise to raise capital depends, in part, on its current capital structure. For government enterprises that cannot issue equity (e.g., common stock), an analysis of the enterprise's capital structure usually means measuring the degree to which it relies on *debt*.

Enterprises that are heavier users of debt are generally considered to be financially riskier than those that borrow less (recognizing that average levels of debt vary across industries). The use of debt, *per se,* is not a signal of poor financial condition, but all else being equal, the level of enterprise debt, the greater the possibility that unexpected changes in enterprise revenues and expenses may require general fund contributions to the payment of the enterprise's debt service. Moreover, in terms of capital expansion, all else being equal, the greater the debt carried by the enterprise, the greater the difficulty of raising additional debt. For these reasons, we need to examine the stock of debt outstanding and debt service flows to assess an enterprise's capital structure.

The likelihood that an enterprise will be able to repay its debt depends on the annual payments required by existing debt levels. A ratio that is commonly used in this assessment is the *debt service coverage* ratio, which is used to compare the funds available in a given period (normally a year) for the repayment of debt with the amount of debt and interest on the debt that must be repaid over that period.

For an enterprise, the debt service coverage ratio can be defined as [Total net income plus depreciation plus interest payments] divided by [Principal payments plus interest payments]. The numerator represents the annual cash flow available to pay debt service (depreciation is included in the numerator because although it is an expense, it is not a cash flow), and the denominator is the annual debt service. Higher values of the debt service coverage ratio indicate that the enterprise has more funds available in any given year (more coverage) to pay back the debt, so that the risks of not being able to pay debt service are less.

For an enterprise, a measure of the amount of debt outstanding is the *debt to assets* ratio, the stock of long-term debt outstanding to the total fixed assets of the enterprise.[15] This ratio measures the proportion of the fixed assets of the enterprise that is financed by long-term debt but again suffers from the use of assets measured by historical costs.

### Levels and Liquidity of Internal Resources

Analysis of the levels and liquidity of internal resources for enterprises follows the same approach presented earlier for other government funds, with a few exceptions noted shortly.

---

[15] Ibid., p. 33.

To analyze levels of internal resources, we examine the levels and trends of fund balances (sometimes termed *net worth* or *retained earnings* in government enterprises), but we also use debt to asset ratios (rather than a fund balance to revenue ratios) to determine the adequacy of this "equity" (nonborrowed) capital cushion. Too high a debt to asset ratio implies that the enterprise needs more internal resources in the form of net worth or retained earnings, relative to its debt. Internal resources can increase by transfers from other funds and/or surpluses ("profits") earned by the enterprise. Thus enterprise fund surpluses and deficits are analyzed as a primary source of the increases or decreases in the enterprise's fund balances or net worth.

To analyze the liquidity of the enterprise's internal resources, we start by estimating the expected levels and timing of cash flows to and from the enterprise, and the probability of cash flow problems, using cash budgets (if available) and information on past surpluses and deficits and sources and uses of cash from existing financial statements. We also employ liquidity measures such as net working capital, and the current and quick ratios.

We next try to assess the extent to which the enterprise can change the magnitude of its cash flows, through additional borrowing or increasing revenue and/or decreasing its expenditures, and the timing of its cash flows by speeding up cash inflows (like collections of water bills), and/or slowing down cash outflows (like payment of bills). In the last case, we again turn to collection rates and payment rates, as we did in our earlier analysis.

Finally, standard methods of comparing changes in current assets and liabilities over time and/or between organizations can be used for evaluating the liquidity of government enterprises.

### An Application

In this final part we conduct a financial analysis of one of the government enterprise funds in Dyer Straits, the water and sewer fund. The analysis of the second enterprise fund, the municipal parking fund, is presented as an exercise for the reader at the end of the chapter. For the water and sewer fund, we present the basic financial data and then conduct the four-part analysis. Our ultimate concern is how the financial condition of the enterprise affects the overall financial strength of Dyer Straits.

The balance sheets for the water and sewer fund (and the reference group) over the 1979–83 period are presented in Table 8–14 and the revenues and expenses are reported in Table 8–15. (The most recent data for the funds in Dyer Straits appeared in Chapter 2.) Finally, Table 8–16 presents relevant receipts and disbursements data.

The water and sewer systems in Dyer Straits and the reference group are enterprises that provide essential services for their respective jurisdictions. From the supply point of view, both systems are monopolies. Individuals and organizations in the particular jurisdictions we are analyzing have no other options for the

TABLE 8–14  Balance Sheets—Water and Sewer Fund, City of Dyer Straits and Reference Group, End of Year, 1979–83 ($ Thousands)

| | DYER STRAITS | | | | | REFERENCE GROUP | | | | |
|---|---|---|---|---|---|---|---|---|---|---|
| | 1979 | 1980 | 1981 | 1982 | 1983 | 1979 | 1980 | 1981 | 1982 | 1983 |
| *Assets:* | | | | | | | | | | |
| Current assets | | | | | | | | | | |
| Cash | 622 | 577 | 531 | 517 | 580 | 32,000 | 32,500 | 35,000 | 35,400 | 36,400 |
| Time deposits | 1,467 | 1,374 | 1,186 | 886 | 556.9 | 15,900 | 23,300 | 28,800 | 37,800 | 42,300 |
| Accounts receivable | 263 | 272 | 251 | 123 | 183 | 6,400 | 6,800 | 7,200 | 7,400 | 8,300 |
| Due from other funds | 41 | 37 | 19 | 4 | 0 | 1,900 | 3,900 | 4,700 | 3,100 | 1,200 |
| Inventories | | | | | | | | | | |
| Materials | 33 | 29 | 22 | 17 | 17 | 1,100 | 1,200 | 1,100 | 900 | 900 |
| Fixed assets | | | | | | | | | | |
| Equipment (net of depreciation) | 141 | 149 | 180 | 183 | 203 | 9,700 | 10,200 | 10,400 | 11,700 | 12,800 |
| Land | 703 | 703 | 768 | 768 | 768 | 48,500 | 49,100 | 49,100 | 49,500 | 49,700 |
| Buildings (net of depreciation) | 2,132 | 2,948 | 3,774 | 4,219 | 4,282 | 126,300 | 138,400 | 143,300 | 152,900 | 161,000 |
| Total Assets | 5,402 | 6,089 | 6,731 | 6,717 | 6,589.9 | 241,800 | 265,400 | 279,600 | 298,700 | 312,600 |
| *Liabilities:* | | | | | | | | | | |
| Current liabilities | | | | | | | | | | |
| Vouchers payable | 57 | 151 | 79 | 77 | 92 | 3,188 | 4,461 | 110 | 2,673 | 12,000 |
| Bond interest and matured bonds payable | 12 | 8 | 21 | 22 | 22 | 2,800 | 3,300 | 1,900 | 2,800 | 1,700 |
| Salaries payable | 47 | 142 | 81 | 82 | 127 | 4,900 | 5,100 | 2,000 | 4,500 | 6,800 |
| Due to other funds | 54 | 28 | 39 | 161 | 91 | 3,000 | 2,800 | 300 | 1,900 | 3,300 |
| Bond anticipation notes payable | 1,767 | 1,889 | 1,902 | 1,838 | 2,133 | 43,569 | 42,821 | 50.540 | 48,766 | 46,344 |
| Capital notes payable | 100 | 0 | 225 | 175 | 90 | 7,393 | 7,204 | 6,407 | 6,399 | 7,482 |
| Long-term liabilities | | | | | | | | | | |
| Revenue bonds payable | 1,251 | 1,812 | 2,418 | 2,585 | 2,528 | 44,403 | 57,467 | 68,496 | 75,615 | 74,737 |
| Total Liabilities | 3,288 | 4,030 | 4,765 | 4,940 | 5,083 | 109,253 | 123,153 | 129,753 | 142,653 | 152,353 |
| *Retained earnings* | 2,114 | 2,059 | 1,966 | 1,777 | 1,506.9 | 132,547 | 142,247 | 149,847 | 156,047 | 160,247 |

TABLE 8-15   Statements of Revenues and Expenses—Water and Sewer Fund, City of Dyer Straits and Reference Group, 1979–83 ($ Thousands)

| | DYER STRAITS | | | | | REFERENCE GROUP | | | | |
|---|---|---|---|---|---|---|---|---|---|---|
| | 1979 | 1980 | 1981 | 1982 | 1983 | 1979 | 1980 | 1981 | 1982 | 1983 |
| *Operating Revenues:* | | | | | | | | | | |
| Sale of water | 1,403 | 1,471 | 1,504 | 1,592 | 1,711 | 65,900 | 72,000 | 76,200 | 82,400 | 90,300 |
| Sewer charges | 272 | 288 | 303 | 321 | 337 | 10,500 | 11,400 | 12,500 | 13,900 | 15,400 |
| Interfund transfers | 69 | 49 | 52 | 29 | 80 | 3,600 | 4,100 | 4,300 | 4,800 | 3,100 |
| Total Operating Revenues | 1,744 | 1,808 | 1,859 | 1,942 | 2,128 | 80,000 | 87,500 | 93,000 | 101,100 | 108,800 |
| *Operating Expenses:* | | | | | | | | | | |
| Salaries | 614 | 606 | 616 | 725 | 729 | 22,900 | 24,300 | 27,000 | 30,300 | 34,900 |
| Materials and supplies | 409 | 418 | 421 | 431 | 448 | 14,900 | 16,200 | 17,500 | 19,400 | 21,500 |
| Repairs and maintenance | 169 | 189 | 197 | 209 | 257 | 8,200 | 9,100 | 10,400 | 12,000 | 13,400 |
| Utilities | 51 | 63 | 60 | 65 | 74 | 1,900 | 2,200 | 2,700 | 3,200 | 3,800 |
| Depreciation | 224 | 274 | 280 | 303 | 352 | 6,300 | 6,900 | 7,800 | 8,400 | 9,200 |
| Other expenses | 94 | 110 | 113 | 117 | 121 | 4,100 | 4,600 | 5,100 | 5,700 | 6,200 |
| Interfund transfers | 143 | 141 | 179 | 191 | 222 | 6,000 | 6,400 | 7,900 | 8,900 | 9,800 |
| Total Operating Expenses | 1,704 | 1,801 | 1,866 | 2,041 | 2,203 | 64,300 | 69,700 | 78,400 | 87,900 | 98,800 |
| Net Operating Income (Loss) | 40 | 7 | (7) | (99) | (75) | 15,700 | 17,800 | 14,600 | 13,200 | 10,000 |
| Net Income (Loss)* | (17) | (55) | (93) | (189) | (270) | 8,200 | 9,700 | 7,600 | 6,200 | 4,200 |

Negative numbers in parentheses.

*Including non-operating revenues and expenses.

TABLE 8-16  **Statements of Receipts and Disbursements, Water and Sewer Fund, City of Dyer Straits and Reference Group, 1979–83 ($ Thousands)**

| | DYER STRAITS | | | | | REFERENCE GROUP | | | | |
| | 1979 | 1980 | 1981 | 1982 | 1983 | 1979 | 1980 | 1981 | 1982 | 1983 |
|---|---|---|---|---|---|---|---|---|---|---|
| Water and Sewer Fund | | | | | | | | | | |
| Receipts | 3,712 | 4,036 | 4,344 | 4,499 | 4,797 | 151,300 | 165,300 | 176,400 | 181,800 | 175,300 |
| Disbursements | 3,703 | 4,174 | 4,578 | 4,813 | 5,063.1 | 143,800 | 157,400 | 168,400 | 172,400 | 169,800 |

provision of water and disposal of sewerage. This is common in the case of operations that have significant economies of scale where there are substantial cost savings if the service is provided by only one producer. Therefore, from a supply point of view, competition is not a concern.

What could be a problem from a supply point of view is inadequate capacity of the respective systems. In the case of water, Dyer Straits has both wells and reservoirs that have significantly more capacity than is currently needed. The sewer system, because of significant capital construction over the past five years (see Table 8-14, buildings and revenue bonds payable) has been upgraded and now substantially meets all federal and state government requirements.

In terms of demand, in the short run both systems have relatively inelastic relationships between price and quantity. Because of the nature of water consumption and sewage disposal, there are only limited opportunities to alter the quantity of the output consumed in response to changes in price. Over the long run, however, the price of water and sewer services may affect who lives and works in Dyer Straits and may eventually affect the revenues of the water and sewer systems. Since, however, the rate structure in Dyer Straits is similar to rates in the reference group, there do not appear to be any significant problems from a supply and demand perspective for the water and sewer systems.

When we analyze the operational performance of the water and sewer systems, however, the conclusions are somewhat different. Five measures of the operational performance of the water and sewer funds developed from Tables 8-14 and 8-15 are presented in Table 8-17. First, operating income, the difference between revenues and expenses from operations, is negative in three of the five years and the trend appears to be worsening. In 1982 and 1983, for example, the operating losses are around 3.5 to 5.0 percent of revenues. These losses are troubling in and of themselves, but they stand in contrast to the significant operating profits in the reference group. Although reference group operating profits as a percentage of revenues are declining, in the most recent year they are still over 9 percent. This performance of the water and sewer systems in Dyer Straits may be problematic if it continues.

The more-detailed revenue and expense statement presented in Chapter 2 showed that interest earnings and interest expense are the only nonoperating revenues and expenses, respectively. When these nonoperating items are added to the net income from operations for the water and sewer fund, the losses are significantly greater and occur in *all* five years. Moreover, the gap between operating income and net income is widening because interest earnings are decreasing and interest on debt is increasing. The net income in the reference group is positive in all of the five years.

The poor operating performance is also reflected in the return on investment data in Table 8-17 which shows the return to all sources of capital, including debt. In four of the five years the return on investment is below 4 percent, and in those years the return on investment is less than half the return on investment in the reference group. Part of the poor performance in Dyer Straits is due to the lower

TABLE 8-17  Measures of Operational Performance and Capital Structure, Water and Sewer Fund, City of Dyer Straits, and Reference Group, 1979–83

| | DYER STRAITS | | | | | REFERENCE GROUP | | | | | LOCATION QUOTIENTS* | | | | |
|---|---|---|---|---|---|---|---|---|---|---|---|---|---|---|---|
| | 1979 | 1980 | 1981 | 1982 | 1983 | 1979 | 1980 | 1981 | 1982 | 1983 | 1979 | 1980 | 1981 | 1982 | 1983 |
| Operating Income† | 40 | 7 | (7) | (99) | (75) | 15,700 | 17,800 | 14,600 | 13,200 | 10,000 | NC | NC | NC | NC | NC |
| Net income† | (17) | (55) | (93) | (189) | (270) | 8,200 | 9,700 | 7,600 | 6,200 | 4,200 | NC | NC | NC | NC | NC |
| Operating income/ revenues | .0229 | .0039 | (.0038) | (.0510) | (.0352) | .1963 | .2034 | .1570 | .1306 | .0919 | NC | NC | NC | NC | NC |
| Return on investment‡ | .0361 | .0346 | .0462 | .0398 | .0281 | .0846 | .0893 | .0836 | .0797 | .0627 | .4267 | .3875 | .5526 | .4994 | .4482 |
| Total asset turnover§ | .3228 | .2969 | .2762 | .2891 | .3229 | .3309 | .3297 | .3326 | .3385 | .3480 | .9755 | .9006 | .8304 | .8541 | .9279 |
| Debt/assets | .5772 | .6079 | .6770 | .6845 | .7209 | .3944 | .4050 | .4487 | .4378 | .3997 | 1.4635 | 1.5009 | 1.5088 | 1.5635 | 1.8036 |
| Debt service coverage‖ | .7956 | .8246 | .6219 | .6271 | .5080 | 1.1359 | 1.1441 | .9884 | .9282 | .9133 | .7004 | .7207 | .6292 | .6756 | .5562 |

NC = Not calculated. Negative numbers in parentheses.

*Dyer Straits/Reference Group.

†Thousands of dollars.

‡(Operating income + interest expense)/total assets.

§Operating revenues/total assets

‖(Net income + depreciation + interest expense)/(principal payments + interest payments)

361

level of asset turnover in Dyer Straits compared with the reference group. Every dollar of assets in Dyer Straits in 1983 generates only 93 percent of the revenues generated in the reference group in the same year. But our interpretation of both the return on investment and asset turnover must be somewhat cautionary because Dyer Straits' assets are newer and thus are measured in more current dollars. The other measures of operating performance are not subject to the same caveat.

Note that we are focusing on the meaning of the operating performance measures strictly from the financial perspective. For a service like water and sewer, when the users of the enterprise are the same as the "owners," the enterprise may be run with a low return on investment as a goal. Even though the owners receive a lower financial return on investment from the enterprise, they receive other benefits from lower charges. If this strategy is used, the social performance may differ from the financial performance.

The operational performance of the water and sewer funds raises concerns for the overall financial condition of Dyer Straits. Although the internal resources of the water and sewer fund have been sufficient to avoid the need for operating subsidies from the general fund of Dyer Straits, current trends suggest that the poor operating performance, if not corrected through some combination of increased revenues and decreased expenses, may put financial pressure on the government.

Two capital structure ratios are shown in Table 8-17. First, the water and sewer fund's ability to pay its debt service as measured by the debt service coverage ratio has declined because operating performance has declined and outstanding debt has increased. There has also been a decline in the debt service coverage ratio in the reference group, but not as drastic as the decline in Dyer Straits. Since the debt service coverage ratio is substantially below one in Dyer Straits, this indicates that the enterprise's internal resources are being drawn upon to pay the debt service. This may have an effect on the liquidity of Dyer Straits.

Second, the debt to asset ratio is higher in Dyer Straits than in the reference group and is rising in Dyer Straits compared with a stable ratio in the reference group. Although both Dyer Straits and the reference group have increased their fixed assets over the period, Dyer Straits has had to rely more heavily on debt in part because profits were not provided from operating performance.

From the capital structure analysis, we can conclude that the water and sewer fund has increased its use of debt and that its ability to pay debt service from resources generated from operations has declined. When combined with the conclusions on operational performance, the possibility that the water and sewer fund will draw on the resources of other funds cannot be overlooked.

To assess the levels and liquidity of internal resources in the water and sewer fund, we begin by returning to the fund's balance sheet (Table 8-14). The fund balance (retained earnings) has fallen steadily since 1979, reflecting losses over this time period. The fact that retained earnings were rising in the reference group during this period makes this reduction in internal resources even more ominous.

Table 8-18 shows the cash flows in the water and sewer funds for Dyer Straits and the reference group. It is clear from this table that there has been a decline in cash in Dyer Straits, both absolutely and compared with the reference group. Despite this decline, however, Table 8-18 shows that there is still considerable cash in the water and sewer fund in 1983.

The fact that enterprise funds include both capital and operating activities must be kept in mind when examining liquidity. In the case of Dyer Straits' water and sewer fund, some of the cash in each year consists of the proceeds from bond anticipation and capital notes that are intended for capital additions and replacements. Since we know from other information that by 1983, roughly $600,000 of capital projects remains to be completed for which funding has been received in Dyer Straits' water and sewer fund, roughly $500,000 of cash is available for other purposes. Thus, despite the poor operating performance and the decline in cash, the water and sewer fund in Dyer Straits does not face a liquidity crisis.

The decline in the liquidity position in Dyer Straits' water and sewer fund is also illustrated in Table 8-19 where three liquidity measures are shown. All three measures have declined and, most recently, have become quite low: net working capital is negative, and both current and quick ratios are close to or less than 0.5. Again, however, the fact that both operating and capital activities are accounted for in the fund should be taken into account in the interpretation of these ratios.

One approach would be to separate, at least approximately, the capital transactions from the operating ones. For example, in Dyer Straits in 1983 we could assume that the $600,000 earmarked for capital is "unavailable." Furthermore, we could assume that the revenue anticipation and capital notes will be converted into long-term debt. With these two assumptions, the three liquidity measures for 1983 in Dyer Straits are $405,000, 2.2199, and 1.6175 for net working capital, current ratio, and quick ratio, respectively. Thus, after separating the capital transactions, the liquidity of the operating component of the water and sewer fund does not appear to be a problem. But if the assumptions behind this adjustment are not correct, for example if the fund for some reason cannot convert the short-term debt into long-term debt, then the lower ratios shown in Table 8-19 are relevant. In summary, if the separation of the capital items is valid, the water and sewer fund in Dyer Straits does not face a liquidity problem despite the fact that levels of liquid assets have declined considerably over the five years.

The common size balance sheets for the water and sewer fund for Dyer Straits and the reference group are shown in Table 8-20 to determine whether some additional factors should be taken into account. This table confirms the loss of cash in Dyer Straits, both absolutely and compared with the reference group. The common size balance sheet also points out that Dyer Straits relies more heavily than the reference group on the use of short-term borrowing. This may be due to the size of the capital program underway in Dyer Straits.

Although the common size balance sheet does not indicate that the receivables in Dyer Straits are out of line with those in the reference group, in

TABLE 8-18  Cash, Cash Flows, and Net Income, Water and Sewer Fund, City of Dyer Straits and Reference Group, 1979–83 ($ Thousands)

| | DYER STRAITS | | | | | REFERENCE GROUP | | | | |
|---|---|---|---|---|---|---|---|---|---|---|
| | 1979 | 1980 | 1981 | 1982 | 1983 | 1979 | 1980 | 1981 | 1982 | 1983 |
| Opening cash | 2,080 | 2,089 | 1,951 | 1,717 | 1,403 | 40,400 | 47,900 | 55,800 | 63,800 | 73,200 |
| Receipts | 3,712 | 4,036 | 4,344 | 4,499 | 4,797 | 151,300 | 165,300 | 176,400 | 181,800 | 175,300 |
| Disbursements | 3,703 | 4,174 | 4,578 | 4,813 | 5,063 | 143,800 | 157,400 | 168,400 | 172,400 | 169,800 |
| Net cash change | 9 | (138) | (234) | (314) | (266) | 7,500 | 7,900 | 8,000 | 9,400 | 5,500 |
| Closing cash | 2,089 | 1,951 | 1,717 | 1,403 | 1,137 | 47,900 | 55,800 | 63,800 | 73,200 | 78,700 |
| Net income (loss) | (17) | (55) | (93) | (189) | (270) | 8,200 | 9,700 | 7,600 | 6,200 | 4,200 |

**Negative numbers in parentheses.**

TABLE 8-19 Liquidity Measures, Water and Sewer Fund, City of Dyer Straits and Reference Group, 1979–83

| | DYER STRAITS | | | | | REFERENCE GROUP | | | | | LOCATION QUOTIENTS* | | | | |
|---|---|---|---|---|---|---|---|---|---|---|---|---|---|---|---|
| | 1979 | 1980 | 1981 | 1982 | 1983 | 1979 | 1980 | 1981 | 1982 | 1983 | 1979 | 1980 | 1981 | 1982 | 1983 |
| Net working Capital† | 389 | 71 | (338) | (808) | (1,218) | (7,550) | 2,314 | 15,534 | 17,562 | 11,484 | NC | NC | NC | NC | NC |
| Current ratio‡ | 1.1910 | 1.0320 | .8560 | .6569 | .5233 | .8836 | 1.0354 | 1.2537 | 1.2620 | 1.1480 | 1.3479 | .9967 | .6828 | .5205 | .4558 |
| Quick ratio§ | 1.0255 | .8796 | .7316 | .5958 | .4450 | .7386 | .8534 | 1.0425 | 1.0919 | 1.0140 | 1.3884 | 1.0307 | .7024 | .5457 | .4389 |
| Days Outstanding: Accounts receivable | 57.3 | 56.4 | 50.7 | 23.5 | 32.6 | 30.6 | 29.8 | 29.6 | 28.0 | 28.7 | 1.87 | 1.89 | 1.71 | .84 | 1.14 |

NC = Not calculated.

*Dyer Straits/Reference Group.

†(Cash plus time deposits plus accounts receivable plus due from other funds plus inventories) less (vouchers payable plus bond interest and matured bonds payable plus salaries payable plus due to other funds plus bond anticipation notes payable plus capital notes payable). (In thousands of dollars).

‡Current assets divided by current liabilities as defined in preceding footnote.

§(Cash plus time deposits) divided by current liabilities.

TABLE 8–20 Common Size Balance Sheets, Water and Sewer Fund, City of Dyer Straits and Reference Group, 1979–83 (total assets equal 100%)

| | DYER STRAITS | | | | | REFERENCE GROUP | | | | | LOCATION QUOTIENTS* | | | | |
|---|---|---|---|---|---|---|---|---|---|---|---|---|---|---|---|
| | 1979 | 1980 | 1981 | 1982 | 1983 | 1979 | 1980 | 1981 | 1982 | 1983 | 1979 | 1980 | 1981 | 1982 | 1983 |
| *Assets:* | | | | | | | | | | | | | | | |
| Current Assets | | | | | | | | | | | | | | | |
| Cash | 12 | 9 | 8 | 8 | 9 | 13 | 12 | 13 | 12 | 12 | .92 | .75 | .62 | .67 | .75 |
| Time deposits | 27 | 23 | 18 | 13 | 8 | 7 | 9 | 10 | 13 | 14 | 3.86 | 2.56 | 1.80 | 1.00 | .57 |
| Accounts receivable | 5 | 4 | 4 | 2 | 3 | 3 | 3 | 3 | 2 | 3 | 1.67 | 1.33 | 1.33 | 1.00 | 1.00 |
| Due from other funds | 1 | 1 | 0 | 0 | 0 | 1 | 1 | 2 | 1 | 0 | 1.00 | 1.00 | 0 | 0 | NC |
| Inventories Materials | 1 | 0 | 0 | 0 | 0 | 0 | 0 | 0 | 0 | 0 | NC | NC | NC | NC | NC |
| Fixed Assets | | | | | | | | | | | | | | | |
| Equipment (net of depreciation) | 3 | 2 | 3 | 3 | 3 | 4 | 4 | 4 | 4 | 4 | .75 | .50 | .75 | .75 | .75 |
| Land | 13 | 12 | 11 | 11 | 12 | 20 | 19 | 18 | 17 | 16 | .65 | .63 | .61 | .65 | .75 |
| Buildings (net of depreciation) | 39 | 48 | 56 | 63 | 65 | 52 | 52 | 51 | 51 | 52 | .75 | .92 | 1.10 | 1.24 | 1.25 |
| Total Assets† | 100 | 100 | 100 | 100 | 100 | 100 | 100 | 100 | 100 | 100 | 1.00 | 1.00 | 1.00 | 1.00 | 1.00 |

| Liabilities: | | | | | | | | | | | | | | | |
|---|---|---|---|---|---|---|---|---|---|---|---|---|---|---|---|
| **Current Liabilities** | | | | | | | | | | | | | | | |
| Vouchers payable | 1 | 2 | 1 | 1 | 1 | 1 | 2 | 0 | 1 | 4 | 1.00 | 1.00 | NC | 1.00 | .25 |
| Bond interest and matured bonds payable | 0 | 0 | 0 | 0 | 0 | 1 | 1 | 1 | 1 | 1 | 0 | 0 | 0 | 0 | 0 |
| Salaries payable | 1 | 2 | 1 | 1 | 2 | 2 | 2 | 1 | 2 | 2 | .50 | 1.00 | 1.00 | .50 | .50 |
| Due to other funds | 1 | 0 | 2 | 2 | 1 | 1 | 1 | 0 | 1 | 1 | 1.00 | 0 | NC | 2.00 | 1.00 |
| Bond anticipation notes payable | 33 | 31 | 28 | 27 | 32 | 18 | 16 | 18 | 16 | 15 | 1.83 | 1.94 | 1.56 | 1.69 | 2.13 |
| Capital notes payable | 2 | 0 | 3 | 3 | 1 | 3 | 3 | 2 | 2 | 2 | .67 | 0 | 1.50 | 1.50 | .50 |
| **Long-term Liabilities** | | | | | | | | | | | | | | | |
| Revenue bonds payable | 23 | 30 | 36 | 41 | 38 | 18 | 22 | 24 | 25 | 24 | 1.28 | 1.36 | 1.50 | 1.64 | 1.58 |
| Total Liabilities† | 61 | 65 | 71 | 74 | 77 | 45 | 46 | 46 | 48 | 49 | 1.36 | 1.41 | 1.54 | 1.54 | 1.57 |
| *Retained Earnings* | 39 | 34 | 29 | 26 | 23 | 55 | 54 | 54 | 52 | 51 | .71 | .63 | .54 | .50 | .45 |

NC = Not calculated.

*Dyer Straits/Reference Group.

†Totals may not add due to rounding.

order to assess the condition of the receivables, the days outstanding are calculated and these are shown in Table 8–19. In Dyer Straits the days outstanding have improved substantially over the five-year period, and in 1983 they are only 14 percent higher than the reference group's.

Thus the primary problem of the water and sewer fund in Dyer Straits is its poor operating performance. The fund has adequate liquidity, assuming that it can convert its high level of short-term debt into long-term debt. But, if the poor operating performance continues, Dyer Straits' other funds may be drawn upon to pay debt service and other expenses.

## QUESTIONS

1.  What major questions are addressed by internal resource analysis? Discuss the principal differences between internal resource analysis and the other components of financial analysis. How is internal resource analysis related to the other components of the analysis?
2.  Identify and discuss several ways to organize a government's fund structure for internal resource analysis. What are the advantages and disadvantages of the organization of funds for internal resource analysis of Dyer Straits?
3.  Differentiate between the level of internal resources and the liquidity of internal resources. Can a government have both a liquidity problem and a high level of internal resources at the same time? Can a government have a very low level of internal resources without having a liquidity problem?
4.  Why are balance sheets an important source of information for internal resource analysis? What problems are encountered when using balance sheet information in the analysis of internal resources? What are important sources of information for internal resource analysis other than balance sheet information?
5.  What are the principal measures of a government's level of internal resources? How are these measures interpreted? How do intergovernmental transfers, budgeting biases, and accounting adjustments affect the measurement of the level of internal resources?
6.  Why is the analysis of the internal resources of a government's capital projects fund different from the analysis of such operating funds as the general, debt service, and special revenue funds? What are the primary concerns of the financial analyst when analyzing the level of internal resources in the capital project funds?
7.  Why is the analysis of a government's liquidity an important part of financial condition analysis?
8.  True or false: "A government that is illiquid is in poor financial condition." Defend your answer.
9.  What are the principal measures of the liquidity of internal resources? Discuss the strengths and weaknesses of each measure.
10. What options are available to a government to change the liquidity of its internal resources? What are the advantages and disadvantages of the various options?
11. Discuss how the liquidity analysis of capital projects funds differs from the analysis of the operating funds of the government.
12. Why are government enterprises analyzed separately from the other activities of a government? How might government enterprise activities affect the financial condition of the entire government?

13. What measures are used to assess the likelihood that a government enterprise will affect the financial condition of the government? What are the strengths and weaknesses of the various measures?

———————————————————**PROBLEMS**———————————————————

1. The performance of Dyer Straits' water and sewer enterprise fund was analyzed in this chapter. In this problem, information is presented so that the performance of the second enterprise fund, the municipal parking fund, can be analyzed.

The municipal parking fund maintains and services parking meters and operates a number of parking lots and garages in downtown Dyer Straits. In contrast to the water and sewer system, the parking facilities are not monopolies. The numerous private parking facilities in Dyer Straits compete with both the on-street and off-street parking provided by the municipal parking fund. In addition, other forms of public transportation are available for people who travel to downtown Dyer Straits so that the use of the automobile can be avoided. Finally, shopping malls outside of Dyer Straits provide an alternative to downtown shopping.

The balance sheets for the municipal parking fund in Dyer Straits and the reference group are presented in Table 8–21 for 1979–83. Note that virtually all the cities in the reference group operate municipal parking funds as enterprises. Table 8–22 presents the revenues and expenses for the municipal parking funds for Dyer Straits and the reference group for 1979–83, and the receipts and disbursements for the same period are presented in Table 8–23.

Using this information, analyze the performance of the municipal parking fund in Dyer Straits. In particular, discuss the effects that the municipal parking fund is likely to have on the financial condition of Dyer Straits.

2. Information on the city of Red Lion and a reference group was presented in the problems at the end of Chapter 4.
   a. Using this information, assess the level of internal resources in Red Lion.
   b. Assess the liquidity of internal resources in Red Lion. Are the conclusions on level and liquidity of internal resources similar?
   c. Overall, would you conclude that Red Lion's internal resources are a positive or a negative influence on its financial condition? Does the level and/or liquidity of internal resources appear to be a trouble spot for Red Lion? Is this condition moderated or exacerbated by the conclusions from the revenue, expenditure, debt, and pension analyses in Red Lion?

TABLE 8-21 Balance Sheets, Municipal Parking Fund, City of Dyer Straits and Reference Group, End of Year, 1979-83 ($ Thousands)

| | DYER STRAITS | | | | | REFERENCE GROUP | | | | |
|---|---|---|---|---|---|---|---|---|---|---|
| | 1979 | 1980 | 1981 | 1982 | 1983 | 1979 | 1980 | 1981 | 1982 | 1983 |
| *Assets:* | | | | | | | | | | |
| Current assets | | | | | | | | | | |
| Cash | 183 | 171 | 201 | 208 | 148.9 | 8,300 | 7,500 | 7,600 | 8,000 | 8,300 |
| Time deposits | 200 | 218 | 256 | 259 | 200 | 4,100 | 4,100 | 5,000 | 8,000 | 12,000 |
| Accounts receivable | 16 | 21 | 26 | 16 | 8 | 1,000 | 800 | 900 | 600 | 700 |
| Due from other funds | 13 | 9 | 10 | 31 | 121 | 1,400 | 1,900 | 1,100 | 5,100 | 2,900 |
| Inventories | | | | | | | | | | |
| Materials | 7 | 5 | 7 | 4 | 4 | 300 | 300 | 400 | 400 | 300 |
| Fixed Assets | | | | | | | | | | |
| Equipment (net of depreciation) | 12 | 25 | 25 | 26 | 34 | 1,800 | 1,900 | 2,000 | 2,100 | 2,200 |
| Land | 261 | 314 | 377 | 377 | 377 | 24,500 | 25,000 | 25,300 | 26,400 | 26,400 |
| Buildings (net of depreciation) | 1,554 | 2,038 | 2,738 | 2,762 | 2,774 | 103,800 | 111,300 | 116,200 | 118,800 | 120,800 |
| Total Assets | 2,246 | 2,801 | 3,640 | 3,683 | 3,666.9 | 145,200 | 152,800 | 158,500 | 169,400 | 173,600 |
| *Liabilities:* | | | | | | | | | | |
| Current liabilities | | | | | | | | | | |
| Vouchers payable | 25 | 21 | 27 | 16 | 18 | 5,424 | 4,525 | 1,432 | 2,346 | 1,200 |
| Bond interest and matured bonds payable | 6 | 11 | 12 | 7 | 7 | 1,500 | 1,200 | 700 | 1,100 | 1,000 |
| Salaries payable | 23 | 29 | 32 | 27 | 58 | 5,100 | 3,900 | 900 | 3,300 | 3,600 |
| Due to other funds | 4 | 8 | 14 | 12 | 12 | 1,100 | 1,900 | 1,800 | 200 | 100 |
| Bond anticipation notes payable | 995 | 1,274 | 1,339 | 1,331 | 1,307 | 18,672 | 18,352 | 21,660 | 20,900 | 19,858 |
| Capital notes payable | 0 | 0 | 150 | 100 | 60 | 3,168 | 3,088 | 3,346 | 2,742 | 3,206 |
| Long-term liabilities | | | | | | | | | | |
| Revenue bonds payable | 663 | 921 | 1,526 | 1,653 | 1,686 | 19,030 | 24,629 | 29,356 | 32,406 | 32,030 |
| Total Liabilities | 1,716 | 2,264 | 3,100 | 3,146 | 3,148 | 53,894 | 57,594 | 59,194 | 62,994 | 60,994 |
| *Retained Earnings* | 530 | 537 | 540 | 537 | 518.9 | 91,306 | 95,206 | 99,306 | 106,406 | 112,606 |

TABLE 8-22  Statements of Revenues and Expenses, Municipal Parking Fund, City of Dyer Straits and Reference Group, 1979–83 ($ Thousands)

|  | DYER STRAITS | | | | | REFERENCE GROUP | | | | |
|---|---|---|---|---|---|---|---|---|---|---|
|  | 1979 | 1980 | 1981 | 1982 | 1983 | 1979 | 1980 | 1981 | 1982 | 1983 |
| *Operating Revenues:* | | | | | | | | | | |
| Parking charges | 793 | 882 | 893 | 931 | 962 | 37,200 | 40,900 | 44,600 | 49,300 | 52,900 |
| Interfund transfers | 64 | 96 | 94 | 103 | 142 | 5,100 | 5,800 | 6,200 | 6,800 | 7,400 |
| Total Operating Revenues | 857 | 978 | 987 | 1,034 | 1,104 | 42,300 | 46,700 | 50,800 | 56,100 | 60,300 |
| *Operating Expenses:* | | | | | | | | | | |
| Salaries | 438 | 447 | 448 | 479 | 491 | 16,300 | 17,900 | 19,700 | 21,600 | 24,000 |
| Materials and supplies | 31 | 29 | 24 | 27 | 32 | 900 | 1,000 | 1,100 | 1,300 | 1,500 |
| Repairs and maintenance | 63 | 50 | 53 | 60 | 63 | 1,900 | 2,000 | 2,300 | 2,600 | 2,900 |
| Utilities | 41 | 29 | 27 | 33 | 38 | 1,400 | 1,600 | 1,700 | 1,900 | 2,000 |
| Depreciation | 173 | 194 | 204 | 207 | 240 | 8,900 | 9,300 | 10,000 | 10,400 | 10,800 |
| Other expenses | 39 | 35 | 32 | 31 | 43 | 1,500 | 1,600 | 1,800 | 1,900 | 2,200 |
| Interfund transfers | 43 | 52 | 50 | 52 | 60 | 2,600 | 2,900 | 3,100 | 3,200 | 3,700 |
| Total Operating Expenses | 828 | 836 | 838 | 889 | 967 | 33,500 | 36,300 | 39,700 | 42,900 | 47,100 |
| *Net Operating Income (Loss)* | 29 | 142 | 149 | 145 | 137 | 8,800 | 10,400 | 11,100 | 13,200 | 13,200 |
| *Net Income (Loss)* | (74) | 7 | 3 | (3) | (18.1) | 2,400 | 3,900 | 4,100 | 7,100 | 6,200 |

TABLE 8-23  Statements of Receipts and Disbursements, Municipal Parking Fund, City of Dyer Straits and Reference Group, 1979–83 ($ Thousands)

|  | DYER STRAITS | | | | | REFERENCE GROUP | | | | |
|---|---|---|---|---|---|---|---|---|---|---|
|  | 1979 | 1980 | 1981 | 1982 | 1983 | 1979 | 1980 | 1981 | 1982 | 1983 |
| Municipal Parking Fund | | | | | | | | | | |
| Receipts | 1,951 | 2,171 | 2,389 | 2,513 | 2,745 | 72,000 | 76,300 | 88,100 | 90,800 | 92,000 |
| Disbursements | 1,972 | 2,165 | 2,321 | 2,503 | 2,863.1 | 73,300 | 77,100 | 87,100 | 87,400 | 87,700 |

# CHAPTER
# 9

# Summary
# and Conclusions

Chapters 3 through 8 have presented a framework, concepts, and techniques for analyzing the financial health of a government and have applied this approach in a comprehensive way to a hypothetical city, Dyer Straits. This chapter reviews the methods described in these earlier chapters and presents an integrated approach to evaluating the financial condition of governments. This approach is illustrated by summarizing the overall financial evaluation of Dyer Straits, drawing on the individual analyses of earlier chapters. The next chapter applies the full analysis to an entirely new case study to enable the reader to gain additional experience in financial analysis.

The first of the two sections in this chapter reviews the methodology used to evaluate the financial condition of a government, and the second synthesizes the analysis of Dyer Straits. This chapter is not intended as a substitute for the detailed exposition contained in the earlier chapters; instead, this chapter and the next should help the reader digest and integrate the ideas contained in Chapters 3 through 8.

## I. THE ANALYSIS OF FINANCIAL CONDITION

### A Definition and Framework[1]

The basic focus of this book is the financial well-being of governments—all types of government at the state level and below, including counties, munici-

---

[1] Readers who are familiar with the analysis presented in Chapters 4 through 8 may wish to read most of section I quickly and concentrate on the last part, "Overall Conclusions of Financial Condition," and Table 9-1. For those readers who have not read Chapters 4 through 8 recently, this entire section should serve as a useful review.

palities, towns, school districts, special districts, and government enterprises. All of these entities serve the public interest, and their financial viability is crucial in the U.S. federal system of government.

We look at the finances of governments at the total organizational level; it is the government as a whole that is being evaluated, not a particular revenue source, program, or department. Our analysis addresses the basic question, what is the financial condition or health of the government? Or, more precisely, what is the probability, both now and in the future, that a government will meet its financial obligations to creditors, consumers, employees, taxpayers, suppliers, constituents, and others as these obligations come due?

This definition has a time dimension since financial well-being may vary between the short run and the long run; it is multidimensional because of the diverse groups to whom the government is obligated and because of the diverse revenue and expenditure pressures that shape its finances; it incorporates implicit obligations and resources, which may not show up as explicit accounting or legal claims; and finally, it treats overall financial condition both as a composite and as a continuous variable, with governments likely to have both financial strengths and weaknesses, and an overall financial condition that ranges from very sound to very poor.

Financial condition is a complex concept, reflecting a myriad of factors and requiring analysis and measurement along many dimensions. No single measure, formula, or rule of thumb is adequate to evaluate the financial complexities of governments. A multifaceted approach is needed. Consequently, we organize the analysis into five specific components of financial analysis: revenue, expenditure, debt, pension, and internal resource analyses. All of these components need to be studied separately and then integrated.

### Revenue Analysis

Revenue analysis occupies a central position in financial condition analysis. The ability of a government to increase its revenues now and in the future is critical to its overall financial well-being. To evaluate this ability we examine the government's economic base, revenue base, actual revenues, revenue capacity, and the way in which these components interact to determine the government's revenue-raising ability (revenue reserves).

**Economic Base.**     All the revenues of governments are derived from some type of economic stocks and flows—income, land and property values, retail sales, etc.—which, in turn, reflect economic activity within the government's jurisdiction or other relevant geographical area. Consequently, revenue analysis begins with a look at a government's economic base, the underlying economic conditions faced by a government.

Theories of supply and demand are used to develop alternative approaches to assess the economic strength of a particular area. Rather than choosing a single approach, we use different approaches to identify key factors affecting the economic strength of a locality. Income is one of the best measures of economic activity among those that describe the economic base, and in most cases, data are available for a measure of personal income, either per capita or per family (or household). Factors that determine income are also important, such as population growth and characteristics; labor force and employment levels, changes, and composition; and productivity measures. Income has both direct and indirect effects (through other tax bases) on government revenues.

Income stability and distribution are other important measures of economic strength that affect government finances. National downturns and upturns may be exaggerated in the local economy, and this affects the government's ability to raise additional revenues or to rely on its existing revenues. The diversification of the economy and the nature of the principal products produced locally, along with past performance, are often viewed as the best indicators of future stability. Also, since differences in income distribution may affect governmental revenues and expenditures, measures of income distribution, such as the percentage of the population with incomes below a poverty level, are also important.

**Revenue Base.**    Only selected economic stocks or flows that constitute the economic base can be tapped to provide governmental revenues. Revenues generated from the local economy primarily include taxes on property, sales, and income, as well as fees and user charges for certain government goods or services. Revenues not derived directly from the local economy (nonlocal revenues) come from such sources as the federal and state governments. These sources of revenues taken together represent the government's revenue base. The uses of these revenue bases vary considerably across governments.

The property, sales, and income tax bases are the most important local revenue bases, and this part of the analysis concentrates on the levels and changes in these tax bases. The base for other local revenues, such as fees, is harder to establish, but income levels often serve as a proxy for this revenue base. For intergovernmental revenues, the basis for the distribution of the aid can generally be used to represent this revenue base. All else being equal, high and rising revenue bases contribute to stronger financial health.

**Actual Revenues.**    An examination of the government's actual revenues is the third component of revenue analysis. Actual tax revenues, fees, user charges, and intergovernmental aid are examined to determine what their relative importance is to the government and how they are changing over time. Unique revenue features can be uncovered by comparing the government's revenues per capita with a reference group's. This analysis also shows how heavily the government is relying on intergovernmental aid. Although, all else being equal, more intergovernmental aid is better than less, the problem with intergovernmental aid is the lack of control of this revenue source by the receiving government. Thus a government's vulnerability to changes at the state and federal levels increases as the levels of intergovernmental aid increase.

**Revenue Capacity.**   The next step in determining a government's ability to raise additional revenues is to measure the government's revenue capacity. Revenue, or fiscal, capacity is the ability of the government to tap a particular revenue source or set of revenue sources—a reasonable upper limit on money that can be raised from that source or sources regardless of current revenue levels. In our analysis revenue capacity is applied primarily to tax revenues, although conceptually it can be applied to non-tax revenues as well.

Revenue capacity is defined and measured through legal limits and comparative analysis. Most states have some form of legal constraint on their major local taxes, and the tax limitation movement of the past decade has tightened some of these limits. These legal limits are one form of revenue capacity. When examining legal limits, however, it is important to realize that these limits are not absolute; legal limits can change, in either direction, as a result of legislative actions, tax levy votes, and referenda.

Comparisons with other governments constitute a second method to calculate revenue capacity. Most comparative measures of fiscal capacity are based on the average behavior of the reference group and treat this average level of taxation in the reference group as a relevant benchmark or standard. While a useful guide, average levels should obviously not be interpreted as an upper limit on revenue-raising potential.

Both single and multifactor comparative measures of revenue capacity are available. There is no single best measure, and it is useful to know the advantages and disadvantages of different approaches. Revenue capacity based on total taxes per capita (one measure of ''tax burden'') is commonly used, although it fails to account for differences in economic and tax bases. Another single-factor method that takes these differences into account more completely is total taxes as a percentage of income.

The Advisory Commission on Intergovernmental Relations (ACIR) has developed a multifactor method that applies the average tax rate for each tax in the reference group to the appropriate base of the government under study. Multiple regression techniques are also used to develop multifactor methods that differ from the ACIR methods both conceptually and methodologically.

Given the alternative revenue capacity methods, it is probably advisable to compute more than one measure in financial condition analysis. Then the different dimensions captured by the various measures can be used to gain a more complete understanding of a government's revenue capacity.

**Revenue Reserves.**   The final step in revenue analysis is the calculation of revenue reserves, our measure of a government's ability to raise additional revenues. Revenue reserves are defined as the difference between a government's revenue capacity and the actual revenues it is raising. The greater the revenue reserves, the higher the probability that the government can extract additional revenues from the revenue base without adverse consequences.

Besides a direct dollar measure of annual revenue reserves, the extent of revenue reserves can also be estimated as a ratio such as actual revenues/revenue capacity. The basis for the calculation of the revenue capacity measure must always be kept in mind when interpreting the revenue reserves. Finally, other measures, such as local revenues/index of community resources, per capita revenues/per capita income, different tax revenues/tax bases (i.e., the actual tax rates), can be used to estimate revenue reserves.

**Conclusions from Revenue Analysis.**    The preceding five steps provide the input to evaluate a government's revenue prospects. High and rising levels of economic activity are desirable for long-run financial health from the revenue perspective. Moreover, it is important that the positive signs in the economic base be captured in the revenue bases. Consequently revenue reserves, the difference between revenue capacity and actual revenues, provide a more immediate assessment of the government's revenue prospects than economic measures alone. In addition, the role of intergovernmental revenues and their characteristics must be considered.

### Expenditure Analysis

Expenditure analysis estimates the pressures on the government for additional expenditures, the extent to which current needs of the community normally met by government are not being met. High expenditure pressures threaten the government's financial condition. Conversely, fewer unmet needs provide a source of financial strength if a government can reasonably cut back on its expenditures or slow the growth in expenditures.

Estimating expenditure pressure is the most subjective and difficult of all the components of financial condition analysis. The importance of this component, however, requires that at least some effort be made to measure expenditure pressure. To estimate the pressure on government for additional expenditures, we look at actual expenditures, input prices and quantities of inputs, and the relationship of inputs to outputs, production and service conditions and community needs.

**Actual Expenditures.**    The first task in expenditure analysis is to determine which expenditures are to be examined. Current and, to a lesser degree, capital expenditures are usually the focus of this part of the analysis. If comparisons are being made with a reference group, direct, current expenditures are divided into common functions, noncommon functions, and enterprises. Most of expenditure analysis focuses on common functions, although separate analyses can be applied to noncommon functions. Enterprise expenditures are discussed in "Internal Resource Analysis."

Actual expenditures and components of expenditures are examined in total and per capita terms, both over time and compared with a reference group's, to determine the government's expenditure priorities, expenditure growth, and "fixity" of expenditures. Comparisons of the growth rates in revenues and expenditures can reveal potential imbalances, and per capita expenditure trends and comparisons can provide initial insights into the government's expenditure pressures. Per capita expenditure comparisons are limited because expenditures on resources do not necessarily measure the outputs from government activities that meet community needs. The way in which governments provide outputs and meet these needs is considered in the next three steps in expenditure analysis.

**Input Prices and Quantities of Inputs.** Expenditures are of limited use in financial analysis, in part because they are measured in dollars that differ in value both over time and across locations. Thus, to improve estimates of actual resources (inputs) purchased in expenditure analysis, we need to adjust them for price differences. In general, all else being equal, a government that faces higher input prices will have greater expenditure pressure and poorer financial condition.

Price indexes are beginning to be developed to adjust for changes over time and across locations in the prices that governments pay for the resources they use. These indexes, however, have not yet been developed to the point where they are likely to be readily available for financial analysis for most governments.

Rather than using price indexes to eliminate the effects of prices, in some cases it may be possible to use direct measures of actual inputs, such as the number of employees per capita. These measures, however, have their own methodological limitations.

**Inputs, Outputs, and Efficiency.** The way in which inputs are translated into the outputs that eventually meet community needs depends on the efficiency of government operations. Therefore, to the degree possible, an examination of government efficiency should be included as a part of expenditure analysis. Both technical efficiency, the ratio of physical units of inputs to physical units of outputs, and cost efficiency, the ratio of the dollar value of inputs to physical units of output, are helpful in expenditure analysis. Whenever the efficiency of a government's operations can be improved, expenditure pressures will be reduced. With greater efficiency, less expenditures are necessary to provide the same level of output, or more output can be produced with the same level of expenditure.

Since detailed production and cost functions are not likely to be available for expenditure analysis, ratios of inputs to outputs and of dollars of expenditures to outputs are often the only feasible ways to assess efficiency. Even these ratios, however, require data that are often unavailable for many governments.

**Production and Service Conditions and Community Needs.**    Two additional concepts need to be incorporated into expenditure analysis. First, there may be certain environmental factors, observable at the organization level, that suggest it is more difficult to produce and distribute public goods and services in some localities (at some points in time) compared with others. Weather conditions, population density, total population, and housing density are examples of production and service conditions that may increase the costs of government services. Second, governments may face different levels and types of needs that must be met with governmental outputs. Concentrations of low-income populations, high proportions of dependent populations, and poor housing conditions are examples of need measures. All else being equal, more stringent production and service conditions, and higher local needs for government services, mean greater expenditure pressures and poorer financial condition.

Three problems must be overcome before production and service conditions and needs can be used in expenditure analysis. First, these factors need to be identified. Empirical and conceptual studies of government expenditure determinants, and research on social indicators, provide a useful starting point. Second, these factors need to be measured. Data are available to measure only some factors without surveys or special data collection efforts. Finally, these factors need to be incorporated systematically into expenditure analysis. Alternative methods include a qualitative assessment of a series of individual measures, the construction of an index, and/or the utilization of multiple regression analysis. In all cases the goal is to determine the extent to which government expenditures ultimately meet local needs.

**The Assessment of Expenditure Pressures.**    Several factors operate to increase expenditure pressures, which in turn worsen financial condition:

> Higher prices increase expenditure pressures because more inputs are required for a given level of output.
>
> Inefficiencies create expenditure pressures because more inputs, or inputs costing more dollars, are needed to produce a given level of output.
>
> More severe production and service conditions mean that more expenditures are required to provide a given level of output.
>
> Higher community needs require more outputs (and consequently more inputs and higher expenditures).

Thus high input prices, inefficiencies, severe production and service requirements, and high needs generate the most expenditure pressures on a government.

Although these factors can be examined individually or as a group, a more valid assessment of expenditure pressures is produced by relating some or all of these factors to actual expenditures. For example, an index of production and service conditions and needs can be used to group governments in a reference group into low, medium, and high categories. If actual expenditures per capita in the government are low (high) relative to the appropriate category determined by the index, then the government is more (less) likely to have pressures for additional expenditures. The use of price-adjusted expenditures per capita would make this comparison even more precise.

Instead of categories of the factors, ratios of expenditures per capita to an index of production and service conditions and needs can be developed. Lower (higher) values of these ratios are indicative of greater (lesser) expenditure pressures. Finally, with more-sophisticated statistical techniques such as multiple regression, expenditures per capita can be predicted with the relevant production and service condition and community need factors taken into account, and this predicted value can be compared with the actual value to provide an estimate of expenditure pressures.

### Conclusions from Expenditure Analysis.

Inadequate conceptual and methodological development and limited data make expenditure analysis more difficult and less reliable than revenue analysis. Nevertheless, the steps we outline provide an approach to examining those factors that affect the government's expenditure pressures and financial condition.

In addition to this approach to the assessment of a government's "common" functions, the noncommon functions should be examined. Of course, public elementary and secondary education should be analyzed either separately or combined with the government in a consistent fashion. But beyond education, if the government carries out other functions that are not organized as enterprises, then these, too, can increase expenditure pressures. Analyses of capital expenditures are also important. The results from an examination of noncommon functions and capital should be combined with the common function expenditure analysis to estimate more fully the expenditure pressures on a government.

### Debt Analysis

Two types of decisions by governments, borrowing and providing pensions for employees, have long-term implications. Debt and pension analyses are considered separately, debt analysis in this part and pension analysis in the next.

Debt analysis examines the actual levels of the government's debt, the capacity of the government to carry debt (the maximum level of debt it can reasonably carry), and the way in which the actual debt compares with its capacity to carry debt. We are interested in determining whether the government is carrying too much debt, and its ability to issue additional debt. The three steps in debt analysis include examinations of actual debt and debt service levels, debt burden measures, and debt capacity and reserves.

### Actual Debt and Debt Service.

The first step in debt analysis is to assemble and assess the actual outstanding debt and debt service of the government under study (and, if possible, of any governments with overlapping jurisdictions).

Generally, this is accomplished by examining the government's outstanding debt and debt service (and debtlike obligations such as leases) both over time and compared with a reference group's. As a general rule, all government long-term debt except self-supporting long-term debt should be included in the analysis. In most cases the debt to be included in the analysis will be general obligation debt, and the excluded self-supporting debt will be revenue or limited obligation debt. Self-supporting debt is repaid from the revenues of an activity that utilizes the borrowed funds without drawing on the government's tax or other revenue bases.

Outstanding debt should include short-term debt if the short-term debt is issued in anticipation of the type of long-term debt that would be included. Revenue and tax anticipation borrowing is only included if it is rolled over or otherwise kept outstanding on a continuing basis, and thus essentially serving as long-term debt. Outstanding debt of overlapping jurisdictions when included in the analysis should be calculated using the same criteria established for organizational debt.

Similar criteria are used to identify the debt service included in the debt analysis. Debt service includes the principal and interest payments on the long-term debt included above. Principal on short-term debt should not be included unless the short-term debt is being refinanced on a continuing basis and thus equivalent to long-term debt. All interest on short-term debt should be included in the debt service total unless it is being repaid from specific self-supporting project revenues. In almost all cases debt service refers to the government, but if data on overlapping debt service are available they should be analyzed as well.

By defining debt in this way and examining it over time and compared with a reference group, the levels and trends in outstanding debt and debt service can be examined and any unusual features identified. In addition, the relative importance of the debt of the organization being studied compared with overlapping debt can be determined.

**Debt Burden Measures.**    The second step in debt analysis corresponds to the traditional debt analysis conducted by municipal bond analysts. Debt burden measures generally compare the level of outstanding debt or debt service with a variable that attempts to capture the government's ability to repay debt. If the debt burden ratio is too high, then the government is viewed as carrying too much debt, indicating it may have trouble issuing new debt or even repaying its existing debt.

There are two broad groupings of debt burden measures, one based primarily on financial stocks and the other on financial flows. Measures based on outstanding debt include the ratios of outstanding debt to full assessed value of taxable property, population, personal income, and fiscal capacity. Each of these measures has strengths and weaknesses.

Debt burden measures based on flows typically compare debt service with different measures of governmental revenues, such as total revenues, own source revenues, and property tax revenues. A less common but more precise measure is the ratio of debt service to fiscal capacity, since it uses a broader measure of the government's ability to repay its debt than just its current revenues.

Debt burden measures are interpreted in three ways. First, they can be computed over time and compared with a reference group's to see if the government's debt levels are growing or declining, and high or low, relative to comparable governments. Second, they can be compared with standards developed by municipal bond analysts. Finally, they can be compared with legal limits on government debt where they exist. With these three bases for comparison and a range of debt burden ratios, traditional debt analysis, expanded to include fiscal capacity measures, provides a reasonable assessment of whether or not the level of debt in the government is too high.

**Debt Capacity and Reserves.**     Traditional debt burden measures, however, capture only a subset of the factors that should enter a determination of whether the government can borrow additional funds. A more complete debt analysis can be obtained by comparing the previously developed measures of revenue reserves and expenditure pressures. The higher the revenue reserves and the lower the expenditure pressures, the greater the ability of the government to pay off its existing debt and/or to borrow additional funds.

This approach may lead to different results than those provided by traditional debt burden measures. For example, it is possible for a government to have negative revenue reserves and high expenditure pressures while simultaneously having very little outstanding debt. The opposite may also occur. These cases show that total reliance on the debt burden ratios may be misleading and justifies the inclusion of the results from revenue and expenditure analysis in debt analysis to determine whether the level of debt in the government is too high.

**Conclusions from Debt Analysis.**     Traditional debt analysis that relies on debt burden ratios based on both stocks and flows is relatively straightforward. Yet debt burden ratios can be misleading at times, and they should be supplemented with the findings from revenue and expenditure analysis. When both of these approaches are utilized, the analyst is able to determine whether the government is capable of borrowing additional amounts without jeopardizing its financial health.

### Pension Analysis

When governments participate in pension systems, they promise to compensate employees during retirement. Because demographic factors, inflation, investment returns, and salary increases are subject to uncertainty, the government's actual future pension liability is uncertain. Moreover, because of the long-term and perpetual nature of pension systems, governments have considerable leeway in their decision on how to fund their pension systems. This uncertainty and apparent flexibility can create problems for governments in the future if their pension systems are not adequately funded.

The purpose of pension analysis is to determine the extent to which the pension system is generating current and future expenditure pressures on the government. These pressures are closely related to the financial condition of the pension system. In general, the poorer the financial health of the pension system now, the greater the resources the government will have to devote to the pension system in the future. If, in the future, a government must devote more of its resources to pensions, then fewer resources will be left to meet other needs and, as a result, financial condition will suffer.

There are three general methods to assess the financial condition of a pension system and the likely future expenditure pressure that the pension system will generate. These methods involve examinations of (1) the assets and liabilities of the pension systems, (2) the actuarial assumptions and funding methods, and (3) the cash flows of the system.

**Assets and Liabilities.**    Since pension funds receive assets and pay out benefits in the future, present value concepts are often used to assess the financial status of a pension system. A common measure of the pension system's financial health is its unfunded liabilities, the difference between the present value of all future benefits that must be paid to retirees (and disabled workers, etc.) and the present value of all pension assets, including assets expected as normal contributions in the future.

Since almost all pension systems have some unfunded liabilities, the critical question is, how much is too much? There is no simple answer to this question because different pension systems use different funding methods and actuarial estimates and have different clientele groups, and because governments often have many years over which the unfunded liability can be met if it has to be met at all.

Guidelines can be used to assess the unfunded liability. Often it is not the size of the unfunded liability alone that is a concern but whether it is growing or declining. Useful measures of pension obligations include the funded ratio, the ratio of unfunded liability to payroll, per capita unfunded liability, and the ratio of unfunded liability to full value of property. When these measures are examined over time, compared with a reference group's, and assessed against industry standards, a reasonably good reading of the pension system's financial status and the expenditure pressures it will create for the government in the future can be obtained. The calculation of these measures is, however, dependent on the pension system's funding methods.

**Actuarial Assumptions and Funding Methods.**    An examination of the pension system's actuarial estimates and funding methods can serve as a supplement to or substitute for an analysis of the pension system's assets and liabilities. Even when these estimates are made by actuaries, significant differences can emerge that may affect the pension system's financial health. Consequently, it is useful to examine the actuarial estimates, particularly estimates of inflation rates, yields on investments, and salary increases.

Besides the actuarial estimates, the actual funding method can be examined to help evaluate the pension system's financial health. A system funded on a pay-as-you-go basis, rather than some form of advance funding, is often a sign that the resources required by the pension system will increase in the future. The relationship between financially stressed pension systems and pay-as-you-go financing is relatively close.

All advance funded systems, however, are not immune from funding problems. One distinction among advance funded systems is whether or not the system is actuarially based. The risk of poor funding is greater with nonactuarially advance funded systems. Even for actuarially based advance funded systems, funding options for normal and supplemental costs can affect the financial status of the pension system. Finally, it is worthwhile to assess whether the required pension contributions are actually being made by the government.

**Cash Flows.**  Cash flows to and from pension systems represent only current transactions, and this is a shortcoming. Although only proxy measures, cash flow measures are still helpful because they are not complicated by actuarial estimates, they are related to measures based on assets and liabilities, and the data they require tend to be more readily available.

The ratio of cash receipts to cash disbursements is a useful cash flow measure. In pay-as-you-go systems, receipts equal disbursements (a ratio of one); in advance funded systems, receipts exceed disbursements, enabling the system's asset base to grow (ratio greater than one). A second cash flow measure is investment earnings as a percentage of benefits. A better-funded system will typically have investment earnings that are significantly higher than benefits paid out by the system.

The ratio of assets to benefits is not a pure cash flow ratio, since assets are a stock rather than a flow, but it has been cited by analysts as a useful proxy measure because it tends to be correlated with the measures based on assets and liabilities. The final cash flow measure is contributions to the pension system as a percentage of total salaries. This is a current measure of the burden that pensions are placing on expenditures, but it must be interpreted with other findings to know whether, for example, a high ratio signifies excellent funding or an attempt to compensate for deficient funding in the past.

**Conclusions on Pension Analysis.**  For many governments, pensions are not likely to cause serious expenditure pressures in the future. Pension analysis as a part of financial condition analysis is important, nevertheless, because some governments now have or will have problems related to their pensions and occasionally the problems may be severe.

Pension analysis is difficult due to the complexity and time dimension inherent in pensions themselves and the limited information available for analysis. Yet measures that represent the system's assets and liabilities, actuarial practices and funding methods, and cash flows provide reasonably good estimates of the likely future impact of pensions on the government's financial condition.

### Internal Resource Analysis

The final component of our analysis of financial condition assesses the government's ability to draw on internal resources to meet financial obligations. This is a short-run concern, with governments having fewer options to modify their internal resources than they have to influence their long-run financial well-being. While the government's internal resources may reflect its long-run financial condition, in the short run internal resources can vary somewhat independently from longer-term financial condition, so that they must be examined separately.

Both the levels and the liquidity of the government's internal resources are assessed to measure the government's ability to meet expected and unexpected needs for cash. Levels refer to the amount of resources that a government has on hand at a point in time, and liquidity refers to its ability to convert those resources to cash.

The analysis of internal resources is applied separately to different funds or groups of funds. Most major operating funds are examined together; this includes the general and debt service funds, and possibly special revenue funds. Due to the special nature of capital projects and their financing, and to the self-sustaining character of government enterprises, these funds are usually analyzed separately on an individual basis.

**Levels of Internal Resources.**    All else being equal, a government with higher levels of internal resources is in better financial condition. Internal resources are measured principally by fund balances (or retained earnings for enterprise funds), adjusted to include certain reserve funds and designations. Ratios of fund balances to revenues or expenditures and fund balances per capita can be computed over time and compared with a reference group's. Furthermore, whether the fund balance is positive or negative is important in and of itself.

Changes in the levels of the internal resources are measured by the differences between revenues and expenditures, i.e. surpluses and deficits. Ratios of surpluses and deficits to revenues or expenditures, or to population, are useful. Whether there is a surplus or a deficit is important, and trends over time and comparisons with a reference group are also helpful.

Other factors may influence these measures of internal resources. Appropriations of previous surpluses represent a revenue source that affects current surpluses and deficits and may mask a current operating deficit. Interfund transfers can affect both fund balances and surpluses and deficits and should be scrutinized carefully. The budgeting biases of the government should be examined, and finally, accounting changes and adjustments should be checked to determine their influence on the measures of levels of internal resources.

**Liquidity of Internal Resources.**   Liquidity analysis is concerned with the government's cash balances, the extent to which other short-term assets can or will turn into cash shortly, and the extent to which short-term liabilities will convert into demands for cash. If a government has cash on hand plus cash inflows that exceed cash outflows, or can adjust its stocks and flows of resources to achieve such an outcome, then the government has adequate liquidity.

Although useful, monthly or quarterly cash flow statements and forecasts are seldom available. In their place, annual estimates of receipts and disbursements are a good starting point for liquidity analysis. Working capital (current assets less current liabilities) and the current ratio (current assets over current liabilities) measure the government's short-term expected inflows and outflows at a point in time. The quick ratio, which compares more liquid current assets with current liabilities, is a more conservative measure of liquidity that takes the timing of the cash flows into account to some degree.

A government may, however, be able to alter its current liquidity, and one measure of this possibility is the "fixity" of receipts and disbursements. Contracted expenditures for personnel, leases, debt, and pensions may limit the government's flexibility considerably. A high level of short-term debt not only means more fixed payments but also limits the use of additional short-term borrowing to increase liquidity. Receivable collection rates and current liability payment rates influence liquidity, and cost-effective policies in these areas have the potential to improve liquidity.

**The Special Case of Enterprises.**   Since enterprises are separate governmental activities that are intended to be self-sustaining, we have not included them in the previous analyses. Government enterprises, however, may affect the government's financial condition. We have included the analysis of enterprises as part of internal resource analysis, since an enterprise's surplus funds or need for subsidy is likely to affect the levels and liquidity of the government's internal resources.

The analysis of a government enterprise is analogous to the financial analysis of a private corporation operating on a break-even basis. The objective is to determine whether the enterprise is likely to draw on the resources of the government. To do this, we analyze four aspects of the enterprise: market, operational performance, capital structure, and liquidity.

The market for the goods or services of the enterprise affects the enterprise's performance. On the supply side, competition, both direct and indirect, should be examined along with the particular regulations in the industry in question. On the demand side, the price elasticity for the product or service produced is a critical concern. All else being equal, an inelastic demand increases the probability that price increases can be used to keep the enterprise on a break-even basis and not draw on the internal resources of the government.

Operational performance focuses on revenues and expenses. Measures of earnings compare revenues and expenses, and the return on investment compares earnings with the asset base generating these earnings. Any measure that contains assets such as return on investment is subject to the problems of asset measurement. All else being equal, the better the operational performance of the enterprise, the less likely the enterprise will draw on the internal resources of the government.

Capital structure is concerned with the enterprise's use of debt. The higher the level of debt, the greater the possibility that the rest of government may have to contribute to the enterprise's debt service. Both the debt service coverage ratio and the debt to assets ratio are useful indicators of the debt structure of the enterprise.

Liquidity analysis of an enterprise is very similar to the liquidity analysis of other major government funds. Liquidity analysis is important because if the enterprise runs short of cash, the rest of government may be called upon to make up the shortfall. An examination of the enterprise's receipts and disbursements, measures such as net working capital, current ratio, and quick ratio, and changes in balance sheet items, particularly receivables, provide an assessment of the liquidity position of the enterprise.

By combining these four analyses, an assessment of the likelihood that the enterprise will draw on the internal resources of the government can be estimated. If the enterprise has been drawing on, or is expected to draw on, the government's internal resources, this is a negative finding in the assessment of the government's financial condition.

**Conclusions on Internal Resource Analysis.**    Internal resource analysis may reveal short-term financial weaknesses, regardless of the government's long-term financial prospects. Liquidity problems, however, are often highly visible, and long-term financial strengths may not be enough to avoid a crisis. Consequently, both short-term and long-term financial health have to be studied together, joining concerns about the levels and liquidity of internal resources with longer-term concerns about revenue reserves and expenditure pressures facing the government.

### Overall Conclusions on Financial Condition

The final step in the analysis of financial condition is to combine the results of revenue, expenditure, debt, pension, and internal resource analyses. Only when the results of all the components are examined together can a complete assessment of the government's financial condition be made. Table 9–1 summarizes the measures that might be assembled to provide such a synthesis.

TABLE 9-1    Key Measures for Financial Condition Analysis

**Revenue Reserves**

Individual tax rates
Percentage of legal tax limit used
Tax revenues/population
Tax revenues/tax capacity
Tax revenues/index of community re-
  sources
(similar measures for each major tax
  and for nontax revenues)

**Internal Resources**

Fund balance/population
Fund balance/total expenditures
Surplus (deficit)/total expenditures
Current assets less current liabilities
Current assets/current liabilities
Quick assets/current liabilities
"Fixed" expenditures/total expenditures
Collection and payment rates
(similar measures for each fund; plus oper-
  ating performance and capital structure
  measures for enterprises)

**Current and Capital Expenditure Pressures**

Expenditures/population
Real expenditures/population
Real per capita expenditures/index of
  needs and service conditions
Government employees/population
Government employees/index of needs and
  service conditions
(similar measures for specific expendi-
  ture types, functions)
Capital expenditures/population

**Debt Reserves**

Debt/population
Debt/income
Debt/property value
Debt/legal limit
Debt service/annual revenues
Debt service/tax revenues
Debt service/revenue capacity
Debt service/(revenue reserves less expend-
  iture pressures)
Bond ratings; yields
(similar measures for overlapping debt)

**Pension Expenditure Pressures**

Unfunded liabilities/population
Unfunded liabilities/property value
Unfunded liabilities/annual payroll
Pension assets/benefits
Pension contributions/salaries
Pension receipts/disbursements
Annual earnings/annual benefits
Funded ratio
Plan termination liability
Quick pension liability ratio
Plan continuation liability
Reserve ratio

For some governments, the synthesis is likely to be relatively straightforward—many of the components will point in the same direction, either good or
bad financial condition, and the individual analyses will be mutually supportive.
For other governments, and these are likely to be the majority, there will not be a
single finding that emerges from the various analyses. Instead the findings will
point to some strengths and some weaknesses, some areas that are improving and
others that are worsening, and the final conclusion will be a series of findings on
the positive and negative aspects of the government's financial condition.

We believe that analyzing the major components separately, and then combining the results, is more useful for many (but not all) purposes than reducing the various findings to a single number or index of financial condition. This is largely because the separate analyses often provide clues to why the financial condition is the way it is, and where policies need to be changed to achieve a more desirable financial condition. For those who wish to develop a single index of financial condition, there is no reason why the measures used in the various components cannot be combined to provide such an index.

## II. THE FINANCIAL CONDITION OF DYER STRAITS

A second way to summarize the financial condition methodology is to review the analysis of the city of Dyer Straits. The Dyer Straits example was used in Chapters 4 through 8 to illustrate different components of the analysis. We now combine these analyses to draw conclusions for Dyer Straits based solely on the results developed in the earlier chapters. In an actual analysis there will be additional information about the specific government under investigation that can supplement the analyses presented here, such as the plans of major employers, new housing and commercial development, and specific tax and bond initiatives.

The analysis and conclusions for Dyer Straits are organized according to the five components of the analysis summarized in the first part of this chapter. Table 9-2 presents an initial tabulation of key measures from each of these components to provide input for the conclusions about Dyer Straits. This table presents only selected measures and one year of data, but it helps pull the analysis of Dyer Straits together.

### Revenue Analysis in Dyer Straits

Economic base analysis points out weaknesses in Dyer Straits, primarily in the trends. Over twenty years ago, Dyer Straits' economic base was in relatively good condition relative to the reference group's. Between 1960 and 1980, however, population, employment, and income moved downward relative to the reference group's, and other measures of the economic base showed similar signs. If these trends continue, then the economic base could be significantly weaker than the reference group's in a few years.

The trends in the revenue bases in Dyer Straits mirror those found in the economic base. The per capita property and sales tax bases relative to the reference group's have declined about 5 and 4 percent, respectively, although both are about 4 percent higher than the level in the reference group. The per capita income base has also declined slightly relative to the reference group's from 1979 to 1983 and is about 1 percent higher in Dyer Straits in 1983. Thus all three tax bases in Dyer Straits show some weakness relative to the reference group. A strength, however, is the absolute levels of the per capita bases relative to the reference group.

TABLE 9-2  **Selected Financial Measures for Dyer Straits and Reference Group, 1983**

| AREA OF FINANCIAL ANALYSIS | DYER STRAITS | REFERENCE GROUP |
|---|---|---|
| Revenues | | |
| Per capita property taxes | $141.72 | $100.42 |
| Per capital sales tax | $ 41.13 | $ 29.02 |
| Per capita total taxes | $182.83 | $129.44 |
| Per capita total revenues | $298.65 | $238.09 |
| Property taxes/property tax capacity | 135% | 100% |
| Sales tax/sales tax capacity | 135% | 100% |
| Total taxes/total tax capacity | 135% | 100% |
| Total tax capacity less total tax revenues | $(47.85) | $0 |
| Expenditures | | |
| Per capita expenditures | $308.18 | $238.00 |
| Per capita real expenditures | $218.87 | $172.50 |
| Government employees per 10,000 population | 111 | 92 |
| Per capita expenditures/index of production and service conditions | $1232* | $1096* |
| Per capita real expenditures/index of production and service conditions | $875* | $795* |
| Per capita expenditures/index of community needs | $512* | $474* |
| Per capita real expenditures/index of community needs | $363* | $344* |
| "Needed" per capita real expenditures less actual per capita real expenditures | $(29.00) | $0 |
| Debt | | |
| Debt/population | $325.00 | $308.00 |
| Debt/property value | 5.4% | 2.9% |
| Debt/income | 7.4% | 3.8% |
| Debt/debt limit | 84.1% | 45.1% |
| Debt/fiscal capacity | 2.4% | 1.3% |
| Debt service/total revenues | 11.4% | 10.6% |
| Debt service/own (local) revenues | 16.0% | 15.9% |
| Debt service/fiscal capacity | 25.3% | 19.4% |
| Pension | | |
| Unfunded liability/population | $892.00 | $308.00 |
| Unfunded liability/property value | 14.8% | 5.3% |
| Pension receipts/disbursements | 121.6% | 276.3% |
| Investment earnings/annual benefits | 24.5% | 101.4% |
| Pension assets/annual benefits | 348.1% | 1484.4% |
| Government contributions/annual payroll | 24.2% | 17.2% |
| Internal Resources | | |
| Fund balance/total revenues | 2.4% | 8.0% |
| Surplus (deficit)/total revenues | (3.2)% | .04% |
| Working capital/total expenditures | 2.4% | 8.0% |
| Current assets/current liabilities | 119.7% | 166.6% |
| Quick assets/current liabilities | 7.8% | 69.2% |
| Collection rate for property taxes | 87.8 days | 49.9 days |
| "Nonfixed" expenditures/total expenditures | 14.89% | 18.75% |

For more details on these measures, see Chapters 4 through 8. Negative numbers are in parentheses.
*dollars per unit of index.

Despite the trends in the economic and revenue bases, Dyer Straits' per capita revenue growth has exceeded the reference group's by a considerable margin. By 1983, per capita total revenues in Dyer Straits were over 25 percent higher than in the reference group; per capita property and sales taxes in Dyer Straits were over 41 percent higher than in the reference group. Per capita state and federal aid have also grown more rapidly in Dyer Straits than in the reference group; the levels of per capita aid were roughly 5 percent higher in Dyer Straits than in the reference group in 1983.

The analysis of fiscal capacity, when combined with actual revenues to estimate revenue reserves, shows that Dyer Straits is tapping its base more than similar cities. For example, when the ACIR tax capacity measure is compared with actual revenues, the per capita revenue reserves in Dyer Straits decrease from negative $24 in 1979 to negative $48 in 1983 where the reference group is at zero reserves, by definition. In percentage terms, Dyer Straits is using its (ACIR) tax capacity by 35 percent more than the average of the reference group. Similar findings emerge from the income-based and regression-based fiscal capacity measures.

The conclusions from revenue analysis are not very positive. Dyer Straits has very limited ability to raise any additional revenues from its own sources, since the economic and revenue bases are not keeping pace with the reference group's and the existing revenue base is already being severely tapped. Unless state and federal aid increase for Dyer Straits, there are no sources of new revenues and the existing sources are not guaranteed. Dyer Straits would be in even greater difficulty if it did not have the relatively high levels of its revenue base, but these are being utilized quite heavily. Of course, there could be specific information about new development, industrial expansion, and so forth, that would modify these findings, but based on the data that are available for all the cities in our reference group, Dyer Straits does not have any slack on the revenue side.

### Expenditure Analysis in Dyer Straits

Several conclusions can be drawn from an analysis of actual expenditures in Dyer Straits. First, expenditures per capita in Dyer Straits are over 30 percent higher than in the reference group, which is a substantial difference. In addition, per capita expenditures in Dyer Straits are growing more rapidly than in the reference group. The high and rapidly growing expenditures in Dyer Straits suggest the tentative finding that Dyer Straits can reduce its expenditures and thus lessen its expenditure pressure, improving its financial condition as a result.

Per capita expenditure growth is a particular cause for concern. Per capita expenditures have grown 51.7 percent over the five-year period 1979–83 while per capita revenues grew by only 48 percent. A continued imbalance between expenditures and revenues could cause problems for Dyer Straits. The high-expenditure elasticity (with respect to income) in Dyer Straits is problematic and indicates that an increasing share of income is being used for government expenditures.

Finally, the analysis of expenditures in Dyer Straits shows that salaries, fringes, and debt service warrant attention. From a functional standpoint, police, fire, administration, and social services expenditures are high and rising relative to the reference group. These findings may provide a starting point for reducing expenditures if the analysis shows that this is possible and desirable.

Price differences affect the assessment of actual expenditures. While per capita expenditures in Dyer Straits in 1983 are 1.3 times those of the reference group, price-adjusted per capita expenditures in Dyer Straits in 1983 are 1.27 times those in the reference group, suggesting that price differences account for only a small part of the higher expenditures in Dyer Straits compared with the reference group.

Dyer Straits' price-adjusted expenditures for 1979–83 show that most of the expenditure increases observed in Dyer Straits over the five-year period were due to price increases. While total expenditures unadjusted for prices increased 47.1 percent, price-adjusted (''real'') expenditures increased only 4.5 percent over the five-year period. The implication is that the expenditure increases may not have gone to meet more of Dyer Straits' needs because most of the increases were due to price increases.

Employees per capita in Dyer Straits, a proxy for real expenditures, increased by 16.5 percent over the five-year period, again considerably lower than the increase in dollar expenditures. Compared with the reference group, Dyer Straits' per capita employees were 8 percent higher in 1979 and 21 percent higher in 1983, providing additional evidence that real expenditures per capita were higher in Dyer Straits than in the reference group.

Two major conclusions emerge from the analysis of price indexes and inputs. First, price increases account for a significant part of the increase in dollar expenditures in Dyer Straits and the reference group for 1979–83. Second, after adjusting for prices, real expenditures per capita are considerably higher in Dyer Straits than in the reference group.

The two final factors that influence expenditures and expenditure pressures are production and service conditions and needs. All else being equal, more stringent production and service conditions and higher needs increase expenditure pressures. An index of production and service conditions indicates that Dyer Straits has slightly more demanding conditions compared with the average in the reference group. When per capita dollar and real expenditures are examined simultaneously with this index, it appears that Dyer Straits expenditures are high, given its production and service conditions, even correcting for input prices. The explanation for this finding may lie with Dyer Straits' greater needs or inefficiencies in the operations of the Dyer Straits government.

A similar analysis using a needs index shows that compared with the reference group, Dyer Straits' needs index is very high, but its real expenditures per capita are even higher. Given Dyer Straits' input prices, production and service conditions, and needs, we conclude that Dyer Straits is either operating inefficiently or providing more output relative to its needs than are comparable jurisdictions. If there are inefficiencies that Dyer Straits can eliminate or outputs that can be reduced and needs still met, then expenditure pressures can be reduced.

The final part of the expenditure analysis is an assessment of expenditure pressures. All else being equal, higher prices, lower efficiency, more stringent production and service conditions, and higher needs increase expenditure pressures and thus worsen financial condition. In Dyer Straits we found that two of these factors, higher prices and higher needs, were present. Production and service conditions were slightly more demanding than average, and very little information was available on efficiency. Thus there is some indication that Dyer Straits will have to spend more than the average city in the reference group to meet its needs, but whether there are expenditure pressures depends on its actual level of expenditures.

When Dyer Straits' real per capita expenditures are assessed against an index of production and service conditions and community needs and compared with a reference group's, we find that Dyer Straits ranks considerably lower on its combined index than it does on its real expenditures, suggesting that Dyer Straits is overspending compared with its reference group. Similar findings emerge from a regression analysis. Therefore Dyer Straits does not have pressures for additional expenditures and may even be able to cut back on its expenditures, either by improving efficiency or by reducing the level of output or both, and still meet its needs. Expenditure reductions will also bring expenditures more into line with revenues. These findings are more positive than if we found that even with no slack in Dyer Straits' revenues, more expenditures were needed to meet needs adequately.

### Debt Analysis in Dyer Straits

When organizational debt in Dyer Straits and the reference group for the five years from 1979 through 1983 is examined, we find that total outstanding long-term debt has increased more rapidly in Dyer Straits than in the reference group, and this holds for both general and limited obligation long-term debt, as well as short-term debt. In addition, debt service payments in Dyer Straits have increased more rapidly than in the reference group for total long-term debt and total short-term debt. Finally, outstanding overlapping general obligation debt and debt service increased more rapidly over the period for Dyer Straits compared with the reference group. Thus the data on the debt and debt service in Dyer Straits and the reference group show rather clearly that Dyer Straits has been increasing its debt and debt service relative to the reference group.

The most traditional form of debt analysis uses various forms of debt burden measures. If the debt burden measures are high, this is usually interpreted to mean that the government is carrying too much debt, will probably have some difficulty borrowing additional amounts, and may have difficulty repaying the debt.

The ratio of debt to full assessed value of property is much higher in Dyer Straits than in the reference group for both organizational and overlapping debt. The level of this ratio in 1983 for direct and overlapping debt, 16.44 percent, is rather high when compared with industry standards as well. Similar findings emerge from the analysis of three other debt burden ratios: per capita debt, debt to income, and debt to fiscal capacity. In the former case, Dyer Straits' direct and overlapping debt is approaching the $1,000 figure, which is considered a sign of trouble. One additional finding that can be drawn from these debt burden ratios is that a significant part of Dyer Straits' debt is comprised of overlapping rather than organizational debt.

Another assessment of debt burden is obtained by examining debt burden measures based on flows rather than stocks. The ratios of debt service to total revenues and debt service to own source revenues reveal that for organizational debt, Dyer Straits and the reference group are at similar levels. For organizational debt plus overlapping debt, however, these ratios in Dyer Straits are considerably higher than in the reference group, but none of these flow measures approach the industry benchmarks.

One reason why the debt burden measures based on outstanding debt are relatively higher in Dyer Straits compared with the debt burden ratios based on debt service is that Dyer Straits stretches its debt repayment over a longer period compared with the reference group. Although Dyer Straits' higher level of debt places a lower burden on current revenues compared with the reference group, the more rapid repayment schedule in the reference group will permit a higher level of new borrowing.

A second reason for the lower debt service ratios in Dyer Straits relative to the outstanding debt ratios is that Dyer Straits is drawing high levels of revenues from its existing revenue bases. This is confirmed by computing the ratio of debt service to fiscal capacity. This debt service ratio is 30 percent higher in Dyer Straits than in the reference group in 1983.

Aside from the high levels of debt and, to a somewhat lesser degree, debt service in Dyer Straits, other aspects of its debt practices do not raise particular problems. Short-term borrowing appears to be limited to bond anticipation purposes, and its capital program is commensurate with its borrowings. One hypothesis is that Dyer Straits needs high levels of debt to rebuild its old and poorly maintained infrastructure. Thus, based on the traditional debt burden approach, with some elaborations, Dyer Straits appears to be at or close to its debt capacity and additional borrowing may be difficult.

By examining the results of the revenue and expenditure analyses in Dyer Straits, we can produce a second estimate of Dyer Straits' ability to borrow additional amounts. The revenue analysis showed that it is unlikely that significant additional revenues can be raised. Own source revenues, particularly taxes, are being utilized quite heavily, while state and federal aid increases are not to be expected. At the same time, however, there is some slack on the expenditure side, and if this slack can be converted to funds to pay debt service, then Dyer Straits may be able to borrow additional amounts without necessarily raising additional revenues. Consequently, if Dyer Straits can improve its efficiency or cut back expenditures where needs are being "overmet," then the funds that are freed up as a result can be used to pay additional debt service, meaning that Dyer Straits can borrow additional amounts.

Thus, although the traditional analysis suggests that the levels of debt are rather high in Dyer Straits, the expenditure analysis raises the possibility that with some expenditure reductions, additional borrowing may be possible for Dyer Straits.

### Pension Analysis in Dyer Straits

Dyer Straits and all cities in the reference group administer their own pension systems for their employees. These pension systems involve no employee contributions and only six systems in the state, including Dyer Straits, automatically adjust benefits according to the cost of living. Dyer Straits is moving toward an actuarially based advance funded system and hopes to achieve this in six years.

The unfunded liability is a measure of the pension system's liabilities less assets. In Dyer Straits the unfunded liability remained constant over the five-year period 1979–83 while in the reference group the unfunded liability declined by about 20 percent, indicating that Dyer Straits' pension funding may not be as sound as the reference group's. The funded ratio compares pension assets with assets plus unfunded liabilities, and this ratio increased from 11 to 14 percent in Dyer Straits over the five years. While the increase is a good sign, the absolute level is quite low judging by all state and local pension systems. Moreover, the funded ratio is higher and grew more rapidly in the reference group.

A second ratio, unfunded pension liabilities per capita, is almost three times higher in Dyer Straits compared with the reference group and is growing slightly while the value in the reference group is declining. The ratio of unfunded pension liabilities to full assessed value of property is, again, over two and one-half times as high in Dyer Straits compared with the reference group and has risen considerably relative to the reference group, although it declined slightly in Dyer Straits.

Thus, based on the pension asset and liability measures, serious questions are raised. The high levels of the unfunded liabilities suggest that in the future the pension expenditures may have to increase; this translates to additional expenditure pressures in the future.

Only limited information is available on the funding characteristics of Dyer Straits' pension system. Most important, Dyer Straits is not now using an actuarially based advance funded system, although it is legally mandated to do so by 1989. In 1983 Dyer Straits was contributing normal costs, interest on the supplemental liability, and a small part of the supplemental liability. Since Dyer Straits is an older, declining city with a fairly mature work force, the switch to a fully funded system could be a significant burden. The automatic increases in benefits based on the inflation level will further increase expenditure pressures compared with the reference group where only *ad hoc* adjustments are provided.

The results from the cash flow measures are consistent with the previous analyses. The ratio of cash receipts to disbursements is greater than one in Dyer Straits but less than half as large as the value in the reference group and considerably below the average value calculated by the U.S. Bureau of the Census for locally administered systems. The analysis of the second and third ratios in this group, investment earnings as a percentage of benefits and the ratio of assets to benefits, leads to similar findings.

The final ratio, government contributions as a percentage of payroll, must be examined in conjunction with the other ratios. For Dyer Straits' pensions, the measures based on assets and liabilities and on cash flows indicate that the funding status needs to be improved, and this will require a larger contribution of resources from Dyer Straits in the future. This, combined with the finding that the ratio of government contributions to payroll is already higher in Dyer Straits than in the reference group, indicates that by postponing its pension obligations, contributions as a percentage of payroll are likely to go even higher in the future.

These findings can be related to the earlier analyses on revenues, expenditures, and debt. It will be difficult for Dyer Straits to meet the future pension contributions from the existing revenue base, since it is already being tapped extensively. But, in the expenditure area, there may be some slack. These findings on pensions, however, force us to modify the conclusions on debt to some degree because if the expenditure slack can be converted into usable resources, the future expenditure pressures from pensions may fully utilize this slack, leaving no additional resources for new borrowing.

### Internal Resource Analysis in Dyer Straits

Most of the "normal" ongoing activities of Dyer Straits, with the exception of enterprises, are accounted for in the general and debt service funds. The analysis of the levels and liquidity of internal resources in these two funds shows that Dyer Straits may have problems in this area, particularly if the trends observed over the past few years continue.

The decline in the level of internal resources in the general and debt service funds is documented by the deficits of the combined funds. Dyer Straits had a deficit in four of the five years under study while the reference group, as a whole, had a very small surplus. In the most recent year when the deficit was the largest, it represented over 3 percent of revenues in Dyer Straits. For 1979 through 1983, Dyer Straits' fund balances for the general and debt service funds declined from 11 percent to less than 3 percent of revenues. If these trends continue at their current level for one or two more years, Dyer Straits could have a negative fund balance, a very bad sign for its level of internal resources.

The findings on the liquidity of internal resources in the general and debt service funds are equally negative. The two funds combined had a negative cash flow in four of the five years from 1979 through 1983 while the reference group had a positive cash flow in four of the five years. From 1979 through 1983, cash in the two funds in Dyer Straits declined from $672,000 to $91,000, and with the largest cash deficit in 1983, a cash problem in the near future is very probable unless the current trends reverse.

The liquidity ratios confirm the findings from the cash flows. The fact that Dyer Straits' expenditures are relatively fixed, that receivables have increased over the five years and most recently are at very high levels, and that the end of the fiscal year is not the low point in terms of cash availability are further bad signs. Although it does not show up in the year-end financial statements, the cash flows indicate that Dyer Straits had to borrow at certain times during the year to have positive cash balances; up until 1983 it has been able to pay back this short-term borrowing before the end of the fiscal year.

Thus the internal resources in the two funds that cover most of the current activities in Dyer Straits are low and have been declining over the past five years. If the combined revenue and expenditure deficits and decreases in cash continue much longer, Dyer Straits will have serious internal resource problems. Either it will have to borrow short term to have enough cash to operate or some of its creditors may have to wait longer than they expect to receive what is owed to them by Dyer Straits. But steps such as short-term borrowing are stopgap measures; longer-term solutions are needed and we will discuss these in the next section.

The pattern of inflows and outflows in the capital projects fund is typically uneven. From an internal resource perspective in the capital projects fund, it is important to know whether the resources on hand are sufficient to fund the projects for which commitments have been made. This is the case in Dyer Straits. From a liquidity perspective, Dyer Straits is in good shape in the capital projects fund, since most of the assets are in cash or time deposits.

One practice that could become a problem in the capital projects fund is the use of short-term debt, in this case bond anticipation notes and capital notes. While in some circumstances the issuance of short-term debt prior to the issuance of long-term debt is cost effective, if Dyer Straits' financial condition deteriorates to the point where its ability to pay creditors is seriously questioned, then it may not be able to convert the short-term debt into long-term debt except under very unfavorable circumstances. Thus the high level of short-term bond anticipation debt leaves Dyer Straits somewhat vulnerable.

The internal resource analysis of an enterprise fund examines the fund's performance to assess whether the enterprise is likely to draw on the financial resources of other government funds. In the case of Dyer Straits' water and sewer fund, certain negative trends are apparent. Although the water and sewer systems are virtual monopolies and their services are relatively price inelastic, the operating performance of the water and sewer fund is not very positive. Operating income is negative in three of the five years, and net income is negative in all five years. The return on investment for the fund is under 3 percent in 1983, less than half of that for the water and sewer funds in the reference group.

In terms of capital structure, the water and sewer fund in Dyer Straits has a much higher debt to assets ratio and a much lower debt service coverage ratio than comparable funds in the reference group. The poor operating performance led the fund to borrow more heavily for its needed capital improvements than if more internal resources had been available. Debt service coverage in 1983 was around 0.5, indicating that resources from current operations were not sufficient to pay debt service. Although the water and sewer fund in Dyer Straits has not been subsidized to date, if the poor performance continues the possibility of subsidies from the general fund must be raised.

The liquidity analysis of the water and sewer fund shows that while cash has declined, a cash crisis does not appear to be imminent. The liquidity ratios are quite low for the fund as a whole, but once the capital transactions are separated, the operating component appears to be satisfactory for the short term. But if the poor operating performance and negative cash flow continue for several more years, a liquidity crisis could occur and the water and sewer fund would more than likely have to draw on the resources of Dyer Straits. Again, the use of short-term debt in this case could end up being problematic. Overall, the analysis of the water and sewer fund in Dyer Straits shows that it is a concern.

The analysis of the second enterprise fund in Dyer Straits, the municipal parking fund, was left as an exercise for the reader. Instead of providing the results of the analysis of the municipal parking fund here, we will assume that the municipal parking fund's performance will not affect the financial condition of Dyer Straits.

To conclude, the internal resource analysis in Dyer Straits points out several weaknesses. Perhaps the most troubling aspect is the low and declining levels and liquidity in the combined general and debt service funds which account for most of current activities. Dyer Straits is rapidly approaching a point where new actions will be required to provide sufficient resources for Dyer Straits' operations. The capital projects fund appears to have sufficient resources for the unfinished, but committed, projects. One potential problem in the capital projects fund, which is shared by the two enterprise funds, is the extensive use of short-term borrowing, which may be difficult to convert into long-term borrowing if the internal resources of Dyer Straits deteriorate further. The poor operating performance of the water and sewer fund is also a problem, and if this continues, there may be a need for subsidies from the general fund within several years.

### Overall Conclusions for Dyer Straits

The analysis of the financial condition of Dyer Straits identifies many more weaknesses than strengths. The most serious negative factors include the deterioration in the economic and revenue bases along with revenue reserves that are becoming more negative, the high levels of outstanding debt, particularly overlapping debt, the increased expenditure pressures that will be caused when the pension system's funding moves to a more acceptable method, the decline in the levels of internal resources in Dyer Straits, and the deteriorating liquidity. When viewed together, these factors strongly suggest that Dyer Straits is approaching a financial crisis, although there may be time to avert it.

A potential source of strength was found in the expenditure analysis. Given Dyer Straits' input prices, production and service conditions, and needs, it appears that expenditures are higher than necessary. Consequently, if Dyer Straits can cut back its expenditures either by improving its efficiency or by reducing its outputs in areas where its needs are being "overmet," then this may free up resources to meet pension requirements and bring revenues and expenditures more closely into balance. If this cannot be done, and the trends that were uncovered for 1979 through 1983 continue, serious problems could ensue. Moreover, even if the necessary steps are taken, a sudden downturn in the economy could reduce own source and intergovernmental revenues to the point where the actions taken by Dyer Straits are too little, too late. If the problems had been identified earlier, more options might have been available to Dyer Straits. But even with earlier diagnosis, some of the problems facing Dyer Straits may be beyond its control.

## QUESTIONS

1. Why do the results of revenue, expenditure, debt, pension, and internal resource analysis need to be brought together and compared to provide a comprehensive analysis of a government's financial condition? Illustrate how the conclusions from one component of the analysis (for example, debt) might be modified or even reversed based on the results of the other financial analysis components.

2. Can a government with serious financial problems in one area, such as revenues or pensions, still be considered financially strong overall? Conversely, can a government financially strong in one area be in serious financial difficulty overall?

3. Integrating and presenting results from the five areas of financial analysis is a difficult but essential task. Develop your own method for presenting diverse conclusions about a government's finances—table, graph, summary chart—that shows both financial strengths and weaknesses, and an overall assessment of the government's financial condition. Tables 9-1 and 9-2 in the text may be of help to you in this task.

## —————————————————————PROBLEM—————————————————————

1. Drawing on your analysis of Red Lion in preceding chapters, present a summary of your findings and an overall evaluation of the city's financial condition. Your summary should include a final overall evaluation as well as a review of major financial strengths and weaknesses. You may wish to develop a table like Table 9-2 in the text to help summarize your findings and conclusions.

# CHAPTER
# 10 A Final Case Example

The city of Dyer Straits was used as a hypothetical example throughout the book to illustrate the analysis of financial condition as each analytical approach was introduced. This final chapter is designed to illustrate further our approach to the analysis of financial condition through the use of a second example, the city of Ferndale.

The example is presented so that you can use the data to assess the financial condition of Ferndale on your own, *prior* to reviewing the analysis presented in the chapter. This will provide you with a measure of how well the methodology is understood. Many, but not all, of the concepts included in Chapters 3 through 8 are incorporated into the Ferndale case. If you want to assess the financial condition of Ferndale as an exercise before reading the analysis in the chapter, you should read through section I, "The Data," and then do the analysis before reading the rest of the chapter.

The data that we use for the evaluation are meant to be representative of what might be available for an actual financial analysis. In a few cases, however, exceptions are made, primarily for pedagogical reasons. As in the analysis of Dyer Straits, many of the idiosyncratic and qualitative data on Ferndale, such as information on a new urban renewal project or a pending plant closing, are not presented and, consequently, are not used in the example. These kinds of data would be available to the analyst in an actual assessment of financial condition.

The analysis follows the approach developed in the book and includes revenue, expenditure, debt, pension, and internal resource analysis. The data are presented in the first section of the chapter, and each of the five analyses is the subject of sections II through VI. The conclusions, based on the five individual analyses, are contained in section VII, the last section.

## I. THE DATA

The available data for this analysis include selected financial, economic, social, and demographic characteristics of Ferndale and a reference group. The reference group is comprised of ten cities located in the same state as Ferndale. As is often the case in actual analyses, more data are available for the city being analyzed, Ferndale, than for the cities in the reference group. Virtually all the data are examples of what would be available in published form. Other data elements that would be useful beyond those that are provided are discussed at various points of the analysis.

Two typical financial statements are available for Ferndale, and these are presented in Tables 10-1 and 10-2. Table 10-1 shows three statements of revenues and expenditures, consolidated for the general and debt service funds. Ferndale has one other fund, a capital projects fund, but this fund is not included in Tables 10-1 and 10-2. Data are presented for 1983, 1984, and 1985; 1985 data are the latest available.

TABLE 10-1    Operating Expenditures and Revenues, City of Ferndale (all funds consolidated except capital projects fund) ($ millions)

| EXPENDITURES | 1983 | 1984 | 1985 |
|---|---|---|---|
| Police | 6.0 | 7.0 | 8.2 |
| Fire | 6.0 | 7.0 | 8.2 |
| Streets | 7.0 | 8.0 | 9.0 |
| Public transportation | 2.0 | 2.5 | 3.0 |
| Recreation | 3.0 | 3.3 | 3.7 |
| Health | 2.0 | 2.0 | 2.1 |
| Refuse | 2.0 | 2.4 | 2.9 |
| Sewer | 2.0 | 2.2 | 2.4 |
| Water | 3.0 | 3.3 | 3.7 |
| Administration | 2.0 | 2.5 | 3.0 |
| Debt service | 4.0 | 4.5 | 5.0 |
| Total Expenditures | 39.0 | 44.7 | 51.2 |
| **REVENUES** | **1983** | **1984** | **1985** |
| Property tax | 15.0 | 16.0 | 17.0 |
| Sales tax | 5.0 | 6.0 | 6.0 |
| Income tax | 2.7 | 2.8 | 3.0 |
| Water charges | 3.5 | 3.75 | 4.0 |
| Sewer use charges | 2.5 | 2.75 | 3.0 |
| Public transportation charges | 2.0 | 2.5 | 2.75 |
| State aid | 6.0 | 7.0 | 8.5 |
| Federal aid | 2.3 | 3.2 | 4.75 |
| Total Revenues | 39.0 | 44.0 | 49.0 |
| Revenues less expenditures | — | (0.7) | (2.2) |

Negative numbers are in parentheses.

TABLE 10-2  **Balance Sheets, Year-End, City of Ferndale (all funds consolidated except capital projects fund) ($ millions)**

|  | 1982 | 1983 | 1984 | 1985 |
|---|---|---|---|---|
| *Assets:* | | | | |
| Cash | 5.5 | 4.5 | 4.5 | 3.0 |
| Property tax receivable | 1.5 | 2.0 | 2.5 | 3.0 |
| Sales tax receivable | 1.0 | 1.0 | 1.2 | 1.5 |
| Due from state | 2.5 | 2.5 | 2.1 | 2.0 |
| Due from federal | 2.5 | 2.0 | 1.0 | 0.6 |
| Total Assets | 13.0 | 12.0 | 11.3 | 10.1 |
| *Liabilities, Reserves, and Fund Balance:* | | | | |
| Accounts payable | 6.0 | 5.0 | 5.0 | 6.0 |
| Reserve for encumbrances | 5.0 | 5.0 | 5.0 | 5.0 |
| Fund balance | 2.0 | 2.0 | 1.3 | (.9) |
| Total Liabilities, Reserves, and Fund Balance | 13.0 | 12.0 | 11.3 | 10.1 |

**Negative numbers in parentheses.**

Ferndale uses an accrual system for revenues and expenditures in its general and debt service funds. It has three activities that operate with user charges —public transportation, the water system, and the sewer system—but these activities are accounted for in the general fund using the revenue and expenditure accrual basis of accounting. The debt service included in Table 10-1 includes all of Ferndale's general obligation debt. Ferndale has no revenue debt outstanding.

Table 10-2 consists of four consolidated balance sheets for Ferndale covering the general and debt service funds. Again, 1985 is the latest year for which data are available.

Table 10-3 lists additional fiscal data plus economic and demographic information for Ferndale and a reference group. The data are shown for 1985, and the percentage change from 1979 for each item is indicated in parentheses. For example, the population in Ferndale in 1985 was 240,000 and in 1979 it was 220,183, or 240,000 divided by 1.09. Again it should be assumed that 1985 is the latest year for which these data are available.

Table 10-3 also lists comparable data for the reference group comprised of the ten cities located in the same state as Ferndale. The actual data shown in Table 10-3 are for the average of the ten reference group cities. In each case the average figure is calculated as the sum of the item for each of the ten cities divided by ten. For example, the total population of the ten cities is 2,000,000, and the average population of the ten cities listed in Table 10-3 is 2,000,000 divided by 10, or 200,000. Although the actual data for each of the cities in the reference group are not shown, these are occasionally used in our analysis. (The reader who carries out the analysis prior to reading Sections II through VII will not have access to these individual items, but this should not have a major impact on the exercise.) Finally, it is assumed that the data for Ferndale and the reference group are computed com-

TABLE 10-3    Selected Fiscal, Economic, and Demographic Information for 1985, City of Ferndale and Average for 10 Other Cities in State (Numbers in parentheses are percentage change from 1979 to 1985)

| | FERNDALE | AVERAGE FOR 10 OTHER CITIES IN STATE* |
|---|---|---|
| Population | 240,000 (+9%) | 200,000 (+12%) |
| Population density (pop/sq mi) | 3,000 (+9%) | 2,400 (+12%) |
| Full assessed value of property | $850M (+18%) | $800M (+20%) |
| Taxable retail sales | $120M (+22%) | $108M (+26%) |
| Taxable income (individual) | $1,000M (+24%) | $900M (+30%) |
| Revenues from property tax | $17.0M (+31%) | $13.6M (+20%) |
| Revenues from sales tax | $6.0 M (+33%) | $5.2 M (+30%) |
| Revenues from income tax | $3.0 M (+24%) | $3.6 M (+30%) |
| Outstanding debt† | $50 M (+36%) | $75 M (+42%) |
| % Population with family income below $5,000 | 8.4% (+5%) | 6.2% (+3%) |
| % Housing stock over 30 years old | 38% (+12%) | 32% (+8%) |
| Municipal employees | 2,400 (+16%) | 1,800 (+20%) |
| Average municipal salary (yearly) | $14,500 (+48%) | $13,500 (+40%) |
| Employment | 75,000 (+3%) | 67,000 (+10%) |
| Unemployment rate | 8.7% (+71%) | 8.0% (+60%) |
| Composition of employment | | |
| Construction | 2.9% (−3%) | 4.4% (+10%) |
| Finance, insurance, real estate | 7.3% (+4%) | 7.2% (+4%) |
| Government | 5.7% (+4%) | 4.2% (−13%) |
| Manufacturing | 30.0% (−3%) | 36% (+6%) |
| Services and other | 21.0% (+1%) | 16% (−) |
| Transportation, communication, and utilities | 7.1% (−10%) | 8.2% (−7%) |
| Wholesale and retail | 26.0% (+4%) | 24.0% (−6%) |
| Median age of population | 31.4 (+2%) | 29.7 (+.7%) |
| Median years of education | 11.8 (+3%) | 12.6 (+3%) |
| Government expenditures | 51.2M (+50%) | 38.7M (+40%) |
| Fixed assets (at cost) | 60 M (+12%) | 80 M (+20%) |
| Debt service‡ | 4.5 M (+20%) | 4.9 M (+16%) |
| Government contribution to pensions | 5.3 M (+112%) | 4.4 M (+26%) |
| Pension investment earnings | 1.8 M (+6%) | 5.2 M (+58%) |
| Pension benefits paid | 5.7 M (+138%) | 4.8 M (+50%) |
| Pension assets | 20.0M (+25%) | 52.0M (+69%) |
| Price index § | 143 (+40%) | 136 (+36%) |
| Needs index § | 121 (+9%) | 106 (+6%) |

M = millions; (−) indicates no change.
*10 cities range in population from 75,000 to 380,000.
†Including overlapping debt, excluding short-term borrowing.
‡Organizational debt service excluding principal on short-term borrowing.
§ 1979 = 100 in reference group.

parably. For example, all cities operate separate school districts and all education-related information has been removed except for overlapping debt. Furthermore, all cities have comparable fund structures and bases of accounting.

In the next five sections, we use the data presented in Tables 10-1, 10-2, and 10-3 to carry out the five components of financial condition analysis for Ferndale. Throughout the analysis two particular comparisons are stressed: a comparison between Ferndale and the reference group, and a comparison of Ferndale with itself, over time. Clearly the analysis is limited by these comparisons, and a more complete picture could be drawn if we knew the position of the reference group relative to other cities in the region or nation. The analysis that follows could be expanded to take this larger frame of reference into account, but for our purposes we will assume that the results presented below would remain unchanged in the larger context.

## II. REVENUE ANALYSIS

The five components in the revenue analysis for Ferndale include an evaluation of the economic base, revenue base, revenue capacity, actual revenues, and revenue reserves.

### Economic Base

Although data are not available to assess the economic base of Ferndale thoroughly, the data in Table 10-4 give us an indication of certain key factors and trends. First, the income data are limited but still useful. Taxable income of the residents of Ferndale is only a proxy for a more comprehensive measure of income that would include taxable and nontaxable income of all individuals who reside in Ferndale. The available income data indicate that the level and growth of per capita income are lower in Ferndale than in the reference group. Furthermore, the low-income group is larger and is growing more rapidly in Ferndale than in the reference group. Growth in taxable income per worker is somewhat higher in Ferndale than in the reference group, but this is partly explained by the changes in employment compared with population (see below). It would be helpful to have access to more-representative income data, but using existing data it does not appear that Ferndale residents have high incomes or are experiencing high growth in income.

The data on population show that Ferndale is experiencing slightly below average growth, the population is older, and the median age is increasing more rapidly than in the reference group. If the age data mean that either the younger (and presumably more productive) segment of the population is leaving, or that Ferndale has a higher than average over-65 population, then the age composition may be a cause of the current slower growth in the economic base. On the other hand, the population data may result from smaller family size (i.e., fewer children per family), which would not have the same implications for the economic base.

TABLE 10-4    **Measures of Economic Base, 1985, City of Ferndale and Average for 10 Other Cities in State (Numbers in parentheses are percentage change from 1979 to 1985)**

|  | FERNDALE | AVERAGE FOR 10 OTHER CITIES IN STATE |
|---|---|---|
| Income |  |  |
| Taxable income | $1,000M (+24%) | $900M (+30%) |
| Taxable income per capita | $4,167 (+14%) | $4,500 (+16%) |
| % Population with family income below $5,000 | 8.4% (+5%) | 6.2% (+3%) |
| Taxable income per worker | $13,333 (+20%) | $13,432 (+18%) |
| Population |  |  |
| Population | 240,000 (+9%) | 200,000 (+12%) |
| Median age of population | 31.4 (+2%) | 29.7 (+7%) |
| Labor Force |  |  |
| Employment | 75,000 (+3%) | 67,000 (+10%) |
| % Labor force unemployed | 8.7% (+71%) | 8.0% (+60%) |
| % Population employed | 31.3% (−5%) | 33.5% (−2%) |
| Sectors of employment |  |  |
| Construction | 2.9% (−3%) | 4.4% (+10%) |
| Finance, insurance, real estate | 7.3% (+4%) | 7.2% (+4%) |
| Government | 5.7% (+4%) | 4.2% (−13%) |
| Manufacturing | 30.0% (−3%) | 36% (+6%) |
| Services and other | 21.0% (+1%) | 16.0% (−) |
| Transportation, communication, and utilities | 7.1% (−10%) | 8.2% (−7%) |
| Wholesale and retail | 26.0% (+4%) | 24.0% (−6%) |

M = millions; (−) indicates no change.

The labor force data are more pessimistic than either the income or the population data. First, the number of jobs (employment) in Ferndale has grown much more slowly than the comparable figure in the reference group and much more slowly than the population growth in Ferndale. This is more obvious when employment is compared with population. The percentage employed has declined more rapidly in Ferndale than in the reference group and is at a somewhat lower level. Simultaneously, the unemployment rate has increased more rapidly and has reached a higher level in Ferndale than in the reference group. Thus the trends and levels of employment indicate that Ferndale is not gaining jobs as rapidly as it might, and this may account for the slower growth in income.

Finally, data are available on the segments of the economy for the employment in Ferndale. The mix of employment is not drastically different than in the reference group, although the jobs in Ferndale are oriented more toward services compared with manufacturing. The relative loss of manufacturing employment that Ferndale has experienced may be a problem, since slower growth in this sector is often associated with slower growth in the economic base in general. The figures on construction employment are consistent with this interpretation. Moreover, in two sectors of employment where the share of employment in Ferndale exceeds the share in the reference group, government and services, much of the property base associated with this employment is tax-exempt government property, educational institutions, and hospitals.

While in this analysis, as always, it would be desirable to have more-detailed information on Ferndale's economic base, particularly more accurate and detailed income data, the available data indicate that the economic base of Ferndale is not keeping pace with that of the reference group, and furthermore, its current economic potential appears to be at a lower level compared with the reference group's. Although the situation may change in the future, it seems reasonable to conclude that Ferndale should not expect substantial increases in revenue potential in the short or intermediate term if the trends observed over the past few years continue. Finally, if changes in income lag somewhat behind changes in employment, then continued erosion of the income base may take place in the future. In general, the economic growth potential does not appear to be strong.

### Revenue Base

The economic base of a government is translated into available resources through specific revenues. Table 10-1 shows that the principal tax revenues of Ferndale are the property, sales, and income tax. In this part we examine the corresponding tax bases. Information on these bases, obtained from Table 10-3, is shown in Table 10-5 for Ferndale and the reference group.

The property tax base is considerably lower on a per capita basis in Ferndale than in the reference group. On a per capita basis the growth in the property tax

TABLE 10-5  Measures of Revenue Bases, City of Ferndale and Average for 10 Other Cities in State (Numbers in parentheses are percentage change from 1979 to 1985)

|  | FERNDALE | AVERAGE FOR 10 OTHER CITIES IN STATE |
|---|---|---|
| Property tax |  |  |
| Full assessed value of property | $850M (+18%) | $800M (+20%) |
| Full assessed value per capita | $3,542 (+8%) | $4,000 (+7.2%) |
| Elasticity* | .75 | .67 |
| Retail Sales |  |  |
| Retail sales (taxable) | $120M (+22%) | $108M (+26%) |
| Retail sales per capita | $500 (+12%) | $540 (+13%) |
| Elasticity* | .92 | .87 |
| Income |  |  |
| Taxable income | $1,000M (+24%) | $900M (+30%) |
| Taxable income per capita | $4,167 (+14%) | $4,500 (+16%) |
| Elasticity* | 1.0 | 1.0 |

M = millions.
*(% Change in base)/(% Change in income tax base) for 1979–85.

base is keeping pace with the reference group's, although property assessment procedures often contribute to the value of the property tax base lagging behind changes in income and employment. A rough elasticity is calculated by dividing the percentage change in the total base by the percentage change in the taxable income base. This shows that the growth (or decline) in the property tax base is generally lower than for the income tax base, but Ferndale's elasticity is comparable with that of the reference group. Perhaps the most salient finding for the property tax base is its lower absolute level relative to that of the reference group. Additional information on the composition of the property tax base would indicate the extent to which Ferndale or the reference group exports significant amounts of its property taxes.

For both the sales tax base and the income tax base, the level and growth on a per capita basis are somewhat lower in Ferndale than in the reference group. Consequently, each resident of Ferndale has an "available" revenue base that is lower than that of the average resident in the reference group, although the growth of the tax bases compared with income is roughly the same.

Again, as in the economic base, the revenue bases for Ferndale are relatively low and there are no signs that would suggest extraordinary future growth. In fact, if the economic base continues its relative decline, the revenue bases may deteriorate as a result. Furthermore, even if the economic base begins to grow more rapidly, it may be some time before the effects are reflected in the tax bases. Since the property base is so important, additional data on housing starts, commercial and industrial construction, and rental prices and occupancy rates, as well as the composition of the property tax base, would be helpful.

### Revenue Capacity

The revenue capacity measures attempt to quantify the ability of a government's revenue base to generate revenues. For Ferndale we have computed a multifactor measure and a single-factor measure, and these are shown in Table 10-6. The basic data that are required to compute the revenue capacity measures are listed in the first part of the table. Included are the tax bases and revenues for Ferndale and the reference group for 1979 and 1985.

The first revenue capacity measure computed for Ferndale is a multifactor measure constructed along the lines suggested by the Advisory Commission on Intergovernmental Relations (ACIR). First, from the basic data, the average tax rates for the reference group plus Ferndale are computed. Second, these average tax rates are applied to the Ferndale revenue bases to yield a revenue capacity measure for Ferndale: $19.94 million in 1979 and $24.11 million in 1985.

The second revenue capacity measure is the single-factor measure based on income. First, the total taxes for the reference group plus Ferndale are divided by total income in the reference group plus Ferndale to obtain an implicit "tax rate." In this case the "tax rate" is taxes as a percentage of taxable income. To obtain the capacity measure, this implicit tax rate is applied to Ferndale's income tax

TABLE 10-6   **Calculation of Revenue Capacity, 1979 and 1985**

| | FERNDALE | | AVERAGE FOR 10 OTHER CITIES IN STATE | | TOTAL FOR 11 CITIES IN STATE | |
|---|---|---|---|---|---|---|
| | 1979 | 1985 | 1979 | 1985 | 1979 | 1985 |
| *Basic Data (all figures in millions of dollars)* | | | | | | |
| Property tax base | 720 | 850 | 667 | 800 | 7,390 | 8,850 |
| Property tax revenue | 13.0 | 17.0 | 11.3 | 13.6 | 126 | 153 |
| Income tax base | 807 | 1,000 | 692 | 900 | 7,727 | 10,000 |
| Income tax revenue | 2.4 | 3.0 | 2.8 | 3.6 | 30.4 | 39 |
| Sales tax base | 99 | 120 | 86 | 108 | 959 | 1,200 |
| Sales tax revenue | 4.5 | 6.0 | 4.0 | 5.2 | 44.5 | 58 |
| Total tax revenue | 19.9 | 26.0 | 18.1 | 22.4 | 200.9 | 250 |

*ACIR Method—Ferndale*
  a) Average tax rate

| | 1979 | 1985 |
|---|---|---|
| Property tax | .017 | .017 |
| Sales tax | .046 | .048 |
| Income tax | .0039 | .0039 |

  b) Average tax rate × Ferndale base = Revenue capacity

| | 1979 | 1985 |
|---|---|---|
| Property | .017 × 720 = 12.24 | .017 × 850  = 14.45 |
| Sales | .046 × 99  =  4.55 | .048 × 120  =  5.76 |
| Income | .0039 × 807 =  3.15 | .0039 × 1,000 =  3.90 |
| Total revenue capacity | $19.94M | $24.11M |

*Income Base Method—Ferndale*
  a) Average "income" tax rate

| | 1979 | 1985 |
|---|---|---|
| | 200.9/7,727 = .026 | 250/10,000 = .025 |

  b) Average tax rate × Ferndale base = Revenue capacity

| | 1979 | 1985 |
|---|---|---|
| Revenue capacity: | .026 × 807 = $20.98M | .025 × 1,000 = $25.0M |

base to obtain a revenue capacity measure of $20.98 million in 1979 and $25.0 million in 1985.

Note that while the two capacity measures differ somewhat for the two years, the increase in capacity is roughly $4 million for both measures. Other capacity measures such as legal limits or more-complex regression measures could have been computed if additional information had been available. Before we can interpret these capacity measures, however, the actual revenues of Ferndale and the reference group need to be examined.

### Actual Revenues

Complete revenue data for Ferndale and the reference group are not available. Certain conclusions can, however, be drawn from the data in Tables 10-1, 10-3, and 10-6. Ferndale's actual revenues for 1983 through 1985 are shown in Table 10-1, and the actual tax revenues for Ferndale and the reference group for 1979 and 1985 are shown in Table 10-6.

When Ferndale's revenues for 1983 through 1985 are examined, certain trends become apparent that were not detected in the other revenue analyses. Table 10-7 shows Ferndale's revenues in index number form (1979 = 100) and in common size form (total revenues = 100 percent). Both parts of Table 10-7 illustrate the important effect of outside aid on the revenue structure of Ferndale. The index numbers show that state and federal aid have increased 41.7 percent and 106.5 percent, respectively, whereas total revenues have increased by only 25.6 percent. Similarly, state and federal aid constituted 27 percent of revenues in 1985, up from 21.3 percent of revenues in 1983. The greater importance of outside aid can also be seen from the fact that $4.95 million of the $10 million increase

TABLE 10-7   **Revenues in Index Number and Common Size Forms, City of Ferndale, 1983–85**

1. REVENUE DATA, CITY OF FERNDALE, INDEX NUMBER FORM

|  | 1983 | 1984 | 1985 |
|---|---|---|---|
| Property tax | 100.0 | 106.7 | 113.3 |
| Sales tax | 100.0 | 120.0 | 120.0 |
| Income tax | 100.0 | 103.7 | 111.1 |
| Water charges | 100.0 | 107.1 | 114.3 |
| Sewer use charges | 100.0 | 110.0 | 120.0 |
| Public transportation charges | 100.0 | 125.0 | 137.5 |
| State aid | 100.0 | 116.7 | 141.7 |
| Federal aid | 100.0 | 139.1 | 206.5 |
| Total | 100.0 | 112.8 | 125.6 |

2. REVENUE DATA, CITY OF FERNDALE, COMMON SIZE STATEMENT FORM

|  | 1983 | 1984 | 1985 |
|---|---|---|---|
| Property tax | 38.5 | 36.4 | 34.7 |
| Sales tax | 12.8 | 13.6 | 12.2 |
| Income tax | 6.9 | 6.4 | 6.1 |
| Water charges | 9.0 | 8.5 | 8.2 |
| Sewer use charges | 6.4 | 6.2 | 6.1 |
| Public transportation charges | 5.1 | 5.7 | 5.6 |
| State aid | 15.4 | 15.9 | 17.3 |
| Federal aid | 5.9 | 7.3 | 9.7 |
| Total | 100.0% | 100.0% | 99.9% |

in revenues for Ferndale from 1983 through 1985 came from increases in outside aid.

It would be helpful to compare per capita revenue from outside aid for Ferndale with that for the reference group, and to examine the basis of distribution in order to assess the changes in Ferndale compared with those in the reference group. But even without these comparisons, the importance of state and federal aid in Ferndale's revenue structure is apparent. Similarly, it is difficult to assess the user charges in Ferndale without comparable data from other jurisdictions, although the changes in Ferndale seem to be minor.

We can, however, compare the tax revenues in Ferndale with those in the reference group. Total taxes for Ferndale and the reference group are shown in Tables 10-3 and 10-6 and per capita taxes are shown in Table 10-8. Per capita taxes increased more rapidly in Ferndale than in the reference group, and the level of per capita taxes is higher in Ferndale for property taxes but lower in Ferndale for sales and income taxes compared with the reference group's. Total per capita taxes are lower in Ferndale than in the reference group, although the gap has narrowed considerably over the 1979–85 period. To further assess the level of these revenues, actual revenues are compared with measures of revenue capacity to estimate revenue reserves.

### Revenue Reserves

The difference between a government's revenue capacity and its actual revenues is a measure of the government's revenue reserves. The two capacity measures computed in Table 10-6 can be used to estimate Ferndale's revenue reserves, and these calculations are shown in Table 10-9. The ACIR measure indicates that Ferndale was roughly at the revenue capacity mark in 1979 but was "overtaxing" its base by $1.89 million, or approximately 8 percent in 1985. Since the capacity level is at the average tax rate point, Ferndale is not necessarily at any maximum. In fact, when the ACIR fiscal capacity measures are calculated for all ten cities in the reference group, it turns out that two other cities are taxing their base at a higher percentage of their fiscal capacity compared with Ferndale. The

TABLE 10-8   **Per Capita Tax Revenues, City of Ferndale and Average for 10 Other Cities in State, 1979 and 1985**

|  | FERNDALE | | AVERAGE FOR 10 OTHER CITIES IN STATE | |
|  | 1979 | 1985 | 1979 | 1985 |
|---|---|---|---|---|
| Property tax | $59.0 | $ 70.8 (+20%) | $ 63.5 | $ 68.0 (+7%) |
| Sales tax | 20.5 | 25.0 (+22%) | 22.4 | 26.0 (+16%) |
| Income tax | 11.0 | 12.5 (+14%) | 15.5 | 18.0 (+16%) |
| Total | $90.5 | $108.3 (+20%) | $101.4 | $112.0 (+10%) |

Numbers in parentheses indicate changes from 1979 to 1985.

TABLE 10–9    **Revenue Reserves for City of Ferndale, 1979 and 1985**

| FISCAL CAPACITY MEASURE | 1979 | | | 1985 | | |
|---|---|---|---|---|---|---|
| | Fiscal Capacity | Actual Revenues | Revenue Reserves* | Fiscal Capacity | Actual Revenues | Revenues Reserves* |
| ACIR | $19.94M | $19.90M | $ .04M | $24.11M | $26.0M | $(1.89M) |
| Income base | 20.98M | 19.90M | 1.08M | 25.0M | 26.0M | (1.0M) |

*Negative reserves are in parentheses.
M = millions.

income base method shows that Ferndale was undertaxing its base in 1979 and overtaxing it in 1985, but by less than indicated with the ACIR method.

Two conclusions can be drawn from this analysis of revenue reserves. Both measures of fiscal capacity indicate that Ferndale has increased its utilization of the tax base compared with the reference group between 1979 and 1985; and both measures indicate that Ferndale does not have a substantial revenue reserve. The difference between the findings for the two fiscal capacity measures is due, in part, to the relative differences among the tax bases in Ferndale compared with the reference group. The lower property tax base in Ferndale relative to the income tax base results in a larger overtaxing amount with the ACIR method.

Note that the per capita revenue figures shown in Table 10–8 could be interpreted as a population-based capacity measure. Using this measure, Ferndale appears to be undertaxing its population, but this may be misleading because Ferndale has low per capita tax bases. Also, the tax rates themselves can be examined as a rough indicator of fiscal capacity and reserves, although a precise interpretation is difficult. The tax rates for Ferndale and the reference group are listed in Table 10–10, and this shows the higher tax rates for the two most important taxes, property and sales. Finally, if legal limits exist and are available, the situation in Ferndale should be compared with these limits as a measure of revenue reserves.

### Conclusions from Revenue Analysis

The findings from the five steps can be combined to assess Ferndale's ability to raise additional revenues. First, additional revenues do not appear to be forthcoming from growth in the economic base and, subsequently, growth in the revenue base. The economic base appears to have stagnated while the tax bases are low, at least on a per capita basis. It seems reasonable to assume that major changes in the economic structure of Ferndale would be required for short- or intermediate-term economic base or revenue base growth. Second, while Ferndale may have some room to further tax its revenue base, its revenue reserves have declined significantly during the study period, and probably only moderate amounts of additional revenues can be generated by raising taxes without altering Ferndale's position relative to the reference group's. Third, it is difficult to assess

TABLE 10-10   Tax Rates, City of Ferndale and Average for 10 Other Cities in State,
1979 and 1985

|  | FERNDALE | | AVERAGE FOR 10 OTHER CITIES IN STATE | |
|---|---|---|---|---|
|  | 1979 | 1985 | 1979 | 1985 |
| Property tax | .018 | .020 | .017 | .017 |
| Sales tax | .046 | .050 | .047 | .048 |
| Income tax | .003 | .003 | .004 | .004 |

the likelihood of increases in future outside aid without additional information, but growth similar to the rate over the 1983–85 period is unlikely to be sustained.

Thus Ferndale is not facing a revenue crisis in 1985 but may be headed for trouble. Only if economic and revenue bases continue to hold their own and outside aid continues at least at the existing level will Ferndale be able to continue moderate revenue growth without creating a significant negative revenue reserve. This may not present a serious problem if there is slack on the expenditure side, and we turn to this next.

## III. EXPENDITURE ANALYSIS

Before we discuss the five steps that constitute expenditure analysis, a comment on the available data is needed. First, the examination of expenditures focuses on total city expenditures, excluding only capital expenditures. Since capital expenditures occur unevenly, it is assumed that debt service more accurately reflects the use of capital in operations, but it is recognized that an alternative approach would have been to exclude debt service as well. Second, three enterpriselike activities are included in the examination, since the data are not available to separate them. As it turns out, all cities in the reference group operate water, sewer, and public transportation systems, so that the data for Ferndale and the reference group are comparable. In the next five parts we assess actual expenditures, input prices, needs, real expenditures, and expenditure pressures.

### Actual Expenditures

The first step in expenditure analysis is the analysis of actual expenditures. Expenditure data and the available information on the components of expenditures are listed in Table 10-11. Both total expenditures and expenditures per capita have grown more rapidly in Ferndale than in the reference group. The growth in expenditures is further highlighted by the expenditure elasticity; the percentage change in expenditures compared with the percentage change in taxable income is 2.1 in Ferndale and 1.33 in the reference group. Not only have ex-

TABLE 10-11   **Expenditures and Expenditure Components, City of Ferndale and Average for 10 Other Cities in State, 1979 and 1985**

| | FERNDALE | | | AVERAGE FOR 10 OTHER CITIES IN STATE | | |
|---|---|---|---|---|---|---|
| | 1979 | 1985 | % Change | 1979 | 1985 | % Change |
| Expenditures | $34.1M | $51.2M | +50% | $27.6M | $38.7M | +40% |
| Expenditures per capita | $155 | $213 | +37% | $155 | $194 | +25% |
| Municipal employees | 2,069 | 2,400 | +16% | 1,500 | 1,800 | +20% |
| Municipal employees per capita | .0094 | .010 | +6% | .0084 | .009 | +7% |
| Average municipal salary | $9,797 | $14,500 | +48% | $9,642 | $13,500 | +40% |
| Total salaries | $20.27M | $34.8M | +71.7% | $14.46M | $24.3M | +68% |
| Salaries as % of expenditures | 59.4% | 68% | +14.5% | 52.4% | 62.8% | +19.8% |
| Nonsalary expenditures | $13.83M | $16.4M | +18.6% | $13.14M | $14.4M | +9.6% |
| Nonsalary expenditure per capita | $62.8 | $68.3 | +8.8% | $73.6 | $72.0 | −2.2% |
| Nonsalary expenditure per municipal employee | $6,684 | $6,833 | +2% | $8,760 | $8,000 | −8.7% |
| Fixed assets (at cost) | $53.57M | $60M | +12% | $66.67M | $80M | +20% |
| Fixed assets per capita | $243 | $250 | +3% | $373 | $400 | +7.2% |
| Fixed assets per municipal employee | $25,891 | $25,000 | −3.4% | $44,444 | $44,444 | — |

M = millions

penditures in Ferndale grown more rapidly than income, but they have also grown more rapidly than revenues. From Table 10-1 total revenues in Ferndale have increased 26 percent from 1983 to 1985, while total expenditures have increased 31 percent over the same period. In addition to these troubling trends, the level of per capita expenditures is higher in Ferndale than in the reference group.

The data in Table 10-11 show that the higher level of per capita expenditures in Ferndale is due, in part, to higher per capita government employees and the higher average salary. Although it is difficult to assess the quality of the fixed asset data, it appears that Ferndale is operating with less "capital," in per capita or per employee terms, than the reference group. This *may* raise expenditures if the introduction of more capital would have been more efficient. Here, however, the data are only suggestive; more-refined data and analysis are necessary to determine whether this observation regarding efficiency is correct.

  We can also examine the limited data on expenditure functions to determine which categories are more responsible for the growth in expenditures. These data are shown for Ferndale in Table 10–12, and while there are some large percentage changes over time (public transportation, refuse, and administration), these are not large enough to change the relative importance of different expenditure categories significantly in Ferndale from 1983 to 1985.

  Thus the major findings are the high level of expenditure growth and the

TABLE 10-12    **Expenditures in Index Number and Common Size Forms, City of Ferndale, 1983–85**

| 1. EXPENDITURE DATA, CITY OF FERNDALE, INDEX NUMBER FORM | | |
| --- | --- | --- |
| | 1983 | 1984 | 1985 |
| Police | 100.0 | 116.7 | 136.7 |
| Fire | 100.0 | 116.7 | 136.7 |
| Streets | 100.0 | 114.3 | 128.6 |
| Public transportation | 100.0 | 125.0 | 150.0 |
| Recreation | 100.0 | 110.0 | 123.3 |
| Health | 100.0 | 100.0 | 105.0 |
| Refuse | 100.0 | 120.0 | 145.0 |
| Sewer | 100.0 | 110.0 | 120.0 |
| Water | 100.0 | 110.0 | 123.3 |
| Administration | 100.0 | 125.0 | 150.0 |
| Debt service | 100.0 | 112.5 | 125.0 |
| Total | 100.0 | 114.6 | 131.3 |

| 2. EXPENDITURE DATA, CITY OF FERNDALE, COMMON SIZE STATEMENT FORM | | |
| --- | --- | --- |
| | 1983 | 1984 | 1985 |
| Police | 15.4 | 15.7 | 16.0 |
| Fire | 15.4 | 15.7 | 16.0 |
| Streets | 17.9 | 17.9 | 17.6 |
| Public transportation | 5.1 | 5.6 | 5.9 |
| Recreation | 7.7 | 7.4 | 7.2 |
| Health | 5.1 | 4.5 | 4.1 |
| Refuse | 5.1 | 5.4 | 5.7 |
| Sewer | 5.1 | 4.9 | 4.7 |
| Water | 7.7 | 7.4 | 7.2 |
| Administration | 5.1 | 5.6 | 5.9 |
| Debt service | 10.3 | 10.1 | 9.8 |
| Total | 99.9% | 100.2% | 100.1% |

higher levels of expenditures in Ferndale compared with the reference group's. These findings do not take prices into account, which we turn to next.

### Input Prices

The ability to adjust for input prices depends to a large degree on the availability of a price index. For this case, it is assumed that a municipal price index that assesses prices both over time and across locations is available. This index is standardized at 100 for the reference group in 1979 and equaled 136 for the reference group in 1985 (see Table 10–3). The value of the price index for Ferndale was 102 and 143 in 1979 and 1985, respectively. Thus in 1979 the prices for municipal inputs in Ferndale were slightly higher than in the reference group, and prices in Ferndale grew somewhat more rapidly than in the reference group during the next six years. All else being equal, high and rising prices increase expenditure pressures.

Although the price index theoretically includes all inputs used by a government, a simpler index may be computed by assuming that all input prices can be summarized by the average salary of government employees. This, of course, ignores the quality differences that should be produced by higher salaries. In this case the average salary in Ferndale and the reference group was $9,797 and $9,642 in 1979 and $14,500 and $13,500 in 1985. If the reference group salary in 1979 is set to 100, these Ferndale "price indexes" are 102 and 150 in 1979 and 1985, respectively. The figures for this particular case turn out to be fair approximations of the price indexes, although actual empirical research is needed to test this assumption. The overall conclusion is that prices in Ferndale appear to be higher than the average for the reference group.

### Expenditure Needs

In financial condition analysis, the assessment of needs is a difficult step. In the case of Ferndale, however, there are available measures that appear to be related to need, and these are summarized in Table 10–13. While each of these measures may not be the most-preferred measure of community needs (some variables also incorporate aspects of production and service conditions), measures of crowding, income levels, housing condition, low education, old age, and unemployment have often been cited in the literature on needs.

The general conclusion drawn from Table 10–13 is that Ferndale has somewhat higher needs than the reference group. If we assume that low income, old housing, and high unemployment are the least-ambiguous needs measures, Ferndale's high needs relative to the reference group's are apparent. Furthermore, the individual data on each measure (data not indicated) show that Ferndale has the highest percentage of older-housing and low-income population and is second highest in terms of unemployment. The age and education measures are harder to interpret, since we are more concerned with the tails of the distribution

TABLE 10-13   Measures of Expenditure Needs, City of Ferndale and Average for 10 Other Cities in State, 1979 and 1985

|  | FERNDALE | | | AVERAGE FOR 10 OTHER CITIES IN STATE | | |
|---|---|---|---|---|---|---|
|  | 1979 | 1985 | % Change | 1979 | 1985 | % Change |
| Population density | 2,752 | 3,000 | +9% | 2,143 | 2,400 | +12% |
| % Population with family income below $5,000 | 8.0% | 8.4% | +5% | 6.0% | 6.2% | +3% |
| % Housing stock over 30 years old | 33.9% | 38% | +12% | 29.6% | 32.0% | +8% |
| Median years of education | 11.5 | 11.8 | +3% | 12.2 | 12.6 | +3% |
| Median age | 30.8 | 31.4 | +2% | 29.5 | 29.7 | +7% |
| Unemployment rate | 5.1% | 8.7% | +71% | 5.0% | 8.0% | +60% |
| "Needs index" | 111 | 121 | +9% | 100 | 106 | +6% |

(i.e., percentage over 65) than the mean or median, but these data are at least consistent with the conclusion of higher needs.

Some or all of these needs measures could be combined into a needs index using any of several methodological assumptions. For illustrative purposes, a hypothetical needs index is presented in Table 10-13, and indicates higher and more rapidly growing needs in Ferndale than in the reference group.

The general conclusion is that Ferndale has higher needs than most other cities in the reference group. Perhaps a limited conclusion is that if the eleven cities are grouped into three groups categorized as high, moderate, and low needs, Ferndale would probably fall in the high-needs group regardless of the methodology employed to measure needs.

After analyzing actual expenditures, input prices, and needs, the final two steps combine these findings to assess expenditure pressures.

### "Real" Expenditures

The actual expenditures shown in Table 10-11 can be converted into a measure of "real" expenditures by dividing expenditures by the municipal price index. These real expenditures are shown in Table 10-14. Note that total real expenditures grew in Ferndale and the reference group between 1979 and 1985, but per capita real expenditures declined in both Ferndale and the reference group over the period. Thus, on a per capita basis, fewer real inputs per capita are being utilized by Ferndale and the reference group in 1985 compared with 1979. The level of per capita real expenditures is somewhat higher in Ferndale than in the reference group in 1985, but the difference is only 4 percent. In fact, using data that are not shown, Ferndale ranks fifth from the highest in terms of real per capita expenditures among the eleven cities.

TABLE 10–14   "Real" Expenditures, City of Ferndale and Average for 10 Other Cities in State, 1979 and 1985

| | FERNDALE | | | AVERAGE FOR 10 OTHER CITIES IN STATE | | |
|---|---|---|---|---|---|---|
| | 1979 | 1985 | % Change* | 1979 | 1985 | % Change* |
| "Real" expenditures | $33.4M | $35.8M | 7% | $27.6M | $28.5M | 3% |
| "Real" expenditures per capita | $152 | $149 | (2%) | $155 | $143 | (8%) |

*Negative changes in parentheses.
M = millions.

A second and somewhat different assessment of "real" per capita expenditures can be obtained by examining municipal employees per capita that were shown in Table 10–11. Again the conclusion is reached that real per capita expenditures are somewhat higher in Ferndale than in the reference group.

### Expenditure Pressures

To estimate the pressure on Ferndale for additional expenditures, real expenditures are compared with expenditure needs. Given the quality of the data and techniques for analysis, this must be done in a subjective fashion.

First, the examination of expenditure needs showed that for most measures of needs and a somewhat arbitrarily constructed needs index, Ferndale has very high needs compared with the other cities in the reference group. Second, the analysis of real expenditures in Ferndale indicated that per capita real expenditures were somewhat higher in Ferndale than in the reference group. When these two observations are combined, there appears to be moderate expenditure pressure in Ferndale. That is, based on the real expenditures in comparable jurisdictions, Ferndale may have to spend more to meet its needs. While this is admittedly a subjective assessment, it seems fairly safe to assume that there is little or no room for Ferndale to cut back on its existing expenditures if it is to meet its needs to the extent that needs are being met by other cities in the reference group. There is also the possibility that through efficiency improvements, Ferndale may be able to increase its outputs without increasing its inputs. The potential for such improvements is not known.

### Conclusions from Expenditure Analysis

This expenditure analysis has highlighted several findings. First, actual expenditures per capita are growing more rapidly than income, revenues, and per capita expenditures in the reference group. This high growth, particularly in relation to revenues, will have an effect on internal resources. Second, Ferndale has moderate expenditure pressures. Ferndale's high levels of needs make it unlikely that Ferndale will be able to free up resources by cutting back on expenditures, and there may actually be pressures for additional expenditures. This latter conclusion is reinforced by the finding that per capita real expenditures have actually declined in Ferndale between 1979 and 1985. These findings on expenditure pressures will have an impact on debt and pension analysis. Finally, there is the possibility that Ferndale can generate additional resources by improving efficiency, but additional analysis is needed to evaluate this possibility.

## IV. DEBT ANALYSIS

The debt analysis component is comprised of three interrelated parts. First, the concepts of revenue reserves and expenditure pressures are used to estimate Ferndale's debt capacity. Second, existing debt is examined; and third, debt burden is assessed. All three steps contribute to our assessment of Ferndale's ability to borrow additional funds.

### Debt Capacity

The traditional debt capacity measures used in debt analysis are based on sources of revenues, such as property value or fiscal capacity, or the revenues themselves. These revenue measures, which were discussed in the revenue analysis section, will be related to Ferndale's actual debt in the next part.

Another way to assess Ferndale's capacity to borrow additional funds is to examine its revenue reserves and expenditure pressures. From Table 10-9 and our earlier analysis, Ferndale does not have excess capacity on the revenue side, although it is not taxing its base to the "maximum." On the expenditure side, there is already moderate pressure given the current level of actual expenditures and existing needs (Tables 10-13 and 10-14). This absence of slack in both its revenues and expenditures means Ferndale does not have the ability to borrow additional funds easily. Only if Ferndale taxes its base further beyond its fiscal capacity without diverting any of the new revenues to current expenditures could additional monies be generated for debt service.

### Actual Debt and Debt Service

Comparing revenue reserves to expenditure pressures is a method to assess the capacity for additional borrowing without considering Ferndale's actual debt. The conventional method to evaluate the extent of Ferndale's indebtedness, however, compares existing debt with a measure of revenue capacity. Following this approach Table 10-15 provides data on outstanding debt and debt service for Ferndale and the reference group, and various debt burden measures. Outstanding debt includes overlapping debt but excludes limited obligation debt and short-term debt. Debt service includes the principal and interest on organizational

TABLE 10-15    General Debt Measures, City of Ferndale and Average for 10 Other Cities in State, 1979 and 1985

|  | FERNDALE | | | AVERAGE FOR 10 OTHER CITIES IN STATE | | |
|---|---|---|---|---|---|---|
|  | 1979 | 1985 | % Change | 1979 | 1985 | % Change |
| Outstanding debt | $36.76M | $50M | +36% | $52.82M | $75M | +42% |
| Outstanding debt/ full assessed value | 5.1% | 5.9% | +15.7% | 7.9% | 9.4% | +19.0% |
| Outstanding debt per capita | $167 | $208 | +24.6% | $296 | $375 | +26.7% |
| Outstanding debt/ taxable income | 4.6% | 5% | +8.7% | 7.6% | 8.3% | +9.2% |
| Debt service | $3.75M | $4.5M | +20% | $4.2M | $4.9M | +16.7% |
| Debt service/taxes | 18.8% | 17.3% | −8.0% | 23.2% | 21.9% | −5.6% |
| Debt service/ACIR fiscal capacity | 18.8% | 18.7% | −0.5% | 23.2% | 21.9% | −5.6% |

M = millions.

general obligation long-term debt and the interest on organizational general obligation short-term debt. Both outstanding debt and debt service increased more rapidly in Ferndale than in the reference group from 1979 to 1985. We can now use this information on actual debt to measure Ferndale's debt burden.

### Debt Burden

Since data are not available on legal debt limits, the debt burden measures for Ferndale are analyzed by comparing them with the measures in the reference group and with rules of thumb. The three measures of debt burden based on outstanding debt—debt to full assessed property value, per capita debt, and debt to income—all indicate that Ferndale has borrowed considerably less than the reference group. Moreover, none of the measures appear to be approaching the "danger" levels established as rules of thumb. Similar conclusions emerge from the two debt burden measures based on debt service. Here again the levels of debt service to taxes and debt service to ACIR fiscal capacity are considerably lower in Ferndale than in the reference group, and the benchmarks suggested for these measures are not exceeded.

### Conclusions from Debt Analysis

Despite the traditional debt burden measures that indicate that Ferndale is somewhat below the average in the reference group in its use of debt, our earlier examination of Ferndale's revenue reserves and expenditure pressures indicated that the issuance of additional debt would stretch already low or nonexistent revenue reserves and/or increase existing expenditure pressures to meet the additional debt service requirements. These somewhat contradictory findings point up the importance of combining revenue and expenditure analysis with the traditional debt burden analysis. Based solely on the debt burden measures, the findings suggest that increases in debt are possible for Ferndale. The more complete analysis shows that Ferndale may be too constrained to carry any additional debt.

## V. PENSION ANALYSIS

Ferndale, as well as the other cities in the reference group, operates its own individual pension system for all local government employees. Since each local government is responsible for the pension system, these systems must be analyzed to determine the pressures they will place on future expenditures. Only limited data are available on pensions for Ferndale and the reference group. Table 10–3 listed data on government contributions to pensions, pension investment earnings, pension benefits paid, and pension assets. This is typical of the amount of information available on local government pensions, although it would definitely be more desirable to have data on the actuarially computed unfunded liabilities as well. In this section the available information is used to estimate future expenditure pressure due to pension systems.

### Pension-Funding Measures

To assess the likely impact of the pension system on local government expenditures, comparisons can be made between Ferndale and the reference group, and between Ferndale and national averages available from the U.S. Census. In this case the latest census data are from 1982, although it is assumed that these can be compared with the 1985 data in the example without adjustments.

The pension measures that can be computed with the data on hand are the cash flow measures identified in Chapter 7. First, Table 10-16 shows the ratio of

TABLE 10-16    **Pension System Measures, City of Ferndale and Average for 10 Other Cities in State, 1979 and 1985**

|  | FERNDALE | | | AVERAGE FOR 10 OTHER CITIES IN STATE | | |
|---|---|---|---|---|---|---|
|  | 1979 | 1985 | % Change | 1979 | 1985 | % Change |
| Cash receipts/ disbursements | 1.75 | 1.25 | −29% | 2.13 | 2.00 | −6% |
| Investment earnings as a percentage of benefits | 70.8% | 31.6% | −55% | 103% | 108% | +5% |
| Assets/benefits | 6.67 | 3.51 | −47% | 9.59 | 10.83 | +13% |
| Government contributions as a percentage of payroll | 12.3% | 15.2% | +24% | 24.2% | 18.1% | −25% |

cash receipts to cash disbursements. Since this ratio exceeds one for both years for Ferndale and the reference group, this indicates that Ferndale's pension system and the average for the reference group are accumulating assets. Ferndale's ratio of cash receipts to disbursements, however, has declined significantly over the six years and is considerably lower in 1985 compared with the reference group's. This may be a sign that the contributions to Ferndale's pension system in the past have been at a level that will require higher pension contributions in the future. In addition, the fact that the average ratio of cash receipts to disbursements for all locally administered pension systems in the United States is 2.29 reinforces the finding that Ferndale may be underfunding its pension system.

The second measure in Table 10–16, investment earnings as a percentage of benefits, further supports the finding from the ratio of cash receipts to disbursements. Ferndale's investment earnings as a percentage of benefits are less than one-third of the value of the reference group in 1985, and while this measure has grown slightly from 1979 to 1985 in the reference group, it has declined by 55 percent over the same period in Ferndale. Moreover, the national average of 83 percent for investment earnings as a percentage of benefits for all locally administered pension systems is over two and one-half times as high as the 31.6 percent in Ferndale in 1985. These measures suggest that Ferndale's accumulated assets are not contributing as substantially to the fund compared with both the reference group and the national average, and inflows to the pension system in Ferndale do not exceed outflows by expected margins, leading to the general conclusion that Ferndale has not been contributing adequately to its pension system.

The third measure, the ratio of assets to annual benefits, adds further support to these conclusions. This ratio, which is known to be related to the funding status of pension systems, is over three times higher in the reference group than in Ferndale, and even the value in the reference group is somewhat below 12.23, the national average for locally administered pension systems. Furthermore, this ratio has declined dramatically in Ferndale while it has increased in the reference group.

The final measure presented in Table 10–16 is governmental pension contributions as a percentage of payroll. This measure has increased in Ferndale from 1979 to 1985 and has declined in the reference group, although the value in Ferndale is below the value in the reference group in 1985. Apparently, the funding in the reference group is good enough that measures such as the ratio of assets to benefits increased even while the contributions as a percentage of payroll decreased. On the other hand, Ferndale's contributions as a percentage of payroll increased, but the measures of the well-being of the pension system still deteriorated over the 1979–85 period.

### Conclusions from Pension Analysis

Actuarial valuations and computations of unfunded liabilities are key inputs to the assessment of the financial condition of pension systems. In the absence of such information, the analysis must be based on less-precise measures, derived primarily from information on the cash flows and assets of the pension system. Using this information, there are evidently serious questions concerning the financial condition of Ferndale's pension system. Cash receipts to disbursements, investment earnings as a percentage of benefits, and assets to benefits have all been declining to low levels despite the increase in government contributions measured as a percentage of payroll. This suggests that the funding level is poor, and that contributions may have to increase in the future just to maintain its current condition. If Ferndale decides to strengthen the financial condition of its pension system, the contribution rate will probably have to increase even further.

Considering the absence of revenue reserves and the existence of moderate expenditure pressure, this is more bad news. Since pension contributions are likely to continue to increase, this demand for funds will compete with the need for other current expenditures and additional borrowing. The results of the pension analysis further reduce Ferndale's options, which were already very limited.

## VI. INTERNAL RESOURCE ANALYSIS

The final component in the examination of Ferndale's financial condition is internal resource analysis. The magnitude of internally available funds is examined first, followed by an assessment of Ferndale's liquidity position.

### Magnitude of Internal Funds

The analysis to this point has not specifically examined the magnitude of revenues and expenditures simultaneously. It is the excess of revenues over expenditures that generates potential funds that can be utilized by Ferndale. Complete data for Ferndale and the reference group are not available, but limited information for Ferndale for 1983 through 1985 is available and is shown in Table 10-17.

Including all organizational revenues and expenditures except capital expenditures and proceeds from borrowing, Table 10-17 shows that Ferndale's expenditures exceeded revenues by $700,000 in 1984 and $2,200,000 in 1985. By 1985 these deficits produced a *negative* fund balance of $900,000, as shown in Table 10-2. This is an unambiguously bad sign.

An examination of the activities that are funded by user charges (but not accounted for as enterprises) shows that these are not the principal source of the deficit. In fact, using the expenditure accrual basis of accounting the net result of these activities is a surplus, as can be seen in Table 10-17. (If these activities were accounted for on an expense accrual basis, changes such as the addition of depreciation could alter the difference between revenues and expenses.)

Thus Ferndale has a revenue-expenditure imbalance that is seriously eroding the city's internal resources and will create severe problems if it continues. Although the three user charge activities do not appear to be a cause of the deficit, more detailed information would be desirable. Whether the declining level of internal resources is accompanied by a liquidity problem is the next question addressed.

TABLE 10-17    **Comparisons of Revenues and Expenditures, City of Ferndale, 1983–85**

OPERATING SURPLUS OR DEFICIT—FERNDALE ($ MILLIONS):

|  | 1983 | 1984 | 1985 |
|---|---|---|---|
| Revenues | 39.0 | 44.0 | 49.0 |
| Expenditures | 39.0 | 44.7 | 51.2 |
| Surplus or (deficit) | — | (0.7) | (2.2) |

OPERATING SURPLUS OR DEFICIT—FUNCTIONS WITH USER CHARGES ($ MILLIONS):

1. Public Transportation

|  | 1983 | 1984 | 1985 |
|---|---|---|---|
| Revenues | 2.0 | 2.5 | 2.75 |
| Expenditures | 2.0 | 2.5 | 3.0 |
| Surplus or (deficit) | — | — | (.25) |

2. Sewer

|  | 1983 | 1984 | 1985 |
|---|---|---|---|
| Revenues | 2.5 | 2.75 | 3.0 |
| Expenditures | 2.0 | 2.2 | 2.4 |
| Surplus or (deficit) | .5 | .55 | .6 |

3. Water

|  | 1983 | 1984 | 1985 |
|---|---|---|---|
| Revenues | 3.5 | 3.75 | 4.0 |
| Expenditures | 3.0 | 3.3 | 3.7 |
| Surplus or (deficit) | .5 | .45 | .3 |

**Negative numbers in parentheses.**

### Liquidity of Internal Funds

While the magnitude of internal funds has decreased in Ferndale, it is important to determine whether Ferndale faces or is likely to face a liquidity problem. Table 10–18 presents a number of measures that assess Ferndale's liquidity. In addition, the balance sheets in Table 10-2 include important information.

All measures show a decrease in Ferndale's liquidity over the 1983–85 period. Although the year-end is only one point in time, despite a substantial drop in the level of cash, there is still not a cash crisis in Ferndale at year-end. At the same time, tax receivables have increased dramatically. When the receivables are converted into days outstanding at the bottom of Table 10-18, a reason for the relative increase in receivables becomes clear. This is one cause of the decrease in liquidity, and some analysts believe that increased tax delinquency is a predictor of greater financial problems. Note that Ferndale has been able to maintain its cash position by "speeding up" its collections from the federal government, and to a lesser degree from the state government. But Ferndale may not be able to speed up these payments further in the future. The balance sheets indicate that liabilities (including the prospective liabilities represented by encumbrances) have not changed dramatically over the period and thus have not affected liquidity. The financial statements do not show any short-term debt outstanding at the end of the

TABLE 10-18   **Measures of Liquidity, Ferndale, 1982–85**

**A. Comparative Balance Sheets—City of Ferndale**
  **1. Index Number Form**

|  | 1982 | 1983 | 1984 | 1985 |
|---|---|---|---|---|
| *Assets:* | | | | |
| Cash | 100.0 | 81.3 | 81.8 | 54.5 |
| Property tax receivable | 100.0 | 133.3 | 166.7 | 200.0 |
| Sales tax receivable | 100.0 | 100.0 | 120.0 | 150.0 |
| Due from state | 100.0 | 100.0 | 84.0 | 80.0 |
| Due from federal | 100.0 | 80.0 | 40.0 | 24.0 |
| Total Assets | 100.0 | 92.3 | 86.9 | 77.7 |
| *Liabilities, Reserves, and Fund Balance:* | | | | |
| Accounts payable | 100.0 | 83.3 | 83.3 | 100.0 |
| Reserve for encumbrances | 100.0 | 100.0 | 100.0 | 100.0 |
| Fund balance | 100.0 | 100.0 | 65.0 | (45.0) |
| Total Liabilities, Reserves, and Fund Balance | 100.0 | 92.3 | 86.9 | 77.7 |

  **2. Common Size Statement Form (Percent)**

|  | 1982 | 1982 | 1984 | 1985 |
|---|---|---|---|---|
| *Assets:* | | | | |
| Cash | 42.3 | 37.5 | 39.8 | 29.7 |
| Property tax receivable | 11.5 | 16.7 | 22.1 | 29.7 |
| Sales tax receivable | 7.7 | 8.3 | 10.6 | 14.9 |
| Due from state | 19.2 | 20.8 | 18.6 | 19.8 |
| Due from federal | 19.2 | 16.7 | 8.8 | 5.9 |
| Total Assets | 99.9 | 100.0 | 99.9 | 100.0 |
| *Liabilities, Reserves, and Fund Balance:* | | | | |
| Accounts payable | 46.2 | 41.7 | 44.2 | 59.4 |
| Reserve for encumbrances | 38.5 | 41.7 | 44.2 | 49.5 |
| Fund balance | 15.4 | 16.7 | 11.5 | (8.9) |
| Total Liabilities, Reserves, and Fund Balance | 100.1 | 100.1 | 99.9 | 100.0 |

**B. Short-Run Liquidity Measures—City of Ferndale**

|  | 1982 | 1983 | 1984 | 1985 |
|---|---|---|---|---|
| Current assets/current liabilities | 1.18 | 1.20 | 1.13 | .92 |
| Cash/current liabilities | .500 | .450 | .450 | .273 |
| Working capital (current assets − current liabilities) | $2.0M | $2.0M | $1.3M | ($.9M) |

**C. Collection Information—City of Ferndale**

|  | 1983 | 1984 | 1985 |
|---|---|---|---|
| "Days" Outstanding: | | | |
| Property tax | 48.7 | 57.0 | 64.4 |
| Sales tax | 73.0 | 73.0 | 91.3 |

Negative numbers in parentheses.
M = millions.

year, so that if Ferndale is using short-term debt it has been paid back by year-end.

The short-run liquidity ratios confirm the conclusions drawn from the balance sheets. All three ratios show a decrease in Ferndale's liquidity, and by 1985, judging by the negative working capital and the current and quick ratios that are below one, the decrease is to a point where it is a serious problem. If these trends continue much longer, Ferndale could be in danger of running out of cash.

### Conclusions from Internal Resource Analysis

The figure that dominates the internal resource analysis is the excess of expenditures over revenues. This trend cannot continue much further without causing a severe financial crisis. Ferndale's liquidity trends are equally ominous, although a cash shortage has not yet developed. If the deficits and lagging receivables continue, however, a cash shortage is not out of the question in the near future.

## VII. OVERALL CONCLUSIONS

The various components of financial analysis strongly suggest that Ferndale's financial condition is very close to a crisis stage, and that the trend is still downward. Ferndale faces a number of severe constraints. Ferndale has little in the way of revenue reserves, is experiencing moderate expenditure pressure, will probably have to increase its pension contributions in the future, and its level of internal resources and liquidity is poor and worsening. Although Ferndale has not over-borrowed, its ability to borrow additional funds is highly questionable.

While Ferndale's situation is not beyond repair, if policies and/or external events do not halt or even reverse the trends that are apparent over the 1979–85 period, financial insolvency could result. There may be some steps that Ferndale's administration can take, but the troubles facing Ferndale may be built into the system; certain needs may not be capable of being met at the local level. Within our framework, even some governments that do everything they should or can may still turn out to be financially pressed.

# Index

capital structure and, 355
demand and supply, 352–53
example of, 356–68
levels of liquidity, 355–56
operational performance and, 353–55
level and liquidity of, 316–17
levels of, 324–35, 384–85
analysis of, 328–30
determinants of, 326–28
example of, 331–35
measures of, 324–36
summary of, 330–31
liquidity of, 336–51, 385
cash flows and, 336–38
creation of, 341–44
example of, 345–51
measures of, 338–41
summary of, 344–45
nature of, 315–17
Internal service funds, 25
Inventories, reserves for, 32

**L**

Liabilities:
current, defined, 21
long-term, defined, 22
Liability:
defined, 16, 23
Liquidity:
internal resources and, 336–51
cash flows and, 336–38
creation of, 341–44
example of, 345–51
levels of, 355–56
measures of, 338–41
summary of, 344–45
Location quotients, 90
Long-term assets, defined, 22
Long-term liabilities, defined, 22

**M**

Modified accrual system, 21

**N**

National Council on Governmental Accounting (NCGA), 27, 28, 29
statement 1, 27–28
statements required by, 39
Net income from operations, 354
Net working capital as liquidity measure, 340
Nonexpendable funds (*see* Proprietary funds)

**O**

Operating budgets, 55–58
Operating income, 354
Outflows, 17, 20, 23
stages of, 19
Outputs, measuring, 202–3
Outstanding debt (*see* Debt outstanding)

**P**

Pension analysis, 279–82, 381–84
example of, 304–11
introduction to pensions, 275–77
measures of, 291–304, 382–83
actuarial estimates and funding methods, 297–300, 382–83
assets and liabilities, 292–97, 382
cash flows, 300–304
nature of, 275–82
need for, 277–79
pension funding, 282–91
alternative methods of, 287–90
disclosure of information, 290–91
normal and supplemental costs of, 286–87
pay-as-you-go versus advanced, 282–84
role of uncertainty in, 284–86
present value and, 280
Pension funding, 282–91
actuarially-based, 285
disclosure of information, 290–91
nonactuarially-based, 285